THE SLAVE SYSTEMS OF GREEK AND ROMAN ANTIQUITY

Memoirs of the

AMERICAN PHILOSOPHICAL SOCIETY

Held at Philadelphia

for Promoting Useful Knowledge

Volume 40

THE SLAVE SYSTEMS
OF
GREEK AND ROMAN ANTIQUITY

WILLIAM L. WESTERMANN

Professor Emeritus of History
Columbia University

THE AMERICAN PHILOSOPHICAL SOCIETY

INDEPENDENCE SQUARE

PHILADELPHIA

1955

Library of Congress Catalog
Card No. 54–9107
ISBN 0-87169-040-3

Reprinted 1984

TO THE MEMORY
OF
MICHAEL IVANOVICH ROSTOVTZEFF

CONTENTS

PREFATORY STATEMENT AND ACKNOWLEDGMENTS

The beginning of my interest in the problems of ancient slavery lies many years in the past. The impulse behind this attempt to write a comprehensive study of the experience of the Greek and Roman peoples with the institution of slave labor and its results in antiquity is more recent. It originated in a recommendation made by Professor Michael Ivanovich Rostovtzeff to Professor Wilhelm Kroll of Breslau University that I should prepare a synthesis of the history of Greco-Roman enslavement for the *Pauly-Wissowa-Kroll Real-Encyclopädie der classischen Altertums-wissenschaft*. The resulting article upon *Sklaverei* appeared in 1935 in Supplementary Volume six of that invaluable German series. Toward the accomplishment of the primary task I was helped by a grant of money made by the Council of Research in the Social Sciences of Columbia University. This is the first opportunity I have had to make a public acknowledgment of the important assistance which the funds supplied out of the resources of Columbia University by the Council meant to me. The grant enabled me to secure the services of a small group of capable and enthusiastic graduate students, all equipped with the necessary knowledge of the ancient languages, to assist me in the collection of the materials upon Greek and Roman slavery which are so widely scattered in the ancient literature and the supplementary evidence of the inscriptions and the papyri.

The generous idea of bringing up to date the Pauly-Wissowa-Kroll article entitled *Sklaverei* and presenting it in an English version occurred to some of my colleagues in the Department of History toward the close of my active teaching career at Columbia. The department supplied me with sufficient funds, out of the endowment left to it by the will of the eminent Professor William H. Dunning, to secure help in the revision and the typing of this new version of the original article upon slavery written in German. To the American Philosophical Society my indebtedness is great for its generosity in providing for the publication of this volume.

The first four chapters of this new synthesis (chapters I-IV) cover the history of enslavement practice in the period of the free Greek polities. This will not be found to deviate greatly from the presentation available in the *Sklaverei* treatment, except in one respect. Additional knowledge upon Jewish slavery in a colony in upper Egypt during the second half of the fifth century B. C. has been made available to me through the generous and scholarly attitude of Dr. Emil G. Kraeling of New Canaan, Connecticut. He supplied me, in advance of their definitive publication, with his translations and explanation of three new documents written in Aramaic which deal with enslavement practice in the well-known Hebrew colony of Elephantine. As the discussion of them in chapter III should indicate, their contents are of unusual importance in establishing marked contrasts in the fundamental attitude and the procedures of Hebrew and older Semitic slavery as compared with those of the Greeks. Awaiting the discussions of the Aramaic scholars which this new material will inevitably provoke, my treatment of it is only tentative, a mere indication of its importance for the slavery problem of the eastern Mediterranean area in the Greek polity period. My indebtedness to Dr. Kraeling for his generosity in making this new material available to me sometime before its publication is very great indeed.

The four chapters upon slave labor and the treatment of slaves as these presented themselves in the eastern Mediterranean area after the conquest of Egypt and southwestern Asia by Alexander of Macedon (chapters V-VIII inclusive) are quite fully recast and rewritten. In them I have tried to approach the problems of slave legislation and employment as displaying, in their own way, in an age conspicuously marked by cosmopolitanism and syncretism, the results of acceptances and rejections in the field of slave-labor economy. I am fully aware that the ideas there advanced must be subjected to further study and will call for discussion and probable revision.

The account of slavery in the lands of the western Mediterranean during the period of the rise of the Roman republic will be found in chapters IX-XII. It has been added to by numerous details and changed in some of its conclusions. But it did not require a drastic revision of the original treatment as given in the Pauly-Wissowa-Kroll encyclopedia.

The discussion of the slave systems of the Roman imperial world of the first three centuries after Christ appears in chapters XIII-XIX. This has been greatly extended and deepened, I hope, in its understanding of the relation of slave labor to the larger political and cultural movements of that time. The final chapters, XIX-XXIV, dealing with slavery in a world of aggressive and ultimately dominant Christianity are entirely new as contrasted with the brief statement made in the Pauly-Wissowa-Kroll treatment. In the chronological setting of the two and a half centuries from the accession of Diocletian to the death of Justinian two problems projected themselves out of the materials upon slavery. Neither the one nor the other is new; but each is culturally important and each deserves a restatement and a new evaluation of precisely what it

ix

signified in the setting of the culture of which it was a part.

The first of these arises out of the observation of the lessening of the space which throughout the previous history of antiquity had separated the free from the enslaved, both legally and in public esteem, especially in the field of labor. This I have thought of in terms of a levelling process which lowered the legal and social status of the free and at the same time raised the standing of the slave group.

The second problem has been that of the attitude of Christianity toward the system of slavery. Why did Christianity reject, in its internal organization and its membership, the inequalities implicit in the doctrine of human enslavement, and still, externally, accept its practice without condemnation?

Throughout the entire book it has been a constant effort on my part to look out of the windows of the slave structures, as I have entered into them, upon the changing scenery of the Greek and Roman Mediterranean cultures in which they stood. At the expense, no doubt, of a more colorful presentation of the entire subject of enslavement I have consciously avoided the use of terms to characterize the enslaved classes of antiquity and their condition which are charged with emotional connotations — such, for example, as " the horrors of slavery," or the descriptive phrases applied to the slave as " servile beast " or as " human merchandise." Though they may have been true in instances, they seem to me, in the main, to distort the picture of slave labor and its practices in antiquity.

It remains for me a pleasant duty to make a few brief acknowledgments of the interest shown by my colleagues in history, at Columbia University and elsewhere, in the development of this study as it progressed and for the many suggestions which came from them which have been valuable to me. In three successive years I had the advantage of working in collaboration with three of my colleagues in history and their graduate students upon general and specific aspects of the slave institutions as these displayed themselves in different parts of the world. Professor Frank Tannenbaum, to whom my personal indebtedness is especially great, and his students presented the problems of slavery in Brazil. Slavery in North America fell to the students in Ameri-

can history under the direction of my friend, Professor John Krout, now Vice President of Columbia University. Professor Geroid Robinson and his group were interested in the broader aspects of bondage as represented in the Russian serf system. The students enrolled with me dealt with the practices of slavery in Greek and Roman antiquity. Since his connection with Columbia University began I have had the benefit, also, of many conversations with Professor Richard Morris upon contrasts and likenesses between the structure of American slavery, in which he is well versed, and the slave institutions of antiquity.

The task of reading and assessing the entire manuscript of this study was undertaken by Professor Thomas R. S. Broughton of Bryn Mawr College. I am grateful to him for the meticulous care with which he did this and for the scholarly knowledge and judgment which enabled me to accept so many of his suggestions.

To M. Georges Daux I am beholden for keeping me in touch with his new publications of Delphic manumissions under the system of the trust sale to Apollo as they appeared and with his admirable revisions and restorations of the documents which had been published in the past. His study of the chronological setting of the Delphic material, in his *Chronologie Delphique*, has been invaluable to me. Professor Rafael Taubenschlag of Warsaw University, through a number of years of daily contact in the Papyrus Room in the Columbia University Library, gave me the benefit of his knowledge of the legal as well as the social problems of slavery in Hellenistic Egypt and during the Roman Empire.

This preface began with mention of the name of the late Michael Ivanovich Rostovtzeff. It is fitting that it should also end with his name. His grasp of ancient economic history in all of its phases naturally included a deep interest in its slave-labor problems. The dedication of this study to his memory is, of course, a tribute to the complete honesty and to the amazing breadth and depth of his scholarship. Quite as much it is a token of gratitude for the gift of friendship which he always displayed and for the generosity with which he used that gift.

W. L. W.

Scarsdale, New York,
June 30, 1954

EDITOR'S NOTE:

Following the death of Dr. Westermann on October 4, great care by Professor John Day, of Barnard College.

1954, the printer's proof of this publication was handled with

ABBREVIATIONS

AJA: American Journal of Archaeology.

AJP: American Journal of Philology.

Abh. Bayer. Akad.: Abhandlungen der Bayerischen Akademie der Wissenschaften, philosophische-philologische Klasse.

Abh. Ber. Akad.: Abhandlungen der Preussischen Akademie der Wissenschaften (Berlin).

Annales du Service: Annales du Service des Antiquités de l'Égypte.

Anuario Español: Anuario de Historia del Derecho Español.

Arch. f. Pap.: Archiv für Papyrusforschung.

Ath. Mitt.: Mitteilungen der deutschen archaeologischen Instituts, athenische Abteilung.

BCH: Bulletin de Correspondance Hellénique.

Berl. Sitzb.: Sitzungsberichte der Preussischen Akademie der Wissenschaften (Berlin).

Bull. Inst. Franc.: Bulletin de l'Institut Français d'Archéologie Orientale du Caire.

Bull. Soc. Alex.: Bulletin de la Société Archéologique d'Alexandrie.

CAF: Comicorum Atticorum fragmenta (ed. Th. Kock).

CAH: Cambridge Ancient History.

Chron. Pasch.: Chronicon Paschale.

CIA: Corpus Inscriptionum Atticarum.

CIL: Corpus Inscriptionum Latinarum.

CIL 1²: Corpus Inscriptionum Latinarum, 2d edition, 1 (parts 1 and 2).

Class. Phil.: Classical Philology.

Class. Quart.: Classical Quarterly.

Class. Rev.: Classical Review.

Ét. de Pap.: Études de Papyrologie. Société Royale égyptienne de Papyrologie.

FCG: Fragmenta Comicorum Graecorum (A. Meineke, Poetae Comici).

FGrH: Fragmenta der griechischen Historiker (ed. F. Jacoby).

FHG: Fragmenta Historicum Graecorum, ed. Carl Müller.

FIR: Fontes Iuris Romani Antiqui (ed. Bruns-Gradenwitz).

GDI: Sammlung der griechischen Dialektinschriften (ed. H. Collitz, Baunack, Bechtel et al.).

Gött. Gel. Anz.: Göttingische Gelehrte Anzeigen.

Harv. Theol. Rev.: Harvard Theological Review.

IG: Inscriptiones Graecae.

IG²: Inscriptiones Graecae (editio minor).

IG Rom.: Inscriptiones Graecae ad Res Romanas Pertinentes, ed. Cagnat, R. et al.

ILS: Inscriptiones Latinae Selectae, ed. Hermann Dessau.

Inscr. Magn.: Die Inschriften von Magnesia am Maeander, ed. Otto Kern.

JEA: Journal of Egyptian Archaeology.

JHS: Journal of Hellenic Studies.

JRS: Journal of Roman Studies.

Just. Codex: Justinian, Corpus Juris Civilis, Codex.

Just. Digest: Justinian, Corpus Juris Civilis, Digesta.

Just. Inst.: Justinian, Corpus Juris Civilis, Instituta.

Just. Nov.: Justinian, Novellae.

Klio: Klio. Beiträge zur alten Geschichte.

MAMA: Monumenta Asiae Minoris Antiqua.

Mél. Bidez: Mélanges Bidez. Annuaire de l'Institut de Philologie et d'Histoire Orientale 2.

Mél. Glotz: Mélanges Gustave Glotz.

Mnemos.: Mnemosyne.

Mon. Ant.: Monumenti Antichi. Reale Accademia dei Lincei.

Münch. Beitr.: Münchener Beiträge zur Papyrusforschung und antiken Rechtsgeschichte.

Mus. Belg.: Musée Belge.

NT: New Testament.

OGI: Orientis Graeci Inscriptiones Selectae, ed. W. Dittenberger.

OT: Old Testament.

Pr: in references to the Corpus Juris Civilis of Justinian, the "beginning," or "initial paragraph."

P. Aberd.: Catalogue of Greek and Latin papyri in the Univ. of Aberdeen, ed. Eric G. Turner.

P. Baden: Veröffentlichungen aus den badischen Papyrus-Sammlungen, by W. Spiegelberg and Gerhard Bilabel.

BGU: Aegyptische Urkunden aus den staatlichen Museen zu Berlin, Griechische Urkunden.

P. Cairo Maspero: Catalogue général des antiquités égyptiennes du Musée du Caire. Papyrus grecs d'époque byzantine, ed. Jean Maspero.

P. Cairo Zenon: Catalogue général des antiquités égyptiennes du Musée du Caire. Zenon papyri, ed. C. C. Edgar.

P. Col.: Columbia Papyri, ed. W. L. Westermann, Clinton Keyes, Elizabeth Hasenoehrl, Herbert Liebesny.

P. Corn: Greek papyri in the library of Cornell University, ed. W. L. Westermann and C. J. Kraemer.

CPR: Corpus papyrorum Raineri.

P. Eitrem 7, in JEA 17: 44-47.

P. Flor.: Papiri greco-egizii, by D. Comparetti and G. Vitelli.

P. Freib: Mitteilungen aus der Freiburger Papyrussammlung, by W. Aly, M. Gelzer, Wilcken and Partsch.

P. Giss.: Griechische Papyri im Museum zu Giessen, by O. Eger, E. Kornemann, P. M. Meyer.

P. Giss. no. 20, in Schriften der hessischen Hochschulen, Univ. Giessen, by H. Büttner.

P. Goodspeed: Greek papyri in the Cairo Museum, by E. Goodspeed.

P. Grenf. 1: An Alexandrian erotic fragment, etc., by Bernard P. Grenfell.

P. Grenf. 2: New classical fragments and other Greek and Latin papyri, by B. P. Grenfell and A. S. Hunt.

P. Gron.: Papyri Groninganae: Griechische Papyri der Universitätsbibliothek zu Amsterdam, ed. A. G. Roos.

P. Hal.: Dikaiomata, Auszüge aus Alexandrinischen Gesetzen und Verordnungen, by the Graeca Halensis.

P. Ham.: Griechische Papyrusurkunden der Hamburger Staats- und Universitätsbibliothek, ed. P. M. Meyer.

P. Harris: The Rendel Harris Papyri of Woodbrooke College, ed. J. E. Powell.

P. Jand.: Papyri Jandanae, ed. C. Kalbfleisch and students.

P. Leipz.: Griechische Urkunden der Papyrussammlung zu Leipzig, ed. L. Mitteis.

P. Lille: Papyrus grecs, by Jouguet, Pierre, P. Collart, J. Lesquier, M. Xoual.

P. Lond.: Greek papyri in the British Museum, F. G. Kenyon and H. I. Bell.

P. Mich.: Michigan papyri, ed. A. E. R. Boak, J. G. Winter, E. M. Husselman, W. F. Edgerton, H. C. Youtie, O. M. Pearl.

P. Mich. Zenon: Zenon papyri in the Univ. of Michigan collection, ed. C. C. Edgar.

P. Oxy: Oxyrhynchus papyri, ed. B. P. Grenfell, A. S. Hunt, H. I. Bell, E. Lobel, and others, 21 v.

P. Paris: Notices et extraits des papyrus grecs du Musée du Louvre, ed. Brunet de Presle.

Pauly-W., RE: Pauly-Wissowa-Kroll-Mittelhaus, Real-Encyclopädie der classischen Altertumswissenschaft.

P. Petrie: The Flinders Petrie papyri, ed. J. P. Mahaffy and J. G. Smyly.

P. Prin.: Papyri in the Princeton University collections, ed. A. C. Johnson, H. B. Van Hoesen, E. H. Kase, Jr.

SLAVE SYSTEMS OF GREEK AND ROMAN ANTIQUITY

P. Rev.: Revenue laws of Ptolemy Philadelphus, by Bernard
P. Grenfell.

P. Ross. Georg.: Papyri russischer und georgischer Sammlungen, by G. Zereteli, Krüger, P. Jernstedt.

P. Ryl.: Catalogue of the papyri in the John Rylands library,
ed. A. S. Hunt, J. de M. Johnson, V. Martin, C. H. Roberts,
E. G. Turner.

PSI: Pubblicazioni della Società Italiana, Papiri greci e latini,
ed. G. Vitelli, Medea Norsa.

P. Schow: Charta graece scripta Musei Borgiani, ed. N. Schow.

P. Strassb. inv. no. 1409: Friedr. Preisigke, Ein Sklavenkauf
des 6 Jahrhunderts, Arch. f. Pap. 3: 419.

P. Strassb.: Griech. Papyrus der kaiserl. Universitäts- und
Landesbibliothek zu Strassburg, ed. Fr. Preisigke.

P. Teb.: Tebtunis papyri, by B. P. Grenfell, A. S. Hunt, J. G.
Smyly, E. Goodspeed, C. C. Edgar.

P. Thead.: Papyrus de Théadelphie, by P. Jouguet.

Phil.: Philologus.

RE: See Pauly-W., RE, above.

Rev. Ét. Anc.: Revue des Études Anciennes.

Rev. Ét. Grec.: Revue des Etudes Grecs.

Rev. Phil.: Revue de Philologie.

Rh. Mus.: Rheinisches Museum.

Rom. Mitt.: Mitteilungen des deutschen archäologischen Instituts, römische Abteilung.

Rüsch Gram.: Grammatik der delphischen Inschriften, by E.
Rüsch.

Scrip. Hist. Aug.: Scriptores Historiae Augustae.

SIG²: Sylloge Inscriptionum Graecarum, 2nd ed. by W. Dittenberger.

SIG³: Sylloge Inscr. Graecarum, 3d ed., Dittenberger.

Suppl. Epigr.: Supplementum Epigraphicum Graecum, ed. J. J.
E. Hondius.

Sitzb. Heidelb. Akad.: Sitzungsberichte der Heidelberger Akad.
der Wissenschaften, phil.-hist. Klasse.

Stud. Pal.: Studien zur Paläographie und Papyruskunde, ed.
C. Wessely.

TAPA: Transactions of the American Philological Association.

UPZ: Urkunden der Ptolemäerzeit, by Ulrich Wilcken.

WkP: Wochenschrift für klassische Philologie.

Wien. Sitzb.: Sitzungsberichte der kaiserl. Akademie der Wissenschaften in Wien, phil.-hist. Klasse.

Yale Class. Stud.: Yale Classical Studies.

Ztsch. d. Sav.-Stift.: Zeitschrift der Savigny-Stiftung für Rechtsgeschichte, romanistische Abteilung.

I. GREEK SLAVERY FROM HOMER TO THE PERSIAN WARS

Slavery existed throughout the history of antiquity side by side with free labor as a constant factor of the changing social and economic order. Both by masters and by slaves it was regarded as an inevitable and unavertable condition.[1] In his discussion of the origins of the state, at the beginning of the *Politics*, Aristotle gives the connections between master and slave, husband and wife, father and children as the three fundamental social expressions of the relationship between rulers and ruled in any organized society. His decision that the master-slave relation is consistent with nature stands in opposition to another philosophic explanation which regarded slavery as expedient, but justified only by man-made law, not by nature. Neither Aristotle nor those whom he opposed conceived the possibility of the abolition of slavery, the discussion being merely an academic one regarding the genesis of the institution. This attitude of complete acceptance of slavery, despite the continuance of the debate as to its genesis in nature or through human agency, is characteristic of the literary attitude toward it as an institution throughout antiquity.

The quantitative proportion between the free and the slave populations varied greatly according to the economic conditions which favored or were adverse to the use of slaves in each locality at a particular period. Occasional statements regarding the numbers of slaves in given places are available; but these are scattered and untrustworthy. Statistical treatment of such scattered numbers is impossible. Considering the constant presence of slavery and its inherent importance in ancient life, there is surprisingly little literary discussion of the subject from antiquity. This attitude of complete and unquestioning acceptance goes so far that no single ancient author has written specifically and separately upon slave life or slave problems.

The treatment and the living conditions of slaves varied according to individual owners and to the changing economic uses of slave labor, to the extent that no general rule can be laid down. Comparisons and inferences taken from modern slavery are dangerous and misleading, particularly in view of the Christian-moralistic attitude which became dominant in the anti-slavery discussion of the nineteenth century. Slavery was in antiquity purely a practical problem. Ethical considerations entered, of course, into the relations between individual masters and their slaves; but these moral standards were not applied in the consideration of the slave system *per se* until the Christian literature of the post-Diocletian era appeared. Even then any criticisms of the institution of slavery are implied rather than boldly expressed. This peculiarity does not preclude the constant feeling from Homer onward that when the day of slavery had overtaken a man, fate had deprived him of the half of his capacity,[2] and that slave status was a wretched and degrading condition for one who had known freedom. In the Greek and in the Roman legislation affecting slaves a constant paradox appears which is inherent in the very nature of the institution itself, that the slave, theoretically considered, was a chattel and as such was subject only to the laws governing private property, but that he was, in actuality, also a human being and subject to protective legislation affecting human individuals.

In the discussion of slavery which follows, a sharp distinction has been maintained between actual slavery and serfdom in the various forms in which this type of bondage appeared in antiquity, such as helotry,[3] the Roman colonate,[4] and the system of indentured service called *paramonē* in the Greek world which still applied to some of the manumitted slaves. Slavery is to be distinguished from serfdom in that the slave is the property of another man, whereas the serf is bound to the place of his labor obligations, not to a man, and owes to his lord only specified annual services. In the Greek *paramonē* relation the duration of the duties to be exacted of the person involved was temporarily limited and the condition, therefore, was not complete slavery (*douleia*; Latin *servitudo*). The peculiar conditions of ancient slavery demand, however, that the state slaves (*demosioi*; Latin *servi publici*)[5] be included in the discussion as well as those owned by the religious organizations.

GREEK SLAVERY IN THE HOMERIC PERIOD

The statement of Hecataeus[6] that the Greeks had no slaves in the primitive period of the construction of the walls of Athens has no value as evidence. We can only theorize regarding the beginnings of slavery in the Greek as well as in the Roman world. Factually, in both areas, its origins are completely closed to our view. In the period of the Homeric poems, slave-owning by individuals, as one element of the private ownership of property, was already fully developed.[7] The number of

---

[1] Meyer, Ed., Die Sklaverei im Altertum, *Kleine Schriften*, 2nd ed., 1: 211, 1924.

[2] Homer, *Odyssey* 17: 322-323.

[3] Pauly-Wissowa-Kroll, *Real-Encyclopädie der classischen Altertumswissenschaft* (= *RE*) 8: 203-206.

[4] *Ibid.* 4: 483-510.

[5] *Ibid.* 5: 161.

[6] It appears in Herodotus 6: 137.

[7] Swoboda, H., *Zeitschrift der Savigny-Stiftung, Rom. Abt.* 26: 241.

the slaves owned, even by the wealthiest chieftains, was surprisingly limited;[8] and the type of slavery was so mild that it is difficult to distinguish it at times from patriarchal clientage or serfdom.[9] The Homeric designation for "slave" is *dmōs*, feminine plural *dmōai*. The customary Greek word *doulos* appears but twice in the *Iliad* and *Odyssey*.[10] The *dmōes* as slaves are distinctly contrasted with the *amphipoloi*, free servants, in the *Odyssey* 9: 206; but the essential meanings of the two terms are not strictly maintained by the epic writers.[11] For princely households such as the palace of Alcinous [12] and that of Odysseus [13] fifty female slaves seem to have represented the standard number. Indefinite references occur to male slaves owned by Odysseus;[14] but their number was certainly not large. Definitely known are only Eumaeus, the swineherd,[15] and Dolius,[16] the latter married to a Sicilian woman who was also apparently a slave.[17] Confirmatory evidence upon the relatively small number of slaves in the Homeric period is to be found in the negative observation that slaves do not appear as body servants (*therapontes*) and military attendants of the fighting men; that slave dealers do not appear in the epics; that there is no wholesale raiding for slaves; and that even the common labors of agriculture and herding are supplied in considerable part by hired labor.[18]

Slaves in the Homeric period were obtained by capture in war and by casual and sporadic, rather than organized, stealing of men, women, and children.[19] Armed raids for the express purpose of capturing slaves were not customary. Henri Wallon's idea that the capture of slaves was a distinct purpose of Homeric warfare was the cause of his exaggeration of the importance of slavery until it became the entire background of the Homeric scene.[20] Men of fighting age when captured alive, an occurrence which was regarded as unusual,[21] were customarily ransomed;[22] but Achilles boasts that he had captured alive and sold many Trojan men.[23] Women and children taken during the capture of a town were spared, and the fate of slavery was expected for them.[24] Agamemnon alone received as his share of the booty from the capture of Lesbos seven women as slaves; and such female slaves were passed about as gifts between chieftains.[25] Young and comely female captives were used as concubines by the Homeric chieftains, both under conditions of warfare and in time of peace. Out of this situation, in rare instances, the slave concubine might rise to the position of legal wife, as in the promise to Briseis.[26] Captive women were equally prized for their knowledge of the household labors of spinning and weaving;[27] usefulness of this kind was the lasting service of such captives after their physical attractiveness had passed. Houseborn slaves do not appear at all in the epics. The false story told by Odysseus, that he was the child of a slave concubine,[28] yet had inherited from his father along with his legitimate half-brother, suggests that houseborn children of master and slave women were regarded as free. No case of formal manumission appears, nor any example of limited bond service, *paramone*. The incident of Poseidon and Apollo in the *Iliad* 21: 444-445 is a simple contract of labor for hire for one year which has been wrongly interpreted by Beauchet as a *paramonē* agreement.[29]

There is no example of enslavement or self-sale because of debt in the two epics. It is probable, however, that this old institution had already established itself among the Greek tribes. The Phoenicians twice appear as traders in slaves,[30] the Taphians twice.[31] Slaves captured about Troy were sold to the islands of Samos and Imbros as well as to Lemnos.[32] Only two cases occur in which the purchase price of slaves is given, both involving females.[33] The difference in price in these two cases may be explained in the first instance by evaluation at the source, i. e. upon the war front,

---

[8] This is correctly assessed by Ed. Meyer in his *Kleine Schriften* 1: 183, as against Francotte's view in *RE* 9: 1386.

[9] Seymour, Th. D., *Life in the Homeric Age*, 260, New York, Macmillan, 1907.

[10] *Doulē, Iliad* 3: 409; *Odyssey* 4: 12. Compare the derivative *doulosunē, Odyssey* 22: 423 and the adjectival form in *doulion ēmar*, "the day of enslavement" in *Iliad* 6: 463 and 24: 729.

[11] The *dmōai gunaikes* (slave women) of *Odyssey* 7: 103 and the *amphipoloi gunaikes* of *Odyssey* 6: 51-52, for example, do the same work.

[12] *Odyssey* 7: 103.

[13] *Ibid.* 22: 420-423.

[14] *Ibid.* 1: 398; 14: 399.

[15] *Ibid.* 14: 115; 15: 364-366.

[16] *Ibid.* 4: 735-736.

[17] *Ibid.* 24: 365-366, 389-390; the status of their six sons is doubtful.

[18] *Ibid.* 10: 84-85; 13: 222, Athena as free herdsman; 18: 357-358, Odysseus desired as free hired man to build walls and plant trees; *Iliad* 11: 676, the herders of cattle in Elis are country folk, *laoi agroiokoi*, obviously free; *Iliad* 13: 390, the cutting down of trees is done by carpenters, not by slaves. *Cf.* Beloch, Jul., *Die Bevölkerung der griechisch-römischen Welt*, 493, Leipzig, Duncker und Humblot, 1886.

[19] *Iliad* 21: 453-454; *Odyssey* 14: 264-265, where the men were slain; *ibid.* 14: 340 and 415-484, where the slave snatchers were Phoenician traders.

[20] Wallon, Henri, *Histoire de l'esclavage dans l'antiquité* 1: 60, 66, 70, Paris, Librairie Hachette, 1879.

[21] *Iliad* 9: 592-593.

[22] *Ibid.* 9: 104-106; 21: 35-42, 78-79, where the purchase price of Lycaon, a prince, in expectation of a large ransom, was extraordinarily high.

[23] *Ibid.* 21: 102.

[24] E. g. *Iliad* 6: 455; 9: 594; 16: 830-832; *Odyssey* 8: 527-529.

[25] *Iliad* 9: 128-131; *Odyssey* 24: 278-279; *cf.* the male slave, Dolius, given to Penelope by her father, *Odyssey* 4: 736.

[26] *Iliad* 19: 297.

[27] *Ibid.* 10: 128; 19: 245.

[28] *Odyssey* 14: 200-204: ἐμὲ δ' ὠνητὴ τέκε μήτηρ.

[29] Daremberg-Saglio, *Dictionnaire des antiquités* 4²: 1261.

[30] *Odyssey* 14: 297; 15: 473-483.

[31] *Ibid.* 14: 452; 15: 427-428.

[32] *Iliad* 7: 475; 24: 753.

[33] *Ibid.* 23: 705, a woman worth four cattle; *Odyssey* 1: 430, where Laertes paid twenty cattle for the nurse, Euryclea.

and by eventual sale price upon delivery at a distant island in the second case.

Making necessary allowance for the aristocratic point of view intrinsic in the epic poems and its consequent master morale, it is still clear that the treatment of slaves by their owners was notably mild and kindly. It was based fundamentally upon the solidarity of the *familia* as represented in the economic household organization characteristic of the period. Conversely, the Homeric poems represent the slaves, on the whole, as loyal and devoted, often to the point that relations of marked affection existed between them and members of the households of which they were a part.[34] Such examples of good feeling depended, to be sure, upon the individual characters of both slave and master. As instances of evil actions done by slaves one need only recall the betrayal of Eumaeus when a child to Phoenician traders by a slave woman,[35] and the disloyalty of the young female slaves of Odysseus to his household which resulted in the hanging of them.[36]

Slave-owners did not disdain to do the same type of physical work as was performed by the slaves; but the living conditions of slaves fell, in general, far below those of the masters.[37] Only a slight difference can have existed between the standards of living of the Homeric slaves and the free workmen (*thētes*) of the time. This conclusion is implied in the well-known statement of Achilles that after his death he would prefer to work for hire for a propertyless man than rule in Hades:[38] for he had selected, as typical example of a bitter life on earth, that of a hired farm laborer rather than the life of a slave.

From the legal standpoint, custom gave the master complete and arbitrary control over his slaves, to the power of life and death over them.[39] From the scanty data which we have upon the slave's right to marry or own a house, it appears that these rights depended upon the whim and consent of the slave-owner.[40] The work

performed by slaves did not differ from that done by free servants. Women slaves, used in the work of the master's household, were not drawn into the heavier or outdoor tasks of farm life. They prepared food and served it,[41] prepared the bath of the masters and served them when bathing,[42] acted as chamber servants,[43] spun yarn and ground meal;[44] but such tasks were also attended to by servants who were free.[45]

FROM HOMER TO THE PERSIAN WARS

The Homeric situation has demanded the foregoing elaborate analysis because it establishes the general picture of a mild form of agricultural and household use of slaves which persisted into the second century B. C., though with varying intensity, in those parts of the Greek world which did not become handicraft production areas. In those Greek states in which helotry or other forms of serfdom persisted, such as Sparta and Thessaly, any important development of slavery is not to be expected.

During the eighth and seventh centuries events occurred which had a profound influence upon all social and economic phases of Hellenic life. These were the colonization of the Mediterranean littoral, the introduction of coined money in exchange, and the early stages of the Hellenic industrializing of handicraft production. That these changes gradually increased the use of slaves and eventually altered the whole type of Greek slavery cannot be questioned. The net results of these three relatively concurrent events are known; but the comparative importance and influence of each one of them in spreading and intensifying the use of slaves must remain a problem of speculation. Although adequate contemporary evidence is lacking, the economic and social conditions existing in the Greek world in the seventh century were such as to warrant the assumption that the change to the use of slave labor in the handicraft industries and to a larger application of slave labor in general was well under way before 600 B. C.[46] The existence of a considerable number of debtor slaves in Attica as early as Solon's time, although Athens was still relatively in the background of the commercial trends, and the fact that an export market for these slaves existed in other Greek city-states may be cited in support of the statement above.

[34] Examples of this are: Eurycleia and Penelope, *Odyssey* 4:743-746; Eurycleia and Telemachus, *Odyssey* 19:482, 492; Eurycleia and Odysseus in the moving scene of recognition by the nurse, *Odyssey* 19:467-475. Compare with this the hope of Agamemnon that he might return to his home welcome to his children and his free and slave servants, δμώεσσιν, *Odyssey* 11:431, and the rearing of the slave boy, Eumaeus, in the household of Laertes along with the daughter Ctimene, *Odyssey* 15:365; *cf.* 557: ἀνάκτεσιν ἤπια εἰδώς.

[35] *Odyssey* 15:415-481.

[36] *Ibid.* 22:424-425, 465-473.

[37] This is a view of the situation opposed to that of L. Beauchet, *Histoire du droit privé de la république Athénienne* 2:397, Paris, Librairie Marescq Ainé, 1897, who based his view upon the conditions under which Laertes, father of Odysseus, was living in the company of the slaves, *Odyssey* 11:190. The circumstances in this case were, however, quite untypical.

[38] *Odyssey* 11:489-491.

[39] *Iliad* 23:174-176; *Odyssey* 22:465-473.

[40] *Odyssey* 21:214-215. *Cf.* 14:61-63, where the slave Eumaeus expresses his hope for a *peculium*, house and wife from his master. See M. Weber, *Gesammelte Aufsätze zur Sozial- und Wirtschaftsgeschichte*, 101 n. 1, Tübingen, J. C. B. Mohr,

1924, who correctly uses this incident to prove that no marked line of distinction existed between purchase slaves and clients.

[41] *Odyssey* 3:428.

[42] *Ibid.* 4:49.

[43] *Ibid.* 7:8.

[44] *Ibid.* 7:103.

[45] ἀμφίπολοι, *Odyssey* 6:52.

[46] Glotz, G., *Ancient Greece at work*, 71, 74, London, Kegan Paul, Trench, Trubner & Co.; New York, Alfred A. Knopf, 1926; and the more conservative statement of Hasebroek, J., *Griechische Wirtschafts- und Gesellschaftsgeschichte bis zur Perserzeit*, 82, Tübingen, J. C. B. Mohr, 1931.

For the period 750-600 B. C. we have slight indications of the type of slavery in Boeotia presented in Hesiod.[47] The word for slave is still the Homeric *dmōs*. For Hesiod the essential elements of the life of the small peasant are a house, a wife, and an ox for plowing.[48] Notable here is the complete omission of slaves as a fundamental necessity. The peasant of modest means of the type of Hesiod might well have slaves[49] but he also used hired labor.[50] For Boeotia, therefore, the type of slavery had not changed greatly from that depicted in the Homeric poems.

In the older agricultural colonies established in the Pontic regions, in Thrace, and in the West, there is no reason to suppose that conditions differed greatly in respect to farm labor and slavery, considering the pacific relations generally established between the colonies and the indigenous populations.[51] Sale to the Greek colonists by the native populations of captives taken in their intertribal wars had presumably widened the sources of slave supply open to the Greeks, sufficiently to meet an increase in the demand which may be conjectured because of the development of Greek handicraft industries and the rapid spread of the use of coined money. Because of the collapse of the patriarchal system and the increase in the variety of needs to be satisfied, the family organization could no longer have sufficed to furnish the necessary amount or the variety of aptitudes required in the labor market.[52] In the situation thus created, the Greeks turned increasingly to slave labor, with which they had long been acquainted. The assumption by the *polis*, in the laws of Draco, of the right to inflict the same punishment for the murder of a slave as for the murder of a free man[53] also presupposes some increase in the number of slaves and in the importance of slavery even in Attica. The purchase and manumission of a slave courtesan by Charaxus, brother of Sappho, gives some idea of slavery in the Greek community of Naucratis in Egypt.[54]

Both Theopompus and Posidonius ascribed to the Chians first among the Greeks the use of non-Greek slaves obtained by purchase.[55] The supposition that these slaves were to be used in the small handicrafts of the time, as well as in the winegrowing for which Chios was famous, gains support from the statement of Herodotus[56] regarding the early development of metallurgy at Chios. Periander, tyrant of Corinth, passed a law against the ownership of slaves, which, according to Nicolaus of Damascus,[57] was motivated by the desire of Periander for political reasons to keep the citizens at work.[58] It should not be connected with agitation of the free working population against slavery as suggested by Ed. Meyer, *Kleine Schriften* 1: 198; much less to the alleged desire to protect small domestic industries against "large slave factories."[59] Increased use of slaves, presumably in agriculture, in Attica is suggested by the practice of enslavement of debtors known to us from the abolition of self-sale or sale of members of one's family by Solon in 594 B. C.; by laws ascribed to Solon, one forbidding slaves to anoint themselves with oil or to practice homosexuality,[60] and a second making slave-owners responsible for damage inflicted by slaves.[61] For Crete the treatment of slaves as a class in the laws of Gortyn predicates a fairly large number and their legal formulation into a distinct social group.[62]

The conclusion that slavery increased in importance finds support in the appearance in the sixth century of a characteristic indirect tax for the exchange of slaves by sale in Cyzicus.[63] The abolition by Solon of the right of the individual in Attica to mortgage himself, his wife or his children for debt was far-reaching in its consequences. Solon states that many of the poor had been loaded with shameful bonds and sold into foreign lands[64] and that he had brought back to Athens many who had been sold, justly or unjustly.[65] Plutarch[66] has correctly stated that some of those enslaved for debt had remained in Attica as slaves of Attic masters.[67] There were two ways by which a debtor could be reduced to slavery,[68] by voluntary self-submission to servitude or by judicial decision when the total property of the debtor did not suffice to meet the debt obligation.

The Attic law of Solon prohibiting the sale of one's own person or that of wife or child was widely imitated

[47] Hesiod, *Works and days*.

[48] *Ibid.*, 405, rejecting the following line: κτητήν, οὐ γαμετήν, ἥτις καὶ βουσὶν ἔποιτο as an interpolation after Aristotle's time.

[49] δμῶες, Hesiod, *Works and days*, 470, 573, 597, 766.

[50] θῆτες; and a hired woman, ἔριθος, *ibid.*, 602-603.

[51] Glotz, G., *Histoire ancienne, deuxième partie, Histoire grecque* 1: 155, Paris, Les Presses Universitaires de France, 1925.

[52] Glotz, G., *Ancient Greece at work*, 84.

[53] This rests upon a restoration generally accepted. *Cf.* Dittenberger, *Sylloge*³, 111 n. 18.

[54] Herodotus, 2: 135; Strabo, 17: 808; Athenaeus, 13: 596.

[55] Jacoby, F., *Die Fragmente der griechischen Historiker* (= *FGrH*) **2B**: 654 and **2A**: 249.

[56] Herodotus, 1: 25.

[57] *Frg.* 58, FGrH **2A**: 357.

[58] Laqueur, R., Hellenismus, *Schriften der hessischen Hochschulen, Universität Giessen* 1: 29, 1924.

[59] This modern rationalization is correctly rejected by Ure, P. N., *The origin of tyranny*, 192 n. 1, Cambridge, England, Univ. Press, 1922.

[60] Plutarch, *Solon*, 1, 3.

[61] Hypereides, 5, 22.

[62] Collitz, H. and F. Bechtel, *Sammlung der griechischen Dialekt-Inschriften* (= *GDI*), no. 4991.

[63] ἀνδραποδωνίη, Dittenberger, *Sylloge*³, 4.

[64] Diehl, E., (ed.), *Anthologia Lyrica Graeca* (= Diehl), frg. 3, 23-25; Bergk, Th., (ed.), *Poetae Lyrici Graeci* (= Bergk), frg. 4, 23-25.

[65] Diehl, frg. 24, 8-10; Bergk, frg. 36, 8-10: πολλοὺς δ' Ἀθήνας πατρίδ' ἐς θεόκτιτον ἀνήγαγον πραθέντας; *cf.* Aristotle, *Constitution of Athens*, 6: κωλύσας δανείζειν ἐπὶ τοῖς σώμασιν; Plutarch, *Solon*, 15, 3.

[66] Plutarch, *Solon*, 13, 2.

[67] Swoboda, H., *Zeitschrift der Savigny-Stiftung, Rom. Abt.* **26**: 212 against Ed. Meyer, *Kleine Schriften* 1: 177 n. 1.

[68] Swoboda, *loc. cit.*, 212-213.

or adopted in the Greek world, so that personal mortgage for debt to individuals and its possible consequence of enslavement ceased to exist in most of the Greek city-states, though not in Gortyn in Crete and possibly not in other places. The Solonian legislation applied only to the executory right of persons to enslave others for debt and was limited in its effects because it did not preclude enslavement of free persons through debt to the state.[69] Slavery incurred by debt was thus certainly eliminated as a source of slave recruitment of any consequence to the Greek world until the Hellenistic period.

The fragmentary data available for the sixth century reveal a liberal attitude on the part of the early tyrants

toward the manumission of slaves.[70] This is to be ascribed to personal political reasons rather than to a fear inspired by greatly increased slave numbers. This liberal policy certainly was followed by Cleisthenes in Attica after the overthrow of the tyranny when he enrolled many metics and slaves in the newly organized Athenian tribes.[71] The absence of a rigid social stratification which separated the slaves from the lower class free population is further indicated by their admission into the Orphic and Eleusinian mysteries on a basis of religious equality.[72]

---

[70] Aristotle, *Politics*, 1315a.
[71] *Ibid.*, 1275b.
[72] *Cf.* Willoughby, H. R., *Pagan Regeneration*, 38, Chicago, Univ. of Chicago Press, 1929.

---

[69] Weiss, E., *Griechisches Privatrecht*, 508, Leipzig, Felix Meiner, 1923.

II. FROM THE PERSIAN WARS TO ALEXANDER

SLAVE SUPPLY AND SLAVE NUMBERS

The available data upon slavery, though still unsatisfactory in quantity and continuity of the conclusions to be obtained, become more numerous and more capable of intelligent and detailed treatment, the bulk of the information centering upon conditions in the Athenian city-state. The period as a whole is marked by an increase in the number of slaves relative to that of the free population; by increased employment of slave labor in handicraft industries in those cities which became centers of industrial production through small shop labor and through household labor for sale of the product to distributing agencies; and by the practice of capital investment in slaves for this type of household labor or in slaves which were leased to shop owners as instruments of production and sources of income to their owners. In Attica the extension of mining of silver on the Laurian promontory brought with it the use of slaves leased by their owners for mining labor upon a considerable scale.

The transition of status of individuals from freedom to slave condition[1] and conversely from slavery through manumission to free status occurred with greater frequency and ease. An increased social consciousness of slaves as a class followed upon the increase in their numbers. This social awareness in its turn gave rise to discussions of the origin of slavery, the treatment of slaves, and their place in the political systems of that time. The specific and incontrovertible designations for slaves are: *doulos*, which remained in constant and predominant use throughout the rest of antiquity both in the legal and popular usages; *andrapodon*, a word legally clear and admissible[2] which tended to give way

before *doulos* but was constantly used in the verb and adjectival form and in the noun compounds, such as *andrapodizesthai, andrapodistes, andrapodōniē*; *sōma andreion* and *sōma gunaikeion* which are in constant use in the manumission inscriptions. *Sōma* alone was not sufficiently explicit for legal use,[3] although it sometimes appears singly with the meaning of "slave" in the loose usage of the classical authors.[4] Caution must be used in the translation of the numerous words such as *oiketēs, therapōn, pais, paidarion*, which fundamentally have another significance than "slave" but are often, though loosely, employed by the ancient writers with that meaning.[5] See, however, *oiketas* in the letter of Philip V of Macedon of 214 B. C.[6] used as "slave"; but compare the correct antithesis of *hypēretai* with the meaning of "servants," in opposition to *douloi* "slaves," in Plato, *Statesman*, 289c: *tode de doulōn kai pantōn hupēretōn loipon.*

Slave status might fortuitously be the lot of any person, whether occurring by the accident of birth or in the lifetime of one born free, by captivity in war, by kidnapping or by some misfortune which altered one's economic status.[7] Throughout antiquity slave condition was heritable, in some places through the male, in others through the female parent.[8] The importance of

---

480, διάγραμμα τῶν ἀνδραπόδων, of 198-197 B. C. in Westermann, W. L., *Upon slavery in Ptolemaic Egypt*, New York, Columbia Univ. Press, 1929.
[3] Pollux, 3:78: σώματα δ᾽ οὐκ ἂν εἴποις, ἀλλὰ δοῦλα σώματα.
[4] Xenophon, *Cyropaedia* 7:5,73.
[5] Pollux, 7:78 restricts the use of παῖς as "slave" to the Attic writers.
[6] Dittenberger, *SIG*³ 2 no. 543:32.
[7] Aristophanes, *Plutus*, 147-148: διὰ μικρὸν ἀργυρίδιον δοῦλος γεγένημαι.
[8] Beauchet, L., *Histoire du droit privé de la république Athénienne* 2:404-409.

---

[1] E. g. the Athenian Euxitheus who became a slave by capture in the Decelean War, Demosthenes 57:18.
[2] Herod., 6:19. Columbia papyrus (= *P. Col.*) inventory no.

birth as a source of slavery differed widely according to local laws as to inheritance of status from one parent alone or from both parents, and according to the economic conditions which might at any time favor or discourage marriage between slaves or concubinage of slave-owners with slave women.

Exposure of undesired infants, a practice legally recognized in some of the Greek city-states,[9] became a minor source of slavery.[10] At Thebes certainly,[11] presumably also in other localities, infant exposure was forbidden on penalty of death, with substitution, in the case of Thebes, of legalized sale into slavery of a child by the father on proof of extreme poverty. Where exposure was practiced the rescue of abandoned children for future use as slaves must have been restricted by the expense and hazard entailed by the years of unprofitable outlay upon the rearing of such children. The additional danger was always present that the right of the original owner, in case the child was of slave status, might at any time be brought forward and that an exposed child of free birth might always regain its original status upon proof of free family connection.[12] Information upon infant exposure with resultant slavery was formerly based upon the Attic drama [13] and upon its use as a stock stage device of the New Comedy.[14] The practice is now firmly attested by actual cases supplied by the papyri from Roman Egypt where the legal designation for it was "to rescue from the dung-pile for enslavement."[15] This terminology appears also officially much later in the instructions given to the Idios Logos in Roman Egypt.[16] The adoption of exposed male children by the lower class Egyptians was connected with payments of money, but it was not forbidden to take them as slaves.[17]

The effects of piracy and the varying intensity of piratical activity as contributing to the slave supply can be followed with some degree of accuracy.[18] Its effectiveness as a source of supply varied according to the absence or presence of a dominant sea power both capable of sea control and economically interested in the repression of piracy.[19] It was also influenced, of course, by the prevailing market demand for slave labor. The constant danger of seizure of free persons and the illicit export of them for sale into slavery is apparent from the law of Athens against slave-snatchers and the penalty of death imposed for its infringement.[20] The death penalty was also applied at Corinth for this crime as in the case of the brother of Agoratus in Lysias, 13, 67, dealing with the seizure of the small daughter of a citizen of Corinth. Under the tyrants of the latter half of the sixth and the early years of the fifth centuries conditions along the Greek shores were favorable to enslavement through kidnapping as shown by the incident cited by Herodotus, 6, 16 when Chian refugees, mistaken by the Ephesians for pirates, were attacked and killed. A law of the city-state of Teos is known which called for the death penalty for anyone who harbored a pirate.[21]

The references to slavery for the late sixth and early fifth centuries are exceedingly scant; but they seem to show that the western satrapies of the Persian Empire, rather than the Greek city-states, offered the best market for slaves.[22] The tyrant Polycrates, for example, did not have available at Samos a sufficient number of slaves technically equipped for his building operations and was, therefore, compelled to send for paid workmen from abroad.[23] Herodotus gives no evidence of an increase in slave numbers in the Greek cities due to captures in the course of the Persian wars; and the account given by Thucydides, 1 : 90, of the rebuilding of the walls of Athens in 479 B. C. indicates that there was no large supply of slaves then available in Attica.[24]

A considerable increase in the relative numbers and in the importance of the slave population must be assumed for the period of the so-called pentēkontaëtia at Athens (479-431 B. C.), as well as in the other cities which based their economic welfare on small handicraft

[9] Daremberg-Saglio, Dictionnaire des antiquités 2 (1) : 930. For Crete, Laws of Gortyn, 3, 44-49, Bücheler-Zitelmann in Rh. Mus. 40, Ergänzungsheft.

[10] Glotz, G., Études sociales et juridiques sur l'antiquité grecque, 187-227, Paris, Librairie Hachette, 1906.

[11] Aelian, Varia historia 2 : 7.

[12] Daremberg-Saglio, Dictionnaire 2(2) : 935.

[13] Euripides, Ion, 524; Aristophanes, Clouds, 530-532; cf. Plato, Theaetetus, 160e; Aristotle, Politics 7 : 16, 10.

[14] Menander, Plautus, Terence.

[15] 'Αναίρεσθαι ἀπὸ κοπρίας εἰς δουλείαν. Ägyptische Urkunden aus den Museen zu Berlin, Griechische Urkunden (= BGU) 4 : 1107, 9 of 13 B.C.: δουλικὸν αὐτῆς παιδίον [ἀ]ναίρε[τον]; P. Rein. inv. no. 2111, lines 2-7, a nursing contract of A.D. 26 in Mélanges Gustave Glotz 1 : 243, Paris, Presses Universitaires, 1932; P. Oxy. 1 : 37 of A.D. 41; 1 : 38 of A.D. 49/50; Vitelli, Giacomo, Medea Norsa, Papiri dello Società Italiana (= PSI) 3, no. 203, 3-4 of A.D. 87.

[16] BGU 5, 41 : τῶν ἀναιρουμένων ἀπὸ κοπρ[ίας ἀρσ]ενικά, cf. 107. Petropoulos, G. A., An unpublished Greek papyrus of the Athens collection, Aegyptus 13 : 563-568, 1933.

[17] Schubart, Wilh., Rom und die Ägypter nach dem Gnomon des Idios Logos, Zeitschrift für ägyptische Sprache und Altertumskunde 56 : 84, 1920. See also Maroi, F., Intorno all'adozione degli esposti nell'Egitto romano, Raccolta di scritti in onore di Giacomo Lumbroso, 378-279, Milan, Aegyptus, 1925; Pauly-W., RE 11 : 463.

[18] Ormerod, H. A., Piracy in the ancient world, Liverpool, Univ. Press, 1924. Ziebarth, E., Beiträge zur Geschichte des Seeraubs und Seehandels im alten Griechenland, Hamburgische Universität: Abhandlungen aus dem Gebiet der Auslandskunde 30, 1929.

[19] Ormerod, op. cit., 95, 96, 108, 110, and passim.

[20] Pauly-W., RE 1 : 2134, ἀνδραποδιστής.

[21] Dittenberger, SIG³ 1 : 37-38, lines 21-22.

[22] Herod., 3 : 50, 97, 129, 134, 137 and 9 : 105 where Panionius, a Chian slave dealer, is reported to have sold castrated boys to Sardis and Ephesus.

[23] τεχνίτας ἐπὶ μισθοῖς μεγίστοις, Alexis of Samos in Athenaeus, Deipnosophists 12 : 57.

[24] Gomme, A. W., The population of Athens in the fifth and fourth centuries B. C., 25, n. 5, Oxford, B. Blackwell, 1933.

industries. This supposition arises from the following observations: the charge made by Pericles against the Megarians that they had been guilty of harboring runaway slaves;[25] the expectation of Pericles that in case of war Attica would be harmed by desertions;[26] the provision of the armistice of 423 B. C. that neither signatory would harbor fugitives, either free or slave;[27] and the important statement of Thucydides[28] that, after Decelea in Attica had been permanently occupied in 412 B. C. by a Spartan garrison, more than 20,000 slaves of the Athenians deserted.

Among the causes of the increased demand for slave labor in the fifth century were the expansion in handicraft industries, due in notable part to constant wars and the steady demand for war materials, and the withdrawal of citizen workers from the labor market both by recruitment for service in the field of war and through the increased political demands upon their time arising from the steady course of democratization.[29] Before the beginning of the Peloponnesian war the source of the increase in the slave supply which met this demand must be sought in the customary and legitimate slave trade by purchase from the peripheral non-Greek peoples rather than in war and piracy because of the conciliatory attitude imposed upon Athens in her relations with the revolting members of the Delian League and her strong anti-piratical policy dictated by the necessities of her own commercial interests.[30]

The barbarian lands known to have furnished slaves were Phrygia, Lydia, Caria, Paphlagonia,[31] and Thrace, the Thracians, in fact, being willing to sell their children for slave export;[32] Illyria; and Scythia is proved to have been a source of this human commodity by the use of Scythians as public slaves at Athens. Of sixteen slaves in the group owned in 414 B. C. by Cephisodorus, a wealthy metic resident in the Piraeus, five were Thracians, three were Carians, two were Syrians, two Illyrians; and one came from each of the following countries: Colchis, Scythia, Lydia, and Malta.[33]

During the Peloponnesian war slaughter of the fighting men frequently took the place of the established custom of exchange of prisoners and the release of captured males on payment of ransom.[34] The captive women in such cases were customarily thrown upon the market as slaves. The effects of this inter-Greek bitterness of warfare must have been great; but the traces of these effects upon slave conditions have disappeared. Antiphon, 5, 20, indicates that the ransoming of slaves transported to distant places became a business enterprise carried on by men who made a profit by shipping them back to their homes for a ransom price obtained there. In accordance with an old Greek law, when ransom money was supplied by an individual rather than by the state the ransomed prisoner was obligated to repay the money as a debt incurred.[35]

In 1752 David Hume, in his essay *Of the populousness of ancient nations*,[36] made a determined attack upon the exaggerated number of four hundred thousand slaves at Athens which was based upon a census of Demetrius of Phalerum probably taken in 311 B. C.[37] Since Hume's day all attempts to re-establish confidence in these figures have been in vain.[38] Similarly the 460,000 slaves ascribed to Corinth and the 470,000 in Aegina, as quoted from Aristotle's *Polity of the Aeginetans*,[39] have been generally discarded by modern criticism. Although the numbers given by modern scholars for the Athenian citizens and metics with their families show a certain degree of similarity, the results attained even here cannot lay claim to anything more than probability, without the possibility of statistical foundation. The slave numbers are in much worse case because no statement of the relative proportions of slave to free population has been handed down. Isolated statements available regarding the numbers of slaves placed upon the market must be approached with scepticism. Diodorus, 11 : 62, is our sole source for the report that Cimon of Athens took twenty thousand prisoners in the Eurymedon campaign. There is no statement as to whether these prisoners were ransomed or sold as slaves. If sold they were probably disposed of as soon as possible because of the cost of feeding and transporting them. The effect of the Eurymedon victory of Cimon upon slave numbers and prices at Athens cannot, therefore, be estimated.[40]

Valuable information for the slave numbers in the last quarter of the fifth century is given by Thucydides, 7 : 27, 5, in the statement that, after the Spartan occu-

[25] Thucydides, 1 : 139, 2.
[26] *Ibid.*, 1 : 142, 4, unquestionably with reference to slaves.
[27] *Ibid.*, 4 : 118, 7.
[28] *Ibid.*, 7 : 27, 5.
[29] Oertel, F., Review of Laqueur, R., *Hellenismus*, in *Gnomon* 3 : 95, n. 1.
[30] Against Scyros, Plutarch, *Cimon*, 8; against Thracian pirates in the Chersonese, Plutarch, *Pericles*, 19. *Cf.* the safety of sea-faring, τῆς θαλάττης ὅπως πλέωσι πάντες ἀδεῶς, as a Panhellenic problem proposed by Pericles, *ibid.*, 17.
[31] Euripides, *Orestes*, 1507-1508; *Alcestis*, 675-678. Aristophanes, *Birds*, 763; *Knights*, 44.
[32] Herodotus, 6 : 6.
[33] Dittenberger *SIG*³ 1 : 96, 14-30.
[34] Thucydides, 1 : 29, 5; 2 : 67, 4; 3 : 50, 1; 68, 2; 4 : 48, 4; 5 : 32, 1 etc.

[35] Laws of Gortyn in Crete, 6, 46-56, less fully and specifically known for Athens from Demosthenes, 53, 11 : τοῦ λυσαμένου εἶναι τὸν λυθέντα, ἐὰν μὴ ἀποδιδῷ τὰ λύτρα.
[36] See Hume, David, *Essays moral, political and literary*, edited by Green and Grose 1 : 419-421, London, 1898.
[37] Athenaeus, 6 : 272c, quoting the *Chronica* of one Ctesicles or Stesiclides.
[38] These numbers were defended by Boeckh, Aug., *Die Staatshaushaltung der Athener*, 3rd ed. 1 : 47-49, Berlin, Reimer, 1886, and by Büchsenschütz, B., *Besitz und Erwerb im griechischen Alterthume*, 137-142, Halle, Waisenhaus, 1869.
[39] This is quoted by Athenaeus, 6 : 272 b and d.
[40] Such an attempt was made by Keil, B., *Anonymus Argentinensis*, 84, n. 3, Strassburg, Trübner, 1902.

pation of Decelea, twenty thousand slaves deserted from Attica, of whom the greater part were handicraftsmen.[41] There is no indication of age or sex of the deserters. The time during which the desertions occurred must have covered the full eight years of the "Decelean War," 412-404 B. C. The statement, therefore, can only be used to mean that, in the judgment of a contemporary and careful source who knew Athens at that time, there were not many more than twenty thousand slaves in Attica and that the slave handicraft workers who fled numbered somewhat under the total of the twenty thousand desertions. The report has received support from a passage of the Oxyrhynchus Hellenic history[42] that the Thebans became prosperous after the occupation of Decelea through buying cheaply the slaves and other goods taken in war.

The one thousand slaves allegedly owned by Nicias at Athens at this time and leased by him to silver-mining entrepreneurs, with the six hundred slaves of Hipponicus and the three hundred of Philomenides,[43] deserve small consideration as reliable numbers, since they are reported from a generation later as hearsay evidence[44] by one who can say no more about the slaves leased to the mines in his own day than that there were many of them.[45]

Against these large numbers stands the view of Plato that fifty or more represent the slave possessions of a wealthy man.[46] Plato's idea of the number of slaves which a wealthy man might be expected to possess is borne out with singular exactness by the actual number owned by the orator, Demosthenes. In his prosecution of the guardian of his estate he disclosed to the court that his father had left him an establishment for the manufacture of knives and swords with thirty-two or thirty-three slaves and a workshop for making couch frames with twenty slave workmen trained to this trade.[47] Another Athenian of the same time, a certain Timarchus, had inherited eleven or twelve slaves, including nine or ten leather workers, a woman linen weaver and a leather embroiderer.[48]

The observation that a considerable part of the Attic population had no slaves at all is even more important than the figures given above in proving that the exaggerated numbers which Athenaeus gives must be aban-

doned.[49] The statement should be obvious for the poorer classes of the city.[50] It is, furthermore, definitely proved for the disabled citizen workman for whom Lysias wrote a speech in defense against an action which was brought for the withdrawal of a state dole formerly received by him. The cripple asserted that he could not afford to keep a slave to help him in his trade.[51] It is also to be proven in the case of some individuals of enough means that they became involved in litigation over estate inheritances. One case will be enough to illustrate the fact. One member of a group involved in a complicated litigation did not inventory any slaves in his property. Stratocles, a brother of the defendant in the case, inherited through the death of a daughter a property valued at two and a half talents, or fifteen thousand drachmas in silver. It is listed as consisting of real estate, sixty sheep, a hundred goats and other equipment; but no slaves appear.[52] The inventory of his estate at the time of his death is also given. The estimated total then was put at three thousand drachmas, made up of real property, interest-bearing loans, furniture, sheep, barley, wine, and nine hundred drachmas in silver. Not a single slave appears.

Two extracts from the literature of the period may serve to clinch the argument. In the *Ecclesiazusae* of Aristophanes, produced in 392 B. C., in her proposal for collective ownership of property the feminist, Praxagora, wanted to put an end to a situation in which one person had many slaves and another had not even a single attendant.[53] In respect to the working classes of the population Xenophon makes the significant re-

---

[41] The Greek word is χειροτέχναι.

[42] Grenfell, Bernard P. and A. S. Hunt, *Oxyrhynchus papyri* (= *P. Oxy.*) 5, no. 842, col. xiii, 28-33, 1908; Jacoby, *FGrH* 2: 66, col. xii, 4.

[43] Xenophon, *Ways and means* (= *Poroi*), 4, 14-15.

[44] *Ibid.*: πάλαι μὲν γὰρ . . . ἀκηκόαμεν.

[45] *Ibid.* 4, 16; *cf.* Beloch, J., *Bevölkerung der griechisch-römischen Welt*, 93.

[46] Plato, *Republic* 9: 578e.

[47] Demosthenes, 27, 9 for the knife makers and 24 for the twenty couch makers. In Demosthenes, 37, 4, a loan was made to a mine owner on the security of his mine pit and thirty slaves which he owned.

[48] Aeschines, 1, 97.

[49] Sargent, Rachel L., The size of the slave population at Athens, *Univ. of Illinois Studies in the Social Sciences* 12(3): 101, 1924.

[50] Gomme, A. W., *Population of Athens*, 21, has correctly concluded that the number of domestic slaves in the homes of the lowest class, the thetes, would be negligible because of the expense of keeping them.

[51] Lysias, 24, 6. In the property inherited by the Athenian, Diodotus, in Lysias, 32, 5, amounting to the considerable sum of seven talents, forty minas, and two thousand drachmas, no slaves are included.

[52] Isaeus, 11, 40-41. The defendant and his brother had sufficient means to care for themselves, but not enough to subject them to the liturgical services which fell upon the well-to-do. Since the number of the sheep and goats inherited by the daughter of one of the two men is enumerated, I judge that if the estate had possessed slaves they would be given. I am assuming that the slave inventory of the estate, if there were any slaves, would not be included under the item of "remaining equipment." *Cf.* the further enumeration of the items in the property, *ibid.*, 43. Some of the property, it is true, was not declared in the inventory. Again, however, I do not believe that slave holdings could be concealed in the declaration.

No slaves are included in the modest property holding of Dicaeogenes in Isaeus, 5, 22-23, nor in the dowry of a daughter in 8, 8. In the *Cyropaedia* 1: 1, 1, Xenophon says that some families kept in their homes a considerable number of slaves, others very few. There is no way of determining what proportion of the families in Athens had some slaves and what part owned "very few."

[53] Aristophanes, *Eccleciazusae*, 593.

mark: "*those who can do so* buy slaves so that they may have fellow workmen." [54]

All the evidence which is really significant points toward the conclusion that in Attica the slaves did not comprise more than a third of the total population, possibly not more than a fourth. It must be granted that this statement is no more than a reasonable suggestion. A guess that the slaves in Attica in the earlier period of the Peloponnesian war numbered from sixty thousand to eighty thousand, including both sexes and all ages, would be within the bounds of reason. The consideration must here be emphasized that the slave population in Attica probably exceeded that of any other Greek city-state of the period before Alexander, possibly excepting Chios, for which Thucydides, 7:40, 2, makes the doubtful claim of more slaves than any state except Sparta.[55] Chios, however, could not nourish more than one hundred thousand slaves.[56]

For the numbers of slaves in the Greek world in the fourth century we are even more completely forced back upon rationalized conclusions from insufficient evidence. There is small reason to assume a marked increase in slaveholding in the Greek world although a shift of the type of employment to a greater use of slaves in the handicrafts and in retail selling is probable. In the disturbed conditions of the time kidnapping was rife.[57] A statement in a fragment of Hyperides in a corrupted text [58] which ascribes more than one hundred fifty thousand male slaves, necessarily adults, to the mines in Attica and to the rest of the country, must be discarded as useless for the investigation of the problem.[59] In his well-known proposal for increasing the revenues of the Attic state, assuming the presence of unexplored veins of silver in the Laurian mining district and an unlimited market for increased production, Xenophon presented a plan for the immediate purchase by the state of one thousand two hundred slaves, which number should be increased within five or six years to six thousand slaves to be bought out of the profits of the enterprise. These state-owned slaves were to be leased to the silver mine owners. His immediate plan contemplated an eventual total of ten thousand slaves publicly owned.[60]

Xenophon was aware that the actual supply of slaves available for purchase was limited. This appears from his statement [61] that any outright purchase in large numbers would compel the state to take slaves of poor quality at too high a price. His ultimate dream of three state-owned slaves " to each of the Athenians," [62] if this be restricted to citizens as was probably intended, would represent a state-owned population of about sixty-five thousand slaves, this in a situation in which private capital investment in slaves for leasing purposes was to be superseded in large part by state ownership.[63] None of these ideas of Xenophon presupposes the dominating numbers of slaves in Attica in his time which are given in the ancient writers. Eduard Meyer [64] has long since expressed the view that agricultural production in most parts of Greece remained in the hands of free labor, except where a serf population provided for it. For Attica this view is supported by manumission lists of the years 340-320 B.C. which give only twelve former slaves in agriculture out of 115 males, with no women slaves thus engaged.[65] For the Peloponnesus the remark of Pericles that the Peloponnesians, in contrast to the Athenians, did their own work [66] warns against the conclusion of predominant slavery there. Great slave masses would have produced slave revolts. No slave revolts, as opposed to Helot uprisings, occurred in the eastern Mediterranean area until the late second century B.C.; and the only fear in regard to slaves is that they might be freed and be used in the class struggle between warring elements of the citizen bodies.[67] In the middle period of the fourth century an increase is noticeable in the number of cases of sale of the inhabitants of cities captured in war.[68]

According to categories of ownership, slaves were differentiated by the Greeks as public slaves,[69] temple slaves,[70] and those privately owned. Although the use of state-owned slaves was probably most highly developed in the administration of the Athenian state and is best known in its application there,[71] public owner-

---

[54] Xenophon, *Memorabilia* 2: 3, 3.

[55] His reference is obviously to the helots.

[56] Andreades, A. M., *A history of Greek public finance*, tr. by Carroll N. Brown, 289, n. 7, Cambridge, Mass., Harvard Univ. Press, 1933. For a discussion of the problem of slave numbers in Athens, see Westermann, W. L., Athenaeus and the slaves of Athens, *Harvard Studies in Class. Philology, Special Vol.*, 451-470, 1941.

[57] Isocrates, 4, 115, cf. 17, 36. Death of Lycon, a merchant from Heraclea at the hands of pirates in the Argolic Gulf, Demosthenes, 52, 5, cf. 58, 53, 56. Vote of thanks, of *ca.* 340 B.C., to Cleomis of Lesbos for ransoming Athenians from the hands of pirates in Dittenberger, *SIG³* 1, no. 263 of *ca.* 340 B.C.

[58] Blass, F. and C. Jensen (edd.), *Hyperidis orationes sex cum ceterarum fragmentis*, frg. 29, Leipzig, Teubner, 1917.

[59] Beloch, J., *Bevölkerung der griechisch-römischen Welt*, 97; Gomme, A. W., *Population of Athens*, 21-22.

[60] Xenophon, *Ways and means*, 4, 23-24.

[61] *Ibid.*, 4, 36.

[62] *Ibid.*, 4, 17: τρία ἑκάστῳ ᾽Αθηναίων.

[63] *Ibid.*, 4, 19: τί ἂν ἧττον μισθοῖτό τις παρὰ τοῦ δημοσίου ἢ παρὰ τοῦ ἰδιώτου.

[64] Meyer, Ed., *Die Sklaverei im Altertum*, 39, Dresden, v. Zahn and Jaensch, 1898.

[65] *Inscriptiones Graecae*, Ed. Minor (= *IG²*) 2²(1) 1553-1578; Gomme, A. W., *The population Athens*, 42.

[66] Thucydides, 1:141: αὐτουργοί τε γάρ εἰσι.

[67] Demosthenes, 17, 15, quoting from the treaties of 356 B.C.

[68] The sale of the women and children of Orchomenus in 363 B.C. is recorded by Diodorus, 15:79, 6; of the inhabitants of Sestus in 353 B.C., *ibid.*, 16:34, 3. The people of Olynthus were sold by Philip II of Macedon, *ibid.*, 16:53, 3.

[69] The expressions found are: δημόσιοι οἰκέται, δημόσιοι ὑπηρέται, δημόσιοι ἐργάται, or simply δημόσιοι.

[70] See the article Hieroduloi in Pauly-W., *RE* 8: 1459-1468

[71] Waszynski, S., *De servis Atheniensium publicis*, diss. Berlin,

ship of slaves is well established for other city-states of the Greek world.[72] Athens customarily obtained its public slaves by purchase in the market.[73] The duties performed by them were of many kinds, including service under the street commissioners;[74] in temple construction;[75] as assistants to various officials;[76] in police services such as assistance to the Eleven in the arrest of offenders;[77] as guards in the prison and as actual executioners;[78] as servitors of the Boulé; as assistants to the guardians of weights and measures; and as clerks of the financial officials.[79]

The largest group of public slaves employed at Athens was that of the "Scythians" who first appear as an established body in the early fifth century B. C. as guards of the city district. They were possibly maintained until sometime in the early part of the fourth century.[80] Their number is given by late authorities as 1,000;[81] but it is generally thought that this number is too high and that it should be reduced to about 300.[82] The abandonment of this body was probably not due to lack of effectiveness, but to the heavy cost which forced its elimination in the time of financial depression following the Peloponnesian war.[83] These *dēmosioi douloi* corresponded to petty bureaucrats and they are sharply distinguished from privately owned slaves in that they received a daily wage,[84] available for their own disposal, of three obols per day,[85] and that they enjoyed a high degree of freedom of movement. The state, as owner, unquestionably had the eminent right of providing for their enfranchisement.[86] Once freed there was no legal

hindrance to their advancement, if the state so willed, to complete citizen rights. Although the *dēmosioi* formed a relatively small portion of the slave class, the consideration of them is important as showing the wide variations in privileges and in treatment of slaves, resulting in recognized degrees of slave status which characterized the Greek and Hellenistic types of slavery and left no single sharp line of distinction between free and slave.

The direction of the religious worship of their states was always regarded as a function of statehood both by the Greeks and Romans. It is true that the early Greeks were accustomed to the practice of attaching to their temples servants who stood in a condition somewhat analogous to slavery, although "bondage" expresses their status more precisely. The suggestion must, however, be rejected that this quasi-servile relationship to the Greek temples had its origins in oriental influences upon a people instinctively averse to the practice of divine servitude.[87] The evidence for slavery in relation to the Greek gods themselves, as distinguished from the temples as organizations, is not convincing. An architect named Demetrius has been cited in connection with the building of the temple of Artemis at Ephesus who was called a slave of Diana by Vitruvius.[88] If the designation as slave is correct it is to be explained as an example of the early and persistent penetration of Oriental influences at this particular Artemis sanctuary.

In 481 B. C. the Hellenes in assembly at the Isthmus of Corinth decreed that those Greeks who Medized should be dedicated to Apollo.[89] Further examples of this type of punishment by temporary consecration to the gods are to be seen in the desire of the Athenians in 371 B. C. that the territory of the Thebans be thus condemned,[90] and in the dedication of the territory of the Cirrhaens, to remain as waste lands, to Apollo, to Artemis and Leto, and to Athena Pronoia, at the behest of the Delphic Amphictyony. This occurred just preceding the battle of Chaeronea.[91] To Euripides corporate possession by the temples of dedicants as assistants in the cleaning of the sacred buildings was an accepted fact of Hellenic life. Although they were bound to the god and although the *temples* of the Greek

1898; Jacob, O., Les esclaves publics à Athènes, *Bibliothèque de la Faculté de philosophie et lettres de l'Université de Liège* 35, 1928.

[72] It is found in Eleusis, *Corpus Inscriptionum Atticarum* (=*CIA*), 834b add. 2: 31; in Miletus, Haussoullier, B., Études sur l'histoire de Milet et du Didymeion, *Bibliothèque de l'École des Hautes Études* 138: 158, 162, 167, 172-177, 241-243, Paris, Émile Bouillon, 1902; in Epidamnus, Aristotle, *Politics* 2: 4, 13. In Crete the public slaves were called μνοΐα, Sosicrates in Müller, *Fragmenta Historicorum Graecorum* (= *FHG*) 4: 399.

[73] Jacob, O., *op. cit.*, 9-10.

[74] ὁδοποιοί,. Aristotle, *Constitution of Athens*, 54, 1.

[75] *IG* 2²(1), 1672 (= Dittenberger, *SIG²*, no. 587) where the δημόσιοι are public slaves.

[76] Dittenberger, *SIG³*, no. 971, 29, in which a public slave appears as representative of the ἐπιστάτης or of the ἀρχιτέκτων in the building account dealing with the construction of the portico of Philon at Eleusis, τῷ ἀεὶ παρόντι τῶν ἐπιστατῶν ἢ τῷ δημοσίῳ ἢ τῷ ἀρχιτέκτονι.

[77] Xenophon, *Hellenica* 2: 3, 54-55.

[78] Plato, *Phaedo*, 63d, 116b and c, ὁ τῶν ἕνδεκα ὑπηρέτης.

[79] Jacob, O., Les esclaves publics à Athènes, 87-139.

[80] Waszynski, S., *De servis Athen. publicis*, 26.

[81] Suidas, τοξόται, φύλακες τοῦ ἄστεος τὸν ἀριθμὸν χίλιοι. Cf. scholium to Aristophanes, *Acharnians*, 54.

[82] Jacob, O., *op. cit.*, 64-73.

[83] Andreades, A. M., *A history of Greek public finance*, 215.

[84] The Greek term is τροφή.

[85] *IG* 2(1): 1672, 4-5: δημοσίοις τροφήν - - - τῆς ἡμέρας τῷ ἀνδρὶ Ι Ι Ι.

[86] This happened in the case of Pittalacus, Aeschines, 1, 62. Cf. Jacob, O., *op. cit.*, 177. In *IG* 2(1): 1566, 33-34 a public slave seems to have manumitted a slave belonging to himself.

[87] This is suggested by Hild, J.-A., in Daremberg-Saglio, *Dictionnaire des antiquités* 3(1) : 171.

[88] Vitruvius, *De architectura* 7: 16 (ed. Krohn): *ipsius Dianae servus*.

[89] Herodotus, 7: 132. The technical term δεκατεύειν means that one tenth of the movable goods of the condemned became the property of the god and their persons were paroled, one might say, to the god, but only until the religious pollution which they had incurred should be expiated in a purification ceremony. See the sacred law of Cyrene, *Rivista di Filologia* 55 (N. S. 5) : 196, 1927; von Wilamowitz-Möllendorff, Heilige Gesetze, *Sitzb. Akad. Berlin, philos.-hist. Klasse, n. f.* 29 (19) : 163, 1927

[90] Polybius, 9: 39, 5.

[91] Aeschines, 3, 108.

gods held slaves, the gods themselves did not do so. The relation of their dedicates was rather one of *nexus*.[92]

Sacred prostitution is known at the temple of Aphrodite at Corinth early in the fifth century.[93] Yet little is otherwise heard of the practice in the period under discussion. It may well have been confined to the Corinthian Aphrodite. In view of the promise of a Corinthian named Xenophon to dedicate fifty girls to Aphrodite [94] the thousand temple courtesans assigned to the Corinthian Aphrodite by Strabo [95] may not be excessive and may be ascribed to the special position of Corinth as harbor town, constantly visited by travelers and sailors. The large number involved would here be explained as the development of a long established local peculiarity which attained its height in the Hellenistic period preceding 146 B. C. The presence of the practice at Corinth is wrongly assigned to Oriental influence by Hepding,[96] since the Greek attitude toward prostitution was thoroughly candid and uncritical.[97] For the period preceding Alexander temple slavery, as opposed to divine enslavement, in the Greek communities of the Aegean Sea and of the West cannot be compared in numbers or in economic and social importance with the influence it attained in the temple organizations of Asia Minor during the Hellenistic and Roman periods. The Delian temple accounts of the year 279 B. C. for example [98] show but two slaves in the service of the temples, increased to three, then to four in 201 B. C. and the following years.[99] It is to be assumed that Greek dedication to a god was not legally regarded as enslavement and was in practice quite different from private slavery in respect to the conditions which surrounded it.

Household employment was one particular field of labor in which slaves may have been used more generally than free servants; and in some communities mining laborers were largely recruited from the slave class. Generally speaking, however, there were few economic services which were closed to the slave class, and few which were in practice, as opposed to political-economic theory, marked as low-class labor fitting only for slaves. This peculiarity is probably grounded in the two factors of ancient slavery represented by the acci-

dental nature of slave recruitment from any social class and by the lack, in antiquity, of the fundamental race distinction which became a marked characteristic of American negro slavery of the eighteenth and nineteenth centuries. Already in the sixth century B. C., as has been noted above, Demetrius, a temple slave of Artemis, appears as one of the builders of the Artemisia at Ephesus along with Paeonius of Ephesus.[100]

Regarding the actual conduct of the trade in slaves in the period preceding Alexander little information has come down, and slaves appear rarely in the cargoes of ships. There is no adequate evidence that any Greek city had, in this period, a special position as center of the slave trade to which slaves were brought for sale and for export to other parts of the Greek world. An incident of mortgage taken by an Athenian upon a ship lying in the harbor at Athens [101] indicates that merchants brought slaves in small numbers to that city. In this case attachment was served upon the slaves in the cargo merely as a precaution to meet the possibility that the mortgage upon the ship might not, on forced sale, cover. the forty minas of the loan.[102] The ship-owner, Apaturius, tried to get his slaves out of Athens secretly and to sail to Sicily but was prevented. Out of this simple incident has grown the modern view of Athens as a slave market with re-exportation to Sicily,[103] whereas a suggestion in Aristophanes [104] would indicate that the business of slave dealing was chiefly undertaken by Thessalians.

The somewhat haphazard nature of the trade in slaves is clearly seen in the report of Herodotus, 7: 156, that Gelon of Syracuse, when he captured Hyblaean Megara, sold the poorer captives into slavery for export out of Sicily. The reasons for the export provisions of his sale were obviously political. That sales of slaves could only be consummated in the market place is certainly proved for Gortyn in Crete [105] and for Thurii in Italy.[106] The practice may be generalized for all the Greek city-states of this period because of the local necessity of previous publication in some central location, preferably the agora, of the intended transfer of the slave; because of the increased security of collection of the slave-sale tax by the state if they were sold elsewhere, and because of the increased security for the purchaser if the sale were openly consummated in the agora as center of the city's business activity.[107]

---

[92] Euripides, *Phoenissae*, 202-225; *Ion*, 102-111, 309-310. See Otto, W. (posthumously), Beiträge zur Hierodulie im hellenistischen Ägypten, *Abh. Bayer. Akad der Wissensch., philos.-hist. Klasse, n. f.* **29**: 10-11 and n. 22, 1950.

[93] Pindar, frg. 107 (ed. Bowra).

[94] Kroll, Wilh., *Zeitschrift für Sexualwissenschaft* **17** : 159.

[95] Strabo, 8: 378; 12: 559.

[96] Hieroduloi in Pauly-W., *RE* **8**: 1465. The institution is probably Anatolian in origin. For the Aphrodite temple at Paphos, see Burmester, O. H. E. Khs., The temple and cult of Aphrodite at Paphos, *Farouk I University: Bull. Faculty of Arts* 4 (3), Alexandria, 1948.

[97] Kroll, *Zeits. für Sexualwissenschaft* **17** : 159-160.

[98] *IG* 11 (2) : 161, 83: τῇ ἀνθρώπῳ; τῷ ὑπηρέτῃ.

[99] Homolle, Th. Comptes et inventaires des temples Déliens, *Bulletin de correspondance hellénique* (*BCH*) **14**: 480-481, 1890.

[100] Hogarth, D. G., The archaic Artemisia, *British Museum excavations at Ephesus*, 4-6, London, 1908.

[101] Demosthenes, 33, 8-10.

[102] *Ibid.*, 33, 10: κατηγγύησα τοὺς παῖδας ἵν' ἔι τις ἔνδεια γίγνοιτο τὰ ἐλλείποντα ἐκ τῶν παιδῶν εἴη.

[103] Büchsenschütz, B., *Besitz und Erwerb*, 122, followed by Beauchet, L., *Histoire du droit privé*, 2: 420.

[104] Aristophanes, *Plutus*, 521.

[105] Laws of Gortyn, 7, 10-11 in Bücheler-Zitelmann, *Rh. Mus.* **40**, *Ergänzungsheft*.

[106] Theophrastus in Stobaeus, *Florilegium* 44: 22.

[107] Partsch, J., Die griechische Publizität der Grundstücks-

The calling out of a projected slave sale by the public herald was a primitive form of publication designed to permit the entering of objections by third parties whose possible rights in the particular slave might be injured. Use of the herald in publication of projected manumissions is definitely known for Mantinea, Athens and Calymna.[108] It may be assumed that a particular place in the agora was selected for slave sales.[109] The sug-gestion that public sales of slaves at Athens were restricted to the first day of the month [110] is thinly supported and in itself not probable. In the case of a slave sale the Athenian law demanded that any concealed sickness, such as epilepsy, be declared beforehand by the vendor, with right of prosecution if such a sickness should later appear.[111]

---

verträge, *Festschrift für Otto Lenel*, 86-87, Leipzig, 1923; Schönbauer, E., *Beiträge zur Geschichte des Liegenschaftsrechts im Altertum*, 126-127, Leipzig, Graz, 1924.
[108] Weiss, E., *Griechisches Privatrecht*, 289.

[109] Hesychius: κύκλος; Diodorus Siculus, 15: 7: πρατήριον; Pollux, 3: 78: πρατῆρος λίθος.
[110] Büchsenschütz, B., *Besitz und Erwerb*, 123, based upon Aristophanes, *Knights*, 43 and the scholium thereto.
[111] Hypereides, 5, 15.

III. FROM THE PERSIAN WARS TO ALEXANDER

SLAVE EMPLOYMENT AND LEGAL ASPECTS OF SLAVERY

So far as known, the laws of the Greek city-states placed no restrictions upon the use to which male or female slaves might be put by the owner. Slaves are correspondingly to be found in all the fields of economic service of that time. According to the method of their employment slaves were distinguished as *douloi* or *oike-tai*, who worked directly for their owner, and the *andra-poda misthophorounta*[1] or *douloi misthophorountes* who are to be identified with the *chōris oikountes*, those who lived apart from the owner's residence, working at occupations of any sort and paying to their owners all or some percentage of their earnings. The measure of the employment of slaves in one or another economic occupation differed widely in different localities of the Greek world. In Corcyra the greater part of the slave population was engaged in agriculture.[2] In Crete the cultivation of the land fell to a type of field slaves called *aphamiōtai* by Sosicrates.[3] They appear in the laws of Gortyn as the *oikeis*, a class of privately owned slaves which was distinctly separated from the household slaves of the town and was possessed of subsidiary rights of inheritance in the land which they worked.[4]

In Attica, Corinth, and Megara the employment of slaves in industrial work far outweighed their use in agricultural production.[5] In these city-states a rapid development of the custom of capital investment in slaves as instruments of production, earning money for their owners under the lease system, and the wide diversification of such labor, are clearly apparent. The alleged one thousand slaves of the Athenian general Nicias, the six hundred of Hipponicus, the three hundred of Philomenides,[6] and the thousand of Mnason,[7] although greatly exaggerated as to the actual numbers, give evidence of the wide application of the system. In the classical authors slaves appear in transportation services, as muleteers[8] and as transporters of copper;[9] in distributive services as retailers of unguents;[10] in handicrafts as sword makers and couch makers,[11] as shield makers,[12] as fullers,[13] and as charcoal burners.[14] It is not to be doubted that merchants sailing their own ships to foreign ports used slaves as oarsmen,[15] although no trace of this as a slave occupation has appeared in the literature or in manumission inscriptions.

In the building accounts of the Erechtheum at Athens of 409-408 B. C. sixteen slaves appear as skilled work-men as against thirty-five metics and twenty citizens, receiving equal pay for similar types of work with the free. Simias, an Athenian citizen and a stonemason by trade, appears along with five slaves belonging to him, the six receiving like pay as individuals, each separately listed, so that the slave-owner is not to be regarded as contractor or overseer of the labors of his slaves.[16] Phalakros, a citizen, works upon the same basis with

---

[1] Isaeus, Or. 8, 35.
[2] Thucydides, 3: 73.
[3] Müller, *FHG* 4: 399.
[4] Laws of Gortyn, 5, 25-28.
[5] This is implied for the time of the Decelean War by Thucydides, 7: 27. For the years 340-320 B. C., *cf.* Gomme, A. W., *The population of Athens in the fifth and fourth centuries B. C.*, 42.

[6] Xenophon, *Ways and means*, 4, 14-15.
[7] Athenaeus, 6: 264d.
[8] δοῦλοι ὀρεωκόμοι, Aristophanes, *Thesmophoriazusae*, 491. *Cf.* Plato, *Lysis*, 208b.
[9] Demosthenes, Or. 49, 51-52.
[10] Hypereides, Or. 5, 5-6, where Midas, a slave, managed an unguent shop for his owner.
[11] Demosthenes, Or. 27, 9.
[12] Demosthenes, Or. 26, 11.
[13] Lysias, Or. 23, 2.
[14] Aristophanes, *Acharnians*, 273.
[15] Wilamowitz-Möllendorff, U. von, *Staat und Gesellschaft der Griechen und Römer bis zum Ausgang des Mittelalters*, 2nd ed., 69-70, Leipzig, Teubner, 1923.
[16] *IG* 1²: 374, 5-10; *cf.* 202-207.

three slaves,[17] Laossos, a citizen, with two slaves.[18] Axiopeithes, a metic who received a contract for completion of a part of the work,[19] carried out his contract by means of two of his slaves;[20] but the metic Aminiades worked beside his slave.[21] In the broken account of receipts and expenditures upon temple construction at Eleusis and the repairing of the Eleusinium at Athens the work was let to contractors who used a group of skilled laborers so that free and slave workmen cannot be distinguished.[22] Most of the supplies, including pitch, wooden beams, olive wood for wedges, and the like, were bought from slaves who had booths in the precinct of the Theseum.[23]

Trustworthy information upon the occupations of former slaves (now freedmen and freedwomen) is also obtained from a group of documents from Athens, datable 349-320 B. C., which list, year by year, the slaves. manumitted under a special procedure before the polemarch.[24] These show seventy-nine males whose occupations are given and fifty-six females,[25] distributed as follows:

	Agriculture	Manufacture	Transport	Distributive Services	Miscellaneous
Men	12	26	10	21	10
Women	0	48	0	7	1

The number engaged in farm work, which includes two specialized vineyard workers, is surprisingly small. The manufacturing group includes: a bronze worker, three goldsmiths, an ironsmith; in the leather trades, two tanners, nine leather cutters, two sandal makers, a cobbler; in the pottery industry, an amphora carrier (water carrier) and a pail maker; in furniture, a sofa maker. To these may be added a glue boiler and an engraver. The women engaged in industry show some forty wool workers.[26] The distributive, or selling, services show six males and three women listed as retail dealers[27] without further explanation as to what they sold.

The following specialized retail dealers appear among the men: sellers of bread, of pickled meats, of incense, of sesame, of fish, of wool, two or three dealing in rope, and three mageiroi;[28] among the women, two sesame vendors, one seller of vegetables, one of honey. Among the men three larger-scale dealers[29] appear. The female workers show also a cithara player, a nurse, and a seamstress.[30] Miscellaneous trades of males include two clerks, a money lender, and a barber. In the household services the work done by slaves was of many kinds, the number of slaves employed varying widely according to the wealth and the desire for display of the individual concerned.[31] Aeschines[32] had seven slaves for the personal service of the six members of his family and two friends; but it is also evident from inventories of properties appearing in the Attic orators that some prosperous families had no household slaves.[33] The household work in such cases must have been done by hired servants.

Plato, in the Laws,[34] expressed the actual situation in the Athens of his day when he said that the poorer citizens must do their own work without slaves. In the households of Athens slaves served as doorkeepers;[35] as attendants of children;[36] as personal attendants of adults;[37] as valets;[38] as porters and messengers doing odd jobs in connection with the master's business affairs;[39] the women as wet-nurses.[40] Slaves were also represented in the more responsible and exacting affairs of the business world, in clerical work,[41] as employees in banks,[42] and as physicians and educators.[43] In the miscellaneous technai having to do with luxury pleasures, slave girls were prominent as entertainers hired for special occasions;[44] and as prostitutes, plying the ancient trade in the financial interests of their owners. Demosthenes tells of the freedwoman, Nicarete, who reared and trained to this profession seven young girls.

---

[17] Ibid., 230.

[18] Ibid., 226.

[19] IG 1²: 373, 98.

[20] Kerdon in IG 1²: 374, 74 and Sokles in line 204.

[21] Ibid., 197, 200.

[22] The same is true in the case of the seventeen day hands (μισθωτοί), IG 2²: 1672, 33.

[23] The Greek term is σκηνῖται, ibid., 9-10, 63, 64. The nail seller, Philon, whose booth was in the Theseum, ibid., 30, cf. 174, was a metic.

[24] IG 2²: 1553-1578. Marcus N. Tod, in Epigraphica 12: 14, 1950, has correctly assumed that these former slaves would usually carry on the same occupations when freed.

[25] See Gomme, A. W., The population of Athens, 42.

[26] For the ἀμφορεαφόρος as "water-carriers" see Tod, Epigraphica 12: 5, 1950. For the ταλασιοῦργοι (wool workers) as not restricted to spinning wool, ibid., 10.

[27] Greek: κάπηλος, καπηλίς.

[28] These appear to be sellers of foods which they cooked, whether meats or cakes; Tod in Epigraphica 12: 8 designates them, in general terms, as "cooks."

[29] Greek: ἔμποροι, translated by Tod, ibid., 6, as "merchant."

[30] They appear in Gomme's tables under "manufacture" and "miscellaneous."

[31] Xenophon, Cyropaedia 1: 1, 1.

[32] Aeschines, Epistles, 12, 11.

[33] Isaeus, Or. 2, 29, 35; 9, 42, 44.

[34] Bissinger, Klio 14: 83, 1914.

[35] Aristophanes, Acharnians, 395; Frogs, 35.

[36] παιδαγωγοί: Plato, Lysis, 208; Gorgias, 452c.

[37] Aristophanes, Acharnians, 1097; Andocides, 1, 11-14.

[38] διάκονος in IG 2²: 1554, 57.

[39] Demosthenes, Or. 37, 22, 24.

[40] IG 2²: 1559, 59-60. The nurse of Alcibiades, a Spartan woman, was probably free, Plutarch, Alcibiades, 1.

[41] γραμματεύς: IG 2²: 1556, 14; ὑπογραμματεύς: ibid.: 1561, 31.

[42] Phormio, who worked his way upward from slavery as clerk in the bank of Pasion, Demosthenes, Or. 45, 82; Kittos, a slave employed in the bank of Pasion, Isocrates Or. 17: 7.

[43] Plato, Gorgias, 452c.

[44] Flageolet player, Aristophanes, Wasps, 1358, 1368; cithara player, IG 2²: 1557, 63; dancer, Aristophanes, Thesmophoriazusae, 1177. Presumably, though not necessarily, the flageolet players of Plato, Symposium, 176e and 212d were of this class.

They provided a living for her as "madam" of a brothel.[45]

Many of the handmaidens who appear in the Attic grave stelae in attendance upon the wives of Athenian citizens and metics were probably unfree; but they are in no way specifically marked as slaves, nor are they distinguished by the sculptors, in dress or features, from their mistresses. Modern attempts to distinguish slaves from free in the vase paintings which present views of the handicraft shops, by features or by strong body hair, are quite unconvincing. In a speech justifying the use of monies of the Delian League for public construction work at Athens, Pericles enumerated the types of workmen (technical specialists, transporters, etc.) who would be benefited by the required expenditures.[46] Each trade, he says, has its own group of attendant menial labor[47] and the requirements for the public works bring prosperity to every age and type. There is no mention of economic or social classification in the grouping of workmen, although slaves and free worked together upon the Parthenon as they did upon the Erechtheum. Even in Athens, one of the few cities in which handicraft slavery was highly developed, it is more than doubtful that slave labor dominated over free labor except in mining and perhaps in household and in retail distributive services. It is also necessary to remember that in numerous polities which were basically agricultural, serfdom in different forms supplied in large measure the labor requirements of the state, and to point to the specific statement of Herodotus[48] that among the Hellenes the glorification of the warrior class and the corresponding contempt for the handicraft workman was strongest under the serf system of Lacedaemon and least apparent at Corinth where handicraft economy was highly developed. The statement of Athenaeus that the Chians introduced the custom of working bought slaves whereas the majority of the Greeks were self-dependent in their business affairs[49] is correct as a generalization for the Greek world.

The actual slave prices which are known from the period are very few. At the time of the Persian invasions the ransom price of two minas per prisoner was generally established for war captives in the Peloponnesus.[50] This may be regarded as the equivalent of a high market price for an able-bodied and physically select slave, the average slave price probably being lower. In an inscription recording the sale in 414 B. C. of the confiscated slaves of the Hermocopids[51] the following prices were realized at public auction upon the slaves of the metic Cephisodorus: upon eastern and southern slaves—a Carian male slave, 150 dr.; a Carian boy, 174 dr.; a Carian child, 72 dr.; a Lydian female slave, 170 dr.; a Melitenean from Cappadocia (sex not determined), 106 dr.; two Syrian male slaves, 240 dr. and 301 dr.; upon slaves of northern extraction—two Thracian males, 165 dr. and 175 dr.; Thracian women, 135 dr., 165 dr., 200 dr.; two Illyrian men, 121 dr. and 161 dr.; a Scythian male, 144 dr.; and a Colchian male, 153 dr.

This range of prices helps to explain the price variations given by Xenophon[52] for his own time as one-half to ten minas. The lowest price of fifty drachmas was probably that for a child,[53] to be explained by the element of risk and expense of rearing to a profit-bearing age which entered into the price. The average of prices of male and female slaves, as they appear in the manumission inscriptions, was about equal—180 dr. in the cases of four women, 178 dr. in the cases of ten men. The facts that the Syrian slaves brought the highest prices, 301 and 240 dr., and that the northern slaves, with nine samples, averaged 162 dr. as against an average of 139 dr. for the four Asia Minor slaves, may be the result of chance or of individual differences in aptitudes, physical fitness, or training in the particular groups. For the first half of the fourth century the average price of mine slaves, as deduced from Xenophon,[54] was about 180 dr., wherein one must reckon with mining slaves as representing unskilled labor of low market value.[55] This price of mining slaves finds some support in the statement of Demosthenes[56] that twenty couch makers left in his father's estate were mortgaged against a loan of 4,000 dr., which would necessitate the conclusion of a higher average value for these skilled workmen than 200 dr. each.

The following additional fixed prices have been reported for the fourth century B. C. preceding Alexander: forced sale of fifteen skilled workmen at an average of 200 dr.;[57] an *oiketēs* priced at 200 dr.;[58] a professedly low valuation placed upon two slaves at 125 dr. each;[59] and 300 dr. paid for a slave girl used as a prostitute.[60] The talent reputed to have been paid by Nicias at

[45] Demosthenes, Or. 59, 18: τέχνην ταύτην κατασκευασμένη καὶ ἀπὸ τούτων τὸν βίον συνειλεγμένη.

[46] Plutarch, *Pericles*, 12, 6.

[47] *Ibid.*: ἑκάστη δὲ τέχνη . . . τὸν θητικὸν ὄχλον καὶ ἰδιώτην.

[48] Herodotus, 2: 167. R. Schlaifer, Greek theories of slavery, *Harvard Studies in Class. Philol.* 47: 165-204, 1936, is wrong in his conclusion, p. 201, that "all labor which was performed by slaves or serfs" in the Greek World was brought "under a stigma from which it never recovered." The author has taken the political theorists of the philosophical schools too seriously as having established "the main line of Greek thought concerning slavery."

[49] Athenaeus, 6: 91: τῶν πολλῶν αὐτουργῶν ὄντων κατὰ τὰς διακονίας.

[50] Herodotus, 6: 79; 5: 77.

[51] *IG* 1²: 249.

[52] Xenophon, *Memorabilia* 2: 5, 2.

[53] *Cf.* the seventy-two drachmas above.

[54] Xenophon, *Ways and means*, 4, 4-16; 23.

[55] Oertel, F., *Rheinisches Museum* 79: 236; 237, n. 1.

[56] Demosthenes, Or. 27, 9.

[57] *Ibid.*, 18.

[58] Demosthenes, Or. 41, 8.

[59] Demosthenes, Or. 53, 1.

[60] Hypereides, Or. 5, 2.

Athens for an overseer in the mines,[61] if true, represents a special and extraordinary purchase of managerial competence. The rather fixed range of prices for the hundred years from the Peloponnesian war to Alexander, from about 120 dr. to 300 dr. for adult slaves, may be due entirely to the limited amount of data at hand, which may fail to indicate fluctuations of price which actually occurred.

Xenophon had information from a source not given that the laborers let out by Nicias to the Thracian mine exploiter, Sosias, and by Hipponicus and Philomenides, toward the end of the fifth century, brought in to their owners a net earning of one obol per day.[62] This one obol a day net from rented slaves is also the basis of Demosthenes' reckoning of the fixed yearly income from the couch makers of his father. In neither case does any deduction for amortization appear.[63]

Since free labor was unquestionably at hand in the Greek city-states and slaves were not subject to military service, definite influence of slave labor upon the work available to free men cannot be denied,[64] with the probability a priori that the competition resulted in a lowering of general wages. The constant presence of satisfactory slave workmen must, for example, have emphasized the difficulty of re-absorbing into the activities of civil life those free workmen who had been displaced from their trades by the requirements of service in war. How far slavery was responsible for the feeling, prevalent in the aristocratic literature of the fourth century B. C., that manual labor was "banausic," cannot be determined. It is expressed most strongly in the writings of the political theorists, and is to be ascribed in considerable degree to the increasing democratization of the Greek city-states with the growing demands which it imposed upon the time and energies of the citizen class.[65]

There is also no satisfactory proof available for the theory of a lower productivity of slave labor as compared with free labor.[66] The fact of equal pay for work contracted for by the day must certainly be regarded as a contradiction of this theory.[67] No evidence is at hand which shows a difference of treatment in point of working hours between free and slave labor doing the same type of work. The agreements made in connection with the Eleusis temples[68] were in part based upon the delivery of a definite quantum per day[69] where the time element depends upon the laborer. There is no sign of any effort to obtain increased production by the process of speeding up the workmen, whether free or slave.[70]

Xenophon, in presenting his project of capital investment to be made in mining slaves by the state, reckoned the income from these slaves upon the basis of 360 working days per year;[71] but a warning against the assumption that slaves were worked without cessation lies in the fact noted by Schwahn[72] that in the Eleusis building inscriptions stone-sawyers paid on a daily wage arrangement were also paid during the Lenaean festival period when there was no work going on.[73] That free labor was employed in the mines may safely be deduced from the known fact that mine owners themselves worked in person in their own concessionary pits.[74] The work done by the slaves mining in the Laurian pits was without doubt hard labor, carried on under the dangerous conditions which have always characterized the mining industry; but the danger was the same for the slave miner and the free. The horrible conditions commonly assumed for the Laurian mine work have come from too great stress upon the criticism aimed at Nicias,[75] the Athenian General, that his wealth was founded upon the labor of miners. For a corrective against this tendency note the ventilation arrangements in the Laurian mines[76] and Ardaillon's estimate of a ten-hour working day with two-hour shifts, or change of occupation, for laborers using pick and shovel.[77]

The statement of Aristotle that the slave is a kind of possession with a soul,[78] although his approach was entirely from the political-economic point of view, is the closest approximation to a definition of the legal status of slaves that has come down to us from any Greek source. As property, slaves were necessarily an object of concern for civil legislation; but they were not, in principle, a subject for political legislation.[79] The slave-owner was protected in his ownership rights at Corinth and Athens by a drastic law against the stealing of another man's slave, the punishment for which apparently fell under the procedure called graphē andrapodismou[80] (indictment for false enslavement).

Slaves, as a consequence of their complete political disability, according to a rule both among the Greek

---

[61] Xenophon, Memorabilia 2 : 5, 2.

[62] Xenophon, Ways and means, 4, 23: ὀβολὸν ἀτελῆ.

[63] Oertel, F., Rheinisches Museum 79 : 233.

[64] Oertel, F. in Pöhlmann, Robert von, Geschichte der sozialen Frage und des Sozialismus in der antiken Welt, 3rd edition, 548, München, C. H. Beck, 1925. Francotte in RE 9 : 1429.

[65] Oertel, F., Gnomon 3 : 94, n. 1.

[66] This view was adopted by Cicotti, E., Il tramonto della schiavitù nel mondo antico, 129, Torino, Fratelli Bocca, 1899.

[67] Francotte in RE 9 : 1429.

[68] IG 2² : 1672, 32-36.

[69] Schwahn in Rheinisches Museum 79 : 177.

[70] Oertel, F. in Rheinisches Museum 79 : 249.

[71] Xenophon, Ways and means, 4, 24.

[72] Schwahn, loc. cit.

[73] Cf.: τὰ δ' ἄλλ' ἑορτή with respect to slave girls in Herondas, 6, 17.

[74] Demosthenes, Or. 42, 20: αὐτὸς τῷ ἐμαυτοῦ σώματι πονῶν. Cf. Xenophon, Ways and means, 4, 22.

[75] Plutarch, Crassus, 34.

[76] Ardaillon, E., Les mines du Laurion dans l'antiquité, 49-53, Paris, Thorin et fils, 1897.

[77] Ibid., 93.

[78] Aristotle, Politics 1 : 2, 4: ὁ δοῦλος κτῆμά τι ἔμψυχον.

[79] Beauchet, L., Histoire du droit privé de la république Athénienne 2 : 421.

[80] Lysias, Or. 13, 67. Bekker, Anecdota 1 : 219, 344.

city-states and later with the Romans, did not participate in the actual fighting as combatants in warfare,[81] since military service, both by land and sea, was a privilege fundamentally connected with citizenship.[82] For Athens it is implied by Xenophon[83] that citizens and metics were used in the navy, but not slaves.[84] The fact that in the heat of passion in civil wars and under the ultimate necessity of preservation of the state this basic theory was frequently abandoned, does not invalidate the general rule. In the naval battle between the Corcyraean and Corinthian fleets in 433 B. C. the Corcyraeans used a large number of slaves upon their vessels.[85] In the hasty preparation of an auxiliary fleet before the battle of the Arginusae Islands in 406 B. C., by vote of the Athenian assembly, 110 vessels were manned with all available persons whether slave or free;[86] and the slaves who took part received pay, their freedom, and equality with the Plataeans in respect to Athenian citizenship.[87] With this incident Alfred Körte has connected a list of sailors from five or more triremes preserved in IG **2²**: 1951 which contains 181 slaves.[88]

Contrary to the view of Boeckh[89] based upon a misinterpretation of Xenophon, *Ways and Means*, 4, 25, and followed by Lécrivain,[90] an ownership tax upon slaves cannot be proved for Athens or Priene.[91] The taxes derived from slaves at Athens were those on import amounting to two per cent,[92] on export, and the tax on slave sales, including the manumission tax which is to be regarded as an integral part of the sale tax.[93] The amount of the sales tax at Athens is not known, the 1/500 of Aristophanes[94] being merely a stage jest; but the total of the indirect taxes derived from slaves which came to Athens and were sold there in the years

before the Decelean war made the sales tax on slaves an important source of revenue.[95]

Both in the interest of its tax collecting and as guarantee of the ownership rights obtained by the purchaser, the Greek law of Athens and of other city-states demanded the publication, by previous posting of a notice[96] or by herald's call, of all sales of *immobilia*, under which fell the sales of slaves. In addition to an affidavit of the vendor that the slave as property was free from ownership claim of a third party,[97] the Athenian law required that the vendor must make it clear if the slave were suffering from any sickness.[98] The diseases which must be declared included tuberculosis, strangury, and epilepsy.[99] The Greek states, by inclusion of a clause in their treaties with other city-states regulating the return of runaway slaves,[100] attempted to protect the private property holdings of their subjects in that peculiarly elusive form of capital investment.

Although, under the general Greek view of the slave as thing and possession of his master,[101] a slave should be legally incapable of property holding, this was not the case with the Cretan agricultural slave called *oikeus* or *dōlos* who could own property in which the dowry rights of the female slave (*oikeia*) were legally protected.[102] Whereas any legal recognition of property ownership by slaves cannot be proved for other states than Gortyn, the master in return for efficient service was accustomed to set aside a part of the earnings of the slave which might ultimately serve for the purchase of his liberty. Differing from the Roman *peculium* in that the Roman *practise*, as opposed to the law, recognized *de facto* the possessory rights of the slave in the property granted or acquired, it produced the result intended by the *peculium* because custom and the self-interest of the owner urged its application toward the ultimate freedom of the slave.[103] The activities of the slaves whose services were leased by their masters[104] and of the slave *emporoi* who traveled overseas in the interests of their owners necessarily entailed some degree of responsibility in the handling of their masters' property as his legal representatives.[105]

As a result of these business activities the right of

[81] Xenophon, *Ways and means*, 4, 41-42, only suggests that slaves might be used as combatants.

[82] For a different view, see Delbrück, H., *Geschichte der Kriegskunst im Rahmen der politischen Geschichte* 1: 110, Berlin, G. Stilke, 1900. There is a statement in Pausanias, 1: 32, 3, that slaves, presumably those owned by Athenians, fought for the first time in battle at Marathon. It may be true; but Herodotus doesn't mention it. The matter is discussed by J. A. Notopoulos in *AJP* 62: 352-354, 1941.

[83] Xenophon, *Constitution of Athens*, 1, 11-12.

[84] Beloch, J., *Die Bevölkerung der griechisch-römischen Welt*, 21.

[85] Of the 1,050 Corcyraeans captured, eight hundred were slaves, according to Thucydides, 1: 55.

[86] Xenophon, *Hellenica* 1: 6, 24.

[87] Aristophanes, *Frogs*, 33, 191, 693-694.

[88] Körte in *Philologische Wochenschrift* **52**: 1027-1031.

[89] Boeckh, A., *Die Staatshaushaltung der Athener*, 2nd ed., 2: 79.

[90] Daremberg-Saglio, *Dictionnaire des antiquités* **4¹**: 704.

[91] Andreades, A. M., *A history of Greek public finance*, 154, 158, 281-282. The tithe on slaves, δεκάτη ἀνδραπόδων, of IG 1²: 310, 222 is too small in amount to be ascribed to an ownership tax.

[92] ἀνδραπόδων πεντηκοστή, Bekker, *Anecdota* 1: 297.

[93] Cf. Westermann, W. L., *Upon slavery in Ptolemaic Egypt*, 61.

[94] πεντακοσιοστή: Aristophanes, *Ecclesiazusae*, 1007.

[95] Xenophon, *Ways and means*, 4, 25.

[96] This is the ἀναγραφὴ τῶν κτημάτων of Theophrastus in Stobaeus, 44: 22.

[97] ἀνέπαφα: Theophrastus in Stobaeus, *loc. cit.*

[98] Hypereides, Or. 5, 15.

[99] Plato, *Laws* 11: 916, presumably copied from the existing law at Athens.

[100] Thucydides, 5: 32 in the armistice of 423 B.C.

[101] Beauchet, L., *Histoire du droit privé de la république Athénienne* 2: 444.

[102] Laws of Gortyn, 3, 40-44.

[103] Beauchet, L., *op. cit.*, 445. Xenophon, *Oeconomicus*, 14, 9: οὐ μόνον πλουτίζων (scil. τοὺς οἰκέτας) ἀλλὰ καὶ τιμῶν ὡς καλούς τε κἀγαθούς.

[104] Greek: ἀνδράποδα μισθοφοροῦντα.

[105] Wenger, L., *Die Stellvertretung im Rechte der Papyri*, 167-168, Leipzig, 1906.

participation in civil actions, in a representative capacity, was necessarily conceded to such slaves.[106] Although the laws of Gortyn show in general less rigid lines of stratification between slaves and free than those known from Athens, the master must in Cretan law appear in court for his slave in all cases.[107] For delicta committed by slaves at Athens, as a general rule, the persons who received benefit from these acts, customarily the owners, were legally responsible, though the slaves might be cited as defendants.[108] How seriously those slaves who lived apart could involve their owners by their business activities cannot be determined with certainty.[109]

The taking of testimony from free persons and from slaves differed in that, with the consent of the slave owner, the slave might be subjected to interrogation under the use of the bastinado[110] or the rack.[111] This difference between free and slave is paralleled in many Greek states by a difference in the law of punishments, that the slave might pay for minor misdeeds with corporal punishment, but the free man was exempt from this indignity.[112] The right of the slave-owner to punish his own slaves was not restricted; but beating a metic or the slave of another person was forbidden at Athens.[113] The legal inequality of slaves is also apparent in the heavier penalties imposed upon them in comparison with the free for the same torts and in the lower indemnities granted by the laws for the same injury when inflicted upon a slave. Homosexual or heterosexual rape in Crete, if committed upon a free person, was penalized by a fine double that imposed if the victim was a slave.[114] Adultery of a slave with a free woman was punished with a fine double that which

a free man would pay.[115] In a case of illegal arrest and detention the perpetrator paid ten staters if the man were free, five staters if he were a slave.[116] The law prevailing at Athens by which slaves could not appear before the *boulé* or assembly except under special permission and under assurance of freedom from prosecution,[117] applied also to metics and women and was not, therefore, strictly a servile disqualification.

Against that group of political, legal, social, and, in less degree, economic disabilities inherent in the ideology of any slave structure, in the Greek city-state world, there stood a group of legal measures designed to protect slaves from abuse of the situation created by the theory of complete dependence upon the will of slave-owners. Athenian law assigned to the court of the Palladium the investigation of cases of murder of a slave, a metic, or a foreigner.[118] This protection of slaves from murder is to be assumed for most of the Greek city-states of the time[119] and is favorably contrasted by Isocrates[120] with the supreme power of life and death held by the Spartan ephors over the Helots. A singularly retrogressive spirit is displayed in this respect by Plato in his state of the *Laws* in which the murder of a slave might be expiated merely by purificatory rites[121] and, on the other hand, the right is conceded to the relatives of a man murdered by a slave of exacting blood vengeance from the slave.[122] This reversion in Plato's projected state to a pre-Draconian attitude toward punishment of slaves finds its explanation in the necessity of rigid control in the agrarian state, based upon slave labor, which Plato contemplated in the *Laws*.[123] The fact that Plato's suggestion did *not* find acceptance in pragmatic form in the slavery sanctions of the Greek city-states of his day is a valuable observation. It signifies that the slave institution in the period of the Hellenic city-states was not strongly agrarian economically. In addition, it strengthens the decision already reached that there could not have been any slave majority over the free population in Greece in the fifth and fourth centuries.

Along with the extension of slavery into industrial fields there appears the development of the right of asylum at the altars of the gods[124] in its application to slaves as a protective measure against undue cruelty

[106] Partsch, J., *Griechisches Bürgschaftsrecht*, 136, Leipzig, Teubner, 1909. The view of Ugo Paoli, *Studi di diritto attico*, 106-107, Firenze, Bemporad & figlio, 1930, that slaves appeared in the commercial tribunals with complete independence of action is doubtful, being based upon a questionable interpretation of οἰκέτης and παῖς in Demosthenes Or. 34:5, 10 as slave.

[107] Bücheler-Zitelmann, *Rheinisches Museum* **40**: Ergänzungsheft, 103.

[108] Hypereides, Or. 5, 22: τὰς ζημίας ἃς ἂν ἐργάσωνται οἱ οἰκέται καὶ τὰ ἁμαρτήματα διαλύειν τὸν δεσπότην παρ' ᾧ ἂν ἐργάσωνται.

[109] Wenger, L., *Die Stellvertretung im Rechte der Papyri*, 168; Partsch, J., *Archiv für Papyrusforschung* **4**: 502, 1908, has suggested that the owners were held responsible only when the slaves had received complete right of representing them.

[110] Greek: βασανίζειν.

[111] Antiphon, Or. 5, 32, 40. Right of the master to refuse, Antiphon, Or. 1, 8; Aeschines, 2, 128. Ugo Paoli, *Studi di diritto attico*, 108, denies the custom of applying torture to slaves at Athens in the commercial courts.

[112] Demosthenes, Or. 22, 55. Fifty blows was a customary punishment at Athens from the time of Solon, Aeschines, Or. 1, 39. For dumping refuse in the market place of the Piraeus, IG 2²: 380, dated 320-319 B.C. At Thasos, Dittenberger, *Sylloge*,³ 1217. The Laws of Gortyn, however, cite no punishments by whipping.

[113] Xenophon, *Constitution of Athens*, 1, 10.

[114] Laws of Gortyn, 1, 7-10.

[115] *Ibid.*, 2, 2-7. At Athens the punishment of a slave in such cases was death, Lysias Or. 13: 18, 66.

[116] Laws of Gortyn, 1, 1-5.

[117] Andocides, Or. 1, 12; Thucydides, 6: 27.

[118] Scholium to Aeschines, Or. 2, 87: οἰκέτην ἢ μέτοικον ἢ ξένον ἀποκτείναντι.

[119] Euripides, *Hecuba*, 291-292. For a member state of the Delian Confederacy, Antiphon, Or. 5, 48.

[120] Isocrates, Or. 5, 181.

[121] Plato, *Laws* **9**: 865c-d.

[122] *Ibid.*, 868c. This is in direct contrast to the law prevailing at Athens as in Antiphon, Or. 5, 48.

[123] Bissinger, J., *Klio*, Beiheft **17**: 108, 1925.

[124] Euripides, *Suppliants*, 268.

of their masters.[125] The scope of the protection afforded varied in different localities. At Gortyn in Crete, in a case involving ownership of a slave, the protection of the temple made it impossible for the defeated party in a lawsuit to lay hands upon a slave.[126] At Athens the slave could obtain temporary refuge in the city Theseum or at the altar of the Eumenides.[127] The protective power of temple asylum at Athens, so far as it applied to slaves, consisted solely in the right of the priest to determine whether the slave should be returned forthwith to his master or be granted the protection of the temple pending an action, designated *prāsin aitein*, under which the slave might demand that he be sold to another owner.[128] The generally fair treatment of slaves and their economic and social assimilation toward the poorer free classes of the population may be deduced both from the undeveloped form of the rights of asylum at this time as compared with those attained in the Hellenistic period, and possibly also from the observation that little evidence has come down to us of the use of this refuge by slaves. Protection against a too easy loss of freedom by persons unable to fend for themselves is to be seen in a provision of the Laws of Gortyn[129] to the effect that in a legal dispute as to status the testimony of those who asserted the freedom of the man concerned should be accepted.[130]

The right of manumission which lay with the owners of slaves throughout antiquity was thoroughly established as a custom in the fifth century B. C., developing in the fifth and fourth centuries into a fashion so widespread that the entire aspect of slavery was changed. From a status enduring formally for the lifetime of the enslaved person it was altered to a condition which brought ancient slavery *de facto* into close relationship with contractual service of limited tenure like the Greek system of the freedman *paramonē*. The inconstancy of status and fluidity of movement from slavery to freedom which resulted from the principle and practice of manumission is of vital importance in the situation. Two methods of manumission existed, mass manumissions by the state and manumissions of single slaves or a group of slaves by individual owners. The first was at times resorted to by the ruling power of the state itself using the military support of enfranchised slaves to strengthen the power which a tyrant might hold, as in the cases of Hecataeus of Miletus[131] and of Theron at Selinus in Sicily,[132] or in support of the freedom of the state in time of extreme danger, as at Athens in 490 B. C.[133] and in 406 B. C.[134] or after the battle of Chaeronea when, on motion of Lycurgus, the slaves were freed.[135]

Serious revolts of slaves did not occur during the period 500-320 B. C., which is a significant commentary upon the generally mild treatment of slaves during that time. The incident of the revolt of the Argive slaves reported by Herodotus,[136] although unhistorical,[137] may be taken as proof of the possibility of mass emancipation by direct action of slaves in the period 500-320 B. C. Despite its dubious authority a report of Polyaenus[138] bears every aspect of verisimilitude. He states that during the siege of Syracuse by the Athenians in 414 B. C. the lower classes in the city revolted, including the slaves, but that the slaves were all persuaded to return to their owners except three hundred who deserted to the Athenians.

Individual emancipation by slave-owners, reported in the ancient literature for the first half of the fifth century B. C., as that of the attendant of the sons of Themistocles[139] and of Salmoxis, slave of Pythagoras of Samos,[140] receives a firmer foundation of knowledge through the manumission inscriptions beginning in the latter half of the fifth century. In the fourth century they increase in numbers and testify to an enlargement of the custom of individual manumission.[141] The number of those manumitted by the single procedure of *dikē apostasiou* alone in the years 340-320 B. C. averaged about fifty per year at Athens, according to Gomme.[142] From about the same time comes a religious decree from the Piraeus by which a number of activities were enjoined during the celebration of the Thesmophoria. Among these prohibitions falls that of manumitting slaves during the festivities.[143] While there was no legal compulsion upon the slave-owner which could force him to the act of manumission it may be assumed that in the fourth century and thereafter the pressure

---

[125] Pauly-Wissowa, *RE* 2: 1881-1885.

[126] Laws of Gortyn, 1, 38-50.

[127] Aristophanes, frg. 567 in *Fragmenta Comicorum Graecorum* (= *FCG*), edited by A. Meineke: ἐμοὶ κράτιστόν ἐστιν εἰς τὸ Θησεῖον δραμεῖν ἐκεῖ δ' ἕως ἂν πρᾶσιν εὕρωμεν μένειν. Cf. Aristophanes, *Knights*, 1312; *Thesmophoriazousae*, 224.

[128] Pollux, 7: 13. Eupolis in the *Poleis*, *FCG*, 225: κακὰ τοιάδε πάσχουσα μηδὲ πρᾶσιν αἰτῶν.

[129] Laws of Gortyn, 1, 14-17.

[130] For protection of a freedman at Athens from return to slavery, see Isaeus, frg. 18; Harpocration, *s. v.* ἄγοι.

[131] Diodorus, 10: 25.

[132] Polyaenus, *Strategemata* 1: 28, use of three hundred slaves by Theron to found his power.

[133] Pausanias, 7: 15, 7, the names of the ex-slaves who were killed being commemorated on a separate stele along with those of the fallen Plataeans, Pausanias, 1: 32, 3.

[134] Xenophon, *Hellenica* 1: 6, 24, names of dead ex-slaves again commemorated. Cf. Körte in *Philologische Wochenschrift* 52: 1027-1031, 1932.

[135] Lycurgus, Or., *Against Leocrates*, 41.

[136] Herodotus, 6: 83.

[137] How, W. W. and J. Wells, *A commentary on Herodotus*, 2nd ed. 2: 94-95, Oxford, Clarendon Press, 1928. Cf. Luria, S., *Klio* 26: 212, 220, 1933.

[138] Polyaenus, *Strategemata* 1: 45.

[139] Herodotus, 8: 75.

[140] Herodotus, 4: 93.

[141] Calderini, A., *La manomissione e la condizione dei liberti in Grecia*, 31, 70, Milano, Ulrico Hoepli, 1908.

[142] Gomme, A. W., *The population of Athens in the fifth and fourth centuries B. C.*, 41, n. 2.

[143] Prott-Ziehen, *Leges Graecorum sacrae*, no. 33: [ὅπως ἂν μηδ]εὶς ἀφέτους ἀφιεῖ.

of social custom operated in most cases to compel acceptance of the manumission price upon the part of the master when it was tendered by the slave.

A recent discovery of Aramaic papyri from Syene in Upper Egypt has been made in the Charles Edwin Wilbour collection of the Brooklyn Museum. It contains three documents which deal with slavery as it operated in the well-known Hebrew colony at Elephantine in the second half of the fifth century B. C. The information which they offer upon the Semitic-Hebrew type of enslavement is presented here because of the sharp contrast which it establishes between the enslavement structures of the Greek polities of that time and that of a distant Hebrew community of the Diaspora.

These Aramaic documents were bought in 1893 at Assuan by Charles Edwin Wilbour of Brooklyn. After Mr. Wilbour's death they were ignored for half a century, stored in a trunk in a New York warehouse. Upon the death of Mr. Wilbour's daughter they were left by her will to the Egyptian Department of the Brooklyn Museum.[144] There are seventeen items in the group. Certainly they belong to the same find of Aramaic material from Elephantine which was published in 1906 by A. H. Sayce and A. E. Cowley.[145] Of the Brooklyn discovery thirteen items are well preserved. Fortunately, the three documents which deal with slaves are included among these thirteen.

In the Sayce-Cowley edition of the earlier purchases of the Aramaic group the papyrus cited as K is an official record of a division between two brothers of property inherited from their mother. These brothers were members of the long-established Aramaic-speaking Hebrew military colony at Elephantine. Of these two, one was to receive in full ownership a slave who bore the thoroughly Egyptian name of Petosiris. The slave mother of this Petosiris responded to the equally Egyptian name of Tebo. Important for the comparative relation of Greek slave practice with the Hebrew system of that period is the statement in the recorded version of Sayce-Cowley papyrus K that the male slave, Petosiris, was marked upon the right wrist with the letter *yod*, written in Aramaic. This mark had been tattooed upon the slave's wrist first by the Hebrew woman, the mother of the two heirs, and again with the same sign by the son who was relinquishing the slave to the ownership of his brother.

From this single document two observations can be made regarding the slave system of the Hebrews resident in this "fortress of Yeb." The slaves of this isolated Hebrew community, so far as the evidence carries us, were Egyptians, by name at least. This observation, although it is based solely upon the lack of evidence of slaves of Hebrew extraction, is in line with the accepted conclusion applying to the Semitic enslavement type that membership in the religious community and tribal brotherhood precluded actual enslavement under the ownership of a coreligionist.[146] The second observation is positive. The marking of a slave, whether by tattooing or branding, was a feature of the Semitic-Oriental slave practice. It was not characteristic of the Greeks.[147]

The important differences between the general Hellenic attitude upon enslavement and that of the Hebrews residing in Upper Egypt, and the lesser similarities between them which emerged, are here presented. Both the divergencies and the likenesses between the two systems apply, when viewed in the large, to the general Semitic-Oriental slave practice as contrasted with that of the Greeks.

The main persons who appear in the new Elephantine documents upon slavery are these. (1) Meshullam bar Zakkur, a Jewish member of the colony, who was evidently a man of some standing in the community. (2) Ananiah (Anani) bar Azariah, also a Jewish resident, called " the servitor (?) of Yahu," a sacred office which his father had held before him. (3) Zakkur, a son of Meshullam. (4) A female slave of Meshullam named Tamut. (5) Two children of this Tamut, a son named Palṭ whose father is not designated, and a daughter by Ananiah — the man numbered two above. This girl was called Yehoyishma. (6) A boy slave belonging to Zakkur son of Meshullam. The name given him was Yedoniah. (7) Uriah bar Maḥseiah. The name Uriah is not a compelling indication that his tribal derivation was actually Aramaean, for two more of the principals among these Aramaic-speaking Hebrews specifically designate themselves as Aramaeans.[148]

In so far as they apply to slavery the legal instruments of the Brooklyn Aramaic items range from 449 to 420 B. C. In the document which comes second in point of chronology (449 B. C.)[149] Meshullam gave his female slave, Tamut, obviously an Egyptian woman, in marriage to Ananiah, a Jew. The slave woman remained in this status until formally manumitted by Meshullam in 427 B. C., despite her position for the twenty-two years following 449 B. C. as legal wife of

---

[144] The interesting story of the purchase, the long storage, and the ultimate rediscovery of the new Aramaic material has been set forth by Dr. Emil G. Kraeling, New light on the Elephantine colony, *The Biblical Archaeologist* 15 (3) : 50-67, September, 1952, and in his extensive edition and commentary upon the material in *The Brooklyn Aramaic Papyri*, 9-20, New Haven, Yale Univ. Press.

[145] Sayce, A. H. and A. E. Cowley, *Aramaic papyri discovered at Assuan*, London, Moring, 1906.

[146] Upon the enforced service, for a six-year period only, of Hebrew to Hebrew, and for three years of Amorite to Amorite under old Babylonian law, consult Mendelsohn, Isaac, *Slavery in the ancient Near East*, 32-33.

[147] Restricting his study to the peoples of southwestern Asia Mendelsohn did not draw the comparisons with the Greek practice.

[148] These are Zakkur, father of Meshullam who is also called " the Jew of Yeb," and Ananiah, son of Azariah, who had some official connection with " Yahu, the god in Yeb."

[149] Papyrus 2 in Kraeling, *Brooklyn Aramaic Papyri*, 140-150.

the free man, Ananiah. She brought into the marriage a dowry consisting of a woolen garment, some money, and a mirror. Presumably these goods were her own property, not a dowry gift from her master. As shown by the marriage arrangements, in case she was later divorced by Ananiah these goods were legally protected for her. In case of the death of either husband or wife the survivor was to inherit all the possessions of the deceased one. It is important to note that this arrangement was to apply even should the death of either party occur within the time during which Tamut, the wife, was still owned by Meshullam. The problem remains for a subtle legal solution whether the items of the dowry brought into the marriage by Tamut would, in case of her husband's death, belong to her or to her owner, Meshullam. The indications of the marriage document are that they would be hers.

The instrument of manumission of Tamut by her master, Meshullam, which is cited as Papyrus 5 by Dr. Kraeling, is dated in 427 B. C. In it Meshullam freed not only Tamut, but also her daughter by Ananiah, the girl named Yehoyishma. As I understand the earlier marriage document of Ananiah and Tamut, Meshullam had given up all claim to the son of Tamut who was called Palṭ. The lad does not appear, at least, in the grant of liberty to Tamut. The manumission document contains one arrangement which will be of unusual interest in the comparative study of the Hebrew and Greek institutions of slavery. Tamut and her daughter agree to serve both Meshullam until his death, and his son, Zakkur, thereafter, "as son provides for his father." [150] In the specifically Hebrew manumission as it appears in this document and possibly in the general ancient Babylonian-Levantine manumission practice, this provision supplies the place of the *paramonē* arrangement which is now so well known in the Greek law of slavery from the thousand Delphic manumissions by entrustment sale to Apollo. Another point in the manumission of Tamut and Yehoyishma should be noted. Tamut had been "marked" on the hand, presumably by tattooed signs, just as was the slave in papyrus K of the Sayce-Cowley Aramaic papyri. [151]

There is one further item in the Brooklyn collection which impinges upon slavery. It is dated in September or October of 416 B. C. and numbered eight in Dr. Kraeling's preview of his publication. This is not directly connected with the slaves of the Meshullam-Ananiah group; but it has some bearing upon the contrast between the two types of the slave institution. It records the gift by Zakkur, son of Meshullam, of a slave lad named Yedoniah, to Uriah, son of Maḥseiah. This Uriah, despite his name and his self-designation as Aramean, was doubtless a Hebrew. He agreed to

adopt the slave as his son, and not to enslave him or to permit his enslavement by others. No one was to be allowed to "mark" the lad. Again, therefore, a mark of some kind appears to be the customary outward symbol of an enslaved person in the ancient Near Eastern world.

All slave systems grow around the hard core of a few similarities, deeply imbedded as the central ideas of the structure. These include the right of complete ownership of one human being by another, with control by the master of the physical powers and the mobility of the slave. Ideologically the slave has no individuality, no legal personality apart from that of his owner. Customarily, in the eyes of the law the slave has no male parent. Around this central core of likenesses there is an overlying growth of differences which are, in their nature, determined by political, economic and other environmental factors. These factors may be climatically or otherwise physically determined, or they may, in some cases, be accidental in character. Borrowings and transferences of ideas and practices from a neighboring slaveholding community may, or may not, play their part in the growth of any slave system.

From the point of view of comparative cultures the determination of the divergences between the slave institutions of different peoples seem to the writer to be more important than the consideration of the likenesses, whether these likenesses are basic to the internal structure of all slave systems or are external adaptations to similar conditions. [152]

Assembling the new Aramaic materials dealing with slavery for notation of their similarities and their contrasting features as measured against the systems contemporaneously present in the Greek polities, the following observations may be made. One small similarity in the two systems had not appeared in any Hebrew slave document, at least so far as known to me, until it appeared in the manumission of the slave woman, Tamut, executed by her master, Meshullam. As has been already pointed out by Dr. Kraeling, [153] the Hebrew manumission practice permitted an arrangement for the continuation of some part of the former servile services of the woman Tamut and her daughter, Yehoyishma, for their former owner, Meshullam; and after his death these attentions were still to be available to his son, Zakkur. As the manumission reads, the two freedwomen were to serve these two men, successively, "as a son or daughter provides for his (or

[150] The quoted phrase is taken from the translation of the document given by Kraeling, *Brooklyn Aramaic Papyri*, 181, line 12.

[151] Kraeling, *Brooklyn Aramaic Papyri*, no. 5, p. 181, lines 2-3.

[152] The terms "morphology" and "pattern" of slavery are here consciously avoided as being misleading in reference to systems of slavery. The institution has no single pattern and no single *morphē*. It takes many forms which are determined by the social ideas and external circumstances under which the specific system has developed.

[153] Kraeling's Aramaic manumission, numbered five, lines 11-15.

her) father." [154] This arrangement was clearly designed to meet the same objective as that attained by the Greek *paramonē* type of manumission, now well known from many examples in the world of the Greek polities, notably from the Delphic trust sale system. [155]

A second parallel between the Hebraic slave structure (which was probably commonly found in all the Semitic systems of the time) and that of the Hellenistic polities, again appears in the manumission grant by Meshullam to the two women. This is to be found in a clause which certainly had the same purpose as the "assent" or "approval" feature of the Delphic manumissions by trust sale to Apollo, and elsewhere is found in real estate transfers in the Greek world. In the granting of their freedom to slaves this *eudokēsis* formula of the Greek systems provided a clearance of title for the new freedman or freedwoman to his, or her, newly acquired liberty, against possible future claims of ownership rights in their persons which might endanger the validity of their new status.

The motivating principle back of these two similarities lay, in my judgment, in the inherent necessities which arise in the procedures of release of individual slaves from their status. No transfer from the Levantine-Semitic practice to the Greek need be postulated, nor any borrowing in the opposite direction which might have produced in the one or the other case, either the *eudokēsis* (consent or approval) clause or the continuing service arrangement of the *paramonē*. The chronological sequence speaks strongly for local origins designed to meet legal pressures in the case of the clearance of title to liberty (the Greek *eudokēsis*). For the Aramaic-Hebrew slave legislation, upon which the Elephantine documents are based, must, in fact, be carried back to the early sixth century B. C., or possibly earlier, when active and constant connections between the Hebraic and Hellenic cultures were only beginning to assume their greater importance. To this one may add an observation which further suggests a different, and basically dissimilar, origin of the clearance of the slave's claim to freedom which is common to both procedures and has been recently presented in its Greek appearance as the *eudokēsis* element. [156] In the Aramaic-Hebrew formula the decision upon the clearance of title is unilateral and authoritative, based solely upon the declaration of the slave-owner. In the Greek *endokēsis* the formula is based upon the assent, voluntarily given, of the parties who might, more remotely than the slave-owner, be interested in the slave as property.

Out of the second century B. C., contemporaneously in the Hebrew structure of slavery in Palestine, from the Greek city-state world, and from the latifundian ranch type of slave labor in Sicily, comes the evidence of one inner structural feature common to all slave institutions of which the ancient slave societies seem to have been aware than those more modern. Fortunately it is attested, also, with a precise term of designation, in the Roman prefecture of Egypt of the first century after Christ. This is the necessity, commonly resting upon all slave-owners and grounded in the moral acceptances which surround them, that they feed and house their slaves up to a minimal standard, at least, of living requirements. This demand was probably all the more strictly binding upon the slaveholders because it does not seem to have been a fixed requirement formulated in legislative enactments. This is the social requirement of sustenance payments, or food rations, which must be supplied to slave laborers under any and all economic systems which have employed slaves.

Approaching this problem of slave sustenance in the chronological order of the evidence, the first bit of information comes from a maxim of a Jewish learned "father," living about 200 B. C., named Antigonus who hailed from the Judaean town of Socho. [157] It reads:

> Be not like slaves who serve their master in the expectation of receiving (*peras*) a gratuity, but be like slaves who serve their master in no expectation of receiving (*peras*) a gratuity and let the fear of Heaven be upon you. [158]

The translation of the word *peras* as "gratuity," or gift, as given by Maimonides and followed, in the above translations by George Foote Moore, is not correct. Its actual meaning, as explained by Elias Bickerman, is "ration," that is the *food allowance* of the slave, corresponding to the term *demensum cibum* in the plays of Plautus who lived at the same approximate time as Antigonus of Socho. [159]

In one of the Delphic manumissions of the second century B. C. the reverse of this type of maintenance arrangement appears in the agreement of a newly created freedman to supply old age sustenance for one of his two manumittors who apparently was no longer in condition to act in his own behalf. [160] The Greek verb used for this service by the freedman is *gērotrophēsai*,

[154] Kraeling, *Brooklyn Aramaic Papyri*, 178.
[155] Kraeling, *Biblical Archaeologist* 15 (3): 65; *Brooklyn Aramic Papyri*, 178.
[156] Westermann, Extinction of claims in slave sales at Delphi, *Jour. Juristic Papyrology* 4: 49-61, Warsaw; Society of Sciences and Letters, 1950.
[157] *S. v.* Antigonos von Socho in *Jüdisches Lexicon* 1, Berlin, Jüdischer Verlag, 1927.
[158] The translation is that of George Foote Moore, in his *Judaism* 2: 75, Cambridge, Harvard Press, 1927. As shown by Bickerman in the article cited in the next note the word *peras* is the equivalent of the Greek *trophimon*, meaning "ration," and should so be translated.
[159] Bickerman, Elias, The maxim of Antigonus of Socho, *Harvard Theol. Rev.* 44: 153-165, 1951. See particularly p. 154 and n. 9-11 on p. 155.
[160] *GDI* 2, 1723, 7, καὶ γηροτροφῆσαι, Φαινέαν (the former slave) Ἀπολλόδωρον, and line 18, ἐπεὶ δὲ καὶ γηροτροφήσῃ Φαινέας Ἀπολλόδωρον. Other examples are given by Westermann, W. L., Slave maintenance and slave revolts, *Class. Philol.* 40: 1-10, 1945.

definitely " to nourish So-and-So in old age." [161] In his account of the first of the two desperate slave revolts in Sicily of 135-132 B.C., Diodorus of Sicily ascribes the violent outbreak of the slaves primarily to two causes. These were the failure of the owners to give their slaves the " slave food rations " (*sōmatotropheia* in the Greek) due to them, and the masters' insistence upon branding or otherwise marking the slaves. This was, as noted above, not one of the practices to which the slaves of the Greek world were accustomed.[162]

Still more conclusive for the prevalence in every slave system of some understanding upon the amount and quality of the rations or food payments required for slaves is a group of brief notations of agreements found at Tebtunis in the Nile valley. These records, published by A. E. R. Boak and his colleagues of the University of Michigan,[163] clearly designate a number of the agreements registered in the record office of Tebtunis as being, in each case, " an agreement for

slave sustenance " (*homologia trophimou doulikou*). One example will suffice to illustrate the entire group of ten such entries found in a register dated A.D. 46: " Agreement of Tapontos and her husband with Kronion for slave maintenance." [163]

Some of the more noteworthy differences between the Hebrew and the Hellenic enslavement systems should also be noted. Although they are peripheral to the central structure of slavery they are nevertheless more revealing than the resemblances. The first is the practice of the Hebrew community of Elephantine of marking the slave as an indication of his status. This was alien to the Hellenic polity system. The second lay in the possibility of the legal marriage of a slave woman to a member of the Hebrew community. A third marked divergence is to be found in her retention, under the Hebrew system of Elephantine, of slave status while married to a free man. A fourth dissimilarity is to be seen in the close relation to enslavement of the adoption of children which is characteristically ancient Oriental, but not Hellenic. This practice in the Hebrew community at Elephantine is implicit in the adoption of a boy by the man Uriah, with the express provision, in order to provide against his legal enslavement, that his adoptive father would not mark him as a slave or sell him as such.[164]

---

[161] *Ibid.*, 8-9. The source is Diodorus, book 34-35, 2. C. Müller, *Diodori Siculi bibliotheca*, Paris, Didot, 1842-1844.

[162] Boak, A. E. R., *Michigan papyri* **2** (1), *Papyri from Tebtunis* (*P. Mich.*), Index V under τρόφιμον δουλικόν, Ann Arbor, Univ. of Mich. Press, 1933. Husselman, Elinor M., Boak, W. F. Edgerton, *P. Mich.* **5** (2) : no. 238, *passim*, where ten entries for slave maintenance appear. See General Index (IX), *s. v.* τρόφιμον.

[163] *P. Mich.* **5** (2) : no. 238, 27. My interpretation of these records appeared in an article entitled Slave maintenance and slave revolts, in *Class. Philol.* **40**; where I included in the *trophimon doulikon* both board and lodging for the slave (p. 7).

[164] Kraeling, *The Biblical Archaeologist* **15** (3) : 62; *Brooklyn Aramaic Papyri*, Papyrus 8, 224-231.

IV. FROM THE PERSIAN WARS TO ALEXANDER

THE SOCIAL SETTING OF POLIS SLAVERY

The social effects of slavery in the Greek city-state period are difficult to gauge because of the danger of generalization where local differences, both in the character and extent of slaveholding, were so great. A marked leniency in the treatment and attitude toward slaves certainly prevailed in Attica[1] in contrast with the arbitrary treatment of the Helots in Sparta,[2] possibly also in comparison with the treatment of the slave class in handicraft-industrial city-states other than Athens. The explanation of this mildness of the practice is to be sought in the relatively high development at Athens of slaves as objects of capital investment, living in the semi-independent condition of the *misthophorounta sōmata* (pay-earning slaves) rather than in a greater humanity to be predicated for the Athenian

people.[3] The laws of Gortyn in Crete present a situation in which the rights accorded to slaves assimilated them even more closely to the free population than was the case at Athens.

In ancient slavery, throughout, abuse of the power of the slave-owner must, in some degree, have been a constant accompaniment of the institution. Its amount and incidence would depend upon the character of the individual master or upon the tradition of the particular slave-owning family. Those of long established wealth customarily treated their slaves with greater kindness than the newly rich.[4] At Athens, as elsewhere, a master's power might, of course, be abused to the point of inducing a slave to commit a murder in his behalf.[5]

There is surprisingly little actual evidence, on the whole, of abuse of the right of the owner to inflict cor-

---

[1] Pseudo-Xenophon, *Polity of the Athenians*, 1, 10; Demosthenes, Or. 9, 3.

[2] Isocrates, Or. 12, 181.

[3] As is done in Daremberg-Saglio, *Dictionnaire des antiquités* **4** : 1261.

[4] Aeschylus, *Agamemnon*, 1042-1045.

[5] Isaeus, Or. 8, 41.

poral punishment upon the slave in this period. Plato felt compelled, in the projection of his slaveholding state of the *Laws*,[6] to advocate a more drastic system of punishments for crimes of slaves than was practised in the state of his birth, even though he was convinced that hatred between free and slave classes must be avoided as an insurance against slave revolts.[7] Plato was also aware of the danger of bad results, both upon master and slave, inherent in the indiscriminate practice of the right of corporal punishment.[8] A number of case reports have come down to us of physicians who treated slave patients living with their owners.[9] These offer trustworthy evidence of the attention which slaves received in sickness.[10] In one of these case records the attending physician reports his observation, certainly drawn from a number of visits, that throat afflictions were more severe with slaves than with free persons.[11] One must also note that the Athenian law imposed upon the slave-owner the obligation of burial of a slave who died.[12]

The inferior social status of slaves was not made obtrusive at Athens by enforced differences in dress or by the demeanor of the Athenian public toward them,[13] although certain types of cheaper garments were sometimes bought for slaves and so became associated with them.[14] Runaway slaves were harshly treated when retaken[15] and sometimes branded;[16] but the practice was an Oriental and pre-Greek one which was generally avoided in the Greek world because of the difficulty of selling a slave thus publicly advertised as having the tendency to disappear. Xenophon's proposal upon the marking of public slaves, in his projected plans for new sources of state revenue,[17] was that slaves acquired by the state should be branded. This idea was apparently essential to his plan for government ownership without the necessity of resale; it does not prove the prevalence of the custom in practice among private owners.

Granting that slave status in general was an unenviable condition, there are many indications that deeper racial and class antipathies, such as those based upon differences of skin coloring, were totally lacking in the

Greek world. One should consider that Aristophanes could publicly jest about free women cohabiting with slaves[18] without arousing the indignation of his audience. The lack of the development of such a feeling explains in part the many privileges which, in fact, slaves enjoyed.

Mixed marriages of free and slave were the subject of legislation in Crete which fixed the inheritance of slave status by a peculiar provision that the children of a free woman who married a slave were to be free if the slave came into her house, but they were to be slaves if the free woman went to live with the male slave in his house.[19] The countryside slaves in Crete (*oikeis*) married, had their own personal property, and might be divorced, in which case the property rights of the female slave were legally protected.[20] That the separate-living slaves (*chōris oikountes*) who worked for their owners in Athens and in similar handicraft production centers might marry and found households of their own cannot be questioned; but nothing is definitely known about the legal rights pertaining to their property. It is to be assumed that when the property became large enough they would customarily buy their freedom. Seventeen cases are recorded in Attic manumission lists from the period 340-320 B.C.,[21] in which the ex-slave had purchased his or her freedom with money obtained in part from a group called loan contributors (*koinon eraniston*). The fact of this kind of loan, which was non-interest bearing, offers incontrovertible evidence of a non-hostile relation, if not actually friendly, of slaves with free persons. The lack of any discriminatory stigma attaching to a person who had once been a slave is seen in the careers of Archelaus, who became King of Macedon although he was a son of King Perdiccas by a slave concubine, hence technically a slave,[22] and that of Pasion, the Athenian banker, once a slave of an Athenian named Archestratus. Pasion arranged that his widow marry a slave of his own whom he had manumitted and that this former slave, Phormion, should succeed Pasion himself as manager of the bank which he had founded.[23]

The continuance of the ideals of the primitive family group maintained the tradition of the slave as participant in the family worship.[24] Though forbidden to take part in the Thesmophoria,[25] slaves at Athens were

---

[6] Plato, *Laws* 9 : 868, 872.

[7] Plato, *Republic* 1 : 351*d*.

[8] Plato, *Laws* 6 : 777*a*.

[9] Hippocrates, *Epidemics* 4 : 2 : τῷ στιγματίῃ παρ' Ἀντιφίλου.

[10] *Ibid.* 2 : 3, 4 ; 5 : 35, 41 ; 7 : 35, 112.

[11] *Ibid.* 6 : 7.

[12] Demosthenes, Or. 43, 58.

[13] Pseudo-Xenophon, *Polity of the Athenians*, 1, 10.

[14] Such as the thick κατωνάκη made of wool and sheepskin, Aristophanes, *Lysistrata*, 1155, which was a garment worn by the poorer classes of the population. See the article Κατωνακοφόροι in Pauly-Wissowa, *RE* 11 : 26, and the Megarian sleeveless ἐξωμίς, scholium to Aristophanes, *Wasps*, 444.

[15] Herodotus, 6 : 11.

[16] Aristophanes, *Birds*, 760 : δραπέτης ἐστιγμένος. *Cf.* the branded slave treated by a doctor at Athens in Hippocrates, *Epidemics* 4 : 2.

[17] Xenophon, *Ways and means*, 4, 21.

[18] Aristophanes, *Thesmophoriazusae*, 491.

[19] Laws of Gortyn, 7, 1-4. Bücheler-Zitelmann in *Rheinisches Museum* 40 : Ergänzungsheft, 65-66.

[20] Laws of Gortyn, 3, 40-43.

[21] *IG* 2²(1) : 1553-1578.

[22] Plato, *Gorgias*, 471*a*.

[23] Demosthenes, 36, 43-46. The statement that Pasion had been a slave will be found *ibid.*, section 45. *Cf.* Schäfer, Hans, Pauly-W., *RE* 18 (2) : 2064.

[24] In Aeschylus, *Agamemnon*, 1004-1005, the slave captive, Cassandra, is invited to take part in the family cult of Zeus Ktesios.

[25] Aristophanes, *Thesmophoriazusae*, 294.

initiated into the mysteries [26] and could attend many of the public sacrifices as spectators or as participating suppliants.[27]   But no examples of foreign cults introduced by slaves or specifically associated with them can be established for this period.

Indications are not wanting that the slaves at Athens had a life of their own, with ameliorations and pleasures therewith.   At the noon hour they might be seen sleeping by the spring;[28] and they had their own modes of rhythmic expression quite distinct from those of the free population.[29]

The relation of slavery to sexual morality, in view of the naïve and open acceptance of prostitution and even of homosexual relations in Greece, is somewhat difficult to determine.   As suggested by W. Kroll,[30] concubinage with slave women tended to limit prostitution by making it in part unnecessary.   But slavery also furnished a ready supply of young girls who could be bought and established as prostitutes, as in the case of the freedwoman Nicarete, who earned her living through the harlotry of seven girls trained by her in the *techne*.[31]

It is important to note in the laws of Gortyn and in the law of Athens that slaves were recognized as human beings, to be protected against insult and overbearing acts (*hybris*), and that the laws of Gortyn made a civil offense of carnal violence, whether heterosexual or homosexual, committed against a slave.[32]   The fines imposed for such acts committed against slaves were, however, comparatively so meagre that they must have put a premium upon physical violence perpetrated upon women of that class.[33]   There can be little doubt that slavery was a strong contributing factor toward sexual promiscuity; but the Greek attitude upon sex relations, which was open and not prurient, was not caused by slavery.   Nor did the social acceptance of such promiscuity ever seriously offend the Greek moral sense, Greek religion, or Greek taste.

The figure of the slave, early formulated as a conventionalized type in the Megarian, Doric, and Epicharmean popular comedy,[34] was taken over by the dramatists and writers of ancient comedy.   Though increasingly individualized in point of character delinea-

tion the stage figure of the slave in comedy never lost completely its early characteristics as a standardized type.   In Aeschylus and Sophocles the slave was sparingly used and slavery was presented as a personal affliction of those who suffered it, without moralistic or humanitarian implications,[35] rather than as a social evil, although the dramatists were conscious of its psychological results upon the enslaved person.[36]   Euripides was more alive than his predecessors to the dramatic possibilities and the emotion of pity which could be aroused in his audience by the use of slaves, presenting them as individualized persons whose inferiority to the free man lay solely in the implications of the word " slave."[37]   J. Schmidt in an essay upon slavery in the dramas of Euripides,[38] has overemphasized the humanitarian tendency to be ascribed to Euripides, whose approach was primarily artistic rather than sociological.   Euripides' acceptance of the right of Greeks to rule over barbarians, the Greeks being by nature free, the barbarians slaves,[39] is to be explained as motivated by the strong element of *polis* patriotism combined with pan-Hellenic patriotism in him.[40]

Little is known of the attitude of the Sophists upon slavery.   Their egalitarian position which would eliminate the distinctions commonly made between Greeks and non-Greeks is reflected in the remark of Antiphon the Sophist: " All of us breathe the air through the mouth and the nostrils."[41]   By implication and by sequence of thought this led, as it necessarily must, to a theoretical statement of the natural equality of master and slave such as appears in a fragment of the comic poet, Philemon: " Though a man be a slave he is made of the same flesh as you.   For no one was ever made a slave by nature; but chance has enslaved a man's body."[42]   The famous quotation from the *Messeniacus* written by the sophist Alcidamas, *ca.* 361 B. C., that God had made all men free, nature had made no man a slave, may be explained as a conviction of Alcidamas in the tradition of his master, Gorgias.   It may be understood as a reflection against a society based upon artificial law, or it may be an opportune answer to Isocrates' insistence upon property rights in slave holdings as presented in his argument against the emancipation of the slaves of the Mantineans.[43]   Although the Cynics

---

[26] A slave *hetaira* was personally initiated by Lysias, Demosthenes, 59, 21.

[27] *Idem.* 59, 85.   At the jar feast, on the second day of the Anthesteria festival at Athens, slaves participated in the drinking and the festivities.   It was " the lucky day for slaves," according to Callimachus, *Aetia*, frg. 178, in the edition of Pfeiffer, R., *Callimachus*, Oxford, Clarendon Press, 1949.

[28] Plato, *Phaedrus*, 259a.

[29] Plato, *Laws* 2: 669c.

[30] Kroll, W., *Zeitschrift für Sexualwissenschaft* 17: 159.

[31] Demosthenes, 59, 18; *cf.* Isaeus, 6, 19-20.

[32] Bücheler-Zitelmann, Laws of Gortyn, 1, 2-11, *Rh. Mus.* 40, Ergänzungsheft.

[33] The fine for the rape of a free man or woman is one hundred staters, for the rape of a slave peasant woman five drachmas.

[34] Aristophanes, *Wasps*, 57. Langer, C., *De servi persona apud Menandrum*, 7-8, diss. Bonn, 1919.

[35] Schmidt, J., Der Sklave bei Euripides: *Wissenschaftliche Beilage zum Jahresberichte der Fürsten- und Landesschule zu Grimma*, 99, 1892.

[36] Aeschylus, *Agamemnon*, 359-361, 953; Sophocles, *The women of Trachis*, 298-305; *Philoctetes*, 995-996.

[37] Euripides, *Ion*, 854-856; *cf. Medea*, 54-55; *Helena*, 728-731.

[38] Schmidt, J., *Der Sklave bei Euripides*, 25.

[39] Euripides, *Iphigenia in Aulis*, 1400-1401.

[40] Hettich, E., *A study in ancient nationalism, the testimony of Euripides*, 67, 69, diss. Columbia, 1933.

[41] *P. Oxy.* 11: 1364, frg. 2, 294-298; Gernet, Louis, *Antiphon*, 178, frg. 5, Paris, Belles Lettres, 1923.

[42] Philemon, frg. 95 in Kock, Theodor, *Comicorum Atticorum fragmenta* 2: 508, Leipzig, Teubner, 1884; Glotz, Gustave, *The Greek city and its institutions*, 260-261, New York, Knopf, 1929.

[43] Pauly-W., *RE* 1: 1536.

did not deal with slavery as an institution their attitude toward it is expressed in the maxim which held that slavery was an accident and a matter of indifference, since only freedom of the spirit counted and the slave could be master of himself and of his owner as well.[44]

The statement assigned to Socrates by Plato in the *Gorgias*,[45] that the slave must suffer injustice and has no one to whom he may turn for aid, is not true to the facts of the time, either legally or in point of social custom. It is, in fact, directly contradicted by a passage in a brochure upon the Athenian polity which has come down to us under a false ascription to Xenophon. It is generally accepted by competent scholars, that the actual author was an Athenian conservative who wrote the study during the first, or " Archidamian," phase of the Peloponnesian war.[46] Although this brochure has been considerably corrupted in transmission to us, the meaning of this quotation is abundantly clear: " Among the slaves and the metics, moreover, there exists at Athens a high degree of license and one does not dare there to strike (one of them) ; nor will the slave step out of the way for you."[47] Definite legislation is, indeed, known to us against the beating of a slave belonging to another master, cited under the law as the " indictment for violence " (*graphē hybreōs*).[48]

The best criterion for determining the rigidity and the harshness of any slave system is to be found in the ease and availability of its manumission procedures. It is not to be questioned that the ways were numerous by which slaves in the Greek city-states could inaugurate and bring to completion one or another of several methods of obtaining their liberation. For Athens at the close of the sixth century we have the report of the incorporation by Cleisthenes of a number of freedmen into the citizen body.[49] The very presence in Attica of any considerable number of freedmen is sufficient proof of the currency and frequency of the use of manumission at that time. There is no clear example from fifth-century Greece of the custom of self-redemption of a slave with his own money (*servus suis emptus*) of which we have so many examples in the manumission records from Delphi after 200 B. C.[50] From the fourth century, however, we do have convincing proofs of the employment of the form of manumission with continuing bondage services, that is the grant of freedom with the contractural obligation resting upon the freedman to assist his former owner when called upon for specific

services. Xenophon, for example, in the third chapter of the *Oeconomicus* pictures Socrates as engaged in a conversation about the use of equipment and labor upon an estate. In the discussion Socrates points out that slave workers who are physically bound and otherwise put under constraints are likely to run away whereas those who have been freed are more willing to work for their former masters and remain with them.[51]

From the *Laws* of Plato we gain absolute certainty regarding the use of the *paramonē* method of manumission in the fourth century. Freedmen, Plato says, should in his state of the *Laws* be subject to seizure if they did not perform their services or did not do so sufficiently well. Thrice each month they were to go to the homes of their manumittors to ascertain what their former owners desired them to do as their required services. These demands must be " just and at the same time possible " for them to perform.[52] This restriction of the continuing services of the new freedman who was under *paramonē* obligations to those tasks which he could perform is practically constant in the several hundred manumissions of this type which occur in the Delphic group of manumissions.[53]

Not so decisive for the *paramonē* type of manumission in the fourth century B. C. as the correspondences of Plato's suggestions in the *Laws* with the Delphic *paramonē* grants of freedom is the case of the manumission of the slave girl prostitute in the court speech against Neaera, ascribed to Demosthenes, which involved an Athenian named Stephanus. In Corinth where she was being kept as a slave by two young men for their carnal enjoyment she purchased her freedom from them, partly with money supplied by a later admirer, partly by soliciting a non-interest bearing advance from a group of her former lovers who had formed an *ad hoc* loan company called an *eranos*.[54] There can be no doubt that the girl was then free; but she must have been subject to possible revocation of that freedom so long as the loan had not been fully repaid by her to the *eranos* group. This is abundantly verified by the Delphic manumissions of this type. Decisive evidence for the use at Athens of the *paramonē* manumission, with its provision for continuing services to the manumittor, appears in the simulated trials of slaves who

---

[44] Diogenes Laertius, 6: 74-75.

[45] Plato, *Gorgias*, 483b.

[46] Hohl, Ernst, Zeit und Zweck der Pseudoxenophontischen Athenaion Politeia, *Classical Phil.* **45**: 35, 1950, dates it in the period 445-431 B. C. The argument is not convincing.

[47] Pseudo-Xenophon, *Polity of the Athenians*, 1, 10-12.

[48] Demosthenes, 21, 48; Aeschines, 1, 15.

[49] Aristotle, *Politics* 3: 1275b.

[50] Collitz, Hermann, J. Baunack, F. Bechtel *et al.*, *Sammlung der griechischen Dialekt-inschriften (GDI)* **2**: 1684-2342, Göttingen, Vandenhoeck-Ruprecht, 1899.

[51] Xenophon, *Oeconomicus*, 3, 4. The terms here used are unmistakably those of the *paramonē* system: ἔνθα δὲ λελυμένους καὶ ἐθελόντας τε (τοὺς οἰκέτας) ἐργάζεσθαι καὶ παραμένειν.

[52] Plato, *Laws* 11:915a: ὅτι χρὴ δρᾶν τῶν δικαίων καὶ ἅμα δυνάτων. This passage has been misinterpreted in the study of Morrow, Glenn, Plato's law of slavery, *Univ. of Ill. Stud. in Lang. and Lit.* **25**: 103, 1939. The services (*therapeiai*) here spoken of are precisely the opposite of " specific duties." They are undefined. See Westermann, W. L., The *paramone* as general service contract, *Jour. of Juristic Papyrology* **2**: 24-27, Warsaw, 1948.

[53] E. g. *Fouilles de Delphes, Epigraphie, Inscriptions du Théatre* 3 (6) : 35, 15; 50, 9; 118; 15-16: ποιῶν τὸ ἐπιτασσόμενον τὸ δυνατὸν πᾶν ἀνεκκλήτως.

[54] Demosthenes, 59, 29-32.

were under such *paramonē* obligations. The court decisions rendered in these cases were called " judgments for release," *dikai apostasiou*.[55]

The assumption is sometimes made, even today, that the Greek political theorists of the fourth century accepted human enslavement as a reality of the economic and political order of their time, but that they felt " uneasy " and " unhappy " about it.[56] The idea is an outcropping of the sentimental attitude toward slave institutions and it is fundamentally misleading when postulated as an attitude characteristic of the fourth century Hellenes. In the *Republic* Plato made no clear statement as to whether the ideal state was to eliminate or accept slavery. The fact that he decried the enslavement of Greeks by Greeks assumes, of course, the contemporary reality that every Hellenic city-state would use enslaved barbarians as laborers. Plato's suggestion about Greeks not reducing other Greeks to slavery was diluted by Xenophon[57] to the point of agreeing with the Greek practice of the time, that it was permissible to enslave one's enemies (obviously including Greeks), but not one's friends.

The enslavement of free Greeks captured in war persisted, despite isolated objections, as in the case of the Spartan admiral Callicratidas, who refused, in the Peloponnesian war, to enslave the Methymnians after the capture of their city.[58] This attitude of Callicratidas did not, of course, apply to the slaves of the Methymnians taken as booty.[59] The praise bestowed by Xenophon upon Agesilaus[60] for protecting children and aged captives who were abandoned by the slave merchants attending his army, throws light upon the general callousness which prevailed toward human suffering attending the capture and sale of war prisoners. The slave merchants who followed the army did not hesitate to abandon to their fate the weakest of these captives when the merchants were overstocked or feared to lose money through the heavy cost of feeding or transporting them. The law attributed to the Athenian finance minister, Lycurgus, to the effect that no resident of Attica might buy a free person out of war

booty without the consent of his former ruler[61] is best explained, perhaps, as an opportunistic political measure, possibly connected with the right of ransom arising out of some concrete case in the Macedonian war[62] rather than as an amelioration of the right of enslavement in war among the Greeks themselves.

Despite tentative approaches in previous writers toward an analysis of slavery, centering about the question whether it was grounded in natural law or was contrary to nature, Aristotle was the first Greek student who discussed it critically as a social institution and attempted to determine its place in the political organizations of his time.[63] In Aristotle's view the primitive and natural association is the household (*oikia*), founded upon the triple relationship of master and slave, man and wife, father and children.[64] Out of the uniting of such primitive units grew the community.[65] Out of the combination of villages arose the state.[66] Possessions are defined as instruments for the purpose of living; and a slave is a servant in the sphere of action.[67] Slavery was, therefore, in the Aristotelian conception, not only natural but also necessary for the maintenance of the type of democratized city-state community, with its privileged body of citizens, in which Aristotle lived. Accepting the point of view of Euripides[68] regarding the Greeks as free men, the barbarians as slaves,[69] Aristotle later presents a scientific explanation of slavery.[70] His conclusion, that slavery is justified and necessary, is grounded in the theory of innate differences, both quantitative and qualitative, in the moral and intellectual capacities of individuals which extend to include racial groups. This view goes back to that school of thought of the latter part of the fifth century which believed in the influence of climate and topography in determining physical and mental characteristics and in the inheritance of characteristics thus acquired.[71]

It is, of course, understood both by Plato and by Aristotle that the slave element of the population in any well organized state can have no political status whatsoever. Its role in the social order is a necessary one, but a purely economic one. It has not been suffi-

[55] *IG* 2²(1): 1553-1578; Westermann, W. L., Two studies in Athenian manumissions, *Jour. Near Eastern Stud.* 5: 94-96, 1946.
The statement made by Ch. Picard in *BCH* 45: 150-157, that the manumission from Thasos which he there published presented a solitary example of its type in the fourth century has been repeated by W. W. Tarn in *CAH* 7: 212, n. 1. The inscription is fragmentary, but may safely be read, as published in *IG* 12, *Suppl.*, no. 368. It is a manumission, possibly by dedication to a god of the *paramonē* type.
[56] Michell, H., *The economics of ancient Greece*, 33, 150, New York, Macmillan, 1940.
[57] Xenophon, *Memorabilia* 2: 2, 2.
[58] Xenophon, *Hellenica* 1: 6, 14.
[59] Schück, Ueber die Sklaverei bei den Griechen, *Programm des städtischen Johannes-Gymnasiums zu Breslau*, 10, Breslau, 1875.
[60] Xenophon, *Agesilaus*, 1, 21.

[61] Pseudo-Plutarch, *De vita decem oratorum: Lycurgus*, προτέρου δεσπότου cannot here mean " owner."
[62] *Cf.* article Lykurgos in Pauly-Wissowa, *RE* 13: 2453.
[63] Schiller, Ludwig, Die Lehre des Aristoteles von der Sklaverei, *Jahresbericht von der königlichen Studienanstalt zu Erlangen*, 5-6, Erlangen, 1847, a study still valuable although based upon the then prevailing acceptance of the exaggerated slave numbers from antiquity.
[64] Aristotle, *Politics* 1: 1, 4-5.
[65] κώμη, *ibid.* 1: 1, 7.
[66] *Ibid.* 1: 1, 8.
[67] *Ibid.* 1: 2, 6. Further defined in *Ethics* 8: 13 as an instrument of action with a soul: ὁ γὰρ δοῦλος ἔμψυχον ὄργανον.
[68] Euripides, *Iphigenia in Aulis*, 1400-1401.
[69] Aristotle, *Politics* 1: 2, 5.
[70] *Ibid.* 1: 5, 3-9.
[71] *Ibid.* 7: 6, 1. Hippocrates, *De aere aquis locis*. Cf. Schiller, L., *Die Lehre des Aristoteles von der Sklaverei*, 27.

ciently emphasized that both of these thinkers have thrown free workmen into close proximity with slave labor by their attitude upon the "banausic" trades. Plato's approach in the state of the *Laws* was that all citizens of the polities should be forbidden to engage in handicraft production because the practice of the crafts leads the practitioner away from that freedom of the spirit which the citizen must have.[72]

In the *Politics* Aristotle raised the question of the precise definition of the word "citizen." Did the term include only those who had the right to share in the magistracies of the state? Or were the lower class workmen, the *banausoi*, also to be regarded as citizens? The problem was made even more precise. If such workmen were regarded as citizens, then the *aretē* of citizens, that is, their quality and character, must be redefined, because the "citizen" should be the type of man who can rule through his possession of the character qualities which are summed up in the idea of citizen *aretē*. That the "banausic" workman cannot rule is the obvious thought of the passage.[73] It is in connection with this argument upon citizenship that Aristotle introduces the assertion that in olden times, among some peoples, to be a craftsman in the lower orders of labor was to be an alien or a slave, and that, even in his day, the mass of the workmen of that type *were* analogous to slaves; "and the best state form will not make a banausic workman a citizen."[74] This discussion, basically a political one upon the quantitative, or inclusive, aspects of "citizenship" and its requirements, is readily subject to misinterpretation when parts of it are removed and quoted out of their context. Under this treatment, quotations from Aristotle's theoretical discussion of slavery have been transformed into a proof that the basic work of Greek society was done by enslaved persons who derived from their labors none of the benefits granted by that social organization. Cicero, who reproduces from Panaetius of Rhodes the

traditional attitude taken by the Greek theoreticians,[75] really presents nothing more than the continuation of this Greek attitude into Roman times. This extension of the theory brings about the identical conclusion as applicable to Roman society which had been wrongly postulated for the Greek world, that the free artisan and the small tradesman were despised because they earned their living by labors which were to be ranked among the *artificia sordida*.[76] For the Greek theoretical approach, however, on the whole, the Greek *democratia* as governmental form of the polity was that setting which, in fact, produced the truly free man in the forms of the *polis* citizen. It was Herodotus, one may note, who first stated that the non-Greek monarchies, notably that of Persia, produced men who did not, and could not, understand or appreciate freedom.[77]

The social analysis of the slave institution became traditionalized in the aristocratic literature of antiquity upon the lines laid down by Aristotle. Nature itself had determined that some men were physically and spiritually adapted for slave status and low-class labors as against those who were both spiritually and somatically unfitted for such tasks, but fitted for civilian life and its freedoms. In this theoretical frame of reference Aristotle's views upon slavery must be read.[78] In practice the manumission of his own slaves as preserved in his will completely contradicted his theoretical exposition of the sociological setting of slavery.[79]

The approach to the slave system of the Hellenic polities should be conditioned upon the understanding of the fluidity of its status. The ascent into freedom by the several methods of manumission then available was as easy and as prevalent as the descent from freedom into servitude.

---

[72] Plato, *Laws* 5 : 741*e*; 8 : 846*d*. In the *Laws* 8 : 831*c-e*, Plato regards the desire for gain as necessarily degrading to the spirit and as characteristic of merchants, shipowners and business agents. See Schiller, L., *Die Lehre des Aristoteles von der Sklaverei*, 19.

[73] Aristotle, *Politics* 3 : 3, 1, p. 1277*b*.

[74] *Ibid.* 3 : 3, 2, p. 1278*a*.

[75] Cicero, *De officiis* 1 : 151-152.

[76] This type of reasoning derives from an untenable view that the use of slave labor was basically detrimental to ancient society of which it was, in fact, an integral and valuable part. An example of this false approach is to be found in Walbank, F. W., *The decline of the Roman empire in the west*, 24-25, London, Corbett Press, 1946.

[77] Herodotus, 7 : 135.

[78] Schiller, Ludwig, *Die Lehre des Aristoteles von der Sklaverei*, 5-8.

[79] See Aristotle's testament in Diogenes Laertius, 5 : 1, 9; Bruns, Ivo, *Zeitschrift der Savigny-Stiftung, Rom. Abt.* 1 : 1-52, 1880; Westermann, W. L., *Jour. Near Eastern Stud.* 5 : 99-101, 1946.

V. THE EASTERN MEDITERRANEAN LANDS FROM ALEXANDER TO AUGUSTUS

RECRUITMENT OF SLAVES AND NUMBERS

For a century after Alexander the sale of captives in war could not have been the primary source of slavery in the Hellenistic world. Even before the treasures of the Persian King fell into his hands, which released him from the constant financial pressure of living off the land, Alexander himself avoided the enslavement of captives[1] except when the bitterness of the opposition dictated the sale of the conquered as a measure of military terrorization. The numbers of 30,000 allegedly sold after the capture of Thebes[2] and after the taking of Tyre[3] are stereotyped figures of little value. According to the estimate of W. W. Tarn, perhaps 8,000 prisoners from Thebes were sold.[4] At Granicus 2,000 Greek mercenaries were captured and sent to Macedon in chains; but of this number the Athenian captives were released two years later.[5] After the march into the interior of Asia began, Alexander's policy toward the defeated enemy necessarily became even more conciliatory. A few sales of prisoners are recorded such as that after the capture of some fortified towns in Aria and Sogdiana.[6] These sales could not have affected either the numbers or the prices of slaves in the distant Aegean area.[7]

Polybius implies that the enslavement of the inhabitants of captured cities was not generally resorted to by the successors of Alexander, the custom being replaced by equal exchange of prisoners between the combatants and ransom of the remainder at an agreed price.[8] In the second half of the third century Miletus arranged a treaty with Cnossus and nineteen other towns of Crete, providing that no Milesian subject would knowingly buy a free man from the Cretan towns and no subject of the Cretan towns would purchase as his slave a free person of Milesian origin.[9] This provision would cover both war captives and free men enslaved through seizure by pirates. The report contained in the well known Jewish propagandist letter to Philocrates[10] that more than 100,000 Jewish slaves captured in the wars of Ptolemy I were freed by Ptolemy II at the time of the translation of the Septuagint, is not supported by evidence of enslavement of any large number of war captives under either of the first Ptolemies. Enslavement on such a scale also runs counter to the policy of conciliation imposed upon these rulers in their desire to hold the control of Palestine and Syria.[11] The suggestion made by M. I. Rostovtzeff that many Jewish slaves might have come upon the Alexandrian slave market in consequence of the first Syrian war of Ptolemy II is not supported by the presence of many slaves or of many Jewish names in the Zenon papyri. The acceptance of this idea is dependent upon the reading $a[\iota\chi\mu\acute{a}\lambda\omega\tau]a\ \sigma\acute{\omega}\mu a[\tau a]$ of Papyrus Gradenwitz no. 1, 5, which is only a possible restoration,[12] and upon the report of Callixenus of Rhodes[13] regarding the great procession of Ptolemy II, which is dated by W. Otto at the end of the first Syrian war in 271-270 B. C.[14] There are no slaves mentioned as participating in or exhibited in this procession. A report in Diodorus[15] that Ptolemy I after the battle of Gaza settled 8,000 captured soldiers in the nomes of Egypt is, on the other hand, credible as to numbers and consistent both with the policy of the early Ptolemies of settling soldiers upon the land[16] and with the general policy of that time against the sale of war captives.

Kidnapping and sale of children remained edemic and constant in the eastern Mediterranean. This is clearly demonstrated in the Greek New Comedy and it is incorporated as a dramatic theme from the *Nea Comoedia* into the plays of Plautus and Terence.[17] Despite the efforts of the Hellenistic powers to control piratical

---

[1] Andreades, A. M., Ἱστορία τῆς Ἑλληνικῆς δημοσίας οἰκονομίας, **2** (1) : 39, n. 5, 40, Athens, Tzaka, 1928-1931.

[2] Aelian, *Varia historia* 13 : 7; Polybius, 5 : 10; Plutarch, *Alexander*, 11. The amount raised by the sale is given by Diodorus, 17 : 14, 4, as 440 talents, without a statement of the numbers involved.

[3] Arrian, *Anabasis of Alexander* 2 : 24, 5. Compare with Diodorus, 17 : 46, 4.

[4] W. W. Tarn in *CAH* **6** : 356.

[5] Q. Curtius Rufus, *History of Alexander* 4 : 8, 12.

[6] Arrian, *Anabasis of Alexander* 3 : 25, 7; 4 : 2, 4; 4 : 3, 1; and two instances in India, *ibid.* 6 : 7, 3; 6 : 17, 1.

[7] Andreades, A., Ἱστορία δημοσίας οἰκονομίας, **2** (1) : 39.

[8] Polybius, 8 : 3. See the ransom arrangements between Demetrius Poliorcetes and Rhodes in 304 B. C. as recounted by Diodorus, 20 : 84, 6. Similar conventions between Miletus, Heraclea and Priene appear in Dittenberger, *SIG*³ no. 588, 67-72.

[9] Wiegand, Theodor, *Milet, Delphinium* 3 (1), no. 140 : 18-38, Berlin, Reimer, 1914 (editors of this volume, Georg Kawerau and Albert Rehm).

[10] Pseudo-Aristeas, *Epistula ad Philocratem*, 14, 17-20.

[11] Rostovtzeff, M. I., Seleucid Babylonia, *Yale Class. Studies* **3** : 68, New Haven, Yale Univ. Press, 1932.

[12] Plaumann, Gerhard, Griechische Papyri der Sammlung Gradenwitz, *Sitzungsb. Heidelb. Akad.,* phil.-hist. Klasse **5**, 15, no. 1 : 19 (= *P. Grad.*).

[13] Athenaeus, 5 : 25-35.

[14] Otto, Walter, Beiträge zur Seleukidengeschichte, *Abh. Bayer. Akad., philos.-philol. Klasse* **34** (1) : 7-9, Munich, Oldenbourg, 1928.

[15] Diodorus Siculus, 19 : 85, 4.

[16] See Mahaffy, John P., *The Flinders Petrie papyri* (*P. Petrie*) **2**, no. 29b, Dublin, Academy House, 1893, republished in better form in *P. Petrie*, **3**, no. 104 and in Mitteis, Ludwig, and U. Wilcken, *Grundzüge und Chrestomathie der Papyruskunde* 1 (2), no. 334, Leipzig, Teubner, 1912.

[17] Plautus, *Captivi*, 971 ff.

activities, notably through the efforts of the Ptolemaic kingdom and the city-state of Rhodes piracy was always present in some degree as a method of providing the local market places with the slave numbers which they needed. The extent of kidnapping was accentuated by the fact that mercenary troops were recruited from pirate organizations and that the mercenary bands, after discharge from specific military tasks, frequently reverted to piracy.[18] Trustworthy instances of the close connection betweeen piracy and enslavement are furnished by the inscriptions of the period. One of these, dated about 260 B. C., narrates the retention in captivity in Crete for three years of free inhabitants of Thera, who were eventually released with the slaves captured with them.[19] A second inscription tells of the seizure by pirates of more than thirty persons from the island of Amorgos, of whom all the free persons and a part of the freedmen and slaves were later ransomed.[20] A third tells of the ransom of two hundred eighty inhabitants of Naxos who had been captured by Aetolian pirates.[21] The inscriptions record only successful arrangements for ransom; but the New Comedy, as preserved in the original Greek fragment and as reproduced by Plautus and Terence, gives ample evidence of the sale of these victims into slavery when the pirates failed to obtain a ransom price.[22] The legitimate trade in slaves, also, no doubt dealt in the retail distribution of these kidnapped and unransomed victims of pirates as well as in those obtained from the customary and legally recognized sources of slavery, namely birth, capture in war, and inability to meet debtor obligations.

In the late third century a return to the policy of enslavement through war can be observed, notably in connection with the wars of the Macedonian kings. Mantinea was captured in 223 B. C. and the population was sold into slavery by Antigonus and the Achaeans under Aratus, but the affair was still condemned in the Greek world.[23] In 203-202 Philip V sold the captured populations of Cius, Myrleia, and Thasos.[24] In 172 B. C. Antiochus IV of Syria attempted to use his campaigns against the Jews as an aid to his budget, overburdened by the war indemnity annually due to Rome, by preparing beforehand for the capture and

sale of a large number of prospective Jewish opponents.[25] That the Hellenistic kings owned large numbers of royal slaves is evident from the report that Antiochus IV had 600 of them march in a great parade at Daphne.[26] In the civil wars between Ptolemies VI and VII in Egypt in 167 B. C. the slaves who were captured by the opposing armies became the booty of the soldiers.[27]

With the mass enslavement by order of the Roman Senate in 167 B. C. of 150,000 Epirotes, chiefly Molossians, from seventy towns[28] the full effects became manifest in the Aegean area of the application of the policy of sale of captives on a large scale which had characterized Sicilian warfare since the time of Dionysius I of Syracuse and had become an accepted feature of Roman military policy during the Punic wars. The development in the West of large grain plantations and cattle ranching in Carthaginian North Africa, in Sicily and in the Italian peninsula had created a new type of labor market which showed a great capacity for the absorption of slave labor. During the second century B. C. these factors associated themselves with an insensitiveness on the part of the Roman Senate to the ultimate economic disadvantages of unrestricted piracy and, in the earlier decades of the first century, with an inability on the part of the Roman state to cope with that problem. The concurrence of these four elements created a situation, during the century of the Roman conquest of the East, 171 to 64 B. C., under which slaves were drained westward in large numbers. From the statement made to the Roman Senate by Nicomedes of Bithynia in 102 B. C., that the majority of his subjects available for war had been carried off by Roman tax collectors[29] some idea of the magnitude of the westward slave traffic and its effect upon the Near East may be obtained.

There is no evidence that the states of the Greek homeland area changed their long-established laws or their fixed social attitude against self-sale into slavery in payment of benefits conferred or against sale into

---

[18] Ziebarth, Erich, Seeraub und Seehandel im alten Griechenland, *Hamb. Univ. Abh.* 30 : 21-29; Ormerod, Henry A., *Piracy in the ancient world*, 123-146. For the activities of the Aetolian mercenary captain, Dicaearchus, which verged upon piratical plundering, at about 200 B. C., consult Diodorus, 28 : 1; Polybius, 18 : 7-8; Westermann, W. L., *Upon slavery in Ptolemaic Egypt*, 22-25.

[19] *Inscriptiones Graecae*, 12, 3, no. 328.

[20] Dittenberger, *Syll.*³, no. 521.

[21] *Ibid.*, no. 520.

[22] Instances of this in the Latin comedies are: Plautus, *Menaechmi*, 29; *Curculio*, 645; *Poenulus*, 84; *Captivi*, 7; *Rudens*, 39; and Terence, *Eunuchus*, 115.

[23] Polybius, 2 : 56, 7; 58, 12; Plutarch, *Aratus*, 45, 4.

[24] Polybius, 15 : 23, 24.

[25] *Maccabees* 1 : 3, 41; 2 : 8, 10-11, 34-35; Ginsburg, M., *Rom et la Judie*, 24, Paris, Povolosky, 1928.

[26] Polybius, 31 : 3. In an inscription from Delphi, probably to be dated in 197 B. C., we hear of a royal slave girl of Attalus I, Dittenberger, *Syll.*², no. 846. Compare Rostovtzeff, M. I., *Social and economic history of the Hellenistic World* 1 : 564, 565; 3 : 1465, Oxford, Clarendon Press, 1941, and Magie, David, *Roman rule in Asia Minor* 1 : 149, Princeton, Univ. Press, 1950.

[27] Meyer, Paul M., *Griechische Urkunden der Hamburger Staats- und Universitätsbibliothek*, no. 91, Leipzig, Teubner, 1924. In the Delphic manumissions by trust sale to Apollo in Collitz, Hermann, F. Bechtel, J. Baunack, *GDI 2*, nos. 2167 and 2172, the *lytra ek polemiōn* represent a definite amount paid by the slaves for their freedom which is based upon the current ransom payment for prisoners, but is not, in fact, a ransom price as is generally believed and as stated by Westermann in Pauly-W., *RE, Suppl.* 6 : 930 and Calderini, *Manomissione*, 216.

[28] Polybius, 30 : 16; Livy, 45 : 34; Appian, *Foreign wars* 10 : 2, 9.

[29] Diodorus, 36 : 3. Catullus, 10, 14-20, speaks of Bithynia as a special source of slaves used as litter bearers at Rome.

bondage of members of the family;[30] but the Greek emigrants into western Asia and Egypt and their rulers did not interfere with the old Oriental native custom of sale of their children where the practice was already accepted. In Egypt both self-transfer and transfer of one's children into slavery for benefits conferred had been customary in the Saite period;[31] and the non-Hellenic practice of self-sale and self-lease remained possible into the latest days of the Ptolemaic regime.[32] In Babylonia the use of slaves on a wide scale had always been customary, with pledge of wife, children, or the debtor himself against a debt, followed by eventual slavery in case of non-payment.[33] Numerous clay bullae from Warka (Uruk) of the period 220-180 B. C. recording payment of the tax on slave sales [34] (andrapodikē ōnē in the Greek) indicate the continuance of slavery in Seleucid Babylonia, presumably on much the same scale as previously.

Arrest and eventual enslavement by state action for non-payment of taxes was everywhere possible, as in the previous Greek period. Pledging of children by their parents against private debts remained unacceptable to the feeling of the Greeks of the homeland; but it was certainly taken over from the enchoric custom by the Greek ruling classes in Ptolemaic Egypt.[35] It was presumably a common occurrence in the Seleucid kingdom also.[36] In Ptolemaic Egypt, contrary to the

Solonian decree still prevailing in the Greek homeland cities, executory arrest and eventual enslavement of the debtor himself is now proven. By negative implication this is clear from a series of excerpts from the laws and regulations of Alexandria of the late third century B. C. Among them occurs the provision that Alexandrian citizens, male or female, might not become the slaves of their fellow citizens.[37] The evident assumption is that inhabitants of Egypt who were *not* Alexandrian citizens might be enslaved by other inhabitants of the country. The attitude toward slavery which inspired this decision was surely not Greek. It is in fact the application, in a restricted field, of the old oriental concept that fellow nationals could not be enslaved to persons of their own tribal group.[38]

Rearing of exposed children into slavery continued to be a common practice in Greece as well as in the expanded areas of Hellenistic influence although it is known only from the comedies of the period and from the appearance of θρεπτοί in manumission inscriptions of the time.[39] The problem raised by these abandoned children went back in Asia Minor to a period long preceding Augustus' time.[40] Presumably infant exposure was a practice as common to Asia Minor as to the Greek lands of the earlier period. The rescuer of the child would customarily rear it as a slave; but the original status of the child remained fixed, so that the parent, or the original owner, if the child had been of slave origin, might re-assert his primary right of *patria potestas* or of *dominica potestas* as the case might be.[41]

It is probable that the proportion of slaves to free population did not greatly increase after Alexander's conquests either in the areas penetrated by Greek emigration and colonization or in the older Greek centers around the Aegean Sea [42] in spite of the enlargement

[30] Philostratus in his *Life of Apollonius of Tyana* 8:7, 161, makes a statement about the later Greek attitude toward slavery which is idealized to the point of falsehood: " still even now they are lovers of freedom and a Greek man will not sell a slave beyond the borders [of his state, presumably]."

[31] Griffith, F. L., *Catalogue of the demotic papyri in the John Rylands library*, nos. 3-7: 50-59, Manchester, Univ. Press, 1909. Compare Taubenschlag, R., *Zeitschr. Sav.-Stift., Rom. Abt.*, 50: 154, 1930. Paul Koschaker in *Abh. sächsischer Akad., philol.-hist. Klasse* 42: 1, 64, n. 1, thought that these transfers might be merely into a bondage status (*Halb-freiheit*), expressed by the Egyptian *bk*. In Cairo Papyrus 65739, lines 16 and 19, published by A. H. Gardiner in *JEA* 21: 140-146, the word *bk* certainly means "slave," not a servant in bondage status. See Gardiner, *ibid.*, 145, n. 23.

[32] Vitelli, G., *Papyri Greci e Latini (PSI)* 5, no. 549, is an agreement of self-lease of 42-41 B. C. made by a woman under a *paramonē* contract for a term of ninety-nine years. This represents merely an indefinite period. See Westermann, W. L., The *paramone* as general service contract, *Jour. Juristic Papyrology* (Warsaw) 2: 34, 1947.

[33] Meissner, Bruno, *Babylonien und Assyrien* 1: 375-376, Heidelberg, Winter, 1920-1925; Mendelsohn, I., *Slavery in the ancient Near East*, 5-19, New York, Oxford Univ. Press, 1949.

[34] Rostovtzeff, *Yale Class. Studies* 3: 26-29, 1932.

[35] Vitelli, *PSI*, 4, no. 424. *Cf.* Arangio-Ruiz, *Persone e famiglia nel diritto dei papiri*, 5, Milan, Soc. "Vita e Pensiero," 1930; *PSI*, 5, nos. 529, 532. A Columbia papyrus of the Zenon archive contains an accusation that a creditor had illegally detained a free woman and her son against a debt, Westermann, W. L., Keyes and H. Liebesny, *Columbia papyri* 4, (= *P. Col.*) *Zenon papyri* 2, n. 83, New York, Columbia Univ. Press, 1940.

[36] This is proven for Phrygia in Asia Minor by Philostratus, *Life of Apollonius of Tyana* 8: 7, 161: "for the Phrygians at any rate it is a custom of the country also to sell their own children."

[37] *Papyrus Halensis* (= *P. Hal.*) 1, lines 219-221, in *Dikaiomata. Auszüge aus Alexandrinischen Gesetzen und Verordnungen*, 23, 81, and 163, Berlin, Weidmann, 1913; Lewald, Hans, *Zur Personalexekution im Rechte der Papyri*, 27 ff. Leipzig, Veit, 1910. Debtor slaves, ὑπόχρεα σώματα, occur in *P. Col.* inv. 480, lines 23-24, 27-29, published in Westermann, *Upon Slavery in Ptolemaic Egypt.* Cf. Oertel, Fr., in *Gnomon* 8, 1654-1655. For divergent explanation of the ὑπόχρεα σώματα as persons of slave status pledged by their owners against debts, see Koschaker, P., in *Abh. Sächs. Akad.* 42 (1): 59.

[38] This is discussed above in Chap. 1.

[39] Cameron, A., ΘΡΕΠΤΟΙ and related terms in the inscriptions of Asia Minor, *Anatolian studies presented to Wm. H. Buckler*, 27-62, Manchester, Univ. Press, 1939, has discussed the three different meanings for *threptos* which appear in the Asia Minor inscriptions of the Roman period. These are: foster-child, adopted child and slave child. These differences no doubt were followed in the third and second centuries B. C. For the Roman Empire see Pliny, *Letters* 10 (9): 65-66. The definition of the word as current in the Roman chancellery appears in Trajan's answer, no. 66, as "free born (children) who were exposed, then picked up by certain persons and raised in slave status."

[40] Pliny, *Letters* 10 (9) 65, 3: *edictum quod dicebatur Augusti*. The decree dealt with the θρεπτοί.

[41] Menander, *Epitrepontes*, 70, 108-128; Pauly-Wissowa, *RE* 11: 467-468.

[42] Glotz, Gustav, *Le Travail dans la Grèce ancienne*, 419,

of the area of slave recruitment for the Greek world and the obvious extension into the newly founded Hellenistic industrial centers of Egypt and Western Asia of the Greek practice of capital investment in slaves for labor in handicraft shops. The small-shop system, employing slave and free labor, may have been instituted in some of the newly founded cities which were predominantly Greek, although data from such cities to prove the point are particularly wanting.[43] In the Greek papyri which come predominantly from the towns and villages of Ptolemaic and Roman Egypt the terms used at Athens to designate these handicraft slaves ("those who live apart" and "pay-earning slaves") do not appear. In the field of agriculture in which the greater part of Egyptian labor had always been employed, the teeming indigenous free population, which had always been accustomed to compulsory services, left little room for slave labor.[44]

The characteristic type of Egyptian slavery in the Hellenistic period was that of household service, especially with the dominant class of Greeks,[45] and the numbers of slaves imported for such services may easily be exaggerated. The total number of those who can actually be identified as slaves in the Zenon documents covering the years 258-237 B. C. cannot be estimated as more than forty-five, including the four slave boys sent by the Ammonite sheikh, Toubias, to the finance minister of Egypt.[46] The workmen "sent from Syria" in Cornell papyrus 1 (ἀποσταλέντα σώματα ἐκ Συρίας), if they were slaves, as seems most probable, certainly did not number more than three or four as shown by the lamp oil nightly used by them.[47] The remaining cases of slaves in the Zenon archive, as far as the status is certain in each case, number about twenty.[48] A series of

wills from the reign of Ptolemy III shows the following numbers of slaves in the ownership of Greek military cleruchs: five slaves and a freedman; a female slave and her boy who was a son of the slave-owner; a slave boy, son of the deceased, who was freed by the terms of the will; two male slaves; and a man and woman, with provision for a deferred manumission for them.[49]

In western Asia the prevailing land system of extensive royal domains worked by a plentiful supply of serfs left small economic opportunity for the introduction of slave labor in agriculture.[50] In Lydia the "royal peasants" (βασιλικοὶ λαοί) formed the greatest part of the agricultural population,[51] although the "servants, those dwelling in the locality" (οἰκέται οἱ κατοικοῦντες ἐν τῶι τόπωι) in Sardis 7, 1, no. 17-18, who were alienated with the land, may have included real slaves who were regarded as part of the inventory of the property. The numerous class of the hieroduli (consecrated slaves) attached to the temples in Asia Minor were slaves, as the name implies; but the degree of their dependence varied widely, so that it is often difficult to distinguish them from serfs or clients. The hieroduli, for example, dedicated to a group of gods as musicians by Antiochus I of Commagene, quite specifically were not to be enslaved.[52]

For slave conditions in central Greece in the Hellenistic period the manumission inscriptions at Delphi, which record the granting of freedom through trust sale of the slaves to Apollo, offer certain conclusions upon the numbers and the geographical origin of the slaves

Paris, Alcan, 1920 (Ancient Greece at work, 349-351, New York, Knopf, 1926).

[43] Rostovtzeff, M. I., CAH 7: 135. For the dominant position of the government and temple manufactories in Ptolemaic Egypt see Rostovtzeff, Soc. and Econ. Hist. Hellenistic World 1: 320-322, and for small shop production in the metal industries, ibid. 2: 1222. Préaux, Claire, L'économie royale des Lagides, 305, Brussels, Fondation Égyptologique, 1939, would make Alexandria an exception in respect to the employment of slave labor in the Greek polis manner.

[44] Breccia, Evaristo, Bull. de la Société Royale de Geographie d'Égypte, Cairo, 15: 71-75, 1927. This is more strongly stated by Pirenne, Jacques, Histoire des institutions et du droit privé de l'ancienne Égypte 2: 317, 1934. For Ptolemaic and Roman Egypt consult Wilcken, U., Griechische Ostraka 1: 695-697, 703-704, and Westermann, Upon slavery in Ptolemaic Egypt, 54-59.

[45] Mitteis, L., and U. Wilcken, Papyruskunde, Grundzüge 1 (1): 260; Arch. f. Pap. 6: 449, 1920.

[46] Edgar, C. C., Zenon papyri (P. Cair. Zen.) 1, no. 59076, Catalogue Général des Antiquités du Musée du Caire 15 (1), Cairo, Institut Français, 1925.

[47] Westermann, W. L., and C. Kraemer, Greek Papyri in the Library of Cornell University, no. 1, 222-224, New York, Columbia Univ. Press, 1926.

[48] P. Col. 3, no. 3, several slaves, cf. P. Cair. Zen. 5, no. 59804; PSI 4, no. 329, a cook; ibid., no. 406, four slaves; P.

Cair. Zen. 1, no. 59003, a young girl, possibly a Babylonian; no. 59015 verso, more than three slaves; no. 59077, a girl; P. Cair. Zen. 3, no. 59355, two female slaves; four fugitive slaves in inventory no. 2087 of the London Papyri, sent to me by T. C. Skeat. The wool workers in PSI 7: 854; P. Cair. Zen. 2, no. 59142 and P. Ryl., 4: 556 (Edgar, C. C. in Bull. John Rylands Library 18: 114; Manchester, 1934) are called "girls" (paidiskai). Contrary to Edgar's note, they need not be slaves.

[49] The references, in the order given in the text, are : P. Petrie, 1, no. 12, cf. 3, no. 9' (= Mitteis-Wilcken, Chrestomathie 1 (2), no. 449) ; 3, no. 2; 3: 6a; 3: 7; 3: 11.

[50] For the serf-like position of the tenants in Asia Minor see M. I. Rostovtzeff, Studien zur Geschichte des römischen Kolonates, Arch. f. Pap., Beiheft 1: 258-259, Leipzig, Teubner, 1910; idem, Anatolian studies presented to Ramsay, 368, Manchester, Univ. Press, 1923; S. and E. Hist. Hellenistic World 1: 509; 3: 1441, n. 285. For Mysia, see Rostovtzeff, Anatolian Studies, 373; for Phrygia, Bithynia and Pontus, Rostovtzeff, Annual Brit. School at Athens 22: 11, 1916-1918; in Caria, Athenaeus, 6, p. 271b; for Seleucid Mesopotamia and the laoi in Asia Minor, Bikerman, Elias, Les institutions des Seleucids, 176-179, Paris, Geuthner, 1938.

[51] Buckler, Wm. H., and D. M. Robinson, Sardis 7: 1, no. 1, Leyden, Brill, 1932; and for the Troad, Dittenberger, W., Orientis Graeci Inscriptiones (= OGI), 1, no. 225, Leipzig, Hirzel, 1903.

[52] OGI 1, no. 383: 171-183: μηθενὶ δὲ ὅσιον ἔστω μήτε βασιλεῖ μήτε δυνάστει μήτε ἱερεῖ μήτε ἄρχοντι τούτους ἱεροδούλους — — — αὐτῶι καταδουλώσασθαι μήτε εἰς ἕτερον ἀπαλλοτριῶσαι. For the current indecisive attitude toward the hierodules of Asia Minor see the posthumous work of Otto, Walter, Beiträge zur Hierodulie im hellenistischem Aegypten, Abh. Bayer. Akad., n. f. 29: 44-45 and n. 220-223, Munich, 1950.

in central Greece which have some value. Deductions regarding the numbers of slaves employed in central Greece which one may be tempted to draw from observation of these documents must, however, be accepted with distinct reserve because of missing factors in the labor situation of the localities involved.[53] There is a noticeable progressive decline in the number of slaves freed under this single manumission form as practiced at Apollo's shrine if one compares the half-century periods 201 B. c. to 154-153 B. c. (priesthoods I-V), 154-153 B. c. to *circa* 100 B. c. (priesthoods VI-XII[1]), and the period *ca.* 100 B. c. to *ca.* 53 B. c. (priesthoods XII[2]-XVI inclusive). For the first period about four hundred eighty-three individual cases of manumission were observed. This would give an average of nine per year. For the last five decades of the second century B. c. the total of grants of freedom used in the calculation out of the trust sales to Apollo was three. This reduces the annual average to six and a half manumissions. The most authoritative chronology of the Delphic archonships now available assigns to priesthoods XII[2]-XVI a period of approximately forty-seven years.[54] The number of the grants of liberty by the system of trust sale to Apollo for these years is about ninety-four. This diminishes the average for the approximate period *ca.* 100 to *ca.* 53 B. c. to two instances of the use of the trust sale manumission per year. These calculations have for me no probative value as establishing a general decline in slave numbers in the Greek world in the two centuries before the Christian era because there is no proof whether the same numerical diminution in manumissions would apply for other forms of granting freedom.

With respect to two other observations based upon the Delphic manumissions the results obtainable are much more convincing and they have some historical significance. The first concerns the ratio of the slaves born in the homes of their owners (*oikogeneis, endo-*

geneis, engeneis) in these three periods to those obtained by purchase, whether they were bought in towns of Greece and the Aegean islands or were imported into Greece from foreign countries. The total number of the individuals brought under observation for the calculation was nine hundred twenty-six. In four hundred fourteen instances nothing is said about the origins of the slaves. In five hundred twelve cases the statement of the *origo* is clearly made, either that the slave in question was born in the home (*oikogeneis*, etc.) or that he derived from some Greek town or from some area alien to Greece. Clearly there was no statute at Delphi which required that the origin of the slave be given *in each case of manumission*. There is a strong probability, though absolute proof is not available, that by Delphic law the slaves born in the homes of their owners were to receive recognition of this fact in the inscribed record and were officially registered somewhere as being of that classification. This conclusion rests upon the fact given by Orosius that Diaeus, Achaean strategos in 147 and 146 B. c., " wrote to all the cities (of the Achaean League) to free those of their homeborn and home-raised slaves who were in the prime of life, up to the number of 12,000, and to arm them and send them to Corinth." This clearly means that in Achaea there existed an official list of the *oikogeneis* and the *paratrophoi* which could be checked. For Delphi the number of the *oikogeneis* who are recorded as such in the published notices of the trust sale manumissions seems to demand the same decision.[55]

In tabulated form the record of nine hundred twenty-six cases under control from the Delphic records appears in table 1.

TABLE 1

	Priesthoods I-V 201-153 B. C.	Priesthoods VI-XII[1] 153 B.C. to ca. 100 B.C.	Priesthoods XII[2]-XVI, ca. 100 to ca. 53 B.C.
Origo not stated....	285	89	40
Born in the home (*oikogeneis*, etc.).	63	162	48
From Greek towns or foreign born...	136	97	6

In the first of the three periods the ratio of the bought slaves to those born in the home, out of one hundred ninety-nine cases in which the *origo* is given, was *ca.* three purchased to one homeborn. In the last half of the second pre-Christian century, in the two hundred

[53] These missing factors were not sufficiently considered by A. Calderini in his *Manomissione e la condizione dei liberti*, 358-359, nor were they mentioned by me in the original article in Pauly-W., *RE, Suppl.* **6** : 933. Calderini's use (*ibid.* 359) of the references in Pausanias, 7 : 15, 2 and Polybius, 38 : 15, 2, is misleading (reference to Polybius wrong in Calderini). The total levy of troops by Diaeus, Achaean general in 147 B. c., amounted only to 14,000 foot soldiers and 600 cavalry according to Pausanias, *loc. cit.* Although Polybius was unquestionably present in Greece at the capture and destruction of Corinth in 146 B. c. (Plutarch, *Philopoemen*, 21) the statement that 12,000 homeborn (*oikogeneis*) and house-bred slaves (*paratrophoi*) were enlisted, as the numbers are ascribed to him in a quotation of Orosius, is not credible. The larger number of 14,600 troops is to be regarded as representing the total enlistment of soldiers, both free and slave. One might venture a guess that the contingent of slaves of fighting age was about a quarter of the total levy, or, roundly, about 3,500. The Delphic figures of the manumissions of houseborn and house-nurtured slaves strongly recommend caution regarding their numbers in general and specifically as given in Orosius' quotation from Polybius.

[54] Daux, Georges, *Chronologie Delphique*, 49-71, Paris, de Boccard, 1945.

[55] From the time of the Roman occupation of Egypt documents called *oikogeneiai*, certifications of birth in the home, were required in Egypt for houseborn slaves. See Schubart, Wilhelm, Oikogeneia, *Raccolta di scritti in onore di Giacomo Lumbroso*, 49-74, Milan, Aegyptus, 1925. Schubart discusses the pertinent documents, including *PSI* **6** : 690 and two other *oikogeneiai* previously unpublished. See also the statute no. 67 (published in the group of laws from Roman Egypt called the *Gnomon of the Idios Logos*), *BGU* **5** (1) with the explanation of Uxkull-Gyllenband, von Waldemar, in *BGU* **5** (2) : 66-68.

fifty-nine cases usable, this ratio had almost been reversed, giving about two and one-third homeborn to each of those born elsewhere in Greece or brought in from alien lands. In the first half of the first century B. C., out of ninety-four cases observed, one sees a remarkable change—eight bred in the slave-owner's home to each one brought in from elsewhere and obtained by purchase.

The tabulation of the origins of the freedmen who were *not* born in the homes of their masters, in the cases which were useful for the purpose, offer the results given in table 2.[56]

TABLE 2

	Priesthoods I-V, 201-154/153 B.C.	Priesthoods VI-XII,[1] 154/153 B.C. to ca. 100 B.C.	Priesthoods XII[2]-XVI, ca. 100 B.C. to ca. 53 B.C.
Greek towns and the Balkans, including Thessaly, Macedon, Thrace and Illyria	76	23	6
Lower Russia and Danube regions (Sarmatians, Bastarmians, Maeotians)	2	10	0
Asia Minor and West Asiatic (e.g., Phrygia, Armenia, Paphlagonia, Elam, Cyprus, Syria, Palestine)	48	41	1
Egypt, including Alexandria	2	3	0
North Africa.......	0	1	0
Italy	6	0	0

Several of the changes in the two tables presented are so marked that they cannot be considered as accidental. They permit, indeed, several clear-cut observations which can be accepted without hesitation. Outstanding is the notation that there was no movement of slaves from the West to central Greece, at least as recorded in the Delphian evidence in the period stretching from 171-170 B. C. (end of the third Delphic priesthood) to the defeat of the Roman army at Carrhae in 53 B. C. Three of the six Italians enslaved in the early period, 201-170 B. C., were women.[57] Despite the appearance of these women, the enslavement of the Italians may be ascribed to the capture of Roman soldiers and their female followers in the war with Philip V of Macedon

and in the Greek phase of the war with the Seleucid king, Antiochus III. The disappearance of all manumissions of Italian born slaves after the Delphic archonship of Sosinicus (174-173 B. C.)[58] is to be ascribed to the power position already established in Greece at that time by Roman Italy.

The relatively large increase, in the century between 153 B. C. and *ca.* 53 B. C., in the number of the homeborn slaves and the corresponding decline in the ratio to them of those brought into the central Greek towns from abroad is the striking feature of the first table. This may find a satisfactory explanation in the progressive decline in the economic position of the cities of Greece, with the exception of Athens,[59] caused in the first instance by the material damage which accompanied the Roman intervention in Greece. This material decline was perpetuated in the period of the complete domination of the Roman state over Greece after 146 B. C. The impoverishment and the spiritual depression resulting from the loss of Greek independence are admirably presented in a fragment quoted from Polybius, who was an astute, informed, and honest observer.

Professor Rostovtzeff, the eminent student of the economic development of the Hellenistic and Roman periods,[60] laid special stress upon the importance of the losses in productive manpower in the Greek polities caused by mortality in war and the exportation of artisan slaves from Greece to Italy.[61] He did not deal with the reverse of this picture, the introduction of the Greek type of production into the West, based upon trained craftsmen who might be either free or slave, but were predominantly, in certain industries, of slave classification. This change, which is noticeable in Italy particularly, from dominant praedial slavery to a fairly balanced free and slave labor system in the handicrafts, is of great importance.[62] The relation of cause and effect in this new emphasis upon industrial slavery in the western Mediterranean—whether the importation of

---

[56] Compare the list of the Delphic freedmen from Greek and foreign localities other than the homeborn (οἰκογενεῖς) as given in Calderini, *Manomissione*, 408-410, and the summaries in Bloch, Moritz, *Die Freilassungsbedingungen der delphischen Freilassungsinschriften*, 17, n. 1-5, Strassburg, Singer, 1914.

In the tabulations which I present here three inscriptions from Delphi recording manumissions by trust sale came too late for inclusion in the estimate. They were published by Christine Dunant in *BCH* **75**: 311-315, 1951, as numbers 3-5.

[57] *GDI* **3**: 2043, 2045, 2116. *Cf.* Calderini, *Manomissione* 410. Bloch, *Freilassungsbedingungen*, 17, n. 3, cites two Romans. One of them I could not find.

[58] *GDI* **2**: 1800.

[59] The exceptional position of Athens in the period 200-86 B. C. has been established by John Day, *An economic history of Athens under Roman domination*, particularly pp. 49, 119-120, New York, Columbia Univ. Press, 1942.

[60] Diodorus Siculus, 32: 26, 2, getting his information, no doubt, from Polybius, says: "They (the Achaeans) seeing before (their) eyes the slaughters and the ox-slayings of their friends and relatives, the captures and plunderings of their native city-states, and the enslavements of entire populations with insolent treatment, cast aside all sense of liberty and freedom of speech, exchanging their noblest benefits for the deepest miseries." Rostovtzeff, M. I., *Soc. and econ. hist. Hellenistic world* **2**: 606-607, 616-617; **3**: 1501, n. 4. For the further depression of the Greek fortunes and spirit caused by the Roman civil wars which were fought so often upon Greek soil in the years 49-31 B. C., see Rostovtzeff, *ibid.* **2**: 1012-1014.

[61] *Ibid.* **3**: 1646, note to p. 617.

[62] Johnson, Jotham, *Excavations at Minturnae* **2** (1), Philadelphia, Univ. of Penn. Press, 1953; Westermann, W. L., Industrial slavery in Roman Italy, *Jour. of Econ. History* **2**: 149-163, 1942.

Greek artisans as slaves into the west caused the increase there in the handicraft use of slaves or the growth in handicraft slave employment motivated the slave importations into the west—is a problem which cannot be answered with the data we possess. It is a reasonable supposition that the increase in central Greece in the ratio of the homeborn slaves as compared with those purchased is definitely bound up with the westward movement of most of the marketed slaves in the century from 153 to about 53 B. C. This would have the tendency to make the breeding of slaves in central Greece economically necessary in the case of a people whose prosperity had been shattered at home and whose outlets for their handicraft products were being rapidly closed to them abroad.

The number of slaves maintained by individual Greeks of the prosperous classes during the Hellenistic period, as presented by the Delphic manumission records, shows a decided decline as compared with the numbers ascribed to the ownership of a few persons about 400 B. C. and with Plato's obvious belief that in his time fifty slaves formed a very large holding. The testaments of the heads of the Lyceum at Athens show the following numbers: Aristotle, more than fourteen; Theophrastus, a total of nine, of whom two had been freed and two manumitted by his will; Strato, seven or more; Lyco, who had already freed three slaves, still had a dozen remaining to be disposed of by his will.[63] The report found in Diodorus that a very wealthy citizen of Abdera

about 170 B. C. could furnish a band of 200 slaves and freedmen in defense of the city is not incredible, although not consonant with other figures for numbers owned by single persons in this period.[64] The Delphic manumissions of the years 201–ca. 53 B. C. present, fairly consistently, the granting of freedom to a single slave, with a considerable number of simultaneous grants to two slaves.[65] The number of the grants made at one time to three or more slaves dwindles rapidly as compared with single and double manumissions. Simultaneous grants to six, nine and ten slaves occur, the highest number being eleven; but only one instance of multiple grants is found in each of these numerical groups. There are very few cases of repeated manumissions made by the same person.[66]

The conclusion that about three slaves would cover the average number owned by any one slaveholding family in central Greece seems to be warranted.[67] Nicomedes of Bithynia, at the request of the city of Delphi, sent thirty slaves to be assigned to the service of the god Apollo. Nineteen of these were used to care for the horses and cattle, eleven being assigned to temple services and to the *technai*, possibly as musicians.[68]

---

[63] Diogenes Laertius, *Lives of the Philosophers* 5: 12-16, 53-55, 63; Westermann, W. L., Two studies in Athenian manumissions, *Jour. Near Eastern Studies* 5: 99-104, 1946.

[64] Diodorus Siculus, 30: 6.
[65] Published chiefly in *GDI* 2: 1684-2342 and *Fouilles de Delphes* (*FD*) 3: 1-6.
[66] These are the numbers given by Calderini, *Manomissione*, 206-208.
[67] Compare with this conclusion the three slaves ascribed to an islander of Cos by Herondas, 8.
[68] Dittenberger, W., *OGI* 1: 345, which is dated within the period 92-74 B. C.

VI. THE EASTERN MEDITERRANEAN LANDS FROM ALEXANDER TO AUGUSTUS

THE DELPHIC MANUMISSIONS: SLAVE ORIGINS, ECONOMIC AND LEGAL APPROACHES

After the conquest of Egypt and southwestern Asia by the forces of Alexander a general shifting of the central area of Greek production occurred which was determined by the opening up of western Asia to the superior business acumen and energy of Greek enterprisers. In this movement the older handicraft centers of the Greek mainland, notably Athens and Corinth, were, in the long run and gradually, replaced in their economic importance by old or new towns located on the western periphery of the wide territory now opened up to Hellenic business life. These might be Greek cities or older Oriental urban centers, sparked into a new vitality by the superior organizational ability of Greek immigrants. Whether completely new foundations or older centers now revived, they were towns more advantage-

ously located with respect to the new opportunities offered in western Asia and in Egypt.[1] Prominent in this group were the island city of Rhodes, Antioch on the Orontes River, Seleucia on the Euphrates, and Alexandria in Egypt. The competition offered by these new aspirants for the trade of a widened world may well have caused some decrease in the numbers of the slave population of handicraft workers in the Greek homeland as compared with the total free group. More probable than this is the suggestion that the industrial shift which occurred, along with other causes, was in some degree responsible for an absolute demographic

---

[1] Beloch, Julius, *Griech. Gesch.*, 2d ed., 4: 1, 278-279; W. W. Tarn in *Camb. Anc. Hist.* 7: 212.

decline in Greece itself. This decrease in population was observed and admirably analyzed by Polybius of Megalopolis for the middle period of the second century B. C.[2]

The information at hand upon the economic use of slaves in the Hellenistic period shows no important change in the many types of their employment. Whatever variations from earlier practice developed in this respect, so far as they can be determined, were evidently due to differences in local labor requirements. On the basis of such local variations one can best explain, for example, the singularity upon the island of Cos that women slaves were officially distinguished in the tax records from the slave vine planters peculiar to the place.[3]

Publication in 1950 of one of the few slave documents as yet found in Macedonia has taken away from the Delphic priests of Apollo one distinction which recently had been assigned to them. This lay in the assertion that they had been the first to describe the condition of freedom as consisting of the four elements, of status, personal inviolability, right to work as one pleased, and the privilege of going wherever one wished. These "four freedoms," it has been said, appeared for the first time at Delphi in the formula followed in the published reports of the manumissions by the process of self-purchase through trust sales to the god Apollo.[4] The new Macedonian manumission recently published is dated in the twenty-seventh year of a King Demetrius who, in all probability, was Demetrius II, and the year seems to have been that of his joint reign with his father. Therefore the document may be placed in 235 B. C.,[5] thus antedating the earliest of the Delphic liberations under the system of sale to Apollo by more than thirty years. The differentiation between individual freedom and slavery in the Beroean manumission is expressed in implications, rather than in a clear enumeration of the qualities which now belonged to the new freedom; but the benefits attained by the granting of his liberty are stated. They lay in the possession of a legally recognized position in the community (status), in the privilege of going where he might desire to go,

and in protection from illegal seizure and detention.[6] Despite this new information some merit still attaches to the originators of the Delphic formula. As our information now stands, it was they (presumably the priests of Apollo) who gave a concise and coordinated description of the four principal elements present in the status of freedom and absent in the case of those subjected to personal slavery.

The Delphic manumissions by self-purchase of their liberation by the slaves themselves through the medium of the entrustment sale to Apollo number more than a thousand. The preponderant type in this group is that of the "outright" manumissions. These represent a completed and immediate separation of the former slave from any further control on the part of his owner. These "outright" grants rarely record the economic employment of the slave who had now been raised into the class of free men. The so-called *paramonē* manumissions, on the other hand, are those in which the new freedman contracts to work for his former master over a period of years when he is called upon to do so. These show clearly that in the towns of the area of central Greece, which is chiefly represented in the Delphic manumission records, the slaves seem, in great part, to have been engaged in household work or in some form of immediate attendance upon their owners.[7] In one of the records posted at Delphi, which is dated 157-156 B. C., a boy who obtained his liberty was required to undergo a period of apprenticeship to a fuller and to work later in the house of his manumittor.[8] Similar conditions apply in household woolweaving in a poem of Herondas, mimist of the early third century B. C.,[9] and in the case of a slave freed at Thespiae under the continuing service obligations of the *paramone*. In the case of this latter freedman it was agreed that he was to retain the tools of his trade when the term of these contractual work obligations ended.[10] In the period 170-158 B. C. an owner of Locrian Physcus granted her release to a homeborn slave who was a flageolet player by trade.[11] In other manumissions, also, freedwomen are designated as "handicraft workers" (*technitai*) in the Delphic documents.[12] A marked tendency observable in the Greek

---

[2] In Polybius, 36: 17, 5-11, read the discussion of the population decline and its causes, *apaideia* and *oliganthrōpia*. For the extent of the Rhodian trade in stamped jars which developed in this period see Rostovtzeff, M. I., *Soc. and Econ. Hist. Hellenistic World* 3: 1486-1487; Heichelheim, Fritz, *Wirtschaftsgeschichte des Altertums*, 1072, n. 12.

[3] Reinach, Th., Inscriptions de l'île de Cos, *Rev. des études Grecques* 4: 361-362, 369: τοὶ ἀγοράζοντες ὠνὰν ἀμπελοστατεύντων καὶ τῶν γυναικείων σωμάτων.

[4] Westermann, W. L., Slavery and the elements of freedom in Ancient Greece, *Quart. Bull. Polish Inst. of Arts and Sciences* 2: 11, New York, 1943; Between slavery and freedom, *Amer. Hist. Rev.* 50: 216, 1945.

[5] M. Andronikos, Ἀρχαιαι επιγραφαι Βεροιας, 20, Department of Historical Monuments and Archaeology, Thessalonica, 1950. Professor Charles Edson of the University of Wisconsin informs me that he is inclined to accept the date as given by Andronikos.

[6] Free status appears in the text of the manumission, *ibid.*, p. 9, line 4, expressed in the phrase that the slaves had "paid down for freedom," κατέβαλον ἐπ' ἐλευθερίαι, fifty gold pieces (twenty-five in one case). The mobility concept appears in lines 13-14, and the personal inviolability respecting seizure in lines 14-22, especially in the words, καὶ ὁ ἄγων εἰς δουλείαν ἀπ[ο]-τ[ιν]έτω etc.

[7] Female slaves, for example, agree that they will "remain within" (the home obviously, ἔνδω μένουσαι), GDI 2, no. 1767, 11 and 1775, 11.

[8] GDI 2: no. 1904, 5-9.

[9] Herondas, 8, 11-13.

[10] Dittenberger, *SIG*[3], 1208.

[11] GDI 2: 1842.

[12] GDI 2: 2154, 2157; *Fouilles de Delphes* (= FD) 3 (1),

homeland area is that slavery, probably of the same home-industry type, spread into localities where the use of slaves upon any considerable scale is not provable for pre-Hellenistic times.[13]

The purchase prices paid for slaves show the same wide variations as in the earlier period. These differences are to be ascribed to such factors as age at the time of purchase, technical equipment, physical condition, personal beauty in the case of luxury slaves, and to changes in the status of the slave market. In the middle of the third century B. C. in Egypt slaves, chiefly from Syria, brought the following prices: a slave girl of seven years, purchase price in Birta in the Ammonite district, fifty drachmas;[14] a boy slave at one hundred twelve drachmas;[15] male slave sold in the Hauran, one hundred fifty drachmas;[16] and a slave girl bought in the same locality, 300 drachmas.[17] In the case of a woman slave and her daughter the original purchase price ca. 259 B. C. was 200 drachmas each.[18] The reward paid for the capture and return of runaway slaves in Palestine at this time was 100 drachmas.[19] The price paid for a slave at Cos at about the same period was three minas,[20] which is in accord with the Egyptian prices. In 173 B. C. a slave girl in Egypt was mortgaged as collateral for a loan of 1,200 drachmas,[21] the actual value of the slave no doubt greatly exceeding the loan.

The manumission prices which appear in the Delphic grants of liberty by the religious procedure of the trust sale to Apollo cannot be compared to the prices in slave transfers because they are complicated by several factors which cannot be computed. These include the personal relations which had been established between the owner and the slave during the time of his enslavement, and the fact that when two or more slaves were freed at the same time the manumission price appears as a total, not broken down into individual payments.[22] A further disturbing factor arises in the many instances of release with accompanying *paramonē* services in which the actual terms of the obligations of the freedmen do not appear and their value cannot be estimated.[23]

Disregarding the value of the services of the freed persons in the manumissions with *paramonē* labor agreements, the range of the manumission prices in the "outright" grants varies from one to twenty minas for the period 201 to 53 B. C. These may be regarded as the money prices paid for liberty in the individual instances. Those which, in the designated century and a half, fall within the range of ten to twenty minas are not numerous, being less than ten per cent of the total number.[24] In two cases the high payment for manumission is to be ascribed, one would judge, to the special skills and to special earning capacities of the slaves, the profits from their labor being lost to their owners when they became free. One of these was a Bithynian-born bronze worker who entrusted fifteen minas to the god for his freedom.[25] A second was a Galatian who worked in leather. His manumission price was ten minas.[26]

The greatest number of the payments made by the new freedmen and freedwomen fall within the range of three and five minas.[27] This approximates more closely the ransom paid for war prisoners in the eastern area than the regular market prices of slaves at the same time. Two known instances of ransom prices are the five minas per prisoner paid in an agreement between Demetrius Poliorcetes and the Rhodians in 304 B. C.[28] and the same rate paid for Roman prisoners of the Hannibalic war who were in slavery in Greece and were freed.[29] It is understandable that the ransom and manumission demands would be in excess of the usual market prices for slaves. This is to be explained, in the case of the manumissions, by the position of the manumittor as the party who had the stronger bargaining power.[30] The slave prices which appear in the comedies of Plautus, quoted in silver minas and obviously taken over from the Greek New Comedy,[31]

---

565 of about 150 B. C., a Bithynian bronze worker; 3, 3 (1), 26, a seamstress.

[13] Ehrenberg, Victor, *Der griechische und der hellenistische Staat*, 72, Leipzig, Teubner, 1932. For a general use of slaves in the formerly undeveloped regions of the Epirots, the Perrhaebians and Athamanians, see Polybius, 33: 1.

[14] Edgar, C. C., *P. Cair. Zen.* 1: 59003, 5, of 259 B. C.

[15] *Ibid.*, 59010, 26, ca. 258 B. C.

[16] Vitelli, G., *PSI.* 4: 406, 18-19.

[17] *Ibid.*, 406, 26.

[18] Edgar, *P. Cair. Zen.* 3: 59355, 48-53.

[19] *Ibid.* 1: 59015 verso.

[20] Headlam, Walter, *Herodas. The mimes and fragments*, 5, 21, Cambridge, Univ. Press.

[21] *P. Ham.*, 28, probably copper drachmas which would be the equivalent of twenty drachmas silver, according to Heichelheim, Fritz, *Wirtschaftliche Schwankungen*, 30, 4.

[22] In *Fouilles de Delphes* (FD) 3 (2) : 222, a woman and her daughter are set free for a seven mina payment; in *FD* 3 (2) : 169, two boys and a girl are freed for a total of twenty minas; in 3 (1) : 24, a male and a female slave paid a total of eight minas for their liberty.

[23] Upon the nature of the *paramonē* obligations Paul Koschaker's views are fundamental as given in his study, Ueber einige griechische Rechtsurkunden, *Abh. d. säch. Akad. der Wissensch.*, ph.-hist. *Klasse* 42 : 24-68, 1931. See, also, a new approach in Westermann, W. L., The *paramonē* as general service contract, *Jour. Juristic Popyrology* 2 : 9-43, 1948.

[24] The reason for the twenty-drachma payment by a houseborn slave to his two masters from Chaleia, in *GDI* 2 : 2146, cannot be guessed. The two owners each attest the sale and its result by the phrase: " Purchaser (i. e. the slave)—free." This is unusual, bespeaking some extraordinary circumstances in this case.

[25] *FD* 3 (1) : 565.

[26] *GDI* 2 : 2094.

[27] There is no marked change in this respect brought about by the newly published records at Delphi since the statement and the tabulation of Calderini in *Manomissione*, 213-215.

[28] Diodorus, 20 : 84, 6.

[29] Polybius, as quoted by Livy, 34 : 50; *cf.* Plutarch, *Flamininus*, 13.

[30] Calderini, *Manomissione*, 212.

[31] Frank, T., *Economic survey of ancient Rome* 1 : 100, Baltimore, Johns Hopkins Press, 1933.

range from selling prices of twenty to sixty minas to demand prices of 100 minas.[32] These are based upon standardized comic exaggeration which was probably present in the original Greek comedies. They have no value as evidence for actual prices either in the Greek cities or at Rome.

In the Zenon papyri from Egypt of the third century B. C. Tyre appears as the most important outlet for Syrian slaves exported to Egypt;[33] but other cities of the Phoenician coast also participated in the slave trade.[34] In the third and in the first part of the second century Rhodes no doubt played the part in the commerce in slaves which any other active trading center would have had.[35] Fifty-eight brief epitaphs from the island of Rhodes are extant, to be dated with great probability in the early half of the second century B. C.,[36] which mention the names and nativities of the dead slaves. Out of a total of sixty slaves whose origins are clear seven were homeborn (*engeneis*) or about one to eight of those purchased from non-Rhodian areas.[37] This is to be compared to the ratio of one homeborn to three foreign born in the Delphic manumission records of the years 201-153 B. C. as presented in tabulation in the preceding chapter. The difference in ratio suggests four conclusions: that there was greater wealth at Rhodes than in the towns of the central Greek area represented in the Delphic records;[38] that this greater wealth permitted, and encouraged, the purchase rather than the home breeding of slaves; that the slaves thus purchased were largely used in handicraft employments; and that the rate of self-purchase into freedom by slaves working in Rhodes must have been relatively high. By far the greater number of the imported group, thirty-eight out of fifty-two cases which could be used, were of Asia Minor origin. This is readily understood because of the position of Rhodes. Only two give Egypt as their place of nativity, this small number being rationally explained by Rostovtzeff as caused by Ptolemaic legislation which forbade the exportation of their Egyptian subjects into foreign enslavement.[39]

The number of the slaves recorded in these succinct funerary inscriptions from Rhodes does not warrant the assignment of a special position to that city either as a center of the slave trade or in respect to the numbers of slaves employed there. Byzantium, by virtue of its position, was able to control and extract profit from the slave trade from the Black Sea regions,[40] the city of Tanais being the northern assembly point for slaves from lower Russia.[41] Colchis, according to Sir William Ramsay, was the probable source of many of the slaves classed as Scythians.[42] Nicaea and Nicomedia would be the outlets for the slaves from Bithynia, and Sinope, Amisus, and Trapezus for the slaves emanating from Cappadocia.[43] The idea, which is too widely accepted, of the concentration of the slave trade of the Aegean upon the island of Delos in the century after 166 B. C. is based solely upon an interpretation of a statement of Strabo alleging that 10,000 slaves could be handled there in one day, that is, brought in, unloaded, sold, and reshipped. The evidence for this fantastic idea is a Greek proverb, and solely that, which says: " Merchant, sail in, unload. Everything has been sold." [44] Despite the physical impossibility of this feat it has found credence among modern writers through association with a slave outbreak which occurred at Delos, probably in 130 B. C.[45] In conformity with the general development of trade facilities which characterized the Hellenistic period, the concentration of different marketing activities at different points in the *agorai* of the Greek trading cities would rationally assign special places in them for the slave sales; but so far as known there were no separate slave markets in the sense in which the term was used in the days of North American slavery.[46]

The prevailing rule of the Greeks of the Classical period against the use of slaves as combatants in war, which was more stringently observed by the Romans, was maintained by the Hellenistic states. About 287 B. C. fugitive slaves who had fraudulently enlisted for service as oarsmen in the fleet of the Islanders were returned to their owners by the Nesiarch of the fleet.[47] Exceptionally, slaves might be associated with the armies in noncombatant occupations, as in the case recorded in Ps.-Aristotle, *Oeconomica*, 1352b, where Antimenes the Rhodian used slaves levied from private owners, presumably for corvée labors in and about the camps.

In the legal attitude of the Greek city-states toward

---

[32] Plautus, *Asin.*, 650-651; *Capt.*, 364, 380, 974; *Curc.*, 63-64; *Epid.*, 52; *Merc.*, 429-440 (100 minas asked for a courtesan); *Most.*, 300, 974, 982; *Pers.*, 662; *Pseud.*, 52.

[33] Edgar, *P. Cair. Zen.* 1: 59093, 11. Cf. Herondas 2: 18 ed. Crusius-Herzog, for prostitutes, presumably slave girls, brought into Tyre and exported to Cos.

[34] OT, *Macc.* 2, 18, 11.

[35] van Gelder, H., *Geschichte der alten Rhodier,* 430, Hague, Nijhoff, 1900.

[36] Rostovtzeff, *Soc. and Econ. Hist. Hellenistic World* 2: 675.

[37] *IG* 12: 1, nos. 480-538; Rostovtzeff, *Soc. and Econ. Hist. Hellenistic World* 2: 690; 3: 1484.

[38] *Ibid.* 2: 1149.

[39] *Ibid.* 2: 1262-1263.

[40] Polybius, 4: 38, 1-8.

[41] Strabo, 11: 2, 3 (= C(asaubon), p. 493).

[42] Ramsay, Sir Wm., *Asianic elements in Greek civilization*, 120, New Haven, Yale Univ. Press, 1928.

[43] *Ibid.*, 119, and n. 2.

[44] Strabo, 14: 5, 2 (= C[asaubon], p. 668).

[45] It is reported by Diodorus, 34: 2, 19, and Orosius, 5: 9. A Delian inscription in *BCH* 38: 250-251, dated in the third century B. C., indicates that the trade in slaves at Delos began before the island was made a free port.

[46] See Hesychius, *s. v.* κύκλος and Pollux, 7: 11: κύκλοι ἐν τῇ νέᾳ κωμῳδίᾳ καλοῦνται ἐν οἷς ἐπιπράσκονται τὰ ἀνδράποδα ἴσως καὶ τὰ λοιπὰ ὤνια.

[47] *OGI* 2: 773, 3-4. Note also the enlistment of available metics, priests, freedman and aliens, with no mention of slaves, in Dittenberger, *Syll.*³, 742, 45, of the time of the defection of Ephesus from Mithradates VI.

the slave as property[48] there was no change from the complete right of the owner to use the slave for whatever work he desired, to sell or mortgage the slave, or to lease its earning capacity for the owner's profit. The owner's right of personal chastisement remained unimpaired;[49] and this right of punishment was often specifically retained for the former master during the period of the *paramonē* services after the slave had been freed.[50] The master might still use female slaves as prostitutes for earning purposes as in the case of the harpist, Habrotonon, of Menander's comedy, *The Arbitrants*.[51]

The master had not, however, the legal right of life and death over the slave. The threat made to burn the slave Davus, in a New Comedy fragment[52] was a threat of lynching, not of a legally permitted punishment.[53] The right of the slave to own property, which had been fully recognized in the older Attic law for those who "lived apart" and, in certain directions, for the household slaves, was still operative.[54] The former Greek differentiations in minor punishments between free and slaves—fines alone being imposed upon the free, whipping with double fine for the slave — persisted in the Greek city-states and was taken over into the legal codes of Hellenistic Egypt and western Asia. A papyrus in the Halle collection, for example, sets a fine of 100 drachmas for threat of bodily injury with a deadly weapon made by a free person; but when such a threat was made by a slave not less than 100 blows constituted the punishment.[55] The severe punishments which might be inflicted upon slaves were still cited as the distinctive mark which separated them from the free as in the case of the citizens of Argos who were tortured by the tyrant Nabis.[56]

As compared with earlier Attic law, a decline in the legal protection afforded slaves is to be noted in Ptolemaic Egyptian law in the failure of the *politikoi nomoi* of Alexandria, the city-state laws, to provide protection for slaves against acts of *hybris* perpetrated upon them by free persons.[57]   Against this is to be placed a greater volume of legislation, and of a more precise and detailed character, than that which existed in the fifth and fourth centuries. This development is to be connected with the general movement toward regulative legislation characteristic of the highly regimented Hellenistic monarchies rather than to an increase in the ratio of slaves to free or to a growth in the economic importance of the slave system. The fragmentary extracts from Ptolemaic laws upon slaves which have been preserved[58] cite some provisions regarding procedure and penalties in cases of slave delicts. A provision new to Greek law is that an action might be entered against a slave as against a free man, the owner of the slave playing no part in this type of procedure. In case the slave was condemned the owner might demand a new trial, suffering a heavier penalty if he lost the case; or the older Greek procedure might be followed of entering the complaint from the outset directly against the slave-owner.[59] In case this form of action were instituted, the owner might be proceeded against in two ways, merely as owner of the slave as property or as instigator and accessory, before the fact, with criminal knowledge.[60] Similar action directly against a slave as independent agent or against the master as being instigator of the deed or having guilty knowledge, is provided for in the law of the *astynomoi* of the kingdom of Pergamum.[61] The older Greek restriction upon the taking of testimony from slaves only when the consent of the owner had been obtained was changed in the Ptolemaic-Egyptian procedure, where the owner's right of decision regarding the use of the bastinado in obtaining testimony from his slave was taken away from him and given to the court; but the taking of testimony by the court through torture could be used only when the documentary evidence in the case was inconclusive.[62]

The Ptolemaic royal ordinance just cited, which is of the third century B. C., also forbade the export of slaves out of Egypt.[63] The taxation derived from slaves by the Hellenistic states was obtained in accordance with the older Greek practice of indirect rather than direct taxation, principally through the tax imposed upon

---

[48] In *OGI* 1: 218, 60-62, 110, from Ilium, *ca.* 280 B. C., slaves are listed as property to be sequestered for confiscation.

[49] Ps.-Aristotle, *Oeconomica*, 1344a gives as the three elements which make up the life of slave, as work, punishment, and food.

[50] This is fixed in the *paramonē* agreement of the manumission inscriptions, *GDI* 1: 1707, 8; 1708, 19; 1716; *FD* 3 (1): 304, 9-10 of 94-93 B. C.; 3 (3, 1): 175; 3 (6): 19, 12-13, *etc.*

[51] Menander, *Epitrep.*, 341 in Körte's *editio major*.

[52] *P. Oxy.* 6: 855, col. II, possibly Menander.

[53] This is also true in Aristophanes, *Thesmophoriazusae*, 726-729, where the person to be burned was a free man.

[54] For this right at Athens, see Menander, *Epitrepontes*, 111, and Taubenschlag, *Ztsch. für Rechtsgesch.* 46: 70. In the Pergamene kingdom, we find in *OGI*, 483: 175: ὧν μὲν ἂν ἔχῃ στερέσθω. Cf. Hitzig, *Ztsch. Sav. Stift.* 26: 446.

[55] *P. Halensis (Dikaiomata)* 1: 182-192, edited by the "Graeca Halensis," Berlin, Weidmann, 1913. For an actual injury committed by a slave, not less than 100 blows are specified in *P. Halensis* 1: 196-197. Cf. *J. Partsch, Arch. f. Pap.* 6: 68. At Pergammum, a beating of 150 blows and 10 days in the stocks were meted out to slaves, *OGI*, 483: 180-184. For the punishment of slaves for impious conduct at the Ceres festival on the island of Syros, see Dittenberger, *SIG,*[2] 680: 2-5. At Rhodes, *IG* 12: 1, 1.

[56] Livy, 32: 38, 8: *in servilem modum lacerati atque extorti,* and Polybius, 13: 7, 6-11.

[57] *P. Hal.* 1: 115-120, as noted by Josef Partsch, *Arch. f. Pap.* 6: 35-36.

[58] *P. Lille* 1: 29, republished in Mitteis-Wilcken, *Papyruskunde, Chrestomathie* 2 (2): no. 369, col. 1, 10-11: κατὰ τοὺς νόμους τοὺς περὶ τῶν οἰκέτων ὄντας.

[59] *Ibid.*, col. II.

[60] See E. Berneker, Zu einiaen Pronessurkunden der Ptolemäerzeit, *Ét. de Pap.* 2: 62-64, 1933, and Partsch, Die alexandrinischen Dikaiomata, *Arch. f. Pap.* 6: 72-73

[61] In *OGI* 2: no. 483, 175-79 the crime is committed μετὰ or ἄνευ τῆς τοῦ κυρίου γνώμης.

[62] *P. Lille* 1: 29, col. 1, 21-26.

[63] *Ibid.*, col. 1, 13-14.

sales and manumissions and without recourse to an ownership tax. The sales tax on slaves in Ptolemaic Egypt about 200 B. C. varied somewhat according to the type of sale involved; but it stood in general at about twenty per cent *ad valorem*.[64] It is generally agreed that this tax on slave transfers in Egypt was a Greek innovation.[65] This was probably true also of the *andrapodikon* of the Seleucids which is interpreted as a tax on sales rather than an ownership tax.[66] The flight of slaves, both singly and *en masse* when war or civil disturbances offered them a suitable opportuntiy, was no doubt of frequent occurrence as attested by the legislation upon that topic which chance has preserved in a treaty between Eupolemus and the city of Theangela in Caria of 315-14 B. C. It contains a provision for the return to Eupolemus of slaves, together with free men and mercenaries, who had fled to Theangela from territories appertaining to him.[67]

Except in the case of temples which had the right of asylum, the harboring of fugitive slaves was an offense punishable by requirement of return of the slave with addition of a fine as recompense to the slave-owner [68] and a punitive fine paid to the state.[69] The system developed in the Hellenistic period for obtaining the return of runaways consisted of posting the descriptions of the slaves with an offer of a fixed reward for notification to the owner, or to his agents, of the place where the fugitive might be obtained.[70] Precise descriptions

(*eikones*) of the slaves were given, as means of identification both at the time of recapture and upon the return of the runaway. Two official notices of runaway slaves posted in Alexandria in 156 B. C. have come down to us.[71] The slave-owners themselves in such cases posted the notices and paid the rewards offered for return of the fugitive. The government made an announcement of the loss of the runaway through the public herald but did not, so far as known, use the official machinery for the detection of the slave, as was later done by the Roman government.[72] A statuette in bronze, executed in the Alexandrian style, has recently been discovered in the Princeton University collection [73] which shows an actor with a mask who was representing, from one of the plays of the New Comedy, a seated slave wearing a metal neck-ring from which depended some object, possibly a disk, which displayed in relief an oil flask and bath strigils.

One of the Alexandrian notices of the runaway slaves mentioned above states, in the listing of items serving for his recognition, that he had " a wart at the left of his nose, a scar over the left corner of his mouth, was tattooed on the right wrist with two foreign letters," that he " had three gold mina coins, ten pearls. an iron ring upon which an oil flask and bath scrapers [were depicted]." In the later Roman Empire of the period from Constantine to Honorius similar collars were worn by slaves as recognition pieces in case of fight, with requests for the return of the slaves at given localities if apprehended.[74]

---

[64] This appears in the section upon the slave tax preserved out of a comprehensive *diagramma tōn andrapodōn* published by Westermann, *Upon slavery in Ptolemaic Egypt*.

[65] *Ibid.*, 37; Partsch, Josef, *Festschrift für Otto Lenel*, 79, Leipzig, Tauchnitz, 1921. Rostovtzeff, *Yale Class. Studies* 3 : 67.

[66] *Ibid.*, 65. See, also, San Nicolo, M., *Ägyptisches Vereinswesen*, 92., Munich, Beck, 1913. For further examples of the tax on transfers of slaves, see the inscription from Cos in *Rev. ét. gr.* 4 : 361-362, line 9, and p. 369, and the remissions granted to synoecized citizens of Teos, *Athen. Mitth.* 16 : 292.

[67] The inscription appears in *Rev. ét. anc.* 33 : 8. Note lines 10-14, and *cf.* pp. 15-16.

[68] Dittenberger, *SIG³* 2 : 736, 82.

[69] *P. Par.*, 10 (= *UPZ* 1 : 221 with the introductory comments by Ulrich Wilcken).

[70] Edgar, C. C., *P. Cair. Zen.* 1 : 59015 *verso*, probably 258 B. C.

[71] Meyer, Paul M., *Juristische Papyri*, 165-166, no. 50; (=*UPZ* 1, no. 121, 566-576, de Gruyter, Berlin, 1927). The dating by Meyer in 145 B. C. has been corrected by Wilcken, *ibid.*, p. 567, to 156 B. C., along with the clarification (p. 569) of misunderstandings of the situation in von Woess, Friedr., Asylwesen Ägyptens in der Ptolemäerzeit, *Münch. Beiträge* 5 : 176-178.

[72] Wilcken, *UPZ* 1 : 568.

[73] Bieber, Margarete, Bronze statuette of a comic actor, *Record of the Art Museum, Princeton Univ.* 9 (2) : 5-12, Princeton, 1950.

[74] *CIL* 15 (2) : nos. 7171-7199.

VII. THE EASTERN AREA FROM ALEXANDER TO AUGUSTUS

BASIC DIFFERENCES BETWEEN PRE-GREEK AND GREEK SLAVERY

The cosmopolitanism of the Hellenistic world divested the word " Hellene " of its racial meaning and gave it a cultural content, identifying as Hellenes those who by intellectual aptitudes and by training shared in the Hellenic spirit.[1] This change, supplemented by the level-

ling of class distinctions under the absolutistic rule established in the Hellenistic monarchies, explains how it might have come about that a royal slave of the Seleucid household named Diodotus could dare to seize the royal power in the kingdom of Syria and be accepted, even temporarily, as ruler.[2] The lessening of

---

[1] Eratosthenes in Plutarch, *De fortuna Alexandri*, 1, 6; Schwartz, Eduard, Hekataeos von Teos, *Rh. Mus., n. f.* 40 : 252-253, 1885.

[2] Appian, *Syrian wars*, 11, 68.

class distinctions is also reflected in a new philosophic attitude toward slavery. The Hellenistic theorists abandoned the racial-genetic approach characteristic of Aristotle which rested its explanation of slavery upon acceptance of the idea of national inferiorities and superiorities. It showed a marked interest in the humane handling of slaves and laid much emphasis upon the kind of treatment which would produce the best economic return from them. Epicurus advised his followers not to punish slaves, but to pity them.[3] The Stoic theory of the equalization of all men in the face of a comprehensive and universal law resulted logically in a levelling of the social barriers which separated free men from those unfree. We are told, for instance, that Zeno of Citium, when ill, wished to be treated in the same manner as a slave.[4]

Too much emphasis has been placed upon Zeller's guarded statement[5] that the early Stoics taught that slavery was unjust. As best displayed by Chrysippus, their interest centered upon a correct definition of slavery and freedom.[6] In their view the unwise man was a slave because he lacked the power of self-originated action, this being a quality possessed by the wise man who was free because he possessed it.[7] In this statement one may find the source, in theoretical formulation, of an observation made practical by the Delphic priests in their manumission by sale to Apollo when they listed the privilege of working at whatever one wished as the third point among the four liberties which a free man possessed and a slave lacked.

The complete acceptance of the slave system by the Stoics and their indifference to the reason for the condition of servitude in individual cases is reflected in the statement of Philemon of the *Nea Comoedia* that all men are free by nature but some have been changed into slaves by human greed,[8] and in the thoroughly practical discussion of slaves in the *Oeconomica*, falsely ascribed to Aristotle, as the most necessary and essential of all possessions.[9] This treatise identifies two kinds of slaves, those used as managers, who must be carefully trained, and the working type.[10] The life of a slave, according to this analysis, consists of work, punishment, and food, the latter item corresponding to the pay of free persons. These three requirements are to be supplied to slaves in such quantity as not to lower their efficiency. Slaves, it is further asserted, should

be rewarded as well as punished. It is advantageous to set freedom before them as an ultimate goal and to permit them to marry and produce children in order to bind them to their services.[11] It is noteworthy that no consideration is given here to a possible economic return from the home breeding of slaves.

Menander in his use of slaves in the New Comedy accepted the stereotypes already established by Aristophanes and the Middle Comedy and presented the four standardized slave figures of the Old and Middle Comedy, the rustic slave, the faithful, the clever, and the buffoon type;[12] but he has individualized his slave figures and ascribed moral qualities to some of them, as for example to Davus in the *Hero*, which are quite as admirable as those possessed by his free characters.[13] This investment of his slave *personae* with the attributes of men should be ascribed to Menander's belief in human character as a directing agency in life[14] and to his supreme interest in character delineation, rather than to any awakened appreciation of the human qualities of the unfree which might be regarded as peculiar to the Hellenistic age.

Every Greek temple had intrinsically a certain protective power over its suppliants which for special temples might, in its application to free persons, be increased to the point of complete asylum, protecting the individual even against the civil authority. In the case of asylum for slaves, however, the authority of the temple priests was not complete.[15] This fact finds its explanation in the dual nature of the slave suppliant, as private property in the view of the civil law, wherein the owner's right must be protected, and as human being in the eyes of the gods. Certain temples and shrines attained particular significance for slaves as did the *hērōon* of the slave leader, Drimiscus, at Chios which provided equal sanctity for slaves and masters.[16] In Egypt the right of the temple is envisaged as limited in time in a notification regarding two runaway slaves, and the power of decision by the priesthood in such a case as restricted.[17] In the first Verrine oration Cicero speaks of the right of refuge for slaves in the temple of Artemis at Ephesus;[18] and there is contemporary documentary evidence that the right to harbor slaves in flight was guaranteed by local religious agreement to the temple at Andania in Messene, where the temple authority appears almost in the light of a bulwark against

[3] Diogenes Laertius, 10: 118, reading οὐδὲ κολάσειν οἰκέτας.

[4] Arnim, Hans von, *Stoicorum veterum fragmenta* 1: 287, Leipzig, Teubner, 1921-1924.

[5] Zeller, Eduard, *Philosophie der Griechen*, 3rd ed., 3: 1, 301 and n. 2, Leipzig, Fues's Verlag, 1875-1881.

[6] Arnim, H. von, *Stoic. vet. frag.* 3: 352.

[7] *Ibid.*, 355, ἐλευθερίαν ἐξουσίαν αὐτοπραγίας τὴν δὲ δουλείαν στέρησιν αὐτοπραγίας. Cf. *ibid.*, 360.

[8] Kock, Theodore, *Comicorum Atticorum fragmenta* 2: 508, no. 95, Leipzig, Teubner, 1884.

[9] Pseudo-Aristotle, *Economics* 1: 1344a.

[10] *Ibid.*, 1344a: ἐπίτροπος καὶ ἐργάτης.

[11] *Ibid.*, 1344b: δεῖ δὲ καὶ ἐξομηρεύειν ταῖς τεκνοποιίαις.

[12] Langer, C., *De servi persona*, 48-86.

[13] Körte, Alfred, *Hellenistic poetry*, 35-36, New York, Columbia Univ. Press, 1929.

[14] Menander, *Epitrepontes (The orbitrants)*, 552-558, *editio major* of Alfred Körte, Leipzig, Teubner, 1912.

[15] Wilcken, U., *Arch. f. Pap.* 6: 419; *id.*, *UPZ* 1: 571.

[16] Athenaeus, 6: 90.

[17] *P. Paris*, no. 10 (*UPZ* 1, no. 121). Cf. Wilcken's remark, *ibid.*, 571.

[18] Cicero, *Against Verres* 1: 33, 35.

private harboring of fugitive slaves, which is subject to fine.[19]

The general Hellenistic restrictions upon temple asylum as affecting slaves appear in Philo where the temple rights, in their impingement upon the civil authority, are confined to protection until the slave might be reconciled with his owner or might, as a last resort, be sold.[20] Among the Hellenistic Jews the right of asylum for slaves lay in any temple, altar, or hearth of a Jewish household.[21] A more strict observance of holidays and pleasures for slaves than in the case of free persons is recommended by the author of the pseudo-Aristotelian *Economics*.[22] In Alexandria this was effected in practice in the jar feast of Orestes, certainly a Hellenic festival, which was particularly dedicated to slaves.[23] Significant, also, of the process of levelling of the barriers which separated free from bond is the increasing appearance in the Hellenistic period of social organizations which consisted exclusively of slaves. Such was the club (*eranos*) established in the third century B.C. in connection with the worship of the Asia Minor deity, Men Tyrannos, and the *collegium* of the Diosatabyriastoi at Rhodes consisting of slaves of the city.[24]

More significant of this social equalizing process are those societies in which unfree members appear along with free members, although the slaves in these groups were customarily publicly owned persons to whom some degree of dignity was attached.[25]

An inscription from Philadelphia on the Lydian-Phrygian border in Asia Minor, early first century B.C., gives the cult regulations appertaining to a private shrine. These grant access to the shrine to free or enslaved persons of either sex.[26] The purpose of the founder was to establish a moral standard with respect to married life, conforming closely to the Stoic ideal of marriage as an institution designed for the community in human life and for the rearing of children.[27] The moral requirements for the admission of worshippers are the same for free and unfree men, and intercourse of a married man with a married slave woman was regarded as pollution for the adulterer, just as intercourse with a married free woman was looked upon.[28] It is indicative, however, of the lower expectation then prevailing in respect to sexual morality on the part of women slaves, that the demands placed upon free matrons do not apply to married slave women and that cohabiting with an unmarried slave girl was permissible.[29] The levelling of the eastern Mediterranean world, which accompanied the cosmopolitanizing of its culture, was apparently abetted in some degree by the importing of west Asiatic slaves in larger numbers into the Aegean area. Thus the worship of the Phrygian god Men, particularly beloved by slaves, found its way to Athens in the third century B.C.,[30] and the cult of the Syrian Atargatis was established at Phistyum in Aetolia, presumably also by Syrian slaves.[31]

Individual instances of unjust and brutal misuse of the possessive power of masters over their slaves no doubt continued to occur, such as are bound to happen under any system of slavery at any time. An instance of this kind is reported by Livy in which two Thebans attempted to kill a slave who was cognizant of a murder which had been committed by them.[32] The general impression left by the sources, however, is that the slave system of the Hellenistic period was not of an oppressive or extremely brutal type, either in the area of the Aegean Sea and the Greek homeland or in the conquered countries of the near East.

This impression is supported, rather than refuted, by the little we know of the history of the slave outbreaks which occurred in the new Roman province of Asia and in Delos and the Laurian mining district of Attica about 130 B.C.[33] These should be regarded as repercussions from the great slave revolts of the west in Sicily and Italy with which they are correctly associated both by Diodorus of Sicily and by Orosius;[34] but they were not desperate struggles of the oppressed free and

[19] Dittenberger, *SIG*,[3] 736, lines 80-84, of 92-91 B.C.: φύγιμον εἶμεν τοῖς δούλοις.

[20] Philo Judaeus, *De virtutibus*, 124.

[21] Philo Jud., *On Dreams*, (*de somniis*) 2:294 ff. Probably in the case of the Jews this right of asylum was restricted to Jewish coreligionists, as indicated by Goodenough, Erwin R., *Jurisprudence of the Jewish courts in Egypt*, 53 and 221, New Haven, Yale Univ. Press, 1929.

[22] Ps.-Aristotle, *Economics* 1:1344b.

[23] Callimachus, *Causes* (*Aetia*), col. 1, 1-2 in *P. Oxy.* 11, no. 1362. *Cf.* the scholiast upon Hesiod, *Works and days*, 368.

[24] *IG* 3 (1), no. 74, for Men Tyrannos; 12 (1), no. 31 for the Rhodian college; and see Poland, Franz, *Geschichte des griechischen Vereinswesens*, 328-329, Leipzig, Teubner, 1909. The *hērōon* established in honor of Drimachus, the leader and benefactor of the enslaved at Chios and visited by them (Athaenaeus, 6:89), belongs in this category.

[25] A club of free and unfree in the Athenian harbor town of Piraeus is recorded in *IG* 2 (5):626b. For Cnidas see *GDI* 3:3510. In the case of a social club in Egypt the names of the members indicate that they were of low free class or of slave status, according to C. C. Edgar, Records of a village club, *Raccolta Lumbroso*, 369, Milan, Aegyptus, 1925. In *P. Teb.* 1:224, containing the accounts of a club of similar type, the names have not been given by the editors.

[26] Dittenberger, *SIG*,[3] 985:5-6, 15-16.

[27] Weinreich, Otto, in *Sitz. Heidelberg. Akad.* 10 (16):60.

[28] *SIG*,[3] 985, 25-28.

[29] *Ibid.*, lines 35-39 and Kroll, Wilhelm, in *Zeitschr. f. Sexualwissenschaft* 17:147, 1930.

[30] *IG* 2 (3):1587, 1593, and Perdrizet, Paul, article "Mén," *BCH* 20:75, n. 1, 1896.

[31] The manumission by sale to the Syrian Aphrodite which shows this (*IG* 9:417) is, to be sure, of the Roman period.

[32] Livy, 32:28.

[33] Diodorus Siculus, 34:2, 19, and 34:3; Orosius, 5:9; Magie, David, *Roman rule in Asia Minor* 1:151, Princeton Univ. Press, 1950. For the chronology consult Ferguson, W. S., Researches in Delian and Athenian documents, *Klio: Beiträge zur alten Geschichte* 7:238, 1907.

[34] Ferguson, W. S., *Hellenistic Athens*, 378-379, London, Macmillan, 1911.

the slaves, revolting for the purpose of gaining social reforms.[85] The thousand slaves who rose in rebellion in Attica were readily suppressed by the Athenian general, Heraclitus; the slaves in Delos likewise by the free population of the island without the need of support from Athens.[86] In the alleged Chian slave uprising under Drimachus, reported by Nymphodorus,[87] the relations established between the camp of the revolters and their masters were evidently amicable and the shrine of the slave leader later attained equal sanctity for the local slave population and for their owners. In the case of the masters the shrine of Drimachus became an oracle for the foretelling of slave plots. Comparison of these disturbances with the long-enduring slave outbreaks in the West and the brutality there displayed by both sides give sufficient proof that the large scale plantation and ranch slavery which developed in the area of the western Mediterranean introduced changes which for two hundred years affected the entire attitude of the Mediterranean world toward slaves and gave to its slave system a new economic and social significance.

The syncretic tendencies of the Hellenistic period manifested themselves in the Near and Middle Orient in many forms after Alexander's death. The process of amalgamation of the social attitudes of the dominant Greeks with the traditions and customs of the dominated peoples found its expression in different ways and in varying degrees of assimilation. Sometimes it resulted in complete acceptance of a Greek custom, at other places in complete rejections, and again in compromises on the part of the dominated and their rulers. All of the degrees of syncretistic acceptances and repulsions reflect themselves in the enslavement practice and in the legislation dealing with slaves among the various peoples subjected to the economic and social penetration of the ruling Greeks.

It is difficult to determine the reasons for the local differences which appear in the Hellenistic cultures in the field of enslavement and of liberation from it. Any attempt to do so must depend upon the establishment of the basic assumptions which displayed themselves in the slave institutions which had developed in the lands of the pre-Greek cultures and to compare them with those which prevailed in the conduct of slavery under the Greek *dēmos* governments. The attempt to penetrate to the sources of the unlikenesses which may be established and to clarify the fundamental conceptions which gave rise to the differences, inevitably entails the danger attending any inquiry as to origins.[88]

Necessarily one must resort to generalizations which will throw obscuring shadows over disparities which may originally have been of minor significance, but, in the end, may have assumed major importance and have led to results of some significance.

One important fact seems to lie at the root of all the differences which are discernible between the pre-Greek and the Greek social responses to the institution of slavery. This is that the level of maturity attained in legal thought by the Greeks of the city-state period, as represented in their attitude toward slavery, was much higher than that reached by their predecessors in ancient Egypt and in the Semitic-speaking lands of western Asia. This greater maturity expressed itself in a more logical recognition among the Greeks of the distinctions of status between the free and the unfree and a far greater semantic precision in the terms which expressed the gradations of social classification.

It has been shown in an earlier chapter that the Homeric designations for male and female slave, *dmōs* and *dmoé*, were already vested with a singleness of meaning which distinguished the persons so designated unmistakably form the free servants of the time (*amphipoloi*). The adjectival form meaning "free" is clearly defined. Though the later Greek word for "hired hand" (*misthōtos*) is not used in Homer, the word for slave, "*doulos*," does appear in the Iliad and the Odyssey; and since that time, to this day, it has distinguished for the people of Hellenic speech the nonfree worker from the hireling. In the Homeric usage the abstract idea of "enslavement" appears only in the adjectival form *douleios*, "slave-like";[39] but this adjective shows that the abstract concept of slavery was distinctly formulated in the thinking of the epic poets.

In the fifth-century code of Cretan Gortyn legal phraseology already had made a clear demarcation between three elements among the state subjects upon the basis of their possession of complete status, of restricted freedom, or of their complete lack of personal liberty. These were: the slaves; those of the next higher grade of bondage; and the free.[40] In the Hellenistic period we find that some of the Greek communities had developed a separate section of their legal regulations which were applicable solely to former slaves who had been liberated. In inscriptions discovered on the island of Calymna, for example, these provisions are clearly set apart under the separate designation of "freedman laws."[41]

In sharp contrast to this clarity of differentiation

---

[85] Magie, David, *Roman rule in Asia Minor* 2: 1040, has discussed this most sensibly.

[86] Orosius, 5:9: *oppidanis praevenientibus oppressi sunt.*

[87] Nymphodorus is quoted by Athenaeus, 6:90.

[88] In the study of hierodulism, for exampel, written by Walter Otto of Munich and posthumously published, Professor Otto emphasized the initial difficulty of distinguishing the Greek from the non-Greek origins of religious enslavement in the Hellenistic Egypt. Otto, W., Beiträge zur Hierodulie, *Abh. Bayer. Akad., philos.-hist. Klasse,* n. f., **29**: 5, 1950.

[39] Odyssey, 24, line 252.

[40] Bücheler-Zitelmann, Recht von Gortyn, in *Rh. Mus.* **40**, *Ergänzungsheft*; Kohler, Josef, and E. Ziebarth, *Das Stadrecht von Gortyn*, Göttingen, Vandenhoeck and Ruprecht, 1912. In the order of their appearance here in the text the words used in the Gortyn Code are: *dōloi, aphamiōtai, eleutheroi.*

[41] Dittenberger, *SIG*[2] 2: 864; 866; 867, sections 1, 3, 5; 869, sect. 2. Nos. 864 and 866 of the second edition are reproduced as nos. 1210 and 1211 in *SIG*[3].

between those completely free and those who were enslaved, with a special term for "freedman" (ἀπελεύθερος) and regulations which provided the freedman group with legal directives, stands the blurring and overlapping of these social classifications in the Egyptian and in the Semitic languages. There is no precise word, in fact, for "manumission" or for "freedman" in the ancient Semitic languages. In the "heroic age" of their infiltration into the Tigris-Euphrates lowlands and their production of their epic poetry,[42] corresponding to the Homeric age of the Greek world, the Sumerian language had no specific word for "slaves" which differentiated them as a population group from war captives. The cuneiform signs for "slave" meant, literally, a "man from the mountains," that is, a captive from an alien land.[43] The same indefiniteness prevailed in the early development of the Egyptian language in the use of the term *b'k*, to the point that the Egyptologists still disagree as to the exact status of the persons thus designated.[44] The Hebrew word *'ebed* suffers from the same vagueness, its application ranging through "slave" or "servant of the Lord" in the phrase *'ebed Jahwe*, to the titulary epithet describing a high military or civil official as *'ebed el malek*, "servant of the king."

The highly matured conception of the slave population which had been attained by the Greek tribes is reflected in the legal distinctions which this semantic clarity evoked. The contrasts which established themselves on this basis between the respective attitudes toward the institution of slavery of the Greeks and the pre-Greeks are here briefly mentioned. Among the pre-Greeks the distinction between the slave and the free man was determined by the concept of "religious tribalism" which governed the activities of the Oriental peoples.[45] An instance of this is to be seen in the law code of Lipit Ishtar of Isin. In the prologue of the code Lipit Ishtar declares that he had released the sons and daughters of Nippur, of Isin, and of Sumer and Akkad from the slavery which had been imposed upon them. This he had done at the behest of the god Enlil.[46] This

religious-tribalistic approach furnishes the explanation of paragraph one hundred seventeen of the Code of Hammurabi which provided that if a "seignor" had been forced to sell "his wife, his son, or his daughter, or he has bound them over to service, they shall work in the house of their purchaser or obligee for three years, with their freedom reestablished in the fourth year."[47] The tribal-religious community point of view here shown is confirmed by paragraph 280 of the Hammurabi Code. As regards natives of the Amorite community enslaved in a foreign land, if and when they returned to their homeland, "their freedom shall be effected without any money (payment)."[48] A somewhat different regulation appears in the Middle Assyrian Code in application to a man or woman of higher rank who was held in pledge by another Assyrian of high status. He or she could not be sold outside of the country. An Assyrian who had been purchased at full value could, however, be sold abroad.[49]

The stricter application among the Hebrews of the religious-tribal approach to slavery is too well known to need elaboration. According to the Levitical code a Hebrew might be under bondage restraints to a coreligionist; but after six years of labor for his Hebrew creditor, in the year of Jubilee, he was to be released unconditionally. Included in this release were the children of the victim in the debt relation.[50] Josephus stated the situation with accuracy when he wrote that a Hebrew who was compelled to endure curtailment of his liberty under bondage to another (Hebrew) because of some infringement of the laws was not enslaved. His punishment was inflicted only "under the *form* of enslavement."[51] A similar expression of this solidarity of the members of the Hebrew religious community in the face of all aliens is to be seen in the early prohibition of the taking of interest upon loans from fellow Hebrews. This regulation against usury in its application to coreligionists has recently been ascribed to the "blood brotherhood morality of the Hebrew tribesmen."[52] It is out of this "nationalistic" concept of the Hebrew community in its relation to Jahwe that one understands the provision of the Talmudic law that "Canaanitic" slaves only, meaning Gentile slaves, could be dedicated

[42] Kramer, Samuel Noah, Heroes of Sumer, *Proc. Amer. Philos. Soc.* **90** (2) : 120-130, 1946; *id.*, New light on the early history of the Near East, *Amer. Jour. Archaeol.* (*AJA*) **52**: 156-164, 1948.

[43] Siegel, Bernard, Slavery during the third dynasty of Ur, *Memoirs Series*, no. 66, *Amer. Anthropol. Assoc.* **49**: 8-9, 1947; Mendelsohn, I., *Slavery in the anc. Near East*, 1.

[44] Otto, Walter, Beiträge zur Hierodulie, *Abh. Bayer. Akad., ph.-hist. Klasse* **29**: 30-31, 1950, posthumously edited by Fried. Zucker.

[45] The term "ethnicism" has been used by Baron, Salo W., *Modern nationalism and religion*, New York, Harper, 1947, to express this approach in the case of the Hebrews. It is here avoided because of the connotation of non-Hebrew and non-Christian paganism which the word "ethnicism" has taken on.

[46] I have used the translation of the Lipit Ishtar Code made by Samuel N. Kramer as given in Pritchard, James B., *Anc. Near Eastern texts*, 159, Princeton Univ. Press, 1950.

[47] *Code of Hammurabi* (*CH*), 117 in the translation of T. J. Meek in Pritchard, *Ancient Near Eastern texts*, 170.

[48] *CH* 280. Again the translation is that of T. J. Meek, *ibid.*, 177.

[49] See the translation by Meek in Pritchard, *Ancient Near Eastern texts*, 187, of tablet C G, 32, of the Middle Assyrian Code, and see Siegel, B., in *Memoirs Series*, no. 66, *Amer. Anthropol. Assoc.* **49** (1) : 44.

[50] OT, *Leviticus*, 25, 45-49, 51-54.

[51] Josephus, *Antiq. Jud.* 3 : 12, 3 (282).

[52] OT, *Deuteronomy*, 23, 19. *Leviticus*, 25, 35-37, however, permits by implication the taking of interest from brother Hebrews. See Nelson, Benjamin N., *The idea of usury*, pp. xv and xvi with n. 2, Princeton Univ. Press, 1949.

to the temple or to the priests of the temple, but Hebrew slaves could not.[53]

In direct contrast to the religious-patriotic motivations of the pre-Greek peoples of the eastern Mediterranean area the Greeks in their practice of enslavement paid little, if any, attention to polity patriotism; and they displayed no deference for religious sentiment. With no consideration even of fellow citizenship in the same polity, but with ruthless logic, they "denationalized" the idea of slavery. The individual subjection of Greeks to Greeks was both admissible in theory and widely practiced. Solonian legislation forbidding the contracting of a debt secured upon the person of the debtor and the sale of one's children[54] is sufficient proof of the actuality and legality of the practice before 594 B.c.[55] Even the regulations passed by Solon did not in any way attempt to preclude the enslavement of Greeks to Greeks by other methods of acquisition and disposal than debt. From other city-states similar proofs are available that subjects of a given polity might become the slaves of their own fellow citizens or of coresidents of non-citizen status. According to a Theban law which forbade the practice of abandoning children a Theban father might, on the plea of inability to support a newborn child, appear before the proper city magistrates and from them obtain permission to have the child sold to the highest bidder. The child, although freeborn and a Theban by birth, could then be raised as slave of the person who had purchased him.[56]

Under the law of Cretan Gortyn of the fifth century B.c., if a subject of that city-state had been ransomed out of slave condition by a fellow subject of that polity, he was "to belong to" the man who had released him, "until the debt incurred by the act of ransoming him had been repaid." There is nothing in the Gortyn code based upon citizen or non-citizen classification of the victim which would preclude or restrict the application of this provision.[57] The sole qualification which is im-

posed is that the person who had been enslaved could not be purchased out of his bondage except with his own consent.[58] This suggests no other inference than that the slavery conditions of the Cretan town of Gortyn at that time were not heavily burdensome.

Another well known case in point comes from fourth-century Athens. It involves an Athenian citizen, Nicostratus, who was accused by Apollodorus, a fellow Athenian, of having entered his house and having illegally seized some of the belongings of Apollodorus. In recounting his previous kindnesses to Nicostratus the plaintiff alleged that he had supplied, as a gift, part of the money to ransom Nicostratus when he had been captured by some enemy state. When Nicostratus later asked for further support from the plaintiff, he explained his request by the plea that he might become a slave of his ransomers if he did not repay the advance made for his release: "You know," he said, "that the laws order that the person released from the enemy is [the possession, that is, the "slave"] of the man who released him if he does not repay the ransom money."[59]

In the *Republic*, Plato, through the lips of Socrates, expressed his own conviction that Greeks ought not to enslave other Greeks in their wars with them.[60] If it had been the fact that the law of Athens forbade Athenians to be in slavery to other Athenians, Plato would have cited that provision in support of his broader conviction that the idea of non-enslavement should be extended to cover the entire Panhellenic field. For he was arguing for the much broader application of the principle that Greeks, of whatever polity they might be, should not be permitted to become slaves of other Greeks.

The manumission records from the *temenos* at Delphi have brought indisputable evidence that the Greeks of the second and first centuries B.c. were not at all averse to enslavement, under their personal ownership, of fellow Hellenes. These documents offer more than eighty examples of the enslavement of men of Hellenic origin and blood to other Hellenes. In some instances the Greek slaves who were freed by sale to Delphian Apollo were fellow subjects and fellow residents of the same polities as the masters who accepted from them,

[53] Kraus, Samuel, Sklavenbefreiung in den jüdisch-griechischen Inschriften aus Süd-Russland, *Festschrift zu Ehren des Dr. A. Harkavy*, 55, St. Petersburg, 1908. Fuchs, Karl, in his doctoral dissertation, Die alttestamentliche Arbeitsgesetzgebung im Vergleich zum Codex Hammurabi, 87-88, Heidelberg, Evangelischer Verlag, 1935, ascribes the similarities in the various Near Eastern codes to basic likenesses in legal principles rather than to borrowings.

[54] In Aristotle's *Constitution of the Athenians*, 12, 4, those referred to as "formerly enslaved" who had been freed by the *seisachtheia* were of citizen status. Solon fulfilled his political promises "with the help of the gods" (σὺν θεοῖσιν); but that is as far as the divine help went. See fragment 8, 6 in Linforth, I. M., *Solon the Athenian*, 136, Berkeley, Univ. of California Press, 1919.

[55] Plutarch, *Solon*, 13, 2-3, drew the correct conclusion in his statement that there had not been, before Solon, any statute which forbade the sale of children by their parents; and Aristotle, *Const. of the Athenians*, 4, assumed that loans secured by the debtor's person had been customary.

[56] Aelian, *Varia historia* 2 : 7.

[57] Bücheler, F., and E. Zitelmann, *Rh. Mus.*, Ergänzungsheft

49 (6) : 46-51, 1885; Kohler, J. and Erich Ziebarth, *Das Stadtrecht von Gortyn*, 51.

[58] *Code of Gortyn*, 6, 51-55.

[59] Demosthenes, Or. 53, 11, (Against Nicostratus): οἱ νόμοι κελεύουσι τοῦ λυσαμένου ἐκ τῶν πολεμίων εἶναι τὸν λυθέντα, ἐὰν μὴ ἀποδιδῷ τὰ λύτρα. A previous statement of the plaintiff, *ibid.*, 7, says: "*He urged me to contribute money* to him for the ransom." The same restriction clearly applied as is found in the Gortyn Code, that the ransoming must occur at the request of the person captured by the enemy.

[60] In Plato, *Republic* 5 : 15 (469B and C). In 5 : 16, 471A the assumption that Greeks did enslave Hellenic cities and their inhabitants is clear: "I agree that our citizens ought to deal with their Greek opponents in this way (i. e., by not destroying cities and enslaving their inhabitants), but toward the barbarians to be disposed *as they are now disposed* toward each other."

through the god, the money for their self-redemption.[61] It is true that such slaves as were natives of the same polity as their owners seem always to have been members of the non-citizen group. Whether this was a rule of legal formulation or is a mere accident of the chance which prevails in the transmission of ancient documentary evidence cannot be determined.

The second notable divergence of the Hellenic system of enslavement from the pre-Hellenic institutions becomes clear in the response to the problem of the inclusiveness of the application of enslavement among the Greeks as compared with the restrictions which were placed upon its enforcement before their time. It lies essentially in the relation of the gods toward the practice; and it results again in the conclusion that in the pre-Greek cultures slavery was hemmed in by the application of religious-tribal considerations against it, whereas the Greeks completely disregarded tribal and coreligious considerations in their enslavement system. Out of this arose a surprising contrast. In the area of the Semitic tongues and the dominantly Semitic cultures of the first millennium b. c. the gods themselves could be slaveholders. Among the Greeks the gods, in strict distinction from their temples as organizations, did *not* have slaves. Said in other words, the Greeks secularized their institutions of slavery. Again, therefore, in their understanding of slave labor they displayed that extraordinary quality of mind which led them, in so many fields, to dissociate their enterprises from whatever religious-tribal restrictions these might have had in the early stages of their development.

In the view of the Levitical Code Hebrews could be in bondage for a six-year period to fellow members of the community, but not in a slave relation to them. In a celebrated passage this attitude was justified by a statement ascribed to Jahwe that He had led them out of their enslavement in Egypt. They were, therefore, all of them God's " servants "; and for this reason they could not be subjected to transfer by sale from one Hebrew to another.[62]

It has been stressed above that the inexactness of the bondage terminology in the languages of the ancient Orient, which fails to fix clear lines of demarcation between the words for captive, servant, and slave, is conspicuously present in the Hebrew word *'ebed* which does not establish a distinction between free servants, persons in bondage, and slaves. It is important to repeat at this point that the word is used in the combination *'ebed Jahwe* to express the idea that all the members of the Hebrew religious community were the " slaves of God." It is in this sense that the Jewish exegetes regarded their people as in the condition of aliens and slaves sojourning in a land not theirs.[63] In Mesopotamian documents of the neo-Babylonian and early Persian period the group of persons belonging to various Babylonian gods, the " devotees " of Shamash, Bel, Marduk, and Ishtar, called *shirke*, were in the same anomalous position.[64] It seems to be established that the *shirke* were of two classes. The one group, distinguished with a star brand, was made up of lifelong properties of the god. Those not branded were in a bondage relation to the god which was terminable. The actual possession of these *shirke* by the god as his slaves is evident from the fact that their status was heritable, the children born to them belonging to the deity.[65] For the purpose of this discussion the important observation is that the *shirke* belonged to the *gods* to whom they owed their services, not to the temples of these gods.

W. W. Tarn was the first scholar to note the fact that, under the Greek institution of enslavement when a slave was either dedicated or sold to a god, that god did not become the owner of the slave, " but only a quasi-trustee, so that the slave went free and the god guaranteed his freedom." [66] The god did not, in fact, guaran-

---

[61] This was correctly stated by Bloch, Moritz, *Freilassungs-bedingungen der delphischen Freilassungsinschriften*, 17. Instances of this practise in the Delphic manumissions are rare, but quite specific. To the case in *FD* **3** (2), no. 226, 3 of 138-137 b. c. (ch. 7 above at n. 55), of the female slave of a Delphian citizen who was definitely " from Delphi by birth," I add these examples : *GDI* **2**, no. 2016 of 187 b. c., the master an Amphissan citizen, the slave " from Amphissa by birth " (τὸ γένος ἐξ Ἀμφίσ-σας) ; ibid. 2053, of 184-183 b. c., the same ; *FD* **3** (2) : 226, of 138-137 b. c., the master a Delphic citizen, the slave " from Delphi by birth " ; *FD* **3** (1) : 303, of priesthood 25, first century of the Christian era, the master a citizen of Physcus, the slave, also, γένει Φυσκικόν. In the Athenian manumissions by the roundabout method of a staged trial of the slave, *IG* **2-3** (2, 2) : 1553-1578, the slaves are designated as " Hermaeus, dwelling in Peiraeus," and the like. In a similar way in the Delphic manumissions the non-citizen extraction of the new freedman or freedwoman appears in phrases such as " by birth from Amphissa."

[62] OT, *Leviticus*, 25, 42 ; *cf.* verse 55. The Septuagint version

uses the indecisive Greek word *oiketai* instead of the unmistakable word for slaves *douloi*. In *Deuteronomy*, 32, 36, however, the word *doulos* is used in the statement that God would give judgment upon the Hebrews and relent toward his slaves, ἐπὶ τοῖς δούλοις αὐτοῦ παρακληθήσεται. For Philo's attitude toward the Jews as bondsmen and the Gentiles, only, as slaves see Goodenough, *Jurisprudence of the Jewish courts in Egypt*, 220.

[63] Bickerman, Elias J., The name of Christians, *Harvard Theological Review* **42**: 120, 1949 ; Bonsirven, J., *Le Judaisme Palestinien* **1**: 83, Paris, Beauchesne, 1934 ; Moore, George F., *Judaism* **2**: 135, Cambridge, Harvard Univ. Press, 1927. Upon the Jews as aliens in a land not theirs consult Lieberman, Saul, *Greek in Jewish Palestine*, 61-62, New York, Jewish Theol. Seminary, 1942.

[64] Dougherty, R. P., The shirkûtu of Babylonian deities, *Yale Oriental Series* **5**: 2, New Haven, 1932.

[65] Dougherty, *Shirkûtu*, 88. The cases of slaves who, after dedication to a god, were required to remain with their masters until their owners died, must be explained as " deferred " dedications, similar in their operation to the deferred manumissions and manumissions by testament, which were not operative until the master's death. In a private slave sale published by Ellen W. Moore in *Neo-Babylonian business and administrative documents*, 275, no. 248, Ann Arbor, Univ. of Michigan Press, 1935, the vendor guarantees the purchaser against the requirement of future service as a consecrated slave, called, in this transfer, a *shushanu*.

[66] Tarn, W. W., *The Greeks in Bactria and India*, 68-69, Cam-

tee the liberty which the freedmen had attained through trust sales to Apollo or through dedications to the gods in the many other religious manumissions hailing from central Greek towns. The securities for the freedom which the slaves thus bought for themselves, by self-purchase or by the indirect method of a fictitious dedication, were guaranteed by the customary legal methods long established and accepted in the case of sales in the Greek world. It was the vendors and their heirs and a group of guarantors, called *bebaiōtēres*, who undertook to protect the objects of sale for the purchasers, under prescribed penalties in case of failure to do so.[67] The essential fact in the situation of the trust sales of slaves to Apollo and in the so-called "dedications" of them to many gods is that *the Greek gods were not slaveholders*. In the Delphic manumissions through Apollo, in a half or more of the sales to the god throughout the entire period of the practice of this trust device the unvarying statement occurs that the slave had "entrusted the purchase (as action, in this case) to the god so that he (the slave) was free."[68] Professor

bridge Univ. Press, 1938. In his brilliant analysis of the documents originally published from Delphi, Paul Foucart, in his *Mémoire sur l'affranchisement des esclaves par forme de vente à une divinité*, 15, Paris, Imprimerie Impériale, 1867, saw clearly that the god did not become the possessor of the slave sold to him.

[67] I cannot accept the one part of the discussion of the guarantors by Paul Foucart, *op. cit.*, 15-21, which makes the god a pledge for the liberty of the new freedman. The god could not be sued for failure to secure the liberty purchased by the freedman. Only the human guarantors could be penalized.

[68] The following manumissions by entrustment to Apollo have been selected at random to show the constancy and the unvarying phraseology of the trust clause, from 200 B. C. to the final quarter of the first Christian century. They are here placed in their chronological order. *GDI* 2: 1799, of 174-173 B. C.; 1793; 1914; 2270; 2286; *FD* 3 (6): 10; 3 (3,2): 268; *GDI* 2: 2170; *FD* 3 (6): 95; 3 (3,2): 286; 3 (6); 119; 3 (3,2); 312; 3 (3,2): 318 which is to be placed somewhere toward the middle of the first Christian century. With unimportant differences the clause reads: καθὼς ἐπίστευσε ὁ δεῖνα (always the slave's name) τῶι θεῶι τὰν ὠνάν, ἐφ' ὧιτε ἐλεύθερος εἶμεν.

M. I. Finley called my attention to the fact that, if Apollo had acquired ownership of the slave, he alone could manumit him. We have no manumissions by the Greek gods. Even the releases from *paramonē* obligations undertaken by these freedmen at Delphi were executed by the former owners of the slaves. Automatically, therefore, the slave was free when the god accepted the entrustment, because he had no slaves. It made no difference whether the slave came to the god by way of dedication or by purchase with the money entrusted to the god by the slave. It is this observation which seems to explain why the term *hierodule* is not found at all in Greek literature or in documents of the mother country before the second century B. C., a hundred years after its first appearance in the Greek papyri from Egypt.[69]

His failure to grasp the simple fact that the Greek gods had no slaves has created difficulties for Fritz Pringsheim in his recent study of the Greek law of sale.[70] The sale to the god, according to Pringsheim, results in formal ownership by the god, which means freedom for the slave. "Legal ownership belongs to the god, but in equity the slave is free." If this had been true, in case of any redhibitory action the freedman would have reverted to the god. As a matter of fact the recipient of the purchase price was *not* the god, but the man who had owned the slave at the time of his slave status. The god had received the purchase price as a trust; but the ownership of the slave was never vested in him.

[69] See again the posthumous study of Walter Otto on hierodulism in *Abh. Bayer. Akad., ph.-hist. Klasse*, N. F. 29: 9-10.

[70] Pringsheim, Fritz, *The Greek law of sale*, Weimar, Bohlaus, 1950. In *GDI* 2: 2166, 8, for example, the subject of the verb in the clause "and he has the price in full (καὶ τὰν τιμὰν ἔχει πᾶσαν)" is *not* the god, but the former slave-owner, as it is in so many of the thousand Delphic manumissions of this type. Pringsheim's main contention is that ὠνή means "ownership." In the thousand Delphic manumissions by trust sale to Apollo it means "sale," either as event or as document of sale, and only that.

VIII. SLAVERY IN HELLENISTIC EGYPT

PHARAONIC TRADITION AND GREEK INTRUSIONS

In the discussion presented in the foregoing chapter a marked difference emerged respecting the clarity of analysis of the problem of status and the legal responses regarding the classifications of subject populations as between the pre-Greek cultures and that of the Greek polities. In those primitive societies in which the tribal economy rests, even in part, upon the labor of slaves, controls over this element in the organization must necessarily develop. These controls express themselves in stabilized and generally accepted understandings, no

less compelling because they are unwritten. In more mature social organisms, and especially in literate ones, regulations to control the labor forces of the state will be written and made public; and a fixed system must be devised for the control of the slave class, if a slave group has developed, or of the bondage system if the answer to the labor problem has resulted in helotry or in some other form of serfdom.

In the history of the Nile valley the elements decisive in its economic life have always been the high birth rate which has constantly prevailed there and the low standard of living set by this demographic factor. Always the old Pharaonic government had had available for its service a large supply of laborers impressed out of the deep pool of its peasant population. Without pay they were compelled to work upon the upkeep of the irrigation system for a given number of days each year.[1] In the long tradition of the Pharaonic centuries these two factors, high birth rate and abundant labor, had constantly precluded the development of any large scale ownership and employment of slaves. Within the narrow range permitted to private enterprise they were as decisively operative as they were in the labor relations of the temples and the secular power.[2]

It is not until the period of the Egyptian Empire, according to the abundant sources which we have, that slaves, in any strict definition of a slave system, begin to appear. The earliest contract for the sale of a slave thus far known to us from Pharaonic Egypt comes from the thirteenth century B. C.[3] For the thousand-year period which lies between the Ramessid era and the easy conquest of the Nile valley by Alexander the Great, one must postulate the continued existence of a slave "system," in the sense of an accumulation of government regulations for control of the slave trade and for protection of the private property investment represented by slave ownership. The numbers of the slaves used in Egypt during this millennium should not, however, be rated as impressive quantitatively in comparison with the greater mass of the free laborers in agriculture and in the handicrafts. For throughout these ten centuries the Egyptian tongue still failed to produce the sharp linguistic categories separating " captives " from " slaves " such as the Greeks evolved in their precise linguistic distinctions between *douloi*, *apeleutheroi*, and *eleutheroi* (slaves, freedmen, and men legally free).[4]

In the seventy-five years after Alexander's death the large scale emigration movement occurred which carried thousands of enterprising Greeks from their native

homes into the lands opened up to the superiorities which they had developed in the previous four centuries.[5] With them these Greeks brought the desire to have slaves available for domestic services in their households as had been their custom in their home life in Greece.[6] The use of some domestic slaves in household services and in home handicrafts by the Greek ruling class in Ptolemaic Egypt is, therefore, not to be denied. The habit of using slaves along with free workmen in the handicrafts was, of course, familiar to these immigrants when they lived in Greece. Presumably it would also have commended itself to them in the new land. Nevertheless, it still remains a moot question whether the system of employing slaves in handicraft production could have established itself upon any large scale in Ptolemaic Egypt, or did so.

General agreement has been reached that agricultural production continued to be carried on under the old Pharaonic system, that is, by a free peasantry—free in the legal sense, however heavily the demands of the state and its system of controls lay upon them. The question of slavery in Ptolemaic Egypt has, therefore, narrowed itself down to a quantitative issue confined to one field. What was the amount of the slave labor employed in the manufacture of goods in the workshops of the villages and towns, and more particularly in the metropolitan centers of the Nile valley?[7] It is unfortunate that it is exactly in these larger centers, Memphis and the other larger Greek polities of Naucratis, Ptolemais and Alexandria, that the sources of our informa-

---

[1] Chapter 5, p. 31 above.

[2] Wilcken, Ulrich, *UPZ* 2: no. 157 (3d cent. B. C.), and p. 16.

[3] Wilcken, U., *Griech. Ostraka* 1: 681-704; *idem, Papyruskunde, Grundzüge* 1 (1): 27-28; Meyer, Eduard, Sklaverei im Altertum, *Kleine Schriften* 1: 191, n. 1.

[4] John A. Wilson, *The burden of Egypt*, 187, Univ. of Chicago Press, 1951, has assigned the development of strict linguistic and legal categories in the field of ancient labor " to more modern times." He may have had the Greeks in mind. If so, it would be correct. His use of " slave troops," 201, 226, 256, and 258, is as confusing as the ancient Egyptian linguistic ambiguities were. So, also, is his statement upon page 256 that the Hebrews were taken into Egypt as " captive laborers " and their appearance as " enslaved Israelites " upon the next page (257). His deduction that the temple inventories of the Harris Papyrus " indicate a body of perhaps 450,000 persons belonging to the temples " (p. 271) is indecisive as between slaves and bondsmen. Even under a loose employment of the term " slavery," this does not seem to be an enslaved population.

[5] Westermann, W. L., The Greek exploitation of Egypt, *Political Science Quart.* 11: 517-539, 1925. Fritz Heichelheim, in his study entitled Die auswärtige Bevölkerung im Ptolemäerreich, *Klio, Beiträge zur alten Geschichte, Beiheft* 18 (*n. f.* 5), 1925, has collected the material upon the original homes of these Greek immigrants into Egypt.

[6] Rostovtzeff, *Soc. and econ. hist. Hellenistic world* 1: 321-322, agrees in general that a large-scale use of slaves was not feasible in Ptolemaic Egypt and that slave labor did not reach the proportions which it attained in other Hellenized areas. He feels, however, that slave labor was certainly used in industry and trade in Alexandria. In this decision he is followed by Claire Préaux, with special application to Alexandria, in her *L'économie royale des Lagides*, 305, Brussels, Fondation Égyptologique, 1939. Upon the use of girls in the house industry of weaving in Memphis we have several letters and accounts in the Zenon papyri of the middle of the third century B. C., including *PCZ* 1: 59080; *P. Mich. Zen.*, no. 19; *PCZ* 1: 59088; *P. Ryl. Zenon*, no. 3 (*Bull. of the Rylands Library*, 18, 1934). I find no evidence in these documents which proves that the work of weaving was done either by slaves, necessarily, or in factories, as Rostovtzeff suggested in his *Large estate in Egypt in the third century, B. C.*, 116, Madison, Wisc., 1922. A statement of Addeus, an agent who reported to Zenon, about his " house-to-house (account) "—(ἐν τῷ κατ' οἰκίαν, supplying λόγῳ)—rather points to household industry in this business. See *PCZ* 4: 59690, 27-29.

[7] This is the view adopted by Wilhelm Schubart, *Einführung in die Papyruskunde*, 417, 454, Berlin, Weidmann, 1918; by Westermann, W. L., *Upon slavery in Ptolemaic Egypt*, 54-59; and by Hellebrand, Walter, Arbeitsrechtliches in den Zenon-Papyri, *Festschrift Paul Koschaker* 3: 241, Weimar, Bohlaus, 1939.

tion, as represented by the Greek papyri, are least numerous. Two rationalizations, based upon general conditions, suggest that the incoming Macedonians and Greeks neither would, nor successfully could, alter the old Pharaonic system of handicraft production which had, throughout the three previous millennia of Pharaonic history, successfully used the poorly paid and exploitable free labor available in the land.[8] The first consideration is the mere inertia of human kind which tends to preserve the established institutions from any change so fundamental as the shift from a readily available free-labor group to slave labor would have necessitated. Second, the initial capital investment would have been great which would have been required to bring about a change of the magnitude involved in substituting slave employment for a free-labor system. It would have been a difficult transition to inaugurate as well as a futile one.

Several observations make the assumption seem improbable that anything but a relatively unimportant amount of employment of slave labor could have developed in the handicrafts even in Alexandria, the most completely Hellenized of all the cities of the Ptolemies. Ulrich Wilcken has called attention [8] to an alleged letter of the Emperor Hadrian in which the writer, who was certainly not Hadrian, lauds the vitality of the economic life of Alexandria, a city in which nobody was idle. There, the letter states, one could find people of every craft. The halt of foot, the lame of hand, even the blind, found work to do. Everybody was busy. "For them there is one god—money." Wilcken pointed out that the entire setting here is one of free workmen. The blind, the halt, and the lame among the slaves certainly could not have obtained employment in an economic situation in which an abundance of cheap free labor would have competed with crippled slaves in the same occupations.[9] More conclusive than this is an observation which can be made directly from a document of the third century B. C., the famous *Revenue laws of Ptolemy Philadelphus*. From this series of regulations it is clear that the processing of the oils derived from the seeds of the olive, from the sesame plant and the castor bean, and from sunflower seeds, was completely a government monopoly. The Ptolemaic government dictated everything, including the rate of pay to the manual laborers, called *kopeis*, who cut the crops, and to the shop workers who ground the seeds in mortars and presses which the state monopoly supplied [10] or which the oil workers might, perhaps, themselves possess.[11]

These workers in the factories were, without a doubt, free men, not slaves either in royal ownership or privately owned. The certainty of this lies in three observations in addition to the fact that fixed wages in money were paid them. The first of these is that, in each nome, the oil workers were appointed to their task by the nome officials. Secondly, they were subject to arrest by the oil contractors and the local officials if they crossed over the borders of the nome during the period of their shop service for the state. The third observation is that the fines which were imposed upon any persons who might harbor impressed government workmen who had fled from other nomes did not vary in amount. They would certainly have been differentiated for free and slave workers if slaves, government owned or privately owned, were among them.[12] The government impressment of the labor of these oil workers and the temporary deprivation of their right of physical mobility were no doubt signs of their nearness to slave status; but the fact that these infringements of their rights are mentioned at all are the indications of their legal freedom. From the dispositions in the *Revenue Laws* regarding the collection of the first fruits of the orchard crops one cannot prove the thesis that the work in that field of labor, also, was done by free men; but it is highly probable. In the oil-producing shops of Alexandria the same general condition of free labor existed as in the rest of the country, except for a different wage scale. In the *Revenue Laws* it is stated that this matter of wages was to be fixed in a separate proclamation.[13] So far as the government monopoly offers us information, Alexandria cannot be differentiated from the rest of Egypt in respect to the labor system involved in the state oil monopoly, and presumably, not in other fields of handicraft production.

The decision made by Rostovtzeff that the " sacred slaves" (*hierodouloi*) of the Egyptian temples were not slaves in the Greek sense of the word [14] has received

---

[8] *Cf.* Wilcken, *Griech. Ostraka* 1: 703-704.

[9] *Ibid.*, 681. The quotation, which represents a reliable second or third century view of Alexandrian business life, is from the lives of Firmus, Saturnius *et al.*, 8, 5-6, in the *Script. Hist. Augustae.*

[10] Grenfell, Bernard P., *Revenue laws of Ptolemy Philadelphus*, col. 45, 1-60, Oxford, Clarendon Press, 1896. If the oil workers (*elaiourgoi*) owned their presses and mortars these also were to be sealed with government seals until the time came for their use in the oil-producing shops.

[11] *Ibid.*, col. 49, 6-13.

[12] *Ibid.*, col. 44, 8-13; 14-18. Mlle Préaux, *L'économie Royale*, 305, correctly mentions the government appointment of the workmen as proof that they were not slaves.

[13] *Ibid.*, col. 55, 15-16: " in Alexandria the wages for the production of sesame oil and the brokerage and the pay (of the sale concessionaires) are to be given according to the proclamation to be made at the time of the sale." This tends to weaken the possibility advanced by Rostovtzeff, *Soc. and econ. hist. Hellenistic world* 1: 321-322, that slaves were widely used in the handicraft techniques in Alexandria, though very little in the *chōra*.

[14] Rostovtzeff, *ibid.* 1: 322. The discussion of these " slaves " by Nathaniel Reich, *Mizraim* 2: 44, 1936, based upon the work

strong confirmation in the study of hierodulism by Walter Otto, published after his death.[15] For the writer the investigation of Otto has eliminated the possibility that "temple slavery" could have been the source of any considerable percentage of the labor supply in the handicrafts, whether it be in the villages of the valley or in the large cities of Egypt such as Alexandria. His meticulous treatment of hierodulism has also furnished important information upon the loose organization and the vagueness of the terms used in the field of bondage as these terms had come down from Pharaonic times. It also offers the possibility of distinguishing, in Ptolemaic and Roman times, some of the elements of the system which were old and indigenous from those which were Greek and Roman in inception and attitude.

Temple slaves were known to the Greeks of the pre-Alexander period; but the word "hierodulism" and the concept which it embodied had not yet found acceptance in Greek religious thinking or in its terminology.[16] When, in the Hellenistic age, the word did appear it implied a relationship to a temple and to the god worshipped in it which Otto described as "temple bondage."[17] The bondsmen of the gods, as thus defined, were apparently to be traced back in their origin to that group attached to the temples of the old Egyptian deities who, in the demotic papyri, are called b'k [18] of the gods. In the Greek legal sense of douloi these "servants" of the various gods were certainly not slaves. They were, in fact, free men of different occupations who worked the temple lands in hereditary leaseholds.[19]

A bilingual sale of a house at Tebtunis in A. D. 44, available both in Greek and demotic versions, discloses the cleft which existed between the hierodule's submission to the god whom he served and the Greek failure to comprehend or to express it. In Wilhelm Spiegelberg's translation of the demotic version of this document the four sellers in the transaction and the purchaser are all called b'k of the god Suchus.[20] In the Greek text no corresponding word appears for the b'k title.[21] Again it is worth noting that when the word hieranthesia, meaning "consecration" to a god, appeared in the world of the Greek cities it might formally appear to be similar to the hierodulismus of Egypt; but it had become, in substance, quite dissimilar to that form of divine relation. This may be seen in a manumission from Tithorea in Phocis of the first century after Christ which was carried through by the device of the sale of the god Serapis. The signature of the person who acted as security for the sale, as it is reproduced upon the stone, reads as follows: " Hand of Paramonus, son of Niceratus. In accordance with the law I acted as security for the consecration (the hieranthesia to the god) as written above." [22] The dedication to the god at Tithorea was, therefore, a secular business transaction which required, by law, the security of a guarantor. It served to liberate the consecrate from a servile status rather than to forge a new bond of subservience to a god, as it did in Egypt.

Only one Ptolemaic contract for the purchase of a slave has appeared among the Zenon papyri. In regnal year twenty-seven of Ptolemy II (259-258 B. c.) this Zenon, a Greek from lower Asia Minor, was at the time managing the Syrian business affairs of Apollonius, economic comptroller of Egypt. In a town of the Ammonitis, east of the Dead Sea, he purchased a slave girl seven years of age from another Greek, named Nicanor, who was serving in a cavalry detachment under an Arab chieftain named Toubias. The instrument of sale is in duplicate. In legal form it is a regular Greek six-witness contract. This was to be expected because the two contracting parties were both of Greek birth.[23] We have evidence that the Greeks in Egypt handed down their slave properties by will to their sons or daughters under the same legal formulas which are known from the wills of the Peripatetic philosophers at Athens in the fourth century B. c.[24] As

---

of Kurt Sethe, had shown that the "peasant slave" in a demotic document of 109-108 B. c. was a temple dependent and actually an owner of land, hence a person in bondage status, but not in enslavement.

[15] Otto, Walter, Beiträge zur Hierodulie, Abh. Bayer. Akad., n. f. 29.

[16] Ibid., sect. 9-10.

[17] Ibid., sect. 10-11. The suggestion has been made by Ambrogio Donini, Science and Society 15: 57-60, 1950, that the word hierodulism arose out of a soteriological myth of salvation from sin and only secondarily was applied to slave manumissions. Although he fully understood the importance of the adjective for "sacred" in its combination in hiero-doulos, Walter Otto sedulously avoided entrapping himself in genetic sociological speculations of this kind.

[18] Otto, W., op. cit., 30-31. The Egyptian word b'k has been translated "slave" by the Egyptologists F. Ll. Griffith and Kurt Sethe. Customarily it appears as "servants," sometimes as "slaves," in the translations of W. Spiegelberg. The discussion of hierodulism by Walter Otto has decided for me the problem of the Egyptian b'k, in the sense of a bondage relationship, that is, neither as a free servant connection nor as a slave condition.

[19] Sethe, Kurt, and Josef Partsch, Demotische Urkunden zum aegyptischen Burgschaftsrecht, Abh. sächs. Akad., phil.-hist. Klasse 32: 36, 1920.

[20] PSI 8: 79-83, Appendix to no. 909, line 1.

[21] Ibid., no. 909, 1-2. Cf. Otto, Beiträge zur Hierodulie, Abh. bayer. Akad., phil.-hist. Klasse 29: 30-31.

[22] GDI 2: 1555d, 30-32 (= IG 9 [1]: 193).

[23] PCZ 1: 59003. There are several indications that Zenon purchased slaves frequently when he was engaged in work in Syria and Palestine for Apollonius, the dioikētēs: PCZ 1: 59015, 17. Compare with this an attempt to escape the export tax on a slave shipment from the harbor of Tyre, PCZ 1: 59093, 13-40 and the gift of four slaves sent by the Ammonite sheik, Toubias, to Apollonius, in PCZ 1: 59076.

[24] Compare the will of Pisias, a Lycian, in P. Petrie 2: 22, with the corresponding parts of the wills of the Peripatetic school heads in Diogenes Laertius, Vitae philosophorum 5: 1, 11-16; 5: 2, 51-57; 5: 3, 61-64; 5: 4, 69-74; Westermann, W. L., Two studies in Athenian manumissions, Jour. Near Eastern Studies, 5: 92-104.

employed by the Greek exploiters of Egypt in the third century B. C., testamentary manumission also followed the models of the fourth century B. C. to which they had been accustomed in the Hellenic polities of their upbringing.[25]

Among the native Egyptians, noted as they were for their adherence to traditional forms, the persistence of some of the elements of the Pharaonic structure of enslavement, already firmly founded upon a thousand years of its practice, was to be expected. On the side of the Macedonian-Greek intruders the acceptance of many of the old Pharaonic attitudes can be easily explained. The early Ptolemies, as rulers, were both cautious and rational. Where necessity or advantage did not press them to it they were not inclined to endanger their position of power by alienating the native population through drastic alterations of the labor conditions to which it had so long been accustomed. The Pharaonic labor system had not developed the clear legal and social distinctions which sharply demarked the boundaries between slaves, freedmen, and the free in the world of the Greek polities. The dimming of these outlines began to appear in the three centuries of Lagid rule, to become increasingly vague in the thousand-year period which followed. In the process of incorporation of old Egyptian attitudes respecting labor relations into legislative enactments passed by the Macedonian dynasts, the ready adaptability of the Greeks to new economic and social conditions and to new responsibilities also played its part.

The Zenon papyri of the third century B. C.[26] already display some of the confusions which could easily result from the obscuring of the sharp lines drawn in Greek society between free and slave status. From the year 245-244 B. C. we have a petition found in the Zenon archive which was directed to King Ptolemy by a Greek of Philadelphia named Antipater. It dealt with developments arising out of a default in payment of a loan made to Antipater by another Greek named Nicon.[27] After a series of complications the primary contract of loan to Antipater was replaced by a new instrument in which the interest due upon the old loan was added to the original principal amount. When this was not paid the defendant, Nicon, seized the wife of the debtor and their son. The wife escaped from his detention; but the boy, according to the charge as drawn up in the petition, was still being held by the creditor *on his own authority*.[28] That is to say, the

creditor had not availed himself of the legal recourses open to him to accomplish this purpose. It has always seemed to the writer that the implications of this complaint are clear enough—that the pledging of one's child for debt was sanctioned in Ptolemaic Egypt and that legal measures existed for the detention of free members of the families of debtors if their persons had been pledged.[29] For several of the scholars who have discussed the problem, though not for all of them, a second document coming from the early years of the second century has helped to confirm the conclusion that default of payment did, indeed, in Ptolemaic Egypt lead to enslavement of the person pledged.[30]

Behind the problem of self-pledge and the pledging of one's family members the record as it stands is incomplete, both regarding the Greek tradition in respect to it and that in Egypt. For Athens we have the well-known law of Solon forbidding the practice. For most of the Greek city-states we assume that the law was as at Athens; and it is a reasonable conclusion that the practice of enslavement as an outcome of debt, except for debts to the state, was not wide spread in the Greek homeland.

In pre-Hellenistic Egypt there is one historical tradition which records that in the confused period of the twenty-fifth dynasty a Pharaoh named Bakenranef (Greek: Bocchoris) passed a law forbidding loans upon the person of the debtor. During the Persian rule over Egypt, from 525 to 332 B. C., this decree had fallen into abeyance.[31] The Ptolemies found, therefore, that a regulation against debtor slavery which was widely, though not universally, established in the Greek world,[32]

---

[25] *P. Petrie* 1, no. 14, line 15. Fragmentary though it is, it should be compared with the manumissions by will which appear in the testaments cited from Diogenes Laertius in the preceding note.

[26] They date from 260 B. C. to 239 B. C. There is one document of the year 273 B. C. (*PCZ* 1: 59001) which, although found with it, has no connection with the activities otherwise represented in Zenon's collection.

[27] Westermann, W. L., C. W. Keyes and H. Liebesny, *P. Col.* 4 (*Zenon Papyri* 2), no. 83.

[28] *Ibid.*, 83, line 16: καὶ ὅτι τὸν ἐλεύθερον εἴρξας ἔχει δι' αὑτοῦ.

[29] Royal peasants, and those subjects who were connected with the finance administration (the *hypoteleis*) were exempted from seizure and enslavement for debt. See *P. Teb.* 1, no. 5, 225; Taubenschlag, *Law of Greco-Roman Egypt* 1: 403-404. They were not to be diverted from their compulsory tasks for the state administration. For the *hypoteleis*, consult Wilcken, *Urkunden der Ptolemaerzeit* (*UPZ*) 1, no. 110, note to line 97 with its references.

[30] *P. Col.* 1 (inv. 480, 23) in Westermann, W. L., *Upon slavery in Ptolemaic Egypt*: [τ]ῶν δὲ ὑποχρέων σωμάτων ὅσα ἂν ἐλεύ[θ]ερα ὄντα ἑαυ[τὰ ----]. "Upon the debtor slaves, as many as have free [done something] themselves [about the] debt, the transfer tax shall be collected, *etc.*"

[31] For the native Egyptian practice this is clear in the demotic papyrus no. 17 of 159 B. C. published by Sethe, Kurt, and J. Partsch, *Demotische Urkunden zum agyptischen Burgschaftsrecht*, *Abh. sächs. Akad., phil.-hist. Klasse*, 32: 433-448.

[32] See von Woess, Friedrich, *Asylwesen in der Ptolemäerzeit* 5: 82-84, for the old Egyptian law upon default of payment. For the inability to establish the Solonian prohibition as a general acceptance among the separatistic polities see the article *Exekution* by Egon Weiss in Pauly-W., *RE*, Supplementb. 6: 56-57. Previous discussions of execution upon the person and consequent enslavement for private debts, including that of Egon Weiss just referred to, have failed to deal with the material offered by the Delphic manumissions by trust sale to Apollo. These show that the failure of a freedman to pay a debt contracted in the interest of his liberation under this procedure, might result, by mutual agreement between the parties concerned, in a reversion of the freedman to slave status. Westermann's interpretation of this passage was not accepted by Paul

was a dead letter in the land which they now ruled. In this particular they appear to have followed the indigenous practice, even in application to their Hellenic subjects in so far as these were not citizens of one of the Greek city-states of Egypt, in preference to perpetuating a tradition widely followed in the homeland of Greece. Only in the city-state of Alexandria the Egyptian practice did not prevail. For an Alexandrian citizen could not become a slave of another Alexandrian; but this deviation from the rule had other antecedents.

Strict controls were imposed by the Ptolemaic dynasty over its free subjects who worked the royal domains as tenants (the *basilikoi geōrgoi*) and over those who were otherwise impressed into the monopoly services of the state. The compulsory enactments which were passed to regulate the labor of these elements of the population follow, in general, the forms of control exercised by individual owners over their slaves under any enslavement system. In the case of the government and free labor under its strict authority, the duration of the compulsory services, as exemplified in Ptolemaic Egypt, was customarily restricted to the fixed seasons during which application of the regulations was necessary.

It may here be recalled that the Delphic manumissions under the trust sale to Apollo expressed the difference between slavery and freedom in terms of the lack, or conversely the possession, of four rights: legal recognition, freedom from seizure, choice of work, and freedom of movement.[33] In the Ptolemaic oil monopoly the right of physical mobility of the oil workers (*elaiourgoi*) impressed for the oil-processing operations in each nome was limited to the confines of that administrative unit during the period of the appointed task. Violators of this regulation were subject to punishment, both the workmen themselves and any persons who might harbor them.[34] This limitation upon the movement of its workmen served the governing organization, also, as a check upon a tendency upon the part of the labor group to exercise its right of free choice of occupation during the period of its prescribed labor for the state.

In the interest of the government revenues, whether agricultural or derived from the monopolized industries, a relaxation of the restriction of worker movement and a method of protection from arrest and seizure had to be supplied to those impressed for government work. This was accomplished by giving to the workers for the state certificates of safe-conduct,[35] called *pisteis*.

The purpose of these passes was apparently twofold. Primarily they were designed to counteract the rigidity of the regulations which controlled the right of unhindered movement of these free workmen during the period of their agreement to serve the state. Secondarily, they supplied the workers with government permits to travel, presumably within the bounds of the nome in which their labor was to be used and in their journeyings back and forth to their homes, so that they might not be hindered in their work while in pursuit of their assigned labors or be subjected to arrest or seizure for other government tasks.

The earliest example of this type of administrative safe-conduct as yet available is dated in 187-186 B. C. A memorandum from a commissioner (*epimelētēs*) to a grain collector (*sitologus*) ordered the *sitologus* to give certificates of safe-conduct to a group of workers whose names appeared on a list. The *pisteis* which they received were to protect them, until the commissioner should himself arrive and dispose of the matter in hand, from seizure by the officials and hindrance in their allotted task. The danger which threatened them in this case seems to have arisen from obligations in grain owed by them which had not yet been cleared with the authorities.[36]

Examples of the administrative "safe-conduct" are also known from the middle of the first century B. C. That they protected the entire families of those who obtained them is clear from the following example: "Eurylochus to Xeinus and Artemidorus, both sons of Satyrus, domiciled in Tanchais, and to their wives and children. Safe conducts have been given to you extending for thirty days from the present day, in which period you will not be drawn away [from your work] by anybody."[37] The constant danger of official seizure which threatened the free peasants of Egypt is shown in a fragment of a decree of about the same time. It declared that "those also who have received *pisteis* from us shall not be subject to seizure until they are released from the working of the farm lands."[38] The

---

Koschaker, *Abh. sächs. Akad., phil.-hist. Klasse* 42: 59, who was followed in his objections by Ernst Schönbauer, *Arch. f. Pap.* 10: 182, 1932. Mlle Claire Préaux, *L'économie royale des Lagides*, 539-540, strongly supports my point of view.

[33] This is briefly presented, with references, in chapter 6, note four, above, p. 35.

[34] *P. Rev. Laws*, col. 44, 8-18.

[35] The translation of *pistis* as "safe-conduct" reproduces accurately the economic and fiscal implications of the document. It is taken over from the study of A. A. Schiller, The Coptic

ΛΟΓΟΣ ΜΙΝΟΤΤΕ documents, *Studi in onore di Aldo Albertoni* 1: 305-324, Padua, Tipografia del Seminario, 1935. *Cf.* Schäfer, Diedrich, *Zu den ptolemäischen* ΠΙΣΤΕΙΣ, *Philologus* (= *Phil.*) 88: 296-301, 1933. Confusion was introduced into the discussion of its meaning by an overemphasis of its connection, which in some respects was real enough, with the right of asylum as presented by Friedrich von Woess, *Asylwesen in der Ptolemäerzeit*, 184-192. Von Woess was clearly aware of the numerous types of the *pistis* documents, including the protection document, "*Sicherheitsurkunde*" (p. 184) or "*Schutzbrief*" (p. 185). Diedrich Schäfer, in his article upon the word in Pauly-W., *RE* 20: 1812-1813, has unfortunately reverted to the view that the *pistis* as document always stands in some relation to the right of asylum. This is not correct. The reference to Diodorus Siculus, 11: 89, 8, which he cites in proof of it, is merely a personal pledge of slave-owners, taken on oath to the god, to treat mercifully their slaves who had found asylum in the temple.

[36] *P. Teb.* 3 (1), no. 741.

[37] *BGU* 8: 1811 and compare 1810.

[38] *BGU* 8: 1812.

protections furnished by the administrative *pisteis* are clearly separated from those supplied by temple refuge in an Oxyrhynchus document which is of about the same time as the executive safe-conduct mentioned above.[39]

The lack of any distinct and sharp line which separated the status of freedom among the lower classes of the Egyptian people from that of the slave group found its expression also in Ptolemaic legislation. A decree of Ptolemy II of the year 261-260 B. c. deals with the registration, for taxation purposes, of cattle and slaves in the Egyptian possessions in Syria and Phoenicia. It contains the following requirement: "If any persons living in Syria and Phoenicia have bought *a free native of the lower class* (*sōma laikon eleutheron*) or have carried him off or in any other manner have gained possession of" such a free person, they were to bring him in and register him. Slaves bought at government auctions, however, even if they asserted that they were free persons, were to remain in the possession of their purchasers.[40] Soldiers in active service in Syria and Phoenicia, and Egyptian army personnel who were holding allotments in those places, if they were living with native women, were not required to declare these companions as their slaves. For the future, so the decree continues, no one was to be permitted to purchase or to accept as security for a debt any of these natives who were free except those who had been enslaved by authority of the state for some default to it, chiefly through fiscal trouble, of course.

The lack of a sharp line between freedom and slave status appears in the very phrase "lower class native who is free"; in the ambiguity in the minds of officials and soldiers as to the status of the native concubines of soldiers; and in the intent of the decree to fix the status of such free natives for the future by forbidding their purchase or their use as pledges.[41] The same ambiguity appears again in the official phrasing of an ordinance dated about 198 B. c. which fixes the incidence and the amount of the taxes to be collected in various types of slave transfers. In a passage, unfortunately broken, it speaks of debtor slaves "who when they were free," or possibly "being free men (by birth)," had taken some form of action relating to the debt. In this case the tax imposed fell equally upon the lender and the borrower whose failure to pay had brought him to this "debtor-slave" condition.[42]

The influences exerted by the Greek law, which

came into Egypt with Alexander's conquest, upon the native Egyptian "law of the land" was strong, as was to be expected. This legal borrowing and the reverse process, that of the acceptances from the *enchoric* law of the subjected natives into the legal structure of the Greeks, have been thoroughly studied by competent jurists.[43] Self-enslavement, as has been shown above, was foreign to the cuctomary practice of the Greeks. In many of the Greek states it was, in fact, forbidden. In Ptolemaic Egypt arrangement for a self-commitment into a status which was the equivalent of slavery is definitely established through a Greek translation of a demotic labor agreement of the year 42-41 B. c. In this transaction a woman—her name is lost—contracted her services to another woman, whose name is an Egyptian one, for the period of ninety-nine years. The word for slavery does not appear in this document. Nevertheless, the servile status of the woman work-taker is made clear by her agreement to do any work which might be assigned her; by the restriction of the compensation for the services she rendered to sustenance and clothing allowance; and by the transference of all the possessions of the work-taker into the house of the woman who obtained the labor services.[44] In Greek city-state law the sale of one's children was generally forbidden. The national law of Ptolemaic Egypt permitted this; but no instance of it connected with a *Greek* family resident in Egypt is known to me.[45]

From the third century B. c we have a group of ordinances in Egypt which dealt solely and specifically with slaves as a class distinct from free workers. Their labor relations were subject to other provisions than those applicable to free labor.[46] It has already been shown that this recognition of the differences in status in these two economic groups prevailed also in the contemporary legal development in homeland Greece. Direct evidence of a transference in this respect from the Hellenic polity practice into Ptolemaic Egypt is not to be proven. The assumption seems warranted, however, that recognition of the slave class as something apart was a Hellenistic innovation brought into Egypt through imitation of the Greek legal practice. The picture which emerges from a third-century series of slavery enactments is a clear composite of old Egyptian and Greek elements. One detail reads: " No one is to sell slaves for export or to

[39] *P. Oxy.* 14: 1620, 13-14.

[40] Liebesny, Herbert, Ein Erlass des Königs Ptolemaios II Philadelphos, *Aegyptus* 16: 257-264 (1936); Westermann, W. L., Enslaved persons who are free, *Amer. Jour. Philol.* 59: 1-30, 1938; Segré, Angelo, Liberi tenuti in schiavitù nella Siria, etc., *Archivio Giuridico* 11: 161-182, 1944.

[41] Liebesny, *Aegyptus* 16: 259, lines 16-20.

[42] *P. Col.*, inv. 480, 24-26, in Westermann, W. L., *Upon slavery in Ptolemaic Egypt.*

[43] Mitteis, *Grundzüge und Chrest. der Papyruskunde* 2 (1-2), *Juristischer Teil*; Taubenschlag, Rafael, *Law of Greco-Roman Egypt in the light of the papyri*, and in his earlier study, Das Sklavenrecht im Rechte der Papyri, *Zeitschr. d. Savigny-Stift., Rom. Abt.* 50: 140-169, 193.

[44] *PSI* 5: 549. See the note of F. L. Griffith quoted in the introduction to the text by G. Vitelli, also Taubenschlag, *Law of Greco-Roman Egypt*, 52-53.

[45] Taubenschlag, *ibid.*, 53.

[46] Jouguet, Pierre, *Papyrus de Lille* (*P. Lille*) 1, no. 29, 9-12: " according to the laws dealing with slaves," καὶ ἡ πρᾶξις συντελείσθω κατὰ τοὺς νόμους τοὺς περὶ τῶν οἰκέτων ὄντας. *P. Lille*, no. 29 appears also in Mitteis, *Papyruskunde, Chrestomathie* 2 (2): no. 369.

tattoo them or to beat them." [47] The prohibition of slave export does not appear in any legislation in the Greek homeland which I have encountered.

The tattooing of slaves was an Oriental rather than a Greek common practice, despite the proposal made by Xenophon of Athens in his pamphlet upon the revenues that slaves purchased by the state should be marked with a state sign as a method of identifying them as government property. [48] In Greece there was obviously no need to prohibit tattooing. In Hellenistic Egypt it had to be forbidden by law. In Greece the master was permitted to punish his slaves, with no legal restriction except against excess in the use of that right. The provision found in Lille papyrus no. 29, the document referred to in the preceding paragraph, made punishment by the master illegal in Egypt except in instances of a criminal act committed by the slave. In such cases the slave could, with legal permission, both be beaten and marked upon the forehead. [49]

From the same Lille papyrus it becomes clear that the sharp line of separation between slave and free which characterized the Greek social legislation was not so visibly drawn as in the slave regulations of Ptolemaic Egypt. There a complaint might be entered, for example, against a slave " as against a free person." [50] Under certain circumstances, therefore, a slave could appear in court in Ptolemaic Egypt with legal recognition of his personality. [51]

Quite in the tradition of the nationalistic attitude toward slavery, which was not Greek, is a provision which appears in a collection of excerpts out of the city laws of Alexandria. The papyrus which presents them is dated about the middle of the third century before Christ. Under the heading " Regarding citizens [scil., of Alexandria] that they may not become slaves " this paragraph states: " The Alexandrian may not be a slave to another Alexandrian, nor an Alexandrian woman to a [male] Alexandrian or to an Alexandrian woman." [52] The religious-tribal attitude which forbade the enslavement of a fellow member of the cult community and the political group cannot be duplicated in the slave legislation of the homeland polities of Greece as we know them. The German scholars who edited these laws, called Dikaiōmata, were aware of this fact. They assumed, however, that such laws existed in Greece but have been lost, and that these assumed laws represented a norm of Hellenic legislation dictating that Greeks

were not to enslave fellow citizens of the polis. [53] The Romans of the very early Republic did show something of this attitude in their insistence that a Roman debtor slave must be sold beyond the Tiber, that is, into non-Roman possession; but the idea that slavery and membership in the same religious or political group were incompatible was not accepted by the Greek world.

Without any model known to me in the foregoing Semitic sales of slaves and other legislation regarding them, or in the forms of the slave procedure of the Greeks in the homeland and the early colonization areas, stands a provision contained in an order of Ptolemy Philometor ascribed to the years 176-170 B.C. The decree publishes the demand that all slaves are to be registered when they reach the age of fifteen years, with the addition of the mother's name. It prescribes also that each slave was to be brought in in person and his description officially recorded. [54] Unfortunately we do not know the age at which the registration was fixed in Egypt for the lists of those subject to the monetary levy upon the common people (laikē syntaxis), which was the Ptolemaic equivalent of the poll tax exacted later by the Romans. [55] This listing differed completely from that demanded of the slaves in Philometor's decree in that it applied to males only, whereas the Philometor register took in the slaves of both sexes. The simplest explanation of the Philometor list which might be suggested would be that its purpose was fiscal; but the observations given above throw doubt upon this conclusion. It is clear that the physical description of each slave would be of value to the government in recapturing fugitive slaves, whether that result was the primary purpose of that part of the requirement or not. One important social result of the recording of the names of the mothers of the slaves should be noted. It represents an official recognition of the personalities of slave women; and it must have enhanced generally, in some degree, the respect accorded them by virtue of this official cognizance of their motherhood.

The difference cited above between the city laws of Alexandria and the laws of the Greek homeland polities upon the point of the possibility of the enslavement of

---

[47] Ibid., 13-15.

[48] Xenophon, Upon the revenues, 4, 21.

[49] P. Lille 29: 27-36. The Hellenistic practice of tattooing a slave as punishment is further shown in Herondas (Herodas), Mime 5, 63-68.

[50] P. Lille 29: 1-5.

[51] Meyer, Paul M., Juristische Papyri, no. 71, p. 243; Mitteis, Ludwig, Papyruskunde, Chrestomathie 2 (2): 277.

[52] P. Hal., 1, 219-221, in Dikaiomata: Auszüge aus alexandrinischen Gesetzen, 122-124.

[53] Dikaiomata, 123.

[54] Powell, J. E., The Rendel Harris papyri 61: 1-5, Cambridge, Univ. Press, 1936. I have not found the name of the mother of the slave given in any of the pre-Greek documents recording slave transactions. Always, as in the Greek documents, it is the owner's name. The lines of cleavage between slavery and bondage classifications in the Jewish community at Elephantine in the fifth century were not, in a juridical sense, sharply drawn. Yet even in the slavery documents written in Aramaic, cited in his preliminary report in The Biblical Archaeologist 15: 50-62, 1952, by Dr. Emil Kraeling as his nos. 2, 5 and 8, the child of a slave woman married to a free Hebrew is called " thy daughter." But the child is not spoken of as Yehoyishma, daughter of Tamut." For the importance of these Aramaic papyri consult the closing pages of chapter 3, above.

[55] Bell, Sir Harold I., The Constitutio Antoniniana and the Egyptian poll-tax, Jour. Rom. Studies (JRS) 37: 17-23, 1947.

one citizen to a fellow citizen is undeniable. It is important also. Limited though it is, this single observation brings the refutation of a belief which, in the continuing form of its acceptance, goes back to antiquity. In a papyrus of the third Christian century it appears in one of the examples of the literary type called the *Acta Alexandrinorum*, the anti-Roman propaganda of the time which records the alleged courage of the pagan martyrs in their trials before the Roman Emperors. In this fragmented document the following inquiry and answer appear: "Caesar: 'You mean, then, that the Athenians and the Alexandrians use the same laws?' Athenodorus: 'Yes! For, though being more powerful than all other laws, they have a fine admixture of human affection.'" Among scholars of today the idea of the similarity of the Alexandrian and the Athenian laws is steadily widening the range of its acceptance, both in historical and in juridical studies.[56] It appears in the growing conviction that the city-state codes of the three Hellenic polities of Ptolemaic Egypt, Naucratis, Alexandria, and Ptolemais, were based upon the Greek common law.[57] Or, more specifically, their origin is ascribed to the body of laws of the polity of the Athenians.[58] For the better understanding of the legal acceptances and rejections between the ruling Greeks of the Hellenistic age and the aliens whom they governed this belief must, in each assertion of the alleged transfer, be sharply questioned.[59]

One of the best known and clearest examples of the comingling of the two diverse culture strains of the Greeks and the Near Eastern peoples whom they ruled is to be observed in the development of the worship of the god Serapis in Hellenistic Egypt and its spread over the Greco-Roman world of the Mediterranean area. The cult of Serapis, even the very being of the god himself, was an artificial and purposeful hybridism between the old and obstinate traditionalism of the Egyptian religious observances and the modern and rationalizing spirit of the Greeks who had taken over the rule of the country.[60] In the development of this worship the dual origin of Serapis, a compound of Osiris-Apis and the Greek deities Zeus-Hades and Asclepius, long continued to manifest itself without developing a real mixture of the two natures into one through the process of syncretism. This continued duality, as against unity, found symbolic expression in the maintenance, in the great Serapeum of Alexandria, of separated elements of the temple structure, one for the Egyptian devotees of Osiris-Apis and another distinct part for the worshippers of the Hellenic cults of Zeus-Hades and Asclepius.[61]

In the worship of this god of dual cultural origin a strange type of religious devotee appears who is called a *katochos*. These *katochoi* were consecrates who stood in an unusual kind of religious attachment to Serapis, being confined, in long-term subjection to him, within the area of his temple enclosure. Designated, also, as *katechoumenoi* (those "held down" by the god), they were men who had given themselves over in a self-imposed allegiance to Serapis. Sometimes their self-devotion resulted from a dream inspired by the god which might be beneficent in its promises. At other times it might be frightening in its implications of disasters which would follow upon disobedience to the god's orders.[62]

Many intimate details of the lives led by these devotees in the Serapeum at Memphis are now available in the collection of all the pertinent texts, found for the most part a century ago in that city, as they have been republished by Ulrich Wilcken with an admirable com-

---

[56] *P. Oxy.* 18 (E. Lobel, C. H. Roberts, E. P. Wegener, editors): 2177, 12-18. The idea of the adoption of the Athenian laws in Alexandria is accepted, apparently, by the editors, although with some reserve. Two able discussions of this literary genre, which undoubtedly had a firm historical background, are those of Welles, C. Bradford, A Yale fragment of the Acts of Appian, *Trans. and Proc. of the Amer. Philol. Ass. (TAPA)* **67**: 7-23, 1936, and Bell, Sir Harold, The acts of the Alexandrines, *Jour. Jur. Papyrology* **4**: 19-42, Warsaw. 1950. References to the literary treatments will be found in these two articles.

[57] An example of this is to be seen in the statement of Ernest Barker, *Greek Political Theory*, 307, London, Methuen, 1947: "The influence which that code of laws exercised [Plato's code in the *Laws*] sank deep into the law of the Hellenistic world."

For a sober assessment of the separate strains which composed the body of the enchoric law of the Egyptians in the Ptolemaic period and the polity laws of the city-states see Seidl, Erwin, *Römische Rechtsgeschichte und römisches Civilprozessrecht*, 50, Hannover, Wissenschaftliche Verlagsanstalt, 1949.

[58] The editors of *P. Hal.* 1 helped to spread this idea by assuming the existence of a law in the Greek polities which would prevent a Greek citizen from falling into slavery to a fellow citizen. See *Dikaiomata*, 123. This is more than counterbalanced by their careful assembling of the differences which distinguished the Athenian laws from those of Alexandria, *ibid.* 50-51; 78-79; 115-116; 129-130.

[59] Rafael Taubenschlag has collected and discussed the detailed resemblances between the enchoric Egyptian law and its polity codes with those of the individual Greek city-states in *Actes du Ve Congrès Internationale de Papyrologie*, 471-489, Brussels, Fondation Égyptologique, 1938.

[60] Pauly-W., *RE*, 2d ser., **1**, **A2**: 2406, in the article by Gunther Roeder upon Serapis.

[61] *Ibid.*, 2410-2411.

[62] Westermann, W. L., Alexandria in the Greek papyri, *Bull. Soc. Roy. d'Archéologie d'Alexandrie* **38**: 11, Alexandria, Société Publications Égyptiennes, 1949. The Greek character of the mysteries of Isis, Osiris, and Serapis is emphasized and ably handled, with references, by Youtie, H. C. The *kline* of Sarapis, *Harvard Theol. Rev.* **41**: 11-12, 1948. Youtie adds, on p. 16, a very interesting letter from the Michigan collection of papyri, P. Mich. inv. 4686, mentioning a coming banquet of "lord Sarapis." The letter emphasizes, pp. 27-29, the Greek side of the dual nature of the god.

In *PCZ* **1**: 59034, 8-10, 15-17, of 257 B.C. a Greek named Zoilus informed Zenon, agent of the dioicetes, Apollonius, that he had been commanded by Serapis to build a temple for him. When Zoilus tried to evade the obligation he fell ill. Later, again, he had a relapse because he did not impress upon Zenon the necessity of building the temple.

mentary.[63] A full century of scholarly interpretation of these Serapeum documents which preceded Wilcken's analysis has not yet, even through Wilcken's able discussion, led to agreement upon the nature and meaning of the detention itself (the *katochē*) nor upon the religious and functional relation of the detainees to the god.

The explanations offered have ranged widely. The earlier editors of the Memphis texts regarded the *katochoi* as voluntary recluses. In the later expansion of this belief by Herman Weingarten in 1876 and by Erwin Preuschen in 1903, their self-dedication to the god became the model upon which early Christian monasticism was constructed. Wilhelm Kroll, followed by S. Witkowski, suggested that the detainees were sick persons who sought healing from Serapis. Friedrich von Woess thought that they were suppliants of the god who fled to his temple to find asylum and protection. Kurt Sethe explained them as captives, in a sense, or prisoners who were in divine arrest because of some breach of military or civil discipline. Other scholars, including Ulrich Wilcken, have regarded the " detainees " as persons who had devoted themselves to the service of Serapis and had given themselves over into his detention after a spiritual seizure which resulted in an inner conversion.[64]

Several elements in the terminology employed in the Serapeum texts dealing with the *katochē* have seemed to me to point to a definite correspondence of that religious detention with the form and the method of the *paramonē* in the Greek system of slavery. The *paramonē* was a contractual labor relation of a semi-bondage type which could be arranged with his former master by a slave who had just been manumitted, or by a free workman who entered into a labor agreement, to be at the call of his employer for a fixed term of service. The worker, whether freedman just up from slavery or free laborer, gave up for the term of his services two elements of his liberty of action. One was his free choice of work during the period of his labor contract. The second element which he sacrificed for the term agreed upon was some part of his complete freedom of movement. He had contracted to " remain " available to his employer for the period designated. The worktaker, the *ergolabōs*, still retained two of the essential rights which in the Delphic manumissions distinguished a free man from one in bondage. These were his legal condition of freedom (*eleutheria*) and his defense against unwarranted seizure. The latter protection, which did not apply in the case of one in the ranks of the enslaved, was expressed in the Delphic manumissions by an adjective stating that he was *anephaptos*.[65]

In terms of the fundamental analysis of labor controls, particularly in the power granted to slave-owners over their slaves, complete command of the mobility of this labor group is a powerful agency in ensuring its subservience. The fugitive slave laws, which are a part of every slave system, furnish an explicit recognition of this method of enforcing the legal deprivation of the slave's right to move as he chose. Under the plantation and ranch slavery of Italy and Sicily the use of leg chains to make the flight of slaves difficult is another proof of the importance attached to this control of mobility.[66]

No written contract was necessary in establishing the relations of a devotee of Serapis (*katochos*) to the deity of his devotion. Therefore, no written form appears, or is to be expected, in the relation established in the Egyptian *katochē* between the self-dedicated detainee and his god. There is, nevertheless, a marked resemblance in the situation between the *katochos* and his god and that which existed between a freedman liberated under the *paramonē* provision and his former owner, or between a free workman who had contracted his services and his employer in the case of a labor agreement of the *paramonē* type. In nebulous form something of this understanding of the detention of the *katochos* in the Memphite and other Egyptian temple precincts of Serapis had arisen in the mind of Walter Otto in his early study of the temples and their priests in Hellenistic Egypt.[67] Later in his career, in the development and deepening of his comprehensive knowledge of the religious life of Ptolemaic Egypt, the concept became more sharply outlined. He saw in the *katochē* system the possible development of an ownership relation on the part of the god and an economic-legal bondage under Serapis which was accepted by the detainee.[68]

The indications of this transfer from the field of Greek labor relations to that of a religious subservience to the semi-Hellenic Serapis may be summarized as follows :

1. Restriction of the mobility of the freedman and the free workmen under the *paramonē* contract to the locale of the agreed services is duplicated in the detention of the *katochoi* within the confines of the temple precinct of Serapis.

In the Delphic *paramonē* manumissions by trust sale to Apollo the new freedman usually agreed to " remain " (*paramenein*) with his former owner. This was often

---

[63] Wilcken, U., *UPZ* 1, *Papyri aus Unterägypten.*

[64] Wilcken, Zu den κάτοχοι des Serapeums, *Arch. f. Pap.,* 6: 184-212, 1920. See also the brief summary of Gunther Roeder in Pauly-W., *RE*, 2d ser., 1, A2: 2413.

[65] Westermann, W. L., Between slavery and freedom, *Amer. Hist. Rev.* 50: 215-220, 1945; *idem.,* The *paramone* as general service contract, *Jour. Jur. Papyrology* 2: 9-44, Warsaw, 1948.

[66] Plautus, *Captivi,* 652; Seneca, *Dialogues* 9: 10, 1.

[67] Otto, Walter, *Priester und Tempel* 1: 118-119.

[68] This phase first appeared in a report by Otto of progress in his study of hierodulism. This was published in the *Sitzb. bayer. Akad., ph.-hist. Klasse* 14: 1934. The idea was expanded in his *Beiträge zur Hierodulie, Abh. bayer. Akad., ph.-hist. Klasse*, n. f. 29: 9-12, 1950.

expressed in the imperative form, *parameinatō*, "let him remain," or, in the plural (*parameinantōn*) in multiple manumissions.[69] The sacrifice by the Serapis detainee of his right of movement consisted of the restriction of his mobility within the confines of the Serapeum complex. He was not permitted to leave the precinct.[70]

2. The freedman, or freedwoman, in the Delphic *paramonē* manumissions promised his (her) services either to the former master or to some person to whom the former slave-owner might have assigned them.[71]

If the similarity of the two situations and the idea of the transfer of the restriction of mobility from the labor field to the religious detention under Serapis are valid, there must have been service requirements placed upon the detainees of this hybrid deity, presumably in connection with the cult worship.[72]

3. In the Delphic grants of freedom accompanied by continuous contractual obligations of the freed person the length of the term of services is sometimes fixed at a definite number of years. In the great majority of the *paramonē* manumissions, however, the services are to endure "so long as he (or she, i. e., the former owner) may live." The effect of this life expectancy of the master upon the freedman obligations is, in fact, nothing more than an expression of time indicating an indefinite period.[73]

As in the case of the *paramonē* the length of the submission to Serapis in the *katochē* was not fixed. It might endure for a short period or for as long as twenty years.[74]

4. The closest relation between the economic-legal *paramonē* developed in Greece and the religious binding of the *katochos* in Hellenistic Egypt displays itself

in the release, in both cases, from the connection established.

In the *paramonē* condition established after liberation from servitude under the Delphic trust sale system, the freedman, or freedwoman, was relieved of his, or her, obligations by an official release called an *apolysis*. Always this means the ending of the *paramonē* duties.[75] Never is it a "release" from slave status.

In the Serapeum texts it was the god who "relieved" the *katochos* devotee from his detention. In a letter dated in 168 B. C., the wife of one of the *katochoi* wrote to him: "After Horus, who brought you the letter, announced that you had been released from the detention, I became completely disgusted." Here the verb for the deliverance is the perfect infinitive *apolelysthai* — exactly the same word as was used in the Delphic releases from the *paramonē* contract.[76]

These parallels in the *paramonē* and *katochē* documents in the phrasing of bondage controls and release are impressively confirmed in a letter from the well-known detainee in the Memphite Serapeum, named Ptolemaeus: "Rejoice, all friends of mine. Release (*aphesis*) is coming swiftly for me."[77] The *katochē* condition was not *douleia*, slavery;[78] but the use of *aphesis* brings us much closer to the enslavement status which *preceded* the condition of contractual services entered into by freedmen in the labor contract of the *paramonē* type of manumission. For the substantive, *aphesis*, in its predicate form, *aphienai*, is one of the verbs officially used throughout the history of the Greek enslavement system to express liberation from slave condition.[79]

---

[69] The discussion of the *paramonē* as a contract for services of a general, unprescribed kind will be found in the study by Westermann, *Jour. Jur. Papyrology* 2: 9-32.

[70] Otto, *Priester und Tempel* 1: 120, n. 6; 121, n. 1. Ulrich Wilcken has established the distinction in the Serapeum texts between the Greek expression for the religious detention of the *katochē* and that for temple arrest. For "arrest" the Greek verb ἐγκεκλεῖσθαι is the word in *Arch. f. Pap.* 6: 186-200.

[71] Obligations of a servant for the former owner are expressed in *GDI* 2: 1952 by ὑπηρετείτω. The services of the freedman were turned over to a second party by delegation from the manumittor in *GDI*, 1694, 1-6. In *GDI*, 1904, 5-6, the *paramonē* services were assigned, under apprenticeship, to a weaver.

[72] One must assume or prove that the *katochoi* were obligated to perform some sort of service. This was pointed out to me by my friend, Professor Zaki Aly, now of the University of Cairo. For the actuality of the *katochē* services of the Serapis detainees and for indications of their nature consult Wilcken in *UPZ* 1: 67-69 and 123, n. 4. It may be that the obligations of the detainees were confined to cult practices only, as suggested by Otto, *Tempel und Priester* 1: 125.

[73] In two cases of Delphic manumissions in which life expectancy was fixed for the *paramonē*, the actual duration can be determined. In *GDI*, 1749 the release (*apolysis*) from the obligations occurred after one year (*GDI*, 1750). In *GDI*, 1918 and the *apolysis*, 1919, the *paramonē* duties lasted nine or ten years.

[74] Wilcken, *UPZ* 1: 69-70.

[75] In twenty-three of the releases in the Delphic group the formula reads: ἀπέλευσε τὸν δεῖνα τᾶς παραμονᾶς, or ἀπὸ τᾶς παραμονᾶς, "he (the former owner) released So-and-So (the ex-slave) from the *paramonē*," as in Daux, Georges, and Salac, *FD* 3 (1) : 43, which is the release from the *paramonē* established by *GDI*, 2151; in Daux, Georges, *FD* 3 (3, 2) : 418 and in the *apolysis*, no. 419; and in other examples.

[76] Wilcken, *UPZ* 1: no. 59, 24-26: ἔτι δὲ καὶ Ὧρον ― ― ― ― ἀπηγγελκότος ὑπὲρ τοῦ ἀπολελύσθαι σε ἐκ τῆς κατοχῆς παντελῶς ἀηδίζομαι.

[77] *P. Paris*, 51, line 39, as published by Ulrich Wilcken in *Arch. f. Pap.* 6: 204-206, and in *UPZ* 1: 559-561, no. 78. The restoration, οἱ παρ' ἐμοῦ πάν[τες. ἄφ]εσις μοι γίνεται, is certainly correct.

[78] Brady, Thos. A., Reception of the Egyptian cults by the Greeks, *Univ. of Missouri Studies* 10 (1) : 27, Columbia, Mo., 1935, was mistaken in his statement that the *katochoi* were "enslaved" completely by a religious faith which held them in captivity "until death or the god released them." Wilcken, *UPZ* 1: 55, to whom Brady refers, regarded them as a special group among the *therapeutai*, the private helpers of Serapis, but certainly not as *douloi*, slaves of the god. They had to be released, it is true; but the release was an *apolysis* "out of detention," not out of slavery

[79] *IG* 9, 1: 42, 3: ἀφίητι ἐλευθέρους from Stiris in Phocis; idem. 9, 2: 1268, 6, probably from Doliche in Thessaly; Diogenes Laertius, 5: 2, 55, from the will of Theophrastus: Μανῆν δὲ καὶ Καλλίαν παραμείναντας ἔτη τέτταρα ― ― ― ― ἀφίημι | ἐλευθέρους; idem., 5: 4, 72 and 73, several instances in the will of Lyco. For its use in the Greek papyri see Preisigke, Friedr., *Wörterbuch der griechischen Papyri, s. v.*, Heidelberg, 1925.

These are correspondences which suggested to me that the status of the *katochoi* in Egypt as bondsmen detained by Serapis was a transference from an economic labor relation into a religious connection with the god. If the evidence for this understanding of the institution of the Serapis detainees has been convincing it brings with it an important secondary result. It strengthens the belief in one of the inherent differences in the morphologies of the pre-Greek and the Greek systems of slavery. In the pre-Greek institutions the gods accepted slaves as well as as bondsmen; but the Greek gods did not accept them. The observation from the Serapis worship which seems to confirm this is that within Egypt, and possibly in Smyrna and Priene only among the Greek cities,[80] the *katochoi* appear as detainees of the god. In the rapid expansion of the Serapis worship over the Greek islands and upon the mainland of Greece the existence of such bondsmen of the god is unknown in any other of the twenty-four towns and cities in which the Serapis worship is recorded.[81]

In the dedications of slaves to some god in central and northern Greece quite the contrary result ensued from the consecration. Sale or dedication of a slave, even to Serapis, in the Greek polities meant, not the establishing of a bondage relation to him, but the breaking off of enslavement.

In their acceptance of the Ptolemaic god, Serapis, the Greeks, therefore, had divested him of that one of his Egyptian characteristics which was most completely at variance with the rational basis of their own enslavement practice. Hellenes might become, and often did become, the slaves of fellow Hellenes; but their gods did not have slaves. Even detention (*katochē*) of their dedicates by their gods was an idea unacceptable to the religious practice of the Greeks.

---

[80] Pauly-W., *RE* **10**: 2533, article Katochos by Ganschinietz; Brady, *Univ. of Mo. Studies* **10** (1): 27-28.

[81] Calderini, A., *Manomissione*, 108-113, lists seven city-states of Greece in which slaves were freed by religious dedication to Serapis or to Serapis and Isis. Brady, *Univ. of Mo. Studies* **10** (1): 45-46, enumerates twenty-two places, including Puteoli and Syracuse in the West, which had temples of Serapis, seven with temples of Serapis and Isis, one at Hyampolis in Phocis combining the worship of Serapis, Isis and Anubis. Slave manumissions are not preserved from most of these places.

IX. WAR AND SLAVERY IN THE WEST TO 146 B. C.

The belief of the Roman jurists was that slavery was an institution of the *ius gentium*, that is, common to all peoples, although not according to the laws of nature.[1] This conclusion embodies the assumption that the custom of enslavement of captives in war and of persons snatched from neighboring tribes was practiced from early times by all the indigenous peoples of the western Mediterranean lands. No credence need be given to the tale of Polybius that the city of Locri in lower Italy was founded by slaves accompanied by free-born Lacedaemonian women.[2] It is a point upon which he has followed a statement made by Aristotle and Theophrastus against the testimony of Timaeus;[3] and he was probably ill-advised in doing so. Nevertheless, one may assume that both Greek and Punic colonists in the period 750-550 B. C. must have brought westward with them those habits of slave employment and those methods of obtaining slaves with which they had been familiar in their respective homelands.

For the period following the Ionian revolt Herodotus gives trustworthy evidence that Greek piratical methods, including the sale into slavery of captured persons, were employed in the West by a refugee from Phocaea named Dionysius who aimed his attacks at the Cartha-ginians and Etruscans, but refrained from attacking Greeks.[4] The sale into slavery, on condition of export out of Sicily, of the poorer classes of Hyblaean Megara by Gelon of Syracuse has equally good support.[5] The report of Diodorus may be credited that Gelon, after the battle of Himera, assigned Carthaginian prisoners as slaves to the Sicilian contingents in proportion to the number of soldiers furnished by each community; but the numbers given are rhetorically exaggerated[6] in the statement that many individuals among the Agrigentines received five hundred slaves each, and in the chauvinistic flourish that all of Libya seemed to have been enslaved by the island of Sicily.[7]

This incident serves, however, to mark the beginning of enslavement upon a large scale through war which became a characteristic feature of the western Mediterranean situation at the time of the rise to power of Dionysius I. During the siege of Syracuse by the Athenians a revolt occurred of the hard-pressed Syracusan *dēmos* against their leaders, in which the local slaves were involved, demanding for themselves full citi-

---

[1] Just., *Institutes* **1**: 3, 3.
[2] Polybius, **12**: 5-10.
[3] Pauly-W., *RE* **13**: 1314.

[4] Herodotus, **6**: 17.
[5] Herod., **7**: 156, sale by Gelon ἐπ' ἐξαγωγῇ ἐκ Σικελίας because of his distrust of the *dēmos*. Compare the action of Theron of Acragas in arming three hundred slaves of Selinus as reported by Polyaenus, *Strategemata* **1**: 28.
[6] Diodorus, **11**: 25, 2.
[7] *Ibid.* **11**: 25, 5.

zen rights.[8] Although most of the slaves were tricked into returning to their masters, only three hundred deserting to the Athenians, this slave movement is important as an early symptom of the later development of western slavery which distinguishes it in type and results from the slave system previously described as characteristic of the lands of the eastern Mediterranean. The captives taken by the Syracusans at the end of the Sicilian war were estimated by Thucydides at not less than seven thousand. Of this number the Athenians, Italians, and Sicilians were not sold as slaves, but were otherwise punished.[9]

The total amount of our information upon the slave system existing in Carthaginian North Africa before 146 B. C. is limited, vague in character, and derived from sources far removed from the time under discussion.[10] Appian is authority for the general statement that the Carthaginians owned large numbers of slaves.[11] These were in considerable part employed in agriculture as shown by the slaves from Spain, Sicily, and Italy found working in the fields by Scipio Africanus in 204 B. c.[12] and by the *mancipiorum praedas* captured in the countryside of North Africa by the army of Spurius Albinus in 109 B. c.[13] That the Carthaginians took an active part in the slave trade of the west is indicated in Ps.-Aristotle, *De mirabilibus auscultatibus* (περὶ θαυμασίων ἀκουσμάτων), 88, where the merchants to whom the Balearians delivered slaves were probably Carthaginians, and by the clause of the second Carthaginian-Roman treaty [14] forbidding the Carthaginians to sell in Roman territory any slaves derived from states with which Rome stood in treaty relations.

The long-accepted belief that the Carthaginians employed their field slaves in chained gangs has, from the standpoint of efficient use, little to recommend its acceptance as a fixed practice. The assumption has been based upon two passages, one of which refers to the chains prepared by the Carthaginians for the binding of war prisoners whom they expected to capture.[15] The other is a special penal case of using the captured

soldiers of Agathocles in chains upon the project of reclaiming the Carthaginian countryside which they had devastated.[16] There is also little reason to assume that the Carthaginians were more brutal to their slaves than were other peoples.[17] Carthaginian slaves, just as those in Hellenistic Greece and, in Apulia, could contract legal marriages, a concession which was not possible under Roman slave law.[18]

Among the early Etruscans the agricultural system was one of large farms cultivated by peasants whose status was either completely free or half-free. There is little information available as to slavery; but the presence of slaves is generally assumed for the households of the Etruscan nobles, these serving as domestics, cooks, dancers, and musicians.[19] It is beyond question, however, that the Romanized estates in Etruria in the late third and early second centuries B. C. had begun to employ slave labor upon a large scale as shown by the use of a Roman legion under a praetor to suppress the slave revolt which occurred in that district in 197 B. c.[20]

In the Latin terminology *servus* is the general and most common word for slave, with *serva* as its feminine counterpart, though it is rarely found in the legal texts. The customary term for an adult female slave was *ancilla*.[21] *Mancipium* is used extensively to designate the slave as chattel, *famulus* in relation to the service of the slave. A slave was often addressed or referred to as *puer*.[22] *Verna* designates a home-born slave of either sex. *Novicius* and *veterator* were often used, without further definition, to distinguish an untrained and a trained slave, respectively.[23]

The traditional account of early Roman history where it deals with slaves is a reconstruction, based in part upon survivals of the ancient legislation and the older attitude toward slavery which persisted into the period of the later Republic. Such vestiges are particularly numerous and trustworthy in their bearing upon the Roman *familia*, of which the Roman slaves were an integral part. Since in the Roman legal concept slavery,

[8] Polyaenus, *Strategemata* 1: 43. Thucydides, 6: 103, 4, does not mention the participation of the slaves.
[9] Thucydides, 7: 87, 3-4.
[10] Gsell, Stéphane, *Histoire ancienne de L'Afrique du Nord* 2: 226-227, 299-300; 4: 134-136, 173-174.
[11] Appian, *Punic wars* 9: 59.
[12] *Ibid.* 3: 15.
[13] Sallust, *Bellum Jugurthinum*, 44, 5. Further references upon Carthaginian slavery are: end of the fifth century B. C., Diodorus, 14: 77, 3 and Justinus, 21: 4; prisoners from Tyre exported to Carthage when Alexander the Great captured that city in 334 B. C., Diodorus, 17: 46, 4 (probably a few thousands): Appian, *Punic wars* 1: 3. For 255 B. C., slaves appearing in the mercenary revolt of 240-238 B. C., Polybius, 1: 67, 7 and Zonaras, 8: 17; purchase of five thousand slaves by the Carthaginian state for naval service in 205 B. C., Appian, *Punic wars* 1: 9; the return of Roman prisoners found working as slaves in 202 B. C., *ibid.*, 8: 54.
[14] Polybius, 3: 24, 5-7.
[15] Diodorus, 20: 13, 2.

[16] *Ibid.*, 20: 69, 5.
[17] For the mild treatment of urban slaves at Carthage, see Gsell, *L'Afrique du Nord* 4: 173.
[18] Plautus, *Casina*, 67-77.
[19] Ducati, P., *Etruria antica*, 140, Turin, Biblioteca Paravia, 1925, for which we have the testimony of Posidonius: παρὰ δὲ τυρρηνοῖς . . . δούλων πλῆθος εὐπρεπῶν and a less decisive statement of Timaeus in Athenaeus, 4: 38, 153d. Cf. Diodorus, 40: 3 and Dio Cassius in Zonaras, 8: 7 regarding the town of Volsinii.
[20] Livy, 33: 36, 1. For the later attitude condoning Cato's activities see Cicero, *Against Quintus Caecilius*, 20, 66.
[21] Buckland, W. W., *Roman law of slavery*, 8, Cambridge Univ. Press, 1908.
[22] Plautus, *Mercator*, 936; *Pseudolus*, 170; ; Cicero, *For Sextus Roscius of Ameria*, 77; Horace, *Odes* 2: 11, 18; *Satires* 1: 6, 116. Cf. *por* (= *puer*) in the early names for slaves such as *Marpor* (= *Marci puer*), Dessau, *Inscriptiones Latinae Selectae*, no. 7822; *Olipor*, Dessau, 4405, 7823; *Gaipor*, CIL 6: no. 30914; *Naepor*, CIL 6, no. 9430.
[23] Buckland, *Roman law of slavery*, 9.

and along with it release therefrom by manumission, were conditions inherent in the *ius gentium*,[24] the enslavement of war captives was expected and accepted, either if it resulted in enslavement of their enemies by the Romans or, conversely, if it happened that the Romans themselves were the ones enslaved.[25] Those who endured slavery, being members of the *familia*, fell under the *dominica potestas* of the head of the family just as the children were under the *patria potestas*.[26] Since the Roman laws of manumission granted the status held by the master to any slave who was freed by formal act, there was nothing abhorrent to the Roman mind in the tradition that Romulus established an asylum in his newly founded city to which slaves as well as free men from the neighboring states might flee and find sanctuary and acceptance.[27] Livy's rejection of the story of the servile origin of Servius Tullius was motivated by his doubt that a child of known servile origin could be honored by betrothal to a king's daughter,[28] rather than by any feeling that it was not seemly that a former slave should rule the Roman state. This latter feeling Livy does ascribe to the aristocratic faction among the Romans which supported the royal family of the Tarquins.[29]

Simple and friendly personal relations were later postulated as the characteristics of the slave and master situation in the early Roman household as in the story of the attempt of the slaves of the Latin Turnus to defend their master against the agents of Tarquinius Superbus.[30] Regarding the relations of masters to slaves in the early period of Roman republican development there is no contemporary material which can be cited. Looking backward from the slave conditions which existed in the second and first centuries B.C. it may be assumed that they were of the domestic type common to small slaveholding communities which may be called patriarchal.

The number of the slaves in the early period of the history of Latium was certainly small. According to tradition Regulus in 258 B.C. had but one slave, his foreman, and one hired hand upon his small farm.[31] More important in respect to the development of slavery at Rome is the observation that the first treaty between Rome and Carthage provides only for the protection of the Latin towns against plundering by the Cartha-

ginians[32] with no specific mention of the sale of slaves either to or by the Romans. The second treaty contains a reciprocal provision binding each of the contracting parties not to bring for sale into the harbors of the other party slaves obtained from states with which that party stood in treaty relations.[33] The introduction of slaves into Roman territory upon a scale which would warrant inclusion of the subject in a treaty must, therefore, be placed at the end of the fourth century B.C.

Because of the improbability of important slave numbers in the fifth and fourth centuries[34] the traditional record of slave revolts at Rome in the early period of the Republic must be rejected as reflections of a later situation.[35] Specific instances of enslavement through debt, applying to Roman citizens as well as to others,[36] may be unhistorical; but the fact of enslavement of debtors appears indisputably in the Laws of the Twelve Tables.[37] In case a former citizen was to be sold in satisfaction of a debt the Roman law, like the Jewish law, required that he be sold outside the confines of the state.[38] Mortgage and sale of members of the *familia* were permitted under the *patria potestas*; but even in the period of the publication of the Twelve Tables it was restricted by the provision that a son thrice sold by his father was to be freed from the *patria potestas*.[39] Agitation against slavery for debt is recorded in the sources as occurring in the years 380 to 369 B.C.;[40] and the abolition in the Roman state of the *nexus*, with its possibilities of complete slavery, is assigned by Livy to a *Lex Poetelia*, submitted, it is asserted, by the consuls of 326 B.C.[41]

The reign of Dionysius I of Syracuse may be taken as the period when the characteristic features of later western slavery appear. These are: a great increase in the numbers of slaves resulting from capture in war; use of slaves as agricultural workers and herdsmen; and the necessity, imposed upon Dionysius by his financial situation, of making his wars finance themselves as far as possible. He therefore applied rigorously the policy of ransom or enslavement of war captives and directed his efforts toward an immediate return in money from the prisoners who fell to him, except where

---

[24] Just., *Institutes* 1: 3, 2; *Digest* 1: 1, 4; 5, 4; 12: 6, 64.

[25] Just., *Institutes* 1: 3; *Digest* 1: 5, 4. Pomponius, also in the *Digest* 50: 16, 239, 1, derives *servus* from *servare, quod imperatores nostri captivos vendere ac per hoc servare nec occidere – – – solent*.

[26] Just., *Institutes* 1: 8, *pr*. (*principium*, beginning) and 1.

[27] Livy, 1: 8, 6.

[28] *Ibid.*, 1: 39, 5-6.

[29] *Ibid.*, 1: 40, 3; 47, 10; 48, 2.

[30] Livy, 1: 51, 8. Macrobius, *Saturnalia* 1: 11, 11, *majores nostri omnem dominis invidiam servis contumeliam detrahentes*. Compare Plutarch, *Coriolanus*, 24, 8-10; *Cato the Elder*, 20, 5.

[31] Valerius Maximus, 4: 4, 6.

[32] Polybius, 3: 22, 11-13.

[33] *Ibid.*, 3: 24, 6-8. Date of the second treaty is 306 B.C. according to Schachermeyr, *Rh. Mus.* 78: 371-373, 1930. The interpretation of the clause upon slave sales appears upon page 375.

[34] Beloch, J., *Bevölkerung*, 297.

[35] The recorded instances are: in 501-498 B.C., Zonaras, 7: 13; Dionysius of Halicarnassus, 5: 51, 53; in 460 B.C., Livy, 3: 15, 5; 17, 2-3; 18, 10; cf. Zonaras, 7: 18; and the alleged revolt of 418 B.C. in Livy, 4: 45, 1-2.

[36] Livy, 6: 15, 9; 20, 6.

[37] Bruns-Gradenwitz, *FIR*, 20-21.

[38] *Trans Tiberim peregre venum ibant*, Gellius, *Noctes Atticae* 20: 1, 47.

[39] Bruns-Gradenwitz, *FIR*, 22; Gaius, 1: 132.

[40] Livy, 6: 27, 8-9; 34, 2; 36, 12.

[41] *Ibid.*, 8: 28, 1. *Cf.* Pauly-W., *RE* 21 (1): 1166.

political advantage recommended dismissal of his prisoners.[42] This is best seen in his attempt in 398 B. C. to save the people of Motya from death at the hands of his soldiers by directing them to flee to the Greek temples. We are told that this action was motivated by the desire of Dionysius to sell them as slaves.[43] It is also seen in the business proposal made by him to the Rhegians in 389 B. C. that he would ransom all those who would pay him one mina, the remainder to be sold as slaves.[44] This system Dionysius recommended also to the Lucanians in Italy in the treatment of their captives from Thurii.[45] With this policy went a ready willingness to free able-bodied slaves for enlistment as mercenaries.[46] Later, Agathocles of Syracuse also enlisted slaves in preparation for his African expedition.[47]

The sale of war prisoners is frequently noted in the accounts of the early history of Rome during the slow expansion of the fifth and fourth centuries. It may be assumed that the numbers of their war prisoners increased with the gradual extension of the Roman power, to the point that the seven thousand Samnite prisoners said to have been sold in 307-306 B. C. may closely approximate the truth.[48] The period of the first two Punic wars, however, marks the great increase in slave numbers in the western area [49] for which the wars themselves were in large part responsible.[50] Probably this source of slaves was supplemented in some degree, even in the West, by the piracy of the Illyrian kingdom until their activities were suppressed by Rome in 228 B. C.[51] After that time the pillaging went over to the Aetolians.[52]

The following enumeration of the reports of prisoners of war sold during the sixty-year period covered by the first two Punic wars and the interval between them will serve to emphasize the impressive total of slaves which must have come upon the western market in that time. It will also help to explain the great change in the use of slaves and the shift for the worse both in the Roman attitude toward them and in the conditions of their employment.

It is clear that where numbers are given in the ancient sources they usually appear in rounded thousands and

are open to suspicion; but there is no means of checking them or of establishing any approximate ratio for deduction. In 262 B. C. more than twenty-five thousand inhabitants of Agrigentum are reported to have been deported, probably into Italy, as slaves.[53] Additional records of war captives who were enslaved are these: in 254 B. C. at Panormus fourteen thousand of the captured inhabitants were permitted to ransom themselves at two minas each and thirteen thousand were taken away for sale; [54] about 230 B. C., a sale of slaves into Italy by the Celtic Boli; [55] in 241 B. C. Carthaginian soldiers captured in Sicily were sold at Lilybaeum; [56] and in Spain in 219 B. C. Hannibal distributed among his soldiers the prisoners taken at Saguntum; in 211 B. C. slaves were again available from the capture of Agrigentum; [57] and Scipio set to work at New Carthage in Spain two thousand artisans who were to serve as public slaves of Rome, probably in war production, with a promise of freedom to them in return for diligent service at their trade.[58] After the recapture of Capua in 211 B. C. its citizens were sold, exclusive of the leaders of the revolt. According to the express statement of Livy they were sent to Rome for sale.[59] In 210 B. C. new slaves were available from the capture of Anticyra in Locris [60] and from the taking of Hasdrubal's camp in Spain.[61] From the recapture of the revolted city of Tarentum a large number was sold.[62] In 207 B. C. a few thousand prisoners remained over from the slaughter of Hasdrubal's army; [63] of the prisoners captured by Scipio in Africa during the years 205-201 B. C. the reported total amounting to twenty thousand and seven hundred persons,[64] a large number were shipped to Sicily for sale.[65]

It is also clear that a considerable number of captives taken by the Carthaginians, chiefly Roman citizens and Italian allies, fell into slavery. Their number would obviously be less than the number of those sold by the

[42] Andreades, A., *Greek public finance*, 164-165.

[43] Diodorus, 14: 53, 2.

[44] Diodorus, 14: 111, 4. Ps.-Aristotle, *Oeconomica* 2: 2, 1349b, gives the ransom price at three minas. For the advantages of acceptance of ransom over sale see Andreades, *Greek public finance*, 168 and n. 5.

[45] Diodorus, 14: 102, 2. *Cf.* the sale of captives at Herbita and Catana by Dionysius, *ibid.*, 14: 15, 1-2.

[46] Diodorus, 14: 58, 1, crews of sixty warships recruited from freed slaves. This presupposes 12,000 male slaves capable of such services in Syracuse, according to Beloch, *Bevölkerung*, 280.

[47] Justinus, 22: 4.

[48] Livy, 9: 42, 8. A vague statement of the sale of Samnite slaves in 293 B. C. occurs in Livy, 10: 46, 5.

[49] Beloch, *Bebölkerung*, 299.

[50] *Ibid.*, 415.

[51] Ziebarth, Erich, *Beiträge zur Geschichte des Seeraubs*, 27.

[52] Ormerod, H. A., *Piracy in the ancient world*, 141-142.

[53] Diodorus, 23: 9, 1; without the figures, Zonaras, 8: 10.

[54] Diodorus, 23: 18, 5.

[55] Zonaras, 8: 19.

[56] Polybius, 1: 41, 8. Most of these would quickly come under civilian ownership.

[57] Livy, 26: 40, 13.

[58] Polybius, 10: 17, 9-10, χειροτέχναις. Compare with Livy, 26: 47, 1-3, who adds that other able-bodied slaves were enrolled by Scipio for service in the Roman fleet.

[59] Livy, 26: 16, 6. No numbers are given. A variant source in Appian, *Hannibalic war*, 43, states that only the Carthaginians captured at Capua were enslaved.

[60] Polybius, 9: 39, 2-3; Livy, 27: 26, 3.

[61] A few thousand African troops out of a reported total of twelve thousand prisoners, Livy, 27: 19, 2.

[62] Livy, 27: 16, puts the number at thirty thousand, which is probably exaggerated because there was a scarcity of farm slaves in Latium in the next year, *ibid.*, 28: 11. 9.

[63a] About the same number as that of the Romans captured at Cannae, Appian, *Hannibalic war*, 53.

[64] Appian, *Hann.*, 15; 23; 26; 36; 48.

[65] Livy, 29: 29, 3: *extemplo - - missa in Siciliam; cf. idem*, 29: 35, 1.

Romans because the Carthaginians captured but few cities by siege. Twelve thousand slaves from the Roman armies, found in Achaea, were released at the request of Flamininus in 195 B. C., which, as Livy rightly observes, implies a much greater number in the whole of Greece.[66] The captives of Roman and Italian status who were still found in Crete in 188 B. C.[67] may have come in part from the war with Antiochus; but the majority was probably made up from captives taken by Hannibal. A clause in the treaty with Antiochus III of 187 B. C. stipulated that the former slaves of Roman subjects or allies, and Romans and their allies captured in war, were to be returned to the victors.[68] The presence of Roman prisoners as slaves in Africa is attested by a provision of the treaty with Carthage for the return of Roman captives, as well as deserters, who were found there at the close of the Hannibalic War.[69]

In addition to the actual evidence accumulated above, the importance of the increase in the number of slaves in Italy and Sicily is shown by two facts: by the enlistment of male slaves of the requisite age and physical ability as fighting men during the Hannibalic War, and by the frequency and duration of the slave revolts in Italy and Sicily from 200 B. C. to 70 B. C. The Roman state was compelled to resort to the enlistment of eight thousand slave volunteers in 215 B. C. after the battle of Cannae.[70] These were purchased by the state from private owners with a promise to pay the purchase price when the war was completed.[71] The owners refused to accept, before the end of the war, the price of the slaves who were manumitted by Tiberius Gracchus for the services they had rendered in battle.[72] Although these slave levies displayed a tendency to personal loyalty to particular leaders rather than a state loyalty,[73] their effectiveness as combatants could be compared favorably with that of other Roman levies.[74] Enrollment of slaves was again resorted to in the crisis of the year 207 B. C.[75] Hannibal also is said to have armed slaves and used them as combatants in Bruttium in 204 B. C.[76] and in Africa in the following year.[77]

With such numbers of slave material available for labor purposes, the Roman system of leasing the *ager publicus* together with the constant military services demanded of Roman citizens and Italian allies, from which slaves were customarily exempt, fostered the growth of large plantations and ranches in Italy and the use of slave labor upon them as against the small farm system and the employment of free hired labor.[78] According to Dio Cassius[79] the enormous military losses suffered by the Roman state at the battle of Cannae had brought about instances of mating of free women and slaves for the purpose of producing offspring. Although no battles occurred with comparable losses to the Roman state between 216 B. C. and the battle of Arausio in 105 B. C. when the loss of eighty thousand fighting men under Roman arms is recorded,[80] the mortality among Roman citizens and Italian allies sustained year by year in consequence of the wars of expansion and the civil wars of the first century B. C. were severe. They continued to be a constant drain upon the peasantry, upon free hired labor engaged in agriculture and upon the free laborers occupied in handicraft production. During the years 201 to 151 B. C., for example, the war losses totalled ninety-four thousand as these are recorded by Livy and Appian. This gives an average of 1880 per year, excluding the losses from disease for which no records are given.[81]

Replacement of these losses occurred mainly through the constant supply of slaves which flowed in a swelling or declining stream into Italy and Sicily, sometimes in large numbers owing to the capture and sale of prisoners of war, at other times fed only by the customary traffic in slaves. These recognized sources of supply were expanded to greater proportions in the years 133 to 67 B. C. by the unrestricted activities of pirate organizations centering in Cilicia;[82] by the kidnappings conducted by Roman taxgatherers; and by the necessity imposed upon the inhabitants of the province of Asia of selling their children into slavery to meet the tremendous burdens placed upon them by Sulla in 85-84 B. C.[83] The last two factors explain completely the surprising preponderance of slaves with Greek names and correctly ascribed to Asia Minor, amounting to sixty-seven per cent of the total number, which appear in the *magistri-magistrae* lists from Minturnae of 90 to 64 B. C.[84]

Out of the long list of sales of war captives in this period only a selected group need be cited in proof that the losses in free labor of Roman citizens and allied

---

[66] Polybius in Livy, 34: 50, 4-7.
[67] Livy, 37: 60, 3.
[68] Livy, 38: 38, 7.
[69] Polybius, 15: 18, 3.
[70] Livy, 22: 57, 11; 33: 35, 7-9; Zonaras, 9: 2; Servius Grammaticus, *In Vergilii carmina, Aeneidos* 9: 544. The numbers of the slaves enrolled have been increased in Valerius Maximus, 7: 6, one to twenty-four thousand. For slaves enlisted also among the Roman allies see Livy, 25: 1, 4.
[71] Livy, 22: 57, 11; 34: 6, 12.
[72] *Ibid.*, 24, 18, 12. For the manumission cf. *ibid.*, 24: 14, 1-8; 16, 10; 25: 6, 21.
[73] Livy, 25: 20, 4.
[74] *Ibid.*, 26: 2, 10.
[75] *Ibid.*, 27: 38, 10; 46, 13.
[76] Appian, *Hannibalic war*, 57.
[77] Zonaras, 9: 12.

[78] Appian, *Bella civilia* 1: 1, 7: τοὺς ἐλευθέρους ἐς τὰς στρατείας ἀπὸ τῆς γεωργίας περισπᾶν. For the demand for agricultural slaves in Sicily also, *ibid.*, 1: 1, 9. Cf. Frank, T., *Economic survey of ancient Rome* 1: 100.
[79] Dio Cassius, 1: 224 B, in Tzetz., *Hist.* 1: 785.
[80] Livy, *Periochae*, 67.
[81] Frank, *Economic survey* 1: 110.
[82] Ormerod, *Piracy*, 207-241.
[83] Plutarch, *Lucullus*, 20.
[84] Johnson, Jotham, *Excavations at Minturnae* 2 (1), *Republican Magistri*, 106-113, 1933.

states in Italy through mortality in war were more than counterbalanced by the replacements possible through slavery resulting from war activities. Under this method of approach exact calculations are impossible because of factors which cannot be controlled, such as the increasing enlistment in the Roman armies of peregrine elements from outside of Italy [85] which served to reduce the military losses falling upon the Roman citizen classes.

There are no figures available which can furnish any estimate of population movement, the increase or decrease of birth rate, among the free population of Italy. There is also an unknown percentage of deduction to be made for the numbers of war captives who did not enter into Italy as slaves. This deduction is necessitated by the fact that such prisoners were usually disposed of immediately and near the locality of the beleaguered city in which they were taken. A considerable number of them would, sooner or later, be bought out of slavery by relatives or interested friends and returned to their homes and customary activities as free men.

Although these considerations operated to reduce the amount of the substitution of slave labor for free labor in Italy, the trend toward such replacement becomes obvious. After the battle of Cynoscephalae, in 196 B. C., Titus Flamininus set up for sale a part of the 5,000 prisoners taken, distributing a part also among his soldiers.[86] In the case of the local slave population remaining in Laconia in 189 B. C., in the war of the Achaeans against Sparta, we know that the Romans decided that they were to be turned over to the Achaeans for capture and sale.[87] It is to be presumed, in most cases like this of sale at a distance from Italy, that only a small number would eventually come westward to meet the growing demand in Sicily and Italy, but that of those given as booty to the Roman soldiery the greater part would accompany their new masters to their homes at the end of the campaign. In a punitive expedition against the Istrians in 178 B. C. from three captured towns 5,632 persons were sold at auction.[88] The number, being an uneven one, is apparently exact; and it would far surpass the Roman losses at the beginning of the war.[89]

In 176 B. C. occurred, however, the long-continued auction, apparently held at Rome, of slaves from the revolt in Sardinia which gave rise to the well known expression " Sardinians for sale, one more worthless than another." [90] The number of Sardinians slain or

captured was given at eighty thousand by Tiberius Sempronius Gracchus upon a tablet set up at Rome.[91] In the first year of the war with Perseus a considerable number of prisoners obtained from Boeotian towns fell into slavery, two thousand five hundred from Haliartus,[92] and from Thisbe those who had sided with Macedon.[93] Complaints regarding the rapacity displayed by the Roman commanders in the taking of prisoners for sale which reached the Roman senate from Coronea in Boeotia, from Abdera, and from the Alpine Gauls, received attention in the first two cases. A fine was imposed upon the commander in Boeotia, Licinius Crassus, and the captives found in Italy were bought from their purchasers and restored to their homes.[94] In the case of Abdera a senatorial embassy was sent to that town to restore those who had been enslaved.[95]

The enslavement of 150,000 men from seventy towns of Epirus in 167 B. C. upon direct order of the Roman senate is so well attested that the fact cannot be doubted, despite the enormous numbers handed down and despite our complete ignorance of any adequate motive for so drastic an action.[96] The estimate of a total of 250,000 prisoners of war taken by the Romans in the years 200-150 B. C. does not appear to be too great; [97] but a considerable number of these would soon have been released from permanent servitude by ransom or purchase negotiated by friends and relatives. The number of those enslaved at the time of the destruction of Carthage and Corinth in 146 B. C. is not known. Appian states that fifty thousand remaining alive at Carthage were granted their lives.[98] These may have been sold, although Zonaras asserts that only a few became slaves, the greater part of the men dying in prison.[99] Most of the Corinthian men had fled the city when it was taken. The majority of those who remained were massacred, only the women and children being sold by Mummius.[100]

A discussion by Apuleius of Madaura (in North Africa) in his *Apologia* gives the impression retained by men of the second century after Christ of the number of personal slave attendants who accompanied the Roman *imperatores* of the third and second centuries B. C. when they were upon campaigns. They took pride, according to Apuleius, in the small number of their slaves. Marcus Antonius, a man of consular rank, had but eight slaves in his household. One of the wealthy Carbos had one less. Manius Curius, the conqueror of Pyrrhus

[85] Mommsen, Theodor, *History of Rome* 3: 458. Iberian cavalrymen were given citizenship during the Social War in accordance with the *lex Julia, Bulletino della commissione archeologica comunale di Roma* 36: 169, 1908.
[86] Livy, 33: 10, 7; 11, 2.
[87] *Ibid.*, 38: 34, 2.
[88] *Ibid.*, 41: 11, 8.
[89] *Ibid.*, 41: 2, 9-10.
[90] Festus, *De verborum significatu*, 322, W. J. Lindsay, p. 428.

[91] Livy, 41: 28, 8.
[92] *Ibid.*, 42: 63, 11.
[93] *Ibid.*, 42: 63, 12. For the substitution of the name Thisbe for the name Thebes of the text, see Mommsen, Th., *Ephemeris epigraphica* 1: 290, 1872.
[94] Zonaras, 9: 22.
[95] Livy, 43: 4, 8-11.
[96] Polybius, 30: 15; Livy, 45: 34, 5-6.
[97] Frank, T., *Economic survey* 1: 188.
[98] Appian, *Punic wars*, 19, 130.
[99] Zonaras, 9: 30.
[100] Pausanias, *Periegesis* 7: 16, 8.

of Epirus, had only two slaves in his camp included in his military contingent of personal following. Marcus Cato, the elder, is quoted by Apuleius as having left a document stating that when he went into Spain as proconsul he took with him but five slaves as personal attendants

and assistants to him in his campaigns.[101] The last of these figures is certainly trustworthy. It was quoted directly from Cato himself by Apuleius.

[101] Apuleius, *Apologia*, 17.

X. THE ROMAN REPUBLIC
PRAEDIAL SLAVERY, PIRACY, AND SLAVE REVOLTS

The tremendous loss of life suffered by the Roman forces in 105 B. C. at the battle of Arausio was more than met by the number of the German captives taken by Marius, which Livy gives at ninety thousand of the Teutones and sixty thousand of the Cimbri.[1] Although this huge number is open to suspicion as repeating the exact total of one hundred and fifty thousand Epirotes sold into slavery in 167 B. C., some elements of these Germans were still present in Italy as slaves at the time of the Servile War of 73-71 B. C.[2] The claim that one million Gauls came to Rome as slaves,[3] and a modern variant of this to the effect that one million Celts fell into slavery, in consequence of Caesar's Gallic campaigns of 58-51 B. C., are not to be accepted. The second statement is a distortion of the assertion of Plutarch and Appian that a million Celts were slain or captured during those years.

In the first two years of the conquest of Gaul Caesar's policy was, in this respect, distinctly conciliatory. The only record of a sale of captives in these two years is that in the case of the Aduatuci, when the number reported to Caesar by the purchasers was fifty-three thousand.[5] No other sale is recorded by him until 56 B. C., in the case of the Veneti, where the accepted right of sale of captives was employed as a retaliatory measure.[6] There is no indication in Caesar's account that the expectation of slaves from Britain expressed by Cicero in a letter of 54 B. C.[7] was realized. A large distribution of Gallic prisoners into slavery occurred in 52 B. C., after the siege of Alesia, when Caesar's soldiers each received a captive as booty.[8] A total of one hundred fifty thousand slaves resulting from the Gallic wars of Caesar would constitute an approximate estimate. Because of the custom of immediate sale of prisoners in the locality, as in the case of the Aduatuci above,[9] only a part of those sold would eventually come into slavery in Italy, some with the soldiers, others by the indirect

method of purchase by Italians, resident in Gaul, who would transport them into Italy for sale.[10]

To the figures of military losses of the free male Italian population, as given above, must be added the heavy mortality suffered by this class which resulted from the Social War and the civil wars of the first century B. C. The impression that western slavery in its relation to the total population in the second and first centuries B. C. attained proportions never before known in antiquity, and never to be reached again, is supported by the evidence of the slave revolts which occurred intermittently until 70 B. C.; by the flourishing state of piracy which fed largely upon ransom for kidnapped persons and redemption money paid by relatives for persons enslaved; and by the increase in numbers of slaves in non-productive and luxury services among the higher classes in Italy. The slave revolts, which began in Italy immediately after the close of the Hannibalic War and frequently required the use of legionary forces for their suppression, clearly indicate a large concentration of men of slave status who were of fighting age. In 198 B. C. North African attendants of Carthaginian hostages revolted and were joined by other slaves of the locality.[11] In 196 B. C. a more serious outbreak in Etruria was suppressed by the peregrine praetor with one legion. He crucified the leaders and returned the survivors to their masters.[12]

The increasing frequency of manumissions by Roman citizens and the admission of their freedmen to citizenship aroused antagonism at Rome to the extent that the magistrates were required in 177 B. C. to demand an oath that the motive of manumission was not the mere desire to change the ex-slave from servile to citizen rank.[13] Opposition also arose to the illegal intrusion of freedmen, advanced to membership in the *populus Romanus*, into other than the four country tribes. In 168 B. C. a drastic proposal that all ex-slaves should be removed from the tribal lists was rejected as unconstitu-

---

[1] Livy, *Periochae*, 68.
[2] Caesar, *Bellum Gallicum* 1: 40.
[3] Schneider, A., *Zur Geschichte der Sclaverei im alten Rom*, 15, Zürich, Schulthess, 1892.
[4] Plutarch, *Caesar*, 15; Appian, *Celtic wars*, 2.
[5] Caesar, *Bellum Gallicum* 2: 33.
[6] *Ibid.*, 3: 16.
[7] Cicero, *Ad Atticum* 4: 16.
[8] Caesar, *Bell. Gall.* 7: 89; twenty thousand captives were returned by Caesar to the Aedui and Arverni, *ibid.*, 7: 90.
[9] *Ibid.*, 2: 33.

[10] This is exemplified in the case of Sextus Naevius in 83 B. C. which is recorded by Cicero, *Pro Publio Quinctio*, 6, 24.
[11] Livy, 32: 26, 8; Zonaras, 4: 16.
[12] Livy, 33: 36, 3.
[13] *Ibid.*, 41: 9, 11. Fritz Heichelheim, *Wirtschaftsgeschichte des Altertums* 1: 643, Leyden, Sijthoff, 1938, seems to ascribe to the acceptance of the freedmen of Roman citizens into Roman citizenship the eventual idea of a mass emancipation of Roman slaves. This notion is not valid, either as purpose of the advance of Roman freedmen to citizenship or as eventual result of it.

tional because of its retroactive aspect. A compromise was reached whereby the ex-slaves who were at that time enrolled on the lists and those to be manumitted in the future should all be restricted to membership in a single tribe.[14]

Despite the increasing tendency of the Roman state to apply rigidly the right of the conqueror to enslave its captives taken in war, the Roman senate early in the second century B. C. formulated a policy that runaway slaves of any type of ownership category, whether in royal, municipal, or private ownership, should be restored where possible to their former masters. This action was apparently based upon the theory of the sanctity of private property and designed politically to enlist the support of the propertied classes among their allies and former enemies. Originally formulated after the defeat of Nabis of Sparta in 196 B. C.,[15] it was revived and applied by Sulla in the east in 84 B. C.[16]

The maintenance, within the sphere of Roman political influence, of the status of free-born persons was also expressed as a policy in the case of the Lycians against the Rhodians in 178 B. C.[17] It is significant, however, that the Achaeans three years later refused to take advantage of this precedent, and to accept return of their own runaway slaves from Perseus of Macedon, out of fear of offending the Romans.[18] The total area available for the employment of slaves as against bondage servants and free labor was increased in the second century by the liberation of many of the Lacedaemonian helots by King Nabis of Sparta [19] and the ending of the helotry system after the establishment of Roman control over Greece.[20]

A great increase in the numbers of the slaves introduced into Italy and the Roman province of Sicily must be ascribed to the capture of enemy troops and the looting of cities and towns in the Roman wars of expansion of the second century B. C. and to the organized activities of the Mediterranean pirates in the late second and early first centuries B. C. Thirty-five years have elapsed since Herman Gummerus suggested a connection of the concurrent development of handicraft production in Italy with the swelling stream of slave craftsmen brought to the west from the Hellenistic East.[21] This observation and its rationalization were supported seventeen years later by the discovery of the inscribed lists of slave and freedmen officials elected as leaders of handicraft guilds at Minturnae in Italy.[22] Despite

this increased use of slaves in the manufacturing procedures in the West the accounts which we have of the great slave revolts in Sicily and Italy depict them as inspired by the conditions on the latifundia. These outbreaks found their leaders among the personnel of the agricultural slaves. The evidence does not permit that they be explained as emanations of the new development of handicraft slavery in the West.

The detailed accounts of the two great slave revolts in Sicily which occurred in the years 135 to 132 B. C. and 104 to 101 B. C., as narrated by Diodorus of Sicily, give a direct picture of the extent of the western latifundian slavery in the native island of Diodorus, as they also throw a reflected light upon the conditions in Italy in the last two centuries B. C. After sporadic outbreaks in the middle of the second century the great revolt of 135 B. C. occurred. Its immediate occasion was the hatred engendered among his slaves by the brutal treatment accorded them upon the estate of a landowner at Enna in central Sicily.[23] The larger background behind the real causes was the wealth and greed of the Sicilian landowners. Their desire for greater gain from the exploitation of their praedial slaves led them to abandon the accepted and traditional expectations of the slaves in respect to their maintenance quotas in food allowances (*sōmatotropheia*) and clothing assignments (*himatismos*). The owners of the big estates used their young and vigorous slaves as herders, apparently, letting them make shift for themselves without the supervision of overseers. Contrary to the prevailing Greek and Roman custom, they branded the slaves, and insulted them by unjustified beatings. These were, according to the precise analysis of Diodorus, the basic causes of the revolts.[24]

The original local outbreak in the first insurrection in Sicily involved only four hundred slaves; but the numbers of the slaves swelled within three days to six

---

[14] Livy, 45: 15, 5.

[15] Livy, 34: 35, 4.

[16] Appian, *Mithridatic wars,* 61.

[17] Livy, 41: 6, 11.

[18] Their action is naively motivated by Livy, 41: 23, 8 by the suggestion that the slaves in question were of little value.

[19] Livy, 34: 31-32; Lécrivain in Daremberg-Saglio, *Dictionnaire* 3: 69.

[20] Strabo, 8: 5, 4. See, also, Pauly-W., *RE* 8: 206.

[21] Gummerus, Herman, Industrie und Handel, Pauly-W., *RE* 9: 1454-1455.

[22] Johnson, J., *Excavations at Minturnae* 2 (1), *Republican Magistri*, Philadelphia, 1933. See, also, Westermann, W. L.,

Industrial slavery in Roman Italy, *Jour. Econ. Hist.* 2: 152-154 1942.

[23] Diodorus, 34-35: 2, 10, Dindorf, L.-C. Müller edition, Paris, Firmin-Didot, 2: 531-532. *Cf. Strabo,* 6: 2, 6.

[24] Diodorus, 34-35: 2, 1-4. This passage is *not* an emotional one as it is usually said to be. It is intensely practical—something that might happen under any slave system when the customary acceptances of the slave group are broken down. The word *sōmatotropheia* for "slave maintenance" expectations is exact, as a description of the slave sustenance rations. It offers no difficulty whatsoever. See Westermann, Slave maintenance and slave revolts, *Class. Phil.* 40: 8-10, 1945. The account of Diodorus is usually classed as a psychological portrayal which goes back to Posidonius, Jacoby, F., *FGrH,* 2: 108d, p. 287. *Cf.* Taeger, Fritz, *Untersuchungen zur römischen Geschichte und Quellenkunde: Tiberius Gracchus,* Stuttgart, Kohlhammer, 60, and its notes, 1928.

An idea has been briefly advanced by Bidez, J., *La cité du monde et la cité du soleil,* 49-50, Paris, Belles Lettres, 1932, which should be discarded. It is to the effect that the Sicilian slave revolts were uprisings which represented a new proletarian spirit evoked by Stoic propaganda. With it the word "proletarian" (Latin *proletarius*) should go overboard because of the modern Marxist connotations which are now, unfortunately, inseparable from it.

thousand men.[25] To this group five thousand of fighting age were added by a similar revolt about Agrigentum.[26] An intimation of the numbers of slaves involved and of the conditions engendered by their use as herdsmen and in other forms of labor upon the ranchlike estates may be gleaned from the statement of P. Popilius Laenas, consul in 132 B. C. He reported that, as praetor in Sicily in 135 B. C., he had hunted out and returned 917 fugitives from Italian owners who were found in Sicily.[27] The eventual maximum of the slaves and the free men who adhere to their cause is given by Livy[28] at seventy thousand. This estimate is to be accepted in place of the two hundred thousand given by Diodorus.[29] Even the lower number is impressive in view of the fact that some important city districts did not come under the control of the slave bands. Only Enna, Tauromenium, Catana, and possibly Agrigentum are specifically known to have done so.[30]

The leader of this revolt came from Syria, hence named himself King Antiochus and called his supporters Syrians;[31] but the assumption by Beloch[32] of the national Syrian character of the revolt[33] is unwarranted. It is probable that the slaves derived from many regions, with a strong nucleus of Sicilian-born members.[34] The rough estimate given by Beloch[35] may be accepted as reasonable that Sicily in the second century B. C. had more slaves compared to its area and total population than any other region of that time, if it is associated with his warning that the belief in an absolute majority of slaves over free persons must be discarded. The widespread repercussions of the Sicilian revolt included a slight disturbance at Rome, more serious trouble at Sineussa and Minturnae in Italy,[36] and the rebellions of one thousand slaves at Athens and Delos which Diodorus[37] correctly connected with the Sicilian troubles.

The chronological sequence in respect to the widening of the sphere of activity of the Cilician pirates beyond the older confines of the Syrian and Asia Minor coast and the perfecting and power of their organization can no longer be established. The extension of the radius of their activity must, however, be ascribed to the period before the first recorded expedition to curb their power was made by the Roman state in 102 B. C.[38] Side

in Pamphylia and Delos[39] became centers for the disposal to retail slave handlers of the victims of their kidnapping enterprises. The alleged incident of the kidnapping of Julius Caesar in his young manhood, for whose release, it was said, the sum of twenty talents was demanded and paid,[40] illustrates the fact that ransom, when it could be obtained, was a more lucrative outcome of kidnapping enterprises than eventual sale into slavery. Strabo makes this clear in a statement that the Circassian pirates preferred to accept ransom upon easy terms rather than to sell their captives into slavery.[40a]

The geographic situation of Delos in the Mediterranean Sea, assisted by the preferential treatment in trade relations granted to the island by the Roman senate in 167 B. C., made of it, despite its physical handicaps, an entrepot in the sea trade from East to West from about 130 B. C. to the sack of the island and its treasures by Archelaus, general of Mithradates, in 88 B. C.[41] Particularly for the Cilician pirates, whose kidnapping operations were especially directed against Syria, it offered a most convenient center for the disposal of their pillaged slaves.[42] But a single and unsupported statement of Strabo in the same passage that the island could receive and send away ten thousand slaves upon the same day is without doubt a gross exaggeration of the physical possibilities and of the docking capacity and the business facilities of the island.[43]

After the destruction perpetrated by Archelaus, although the pirates with the active support of Mithradates continued to harass the cities of the islands and of Asia Minor,[44] the island of Delos lost its outstanding importance as a center of the slave traffic. Strabo himself[45] mentions the activity of the tribes of the Cimmerian Bosporus in this field under the Roman Republic, the continued prominence of Tanais on the Don River as emporium in the slave traffic and of Aquileia for the human merchandise supplied by the Illyrians.[46]

The complete and rapid success of Gnaeus Pompey against the Cilician pirates in 67 B. C.[47] shows that the Roman state had been, for more than a half century, criminally negligent of its obligations in permitting the activities of the Cilician pirates to attain the scandalous proportions which they had assumed, rather than that Rome was incapable of meeting the military situation involved.[48] The explanation of the Roman weakness is

[25] Diodorus, 34-35: 2, 16.

[26] *Idem*, 34-35: 2, 17.

[27] Dessau, *ILS* 1, no. 23.

[28] Livy, *Periochae*, 56.

[29] Diodorus, 34-35: 2, 18. See Mommsen, *History of Rome* 3: 310; *Camb. Anc. Hist.* (*CAH*) 9: 15, n. 1.

[30] Diodorus, 34-35: 2, 11; 20: 39, 43. Strabo 6: 2, 6: Καταναῖοι καὶ Ταυρομενῖται καὶ ἄλλοι πλείους.

[31] Diodorus, 34-35: 2, 24.

[32] Beloch, J., *Bevölkerung*, 245.

[33] Frank, T., *Economic survey* 1: 188, wrongly speaks of sixty thousand Syrians and Cilicians.

[34] *Cf.* Last, H., *CAH* 9: 14.

[35] Beloch, *Bevölkerung*, 299-301.

[36] 450 slaves crucified at Minturnae, 4,000 defeated at Sineussa, according to Orosius, 5: 9, 4.

[37] Diodorus, 34-35: 2, 18.

[38] Ziebarth, Erich, *Seeraub und Seehandel*, 32-33.

[39] Strabo 14: 3, 2, ἐπώλουν ἐκεῖ τοὺς ἁλόντας ἐλευθέρους ὁμολογοῦντες and 14: 5, 2.

[40] Plutarch, *Caesar*, 1, 4; 2, 11.   [40a] 11: 2, 12.

[41] For the dates as given see Homolle, Th., Les Romains a Délos, *Bulletin de Correspondance Hellénique* (abbr. *BCH*) 8: 98, 140.

[42] Strabo, 14: 2, 5.

[43] Pauly-W., *RE* 4: 2494.

[44] Iassos, Clazomenae, Samos and Samothrace were captured by them, Appian, *Mithridatic wars*, 63.

[45] Strabo, 11: 2, 12.

[46] *Ibid.*, 5: 1, 8.

[47] Cicero, *De imperio Cn. Pompei*, 35; Plutarch, *Pompey*, 26, 4; 28, 2.

[48] Note the criticism of the Roman governors in handling the pirates of the Caucasus region in Strabo, 11: 2, 12.

to be sought in the insistent and constantly growing demand for slaves in the West and the consequent development of an apathetic attitude among the ruling classes at Rome,[49] perhaps amounting to conscious toleration of kidnapping as an occupation. Their callous indifference may have been associated with the stealing of free people which the tax-farming companies permitted their employees to carry on with impunity, both in the provinces and in adjacent allied territories.[50]

The serious political results of the illicit traffic in slaves became apparent to the Roman senate when the consul, Marius, sent a request for auxiliary troops for the war with the Cimbri to King Nicomedes of Bithynia. He responded that most of his Bithynians had been seized by the Roman *publicani* and were in slavery in the provinces.[51] This information resulted in a decree of the Roman senate providing that the provincial governors should investigate and see to it that no free-born subject of a state allied with Rome should remain in slavery in a Roman province. In pursuance of this order some eight hundred persons were set free within a few days in Sicily;[52] but the actions for freedom were abandoned after a few days because of pressure brought upon the Roman praetor in Sicily by the slave-owners. This fact is highly significant of the political and economic ramifications of the western slave system of that time. Diodorus cites the incident as one of the causes of the second slave uprising in Sicily, which covered the years 104-101 B. C. It involved almost the entire island and required the presence of a Roman army of seventeen thousand men for its suppression.[53] This slave war and its leaders were vividly remembered by the soldiers of Sulla's army twenty years later.[54]

The general economic results which the use of ranch and plantation slaves upon a large scale had produced in Sicily were obviously bad, since the poor free population gave itself over to destruction of the property of the wealthy with as much zest as the slaves.[55] The increase in the number of slaves in Italy and the existence of conditions of slavery upon the large Italian estates similar to those prevailing at the same time in Sicily is attested by an incident which occurred near Capua. The wastrel son of a Roman knight armed four hundred of his own slaves[56] and led them in a revolt. Although this was foredoomed to failure, he nevertheless soon found himself the commander of an army of thirty-five hundred slaves from the neighborhood.[57] The similarity of conditions in Italy and Sicily is also made manifest by the frustrated plan of Spartacus to transport a part of his troops into Sicily and there spread the revolt.[58]

The presence of a growing number of slaves in industrial services in Italy is to be conjectured from the twenty-nine dedications containing names of slave and freedmen *magistri* and *magistrae* which were found at the industrial town of Minturnae.[59] In 90 B. C. the leaders of the revolting Italian allies were able to collect and arm almost twenty thousand slaves against Rome.[60] The fact that Sulla in 81 B. C. could set free and arm ten thousand able-bodied slaves of the proscribed to serve as his bodyguard is significant of the great number of slaves that had been concentrated in the *familiae* of the upper classes in and about Rome.[61] Throughout Italy large numbers of slaves are postulated by the events of the Servile War of 73-71 B. C.[62] Appian gives the army under Spartacus at seventy thousand in 72 B. C. with a rapid increase to one hundred twenty thousand when he marched against Rome, although he refused to accept many deserters who offered to join him.[63] The leaders of this revolt and the chief components of the army were Gauls and Thracians, with a sprinkling of Germans left over from the wars of the Cimbri and Teutones.[64] The plan of Spartacus to make his way through northern Italy to the Alps and the Gallic country[65] indicates the northern origin of the greater number of them. The elimination of these two tribal elements from the slave population of Italy was almost complete[66] until again Celtic slaves appeared through Caesar's conquest of Gaul.

In the last thirty-five years of the Republic slave numbers in Italy may still have been increasing. The fear of an uprising of the slaves could be counted upon to arouse apprehension among the propertied classes as shown at the time of the conspiracy of Catiline,[67] and particularly by the refusal of Catiline to enlist the runaway slaves who came to his camp because of the bad political effects of such an action.[68]

From 60 to 50 B. C. in Rome itself the use of slaves and freedmen to exert political pressure grew to scandalous proportions.[69] Cicero counted upon the support of his friends, with their clients, freedmen, and slaves, in case of violent action against him by Clodius.[70] In

[49] Ormerod, H., *Piracy*, 209.

[50] *CAH* 9: 351.

[51] Diodorus, 36: 3, 1. The incident is to be dated shortly after the battle of Arausio, probably in 104 B. C.

[52] *Ibid.*, 36: 3, 2.

[53] Diodorus, 36: 3, 3 and 8, 1.

[54] Appian, *Mithridatic wars*, 59.

[55] καὶ τῶν ἐλευθέρων οἱ ἄποροι, Diodorus, 36: 2, 6.

[56] *Ibid.*, 36: 2, 3, τοὺς ἰδίους . . . οἰκέτας.

[57] *Ibid.*, 36: 2, 6.

[58] Cicero, *Against Verres* 2: 5, 8 (18); *CAH* 9: 330.

[59] Johnson, J., *Excavations at Minturnae* 2 (1). These inscriptions are dated between 90 and 64 B. C., *ibid.*, 123-124.

[60] Diodorus, 37: 2, 10.

[61] Appian, *Civil wars* 1: 10, 100. *CIL* 1²: 722.

[62] Appian, *Civil wars* 1: 14, 116.

[63] *Ibid.*, 1: 14, 117; ninety thousand in Velleius, 2: 30, 6; seventy thousand in Orosius, 5: 24, 2.

[64] Caesar, *Bell. Gall.* 1: 40.

[65] Appian, *Civil wars* 1: 117.

[66] The six thousand who were taken prisoners were crucified along the highway from Capua to Rome, *ibid.* 1: 120.

[67] Cicero, *Against Catiline* 1: 11; Sallust, *Catiline*, 24, 30; Dio Cassius, 37: 33, 2; 35, 3.

[68] Sallust, *Catiline*, 47.

[69] A plot against Curio, for example, was based upon the use of slaves to assassinate Pompey; Cicero, *Ad Atticum* 2: 24, 2.

[70] Cicero, *Ad Quintum fratrem* 1: 2, 5.

the canvassing for the elections for 56 B. C. the use of armed slaves, both by Milo and Clodius, is attested by Cicero;[71] and the constant presence of armed slaves in the bodyguards of these two enemies is beyond dispute.[72] In 48 B. c., on the eve of the departure of his forces to Greece, Caesar compelled his soldiers to leave their slaves and baggage in Italy.[73] Other isolated bits of evidence indicate that in the exercise of his centralized and personal power he adopted a policy which scrupulously avoided the use of slaves as soldiers.[74] At that time he handled the problems arising from the military use of slaves by his enemies with undisguised but effective brutality.[75]

It is an enlightening commentary both upon the amazing numbers of slaves assembled under the ownership of single Romans of great wealth and upon the willingness of Caesar's opponents to use armed slaves that Pompey's son brought eight hundred of them to his father's standards in Greece, enlisted from his personal attendants and from his slave shepherds.[76] When assassination removed Caesar's firm hand from the guidance of the state, the potential political influence of the city slaves of Rome immediately made itself apparent.[77] The attempts made by both sides in the following period to gain the support of the slaves by enfranchisement or to enlist them as fighting men are well known.[78] In the early period of the struggle for power Sextus Pompey was the outstanding example of departure from the customary Roman attitude opposed to their use in war other than as attendants and in service of transport.[79]

The policy of Octavianus Caesar upon the use of slaves under his command showed a tendency to follow the older tradition of compromising with military exigency by previous manumission of the slaves he enlisted. Thus in 37 B. c. he manumitted twenty thousand slaves whom he had collected through voluntary contribution of his friends or impressment from the unwilling, and had them trained as oarsmen for the impending naval battle with Sextus Pompey.[80] He also freed those slaves who came over to his standards in the ships under

Menas, deserter from Sextus Pompey.[81] Political considerations and traditional Roman ideas regarding the treatment of slaves were the considerations which dictated to Octavianus the return to their owners or the impalement of the slaves captured with the fleet of Sextus Pompey.[82] The number of those returned to their masters for punishment Augustus himself put at almost thirty thousand.[83] This drastic action was contrary to the agreement previously made in 39 B. c. at Misenum that the slave deserters upon all sides should be free.[84]

The available record upon slaves in personal attendance among the wealthier Romans indicates for the last two centuries of the Republic a marked increase in their use in unremunerative luxury services as mere evidence of " conspicuous wealth." In the second century B. c. four or five attendant slaves had sufficed for a well-to-do household.[85] Ptolemy Philometor landed at Rome in 164 B. c. with three slaves and a eunuch, as an earnest of a retinue which would not seem conspicuous.[86] Scipio Africanus, when sent by the Senate to visit the kingdoms of the eastern Mediterranean, was accompanied by five slaves.[87] M. Scaurus' received only six slaves in his inheritance;[88] but when Cato the younger went to Macedon as tribune he was accompanied by fifteen slaves.[89] The growth in the number of attendant slaves is placed by Strabo[90] in the period of the rise of Cilician piracy, after the destruction of Corinth and Carthage. The correspondence of Cicero gives the best available impression of the constant use of slaves in non-productive services such as the carrying of private letters. At Brundisium slaves of Atticus arrived with a letter from their master, followed two days later by others of his slaves bearing another letter from him.[91] The number of slaves owned by Cicero and used in his personal service at Rome and upon his estates was large.[92] His wife, Terentia, had a group owned by herself personally.[93] More significant is Cicero's request to Atticus that he assign some slaves to Cicero's grandson, Lentulus, the number and selection to be left to Atticus.[94] The suite of attendant slaves which accompanied Pompey's friend, P. Vedius, was so large that the tolls which would have fallen upon them in accordance with a *lex*

[71] Cicero, *Ad Atticum* 4: 3, 2, 4.
[72] Appian, *Civil wars* 2: 21, 22.
[73] Caesar, *Civil war* 3: 6.
[74] E. g., the enlistment of slaves by the Alexandrians in their outbreak of 48 B. c., Caesar, *Bellum Alexandrinum*, 2. Use of slaves by Caesar's opponents in Italy, Caesar, *Civil war* 3: 21, 4.
[75] As he did in the crucifixion of three slave spies and the punishment by burning alive of a slave who had murdered his Spanish master; Caesar, *Bellum Hispanicum*, 20. *Cf.* Dio Cassius, 43: 39, 1.
[76] Reading: *pastorum suorum (numcro)*, Caesar, *Civil war* 3: 4, 4. For enlistment of slaves in the African war by Gnaeus Pompey the younger and Marcus Cato, *vide* Caesar, *Bellum Africanum*, 23, 36: *servorum denique et cujusque modi generis hominum*.
[77] Nicolaus of Damascus, 17; 25; 26; 26b; 31; Cicero, *Ad familiares* 10: 33.
[78] See Dio Cassius, 47: 35, 4; 48: 34, 4.
[79] Livy, epitome 123: *collectis . . . proscriptis ac fugitivis*. Velleius, 2: 73, 3.
[80] Suetonius, *Augustus*, 16, 1; Dio Cassius, 48: 49, 1.

[81] Dio Cassius, 49: 1, 5.
[82] *Ibid.*, 49: 12, 4.
[83] Augustus, *Monumentum Ancyranum*, 25.
[84] Dio Cassius, 48: 36, 3.
[85] As in Livy, 39: 11, 2.
[86] Diodorus, 31: 18, 2. Valerius Maximus, 5: 1-2.
[87] Polybius, frg. 63 in Athenaeus 6: 105. The probable date is 141 B. c., *cf.* Pauly-W., *RE* 4: 1452; Kroll, W., *Die Kultur der ciceronischen Zeit* 2: 82, Leipzig, Dieterich, 1933.
[88] Valerius Maximus, 4: 4, 11.
[89] Plutarch, *Cato minor*, 9, 4.
[90] Strabo, 14: 5, 2.
[91] Cicero, *Ad Atticum* 3: 7. *Cf.* 2: 18; 3: 17, 19, etc.
[92] Cicero, *Ad familiares* 14: 4, 4; *Ad Quintum fratrem* 3: 9.
[93] Cicero, *Ad familiares* 14: 4, 4.
[94] Cicero, *Ad Atticum* 12: 28, 30.

viaria proposed by Curio would have amounted to a very considerable item.[95]

The inconsistent Tigellius of Horace sometimes maintained two hundred slaves, at other times only ten;[96] and a man of modest means such as the freedman father of Horace could supply his son with attendant slaves at Rome [97] so that the boy might appear to be a person of inherited wealth. The praetor Tullius was followed by five slaves when traveling on the Tibur road.[98] Modest as his own establishment was, Horace may threaten to send a slave member of his *familia urbana* to work as ninth laborer on his Sabine farm.[99]

H. Gummerus has conclusively proved for the period of Cato [100] as well as for the time of Varro [101] that handicraft production on the small and middle-sized farms of Italy was limited to a few articles, all except the large and isolated *latifundia* depending, on the whole, upon purchase of manufactured articles from the city and upon itinerant free artisans for smaller jobs. It is necessary, therefore, to reckon upon a steady, though moderate, increase in the last two centuries of the Republic in the numbers of slaves employed in handicraft shops in the Italian towns and cities.

The relative numbers of the slaves and free occupied in these industries are not ascertainable. The lists of slave and freedmen *magistri* in cult *collegia* which have been found on the site of the industrial town of Minturnae,[102] and dating in the years 90-64 B. C., show that the slaves of one M. Epidius certainly numbered nine, not counting three freedmen and one slave in whom he had a sharing interest, and the possibility that two more slaves might be ascribed to him and one freedwoman to his wife.[103] Since this total of thirteen and a half, possibly fifteen and a half, slaves and ex-slaves represent only those unfree and freedman members of his *familia* who were selected in their cult colleges as *magistri*, his actual slaveholdings must have been larger, but how much larger cannot be ascertained. The next highest number is the group of three female and three male slave *magistrae* or *magistri* belonging to M. Badius, with one male slave belonging to a Badia who is presumably his wife.[104] By far the largest group of owners appear with only three, two, or one slave or freedman represented among the *magistri*, about twenty slaveholders with three slaves each, about thirty with two each, and about seventy-five with one slave or an ex-slave.[105] The results are vague because of our inability to estimate the ratio of the *magistri* to the number of slaves owned by any single master. It is probable, however, that the greatest number of the slaveholders at Minturnae, those represented by one or two *magistri*, did not own more than one or two to a half dozen slaves,[106] whereas more important citizens such as Epidius and Badius [107] may have owned between twenty and fifty.

For the country districts in the last decades of the Republic we have the testimony of Varro that the farmers preferred to hire itinerant free physicians, fullers, and carpenters to work for them rather than to maintain their own slave artisans, professionally trained to these types of service. The reason given by Varro is that the death of one such specialized enslaved artisan entailed too heavy a capital loss upon the owner. Only the rich possessors of *latifundia*, particularly those who lived far from the towns, were accustomed to own slaves who specialized in handicrafts.[108] In the industries the ease and frequence of manumission in the towns of Italy[109] must be constantly reckoned with as a factor consistently operating to restore the supply of handicraftsmen of free status out of the handicraft class of slaves.[110]

For the labor situation in agricultural production in Italy in the first half of the second century B. C. we have important information in Cato's *De agricultura* which pictures the conduct, upon a profit-making basis, of an olive grove and a vineyard, with subsidiary annual field crops.[111] The word *operarii*, as employed by Cato, has quite generally been regarded as meaning free hired hands [112] except in the case of the five *operarii* mentioned among the permanent labor personnel of the olive grove [113] and the ten *operarii* connected with the vineyard. Varro unquestionably understood these fifteen *operarii* to be slaves.[114] This interpretation has generally been followed since his time [115] although there is reason to believe that they, also, were free laborers, under permanent hire but not living upon the estate. This is indicated by the equipment provided for the olive orchard, consisting of eight beds, eight mattresses, eight bed-spreads, sixteen pillows, ten coverlets.[116] This equipment provides a *lectum in cubiculo* reserved for the visits of the *dominus*, one bed for the slave manager

[95] Cicero, *Ad Atticum* 6 : 1, 25.

[96] Horace, *Satires* 1 : 3, 10-11.

[97] *Ibid.*, 1 : 6, 78-79.

[98] *Ibid.*, 1 : 6, 108-109.

[99] *Ibid.*, 2 : 7, 118. *Cf.* his attendant slaves on the journey to Brundisium, *ibid.*, 1 : 4, 10-11.

[100] Gummerus, H., Der römische Gutsbetrieb als wirtschaftlicher Organismus, *Klio*, Ergänzungsband 1 : 5; 34-38; 41-49.

[101] *Ibid.*, 68-72.

[102] For its industries, see Cato, *De agricultura*, 135.

[103] Johnson, J., *Excavations at Minturnae* 2 (1) : 58.

[104] *Ibid.*, 53.

[105] See the listing of owners by J. Johnson, *ibid.*, 49-77.

[106] *Cf.* the dedication of nineteen slaves in an inscription from Mantua of 59 B. C. in *CIL* 1 (2) : 753, where three masters have two slaves each and thirteen masters only one each.

[107] Johnson, *op. cit.*, 58, 53.

[108] Varro, *De re rustica* 1 : 16, 4. *Cf.* Gummerus, *Klio*, Ergänzungsband 1 : 5, 66.

[109] Daremberg-Saglio, *Dictionnaire* 3 (2) : 1207.

[110] *Ibid.* 3 (2) : 1217 for inscriptional evidence, chiefly of the early empire, upon the occupations of the freedmen.

[111] Brehaut, E., *Cato the Censor on farming*, xxxvii, xxxii, New York, Columbia Univ. Press, 1933.

[112] Cato, *De agricultura*, 145, 1 : *si operarii conducti erunt.*

[113] *Ibid.*, 10, 1.

[114] Varro, *De re rustica* 1 : 18, 1 : *dicit enim (scil.* Cato) *in eo modo haec mancipia XIII habenda.*

[115] *Cf.* Gummerus, H., *Klio*, Ergänzungsb. 1 : 25-27, Frank T., *Economic Survey* 1 : 162-163.

[116] Leaving two extra coverlets, Cato, *De agricultura*, 10, 5.

and his wife, and six beds for the six other slaves.[117] For the four slaves used in the vineyard four mattresses, and four spreads are provided,[118] with no provision of sleeping arrangements for the ten *operarii* attached to the vineyard operations. The total of the slaves attached to the estate is therefore twelve, including the slave *vilicus* and his wife, as against fifteen regular free hands (*operarii*) under permanent hire.

For the seasonal peaks of farm activity, particularly at the harvest period, both in the vineyard work[119] and in olive production,[120] and for all unusual labor demands such as removal of stumpage and erection of new buildings,[121] the owner was advised by Cato to depend upon outside free labor. Although fear had already been aroused among the leaders of the Roman state by the depletion of the Italian stock and the growth in the number of slaves,[122] in Cato's time a strong preponderance of free over slave labor in agricultural production still existed, especially upon the middle-sized estates with which Cato deals, and probably also in general throughout Italy. This becomes evident when one balances the many small peasant farms which employed no slaves[123] against the limited number of the *latifundia* which could advantageously use a large number of them.

An increase in slave labor in the agricultural districts is to be assumed for the period 150 to 50 B. C. both upon the large *latifundia* and upon the middle-sized estates because of the number of slaves which came into Italy and because of Varro's ready acceptance of the idea that the *operarii* of Cato's olive and vineyard properties were

slaves.[124] It is certain, however, that a free peasantry and a plentiful and stable supply of free labor for hire as farm hands still persisted in Varro's day.[125] About 50 B. C. the grandfather of Emperor Vespasian, as a labor contractor for seasonal farm work, still brought farm hands down from Umbria into the Sabine region.[126] In the cattle-raising industry the proportion of slave herders in Sicily was very high from about 150 B. C. onward.[127] The attempt of Julius Caesar to enforce the employment of at least a third of free-born men among the herders used upon the cattle ranches[128] shows that in Italy free labor had, in this field, fallen far behind in competing with slaves. The surmise of Julius Beloch[129] would limit the slave population of peninsular Italy to three slaves to every five free persons, that in the Po Valley to three slaves to every ten free men. For Rome and Ostia, to which he assigns a total population of eight hundred seventy thousand souls in 5 B. C., he would estimate two hundred eighty thousand slaves.[130] Beloch's figures are to be regarded, so far as the slave proportions are concerned, as suggestive estimates. His slave numbers are probably higher, rather than lower, than the actual situation would have warranted. They do stand, however, in close relation to the proportions of slave and free in the slaveholding states of the United States in 1850 when the slaves, as enumerated in the census returns, stood at fifty-one to every hundred free persons.[131]

---

[117] *Bubulcos III, asinarium I, subulcum I, opilionem I, ibid.,* 10, 1. *Cf.* six patchwork cloaks for the last group of six slaves, *ibid.,* 10, 5.
[118] *Ibid.,* 11, 1 and 5.
[119] *Ibid.,* 137.
[120] *Ibid.,* 144, where the contractor is to furnish fifty pickers.
[121] *Klio, Erg.-Bd.* 1: 5, 37-38.
[122] Appian, *Civil wars* 1: 1, 8.
[123] Varro, *De re rustica* 1: 17, 2: *liberis, aut cum ipsi colunt, ut plerique pauperculi cum sua progenie.*

[124] *Ibid.* 1: 18, 1.
[125] *Ibid.* 1: 17, 2: *omnes agri coluntur hominibus servis aut liberis aut utrisque.*
[126] Suetonius, *Vespasian,* 1, 4. *Cf.* Frank, T., *Econ. Survey* 1: 377 and Gummerus, *Klio, Erg.-Bd.* 1: 5, 65.
[127] Diodorus, 34-35: 2, 1.
[128] Suetonius, *Julius Caesar,* 42.
[129] Beloch, J., *Bevölkerung,* 434.
[130] *Ibid.,* 404. *CAH* 9: 787 gives the slave numbers at well over two hundred thousand.
[131] *A century of population growth,* 140, U. S. Dept. of Commerce and Labor, 1909.

XI. THE LATER REPUBLIC

THE SLAVE AND THE ROMAN FAMILIA

Seneca has stated in idealized form the simplicity of the relations and the mutual regard between master and slave which supposedly existed in the early period of the Republic. The slave-owners were called *patres familiae* and the slaves *familiares* and there was neither hatred for the masters nor scorn for the slaves.[1] Discounting his sentimentalized view of the good old days, Seneca's basic assumption of a simple type of slavery which exhibited the close and friendly relations of a

small-scale agricultural community is still probably correct.[2] As in the pre-Solonian community at Athens enslavement of citizens for debt played an important part in the situation.[3] The report in Livy[4] of the seizure of the Capitolium in 460 B. C. by exiles and slaves to the number of twenty-five hundred and the incitement of the slaves by Appius Herdonius[5] to strike for their liberty

---

[1] Seneca, *Epist. mor.,* 47, 14; Macrobius, *Saturnalia* 1: 2, 11; Livy, 1: 51, 8; Plutarch, *Life of Coriolanus,* 24, 4-5 and of *Cato the Elder,* 20, 3-4.

[2] *Cf.* Mommsen, *History of Rome* 3: 305, "slavery that was, in a way, innocent."
[3] Livy, 2: 23, 1, 6; 6: 14, 3-8; 6: 34, 2; 6: 36, 12.
[4] *Ibid.,* 3: 15, 5.
[5] *Ibid.,* 3: 15, 9.

is probably a reflection of Roman conditions of the second and first centuries B. C. so far as any danger from the slaves is concerned. The provision of the laws of the Twelve Tables that debtor slaves must be sold outside the bounds of the state [6] must be explained by the strength of the early tribal cohesion and the feeling of disgrace that a former tribe member be retained in slavery within the community, rather than as an evidence of fear of slave revolts.[7]

The beginning of slavery as an important factor in Roman life was roughly synchronous with the rapid expansion of the state territories in central and southern Italy in the period 350-272 B. C. The imposing of the five per cent tax on manumissions, attributed to the agency of the consul, Gnaeus Manlius, in 357 B. C.,[8] the abandoning of debtor slavery, dated in 326 B. C. by Livy,[9] and the inclusion in the second treaty with Carthage [10] of a restrictive clause upon the sales of slaves in Roman territory are characteristic manifestations of this development toward an economy actually founded upon a combined slave-and-free labor basis.

It is only in the period of developing plantation-ranch and industrial slavery in Roman Italy, from *ca.* 220 B. C. to *ca.* 150 B. C., and the period of the greatest use of slaves in these production forms, *ca.* 150 to *ca.* 30 B. C., that information is available in such quantities as to make a cohesive picture of the system possible. Although these two periods must be treated as one it is clear that great differences existed between them and that the height of western slavery, both in numbers of slaves employed and in the social results of the system, is to be placed in the first century B. C.[11]

Varro defines six methods of legal acquisition of slaves as property. These are: by inheritance; by transfer of possession through purchase from one who has title; by friendly suit (*cessio in jure*); by right of undisputed possession (*si usu cepit*); by purchase of prisoners of war *sub corona*; or by purchase of the confiscated goods of the proscribed. Since enslavement for debt had long been abolished the only unusual feature of Varro's list is his failure to make specific mention of recruitment of slaves through the rescue of exposed infants, which in his list falls under *usucapio*. This omission by Varro is justified by the fact that the rescue of abondoned children does not play an important part in the Roman historical sources of the Republic.[12] Without doubt captivity in war was the primary source of slavery during the last three centuries of the Republic.[13]

The decision whether captives were to be sold as part of the booty derived from the conquered people [14] was a function of the state, vested in the commander in the field by virtue of the *imperium* conferred upon him.[15] The decision taken by the imperator might be reversed by the Senate, as in the case of the slaves brought from Greece in 171 B. C. who were bought back, with public funds, from their owners in Italy and returned as free men to their homes.[16] Having taken the decision to enslave military captives or the population of a town or district, the imperator might assign them to the state as *servi publici*, as was done by Scipio in 212 B. C.; [17] or he might bestow them upon the soldiers [18] or sell them privately in the locality of their capture, which amounts to a method of ransom individually arranged with the families of the captives;[19] or sell the entire group at public auction.[20] The actual conduct of the sale was the duty of the quaestor,[21] the conditions of the sale being determined by the imperator.[22] The proceeds of such a sale were at the disposal of the general, who customarily allocated them to the state treasury; [23] or he might assign them to some public project in the country in which the victory had occurred in case policy or sentiment so dictated.[24] Considerations of state finance, therefore, played an equal part with political and punitive motives in the decisions taken upon the disposal of the captives, as in the case of the immediate sale by Sulla of the slaves owned by Athenians after the siege of Athens.[25]

In 210 B. C., upon the capture of New Carthage in Spain, Scipio assigned two thousand artisans of the captured population as *servi publici* to work upon the production of war materials.[26] State ownership was,

---

[6] "*Trans Tiberim,*" laws of the XII Tables, Bruns, *FIR*, 20-21, tab. III, 5 (Gellius, *Noctes Atticae* 20: 1, 46-47).

[7] As it is motivated by Weber, M., *Gesammelte Aufsätze*, 209.

[8] Livy, 7: 16, 7.

[9] *Ibid.*, 8: 28, 1, 7. It is placed after the battle of the Caudine Forks by Dionysius of Halicarnassus, 16: 9.

[10] Polybius, 3: 24, 6-7.

[11] Meyer, Ed., *Kleine Schriften*, 2d ed., 1: 208; *cf.* M. Weber, *Gesammelte Aufsätze*, 234.

[12] Varro, *De re rustica* 2: 10, 4.

[13] There is a pertinent instance in the case of M. Antonius Gnipho, teacher of Cicero, " a free-born native of Gaul, who was exposed (in his infancy), and (later) was manumitted by his foster-father." Suetonius, *De grammaticis,* 7; *cf.* Pauly-W., *RE* 11: 469-470.

[14] A great number of men and cattle and booty of every kind, Livy, 29: 35, 5.

[15] Just., *Institutes* 1: 3, 3. The commanders give orders to sell the captives, and in this manner they are wont to save and not to kill them.

[16] Livy, 43: 4, 5; Zonaras, 9: 22 C.

[17] The names were enrolled by the quaestor who appointed an overseer for each group of 30 slaves, Livy, 26: 47, 1-2; Polybius, 10: 17, 9-10.

[18] Caesar, *Gallic war* 7: 89; Polybius, 3: 17, 7. A part of the booty was bestowed on the soldiers according to merit, the remainder sold at auction, Livy, 4: 34, 4.

[19] Dio Cassius, 42: 14, 3.

[20] *Sub corona,* Livy, 42: 63, 10.

[21] Polybius, 10: 17, 6-10.

[22] This was the case later in the sale of the Salassi in 25 B. C. Augustus set a prohibition against manumission within twenty years, Dio Cassius, 53: 25, 4.

[23] Livy, 5: 22, 1; 10: 46, 5.

[24] Proceeds from the sale of slaves in Greece were used to rebuild a portico at Megalopolis, Livy, 38: 34, 7.

[25] Appian, *Mithridatic wars,* 38; *cf.* Heichelheim, F., *Hist. Zeitschrift* 143: 95, 1931.

[26] Polybius, 10: 17, 9; Livy, 26: 47, 2.

therefore, known during the Hannibalic War [27]—probably before that time; but the necessity of purchasing slaves from private owners to make up two slave legions after the battle of Cannae [28] indicates how few public slaves were then available. Under conditions of peace during the Republic we may suppose that the *servi publici* were employed in small clerical positions and in other humble routine services of the state of that kind.[29] In the *municipia* of Italy for the early part of the first century B. C. *servi publici* are attested for Minturnae,[30] and for 45 B. C. by a passage of the *lex Julia municipalis* in accordance with which the habitations and places of work assigned them by the local magistrates were protected from encroachment for other public purposes.[31] The passage of a *senatus consultum* in 38 B. C. prohibiting the use of slaves as lictors [32] permits the conclusion that slaves had been previously used in this attendant service upon the magistrates. The enlistment of slaves in army and navy as combatants was recognized as legitimate in times of great crises, but under other circumstances it was strictly avoided.[33] This rule did not preclude the presence of privately owned slaves in the field of war as attendants upon officers and even upon private soldiers.[34]

The revenue accruing to the Roman state from taxation upon the slaves owned by its citizens was derived, under the Republic, solely from the manumission tax of five per cent of the estimated value of the slave which remained at the same figure throughout the period of the Republic.[35] The income derived from this source was deposited in a sacred treasury reserved for use in a time of extremity. In 209 B. C. there were 4,000 pounds of gold available in this chest; [36] and when Julius Caesar laid hold of it in 49 B. C. it contained 4,135 pounds of gold and 900 pounds of silver.[37] The attempts which have been made to estimate the numbers of manumissions at Rome on the basis of the amounts remaining in the sacred treasury, as given above,[38] are beset with

unknown factors and other difficulties to the extent that the results cannot be used.[39]

There is no evidence of any tax on transfers of slaves by sale until it was introduced by Augustus in A. D. 7,[40] nor of any direct ownership tax on slaves exacted from Roman citizens. The attempt of the triumvirs in 40 B. C. to impose an ownership tax aroused bitter opposition in Rome.[41] In 183 B. C. Cato as censor had issued an order that in the new census rating slaves under twenty years of age which had cost ten thousand asses or more should be assessed at ten times their value and that a tax of three *denarii* per thousand asses should be collected upon them; [42] but this is to be regarded as a luxury tax with sumptuary motivation, based upon Cato's well-known dislike and fear of the increasing luxury in all its manifestations,[43] rather than as an application of the idea of direct taxation upon slave ownership.[44] This action of Cato carries with it the implication that declarations of their property holdings by Roman citizens for census rating included an enumeration of their slaves and that a register of transfers of slaves, with the prices paid for them, was available to the censors. In the *lex Julia municipalis* the declarations of properties made by Roman citizens in the towns of Italy certainly included the slaves in the *ratio pecuniae* which was demanded.[45] The direct tax exacted by Lucullus upon the houses and slaves of the subject populations of Asia Minor in 70 B. C. is to be regarded as an extraordinary measure designed to enable local inhabitants to meet the tribute payments due to Rome.[46] The tax upon ownership imposed in Syria by his opponents during the civil war is mentioned by Caesar [47] as one example in a series of extortions.

The information obtainable upon the prices of slaves in the entire western Mediterranean area during the period of the Republic is so scant that little can be done with it. Manumission prices are entirely wanting. It is clear that ransom demands for war prisoners stood in some close relation to slave prices as shown by the opposition of the Roman soldiers to the purchase of slaves for military service by the state as against the alternative of ransoming the captives held by Hannibal in 216 B. C. In this instance the soldiers claimed that the redemption of the captives would be no more expensive than the

[27] *Cf.* Plautus, *Captivi*, 334: *sed is privatam servitutem servit illi an publicam?*

[28] Livy, 22: 57, 11-12; 34: 6, 12.

[29] The attendants of the plebeian tribunes in Livy, 38: 51, 12, were probably their private slaves.

[30] *Publicus servus* in Johnson, J., *Excavations at Minturnae* 2 (1), *Republican magistri*, no. 13, 9.

[31] Dessau, *ILS*, 6085: 82.

[32] Dio Cassius, 48: 43, 3.

[33] See the speech of L. Valerius upon the *lex Oppia* in 195 B. C., Livy, 34: 6, 17-18; *cf.* Servius Grammaticus, *Commentaries on the Aeneid* 9: 544: *lege militari . . . qua servi a militia prohibebantur.*

[34] Caesar, *African war*, 54, 1; *Civil war* 3: 6, 1; Nicolaus of Damascus, 31.

[35] It still stood at 5 per cent (*vicesima*) in 59 B. C., Cicero, *To Atticus* 2: 16, 1.

[36] Livy, 27: 10, 11.

[37] Orosius, 6: 15, 5. In Pliny, *Natural history* 33: 56, the amount is given at fifteen thousand bars of gold, thirty thousand of silver, and an additional thirty million sesterces in coined money.

[38] Dureau de la Malle, Adolph J. C. A., *Économie politique des Romains* 1: 290-294, Paris, L. Hachette, 1840, for the manumis-

sions of the years 357-209 B. C. For the years 81-49 B. C. see Tenney Frank, The sacred treasury and the rate of manumission, *Amer. Jour. Philol.* 53: 360-363, 1932, and *Econ. Surv. Ancient Rome* 1: 101-102, 338.

[39] *Cf.* Beloch's warning, *Bevölkerung*, 414.

[40] Dio Cassius, 55: 31, 4.

[41] Appian, *Civil wars* 5: 67; Dio Cassius, 48: 31, 1.

[42] Livy, 39: 44, 3.

[43] Plutarch, *Cato the Elder*, 18, 2. *Cf.* Cato's bitter statement that handsome slaves cost more than a farm, Diodorus Siculus, 31: 24.

[44] *Cf.* E. Ciccotti, *Tramonto della schiavitù*, 255-256.

[45] Dessau, *ILS*, 6685, 147; Tenney Frank, *Econ. Surv. Ancient Rome* 1: 319.

[46] Appian, *Mithridatic wars*, 83.

[47] Caesar, *Civil War* 3: 32.

cost of the slaves.[48] The ransom offer made by Hannibal was three hundred *denarii* for a Roman soldier, two hundred *denarii* for each Roman ally, one hundred *denarii* for each slave that had been taken,[49] with a five hundred *denarii* demand for each Roman *eques*.[50] Twenty-two years later the Achaeans paid five hundred *denarii* apiece as ransom for some Roman citizens who had been sold into slavery in Greece by Hannibal.[51] As compared with the maximum price of fifteen hundred *denarii* which the elder Cato was willing to pay for his slaves,[52] both the ransom demand of Hannibal and the final payment made by the Achaeans appear to be low; but they stand in close relation to the ransom price of five minas arranged between the Rhodians and Demetrius in 304 B. C.[53] and the average manumission payments of three to five hundred drachmas in the Delphic manumissions of 201 to 50 B. C.[54]

It is evident, however, from the activities of the elder Cato [55] that the luxury prices for slaves had jumped greatly within the two decades following the Hannibalic War. For the last hundred fifty years of the Republic few actual prices paid for slaves are known for the western area.[56] The following general pieces of information occur: Italian merchants, playing upon the love of wine characteristic of the Gauls, were able to trade a *keramion* of wine for a Celtic boy slave; [57] Julius Caesar would pay so extravagantly for a young and capable slave that he would not permit the price to be entered into his accounts; [58] Calenus, a general under Caesar, in 48 B. C. sold Megarian captives to their relatives for a small sum; [59] and a satisfactory bargain was made for slaves, either in behalf of Cicero or of Atticus, in 45 B. C.[60]

A number of statements which appear with reference to the later decades of the Republic vaguely point to a diminution in the oversupply of male slaves of working age provided by external wars; but there is no corresponding information indicating an advance in the market prices. The recorded assertions are: Varro's advice that family life among the agricultural slaves should be encouraged so that the property of the master might be

increased by slave offspring; [61] the fact that home-born slaves begin to appear in the literature and inscriptions; [62] the unwillingness of Varro to recommend ownership of slave craftsmen because the death of one of them might seriously impair the entire profit of an estate; [63] and his admonition that in unhealthy places hired free labor should be used in cultivation instead of the estate slaves.[64] Although an increasing knowledge of the inherent economic weaknesses of slave labor may have played a part in Varro's attitude,[65] this desire to protect one's slaves as valuable property represents an important change from the reckless exploitation of them which was manifested in the treatise of the elder Cato.

From the discussion of numbers of slaves it is clear that the use of them in agricultural labor in Sicily, Italy, and North Africa upon an increasing scale, although not exceeding the employment of free labor except in cattle ranching, was the dominant and distinguishing feature of the labor situation in the West in the last two centuries of the Roman Republic. Legislation which attempted to enforce the hiring of a proportion of free laborers upon the Italian estates is mentioned, without date, by Appian.[66] This poorly authenticated report should not be connected with the Licinian rogations of 267 B. C.,[67] but is more probably a reflection of the legislation of Julius Caesar fixing the ratio of cattle herders at one-third free to two-thirds slave.[68] If the statement of Appian regarding a proportional use of free and slave labor in praedial agriculture is to be accepted as applicable to the period of the Gracchan legislation, its effects upon the situation of Italian agriculture cannot in any case have been great.[69] There is no record of the use of slaves upon a large scale in the Roman provinces of Spain [70] except in the silver mines where forty thousand men were employed in Polybius' time when the mines were owned by the Roman state.[71] Despite the fact that our only testimony that these were slaves is found in Diodorus,[72] this report of their use in the silver mines in Spain may be credited.[73]

---

[48] Livy, 22: 59, 12.

[49] *Ibid.*, 22: 52, 3.

[50] *Ibid.*, 22: 58, 4.

[51] *Ibid.*, 34: 50, 6.

[52] Plutarch, *Cato the Elder*, 5, 4.

[53] Diodorus Siculus, 20: 84, 6.

[54] See Calderini, *Manomissione*, 214.

[55] Livy, 39: 44, 3; Plutarch, *Cato the Elder*, 18, 2; Diodorus Siculus, 31: 24.

[56] In 66 B.C. C. Antonius, consul with Marcus Tullius Cicero in 63 B. C., bought a slave girl for immoral purposes in his home for one hundred fifty drachmas, Q. Tullius Cicero, *De petitione consulatus*, 8, in Eussner, A., *Commentariolum petitionis*, Würzburg, Thein, 1872.

[57] Diodorus Siculus, 5: 26, 4.

[58] Suetonius, *Caesar*, 47.

[59] Dio Cassius, 42: 14, 3. Immediate need of money was probably the motive.

[60] Cicero, *To Atticus* 12: 30, 2; 28, 3.

[61] Varro, *De re rustica* 1: 17, 5.

[62] Cicero, *To his friends* 8: 15, 2. All the slaves of T. Pomponius Atticus were home-born and home-trained, Nepos, *Atticus*, 13, 4. Freedwomen named Verna who were probably home-born slaves, Johnson, Jotham, *Excavations at Minturnae* 2 (1), *Republican Magistri*, nos. 3, 1; 11, 6.

[63] Varro, *De re rustica* 1: 16, 4.

[64] *Ibid.* 1: 17, 2.

[65] *Cf.* Strabo's statement, 5: 2, 7, of the unprofitable nature of the use of Corsican slaves because of their apathy and insensibility.

[66] Appian, *Civil wars* 1: 8.

[67] See the warnings of Beloch, *Bevölkerung*, 413, and of Heitland, *Agricola*, 131.

[68] Suetonius, *Caesar*, 42, 1.

[69] Gummerus, *Klio* 5: 72.

[70] There is no indication that copper mining among the Turdetanians was carried on with slave labor, Strabo, 3: 2, 9.

[71] Polybius in Strabo, 3: 2, 10.

[72] Diodorus Siculus, 5: 36, 4.

[73] *Cf.* Strabo's statement, 12: 3, 40, that the Roman mining contractors who worked the mines of Pompeiopolis in Pontus made use of condemned slaves as labor.

The same conditions which strengthened the use of slave labor in agriculture in Italy during the last two centuries of the Republic,[74] apply in like manner to explain a change from predominant free labor to a greater use of slaves in handicraft production in Italy. Although the penetration of slave labor into the handicrafts may have lagged somewhat behind its spread in the field of agriculture, where from 216 B. C. onward the demand for food production was immediate and pressing and the shortage of free labor insistent, the movements must on the whole have been roughly synchronous.[75]

The first record of the industrial use of slaves on any considerable scale in the West is that which took place in Spain in 210 B. C. when P. Scipio recruited two thousand captured artisans as state slaves under stress of the need for war materials.[76] Later the elder Cato had found it profitable to permit his older slaves to buy slave boys and train them for a year, in order to sell them at a profit.[77]

For an exhaustive study of the labor situation in industrial production in Italy, covering both free and slave labor, see Gummerus' *Industrie und Handel*,[78] which needs only to be summarized here and supplemented. Heavy manual labor, such as grinding meal in bakeries, was relegated to slaves and used as punishment for disobedience or trickery, as shown in frequent references in the Roman comedy,[79] to work in the *pistrinum* corresponding to that in the grinding mills (*mylōnes*) of the New Comedy at Athens.[80] After 150 B. C. the continued introduction, chiefly from the eastern Mediterranean area of slaves technically equipped for handicraft specialties gave a notable impetus to the development of the industries of Italy, affecting primarily the larger handicraft shops, but penetrating also into the economy of the small shop owners.[81] The collection and use of a wrecking and building corps of five hundred competent slaves by Marcus Crassus[82] represents the highest example of organization of slave labor known to us from the West during the Republic. The signatures of the master craftsmen or shop owners which appear upon the relief ceramics from Cales and upon Umbrian beakers are predominantly those of free-born Roman citizens, slave names appearing only exceptionally on the Calenian wares.[83] Allowing for slave labor used for the less exacting manual tasks of this

craft such as tending the ovens, free labor evidently maintained a strong hold in the pottery industry, possibly until about the end of the second century B. C. The *magistri* lists of Minturnae[84] do not indicate the occupations of the slaves and freedmen who are listed except where corporations of the city owned the slaves. Five slaves appear who were owned by the guild of pitch manufacturers,[85] four more who were slaves of the corporation of salt producers;[86] and it is highly probable that most of the remaining slaves and freedmen were industrial workers, with the possibility that a few were engaged in household services.

A warning that free labor still maintained itself strongly in Italy at that time is to be found in the similar *magistri* inscriptions from Capua of the years 112 to 71 B. C.,[87] in which the free-born and freedmen greatly predominate over the slaves.[88] In the Republican lists of similar type,[89] it may be assumed that the majority of the slaves and ex-slaves who appear were engaged in the handicrafts. In the *magistri* lists from Samos[90] and Delos[91] free-born persons and freedmen appear exclusively, except in *CIL* 1[2], 2235,[92] which shows one freedman and four slaves. These *ingenui, liberti,* and *servi* are to be regarded, for the most part, as agents representing large Italian firms.[93] The enumeration of Hatzfeld[94] gives the relative proportions of the classes at about forty-two per cent freedmen, thirty-eight per cent free-born, and twenty per cent slaves. This high percentage of *liberti* over the slaves would in all probability still persist if a larger group of documents were available, because freedmen, representing servants who had already been granted their liberty as capable and trustworthy agents, would be considered more suitable for distant services than persons still in bondage. A large excess of slaves over freedmen appears in the pottery shops of Arretium during the period of the transition from Republic to Empire, 40 to 20 B. C.[95] Additional

---

[74] These were, the military services required of Roman citizens and Italian allies and the influx of slaves derived from war, piracy, and from the regular trade in slaves.

[75] See *CAH* 8: 342.

[76] *Ad ministeria belli*, Livy, 26: 47, 2; Polybius, 10: 17, 9-10.

[77] Obviously apprentice training, Plutarch, *Cato the Elder*, 21, 7.

[78] Gummerus, Industrie und Handel, Pauly-W., *RE* 9: 1450-1459.

[79] *Ibid.* 9: 1452.

[80] Menander, *The Hero*, 2-3; *Periceiromene*, 87.

[81] Gummerus, Industrie und Handel, Pauly-W., *RE* 9: 1454-1455.

[82] Plutarch, *Crassus*, 2, 4.

[83] Gummerus, Industrie und Handel, Pauly-W., *RE* 9: 1450.

[84] Johnson, *Excavations at Minturnae* 2 (1), *Republican Magistri*.

[85] *Ibid., picariorum sociorum servi*, nos. 1, 10; 7, 5; 14, 8; 19, 7.

[86] *Ibid., salinatorum sociorum servi*, nos. 14, 3; 16, 7; 21, 12; 26, 11.

[87] *CIL* 1[2] (2d ed.) part 2, nos. 672-691, Berlin, Reimer, 1918.

[88] Eight slaves, however, out of nine distinguishable names appear in *CIL* 1[2] (2), no. 681.

[89] From Praeneste, *CIL* 1[2] (2): 1443, 1449, 1451, 1453, 1456; from Spoletium, *ibid.*, 2108; from Pompeii, *ibid.*, 777; from Mantua, a dedication to the Lares by nineteen slaves, *ibid.*, 753; from the Spanish town of Nova Carthago, and Tolosa, freeborn, freedmen and slaves in the same organizations, *ibid.*, 2270, 2271, 779 (*cf. Rh. Mus.* 59: 114-115).

[90] *CIL* 1[2] (2), no. 2260.

[91] *Ibid.*, 2235-2253, 2504.

[92] In Dessau, *ILS* this is no. 9236.

[93] Jean Hatzfeld, Les trafiquants Italiens dans l'Orient hellénique, in *Bibliothèque des Écoles Françaises d'Athènes et de Rome* 115: 249, n. 3, Paris, E. de Boccard, 1919.

[94] *Ibid.*, 247.

[95] Park, Marion E., *The plebs in Cicero's day*, 80-84, Cambridge, Cosmos Press, 1921. The conclusion of Park that 123 out of a total of 132 workmen were slaves is to be adopted with

handicraft occupations in which slaves occur are the following: public cooks;[96] fullers;[97] couch makers;[98] and bakers.[99]

In the building trades architecture itself was regarded by Cicero [100] as a profession worthy of free-born men; but Corumbus, a slave or freedman of Balbus, appears in a letter to Atticus as a fine master builder *bellus architectus*.[101]

The *familia* of T. Pomponius Atticus included slaves trained in literature, excellent readers and many copyists.[102] The two *librarioli* whom Atticus sent to Cicero to assist in his library as gluers and in writing title pieces were, therefore, slaves trained in book making.[103] Slaves and freedmen must have been used frequently in the last decades of the Republic as business agents in transfers of money and property [104] and as accountants in large households.[105] They also served as physicians in the households of their owners [106] and as teachers.[107] In the entertainment groups they appear in the last half-century of the Republic as members of musical organizations for public hire;[108] as actors;[109] and as gladia-

tors.[110] Beginning in the second century B. C. the household services of the wealthy Italian families were increasingly supplied by slaves, progressively tending to become, through excess numbers and manner of use, non-productive and luxury appendages of a few outstanding family organizations. Before the great increase in war captives in the first half of the second century B. C. specialist cooks had been hired in the market for unusually festive banquets.[111]

In this period also promiscuous, sometimes brutal, sex indulgence with slave women becomes noticeable in the Roman historical sources.[112] In the following century this freedom of sex indulgence with female slaves becomes more marked [113] and is openly discussed by Horace.[114]

In the closing decades of the Republic slaves appear conspicuously as litter bearers [115] and as letter carriers for private correspondence, as shown so constantly in the letters of Cicero. At Brundisium slaves of Atticus arrive upon one day with a letter from their master, followed two days later by another of his slaves bringing another letter.[116] Slaves were also used in sending confidential and important political messages or money.[117]

The social approach to slavery and the treatment accorded to slaves during the Republic, although subject to all the variations introduced by individual differences among the owners, show certain peculiarities which set Roman slavery apart in the general purview of ancient slave systems. The Romans regarded slavery as an institution common to all peoples without that necessity of explanation of its genesis which appears among the Greeks of the period preceding Alexander. They were

caution in accordance with her warning, *ibid.*, 81, n. 3 and 86, n. 1. Note, also, the caution of Gummerus, Industrie und Handel, Pauly-Wissowa, *RE* 9: 1487.

[96] *CIL* 1² (2): 1447.

[97] *Ibid.* 1² (2): 2108.

[98] *Ibid.* 6 (2): 7988 of 2 B. C.; *ibid.*, no. 9503.

[99] Slave names stamped on loaves of bread, *CIL* 10 (2): 8058, 18; 8059, 30, 34, 98, 99, 153, 154, 160, 412.

[100] Cicero, *De officiis* 1: 42, 7.

[101] Cicero, *To Atticus* 14: 3, 1; *cf.* the slave architect in *CIL* 1: 1216. The building contractors, Diphilus (Cicero, *To his brother Quintus* 3: 1, 1), and Nicephorus (*ibid.*, 3: 1, 5), are more probably freedmen than slaves since Nicephorus was able to abandon a contract which he had made with Quintus Cicero for whom he was acting as *vilicus*.

[102] Nepos, *Atticus*, 13, 3.

[103] Cicero, *To Atticus* 4: 4a, 1; 5, 3; 8a, 2; *cf. ibid.*, 1, 20, and three copyists of Atticus who were to delete a name from all the copies of a speech of Cicero which was being published, *ibid.* 13: 44, 3, Dionysius, Cicero's slave *librarius*, Cicero, *To his friends* 13: 77, 3.

[104] Cicero, *To Atticus* 13: 50, 2. *Cf.* the recommendation of the freedmen or slave business agents of Lamia to the governor of Africa, Cicero, *To his friends* 12: 29, 2.

[105] The freedman Hilarius as *ratiocinator*, Cicero, *To Atticus* 1: 12, 2. Philotimus, the freedman of Terentia, *id., To Atticus* 5: 4, 3; 19, 1; 8, 7, 3; 10, 5, 3. Marcus Tullius, a freedman of Cicero, had assisted the quaestor of Cilicia in 50 B. C. in making up the accounts of the province, *idem, To his friends* 5: 20, 1, 2. This freedman is not to be confused with the faithful M. Tullius Tiro, according to F. Münzer, Pauly-Wissowa, *RE* A1, *Tullius*, no. 15, p. 803.

[106] Suetonius, *Augustus*, 11. A freedman *medicus* appears in *CIL* 10: 388, a slave as a physician's assistant, in Cicero, *In defense of Aulus Cluentius*, 47.

[107] The slave Andronicus, as teacher of the children of Livius Salinator, Hieronymus, *Upon Eusebius' Chronicorum* 2: 125 (ed. Schoene; *cf.* Plutarch, *Cato the Elder*, 20, 3). Cato preferred to instruct his own sons, *ibid.*, 20, 4.

[108] Cicero, *Against Quintus Caecilius*, 17; *Against Verres* 5: 64, who sent six male musicians as a gift to a friend at Rome. The slave musicians belonging to the wife of Milo, Cicero, *In defense of Milo*, 55, were probably kept as private entertainers for the family as in Cicero, *Roscius*, 134.

[109] Antiphon, a freedman, Cicero, *To Atticus* 4: 15, 6; the

actor, Panurgus, owned jointly by Fannius and Q. Roscius, *idem, In defense of Roscius the comedian*, 27-29, 31.

[110] Livy, 28: 21, 2; Cicero, *Pro Sexto*, 134; *To Atticus* 4: 4a 2, where it is clear that the hiring out of trained slave gladiators for the games might be a lucrative business even for a man so prosperous as Atticus; Caesar, *Civil war* 1: 14, 4.

[111] Pliny, *Natural history* 18: 11, 28. Livy, 39: 6, 9 refers to the beginning of the purchasing of slaves who were highly trained in the art of cookery to the early second century when foreign luxury fashions began to appear in Roman society.

[112] Livy, 38: 24, 2-5; 39: 9, 5. For the relations of Scipio Africanus the Elder with a young slave girl see Valerius Maximus, 7: 6, 1. Cato in his old age took a young slave as mistress, Plutarch, *Cato the Elder*, 24, 1, and encouraged paid prostitution of his male slaves with his women slaves in lieu of family ties, *ibid.*, 21, 2.

[113] C. Antonius, consul in 63 B. C., bought a slave girl in the market to serve his desires, Quintus Cicero, *De petitione consulatus*, 8 (see Pauly-W., *RE* 1: 2578). A friend temporarily supplied Marcus Crassus with two slave girls, Plutarch, *Crassus*, 5, 2.

[114] Horace, *Satires* 1: 2, 117; *Letters* 1: 18, 72. *Cf.* Kroll, W., *Ztsch. für Sexualwissenschaft* 18: 149-50.

[115] Catullus, 10, 16.

[116] Cicero, *To Atticus* 3: 7, 1; *cf.* 1: 10, 1; 2: 8, 1; 9, 1; 12, 2; 3: 19, 3; 4: 4a; *To his friends* 8: 12, 4; 14: 5, 1; 16: 9, 2; *To his brother Quintus* 1: 3, 4.

[117] Cicero, *To Atticus* 15: 13, 4; a slave brought news regarding the legion at Alexandria. In Dio Cassius, 40: 8, 2, one of the Nervii offers a slave as messenger; Polyaenus, 8: 23, 1, a slave of Julius Caesar was sent to Miletus to gather ransom money.

unhampered, with respect to the enslavement of their neighbors in wars with the Italians, by any theoretical feeling for the tribal relationship of the peoples of Italy such as found expression among the Greeks of the fifth and fourth centuries with relation to enslavement of fellow Greeks, however ineffective it may have there been in practice.

We have no information regarding the hardships of transportation of slaves. The increased distance of the sea voyages for them, under the adverse conditions of overcrowded boats, from lower Russia, Asia Minor, and Syria to Italy and Sicily, must have added its part to the sufferings of western slavery as compared with that in Greece. Other differentiating characteristics were founded upon the singular and long persisting strength within the Roman state organization of the *familia*, of which the slave was an integral part,[118] subject to its rigid organization and discipline, but sharing in its privileges and protected rights as against the supreme power of the group of *familiae* which comprised the state. In the Greek city-states the freed slave (*apeleutheros*) entered into a separate group of non-citizen subjects, the metics. In the Roman state the *libertus* of a Roman citizen still expressed his relation to the *familia* of his former master by assuming his *praenomen* and *nomen*, and with them, in limited degree, his citizen status and its privileges. For outstanding services the Roman state also granted liberty to slaves, which Cicero equates with citizenship.[119] The Roman citizen body was, therefore, in a constant state of recruitment out of the former slave membership of the Roman *familiae*.

There is no doubt that this situation was already firmly established in the century preceding the great increase of slaves which began with the Hannibalic war; and it may have existed from the earliest period of the Republic. Its political significance received full recognition from Philip V of Macedon when he called attention to the advantages which the Roman state derived from it in an important official letter addressed in 214 B. C. to the *dēmos* of the Thessalian city of Larissa.[120] This liberality of treatment of the ex-slave by the Romans stood in logical correlation with the lack of rigidity and the expansive character of Roman citizenship. In direct contrast to it stood a marked severity of treatment both by the state and by individuals accorded to those of servile status which arose logically out of the strictness of the *familia* discipline. Both attitudes were affected by the increase in slave numbers in the last two centuries of the Republic, manumissions increasing notably

with the growing ease of acquirement,[121] and the state discipline and its punishments developing greater severity through fear of the numbers of the slaves.[122]

The great slave revolts of the second and first centuries B. C. in Sicily and Italy were brought about by three causes. These were: the excess of captured soldiers and the fact that these soldiers had already been hardened to dangers and cruelties by experience in war; the freedom from restraint necessarily permitted these dangerous men when they were employed in ranching;[123] and the neglect and cruelty engendered in the masters both by the brutalized type of the slaves employed and by the method of their employment.[124] To the Roman mind of Livy's day a revolt of slaves was peculiarly heinous and to be met, " not solely in that spirit which we use toward other enemies " (*non eo solum animo quo adversus alios hostes*) but with a special indignation and anger;[125] and the state itself met the danger of their revolts by a system of rewards and punishments, by rewards paid to slaves who might give advance information of threatened uprisings[126] and by the lingering death on the cross as punishment for those who revolted.[127] This form of death, which is but rarely met with in the Greek literature,[128] came to be regarded by the Romans as a terrifying punishment particularly reserved for slaves.[129] As such it appears as a threat often made against them in the Roman Comedy.[130]

Except in cases of revolt which endangered the government the Roman state left the problem of the discipline and punishment of slaves to their owners.[131] Through the *dominica potestas* as conceived by the Roman law the *pater familias* had complete control over all slaves owned in his *familia*, the power of punishment by whipping and by confinement in the *ergastulum*,[132]

---

[118] Wallon, H., *L'esclavage* 2: 177.

[119] *Servos persaepe . . . libertate, id est civitate, publice donari videmus*, Cicero, *Pro Balbo*, 9, 24.

[120] Dessau, *ILS* 2 (2): 8763: ὧν καὶ οἱ Ῥωμαῖοί εἰσιν. οἱ καὶ τοὺς οἰκέτας ὅταν ἐλευθερώσωσιν προσδεχόμενοι εἰς τὸ πολίτευμα καὶ τῶν ἀρχείων με[ταδι]δόντες καὶ διὰ τοῦ τοιούτου τρόπου οὐ μόνον τὴν ἰδίαν πατρίδα ἐπηυξήκασιν ἀλλὰ καὶ ἀποικίας σχεδὸν [εἰς ἑβ]-δομήκοντα τόπους ἐκπεπόμφασιν.

[121] For the fact of numerous manumissions, without accepting his numerical conclusions, see Frank, T., *Amer. Jour. Philol.* 53: 360-363.

[122] The personal severity of Cato was motivated by fear according to Plutarch, *Cato the Elder*, 21, 4.

[123] Diodorus Siculus, 34-35: 2, 2-3. The same type of slavery in Italy, idem, 34-35: 2, 34.

[124] Instances of masters' cruelties given by Diodorus, 34-35: 36-37.

[125] Livy, 21: 41, 10.

[126] Money and freedom granted to informer slaves, Livy, 4: 35, 2; 22: 33, 2; cf. 2: 5, 9; 26: 27, 4, 6; 27: 3, 5; 32: 26, 9, 14.

[127] The leaders alone were beaten and crucified in 196 B. C., Livy, 33: 36, 3. The six thousand captives from the slave revolt in Italy were crucified along the road from Capua to Rome in 71 B. C., Appian, *Civil wars* 1: 120.

[128] Daremberg-Saglio, *Dictionnaire* 1: 1573.

[129] *Servile supplicium* in Tacitus, *Histories* 4: 11, and *Script. hist. Aug., Avidius Cassius*, 4, 6.

[130] E. g. Plautus, *Miles gloriosus*, 359; *Mostellaria*, 557; Terence, *Andria*, 787; cf. Pauly-W., *RE* 4: 1728.

[131] Augustus, *Monumentum Ancyranum*, 25, records that he had returned thirty thousand slaves to their owners *ad supplicium sumendum*, in 36 B. C. after the blame for their actions had been put officially upon Sextus Pompey, Appian, *Civil wars* 5: 77, 80. Trials of charges involving this death penalty were held by the elder Cato in the presence of all his slaves, Plutarch, *Cato the Elder*, 21.

[132] Pauly-W., *RE* 6: 431.

and the right of execution of the death penalty.[133] These powers were held within bounds only by the individual sense of responsibility and of justice of the slave-owner and by the general control over public morals exercised by the censors.[134] Under such conditions many instances of unjust accusations against slaves were certain to arise.[135] Allowing for the unrecorded percentage of cases of considerate treatment of slaves by their owners, increased callousness toward them was probably symptomatic, as shown in the desperation and brutality displayed by the slaves in their reaction during the revolts in Sicily and Italy.[136] The savagery upon their side had been evoked by a disregard of their expectations which is described in detail by Diodorus.[137] The slave-owning psychology of the period is expressed in the completely economic motivation of the conduct of slave employment upon the estates in Italy, as advocated by Cato the Elder in his treatise on agriculture. The slave-driving in his treatment was unmitigated by any consideration of the needs of the slave as human being. The slave manager of the villa was held to account by the owner of the estate, upon his visits of inspection, for complete efficiency in the farm operations, solely with the profit motive in view and with no excuses permitted for slothfulness or flight of the slaves.[138] The slave members of the *familia* were to be adequately fed [139] because this would prevent petty theft of supplies;[140] and the food might be increased when greater physical demands were required from the slaves;[141] but when they fell ill the rations were to be reduced as a measure of economy.[142] For the same reason of economy old and sick slaves were to be sold along with old or worn-out cattle and tools.[143]

There is no provision in Cato's treatise for any family life for the slaves of the *familia rustica* and no suggestion of possible future manumission for them or of responsibility for their care in old age. The slaves were to be used upon holidays in those ways which would observe the letter of religious demands, though they might break the primitive prescription against

certain forms of work upon those days.[144] Provision for the comforts of slaves in respect to clothing are minimal, consisting of a shirt, a cloak, and a pair of heavy wooden shoes each second year.[145] As a necessary corollary to the *dominica potestas* over slaves a jail room, *ergastulum*, was maintained on the estates, in which recalcitrant slaves and those guilty of crimes were confined, often in chains.[146] Although there is no doubt of the existence and constant use of the *ergastula* under the later Republic and in the imperial period [147] and no reason to deny the temptation to individual injustice and cruelty connected with the right of confining slaves in them, their importance has been exaggerated in the modern literature.[148] The elder Cato punished the slaves of his *familia urbana* by whipping for slight mistakes [149] and speaks of the chaining of rural slaves, but only during the winter season.[150]

The numerous differences in the treatment advocated for the rural slaves by M. Terentius Varro from that advised by Cato may be explained in part by temperamental differences between the two; but in their totality they denote a marked alteration in the social attitude toward slavery which had taken place in the century between the two agricultural writers. For Varro the incentive of gain is tempered by the pleasure to be derived through his activities by the landowner.[151] Although the rustic slave is technically considered by Varro as an instrument of production, he is differentiated from animals and farm implements by the distinction that he belongs in a category of speaking instruments (*instrumenti genus vocale in quo sunt servi*) as against the partially vocal and the dumb farm aids (*semivocale [animal] et mutum*).[152] The social approach has passed from a pure profit motivation to one of welfare economics in which the well-being and contentment of the slave are to be considered, although still from the standpoint of enlightened self-interest.[153] Where Cato, as a means of better control, satisfied the sexual instincts of his household slaves through a system of prostitution within the *familia urbana*,[154] Varro advocated a family life so that the slave might be bound to the estate and produce slave sons who would increase the owner's

---

[133] See note 131, above.

[134] Protection of the slave from cruelty as a matter of citizen morals, Dionysius of Halicarnassus, *Antiquities* 20: 20, 3.

[135] A typical, though unhistorical, incident from the early Republic is cited, *ibid*. 8: 69. Verres accused an innocent slave in order to divert attention from himself, Cicero, *Against Verres* 4: 45, 100. Torture and crucifixion of a slave under private authority, Cicero, *Pro Cluentio*, 66, 187; *cf. To Atticus* 14: 15, 1; Horace, *Satires* 1: 3, 80-82. The alleged tortures inflicted by Pomponia, wife of Quintus Cicero, upon the slave who betrayed him were not accredited by Plutarch, *Cicero*, 49, 2.

[136] See ch. X, pp. 64-65.

[137] Diodorus Siculus, 34-35: 2; 36: 5-11.

[138] Cato, *De agricultura*, 2, 2.

[139] *Ibid.*, 56-58.

[140] *Facilius malo et alieno prohibebit, ibid.*, 5, 2.

[141] *Ibid.*, 56.

[142] *Ibid.*, 2, 5, rejecting the suggestion of G. Curcio that this was done to prevent feigned sickness. See Gaetano Curcio, *La primitiva civilta latina agricola e il libro dell'agricoltura di M. Porcio Catone*, 48, Firenze, Vallecchi, 1929.

[143] Cato, *De agricultura*, 2, 7.

[144] *Ibid.*, 2, 4; 138; *cf.* Columella, *De re rustica* 2: 21.

[145] Cato, *De agricultura*, 59.

[146] The building of underground, but healthy, *ergastula* was recommended by Columella, *De re rustica* 1: 6, 3.

[147] Slaves from the *ergastula* were sometimes sold for use as gladiators, Cicero, *Pro P. Sexto*, 134.

[148] See Heitland, W. E., *Agricola*, 146, Cambridge, Univ. Press, 1921, who regards them as barracks in which the rural slaves were constantly confined when not at work.

[149] Plutarch, *Cato the Elder*, 21, 3.

[150] *Cibaria . . . compeditis per hiemem*, Cato, *De agricultura*, 56. The *ergastulum* is not mentioned either by Cato or by Varro. See Heitland, *Agricola*, 185.

[151] *Ad duas metas dirigere debent, ad utilitatem et voluptatem.* Varro, *De re rustica* 1: 4, 1.

[152] E. g. wagons, *ibid.* 1: 171.

[153] *Studiosiores ad opus fieri liberalius tractando, ibid.* 1: 17, 7.

[154] Plutarch, *Cato the Elder*, 21, 2.

property.[155] Good work on the part of slaves was to meet with rewards in food or in exemptions from labor or in permission to own an animal and graze it on the estate.[156] Whereas Cato speaks of the chaining of slaves,

but probably only as punishment for wrongdoing,[157] Varro would not permit the overseer to coerce the slaves with blows where words could accomplish the same result;[158] and he makes no reference to the use of chains.[159]

---

[155] Epirote slaves are cited as examples of the advantages of such relations, Varro, *De re rustica* 1: 17, 5. The shepherd, also, was to have a mate, *ibid.* 2: 10, 6.

[156] A *peculium* for the slave overseer, *ibid.* 1: 17, 5; for the ordinary slave, *ibid.* 1: 17, 7; 19, 3.

[157] Cato, *De agricultura*, 56; *cf.* Plutarch, *Cato the Elder*, 21, 3.

[158] Varro, *De re rustica* 1: 175.

[159] The statement of Suetonius, *On the rhetoricians*, 3, that the chaining of a slave doorman to the door was an ancient Roman custom has no further support in the literature of the Republic.

XII. THE LATER REPUBLIC

SOCIAL AND LEGAL POSITION OF SLAVES

Upon runaway slaves in the West the information is slight although the number of those who attempted to escape from servitude must have been great, particularly in the later period of the Republic when household slaves had become numerous and their detection, when they had once escaped to foreign lands, was difficult.[1] To lessen the danger of escape some masters had metal collars put about the necks of their slaves bearing the names and addresses of slave and master.[2] There is no evidence that the elaborate legal provisions for the apprehension and return of fugitives which prevailed during the Roman Empire[3] had been established during the Republic. The problem of recovering the runaways was, at that time, left to the initiative of the slave-owner with such assistance from his friends and from the magistrates of municipalities and provinces as his influence enabled him to muster.[4] The correspondence conducted by Cicero with two successive governors of Illyricum[5] regarding his slave Dionysius, who had de-

parted with books stolen from Cicero's library, extended over a year and had not brought about the slave's return at the time of the last letter upon the matter. When captured the fugitive might be imprisoned by the magistrate or subjected to hard labor in the mills, upon private or official initiative, awaiting return to the owner.[6]

The attitude of mingled fear, suspicion, and contempt for slaves which is found in the literature of the last two centuries of the Republic[7] was an inevitable outcome of the unlimited powers granted to Roman slave masters under the *dominica potestas* when combined with the great number of slaves available during the period of extreme slave exploitation in the last centuries of the Republic. Where this attitude appears in the early tradition[8] it contradicts the feeling which should arise out of the position of the slaves in the *familia* under the then simple form of slavery and finds little substantiation in the instances of devotion and close relations between masters and slaves and in the examples of confidence in the slaves which are recorded in the dubious narrative of events of the late fourth and third centuries.[9] Even during the period of Roman overseas expansion the general conclusion of rigid severity toward slaves must be modified by considerations of the individual temperaments both of owners and of slaves and by special economic and social circumstances.

Abuse of the power of the master class in inciting

---

[1] Lenaeus, slave of Pompey the Great, successfully concealed himself in Greece, Suetonius, *De grammaticis*, 15. A fugitive slave is reported to have lived for some time with an Epicurean philosopher at Athens as a free man, Cicero, *Ad Quintum fratrem* 1: 2, 14. A slave of Atticus took refuge with a robber leader, Moiragenes, in the Taurus mountains, Cicero, *Ad Atticum* 5: 15, 3; 6: 1, 13. Dionysius, absconding slave of Cicero, fled into the interior of Illyricum, *idem, Ad familiares* 5: 9, 2. *Cf.* the belief still adhered to in the first century after Christ that the Vestal Virgins by a certain prayer could arrest the flight of slaves so long as those were in the precincts of the city, Pliny, *Nat. hist.* 28: 2, 13.

[2] Lucilius, 29, in Nonius Marcellus, *Compendiosa Doctrina*, 36 M, *cum manicis, catulo collarique ut fugitivum deportem.* Compare the inscription upon a bronze disc to be attached to the neckband of a slave in Bruns, *FIR*, 159, 362: *fugi; tene me; cum revocaveris me domino meo Zonio accipis solidum,* and the iron collar found about the vertebra of a skeleton at Brindisi, possibly the collar of a fugitive slave, *Atti. Acad. dei Lincei, Mem.* 1878-79: 215.

[3] Buckland, *Roman law of slavery*, 267-268.

[4] Wilcken, U., *UPZ* 1: 568. Cicero used his influence with his brother Quintus as governor of Asia in behalf of his friend Aesopus. Arrest of the slave awaiting disposition of the case, Cicero, *Ad Quintum fratrem* 1: 2, 14.

[5] Cicero, *Ad familiares* 13: 77, 3; 5, 9, 2; 10, 1.

[6] Cicero, *Ad Quintum fratrem* 1: 2, 14; *Mon. Ancyr.*, 25, return of fugitive slaves to their masters.

[7] *Totidem hostes esse quot servos,* Seneca, *Epist. mor.*, 47, 5; Macrobius, *Saturnalia* 1: 11, 13; Livy, 39: 26, 8; Cicero, *De domo sua* 129; *Pro Caelio* 61-62. The *ludi Megalenses* were turned over to the slaves by the aedile P. Clodius Pulcher in 56 B.C., Cicero, *De haruspicum responsis*, 24; *Post reditum in Senatum*, 13; *In Pisonem*, 9, *ex omni ferce urbis ac servitio.* Even the home-born slaves might be a possible source of danger, Cicero, *Ad familiares* 9: 19, 2; *cf.* Horace, *Epodes*, 4, 3-4, 11-12, with reference to Menos, freedman of Sextus Pompey.

[8] In the speeches ascribed to characters of the early Republic, as in Livy, 4: 3, 7, the later attitude was carried back and applied retroactively as the earlier attitude toward freedmen and their sons. See also Livy, 9: 46, 4.

[9] Valerius Maximus, 4: 4, 6 (*De paupertate*).

their slaves to misdeeds by promises of freedom[10] or in using them to gain illegal advantage[11] was no doubt frequent. In contrast to these cases examples may be cited of a public opinion which was critical of this abuse of power,[12] and instances of genuine personal affection of masters for their slaves. Although the sensitiveness shown by Cicero with respect to the bad fortune and lack of rights of slaves[13] may be unusual among Romans of the late Republic, his willingness to express his admiration for the good qualities of his slaves and the genuine affection in which he held some of them, notably Tiro, were characteristic of his family and equally of his friend Atticus.[14] On the part of the slaves even under the conditions which produced the great slave revolts in the west there is no evidence of a demand for freedom as a natural right of all men[15] nor of any unity of action designed to obtain the abolition of the institution of slavery. Any tendency of this nature was directed merely toward an amelioration of immediate conditions.

It is quite obvious from the frequent examples of loyalty of slaves to their masters which can be cited from this period that the slaves often received and responded to kindly treatment.[16] Fair living conditions must be presupposed in the cases of the slaves sent to the East in connection with the business affairs of their western owners.[17] Under the ordinary conditions of Roman life the close relations of the slaves with the rest of the Roman *familia* and their participation in the household

rites[18] warrants the assumption of considerate treatment in that setting. Except for the years 64-58 B. C., during which all *collegia* were disbanded, except a few which were specifically exempted by the pertinent *senatus consultum*[19] and excepting the time stretching from Caesar's prohibition of the *collegia* during his dictatorship[20] to the establishment of the Empire, the government of the Republic had freely granted the right of association to all subjects, slaves as well as free. For the slaves of the West the social advantages of this attitude of the right of association should not be underestimated.

The development at Rome and in the neighboring towns of central Italy of religious-social organizations of slaves and freedmen may be placed, in want of precise information, in the last half of the second century B. C.[21] The earliest list of *magistri* of the cult associations from Campania which is composed of slaves is dated in 98 B. C.[22] Twenty-nine *magistri* lists from Minturnae, together with inscriptions of a similar kind previously known from other towns of Italy and from Spain and the Danubian regions,[23] represent the attainment by slaves and ex-slaves of both sexes,[24] at about 100 B. C.,[25] of a definite social position in the life of the communities under Roman rule in Italy. They give evidence of social-religious contacts of their own in organizations in which the slave class was customarily, though not necessarily, set apart from free men working in the same crafts or economic services.[26]

Since the names upon the Minturnae lists include only the *magistri* and *magistrae* annually elected out of a more extensive membership of the *collegia*,[27] a considerable body of freedmen and slaves[28] must have participated in the cult worships and in the social life which accompanied them. The spread of the *collegia* among the slave and freedmen classes was rapid before 64 B. C. and became alarming when the ban upon the associa-

---

[10] Incitement of a slave to commit a murder is recorded by Appian, *Mithradatic wars*, 59.

[11] Freedom was sometimes granted in order to place slaves upon the lists for the grain doles, Dio Cassius, 39: 24, 1.

[12] Pompey scrupulously shunned the possibility of criticism regarding his relations with the wife of his freedman, Plutarch, *Pompey*, 2, 4.

[13] Cicero, *Pro Balbo*, 9.

[14] Tiro's facility in taking dictation was praised by Cicero, *Ad Atticum* 13: 25, 3. On his manumission, see *Ad familiares* 16: 10, 2, 15, 2, 16, 1. Concern about an illness of Tiro is expressed in *Ad familiares* 16: 1, 2; 4, 3; 5, 6, etc. Cicero expresses his grief at the death of a boy reader, *Ad Atticum* 1: 12, 4. Quintus Cicero writes of his satisfaction with his slave Statius in *Ad familiares* 16: 16, 2. Cicero consoles Atticus in his grief over a slave, *Ad Atticum* 12: 10.

[15] Schneider, Albert, *Geschichte der Sclaverei*, 20.

[16] Hasdrubal was killed in 221 B. C. by a slave whose master had been put to death by him, Livy, 21: 2, 6. Considerate treatment was shown to the daughter of harsh slaveholding parents in the first Sicilian revolt because of her previous kindness to the slaves, Diodorus Siculus, 34-35: 2, 13. A freedman of Pompey cared for his body after his death, Plutarch, *Pompey*, 80, 2-3. Even under the fear of suspicion of complicity in the murder of their master some slaves would remain with their owner's body, Cicero, *Ad familiares* 4: 12, 3. During the proscription of 43 B. C. several slaves were known to have saved their masters by changing places with them and suffering death in their stead, Dio Cassius, 47: 10, 2-6. Other instances of the devotion of slaves are gathered by Valerius Maximus, 6: 8.

[17] Cicero, *Ad familiares* 1: 3, 2 recommended the freedmen, agents and slaves of A. Trebonius to the proconsul of Cilicia. For slaves at Delos, Samothrace, Pergamum, and Cos, see Hatzfeld, Jean, *Les trafiquants Italiens dans l'Orient hellénique.*

[18] Horace, *Epodes*, 2, 65-66.

[19] Asconius Pedianus, *Ad Ciceronis orationes commentarii*, 67. For the dating in 64 B. C. see Kornemann, Collegium, Pauly-W., *RE* 4: 406. Restoration of the *collegia* by the *lex Clodia* of 58 B. C. is recorded in Cicero, *In Pisonem*, 9; in *Pro Sestio*, 55; and by Asconius Pedianus, 9.

[20] Suetonius, *Julius*, 42.

[21] The rise of guilds of free persons to a position of importance in the industries at Rome is to be placed about the beginning of the second Punic War, Kornemann, Collegium, Pauly-W., *RE* 4: 392-393.

[22] *CIL* 1 (2): 618.

[23] See Johnson, Jotham, *Excavations at Minturnae* 2: 119.

[24] In the Minturnae lists, in the volume cited above, out of 319 names in which the sex can be determined 254 men and 65 women appear.

[25] Cf. J.-P. Waltzing, *Étude historique sur les corporations professionelles chez les Romains* 1: 86, Louvain, Peeters, 1895.

[26] *Ingenui* and *liberti* frequently appear together in the same lists and *liberti* with *servi*. Slaves appear rarely, however, with free-born persons, *CIL* 1 (2): 777 from Pompeii. At Nova Carthago in Spain *ingenui, liberti* and *servi* are found in the same organization, *ibid.*, 2270; possibly also at Tolosa, *ibid.*, 779.

[27] Johnson, J., *Excavations at Minturnae* 2: 120.

[28] Slaves largely predominated at Minturnae if the lists from that city represent the true relations throughout the city.

tions was lifted in 58 B. C.[29] Slaves were not distinguished from freedmen or the free born by compulsory differences of attire except at the time of manumission, when their heads were shaved and they put on a distinctive type of felt skull cap.[30]

The statement of Gummerus [31] that the slaves of Italy were clothed with the coarse weaves of the Insubres [32] means only that the rough wool of the Ligurians and Symbri was made up into cheap clothing sold to the slaves and to others of the poorer population of Italy. The attraction of companionship with others of the same class which the city offered to the slaves had the same appeal over rustic conditions for them as for free men.[33] Although Cato and men of his kind would demand of the *familia rustica*, even upon holidays, such labors as an exact observance of the letter of the religious requirements would permit,[34] there were certain holidays when, by Roman custom, the severities of the labor requirements upon the slaves were either completely set aside or at least greatly mitigated.[35] During the celebration of the Saturnalia the freedmen and slaves were feasted and slaves and free, rich and poor, were on a basis of equality.[36] The slaves had license to jest with their masters with a surprising freedom [37] which was no doubt tempered and controlled by knowledge of a retribution which would follow upon abuse of the privilege.[38] Upon the Matronalia, celebrated upon the Calends of March, mistresses waited upon their slaves.[39] Under the lax discipline of the pleasure villas of the late Republic stormy weather also meant a cessation of the labors of the slaves [40] which the practical farm sense of Cato insisted upon avoiding as far as possible.[41]

In marked contrast with the severity of the Roman treatment of slaves, with the unlimited powers of control which lay with the *pater familias* and with the view, clearly expressed by Cicero,[42] that it was beneath the dignity of a Roman official to grant too great latitude of influence to a slave, stands the broad-minded attitude of the Romans in admitting talented slaves after their manumission into the intellectual life of the Roman community. They were accepted into its political and economic life without any manifestation of prejudice arising from their former status.[43] In the Hellenic East preceding the time of the Roman Empire ex-slaves occasionally, in fact, gained positions of prominence in the economic life of their day.[44] Few freedmen, however, appear among those whose names may be listed as important in the history of Greek culture.

Four features which may help to explain this anomaly of the Roman slave situation are: the secure position which slaves originally held and later maintained in the Roman *familia*; the non-exclusive character of Roman citizenship, which could include slaves after their manumission; the superiority of Greek culture and the appearance at Rome of Greek slaves in the period of the rapid expansion of Roman power over Magna Graecia and Sicily in the period from 290 B. C. to the end of the second Punic War; [45] and the need and lack of teachers to meet the new cultural demands of Roman society, combined with the fact that the principal source of slaves of the period, namely capture in war, furnished a ready supply of adult educated slaves equipped to meet the insistent demand for the instruction of the youth of the Roman upper classes.[46]

The outstanding examples of former slaves who reached high place in the field of Latin literature are Lucius Livius Andronicus from Magna Graecia and P. Terentius Afer. The list of the freedmen who attained a degree of local recognition at Rome under the Republic as writers or as literary assistants includes: Epicadus, who completed the unfinished memoirs of Sulla; [47] Atteius Philologus, who assembled the materials for the historical work of Sallust; [48] L. Voltacilius Pilutus, teacher of Gnaeus Pompey; [49] Tiro, the former slave of Cicero, who assisted him in his literary labors; [50] Lenaeus the grammarian, ex-slave of Pompey, who was commissioned by him to translate into Latin the medical memoranda of Mithradates VI of Pontus; [51] and Apollonius, ex-slave of Crassus, who in 45 B. C. desired to write in Greek an account of Caesar's exploits and was recommended for the task by Cicero.[52] Pliny,

[29] Cicero, *In Pisonem de haruspicis reipubl.*, 24.

[30] Πιλίον, Plutarch, *Flamininus*, 13, 6; Polybius, in Livy, 45: 44, 19.

[31] Gummerus, Industrie und Handel, Pauly-W., *RE* 9: 1471.

[32] Emending οικίας in Strabo, 5: 1, 12.

[33] Horace, *Epistulae* 1: 14, 15.

[34] Cato, *De agricultura*, 2, 4; 140.

[35] Cicero, *De legibus* 2: 9. The feast day of Jupiter Dialis was a holiday for the ox drivers, Cato, *De agricultura*, 132.

[36] Saturnalia in Pauly-W., *RE*, 2d ser., 2: 205; Marquardt, *Staatsverwaltung* 3: 388.

[37] Horace, *Satires* 2: 7.

[38] Similar conditions at the celebration of the *Compitalia* are reported by Cato, *De agricultura*, 57; Wissowa, G., *Religion und Kultus der Römer*, 2d ed., 168, Munich, Beck, 1912.

[39] Article Matronalia in Pauly-W., *RE* 14²: 2307. The Ides of August also was a slave holiday, in Sextus Pompeius Festus, *De verb. significatione*, p. 343, col. a 7 (ed. C. O. Müller).

[40] Horace, *Odes* 3: 17, 14-16.

[41] Cato, *De agricultura*, 2, 3.

[42] Cicero, *Ad Quintum fratrem* 1: 1, 17.

[43] No Roman counterpart existed of the Greek doctrine which explained the genesis of slavery upon theoretical considerations of the inferiority of certain peoples who by virtue of environment and inheritance had become natural objects of enslavement.

[44] Pasion, banker at Athens in the fourth century B. C. is the outstanding example.

[45] Frank, Tenney, *Life and literature in the Roman Republic*, 13-15, 70-72, Berkeley, Univ. of California Press, 1930, and Mommsen, *History of Rome* 3: 112-128, have dealt ably with the cultural reactions of the first and second Punic Wars upon Rome.

[46] *Ibid.* 3: 136.

[47] Suetonius, *De grammaticis*, 12; cf. article Cornelius, Pauly-Wissowa, *RE* 4: 1311.

[48] Suetonius, *De grammaticis*, 10.

[49] He later wrote an account of Pompey's deeds and those of his father, Suetonius, *De rhetoricis*, 3.

[50] Gellius, *noctes Atticae* 13: 9, 1; 15: 6, 2.

[51] Suetonius, *De grammaticis*, 15; Pliny, *Nat. hist.* 25: 2, 7.

[52] Cicero, *Ad familiares* 13: 16, 4; Pliny, *Nat. hist.* 35: 17, 199; cf. Wallon, *L'esclavage* 2: 430-431, 432-434.

35 : 199 mentions as ex-slaves Publilius Antiochius, who introduced the mime at Rome; Manilius Antiochus, an astrologer; and the grammarian, Staberius Eros.[53] To this list Pliny adds the names of eight ex-slaves who attained wealth in the period of the proscriptions of the first century B. C. These are: Chrysogonus, freedman of Sulla; Amphion, freedman of Q. Catulus; Hector, freedman of L. Lucullus; Demetrius, freedman of Pompey;[54] Auge, freedwoman (?) of Pompey;[55] Hipparchus, freedman of M. Antonius; and Menas and Menecrates, freedmen of Sextus Pompey.

The influence which individual slaves had gained in Rome in the middle of the first century B. C. is further attested by the willingness of young Roman advocates to represent them in cases involving freedom.[56] Knowing the secret lives of their masters they were in a position to hurt them by truth or slander[57] and attained in some cases such positions of importance with their masters that even Julius Caesar found it worth while to court their support.[58] Cicero showed deep concern in respect to the fact that Statius, a slave of his brother Quintus, had been permitted to give advice and interfere in the affairs of the province of Asia.[59] He wrote to Quintus admonishing him that it was proper to rely upon a capable slave in domestic affairs, but advisable to divorce him completely from all matters pertaining to affairs of state.[60]

In the last two centuries of the Roman Republic the district comprising Italy, Sicily, and Carthaginian North Africa, primarily because of its extensive employment in agriculture of slaves beside free hired hands,[61] was more completely grounded upon slave labor than any other part of the ancient world at any other period of antiquity. This widespread rise of slaves, supplied in considerable degree from the eastern Mediterranean districts during the wars of expansion of the last two centuries of the Republic, was unquestionably an important factor in shaping the economic and cultural life of Italy and Sicily both at that time and into the first two centuries of the Empire.[62] The trained handicrafts-men introduced as slaves influenced the industrial and technical development of the West and the slaves in agriculture supplied the place of free local labor diverted into military service.[63] Nevertheless, the generalization that Roman civilization was a slave civilization[64] is too strongly phrased, even if applied solely to the central region of the Mediterranean at the height of its slave numbers. The idea is inapplicable even in the restricted sense in which it is used by Max Weber, that slavery caused the differentiations of wealth and poverty and the thinness of the stratum of the propertied classes. Weber's statement arose out of an exaggerated impression of the strength of slavery as against the employment of free labor: and it fails to deal with the impermanence of the slaves in the condition of bondage and the constant recruiting of the semi-free and free laboring classes through widespread manumission out of those of slave status.[65]

Because of the nature of the existing sources upon Roman law it is impossible to establish a division between the Republic and the early centuries of the Empire in the discussion of the Roman legal theory and practice regarding slavery. According to the theory as formulated in the classical period, the institution of slavery was of the *jus gentium* but was at the same time contrary to natural law.[66] Following the division on the basis of the law of nations and natural law, Gaius ascribed personality to slaves under the Roman civil law.[67] The juristic etymology which connected *servus* with *servare*,[68] apparently formulated during the later Republic when captivity in war was the outstanding source of slave supply, is based upon the right of the conqueror in war to slay the captured enemy and upon the view that enslavement of the captive was the merciful action of preserving his life. Fundamentally regarded, however, as an object of ownership, either by a single person, by several persons collectively, or by a corporation such as a *collegium* or the state, the slave was a chattel (*res*),[69] subject to all the economic operations which were applicable to any other commodity, such as sale, mortgage,

---

[53] Pauly-W., *RE*, 2d ser., 3 A2 (1929), col. 1924, *s. v.* Staberius, 4.

[54] For his assumption of political importance see the amusing tale of the elaborate reception of Cato the Younger at Antioch under the misapprehension that Demetrius was arriving, Plutarch, *Cato the Younger*, 13. His suburban villas and expensive gardens at Rome are mentioned by Plutarch, *Pompey*, 40.

[55] Pliny, *Nat. hist.* 35: 18, 200.

[56] Cicero, *Ad familiares* 13: 9, 2.

[57] Cicero, *Pro Caelio*, 57; Juvenal, *Satires* 9: 110-111; 118-119, *vivendum recte . . . ut possis linguam contemnere servi.*

[58] Dio Cassius, 40: 60, 4 and compare Cicero's liberal entertainment, at the time of the Saturnalia, of the slaves and lower class freedmen in the train of Caesar, *Ad Atticum* 13: 52, 2.

[59] Cicero, *Ad Atticum* 2: 18, 4; *Ad Quintum fratrem* 1: 2, 3.

[60] Cicero, *Ad Quintum fratrem* 1: 1, 17. This resentment at the position attained by Statius was shared by the friends of Cicero, *ibid.* 1: 2, 2.

[61] In the ranch and plantation type of slavery which prevailed there.

[62] Persson, A., *Staat und Manufaktur im röm. Reiche*, 54.

[63] The statement is made by Livy, 6: 12, 5, that the use of slaves had saved the Aequian and Volscian districts from becoming a solitude: *locis quae servitia Romana ab solitudine vindicant.*

[64] Weber, M., *Gesammelte Aufsätze*, 293.

[65] Ciccotti, E., *Metron* 9: 34-35, expressed the more credible view that manumission under Roman conditions became a method of revival of the citizen body and of the reintegration of the category of free men.

[66] *Servitus est constitutio iuris gentium qua quis dominio alieno contra naturam subicitur*, Justinian, *Institutes* 1: 3, 2; *Digest* 1: 5, 4, 1; *cf. Digest* 12: 6, 64. The contradiction between the practice of all peoples and natural law is more sharply defined in *Digest* 50: 17, 32 in the statement that all men are equal under natural law.

[67] Gaius, *Institutes* 1: 9, *summa divisio de iure personarum haec est, quod omnes liberi sunt aut servi; cf.* 1: 9, 48, *nam quaedam personae sui iuris sunt, quaedam alieno iuri sunt subiectae, cf.* Affolter, Friedreich, *Die Persönlichkeit des herrenlosen Sklaven*, 1-9, Leipzig, Veit and Co., 1913.

[68] *Digest* 1: 5, 4, 2; 50: 16, 239, 1.

[69] *Codex* 4: 5, 10; 46, 3; 8, 53, 1.

and transference by will and to all the laws which dealt with mobile property.

A reasonable explanation of the comparative severity of the Roman treatment of slaves as compared with that which was practised in Greece is to be found in the strength and sternness of application of the *patria potestas* in the Roman scene. Special treatment of the slave as *res* was necessarily required, however, by the recognition of these human qualities which distinguished him from other objects of use and exchange.[70] The right of an enemy state to enslave Roman captives was accepted as a part of the *jus gentium*. For a Roman citizen who thus became a slave in an enemy land, the fact of his enslavement resulted in a state of suspension of his property rights and of his family relations, pending the end of his condition of slavery. This outcome might be brought about through death or by reason of his return within the boundaries of his native state or within those of a state which stood in friendly relations with Rome.[71] Upon his return his original legal status was restored by a right called *postliminium*. In case he had been redeemed from slavery by a money payment of a second person, the right of *postliminium* did not enter into operation until the ransom money had been repaid.[72]

The marriage relation of a Roman captured and enslaved was dissolved by the fact of his enslavement. It was not automatically restored by *postliminium*, but only through renewed consent.[73] In these cases the human quality of Roman subjects who became slaves through capture in war, even the possibility of their restoration to full citizenship, could not be lost sight of, since their original free status was theoretically in abeyance only while their enslavement lasted. This attitude toward the slave as man as well as *res* lies also inherent in the fact that non-Roman slaves of Roman citizens might be granted full citizen rights by the state after their manumission.[74]

Through conviction under Roman criminal law to complete loss of rights, *deminutio capitis maxima*, which included the ultimate penalty of death or that of condemnation to the mines,[75] free men lost the three essentials which distinguished citizens, namely liberty, family rights, and citizenship,[76] and became *servi poenae*.[77] Under the early law of the Republic con-

demnation to slavery was also used as punishment inflicted for certain breaches of the civil law which later became obsolete either through administrative changes or through changes in the type of penalties imposed. Such were enslavement for evasion of the census,[78] for evasion of military service,[79] for manifest theft according to an article of the Twelve Tables,[80] and, in the two first centuries of the Republic, as a result of a debtor judgment.[81]

Although male and female slaves constantly lived together for the purpose of offspring, and the terms applicable to cognate relationship were regularly employed in actual life with respect to such unions,[82] in principle legal marriage was not recognized as possible for slaves.[83] The union of male and female slaves was consequently differentiated as *contubernium* as opposed to *conubium*.[84] The offspring of the union of *servus* and *ancilla* was of slave status by inheritance, the Roman law following in this respect a principle of the *ius gentium* according to which slavery by birth depended upon the status of the mother,[85] more strictly delimited as the maternal status at the time of the child's birth.[86] A child born of a free father and a slave mother was a slave and property of the owner of the mother, whereas the offspring of a slave father and a free woman inherited the free status of the mother. As a result of the acknowledged freedom of such children, and primarily as a political problem affecting status, cohabitation between free women and slaves became a subject of concern to the state. By a *senatus consultum Claudianum* of A. D. 52 it was enacted that, if a free woman continued to live with a slave belonging to another person after the slave's owner had formally forbidden it, the woman herself and the issue of such a union became slaves of the owner.[87] On the other hand the sexual relations between a free man and his own female slave and the resultant offspring received no attention in legislation since the slave was the property of the master.

In dealing with delicts of slaves the power of punish-

---

[70] This was recognized in the differentiation of agricultural property into *instrumentum mutum, semivocale, et vocale*, made by Varro, *De re rustica* 1 : 17, 1.

[71] Buckland, *Law of Slavery*, 292-295.

[72] *Ibid.*, 304.

[73] *Ibid.*, 296.

[74] Cicero, *pro Balbo* 9 : 24. Philip V of Macedon to the Larissans, Dessau, *Ins. Lat. Sel.*, 8763. The methods of manumission of slaves and the activities of the state necessary to the control of manumission procedure are explained in Pauly-Wissowa, *RE* 14 : 1366-1367; Buckland, *Law of Slavery*, 437-448.

[75] *Damnatio in metallum*, Pliny, *Epistles* 10 : 58; 60; *Digest* 48 : 19, 8, 4.

[76] Just., *Digest* 5 : 4, 11.

[77] *Ibid.* 48 : 19, 8, 4; 17; Mommsen, Th., *Römisches Strafrecht,* 947-948, Leipzig, Duncker and Humblot, 1899.

[78] Cicero, *Pro Caecina*, 34, 99; Dionysius of Halicarnassus, 4, 15, 6; Gaius, *Institutes* 1 : 160; *Ulpian*, 11 : 11, *De titulis*, in Riccobono, S., *et al.*, *Fontes Juris Romani Ante-Justiniani*, 2d ed., 2 : 274, Florence, 1941-1943. This lost its importance in the long period of abeyance of the census after 167 B. C.

[79] This also was abandoned early, see Just., *Digest* 49 : 16, 4, 10.

[80] Cited by Gellius, *Noctes Atticae* 11 : 18, 8; 20, 17.

[81] Livy, 6 : 15, 9; 20, 6, 8; 28, 8; leg. XII Tab., Bruns-Gradenwitz, *FIR*, 21, Tab. 3, 5, from Gellius.

[82] The terms *pater, filius, frater, soror*, etc., occur frequently in the dedicatory inscriptions, see Dessau, *ILS* 1 : 1515, 1516, 1517, 1809, 7430; Just., *Digest* 38 : 10, 10, 5. *Uxor* is used in Columella, *De re rustica* 12 : 1.

[83] Plautus, *Casina*, 67-75.

[84] *Pauli Sententiae* 2 : 19, 6; Just., *Codex* 9 : 9, 23; Ulpian, 5 : 5.

[85] Gaius, *Institutes* 1 : 82.

[86] Ulpian, 5 : 9-10.

[87] Tacitus, *Annals* 12 : 53; Suetonius, *Vespasian*, 11; Tertullian, *Ad uxor.* 2 : 8; Gaius, *Institutes* 1 : 84; *Pauli Sententiae* 4 : 10, 2; Ulpian, 11 : 11; *cf.* Buckland, *Law of Slavery*, 412-413.

ment vested in the head of the family under the *dominica potestas* included corporal punishment, confinement in chains,[88] banishment from Rome or from Italy, and the death penalty.[89] During the Republic abuse of this right by the slave owner was checked by public disapproval, by the power of the censor[90] and by an arbitrator publicly appointed to hear complaints of slaves against poor feeding or too cruel treatment.[91] Under the Empire more definite prohibitions greatly decreased the right of punishment vested in the *pater familias*. Before the state courts, under the alternative of state action for crimes committed by them, slaves had no standing. This legal disability followed logically upon their position as objects of ownership. They were incapable of prosecution as accusers,[92] either in their own behalf or in behalf of others.[93] Although they were permitted to lay information before the magistrates as delators,[94] the opposition to them as informers was marked.[95] In principle the evidence of slaves was not resorted to in civil cases except when other proof was unavailable or insufficient.[96]

The testimony of slaves against their own masters was banned by a decree of the Senate passed under the Republic.[97] Application of this law was evaded, however, under Tiberius by the process of transference of the slaves under question from their owner by enforced sale to a magistrate.[98] The evidence of slaves, when it was admissible, was customarily taken by torture.[99] In cases of murder of a slave-owner torture of the household slaves[100] was provided by a *senatus consultum Silanianum* ascribed to the time of Augus-

tus,[101] and later confirmed by other *senatus consulta*.[102] This practice was later modified in murder cases by a law of Hadrian providing that only those slaves were to be examined who were close enough to the place at the time of the commission of the crime to have been cognizant of it.[103]

Roman slaves owned by Roman citizens were as capable of committing a crime as any Roman who owned them,[104] and from the earliest period they were liable to punishment for what they had done. The slave-owner was liable only in the name of the slave[105] except when the crime was committed with foreknowledge of the act so that he was in a position to hinder it, in which case the owner was responsible in his own name.[106] In case a suit were entered in a civil action against a slave the owner might admit title to the slave and elect to defend him.[107] In this case the owner was subject to payment of the damages inflicted if the guilt of the slave was proven. Or he might refuse to defend his slave. In that case he must transfer the slave to the ownership of the injured party.[108] By a local law enacted in Mylasa in Caria in A. D. 209-211 if a slave broke the banking law of the city the owner had the option of paying a fine or giving in the slave for punishment which consisted of fifty blows and six months' imprisonment.[109] Customarily in cases of serious crimes committed by a slave, such as the murder of the owner or a member of his family, the state would exercise its right of punishment[110] although the original right of the owner to inflict the death penalty[111] still appears in force in the time of the Empire.[112]

From the earliest period of Roman legislation slaves, as possessions of value, were protected from injustice or mistreatment at the hands of others than their owners. By a law of the Twelve Tables[113] breaking a bone of a slave was penalized by a fine which was half that imposed in case the victim were a free man. In case of minor injuries done to a slave, such as insult or physical

---

[88] Affolter, F., *Persönlichkeit des herrenlosen Sklaven*, 155.

[89] *Ibid.*, 133.

[90] Mommsen, Th., *Römisches Strafrecht*, 24, n. 1.

[91] Seneca, *De beneficiis* 3: 22.

[92] Tacitus, *Annals* 13: 10; Just., *Digest* 10: 24; *cf.* Buckland, *Law of Slavery*, 85, n. 5.

[93] Just., *Digest* 50: 17, 107: *servo nulla actio est.*

[94] Buckland, *Law of slavery*, 85.

[95] Julius Caesar was strongly opposed to rewards for slave informers and even to granting them a hearing, Dio Cassius, 41: 38, 3. For the same attitude under the triumvirs see Appian, *Bella Civilia* 4: 29.

[96] Buckland, *Law of slavery*, 86-87. In Pliny, *Epistles* 7: 26, however, the evidence of a slave cleared a suspected freedman of a murder charge.

[97] According to Tacitus, *Annals* 2: 30, 3, this was embodied in a *vetus senatus consultum*; see also Cicero, *De partitione oratoria dialogus*, 118. Cicero tells us of the application of this prohibition in a case affecting the owner's life, *Pro Roscio Amerino*, 41, 120-121. The rule still held in the third century, according to the *Script. hist. Aug., Tacitus*, 9, 4.

[98] Tacitus, *Annals* 2: 30, 3. It was employed again in a case of extortion against Silanus, proconsul of Asia, Tacitus, *Annals* 3: 67, 3. A similar action of Augustus is reported by Dio Cassius, 55: 5, 4.

[99] Cicero, *Pro Cluentio*, 63, 176; In his speech *Pro rege Deiotaro*, 1, 3 Cicero expressed himself as opposed to this practice because it was productive of testimony which was prejudiced by fear. In military trials imposition of the death penalty on the testimony of a single slave was displeasing to the soldiery, *Script. hist. Aug., Pertinax*, 10, 10.

[100] See Tacitus, *Annals* 14: 42-45.

[101] Just., *Digest* 29: 5; *Codex* 6: 35, 11.

[102] Buckland, *Law of slavery*, 95.

[103] *Script. hist. Aug., Hadrian*, 18, 11.

[104] According to a senatus consultum of A. D. 20, *si servus reus postulabitur eadem observanda sunt quae si liber esset*, Just., *Digest* 48: 2, 12, 3.

[105] As in the *senatus consultum* of 11 B. C., Frontinus, *De aquaed. urbis Romae*, 129.

[106] Affolter, F., *Persönlichkeit des herrenlosen Sklaven*, 102.

[107] The slave had the option of defending himself.

[108] See the discussion in Affolter, F., *Persönlichkeit des herrenl. Sklaven*, 103-104, and in Buckland, *Law of slavery*, 103-105.

[109] *OGI* 2: 515, 15-19, 30-34.

[110] Affolter, F., *Persönlichkeit des herrenl. Sklaven*, 140-141.

[111] Mommsen, Th., *Römisches Strafrecht*, 616. This was implied by Cicero, *In Catilinam* 4: 6, 12.

[112] The crucifixion of a slave in 22 B. C. by a *pater familias* was approved by Augustus, Dio Cassius, 54: 3, 7. The death penalty inflicted upon the slaves who murdered their master which is implied in Pliny, *Epistulae* 3: 14, 2-5, was probably imposed by family condemnation and privately administered.

[113] Bruns-Gradenwitz, *FIR*, 29, *Leges XII Tabularum*, Tab. 8, 3.

harm,[114] the master had cause of action for damages against the perpetrator. Action for damages was also available to the owner if the slave had been in some way corrupted by an outsider.[115] If a slave were induced to run away or were forcibly abducted the master might resort to both a criminal and a civil action.[116] Under a *lex Cornelia de sicariis* the murder of a slave, even by his owner, in case he had no legally recognized cause for his action, was punished by deportation, later by death on the cross for those of lower rank, or by the simple death penalty for persons of higher class.[117]

The economic use of slaves by their masters was unrestricted during the Republic. Slaves could be bought or sold, subject to certain rules of sale laid down by the magistrates, or their services could be hired out.[118] The pay for these services accrued to the master who might allow the slave to retain some or all of it. The characteristics of slaves as thinking agents made them usable, however, in activities which necessitated a corresponding adjustment of the laws of property. Thus a slave could receive property, whether by gift or as heir or through business dealings;[119] but since he could not have *dominium*,[120] the ownership of the thing acquired was vested in his master. The object itself was taken by the slave *domini animo*[121] *sed servi corpore*.[122] Under specific consent of his owner for a definite case or under a wider authorization which would include a given transaction a slave was able to deal in the master's name (*domini nomine*) with third parties, either for the purpose of acquiring or of alienating property for his master.[123] In such transactions the slave became a physical extension of his owner's legal person,[124] capable of acting as his owner might act and limited only by his incapacity to engage in fields where civil law forms prevailed. In order that the master might be completely protected, the doctrine developed that unauthorized business activities of slaves were effective only in so far as they benefited the owner.[125] The rights of third parties in such transactions were protected by the prae-

tors who defined in their edicts the liability of the masters for the actions of their slaves. Such liability occurred, and gave a legal motivation to the injured party, whenever a slave acted under definite authorization[126] or when the owner accepted the results of the slave's acts by receiving an addition to his patrimony therefrom.[127] The liability incurred was limited in the first case by the extent of authorization. In the second case it was restricted to the amount acquired.

A slave or a free person might be appointed to act in a representative capacity, as an *institor*, who was legally recognized as authorized to engage in business with the property of his employer or master. If the *institor* was a slave the owner was liable to the extent of the authorization in the articles of appointment,[128] which were an essential element in the arrangement.[129] It became convenient, as a result of this development, for a master to assign to a slave a definite piece of property, of whatever sort, and with it the right to add to this property whatever accrued, even without knowledge of the owner, by way of investment, earnings, gift, interest, produce, or wages. Such assignment was termed a *peculium*.[130] This property became a *quasi-patrimonium* of the slave[131] and was *de facto* the slave's own property, subject however to partial or total recall at the owner's wish.[132] It was not alienable by the slave any more than other property, unless the slave also had the privilege called *libera administratio*.[133] A slave with both *peculium* and *administratio* might engage in almost any industrial or mercantile enterprise, subject to no control except the possibility of having his privileges recalled. In this way he might accumulate a sizable fortune, which, with permission, could be used to purchase his freedom. A bargain struck by a slave with his owner for manumission could be enforced under the Empire. It is not certain that this practice was permitted under the Republic. A slave-owner might be impelled to grant the use of the *peculium* for the purchase of freedom either as an incentive to effective work on the part of the slave or as an investment. From the latter point of view an owner was well protected, since by special recognition of the nature of the *peculium* on the part of the praetors this fund was distinguished from the *patrimonium*. A slave using his *peculium* could render his master liable to a civil action[134] if the case involved only the *peculium* itself.

---

[114] This included the debauching of a female by one not her master, Just., *Digest* 47: 10, 9, 4.

[115] *Digest* 11: 3, 1. In a case reported by Pliny the accusation included bribery of the slave of a man's scribe, Pliny, *Epistulae* 6: 22, 4.

[116] Mommsen, Th., *Römisches Strafrecht*, 780.

[117] *Digest* 48: 8, 1, 2; Affolter, *Persönlichkeit des herrenl. Sklaven*, 141.

[118] For the hire of a *vicarius* see Just., *Digest* 14: 3, 11, 8.

[119] Buckland, *Law of slavery*, 131-144.

[120] *Qui in potestate nostra est nihil suum habere potest*, Gaius, *Institutes* 2: 8, 7.

[121] *Cf*. Just., *Digest* 41: 2, 3, 12.

[122] *Digest* 41: 2; 44: 1; 44: 2; Buckland, *Law of slavery*, 131.

[123] Buckland, *Law of slavery*, 159-186.

[124] As in the instance in which a banker at Puteoli sent a slave to Cicero at Rome in order to convey a property, Cicero, *Ad Atticum* 13: 50, 2.

[125] *Melior condicio nostra per servos fieri potest, deterior non potest*, Just., *Digest* 50: 17, 133. In principle a master could sue, but could not be sued, on the contract of a slave, see Buckland, *Law of Slavery*, 157.

[126] It is called an *actio iussu eius*, Gaius, *Institutes* 4: 70; Just., *Digest* 15: 3, 5, 2; 15, 4.

[127] *Actio de in rem verso*, see Buckland, *Law of slavery*, 176-186.

[128] The *lex praepositionis*, Just., *Digest* 14: 1, 1, 12; 3, 16, 5.

[129] Buckland, *Law of slavery*, 169-174.

[130] For a discussion of the term see Pernice, Lothar A., *Labeo*, 1: 121; Buckland, *Law of slavery*, 187-206.

[131] Just., *Digest* 15: 1, 5, 3.

[132] Partial recall did not abrogate the fundamental right of holding a *peculium*, as the total recall did.

[133] *Digest* 12: 6, 13; 13: 7, 18, 4.

[134] *Actio de peculio*, Buckland. *Law of slavery*, 207-233.

Much more definitely and completely than in the civil law the personality of the slave was, from the earliest period, recognized by the Roman sacral law. It granted them, within circumscribed limits, the capacity of assuming obligations and the right of independent activities which were legally binding.[135] This is to be seen in the following facts: that slaves could bind themselves by vows to the same gods and under the same formulas as free persons [136] and could make dedications in payment of vows undertaken; [137] and in acceptance of the view that burial places of slaves, if clearly marked as such, were *loci religiosi* as dwellings of the *manes* of the dead slaves.[138] Slave members of associations, when once admitted into *collegia* with the consent of their owners,

necessarily carried on certain activities inside these organizations as legal agents who were independent of their owners.[139] No law is known which required that the body of a slave, like that of a free person, must be given burial. If, however, a third party carried out the burial the slave-owner might be subject to action for the expenses incurred. From this fact it may be assumed that the necessity of burying his slave was a religious obligation resting upon the master.[140] Although the magistrates took no action to enforce this ethical and social obligation resting upon the slave-owner, the law did, in fact, give its sanction to a claim to recompense on the part of the person who had carried out the burial in lieu of the slave's master.

[135] For a full discussion see Pernice, A., Zum römischen Sacralrecht, *Sitzungsb. Akad. Berl.*, 1173-1182, 1886.

[136] *Ibid.*, 1174.

[137] *CIL* 1: 1167; *cf.* 602. At Minturnae under the Republic altar dedications were made by servile *collegia* to Venus, Spes, Ceres, and Mercury Felix, Johnson, J., *Excavations at Minturnae* 2: 1, 8, 2; 12, 1; 21, 14; 22, 1; 23, 1; 25, 5.

[138] Just., *Digest* 11: 7, 2: *locum in quo servus sepultus est religiosum*. *Manes* were ascribed to slaves even in Republican

times, Varro, *De lingua latina* 6: 24: *prope faciunt diis manibus servilibus sacerdotes*.

[139] Payment of initiation fees were made, necessarily, and monthly dues and fines were exacted from fellow members.

[140] *Cf.* the *lex collegii Lanuv.* of A. D. 136 in Dessau, *ILS*, 7212, col. 2, 3-4: *quisquis ex hoc collegio servus defunctus fuerit, et corpus eius a domino dominave iniquitatae sepulturae datum non fuerit.*

XIII. SLAVERY UNDER THE ROMAN EMPIRE TO CONSTANTINE THE GREAT

SOURCES AND NUMBERS OF SLAVES

After the reorganization of the Roman state and the establishment of the *pax Romana* by Augustus Caesar external wars which had previously played the primary role in meeting the demand for slaves, and piracy which had been only secondary to it during the years 120 to 66 B. C., lost their outstanding positions in this respect,[1] in comparison with the customary peacetime methods of enslavement. These included slavery by birth, by exposure of infants, by sale of children under stress of poverty, by sale of slave material from border tribes to the slave trade within the boundaries of the Empire, by voluntary submission to slavery, and by penal condemnation to slave status.[2] This shift of emphasis in the sources of supply in the long view of the three centuries here under discussion materially decreased the total numbers of persons available for the slave traffic; and it became a factor also in a change which took place in the prevailing attitude toward the slaves and in their treatment.

During the first two decades after Actium a considerable number of captives taken in the wars waged by Augustus in the West were sold as booty of war.[3] The

eight thousand warriors of the Salassi, an Alpine tribe conquered in 25 B. C., were sold under the condition that they could not be manumitted within twenty years,[4] evidently to avoid future revolts.[5] The Astures and Cantabrians, sold into slavery in 22 B. C., later killed their owners and returned home. Hence they had presumably been sold in Spain. On their reconquest by Agrippa in 19 B. C. no mercy was shown them.[6]

In the eastern sectors of the empire he enslaved the citizens of Cyzicus because they had killed Roman citizens; but Tyre, and Sidon, punished in 20 B. C. for seditions were merely deprived of autonomy; [7] but there was no enslavement of the population.[8] Captured Pannonians were sold in 12 B. C. under condition of export from their home districts.[9] In 11 B. C. the Bessii, a Thracian tribe, were enslaved.[10] Quintilius Varus, when

[1] Wallon, H., *Histoire de l'esclavage dans l'antiquité* 3: 110. Gsell, S., *Mélanges Gustave Glotz* 1: 397-398, Paris: Les Presses Universitaires de France, 1932.

[2] See Mommsen, Th., *Juristische Schriften* 3: 11-20, Berlin, Weidmann, 1907. Buckland, W. W., *The Roman law of slavery*, 397-436, Cambridge, Univ. Press, 1908.

[3] This was the fate of the Alpine tribe of the Salassi in 25 B. C.

to the number of 44,000 of whom 8,000 were fighting men. The sale was held near the Alps in Northwestern Italy at Eporedia, Strabo, 4: 6, 7.

[4] Dio Cassius, 53: 25.

[5] *Cf.* Suetonius, *Augustus*, 21, who regards this proviso as an evidence of *virtutis moderationisque*.

[6] Dio Cassius, 54: 5.

[7] *Ibid.*, 54: 7, 6. *Cf.* Suetonius, *Augustus*, 47.

[8] This is intimated in Barrow, R. H., *Slavery in the Roman Empire*, 4, London, Methuen and Co., 1928.

[9] Dio Cassius, 54: 31, 3.

[10] *Ibid.* 34, 7. *Cf.* the *servus natione Bessus*, in Dessau, H., *Inscriptiones Latinae Selectae* (= Dessau), no. 7492, 3-4, Berlin, Weidmann, 1906.

governor of Syria, sold the inhabitants of Sepphoris into slavery.[11] The total number of the Jews sold as slaves or otherwise assigned to slave labor in the Jewish war led by Vespasian is given at ninety-seven thousand.[12] This total is strongly confirmed by detailed numbers, amounting to about forty-three thousand, which do not include those captured after the fall of Jerusalem.[13] After the Jewish revolt under Hadrian (A. D. 132-135) an unknown number, possibly a large one, was thrown upon the eastern market.[14]

Frequent opportunities must have come to the Roman legionaries during border wars and revolts to purchase captives at military sales which have remained unrecorded in the literature of the time. This is suggested by the appearance of slaves in the possession of active soldiers and veterans in Egypt.[15] When Hadrian changed the frontier policy of the Roman Empire to one of permanent defense along borders strongly protected either by nature or by artificial *limites*,[16] the numbers of those captured in border wars must have declined sharply.[17] Under the quiet regime of Antoninus and the defensive wars of M. Aurelius along the Danube relatively few captives could have been taken. The large numbers of Persians who are reported as having been captured and sold into slavery by Alexander Severus in A. D. 232 [18] were more probably ransomed by the Persian king.[19] Throughout the period of the civil wars of the third century capture of foreign enemies in large numbers would be improbable, and none are claimed in the *Scriptores historiae Augustae*. A limited number of Germans may have been taken captive by Maximinus in A. D. 235-236.[20] The report in the fictitious letter of

Claudius to Brocchus [21] that two or three Gothic women captives were assigned to each Roman soldier after the war of Emperor Claudius with the Goths is utterly worthless. These Gothic captives were apparently settled upon the land as *coloni*.[22] The alleged twenty thousand Sarmatians captured by Carus [23] need not be considered, since they, also, may well have become *coloni*. Suspicion is thrown upon all of these numbers by the modest claim made for Aurelian [24] that, as tribune of the sixth legion in Gaul, he captured and sold into slavery three hundred Franks.[25]

After the defeat in 36 B. C. of Sextus Pompey, whose activities were quite generally classed as piracy by the ancient authorities,[26] and after the suppression of the renewed piratical activities of the Illyrians which was completed with the battle of Actium,[27] security of travel and trade on the sea was maintained throughout the greater part of the Mediterranean for the next two centuries by the establishment and constant maintenance of the imperial standing fleet.[28] With the increase of security upon the sea, piracy in the Mediterranean itself may be eliminated as an important method of meeting the demands of the trade in slaves, although both piracy and kidnapping continued to occur sporadically,[29] particularly in the outlying waters of the Red Sea and Black Sea, which were neglected by the imperial fleets.[30] But the effects of these sources upon the total supply could not have been great. Kidnapping of free persons on land also was greatly reduced in Italy under the efficient imperial government [31] and likewise in the provinces.[32]

A relative increase in the numbers of slaves obtained through the peacetime sources of enslavement finds considerable support in the sources available, although it cannot be established statistically. These methods of enslavement helped to compensate for the losses in slave numbers through the decline of captivity in war. The

---

[11] Josephus, *Jewish War* 2: 5, 11.

[12] *Ibid.* 6: 9, 3.

[13] *Ibid.* 3: 7, 31, 36, 10, 10; 4: 7, 5, 8, 1. *Cf.* 4: 9, 1, 8; 7: 6, 4.

[14] They were sold at Hebron and Gaza, *Chronicon Paschale* (ed. Dindorf) 1: 474. Hieronymus, *Ad Zachariam*, 11, 5; *Ad Jeremiam* 31: 15. "Hadrian's Market" at Gaza remained a vivid memory for centuries, *Chronicon Paschale* 1: 474.

[15] *BGU* 4: 1108 of 5 B. C., alimentation contract in which the soldier was probably father of the slave child. *Cf.* 4: 1033, 2, 9 of A. D. 104-105. *Papiri della Società Italiana* 5: 447, 11-19, of A. D. 167. *BGU* 1: 316 of A. D. 359 = Mitteis, L. and Ulrich Wilcken, *Grundzüge und Chrestomathie der Papyruskunde* 2: 2, 271, Leipzig and Berlin, B. G. Teubner, 1912. *Cf. Studien zur Paläographie und Papyruskunde* 20: 71; *Griechische Papyrusurkunden der Hamburger Bibliothek* (= P. Hamb.), 63. See also the wax tablet found in Egypt containing record of a slave sale to a soldier of the fleet at Ravenna, *Zeitschrift der Savigny-Stiftung, Rom. Abt.* 42: 452-468.

[16] Cheesman, G. L., *Auxilia of the Roman Army*, 107-111, Oxford, Clarendon Press, 1914.

[17] Hadrian had to supply slaves from Cappadocia for service in his camps, *Scriptores historiae Augustae, Hadrian*, 13, 7.

[18] See the forged document, *Scriptores historiae Augustae, Severus Alexander*, 51, 6. For the forgery of the *acta senatus*, see Lecrivain, C., *Études sur l'Histoire Auguste*, 98-99, Paris, Fontemoing, 1904.

[19] *Scriptores historiae Augustae, Severus Alexander*, 55, 3.

[20] The report about them indulges in ridiculous exaggeration, *Scriptores historiae Augustae: Maximinus* 12: 1, and in the fictitious speech, 13, 1.

[21] *Scriptores historiae Augustae, Claudius*, 8, 6.

[22] *Ibid.*, 9, 4: *factus limitis barbari colonus e Gotho.*

[23] *Scriptores historiae Augustae, Carus*, 9, 4.

[24] *Scriptores historiae Augustae, Aurelian*, 7, 1.

[25] *Cf.* the five hundred slaves assigned by him to the estate of Valerian, *ibid.*, 10, 2.

[26] Appian, *Civil Wars* 2: 105; 5: 143; Strabo, 5: 4, 4; Velleius Paterculus, 2: 73, 3: Lucan, *Pharsalia* 6: 421-422; Florus, 2: 18, 1.

[27] Ormerod, H. A., *Piracy in the ancient world*, 254.

[28] Article "*classis*" in Pauly-Wissowa, *R. E.* 3: 2635-2643; Starr, C. G., *The Roman imperial navy*, 114-115, 119-120, 171-174. Ithaca, Cornell Univ. Press, 1941.

[29] Lucian, *De mercede conductis*, 24.

[30] Ormerod, H. A., *Piracy in the ancient world*, 257-260.

[31] Augustus suppressed *grassatores* who had previously seized and turned over free persons and slaves to the landowners who kept them in *ergastula*, Suetonius, *Augustus*, 32, 1. *Cf. Tiberius*, 8, 2.

[32] No complaint of seizure of free persons into slavery appears among the many papyri from Egypt under Roman domination which deal with slavery, although the suppression of illegal enslavement of free persons was never completely effected. See Seneca, *Controversiae* 10: 4, 18; *Digest* 39: 4, 12, 2. For North Africa, see Gsell, *Mélanges Gustave Glotz* 1: 398.

importance claimed by Mitteis [33] for the practice of infant exposure in increasing slave numbers in all parts of the Empire, including Italy itself, has received ample confirmation from the papyri for the province of Egypt.[34] This constant practice must have been accelerated in the different sections of the Empire at each period of special local depressions. To the problem of the civil status of abandoned children who had been reared as foundlings the general attitude of the Roman law was that the finder of the child might rear it either as slave or free, subject to the qualification that proof of free birth might at any time establish the race status of the foundling.[35] In Egypt the assertion of free birth justified the removal of a foundling boy from the house of its owners.[36]

The importance of infant exposure and rescue into slavery in Asia Minor is revealed in the rescript of Trajan in A. D. 112, replying to an inquiry of Pliny the Younger upon the status of such children when free-born.[37] In Bithynia, according to Pliny, it was a problem of importance appertaining to the entire province.[38] From the correspondence of Trajan with Pliny it appears that an edict of Augustus and letters of Vespasian, Titus, and Domitian had previously dealt with the question as it had arisen in Achaea and Lacedaemon.[39] Trajan emphasized the necessity of hearing such claims to freedom and definitely denied the right of the *nutritor* to a claim for the amount expended in the upbringing of the foundling.[40] By a decision rendered in the early third century,[41] in case a slave child were exposed without knowledge or desire of the owner of its mother, the slave-owner might lay claim for its restoration, but he must pay to the one who had reared it the amount expended upon its upbringing or upon its apprentice training to a trade.

The frequency of infant exposure in North Africa, with the probability that slavery would ensue for the abandoned child in a majority of cases, is well attested.[42]

A number of papyri dealing with foundlings in Egypt emphasize the great prevalence of the practice of infant exposure in that province.[43] The adoption of a free-born male foundling in Egypt by a person of Egyptian classification was penalized by legislation which imposed a twenty-five per cent payment upon the estate of the adopter when he died.[44] No restrictions upon the rearing of girl foundlings appears; and the actual occurrences of rearing of foundlings of both sexes into slavery must have been very numerous.

Regarding the number of the homebred slaves in comparison with the *empticii*, the statement in Petronius [45] that thirty boys and forty girls were born in one day on the Cumae property of Trimalchio is purely comic exaggeration; but an indication of actual numbers of *vernae* for central Greece may be gained in the manumission inscriptions from Delphi.[46] Assuming that all the slaves who were homeborn are declared as such and that the slaves who are not specifically mentioned as house-born were purchased, for the period of priesthoods XVII-XXVI (*ca.* 53 B. C. to A. D. 20 as a rough estimate) the homeborn slaves show a decline in proportion to those purchased to the point where the ratio would be about three born in the home to five purchased. This is to be compared with the relation of about one homebred to each purchased slave in the period *ca.* 100 B. C. to *ca.* 53 B. C.[47] The relative number of the house-born slaves is still sufficient to suggest that bearing of children by slave women continued to be encouraged by slave-owners in Greece.

In Egypt the *oikogeneis* appear with great frequency in the papyri of the period of Roman rule.[48] Their

[33] Mitteis, L., *Reichsrecht und Volksrecht in den östlichen Provinzen des römischen Kaiserreichs*, 361, Leipzig, B. G. Teubner, 1891.

[34] *Cf.* Seidl, E., *Kritische Vierteljahrschrift* 25: 311, 1932; Taubenschlag, R., *The law of Greco-Roman Egypt in the light of the papyri*, 53, New York, Herald Square Press, 1944.

[35] Mommsen, Th., *Juristische Schriften* 3: 11. Buckland, W. W., *The Roman law of slavery*, 402.

[36] See *Oxyrhynchus Papyri* 1: 37, 17-18, of A. D. 49.

[37] Pliny the Younger, *Letters* 10: 65-66.

[38] *Ibid.*, 10: 65.

[39] Reading with Mommsen, *edictum . . . Augusti ad Achaeam pertinens* in Pliny, *Letters* 10: 65.

[40] Pliny, *Letters* 10: 66. *Cf.* Mommsen, Th., *Juristische Schriften* 3: 1. The decision regarding alimentation costs was altered by Diocletian. See Just., *Codex* 5: 4, 16 and Pauly-Wissowa, *RE* 11: 469.

[41] Just., *Codex* 8: 51, 1.

[42] Minucius Felix, 31, 4; Tertullian, *Ad nationes* 1: 5; *Apologeticum*, 9; Lactantius, *Institutiones* 6: 20; *cf.* CIL 8: 410, 2394, 2396, 2773, 3002, 3288, 7078, 7754; 8¹: 11576, 12778, 12879, 13328; 8, Suppl. 4: 22928, 22993, 24687; Gsell, S., *Inscriptions latines de l'Algérie* 1: 1810, 3209, 3229, 3771, Paris, Champion, 1922.

[43] *Oxyrhynchus Papyri* 1: 37, 7 and 38, 6; 73, 26. BGU 2: 447, 24 (where among the δουλικὰ σώματα is a women called Κοπρή); 4: 1058, 11; 1106, 22; *cf.* 12: 1107, 9; *Papiri della Società Italiana* 3: 203, 3; *Greek Papyri in the Rylands Library*, 178, and *Papyrus Reinach*, inventory no. 2111, edited by Collart in *Mélanges Gustave Glotz* 1: 241-247. Possibly also BGU 4: 1110, 6; see Taubenschlag, R., *Zeitschrift der Savigny-Stiftung, Rom. Abt.* 50: 146, n. 4, 1930.

[44] *Gnomon of the Idios Logos*, BGU 5: 41 and the difficult section 107. *Cf.* Seckel-Meyer, *Sitzungsberichte der Akademie der Wissenschaften, Berlin*, 453-454, 1928; Maroi, F., *Raccolta di Scritti in onore di Giacomo Lumbroso*, 377-406; Riccobono, Salvatore, Jr., *Il Gnomon dell' Idios Logos*, 47, 178-181.

[45] Petronius, 53.

[46] They are collected in *GDI*, 1684-2342.

[47] The basis of this rough calculation of the priesthoods is that of Georges Daux, *Chronologie Delphique*, 71-79. For the estimated ratio of the home-born to the purchased slaves in the first half of the first century B. C. see the text of chapter five, pp. 32-33.

[48] First century: BGU 1: 297, 16; *Oxyrhynchus papyri* 1: 48, 4; 2: 336; Boak, A. E. R., *Michigan papyri* 2: *Papyri from Tebtunis* (= Pap. Teb. Mich.), 121, *recto* 4, 7, 4, Ann Arbor, Univ. of Michigan Press, 1933; *Papiri della Società Italiana* 11: 1131, 26. Second century: BGU 1: 193, 12, 15, 18, 23; 2: 447, 24-27, five house-born slaves; 3: 859, 3; *Oxyrhynchus papyri* 4: 714, 14; 723, 3; 12: 1451, 26; *The Tebtunis papyri* 2: 407, 7, 8, 18; *Papiri della Società Italiana* 5: 447, 17, 22; 6: 690, 4, 15; 710, 13; *Papyrus Cattaoui*, col. 6 = *Mitteis-Wilcken, Grundzüge und Chrestomathie der Papyruskunde* 2: 2, 372, VI; *Papyrus Berlin*, inventory no. 13295 and *Papyrus*

economic importance in comparison with that of purchased slaves is indicated by section 67 of the *Gnōmōn* of the *Idios Logos*[49] by which the sale for export of house-born children of slaves who were Egyptian nationals was prohibited in principle; and their owners, in case this provision was broken, were punished with heavy property confiscations ranging from twenty-five per cent of their property to the whole of it. Accessories to such a transaction were likewise penalized. The scope of the application of this law was widened by the assumption of the court, where proof of status was not available, that the mothers of the slaves were of Egyptian nationality.[50]

There are no definite statements to be found in the literature of the Empire of the total number of slaves at any given time in any one place; and rare are the indications of their number in relation to the number of the free population. From a statement of the physician Galen,[51] it is to be inferred that Pergamum, his native city, numbered about forty thousand citizens in the last half of the second century and that, if the wives and slaves were added, the population, eliminating all consideration of children, would number more than one hundred and twenty thousand. This indicates a rough estimate on Galen's part of forty thousand adult slaves in Pergamum, or one slave to every two free adults of the citizen class, that is thirty-three and one-third per cent.[52] The inclusion of children and non-citizen inhabitants would further lower the percentage of the total slave numbers. As compared with that in the villages of the Nile Valley this ratio of slaves is extraordinarily high. In relation to the total population of the Egyptian village of Ptolemais Hormos in the year 192 the proportion of slaves has been established at about seven per cent.[53] In a papyrus of A. D. 229-230 [54] out of a total of four hundred sixty-six men subject to the dike corvée

six were slaves. From a daybook giving poll-tax payments at Theadelphia in A. D. 128-129[55] it appears that, out of two hundred eighteen available names of slaves, freedmen, and free men subject to the tax, only two were slaves[56] and two were freedmen.[57] The ratio of slaves suggested by this is one slave and one freedman to each one hundred of free population in the lowest and poorest class in Egypt, which was by far the most numerous element of the population.

Confirmation of the very small percentage of slaves among the lower classes in Egyptian villages and towns is available for Philadelphia in the Fayum in the first century. Two papyri[58] show only one slave as against two hundred eight free persons among those who pay the *syntaximon*. An alphabetical register of poll-tax payments in Philadelphia in A. D. 30,[59] gives two slaves[60] out of a total of fifty-four names of persons whose status is clearly revealed in the document. In a papyrus of A. D. 94,[61] a house-to-house report of males from villages of the Arsinoite nome who are listed as subject to the poll tax, there are about two hundred thirty-two names of persons whose status is quite certain. Among these no slaves appear. The numbers of slaves owned by the poll-tax payers of the towns and cities of Egypt would unquestionably be somewhat higher than the low percentage indicated above for the poorer village inhabitants. This statement is supported by the long but fragmentary account of the *amphodarchos* of the street called *Apollōniou Parembolē* in Arsinoe of the Fayum in A. D. 72-73.[62] The total number of poll-tax-paying males (restricted to those between the ages of fourteen and sixty) living on the street was three hundred eighty-five.[63] The total of the slaves who are listed as living upon the street is fifty-two. Nine slave children who had not yet reached the fourteenth year must be deducted from this number [64] and three more slaves be-

London, inventory no. 2226, ed. by W. Schubart in *Raccolta di scritti in onore di Giacomo Lumbroso*, 49-67. Third century: *Papyrus Oxyrhynchus* 9: 1205, 4; 1209, 15; 12: 1468, 13; *The Tebtunis papyri* 2: 406, 26; *Papyri Fiorentini* 1: 4, 9, p. 27, 7(?) Mitteis-Wilcken, *Grundzüge* 2: 2, 362, 4, 17-18. Early fourth century: *Griechische Urkunden der Papyrussammlung zu Leipzig*, no. 26.

[49] *BGU* 5: 1, 67.

[50] Schubart, W., *Raccolta di scritti in onore di Giacomo Lumbroso*, 59-60; Reinach, Th., *Nouvelle revue historique de droit français et étranger*, 173-174, 1920-1921.

[51] Galen 5: 49 in the edition of Carl Kühn.

[52] Cf. Beloch, J., *Die Bevölkerung der griechisch-römischen Welt*, 236.

[53] Wilcken, U., *Griechische Ostraka* 1: 683, Leipzig and Berlin, Giesecke and Devrient, 1899, where the computation was based upon the list of those engaged in government dike work in the *Charta Borgiana*, N. Schow, *Charta papyracea graece scripta*, Rome 1788 = Preisigke, F., *Sammelbuch griechischer Urkunden aus Ägypten*, no. 5124, Strassburg, Trübner, 1915. Slaves were subject to the dike corvée, if their masters were, see Oertel, F., *Die Liturgie*, 78, Leipzig, B. G. Teubner, 1917, and *BGU* 7: 1634, 11, 15. Slaves of priests of first-class temples were exempt, *BGU* 1: 176 = Mitteis-Wilcken, *Grundzüge und Chrestomathie* 1: 2, 83.

[54] *BGU* 7: 1634, col. I.

[55] P. Col., no. 1, edited by Westermann, W. L. and C. W. Keyes, *Tax lists and transportation receipts from Theadelphia*, New York, Columbia Univ. Press, 1932.

[56] P. Col., no. 1, recto 1a, 36. Taxation on slaves followed the taxes to which their owners were subjected, Mitteis-Wilcken, *Grundzüge und Chrestomathie* 1: 1, 198; Taubenschlag, R., *Zeitschrift der Savigny-Stiftung* 50: 162, 5, 1930.

[57] P. Col., no. 1, recto 1b, 3, 27; 5, 6.

[58] *Papyrus Cornell*, no. 21, Westermann, W. L. and C. J. Kraemer, *Greek papyri in the library of Cornell University*, New York, Columbia Univ. Press, 1926, and *Papyrus Princeton*, no. 2, Johnson, A. C., and H. B. Van Hoesen, *Papyri in the Princeton University collections*, Baltimore, The Johns Hopkins Press, 1931.

[59] *Papyrus Princeton*, no. 9.

[60] Reading Ἡρακλ[είδης] δοῦλ(ος) Πτολεμαίου in col. 2, 2 and Ἡρακλῆς δοῦλος (inserted above the line) Πετεσούχου in col. 2: 10.

[61] *Papyrus London*, no. 257, *Greek papyri in the British Museum* 2: 19-28, London, 1898.

[62] *Papyrus London*, no. 261 + *Papyrus Erzherzog Rainer* + *Papyrus London*, no. 260, published by Wessely, C., *Studien zur Palaeographie und Papyruskunde* 4: 58-83, Leipzig, Eduard Avenarius, 1905.

[63] *Ibid.*, col. 2, 16.

[64] See Wessely, C., *Sitzungsberichte der Wiener Akademie der Wissenschaften, Phil.-hist. Klasse* 145: *Abhandlung* 4, 15-58.

longing to women listed as Alexandrians.[65] Among the poll-tax subjects upon this street, therefore, not above ten per cent were slaves. The proportion of slaves to total free inhabitants, including the Roman and Alexandrian citizens and the Jews, was no more.[66]

The belief formerly held regarding the tremendous numbers of slaves resident in Rome and Italy during the period of the early Empire [67] was founded upon actual instances of large numbers of slaves attached to the households of individual Romans of high rank or of great wealth and upon exaggerated general statements which appear in the literature of the first century. The fact is attested by Frontinus [68] that a group of slaves was selected out of Agrippa's ménage after 33 B. C. to take care of the aqueducts of Rome. In the time of Sextus Julius Frontinus, who was curator of the water supply of the city under Trajan, the number of the slave aqueduct guards which belonged to the state was two hundred forty. It is a plausible assumption that the group of slaves originally turned over by Agrippa to the state out of his slave property did not exceed this number.[69] Pedanius Secundus, *praefectus urbis* in A. D. 61 and one of the richest men in Rome, maintained four hundred slaves.[70] Seneca [71] mentions a proposal once made in the Roman Senate that slaves should be set apart from free persons by a distinctive dress. It became apparent, however, that a great danger would ensue if the slaves should become conscious of their numbers in relation to the free in Rome. Because of the indefiniteness of the time to which this debate in the Senate is to be assigned and because of the general character of the statement as it appears in Seneca, its value upon the size of the slave population is small.

The same skepticism must be applied to the *mancipiorum legiones*, a throng of slaves said to be so large that a *nomenclator* must be used in the Roman household because of them; [72] to the dream of Adeimantus in Lucian,[73] that he is to have two thousand choice and handsome slaves of every age; and to the suggestion of masses of slaves in private possession of a single person implied in the question addressed to a slave by Trimalchio [74] as to the division of the household he belonged to, and in the response that he was of the fortieth *decuria*.[75] It cannot be denied, however, that large numbers of slaves were maintained in the households and retinues of wealthy persons, particularly at Rome, as a matter of vulgar display.[76] An acceptable approximation of the slave numbers attached to a prominent and wealthy Roman *gens* is obtainable from the names of slaves and freedmen of the noble Statilii which appear in the tomb of that family through five successive generations covering approximately the period 40 B. C. to A. D. 65.[77] All of their slaves and freedmen may not, of course, be enumerated in the inscriptions; but the total number which appears, omitting obvious repetitions, is approximately 428, distributed as follows: male slaves 192, females 84, freedmen 100, freedwomen 62. The total of slaves, freedmen and freedwomen who can be definitely assigned to the ownership of T. Statilius Taurus Corvinus, *consul ordinarius* of A. D. 45, is eight.[78] To T. Statilius Taurus Sisenna, consul of A. D. 16, and to his son three slaves and three freedmen can be assigned; to Statilia Messalina, wife of Nero, three or four slaves and one freedman. These numbers have the value of checking fairly closely with the slave figures assigned to the Roman *imperatores* of the third and second pre-Christian centuries by Apuleius of Madaura. He gave eight as the number owned by a consular, Marcus Antonius, seven by one of the Carbos, two maintained as camp servants by Manius Curio, who conquered Pyrrhus, and five slaves as camp assistants taken to Spain by the elder Cato. Completely credible is the statement of Apuleius that he himself traveled to Oea (modern Tripoli) in North Africa with only one slave attendant.[79] This may be accepted as typical for a man of middle class upon his travels in the second century after Christ.

The necessity of avoiding an exaggerated idea of the numbers of slaves maintained by the great Roman families is also seen in the decision of Augustus in A. D. 12 restricting to twenty the number of slaves who might attend their masters into exile.[80] The actual number of attendant slaves who accompanied a prosperous man when traveling is best seen in the eye-witness report of Galen of his overland journey from Corinth to Athens with a friend who was accompanied by two slaves after he had sent others, probably two or three, around to Athens by sea.[81] Seneca, one of the wealthiest men of his day, considered that he was traveling simply and

---

[65] *Papyrus Erzherzog Rainer*, col. 5, in Wessely, C., *Studien zur Paläographie und Papyruskunde* 4: 69.

[66] For a general statement of the small number of slaves in Egypt, *cf.* Meyer, E., *Kleine Schriften* 1: 192, and Wilcken, U., *Griechische Ostraka* 1: 703.

[67] E. g. 900,000 slaves for Rome alone, Marquardt, J., *Römische Staatsverwaltung* 2: 124, Leipzig, S. Hirzel, 1884, taken from the older editions of Friedländer's *Sittengeschichte Roms.*

[68] Frontinus, *De aquaeductibus urbis Romae*, 98.

[69] *Ibid.*, 116.

[70] Tacitus, *Annals* 14: 43, 4.

[71] Seneca, *De clementia* 1: 24, 1.

[72] Pliny, *Natural history* 33: 26. *Cf.* Juvenal, *Satires*, 5, 66-67.

[73] Lucian, *Navigium sive vota*, 22.

[74] Petronius, *Satyricon*, 47.

[75] *Cf.* the comic exaggeration, *ibid.*, 53, that 30 male and 40 female *vernae* were born one day on the Cumaean estate of Trimalchio and the statement that not one slave in ten knew his master by sight, *ibid.*, 37. See also Seneca, *De vita beata* 17: 2.

[76] Seneca, *Epistulae morales* 110: 17: *cohors culta servorum . . . ostenduntur istae res, non possidentur. Cf.* the *grex capillatus* of Martial 2: 57; Juvenal, *Satires*, 6, 141 and 352; Apuleius, *Metamorphoses* 2: 2.

[77] *Corpus Inscriptionum Latinanum* (= *CIL*) 6²: 6213-6640.

[78] Statilius, no. 17 in Pauly-Wissowa, *RE* 3A: 2191.

[79] Apuleius, *Apologia*, 17.

[80] Dio Cassius, 56: 27, 3. *Cf.* the ten slaves originally permitted to Calpurnius Piso when he was exiled by Caligula, *ibid.*, 59: 8, 8.

[81] Galen, *De animi morbis* 5: 18, ed. Kühn.

roughly when accompanied by one cartload of slaves.[82] Even at Rome numerous persons who ranked above the proletariat must have been without any slaves, or at least possessed of no more than one or two.[83]

For the third century the scanty and unreliable sources of information leave a confused record of extravagant numbers of slaves, with conflicting evidence of surprisingly small groups of them owned by provincial governors, by aspirants to the imperial seat, and by actual emperors. Proculus, a rich native of the Maritime Alps, is said to have armed two thousand of his own slaves when he attempted to seize the power in A. D. 280;[84] but the third-century historian, Aelius Cordus, recorded, not the number of the slaves owned by each emperor, but who they were.[85] A revolt in Sicily which occurred in the third century is described as a *quasi quoddam servile bellum—latronibus vagantibus*.[86] In the mind of the writer of a fictitious letter in the *Scriptores Historiae Augustae*, seven slaves and seven other attendants who may be slaves were a sufficient entourage for a proconsul of Syria.[87] The total of the slaves of the Emperor Tacitus, all of whom he manumitted, was less than a hundred.[88] The writers of the history of the Augusti are notoriously untrustworthy. The approach to the slave numbers which they offer must be even more wary and incredulous than that followed above in the discussion of the statements which have come down to us respecting the hordes of slaves owned by individual masters in the first Christian century.

The Augustan legislation upon the subject was embodied in the *lex Fufia Caninia* of 2 B. C. and the *lex Aelia Sentia* of A. D. 4. The *Fufia Caninia* made the number of testamentary grants of freedom permitted to *cives Romani* dependant upon the total number of slaves owned by any one Roman citizen master. One who owned from three to ten slaves was permitted to manumit one half of them in his will; one who owned eleven to thirty, one third of the total. If the slaves of the Roman citizen numbered from thirty-one to one hundred, he might free one fourth of them; if their numbers ran one hundred to five hundred only one in five, or twenty per cent, might be freed by testamentary manumission. The law further provided that no Roman citizen could free by testament more than one hundred, however many slaves he might have.[89]

The *lex Aelia-Sentia*, promulgated six years later, put an age minimum upon the right of manumission by citizens, withholding altogether from Roman youths under twenty years of age the right to free their slaves, if the liberations took place at Rome,[90] and permitting grants of freedom only to slaves over thirty years of age. The rigidity of this enactment was lessened by the provision that the law might be averted in case an acceptable reason for the freedom had been presented, and this reason had been approved by a committee of ten persons made up of five senators and five *equites*.[91]

It has been customary among the modern historians dealing with Augustan social policy to explain these two laws as a part of the total social amelioration policy of Augustus which aimed at the restoration of the *mores majorum* of Rome.[92] This view has the support of two ancient sources. These are: a suggestion made by Dionysius of Halicarnassus antecedent to the passing of the earlier law and a motivation of the act given by Suetonius.[93] Dionysius had left Rome in 8 B. C. and his *History* was published in 7 B. C. Before he left Rome the problem which led to the promulgation of the first of the two laws was already being discussed. His statement is that in the old days of Rome slaves owned by families of Roman citizens, when they were manumitted, were by the fact of Roman liberation admitted to Roman citizenship. This was at that time, according to Dionysius, warranted by their deserts and their uprightness of character. " But in our time," he proceeds, " things do not stand thus. Affairs have come to such a pass of confusion and the fine characteristics of the Roman state have come to such a pass of dishonor and sordidness that some slaves who gather their wealth from robbery, and breaking into houses, and prostitution, or any other vile method of acquiring gain, buy their freedom with these monies, and straightway they are Romans." [94] Dionysius was particularly concerned with the deterioration of the city of Rome alone as shown by his suggestion that these vicious elements, when manumitted, should be ejected from the city and sent into some colony.

The explanation for the passage of the *lex Fufia Caninia* as given by Suetonius in his *Augustus* is that the emperor wished to preserve the Roman citizen body from the infusion, by the right of intermarriage gained by these freedmen, of the alien blood of these former slaves into the pure Roman blood stream. Since this restriction applied only to the one form of granting

---

[82] Presumably four or five slaves, Seneca, *Epistulae morales*, 87, 2.

[83] Juvenal, *Satires*, 3, 286; 9, 64-67, 142-147. A veteran without a slave is mentioned in *Scriptores historiae Augustae Hadrian*, 17, 6.

[84] *Scriptores historiae Augustae, Firmus*, 12, 2.

[85] *Scriptores historiae Augustae, Gordian*, 21, 4.

[86] *Scriptores historiae Augustae, Gallienus*, 4, 9.

[87] *Scriptores historiae Augustae, Claudius*, 14, 7-15.

[88] *Scriptores historiae Augustae, Tacitus*, 10, 7.

[89] Gaius, *Institutes* 1: 40-43; Pauly-Wissowa, *RE* **12**: 2355. This law was still operative in the late third century, *Scriptores historiae Augustae, Tacitus*, 10, 7.

[90] Gaius, 1: 38-41; Ulpian, 1: 13; *Institutiones* 1: 6, 4-7. It was, however, possible in Spanish Salpensa if a *iusta causa manumittendi* has been proven before a council of the *decuriones*. Bruns, C. G., *Fontes iuris Romani antiqui* (= *FIR*), 7th ed. 146, Tübingen, J. C. B. Mohr, 1909: *Lex municipalis Salpensana*, 28.

[91] Gaius, 1: 18; Ulpian, 1: 12. Cf. Partsch, Josef, *Zeitschrift der Savigny-Stiftung, Rom. Abt.* **42**: 246, 1921.

[92] See Last, Hugh, in *CAH* **10**: 432-434, 450, 464.

[93] Suetonius, *Augustus*, 40, 3.

[94] Dionysius of Halicarnassus, *Roman History* 4: 24, 6.

liberty by will, leaving three other legal methods of manumission available to Roman citizens, more credence is to be placed in the suggestion of Dionysius than in the motivation ascribed for it by Suetonius. Certainly it was felt that the number of testamentary manumissions by Roman citizens had become a scandal and a danger, particularly in Rome itself. A rational motive has been presented by Buckland in his book upon the Roman law of slavery. The reason he advances is a fiscal one, namely to prevent too heavy a loss to the

heirs of the manumittor.[95] The jurist Ulpian, moreover, has clearly presented the inheritance motive as that which lay behind the *lex Aelia Sentia*.[96] A *lex Visellia* of A. D. 24, by which freedmen were excluded from the municipal magistracies, was apparently activated by a different desire, that of restricting the public rights of those slaves who had gained their freedom, whatever the method of manumission which had been followed.[97]

---

[95] Buckland, W. W., *The Roman law of slavery*, 546-547.

[96] *Regulae Ulpiani*, 14-15. See Girard, Paul Frédéric, *Textes de droit Romain*, 393, Paris, A. Rousseau, 1895.

[97] Pauly-Wissowa, *RE* 12: 2418.

XIV. THE ROMAN EMPIRE IN THE WEST

ECONOMIC ASPECTS OF SLAVERY

Italy together with the island of Sicily had been the outstanding center of exploitation of slave labor in the two closing centuries of the Roman republic, especially in agricultural production, in comparison with other parts of the Empire. They retained this dubious honor through the first and into the second century after Christ. In Rome and throughout Italy a development of large capital accumulations had taken place which had resulted from the privileged position gained for the peninsula under Rome's leadership in the period from 150 B. C. to A. D. 100. Along with these concentrations of investment money there came a marked increase in the Italian peninsula of handicraft production based upon extensive, though by no means complete, employment of slave labor in the large types of shops. This may have been upon a scale even greater than that which had characterized Athenian manufacturing in the fifth and fourth centuries B. C.[1]

The effects of this development and the relative relation of free and slave labor in all fields of industrial production in the West have been presented in such detail by Herman Gummerus[2] that a recapitulation of his work is unnecessary.[3] In the field of agrarian production Sicily and Sardinia seem to have adhered to the old system of farming by the native peasantry except upon the imperial domains and upon the large estates which were held by rich landowners.[4] In Italy in the early part of the first century after Christ an ample supply of slave labor for use in agriculture and industry was still available.[5] The literature of the first century

increasingly mentions, however, the independent farmer of small holdings.[6]

In respect to the tendency of the landholding system in lower Italy abstracts of mortgage records for the territory of the Ligures Baebiani near Beneventum[7] give interesting information. They contain the designations of the *fundi* by the names of their owners as they existed at a period of land assignment which cannot be placed later than the time of the Triumvirs.[8] They give, also, the owners and assessment valuations of the properties in the time of Trajan when the state loans upon the properties were made. Somewhat less than ninety owners are recorded for the earlier period. This group had shrunk to fifty owners in the time of Trajan (or about fifty-five per cent of the original number).[9] The result for the Beneventine territory is to establish an increase in the size of the large holdings with a marked falling off in their total number, along with a continuation of the small farm holdings at about the same absolute number, as determined by the assessment ratings.[10]

In the region of the Po valley also records of mortgages upon *fundi* near Placentia and Veleia[11] indicate a diminution of the small farm holdings through their assimilation into the *latifundia*. Pliny the Younger gives us a contemporary illustration of this trend in northern Italy in his statement that he was purchasing *praedia* " in the vicinity of my own lands " to the value of three million sesterces.[12] Nevertheless, the surprising fact, even in

---

[1] *Cf.* ch. III.

[2] Gummerus, Herman, Industrie und Handel, Pauly-W., *RE* 9: 1452-1512.

[3] *Cf.* Barrow, R. H., *Slavery in the Roman empire*, 22-129. For a discussion of the slave in the household see *ibid.*, chapter two. His chapter three deals with the agricultural use of the slaves. In chapter four Barrow treats the importance of the slave for commerce and industry.

[4] Rostovtzeff, M., *Soc. and econ. hist. Roman empire*, 196-197.

[5] Frank, Tenney, *Economic history of Rome*, 434.

[6] Lucan, *Bellum civile* (*Pharsalia*) 1: 170; Seneca, *Epistulae morales*, 114, 26; 123, 2; Martial, *Epigrammaton* 1: 17, 3; 3: 58, 33; 7: 31, 9; 11, 14; Tacitus, *Germania*, 25.

[7] *CIL* 9: 1455.

[8] Mommsen, Theodor, Die italische Bodentheilung, *Hermes* 19: 399, 1884.

[9] *Ibid.* 401; Carl, Gertrud, Die Agrarlehre Columellas, *Vierteljahrschrift für Sozial und Wirtschaftsgeschichte* 19: 23-25, 1926.

[10] *Ibid.*

[11] *CIL* 11: 1147.

[12] Pliny the Younger, *Epistulae* 3: 19, 1, 4.

the Po valley, is the persistence of smaller farms directly administered by their owners. Inasmuch as the small farmers had never been responsible for the use of slaves in agriculture upon any impressive scale, the problem of the increase or decrease of agricultural slavery in Italy is dependent upon the methods of production employed upon the larger land complexes. The agrarian writer Columella was concerned with winning back the nobility and the wealthy men of Italy to an active interest in the practice of agriculture.[13] He was convinced that the best and economically most advantageous method of farm organization, if it were possible to enlist the interest of the farm owner and count upon his constant supervision, was that furnished by a strong nucleus of slaves who must be selected with attention to their physical and mental adaptability for their particular work.[14] The tasks assigned to them must be specialized.[15]

The type of farming in which Columella was primarily interested was vineyard culture, with olive cultivation and the raising of cattle as secondary considerations.[16] In his view the cultivation of cereal and fodder crops was essential only for the provisioning of the estate personnel and its cattle.[17] The hiring of free hands to meet the demands of the seasonal peaks of work is to be presupposed for Columella's estate which was based upon slave labor, as well as in the organization advised by Cato[18] in the second century B. C. It is quite clear that cultivation by tenants (coloni) was widely practised in Columella's time;[19] and Columella advised that where tenant leasing was employed the colonus should be one who did his own farm work rather than a city dweller who operated the leased farm by means of slaves.[20] The proportional relation between the use of slaves and the cultivation by coloni is not to be made out from Columella's treatise. The amount of space he gave to the system of farming by slaves is based upon the fact that he accepted the farm work by slaves under direct supervision of the farm owner as the best form of agriculture from the political point of view and that he desired to further that type of organization.[21]

The excavation of villas about Pompeii has brought evidence that slaves were used in wine growing in that region.[22] Estimates of the number of slaves employed in these villas based upon the number of the rooms in a given part of the villa[23] or upon the number of rooms and the calculation of fifteen or sixteen slaves taken from Cato[24] are not valid, because the freedmen and regular hired labor must have been housed in the villa as well as the slaves.[25] In the burial place of the familia of the Epidii at Pompeii,[26] out of twenty-five names covering several generations fifteen, at the most, are names of slaves. The one conclusion, therefore, which can safely be drawn is that upon some of the wine-growing estates about Pompeii a nucleus of slaves was still maintained for the work of the vineyard as in the time of Cato.

In the Po valley at the end of the first century Pliny the Younger and his neighbors were employing outside hired labor rather than using slaves of their own when they were compelled to take their agricultural properties over under the system of direct management.[27] The system of farming under lease to tenants was well advanced[28] and continued to progress in the second century as against the method of farming with slaves. The profitableness of large scale agricultural production with slaves was obviously coming to an end in Italy in the second century.[29] The tenant farmers (coloni) were, as a rule, free men although slaves also must occasionally have appeared as tenants.[30]

Intensified study of the sigillata ware produced at Arretium and found in Italy, of the exported pieces of Arretine pottery found in the Rhenish provinces, and of the local Celtic manufacturing of similar ware,[31] has produced important results which are closely connected with the problem of the decrease in industrial slavery in the West.[32] The period of the predominance of the

---

[13] Columella's protreptic purpose is emphasized by Carl, G., Vjschr. f. Soz.—u. Wirtschaftsgeschichte 19 : 40, 43.

[14] Columella, De re rustica 1 : 9, 19. Cf. Gsell, Stéphane, Esclaves ruraux de l'Afrique romaine, Mélanges Gustave Glotz 1 : 415, n. 1, Paris, Presses Universitaires de France, 1932.

[15] "Ne confundantur opera familiae, sic ut omnes omnia exsequantur"—Columella, De re rustica 1 : 9, 5.

[16] Ibid. 1 : 2, 39.

[17] Gummerus, Herman, Der römische Gutsbetrieb, Klio: Beiträge zur alten Geschichte, Beiheft 5 : 77, 1906.

[18] Cato, De agricultura, 10, 1; 137.

[19] "Hi vel coloni vel servi sunt"—Columella, op. cit. 1 : 7, 1.

[20] Ibid. 1 : 7, 3.

[21] Cf. Heitland, W. E., Agricola, 57, Cambridge, Univ. Press, 1921.

[22] The iron stocks for confinement and punishment of slaves in these villas are pictured in Della Corte, M., Notizie degli

scavi di antichità, 277, fig. 4, 1923. One of them is reproduced in Rostovtzeff, M., Soc. and econ. hist. Roman empire, pl. IX, fig. 2, opp. p. 62. Wooden stocks are shown by Della Corte, Notizie degli Scavi, 1922, 463, fig. 3. The stocks show fourteen apertures and ten apertures for binding the legs, indicating that seven slaves or five slaves might be thus punished at one time, not fourteen or ten slaves as decided by Della Corte.

[23] Rostovtzeff, M. I., Soc. econ. hist. Roman empire, 516.

[24] Cato, De agricultura, 11; cf. Day, John, Agriculture in the life of Pompeii, Yale classical studies 3 : 196, 1932.

[25] Pliny the Younger, Epistulae 2 : 17, 9.

[26] Della Corte, Notizie degli scavi, 303 ff., 1916.

[27] Pliny the Younger, Epistulae 3 : 19, 7. It was necessary at busy seasons to bring hired labor from the towns to supplement hired country labor, ibid., 9 : 20, 2.

[28] Reliqua colonorum, ibid. 3 : 19, 6; necessitas agrorum locandorum, ibid. 7 : 30, 3.

[29] Rostovtzeff, Soc. econ. hist. Roman empire, 190; Frank, Tenney, Econ. hist. Rome, 422-423, 480.

[30] Quidam fundum colendum servo suo locavit, Just., Digest 15 : 3, 16. Possible examples based on the appearance of nomina alone, without praenomina and cognimina, CIL 6; 9276; 10: 7597.

[31] For a brief statement of the decentralization process in the pottery industry see Gummerus, Industrie und Handel, Pauly-W. RE 9 : 1478.

[32] Hermet, Frédéric, La Graufesenque 1, vases sigilles; 2, graffites, Paris, Librairie Leroux, 1934; Oxé, A., Die Töpferrechnungen von der graufesenque, Bonner Jahrbücher 130 : 38-

relief pottery manufactured in Italy at Arretium must be compressed within the brief space of the years 25 B. C. to A. D. 25.[33] Upon the pots made during the first phase of the work at Arretium the names appear of the potters, who seem all to be slaves, along with the stamp of the shop owner. The names of their owners appear in the genitive case after the slave names.[34] In the later phase of the output of the Arretine pottery the workmen no longer sign their names, only the stamp of the firm appearing. The succession of the owners in the control of the Perennius shop has been determined by Oxé as M. Perennius Tigranus followed [35] by M. Perennius Bargathes, who is in turn succeeded by Crescens and Saturnus.[36]

Highly important for the management methods of these potteries and for the social and economic situation of the slave artists is the discovery of Dragendorff that the slaves, in a number of instances, changed their masters as the potteries were sold by one owner to another.[37] This is best seen in the case of the slave Pantagathus, whose signature is ligatured into an unmistakable monogram. He appears first as Pantagathus, slave of the shop owner Rasinius.[38] Later, when Rasinius combined with G. Memmius in the ownership of the pottery works, this slave appears as *Pantagathus Rasini Memmi*, presumably being under the divided slave-ownership of these two proprietors.[39] Later the same Pantagathus goes over both into the pottery works and into the slave-ownership of C. Annius.[40]

This transition of slave-ownership and factory connection can be followed also in the case of Eros who appears under successive shop owners as slave of C. Annius, then of C. Tellius, eventually passing into the ownership and factory of P. Cornelius.[41] Dragendorff

has presented other cases in which corresponding ownership and factory change can be proved by signatures. He was also confident that this corresponding change of factory ownership and slave-ownership can be followed through analysis of the technique of the workmanship in cases of anonymous workmen whose signatures do not appear on the pottery. In such cases the question whether the workmen were free or slave must be left undecided, though the probability for the Arretine shops is that they were slaves.

The fact that the slaves of the early Arretine period were permitted to place their signatures upon their work is in itself of great value in respect to the social and economic position which they had attained as artists of high technical ability and recognized importance. The imprint of the slave's name must have been regarded as an item of value in the sale of the wares produced, inasmuch as it appears conjointly with the trade mark of the firm.

In view of the widespread custom throughout the Empire of assigning Greek or Latin names to slaves whatever their nationality might be [42] the identification of these slave potters as Greeks or Oriental half-Greeks [43] is precarious. The technical skill required for excellent work in the handicrafts could, of course, readily be acquired by craftsmen of any nationality who were trained under the prevalent apprentice system of the time. This is shown by the rapid development of the production of artistic relief ware in southern Gaul where the artists, to a considerable degree, were natives of the locality; and their work successfully competes in quality and beauty with the relief pottery put out at Arretium.[44] The purchase of the slave artisans at Arretium by the new owner of the pottery when the shop changed hands is to be regarded as a rational business procedure which must have been of frequent occurrence.[45] From the several instances of simultaneous change of factory and personnel of the slave craftsmen at Arretium it is apparent that in these shops the connection of the slaves with their work was, to them, economically and socially more significant than their servile subordination to their owners.

99, Bonn, Marcus, and Weber, 1925; Oxé, A., *Arretinische Reliefgefässe vom Rhein*, Frankfurt am Main, J. Baer, 1933; *Frühgallische Reliefgefässe vom Rhein*, Frankfurt am Main, 1934; Dragendorff, H., *Gnomon* 10: 353-363; Dragendorff and Carl Watzinger, *Arretinische Reliefkeramik mit Beschreibung der Sammlung zu Tübingen*, Reutlingen, Gryphius-Verlag, 1948.

[33] Dragendorff, H., *Gnomon* 10: 356-357 and *Arretinische Reliefkeramik*, 15-17.

[34] E. g. *Cerdo M(arci) Perenni, Nicephorus M. Perenni*. For the identification of this Perennius as the shop owner with full name of *M. Perennius Tigranus* see Oxé, *Rh. Mus.* 59: 132-137, 1904; Gummerus, Industrie und Handel, Pauly-W., *RE* 9: 1487; Oxé, *Arretinische Reliefgefässe*, 29.

[35] *Ibid.*, 35.

[36] Dragendorff, H., *Gnomon* 10: 356.

[37] Almost all of the slave artists who made the molds in the workshop of Gaius and Lucius Annius are known to have been previously employed in the Rasinius pottery works. Dragendorff-Watzinger, *Arretinische Reliefkeramik*, 144, identifies the slave artisans Pantagathus, Eros, Chrestus, and Isotimus who appear in the two pottery works as being in each case but one person although working under different shop owners. See also Oxé, *Bonner Jahrbücher* 130: 86, 1925.

[38] Oxé, *Arretinische Reliefgefässe vom Rhein*, 47, vase from the Loeb collection in Boston.

[39] *Ibid.*, 124; cf. *CIL* 10: 8056, 248.

[40] Oxé, *Arret. Reliefgef. vom Rhein*, 39, 50, 121, 122, 126.

[41] Cf. *Cer(do) Ras(ini)*, Oxé, *Arret. Reliefgef. vom Rhein*, 57, and *Cerdo Perenni*, 60, 68.

[42] See ch. XV at the beginning.

[43] Dragendorff, *Gnomon* 10: 358; Gummerus, Industrie und Handel, Pauly-W., *RE* 9: 1507-1510.

[44] Dragendorff, *Gnomon* 10: 360. The Celtic names which appear in the pottery accounts of the Graufesenque may be taken as proof of Celtic nationality because the direction of the alteration of proper names was in this period consistently toward those of Greek or Latin origin.

[45] Cf. mortgage foreclosure on land near Sardis which included the slave labor upon it. Buckler, W. H. and D. M. Robinson, *Sardis* 7: 1, col. 1, 15-18; foreclosure upon a mine pit near Thoricum with its inventory of slave miners, Dittenberger, *SIG*³, 1191; ὅρος ἐργαστηρίου καὶ ἀνδραπόδων πεπραμένων ἐπὶ λύσει; cf., Guiraud, Paul, *La propriété foncière en Grece jusqu'a la conquete romaine*, 440, n. 4: ὑποκεῖθαι τῷ θεῷ τὰ βόσκηματα καὶ τὰ ἀνδράποδα καὶ τὰ [ἐργαλ]εῖα πάντα, Paris, Imprimirie Nationale 1893; Dura-Pergament 23, *Münchener Beiträge* 19: 382-289, 1934; sublease of a slave prostitute to visiting brothel-

No agreement has as yet been arrived at upon the important question whether, in the process of the provincial development of the pottery industry, the system of production by slave labor which prevailed in the Arretine potteries of Italy was transferred into Gaul and into the German provinces. Gummerus leaned to the belief that the Gallic potters were chiefly free men.[46] Oxé leaves the problem undecided,[47] inclining to the conclusion that the craftsmen of the pottery accounts were slaves, serfs or freedmen, because they are designated by single names without patronymic in the genitive.[48] Joseph Loth has followed the unsatisfactory practice of assuming that the workmen were slaves because names such as Cervesa, Vinoulos, Primos, Secundus, Tritos, Tertius, and Moretoclatos sound like slave names.[49] Little evidence, however, has appeared in connection with the Gallic ceramic production to indicate that the workmen were of servile class, except in four cases.[50] The pottery accounts alone do not furnish a firm basis for decision because, as a regular procedure, whether found in Italy or Gaul, they fail to give any indication of the status of the workmen who appear on the lists of payments.[51]

The validity of the view of Oxé that the single *nomina* of the workmen indicate slave status breaks down upon the observation that the names of the owners of the potteries, who must be free men, also appear singly, without patronymics.[52] Most of the general considerations, furthermore, point to the decision that the Gallic potters were to a great extent free men, as advocated by Gummerus and Bohn. In a period, for example, in which the two sources of cheap labor, war and piracy, were being seriously curtailed[53] it is improbable that the type of labor which prevailed in Italy, the center of slave employment in the West of that time, could successfully be transplanted into Gaul and the German provinces where slavery had not previously been strongly

developed. In Italy itself at the same time the habit of slave employment had not asserted itself in all handicrafts or in all parts of the peninsula[54] in the same degree in which it appears in the ceramics industry of Arretium.[55] Slavery undoubtedly had existed among the Gauls before the Roman conquest;[56] but the institution played no conspicuous role in comparison with vassalage and clientage in those parts of the country which were removed from the immediate influence of Roman society.[57] An increase in domestic slavery no doubt took place in the Gallic provinces with the gradual adoption of Roman customs in the century after the conquest;[58] but it is not possible to determine the extent to which it was carried. Vassalage of the several Gallic types still persisted as the dominant feature of labor control; and the total of the slave population in Gaul never approached the proportional strength which it had attained in Italy.[59]

Some of the potters from the Rhine region who appear with signatures on the early Celtic ware were certainly free men.[60] It is also significant that the woodworkers, ironworkers, and stoneworkers of Germania Superior who appear upon two *ex voto* inscriptions from Dijon[61] call themselves *clientes* of the men to whom the dedications are made. They were not slaves.[62] In view of the lack of positive evidence, therefore, to prove the introduction of industrial slavery into Gaul and, negatively, the observation that there was an increasing difficulty in maintaining the supply of slave labor for the Empire, it is little likely that the potters of Gaul and of the Rhine region were of slave class. The failure of industrial slavery to spread from Italy into Gaul when the decentralization of handicraft production began may, indeed,[63] be regarded as an important factor

---

keepers by the lessees of a city brothel in the Arsinoite nome in Egypt, *PSI* 9: 1055a, middle of the third century after Christ.

[46] Gummerus, Industrie und Handel, Pauly-W., *RE* 9: 1513. In this decision A. Grenier, *Festschrift für August Oxé,* 88, Darmstad, Wittich Verlag, 1938, agrees with Gummerus.

[47] Oxé, *Banner Jahrb.* 130: 80-81.

[48] *Ibid.,* 87.

[49] Loth, Joseph. Le graffite de Blickweiler dans le Palatinat, *Académie des inscriptions et belles-lettres, Comptes rendus de seances* 71, 1924.

[50] Mentioned in *CIL* 13: 120, col. 2; *Q. Verri Achillaei Mascurieus fec(it), Asus f(e)c(it) Cigetou, Nasso I( ) s(ervus) f(ecit), Vitalis M. s(ervus) f(ecit)*; see *Germania: Korrespondenz-blatt d. römisch-germanischen Kommission* 7: 67, Frankfurt a. Main, 1923.

[51] See the list of thirteen women weavers from Pompeii with single *nomina, CIL* 4: 1507; the fragmentary account of pottery deliveries from Arretium with four single names of potters without indication of status, *CIL* 11: 6702, 1; and the Blickweiler and Graufesenque accounts from Gaul.

[52] See Oxé, A., Töpferrechnungen von der Graufesenque, *Bonner Jahrb.* 130: 43-58, 1925, *Casti of(ficina),* nos. 5, 8, 10, 16, 20, 22, 23, 25; *[of(ficina) M]odesti,* no. 13; *of(ficina) G[erma . . .]* nos. 32, 33; *ibid.,* 140-141, 2, 380-394, 1936.

[53] See above, p. 84.

[54] Free-born workmen were relatively much more numerous in the smaller country towns than in Rome and in northern Italy. They were strongly represented in the industries, Gummerus, Industrie und Handel, Pauly-W., *RE* 9: 1505.

[55] See the conclusions of Gummerus upon the glass industry, in Pauly-W., *RE* 9: 1500, and his tables upon the goldsmiths and jewellers, based upon the inscriptional materials, with conclusions regarding other types of handicraftsmen, *ibid.* 9: 1504-1506.

[56] Caesar, *Bellum Gallicum* 4: 19.

[57] Note the *clientes et obaerati* of Orgetorix, *ibid.* 1: 4 and the 600 feudal *soldurii* of Adiatunnus, 3: 22. *Cf.* vassalage instead of debtor slavery as the outcome of debt to a wealthy noble, *ibid.* 6: 13, and the *ambacti clientesque* of the *equites,* 4: 15.

[58] Jullian, Camille, *Histoire de la Gaule* 4: 371, Paris, Librairie Hachette, 1913.

[59] Gummerus, Industrie und Handel, Pauly-W., *RE* 9: 1513.

[60] *C. Tigranus, M. Valerius* and *Sex. Varius.* See Oxé, *Frühgallische Reliefgefässe,* 1.

[61] *CIL* 13: 5474, 5475.

[62] The one slave who does appear in *CIL* 13: 5474, *Carantillus serv(us) actor ex voto,* is clearly distinguished as to status. The nameless brickmaker whose account of ten-days' work was found upon a tile in Montenach, Clement, R., Un compte d'un briquetier Gallo-Romain, *Revue des études anciennes* 29: 205-207, 1927, was probably a free hand, not a slave brickmaker.

[63] *Cf.* the failure in Ptolemaic Egypt of the early Greek system of using slaves in the handicrafts to establish itself, pp. 47-48.

in explaining the decline of slavery in the western part of the Roman Empire. Agricultural labor among the Celts before Caesar's conquest of Gaul, as also among the German tribes, had been carried on by men who were vassals of the wealthier elements of their own tribes. Though not totally independent their position must be differentiated from that of the actual slave class.[64] Under the Roman provincial organization the system of peasant vassalage was maintained. The tilling of the soil was in the hands of native peasants who were clients, debtors, or free leaseholders of the aristocracy of the towns and of the owners of the large villas which have become well known through excavations in the regions along the left bank of the Rhine.[65]

Little is known of the system of land tenure in the province of Britain or of the amount of slavery which developed there. Tacitus ascribes to the British chieftain, Calgacus, a knowledge of slavery.[66] This may be either a proof of the existence of slavery in pre-Roman Britain or a reflection in the free areas of Britain of conditions developing in that portion of the island which had already been conquered by the Romans. It has been generally assumed [67] that the peasants of Britain fell into a position somewhat similar to that of the Roman *coloni*.[68] Inasmuch as the Romanization of Britain occurred at a time when the decline in slave employment had already begun in Italy it is a reasonable supposition that industrial slavery, and probably agricultural employment of slaves, never developed to the point where they became important factors in the economic life of the island.

In respect to the Spanish provinces, although the information upon slave employment is again meagre, it is obvious that the type and degree of slavery must have varied greatly in different parts of the peninsula. In the regions along the coasts of Baetica and Tarraconensis and in the lowlands of Lusitania which had been urbanized by Carthaginian and Greek colonists long before the Roman domination [69] we may count upon a much greater intensity of slave employment than in the interior. For inner Hispania had stubbornly resisted domination by Rome until the conquest was completed under Augustus. Mention of freedmen of Roman colonists at Urso in Baetica in 44 B. C.[70] sufficiently indi-

cates, however, the presence of some slaves. The clause upon the retention by the Roman citizens of Salpensa of their rights over their freedmen is to be compared with this,[71] and the provisions, as well, upon the manumission of slaves by those of the inhabitants who were of Latin citizenship.[72]

Except for the gold mines of Spain, the mining properties taken over by the Roman state were sold to private owners [73] who seemed to have worked them chiefly by means of slave labor.[74] Rostovtzeff [75] believes that the mines belonged to the state and were leased to large-scale enterpreneurs. Under the revival of state ownership in the early Empire [76] and the change to a policy of letting out the mines to small lessees [77] slave labor was still used; [78] but the presence of free hired miners along with the slaves is equally evident.[79]

The earlier practice, which had been general throughout the Roman Empire, of condemning criminals, both slave and free, to work in the mines and quarries was still in evidence in Bithynia in the early decades of the second century [80] and in Egypt in A. D. 209.[81] The general tendency, however, noticeable under the early Empire, was to abandon the use both of slaves and of criminals and to turn to a more general use of free miners.[82] In Egypt, in the fourth Christian century, the policy of imposing work in the mines and quarries as

---

[64] Meyer, Eduard, *Kleine Schriften* 1: 179.

[65] Cumont, Franz, *Comment la Belgique fut romanisée*, 40-48, Bruxelles, Lamertine, 1919; Daremberg-Saglio, **5**: 877-881; Dragendorff, Hans, *Westdeutschland zur Römerzeit*, 41-48, Leipzig, Quelle und Meyer, 1912; Rostovtzeff, M. I., *Soc. econ. hist. Roman empire,* 208-211.

[66] Tacitus, *Agricola*, 31, 3: *recentissimus quisque servorum etiam conservis ludibrio est.*

[67] Haverfield, F., *Roman occupation of Britain*, 233-234, Oxford, Clarendon Press, 1924. Collingwood, R. G., *Roman Britain*, 54-56, 80, Oxford, Clarendon Press, 1945.

[68] Ordinance of the fourth century regarding the *coloni* in Britain, *Codex Theod.* 11: 7, 2.

[69] Rostovtzeff, M. I., *Soc. econ. hist. Roman empire*, 198.

[70] Bruns-Gradanwitz, *FIR*, no. 28 (*lex Ursonensis*), 95, 15, Tübingen, Siebeck, 1909.

[71] *Ibid.*, 30; reproduced in Dessau, *ILS*, 6088, 23.

[72] *Ibid.*, 6088, 28.

[73] *CIL* 2: 1001.

[74] Forty thousand slaves were used in the mines of Nova Carthago in the time of Polybius. See above, p. 72; Schulten, A., *CAH* 8: 323.

[75] Rostovtzeff, M. I., Geschichte der Staatspacht in der römischen Kaiserzeit bis Diokletian, *Philologus, Supplementb.* **9**: 448-450, 1904; also in his *Studien zur Geschichte des römischen Kolonates*, 361, n. 1.

[76] Seizure by Tiberius of the silver-mine pits in Spain owned by a certain Marius, Tacitus, *Annals* 6: 19; Pauly-W. *RE* **8**: 2005.

[77] Rostovtzeff, M. I., *Philologus, Supplementb.* **9**: 445-447, 1904; *idem, Geschichte des römischen Kolonates*, 360-361; Hirschfeld, Otto, *Verwaltungsbeamten*, 152-153, Berlin, Weidmann, 1905.

[78] *Lex metalli* of Vipasca in Lusitania, Dessau, *ILS*, 6891; reproduced in Bruns, *FIR*, no. 112, 11-18, 39-40.

[79] *Servos mercennariosque* [*in metallo Vipascensi*], Bruns-Gradenwita, *FIR*[7], 112, 48-49. Compare the punishments for damage to the mining properties which are differentiated for free or slave workmen, *Dessau, ILS*, 6891, reproduced in Bruns, *FIR*, no. 113, 28-31, 33-37, 40-45.

[80] Pliny the Younger, *Letters* 10: 31-32.

[81] Zucker, Friedrich, Urkunde aus der Kanzlei eines römischen Staathalters von Ägypten, *Sitzungsberichte der königlich preussischen Akademie der Wissenschaften* 27: 710-730, 1910, manumission of a condemned slave who had served five years in an alabaster quarry. *Cf.* Fitzler, Kurt, Bergwerke u. Steinbrüche im röm. Aegypten, *Leipziger historische Abhandlungen* 21: 121, Leipzig, 1910. The λειτουργοί in Egypt, so far as the documents permit a decision, appear to have been chiefly free laborers, Oertel, *Liturgie*, 83.

[82] *CIL* 2: 5181, 49; 3: 948-949; Gummerus, Industrie und Handel, Pauly-W., *RE* 9: 1507. Dalmatian tribe of the Pirustae transported to Dacia by Trajan to work the gold mines, Rostovtzeff, *Soc. econ. hist. Roman empire*, 229.

liturgical service demanded of the free population had succeeded in displacing the employment of slaves in this field of work.[83]

In North Africa after the Roman conquest much of the old Carthaginian estates which had been worked by slaves fell into the hands of Italians, veterans of the wars, and emigrants.[84] The reason for this change can no longer be ascertained. Its development displaced the agrarian use of slaves from its primary position as method of farming in North Africa to a secondary place;[85] and the imperial legislation of the second century dealing .with the large estates of North Africa[86] makes it clear that a large part of the farming at that time was done by sublease to peasants with small holdings (*coloni*). Unquestionably the large leaseholders (*conductores*) still used slaves on those parts of their holdings which they worked directly.[87] The *coloni* themselves may have had each his slave or two, as suggested by Gsell.[88] Despite the continued presence of slaves in the third, fourth, and fifth centuries, both in the *familiae urbanae* of the wealthy landowners and upon the landed estates, the day of agriculture slavery as the dominant feature of North African economic life had gone by.[89]

Only a few scattered statements have come down from the imperial period regarding the taxes derived by the Roman state from slaves as property. It did not exact a direct tax upon ownership of slaves, either from the provincial subjects or from Roman citizens. The contributions demanded by Vitellius in A. D. 69 from the freedmen of former emperors was merely a special levy exacted from them in proportion to the number of their slaves. This was made for the specific purpose of meeting the definite promise of largesses to his soldiers,[90] the number of the slaves owned by each person of that group being taken as a rough basis for rating the amount to be exacted from him. The old five per cent tax on manumissions (*vicesima manumissionum*) of the Republican period had been, in effect, a tax upon transfers of slaves to freedman status. This was continued by Augustus at the same rate and the tax was collected by a "procurator of the five per cent on liberation."[91] The increase to ten per cent of the slave's estimated value which was effected under Caracalla[92] was obviously unpopular or unremunerative to the government: for the previous five per cent rate was restored by Macrinus in A. D. 217.[93]

In A. D. 7 Augustus introduced for the first time the sales tax on slaves in its application to purchasers who were Roman citizens, but at the rate of two per cent.[94] This was extremely modest as compared with the slave-sales tax of about twenty per cent known from Ptolemaic Egypt. By the time of Nero the sales tax stood at four per cent. Nero's financial advisers attempted to relieve the purchasers of slaves of this burden and to compel the vendors to pay it. The effort was not successful because the vendors merely added the same amount to the price.[95] Tariffs on export and import of slaves who were bought for sale or use by the purchaser and were introduced into Italy were, presumably, exacted at the Italian harbors just as they were in other parts of the Empire. Failure to declare such slaves for customs duties was punishable.[96]

[83] Fitzler, *Bergwerke u. Steinbrüche*, 121-125. For the general tendency toward development of the compulsory labor system *cf.* Oertel, Fr., *Liturgie*, 87.
[84] Rostovtzeff, *Gesch. des röm. Kolonates*, 317-320; *lex agraria* of 111 B. C., Bruns-Gradenwitz, *FIR* 11, 83: *quem agrum locum populus Romanus locabit, quem agrum locum Latinus peregrinusve ex h(ac) l(ege) possidebit - - - - scripturam populo aut publicano item dare debeto*.
[85] The inadequacy of slaves for grubbing the soil is suggested as one of the causes of this change by Rostovtzeff, *Gesch. des röm. Kolonates*, 319.
[86] *Lex de villae Magnae colonis*, Bruns-Gradenwitz, *FIR*⁷, no. 114; altar dedicated to Hadrian, containing extracts from a *lex Hadriana*, no. 115; letters of procurators dealing with vacant lands, no. 116; decree of Commodus embodying a complaint of the peasants upon the *saltus Burunitanus*, no. 86.
[87] The four hundred slaves of the wife of Apuleius, *Apologia*, 93, presumably worked on her rural properties, Gsell, Stéphane, Esclaves ruraux, *Mélanges Gustave Glotz* 1: 405; *cf.* Just., *Digest* 33: 7, 27, 1; Rostovtzeff, *Soc. econ. hist. Roman empire*, 289.
[88] Gsell, Esclaves ruraux, *Mélanges Glotz* 1: 401.
[89] *Ibid.* 1: 403-407.

[90] Tacitus, *Histories* 2: 94.
[91] See the *proc(urator) XX libertatis* inscribed upon a wine amphora at Pompeii, in della Corte, M. *Pompeii, i nuovi scavi e l'anfiteatro*, 54, Pompei, Sicignano, 1930.
[92] Dio Cassius, 57: 9, 4 in the edition of V. P. Boissevain, 3, Berlin, Weidmann, 1931.
[93] Dio Cassius, 78: 12, 2.
[94] *Ibid.*, 55: 31, 4: τό τε τέλος τὸ τῆς πεντεκοστῆς ἐπὶ τῇ τῶν ἀνδραπόδων πράσει εἰς ἤγαγε.
[95] Tacitus, *Annals* 13: 31, 2; Westermann, *Slavery in Ptolemaic Egypt*, 44, n. 134.
[96] Just., *Digest* 39: 4, 16, 3.

THE PROVENANCE OF SLAVES, HOW SOLD AND PRICES PAID

In view of the ease of reciprocal interchange in Egypt of native Egyptian and Greek names it has long been conceded that attempts to determine the actual nationality of free men in that country after 150 B. C. through the name (as Greek because of a Greek name, as Egyptian because of Egyptian name) must be abandoned.[1] With respect to slaves, after that date the complete lack of authority of the linguistic affiliation of the name as indication of racial strain is evident in several cases in which the actual provenience of the slave is given by an adjectival ethnic designation. Slaves with Greek names whose native homes were in non-Greek localities are frequently mentioned.[2] In the papyri the inadequacy of the name to indicate the *origo* of the slave is attested by the phrase which frequently occurs in the contracts of sale of slaves " named so-and-so, or by whatever other name he (or she) is called."

The following examples are cited from the papyri to show the lack of relation between the provenance of the slave and the name: a German with the Greek name Hermes;[3] a Phrygian girl slave with the Canaanitic name Sambatis, also called by the Greek name Athenais;[4] a non-Italian slave who bears the Latin pet name Anilla, " little mother," whose local connection is indicated by the preserved ending [....]*pyllian*;[5] three generations of house-born slaves, all with Egyptian names except one grandson who was named Apollonius;[6] a Jewish woman ransomed by the synagogue who has the Greek name Paramone, with her child named Jacob;[7] a slave of Italian extraction bearing the Egyptian name Sambas;[8] a boy with the rare name of Greek derivation, Argoutis, who is by race a Gaul;[9] the Moorish or Negro girl called both Atalous and Eutychia.[10]

At Rome the German slaves who appear in the tomb of the Statilii bear for the most part names of Latin derivation such as Castus, Cirratus, Clemens, Felix, Strenuus, Urbanus, with the two Latinized transfers from the Greek, Nothus and Pothus, and a single localizing name, Suebus, which may or may not represent the exact tribal source of the slave.[11] Other countries which furnished slaves who bore Greek names are: Spain, Gaul, Dalmatia, Sardinia, Africa, and Thrace.[12] Numerous Jews of free status have appeared in the Jewish catacombs in Rome of the second and third centuries after Christ whose names were Latin and Greek.[13] There is reason, therefore, to conclude that some Jews may be represented among slaves who would appear, by evidence of the name alone, to be Greeks or of Italian stock. It must further be conceded that slave names derived from cities, districts, or countries (such as Asia, Ephesius, Smyrna, Thraissa, etc.) may only indicate the place of purchase of the slave or some other purely fortuitous association, rather than the nativity.[14]

A safe guide to the derivation of slaves lies, however, in the indication by adjectival *ethnikon* of the *natio* of the slave, because, according to the Roman law, such a statement was required of the vendor when a slave was offered for sale, with right of action by the purchaser for annulment of the sale if this statement was not given.[15] Upon this basis the evidence of the inscriptions and papyri leads to the following conclusions. (1) The number of slaves derived from the peoples living beyond the borders of the Empire was relatively small, in numerical ratio of one to eight of those who were certainly from within the Empire.[16] (2) The great majority of the slaves who appear in any province of the Empire were native to that locality. This fact cannot be taken, however, as proof of racial derivation because of uncertainty as to the original home of the parents of these slaves. (3) The wide displacement and mobility of the free inhabitants of the Empire in the first two centuries of the Christian era were also, in some degree,

---

[1] Strack, M., *Archiv für Papyrusforschung* 1: 208; Otto, W., *Priester und Tempel im hellenistischen Ägypten* 1 (2), 1, Leipzig and Berlin, Teubner, 1905.

[2] Καστα λία, a Syrian woman, *GDI* 2: 1686, 5-6; Διονυσία, an Egyptian woman, *GDI* 2: 1217, 5-6; Ἐργαῖος, a Bithynian, *Fouilles de Delphes* (= *FD*) 3¹: 565, 7-8; Εὐφροσύνα, a Cappadocian woman, *FD* 3³: 21, 7; Σέλευκος, a Syrian, *FD* 3³: 24, 4; Ἀφροδισία, a Sarmatian woman, *FD* 3³: 24, 4-5; Τρύφων, a Syrian, *FD* 3¹: 337, 3-4; Δορύπολις, a Thracian, *FD* 3³: 568, 6-7; Σωτηρὶς τὸ γένος βωτάν, probably from Botion near Ilium, *GDI* 2: 2151, 5-6.

[3] *Papiri della Società Italiana* 5: 447, 7.

[4] *BGU* 3: 887, 3. Cf. Preisigke, F., *Namenbuch*, 524, Heidelberg, 1922.

[5] *Archiv für Papyrusforschung* 11: 110; cf. *P. Oxyrhynchus* 6: 903, 32.

[6] *P. Oxy.* 12: 1468, 11-24.

[7] *Ibid.* 9: 1205, 4-5.

[8] *Papyrus Erzherzog Rainer*, 362, 84 in Wessely, C., *Stud. Pal.* 4: 69.

[9] *BGU* 1: 316, 11-14.

[10] *P. Strassburg*, inv. no. 1404, 25, in *Arch. f. Pap.* 3: 415-424.

[11] *CIL* 6 (2): 6229-6237.

[12] Gordon, Mary L., *Jour. Roman Studies* 14: 103, n. 4, 1924.

[13] E. g. Φλαβίε, Ἐμιλία, Νουμένις (= Νουμήνιος), Nikete, Parecorius (= Παρηγόριος), Eutycheti, Μαρυλλείνα (= Marullina), Νεικόδημος etc., see Leon, H. J., *Trans. Amer. Philol. Assoc.* 58: 210-233.

[14] Varro, *De lingua Latina* 8: 21: *alius appellat a regione quod ibi emit, ab Ionia Ionam, alius quod Ephesi Ephesium, sic alius ab alia aliqua re, ut visum est.* Cf. Gordon, M. L., *Jour. Roman Studies* 14: 98-101.

[15] Just., *Digest* 21: 1, 31, 21: *qui mancipia vendunt nationem cuiusque in venditione pronuntiare debent, plerumque enim natio servi aut provocat aut deterret emptorem.* In slave sales, according to Roman law in Egypt, see *BGU* 3: 887, 3; 1: 316, 13.

[16] See Bang, M., *Archäologisches Institut des deutschen Reichs, Römische Mittheilungen* 25: 246, 1910.

shared by its slave class in the transition of its members from free condition into slavery and, in some cases, after the enslavement had occurred.

Supplementing the collection of the material made by Bang[17] in relation to Egypt, the following certain allocations can be made of slaves who had been imported into that province. From the eastern areas there came: (a) Aethiopians or Negroes who customarily came to Egypt by way of the town Adule, an emporium of the Trogodytes;[18] (b) out of Asia Minor they came from Pamphylia,[19] Phrygia,[20] Lycia,[21] and Pontus;[22] from other parts of the East Mediterranean sector they were obtained from (c) Syria,[23] (d) Parthia,[24] (e) Crete,[25] (f) Cyrene;[26] (g) from the West we find them coming from Italy,[27] Germany,[28] Gaul,[29] and Mauretania.[30] In contrast with the statement of Bang[31] but in accord with the few examples cited in Bang's tabulation,[32] the number of Aethiopian or Negro slaves provable for the Roman Empire was small even in Egypt where they should be found in the largest numbers.[33] The same conclusion is to be drawn regarding slaves imported from countries eastward of the boundaries[34] since Bang cites but two slaves from India,[35]

seven from Arabia,[36] four from Parthia,[37] and one from Persia.[38] For the Oriental countries this is further proved by the lack of importance of the slave trade at the African, Arabian, Persian, and Indian ports, as depicted in the *Periplus Maris Erythraei*. Only Malao[39] on the Somali coast exported a few slaves,[40] and Opone, on the African coast below Cape Guardafui exported slaves of the better type to Egypt.[41] The parts of the Empire outside of Italy which furnished the greatest number of slaves whose places of origin can be strictly determined were Syria[42] and the provinces of Asia Minor.[43]

The explanation of this preponderance lies in the traditional attitude of the peoples of these lands which saw nothing disgraceful in the sale into servitude of members of their families[44] rather than in a predestined tendency to slavery as assumed with respect to the Syrians by Bang.[45] In support of his contention Bang cites passages from Cicero and Livy which imply only a tendency to accept *servitus* in the sense of political subjection.[46] Italy itself, with sixty-four examples takes the highest place in furnishing slaves whose *origo* can be ascertained.[47] Of that number fourteen are specifically given as *vernae*[48] and many more were probably of that class.[49] Spain furnished twenty-five slaves of

[17] *Ibid.* 229-244; cf. 27: 189, n. 1.
[18] See Pliny, *Natural history* 6: 29, 173; κοράσιον δουλικὸν φαιόν, *Papyrus Strassburg*, no. 79, 2, Leipzig, 1912; ibid., no. 1404 in *Arch. f. Pap.* 3: 419; οἰκέτης Αἰθιοπίδος γῆς, a negro with the Greek name Epitynchanon, *Aegyptiaca, Festschrift für Georg Ebers*, 102, Leipzig, 1897. The slave name Μέλας of *BGU* 2: 467, 11, cited as that of a negro by West, L., *Jour. Roman Studies* 7: 54, 1917, proves neither color nor race.
[19] *Papyrus Michigan*, inv. no. 5474, in *Arch. f. Pap.* 11: 110.
[20] *BGU* 3: 887, 3. The name of the slave Σαμβατίς is Canaanitic.
[21] *Ibid.* 913, 8.
[22] *Ibid.* 937, 9.
[23] Lucian, *Toxaris*, 28. The Syrians in *BGU* 1: 155, 178; 2: 618; 3: 816, cited by West, *Jour. Roman Studies* 7: 54, were probably not slaves.
[24] *Greek papyri in the British Museum* 2: xxi, 229: *natione Transfluminianus*.
[25] *Papyrus Leipzig*, 5, 7 in Mitteis, L., *Griechische Urkunden der Papyrussammlung zu Leipzig*, Leipzig, Teubner, 1906. Cf. ibid., 4, 12.
[26] Zereteli, G., and P. Jernstedt, *Papyri russischer und georgischer Sammlungen* 3: 27, 6, Tiflis, 1930.
[27] Wessely, C., *Stud. Pal.* 4: 69, line 366 (= *Papyrus Erzherzog Rainer*, line 88). A slave named Cerinthus attests a document with signature written in Latin, *P. Oxy.* 2: 244.
[28] *PSI* 5: 447, 25.
[29] *BGU* 1: 316, 12-13. Cf. Clement of Alexandria, *Paedagogus* 3: 4, 2.
[30] *CIL* 3: 6618. Possibly *BGU* 3: 728 of the Byzantine period.
[31] Bang, *Archäologisches Institut des deutschen Reichs, Röm. Mitt.* 25: 248. Cf. Rostovtzeff, M., *Social and economic history of the Roman Empire*, 66, Oxford, Clarendon Press, 1926.
[32] Bang, *op. cit.*, 229-230.
[33] In Bang's list there are six slaves from Aethiopia, omitting *Scrip. hist. Aug., Elagabalus*, 32, 5. Three more Aethiopian slaves are to be added from the papyri, see above, n. 18.
[34] This view is opposed to that of Février, J. G., *Essai sur l'histoire politique et économique de Palmyre*, 47, Paris, Vrin, 1931.
[35] Cf. *spadones Indici*, Just., *Digest* 39: 4, 16, 7.

[36] Cf. Strabo's statement, 16: 4, 26, that the Nabataeans had few slaves.
[37] The slavery of the Parthians was of a feudal-militaristic character which did not permit manumission, see Justinus, 41: 2, 5. Slaves from Hyrcania and Scythia, see Philostratus, *Life of Apollonus of Tyana* 5: 20, 203.
[38] *Script hist. Aug., Severus Alexander*, 55, 3: *indigne ferunt Persarum reges quempiam suorum alicui servire*.
[39] See Pauly-W., *RE* 14: 829.
[40] The *Periplus maris Erythraei*, 8, translation by Schoff, Wilfred, p. 25, New York, Longmans Green, 1912: καὶ σώματα σπανίως.
[41] *Ibid.*, 13: δουλικὰ κρείσσονα. The island of Dioscorida imported female slaves, ibid., thirty-one; and Persian Ommana exported them to Arabia and India, ibid., 36.
[42] *Archäologisches Institut des deutschen Reichs, Röm. Mitt.* 25: 232-233: 31 individual cases; cf. Suetonius, *Augustus*, 83. Eight Syrian burden bearers, Martial, *Epigrams* 7: 53, 10; cf. 9: 2, 11 and 22, 9; Juvenal, *Satires*, 1, 104; 6, 351.
[43] Fifty-eight cases including those from the Greek cities of the province of Asia, *Röm. Mitt.* 25: 233-236. Asia Minor slaves at Rome, Juvenal, *Satires*, 7, 15.
[44] For Pontus, Lydia, and Phrygia, see Philostratus, *Life of Apollonius of Tyana* 8: 7, 161.
[45] *Röm. Mitt.* 25: 247.
[46] The word often occurs in this sense in the ancient literature, e. g. the *libido servitutis ut in familiis* ascribed by Tacitus, *Histories* 1: 90 to the Roman Senate; cf. Tacitus, *Germania*, 45, with respect to the German tribe of the Sitones. See also, *idem Agricola*, 30.
[47] *Röm. Mitt.* 25: 242-244.
[48] *Ibid.* 249.
[49] Out of a total of 138 *servi Caesaris* found in inscriptions ascribed to Rome and its vicinity as given in Dessau, thirteen were home-born slaves. It is to be assumed that the relative number of *vernae*, as compared with foreign-born slaves, would be greater in any other kind of organization than in the imperial household.

whom two are distinguished as *vernae*.[50] The North African provinces, Mauretania, Numidia, and Africa, are represented by twenty cases of which three were home-born.[51] Gaul and Germany furnished relatively few slaves.[52] The entire group of the North Balkan and Danubian provinces, including Dacia and the Alpine tribe of the Lepontii, furnished twenty-two of them. No cases of British slaves are cited.

The preponderance of the slaves born in the country in which they were in servitude over the imported slaves is capable of proof in Egypt. There the number of the cases of home-born slaves [53] and of the children picked up as foundlings shortly after birth [54] greatly exceeds the number of the slaves imported. To these home-born slaves and the foundlings it is necessary to add a group of slaves definitely given as deriving from Egypt itself.[55] In the Delphic manumissions of priesthoods XVI-XXXIII [56] out of the total of thirty-four slaves available by condition of the inscriptions, one or two are said to have been brought from abroad,[57] thirteen are called home-born (*oikogeneis*), and the remaining nineteen have no statement as to *origio* and were, therefore, probably bought in the neighborhood of Delphi.[58]

The knowledge obtainable upon the methods of slave sale during the period of the Empire remains more meagre than one would expect from the extent to which the legitimate trade in slaves had developed. Sales of slave materials owned by the state itself decreased with the decline in capture of slaves through war,[59] although the state still had an organization with which to conduct public sales when called upon.[60] The retail slave dealer [61] is a figure now more frequently met in the literature of the time. A noted slave trader of the time of Augustus was a certain Toranius.[62] Slaves continued to be bought

as investment, trained in a particular *technē*, and leased or sold as income-producing property.[63] If one wished to buy a slave of a certain locality in which the trade was not active, it was necessary to send in a special agent for the purpose, as for example into Arcadia in the third century.[64] For the first two centuries, however, a few slaves who are defined as *Graeci* appear in widely separated parts of the Empire, chiefly in its western half.[65]

The customary method employed in the original sales of persons who had newly fallen into slavery or had been imported by the professional slave handlers was that of auctioneering in the regular market.[66] It was the custom of dealers in the West to whiten with chalk the feet of newly imported slaves in order to distinguish these from the slaves derived from the locality,[67] and to exhibit them upon a raised platform,[68] sometimes with a sale placard hung about the neck of the slave. If it was desirable the slave might be compelled to leap about in order to display his agility.[69]

In ordinary transfers of a known slave from one owner to another the agreement to sell would be made informally, presumably by bargaining in the street, as in Egypt.[70] Thereafter, the contract of sale would be consummated in official form and recorded.[71] With the increase in the private trade more stress is laid in liter-

---

[50] *Röm. Mitt.* **25**: 239-240.

[51] *Ibid.* 240-241.

[52] Gaul 14, *ibid.* 239; Germany 8, *ibid.* 248.

[53] Greek: οἰκογενεῖς, see above.

[54] Greek: ἀναίρετοι, see above. Cf. Taubenschlag, R., *Zeitsch. d. Savigny-Stift., Rom. Abt.* **50**: 146, n. 6, 1930.

[55] Two in *P. Freiburg* 8: 2, *Sitz. d. heidelberg. Akad., philos.-hist. Klasse* 7, *Abh.* **10**, 1916; one in *Papyrus Eitrem*, 5, in Preisigke, F., *Sammelbuch griechischer Urkunden aus Ägypten* **3**: 6016, 22, Berlin and Leipzig, W. de Gruyter, 1926; and in *BGU*, 1059, 7.

[56] These priesthoods cover the range of about 60 B.C. to about A.D. 75. See Daux, Georges, *Chronologie Delphique*, 68, 70, 84.

[57] *GDI* **2**: 2151 and possibly 2322.

[58] For *vernae* in the literature of the west, see Martial, 2: 90, 9; 3: 58, 22; Juvenal, *Satires*, 1, 27; 14, 169; Petronius, 53, 2; Apuleius, *Metamorphoses* 11: 18; Statius, *Silvae* 2: 1, 76-88.

[59] Caligula as a finance measure sold gladiators at auction to high Roman officials with compulsory high bidding, Dio Cassius, 59: 14, 1-2.

[60] Conduct of sales in Egypt διὰ κομακτόρων (= *coactores*), *P. Strassburg*, 79, 3; *P. Oxy.* **12**: 1523.

[61] Greek: ἀνδραποδοκάπηλος, Lucian, *Adversus indoctum*, 24; ἀνδραπόδων κάπηλος, Philostratus, *loc. cit.* In Suetonius, *Augustus*, 29, the *mango* is distinguished from the slave exporter. ἀνδραποδιστής in Lucian, *loc. cit.*

[62] Suetonius, *Augustus*, 69; Pliny, *Natural history* 7: 56. Sale through a middleman in Egypt, presumably a slave dealer,

P. Oxy. **1**: 94. Byzantine example of importers of slaves from Aethiopia into Egypt and middlemen *Papyrus Strassburg*, inv. no. 1404, 24-25, 9-10, in *Arch. f. Pap.* **3**: 418-419.

[63] See the complaint in Columella, *de re rustica* 4: 3, 1, that some people spent their money in purchasing slaves, but paid little attention to the care of them.

[64] Philostratus, *Life of Apollonius of Tyana* 8: 7, 161.

[65] In Italy, *CIL* **4**: 4592; **6**: 17448; in North Africa, *ibid.* **8**: 11925; in Spain, **2**: 4319; in Gaul, **12**: 3323; in Dacia, **3**: 940, *tabellae ceratae*, VII.

[66] For the purchase of a slave ἐν ἀγορᾷ in Side of Pamphylia by an Alexandrian for shipment to Egypt, see *BGU* **3**: 887, 1-2. Cf. Lucian, *De mercede conductis*, 23. In Rome sales were conducted in the forum near the temple of Castor, Seneca, *Dialogues* 2: 13, 4; *cf.* Tibullus, 4: 5, 52; Lucian, *Piscator*, 27: καθάπερ τὰ ἀνδράποδα παραγαγὼν ἡμᾶς ἐπὶ τὸ πωλητήριον καὶ κήρυκα ἐπιστήσας ἀπημπόλησεν. Sale of a runaway slave by public crier, Lucian, *Charon*, 2; *Piscator*, 4: ὥσπερ ἐξ ἀγορᾶς ἀποκηρύττων. Caligula when auctioning some of his slaves as gladiators sat upon the sale platform, πρατήριον, and competed in the bidding, Dio Cassius, 59: 14, 1-2. Upon sale by public auctioneer at Vepasca in Spain, see Dessau, 6891, 11-13 = Bruns, *FIR*, 112, 11-13. For market sale by public crier in Baetocaece near Syrian Apamea, see Dittenberger, *OGI* **1**: 262, 19-25, Leipzig, S. Hirzel, 1903.

[67] Pliny, *Natural history* **35**: 199: *pedesque venalium trans maria advectorum denotare instituerant maiores.* Cf. Propertius, 4: 5, 52; Tibullus, 2: 11, 41; Juvenal, *Satires*, 1, 111; Ovid, *Amores* 1: 8, 64.

[68] See article Catasta in Pauly-W., *RE* **3**: 1785-1786.

[69] Propertius, 4: 5, 52: *cretati medio cum saluere foro.*

[70] ἐν ἀγυιᾷ, *P. Oxy.* **1**: 95, 7; **9**: 1209, 9; **14**: 1706, 13; *PSI* **3**: 182, 12, 29. *P. Col.*, inv. no. 551, *verso* 2, 1, see *Aegyptus* 13: 230.

[71] For the registration of slave sales along with other property transfers see the records of the γραφεῖον at Tebtunis in Egypt in Boak, A. E. R., *Papyri from Tebtunis*, Part I, Index VII, *s. vv.* δούλη, δοῦλος, Ann Arbor, Univ. of Michigan Press, 1933.

ary references upon the methods of the dealers, both in purchasing and in disposing of their human wares.[72]

Greater efforts were made to control the trade by legislative enactment and to enforce the declaration of hidden and recurrent diseases affecting the value of the slave. The inspection of prospective purchases by the buyers also became more rigid, and an attempt was made to obtain in the slave the type of physical equipment needed for a particular kind of work.[73] Pliny[74] gives the recipe for a depilatory used upon boys put up for sale in order to increase their attractiveness.[75] When a slave sale was made, the approximate age and a description of the slave by his physical markings[76] were customarily given in the deed of sale as shown in the Egyptian contracts.[77] This description, called in Greek an *eikōn*, in whatever document it appeared, was important to the new owner when the slave passed by sale from one person to another, both for identification purposes and as additional proof of legal ownership.[78]

Under the Roman law the *edicta* of the curule aediles contained a section *de mancipiis vendundis* which required that the placard placed about the slave's neck should state any serious sickness from which the slave was suffering and whether he was a runaway or had a tendency to wander away.[79] The vendor was also required to make a statement if any slave offered for sale were subject to a civil charge involving a possible action for damages[80] because the liability for such delicts was transferred to the new owner along with the *potestas* over the slave.[81] According to the peregrine law of Egypt, although the slave, not the *dominus*, was liable,[82] the warranty that the slave was not subject to legal action at the time was nevertheless inserted in the affidavit of the vendor[83] or embodied in the deed of sale. Under the Roman law purchasers of slaves were protected in case of the development of a serious sickness in the slave by a clause which made the sale revocable, or permitted an action for partial restitution, if *morbus* or *vitium* should appear in the slave.[84]

For the jurists the definition of what constituted a sickness which might invalidate a sale was a difficult problem. In general it was defined as one which would affect the slave's efficiency,[85] which might be an intermittent or recurring ailment such as fevers, agues, or gout, in case these afflictions were severe enough to affect the work of the slave badly.[86] In the slave sales known from Roman Egypt a traditional Egyptian or old Semitic clause appears in the documents of sale which defined those sicknesses which might render the sale invalid. This clause appears in the form that the sale was not revocable except in case a skin infection[87] or epilepsy should manifest itself.[88] In a Byzantine slave sale[89] the statement of the Roman law regarding concealed sickness (*morbus*) and *vitium*, is combined with the specific eastern phraseology which protects the purchaser against epilepsy and leprosy.[90] It is highly prob-

---

[72] In Philostratus, *Life of Apollonius of Tyana* 3: 25, a slave dealer asserts that the slave does not steal.

[73] See the advice given by Varro, *De re rustica* 2 : 10, 3, on the physical requirements of slaves who are to be used as herdsmen. Pliny the Younger bought a group of slaves on the advice of a friend who had inspected them at the sale, Pliny, *Letters* 1 : 21.

[74] Pliny, *Natural history* 32 : 135.

[75] There was a methodical inspection of the physical qualities of slaves by the dealers, *diligenter ac lente mercantium more considerabat*, Suetonius, *Caligula*, 36, 2. Unclothing of slaves for better inspection by the *mango*, Suetonius, *Augustus*, 69. A naked slave set up for sale is depicted upon a grave stele from Capua, see Rostovtzeff, M., *The social and economic history of the Roman Empire*, pl. 11, 2 with explanation on p. 70. Painting of a similar scene from the life of Trimalchio in the peristyle of his house, Petronius, 29, 3. A similar relief from Arlon was published by Laum, B., in *Germania* 2: 108. *Cf.* Seneca, *Epistulae morales* 11 : 1, 9.

[76] Greek: εἰκόνες.

[77] E. g. *BGU* 1: 316, 13-14; 4: 1059, 7, 19-20; *P. Leipzig*, 5, 7-8, cf. 4, 12; *P. Oxy.* 9: 1209, 15. The εἰκόνες sometimes appeared in a separate document, as in *P. Strass.*, 79, 10, where it was given in the tollgate receipt. If the slave had no distinctive markings he was reported as ἄσημος, *BGU* 1: 193, 9; *P. Col.*, Inventory no. 551, *verso* 4, see *Aegyptus* 13: 230; *Papiri della Società Italiana* 3: 182, 17; *P. Freiburg*, 8, 24 in *Sitzungsberichte der Akademie der Wissenschaften, Heidelberg, Phil.-hist. Klasse* 7: Abh. 10.

[78] Preisigke, F., *P. Strass.*, 223, Leipzig, Hinrich, 1912. The occasional necessity of producing the legal documents concerning ownership in order to avoid difficulties which might otherwise arise for the slave-owner is amply illustrated in Papyrus Bibl. Univ. Giss., no. 20 in Büttner, H., *Schriften der hessischen Hochschulen, Universität. Giessen* 3: 7-13, 1931.

[79] Gellius, *Noctes Atticae* 4: 2, 1. Buckland, W. W., *The Roman law of slavery*, 52-58.

[80] Gellius, *loc. cit.*: *quis fugitivus errore sit noxave solutus non sit*.

[81] Buckland, W. W., *Roman law of slavery*, 106.

[82] Taubenschlag, R., *Das Strafrecht im Rechte der Papyri*, 108, Leipzig, Teubner, 1916. *BGU* 4: 1139, 16-17; *P. Oxy.* 2: 283, 16-17; *BGU* 1: 361, col. III, 10, 30; 341, 8; 146, 5. *Cf.* Taubenschlag, R., *Zeitschrift der Savigny-Stiftung, Rom. Abt.* 50: 164.

[83] *P. Col.*, inventory no. 551, *verso* 1, 20.

[84] Buckland, W. W., *Roman law of slavery*, 54-55. In the Dacian affidavit of sale, *CIL* 3, 2: 937, tabella 6, 1, 6; 2, 10, the vendor asserts *eam puellam sanam esse; cf. ibid.*, 940, tabella 7: 1, 5; 2, 8. See Varro, *De re rustica* 2: 10, 5: *sanum esse, furtis noxisque solutum.*

[85] Just., *Digest* 21: 1, 10 pr.

[86] Just., *Digest* 21: 1, 1, 8; h. t. 53.

[87] Greek: ἐπαφή which is presumably leprosy.

[88] E. g. *P. Oxy.* 1: 95, 18-20: ταύτην (sc. δούλην) τοιαύτην ἀναπόριφον πλὴν ἱερᾶς νόσου καὶ ἐπαφῆς. *Cf.* 1: 94, 10; 9: 1209, 19; 14: 1706, 19; *Papiri della Società Italiana* 3: 182, 21; *BGU* 1: 193, col. II, 13; 3: 937, 11; *P. Leipzig*, 4, 19-20; *P. Freib.*, 8: 13, *Sitzungsb. Heidelb. Akad.* 7: *Abh.* 10, 1916. For a discussion of ἐπαφή, whether medical or legal in its significance, and the Semitic background of the phrase, see Westermann, W. L., *Aegyptus* 13: 230-231. Upon the form of the slave sale document see Wilcken, U., *Hermes* 19: 417-431; Mitteis, L., *Reichsrecht und Volksrecht*, 182; Rabel, E., *Die Haftung des Verkäufers wegen Mangels im Rechte*, Leipzig, Veit und Co., 1902.

[89] Maspero, J., *Catalogue des antiquités égyptiennes du Musée du Caire: Papyrus grecs d'époque byzantine* 1, no. 67120, 189, 1911.

[90] *Cf. BGU* 1: 316, 27-28: ἱερὰν δὲ νόσον καὶ σίνος πάλεον (= old physical imperfection = *vitium*) καὶ κρυπτὸν πάθος μεχρὶς μηνῶν ἕξ. *P. Strassb.*, inv. no. 1404, 30-31 in *Arch. f. Pap.* 3: 419.

able that the pamphlet entitled *De emptione servorum* written by the physician, Rufus of Ephesus, of the time of Trajan,[91] dealt with the methods of detecting such hidden diseases and weaknesses of slaves at the time of purchase.

The prices which were paid for slaves during the first three centuries varied, as before, according to the age, condition, training, physical attractiveness, etc., of each slave. The asking prices differed within each country according to the conditions prevailing in the various localities.[92] An attempt to compare the prices prevalent in different parts of the Empire is therefore precarious, at best, in its results. It must be based upon a careful consideration of the disturbing factors noted above [93] and must rest primarily upon evidence furnished by the inscriptions and papyri, using the literary references, always with caution, to supplement the customary prices thus established. At Rome in the period of Augustus five hundred drachmas appears in Horace [94] as a price applicable to a cheap and worthless slave. A clever home-born slave, qualified as a reader through knowledge of Greek, might be obtained for two thousand *denarii*.[95] In Egypt somewhat later a male slave cost one thousand silver drachmas.[96] Another price paid in 5 B.C. was twelve hundred silver drachmas.[97] For the second half of the first century A.D. three moderate prices paid for slaves are available which may be accepted as approximate indications of the customary price level prevailing at Rome: a boy, good at imitation, purchased for three hundred *denarii*;[98] a slave girl of bad moral repute quoted at six hundred *denarii* as a low price;[99] and a male slave bought for twelve hundred *denarii*.[100]

In comparison with these prices stand the following from Egypt for the same period: a girl of about eight years bought for 640 silver drachmas;[101] sale in A.D. 85-86 of an *oikogenēs*, presumably a very young child,

at ten talents, three thousand drachmas copper (= 140 silver drachmas).[102] In close relation to these stand, at the same period,[103] the Egyptian prices for manumission by civil action. The manumission prices in the Delphic emancipations by sale to the god during the priesthoods XVI-XXX stand much higher than the sale and manumission prices for Egypt. They lie in the general range of one to ten minas,[104] with an average of from three to four minas.[105] It is possible that the twenty thousand sesterces paid at Rome for a deformed jester (*morio*),[106] which approximates the Greek manumission prices, may be accepted as representing a luxury price paid for an amusement slave at Rome.

Some slave prices from the Roman literature of the first century cannot be brought into relation with the actual values presented above. They must be explained either as examples of luxury wastage or, in their more extravagant forms, on the basis of manuscript corruption of the numerals involved.[107] However dubious these prices may be [108] there is no doubt that the demand for slaves as objects of luxury in the life of Rome had increased.[109]

For the second century there are no slave prices available for Rome, itself. A trained slave woman, *veterana*, was bought by a sailor of the fleet at Ravenna for 625 *denarii*.[110] Wax tablets from Dacia offer three definite values with exact dates: a slave girl of six years was sold in A.D. 139 for 205 *denarii*;[111] a Greek boy, A.D. 142, sale price 600 *denarii*;[112] a Cretan woman sold in A.D. 160 for 625 *denarii*.[113] These may be regarded as standard, rather than low, prices because in two of these cases they are slaves foreign to the locality.

In Egypt for the same approximate period the following slave values are known from extant documents of sale: a female slave aged twenty-five years, bought for 1,200 drachmas.[114] For a young boy, eight years of age,

---

[91] See Ilberg, J., *Abh. sächs. Akad.* **41**: 1, 45.

[92] For Egypt, see *P. Rylands*, papyrus 244 in *Catalogue of the Greek papyri in the John Rylands Library* **2**: 244, 10-16, Manchester, University Press, 1915, from the Hermopolite nome, of the third century: τὰ δὲ σωμάτια πολλοῦ ἐστιν ἐνθά[δ]ε καὶ οὐ συμφέρει ἀγοράσαι.

[93] *Cf.* Segrè, A., *Circolazione monetaria e prezzi nel mondo antico ed in particolare in Egitto*, 173, Rome, Libreria di Cultura, 1922. For the difference in value of a male and a female slave in Egypt, see *BGU* **4**: 1128, 7, 15: τὸ ἐνλειψόμενο(ν) . . . τῆς . . . . . ἀξίας.

[94] Horace, *Satires* 2: 7, 43.

[95] Horace, *Epistles* 2: 2, 5-6.

[96] *BGU* **4**: 1128, 7 of 14 B.C.

[97] *BGU* **4**: 1114, 16-17: 1 silver drachma = 1 *denarius* at that time, Mitteis-Wilcken, *Grundzüge und Chrestomathie der Papyruskunde* **1**¹: lxv.

[98] Petronius, 68. This was evidently regarded as a good bargain.

[99] Martial, 6: 66, 9.

[100] Martial, 10: 31, 1.

[101] *P. Oxy.* **2**: 263, 14-15 of A.D. 77. This is the equivalent of 160 *denarii*, the Egyptian drachma being reckoned as ¼ *denarius*, Mitteis-Wilcken, *Grundzüge und Chrestomathie der Papyruskunde* **1** (1): lxvi.

[102] *P. Oxy.* **2**: 336.

[103] *P. Oxy.* **1**: 48, 14-15 of A.D. 86: ten silver drachmas and ten talents, 3,000 drachmas copper; **1**: 49 of A.D. 100: ten silver drachmas and two talents, 600 drachmas copper; **4**: 722 of A.D. 91 or 107, one-third ownership part of a slave manumitted for 200 silver drachmas, total 600 silver drachmas.

[104] Calderini, A., *La manomissione e la condizione dei liberti in Grecia*, 214.

[105] *Ibid.*, 213.

[106] Martial, 8: 13.

[107] Pliny, *Natural history* 7: 56, price of two young slaves 200,000 sesterces; Martial 3: 62, 100,000 sesterces for handsome boys; 11: 70 a price of 200,000 sesterces.

[108] The extravagant prices quoted in Pliny, *Natural history* 7: 128-129 are obviously corrupt and cannot be used.

[109] The castration of males was forbidden by Domitian, Suetonius, *Domitian*, 7, with limitation of the price of *spadones* still remaining in the hands of the slave dealers.

[110] Wax tablet of the second century, *Zeitschrift der Savigny-Stiftung, Rom. Abt.* **42**: 453—Preisigke, F., *Sammelbuch der griechischen Papyri*, no. 6304.

[111] *CIL* **3**: 937.

[112] *Ibid.* **3**: 941.

[113] *Ibid.* **3**: 959.

[114] *P. Oxy.* **1**: 95, 21 of A.D. 129.

the price was 700 silver drachmas (= 175 *denarii*).[115] A slave woman was sold for 1,000 silver drachmas[116] a female slave aged about twenty-four, sale price 1,500 silver drachmas;[117] a girl slave bought inside of Pamphylia, price 3,500 dinarii;[118] two-thirds ownership in two young slaves, aged fifteen and eight years, sold for 1,500 silver drachmas, the value of each being about 1,125 drachmas (= 281 *denarii*);[119] slave boy, about seven years, bought by a sailor of the Roman fleet in Seleucia Pieria for 200 *denarii*;[120] 300 silver drachmas paid for a male child about three years of age (low price because of greater risk of the investment).[121] Two prices of the same period from Egypt may be compared with the payment of 625 *denarii* for a grown woman in Dacia:[122] male slave, aged about thirty-eight, bought in A. D. 125-126 for 1,400 silver drachmas (= 350 *denarii*);[123] female slave, aged about twenty-four, sold for 1,500 silver drachmas;[124] cession of a fifth share in a slave girl who is valued at 840 silver drachmas;[125] male slave bought in A. D. 154 for 1,400 silver drachmas (= 350 *denarii*);[126] male slave, again A. D. 154, price 2,800 silver drachmas (= 700 *denarii*);[127] male slave, aged twenty-five, bought in A. D. 160-161 for 1,300 silver drachmas (325 *denarii*).[128] In the text of a sale at Dura on the Euphrates in A. D. 180[129] the price of 500 silver drachmas, Syrian coinage, included a slave and a half share in a vineyard. These data indicate a fairly equal price level for young slaves covering the territory of Dacia, lower Asia Minor, Syria and Egypt, ranging from 175 *denarii* to 600 *denarii*, and for adult slaves covering the territory from Ravenna eastward, prices ranging from 350 to 700 *denarii*.

Slave values available for the western section of the Empire during the third century offer examples

of high luxury prices only.[130] Prices for the third century are available only in Egypt. Those occurring after A. D. 250 reflect the decline in the silver content of the imperial *denarius* as well as that of the tetradrachm of Egypt.[131]

There is no possibility of substantiating by statistical methods the assumption of a progressive decline in the relative number of slaves during the first three centuries of the Roman Empire; but a reduction of the slave population has generally been assumed[132] as a consequence of the closing of the two great sources of slave labor, namely war and piracy.[133] Investment in slaves, either for direct economic employment by the owner or

---

[115] *BGU* 1: 193, col. II, 15-16 = Mitteis-Wilcken, *Grundzüge und Chrestomathie* 2 (2) : 268, of A. D. 136.

[116] *P. Col.* inventory no. 512, unpublished, of A. D. 140.

[117] *BGU* 3: 805.

[118] *BGU* 3: 887, 9—Mitteis-Wilcken, *Grundzüge und Chrestomathie* 2 (2) : 272 of A. D. 151.

[119] *P. Freiburg*, no. 8, 8, 14, in *Sitzungsberichte der Akademie der Wissenschaften, Heidelberg, Phil.-hist. Klasse* 7 : Abh. 10, 1916, of the second century.

[120] *Papyrus London*, no. 229 in Kenyon, *Greek papyri in the British Museum* 1 : London, 1893, of A. D. 166.

[121] *BGU* 3: 859, 10, 20 of the second century A. D.

[122] *CIL* 3 : 959, see above.

[123] *Papyrus Hamburg*, no. 63, 3 in Meyer, P. M., *Griechische Papyrus urkunden der Hamburger Staatsbibliothek*, Leipzig, 1911-1924.

[124] *BGU* 3: 805, 8.

[125] Wessely, *Studien zur Paläographie und Papyruskunde* 22 : 43, 17-18, 20-24.

[126] Preisigke, F., *Sammelbuch*, no. 6016.

[127] *Papyrus Eitrem*, no. 7, 14, in *Jour. Egyptian Archaeology* 17 : 44-45, 1931.

[128] *P. Col.*, inventory no. 551, verso II, 12-13 in *Aegyptus* 13 : 230.

[129] *Parchment Dura*, no. 23, 8-14, 17, in *Münchener Beiträge zur Papyrusforschung und antiken Rechtsgeschichte* 19 : 382-383.

[130] *Scriptores historiae Augustae, Elagabalus*, 25, 5, a prostitute slave girl purchased for 100,000 sesterces. *Cf.* the restriction placed on the ownership of eunuchs by Aurelian because of the high prices attained, *ibid., Aurelian*, 49, 8.

[131] See the tables in Mickwitz, Gunnar, *Geld und Wirtschaft im römischen Reiche des vierten Jahrhunderts, Societas Scientiarum Fennica, Commentationes Humanarum Litterarum* 4 (2) : 40-41, 1932; *Corpus Papyrorum Rainerii* 1: 140, 6, Wien, 1895: a male slave ἀργ[υρ]ίου δραχμὰς [...]χειλίας ἐνακοσίας ἑξήκοντα; *Papyrus Michigan*, inventory no. 5474, in *Archiv für Papyrusforschung* 11: 110, purchase in A. D. 207 of a slave girl aged about eleven; *Papiri della Società Italiana* 3: 182, 23-24 of A. D. 234: a slave woman twenty years of age, 2,200 drachmas silver; *cf.* the payment of 2,200 drachmas silver in a *manumissio inter amicos* of A. D. 211 as manumission price of a home-born slave woman aged about thirty-four years in Mitteis-Wilcken, *Grundzüge und Chrestomathie* 2 (2) : 362, 9-10, 20; *P. Oxy.* 9: 1209, 16, 23: house-born slave woman, aged about twenty-one, with nursing child, 2,000 silver drachmas; *Studien zur Paläographie und Papyruskunde* 20: 71, 11 of A. D 268-270: slave girl of thirteen years, for 5,000 drachmas old Ptolemaic silver coinage; *P. Leipzig*, no. 5, 9 of A. D. 293 in Mitteis, L., *Griechische Urkunden der Papyrussammlung zu Leipzig*, Leipzig, Teubner, 1906: Cretan slave girl twenty years old for 15 talents new imperial coinage in silver. *Cf.* a Roman *manumissio inter amicos* of A. D. 211, from Egypt, of a *verna*, aged about thirty-four, for 2,200 drachmas in Mitteis-Wilcken, *Grundzüge und Chrestomathie* 2 (2) : 362, 10, 20; and the manumission in A. D. 291 of a Jewish woman aged about forty, with two sons aged about four years and ten years, for fourteen silver talents in *P. Oxy.* 9: 1205, 9.—Other documents dealing with slave sales in which the prices either do not appear or are lost are: *Papyrus Strassburg*, no. 79, 5; in *Michigan papyri* 2, *Papyri from Tebtunis*, Part I, Ann Arbor, Univ. of Michigan Press, 1933, among the abstracts of contracts registered in the γραφεῖον of Tebtunis in A. D. 42, out of a total of thirty-two contracts of sale only two are sales of slaves: col. VI, 18 and col. VII, 6; *Oxyrhynchus papyri* 1: 94 of A. D. 83: document empowering to sell a slave; *P. Tebtunis* 3: 561 of the first century; *Papyrus Giessen* 3: 20 of the second century in Büttner, H., *Mitteilungen aus der Papyrussammlung der Giessener Universitätsbibliothek* 3, Giessen, A. Töpelmann, 1931; *BGU* 7: 1162, 14 of A. D. 182; *P. Oxy.* 4: 716 of A. D. 186: a request for public auction of two-thirds ownership parts in a slave, the other one-third part being already free; *Studien zur Paläographie und Papyruskunde* 22: 60; *Papyri russischer und georgischer Sammlungen* 3: 27, 7, second or third century; *P. Oxy.* 14: 1706, 18 of A. D. 207; 12: 1523: receipt for tax on slave sale; *BGU* 3: 937, 11-12.

[132] Ciccotti, E., *Il tramonto della schiavitù*, 282, Torino, Fratelli Bocca, 1899; Barrow, R. H., *Slavery in the Roman Empire*, 4. An increase in the relative proportion of free craftsmen is placed in the second century by Barrow, *op. cit.*, 99. *Cf.* Rostovtzeff, M., *Social and economic history Roman empire*, 539, n. 41.

[133] See above, Meyer, Ed., *Kleine Schriften* 1²: 209.

for the wages to be obtained by renting out the labor of slaves, continued to be a profitable outlet for capital. The profits derived from such investment must, however, have decreased with the gradual shrinkage in the numbers available for purchase.

In general the prohibition against enlistment of slaves in the imperial armies, whether in the land or naval contingents, was more strictly enforced than in the period of the Republic.[134] The Roman commanding officers might,

however, be accompanied into the field by their own slaves, acting in non-combatant services;[135] and an efficient slave was sometimes used in the commissariat department of the army service.[136]

---

[134] Dio Cassius, 67: 13, 1: a slave who had become a centurion was detected and restored to his master by Domitian; Pliny the Younger, *Letters* 10: 30: capital punishment for slaves

who crept into the army was advocated by Trajan if the slaves had enlisted voluntarily.

[135] A *praefectus fabrum* under Marcus Antonius was accompanied into Egypt by his παιδάρια, Dittenberger, W., *Orientis Graeci inscriptiones selectae* 1: 196. Slaves in Pannonia under Junius Blaesus in A. D. 14, Dio Cassius, 57: 4.

[136] Pliny, *Natural history* 7: 40: the slave Tiridates in the Armenian war.

XVI. THE ROMAN EMPIRE

LIVING CONDITIONS AND SOCIAL LIFE OF SLAVES

The degree of improvement of slave conditions under the Empire over those which had prevailed in the last two centuries of the Roman Republic is more marked in the West than in the eastern provinces, where the system had always been characterized by greater mildness,[1] both legally and in practice. In Egypt the welfare of the slave child was, in a number of respects, expressly protected by law. House-born slaves could not legally be sold for the purpose of export beyond the borders of Egypt. Transgression of this law was punishable by partial or total confiscation of property.[2] Purchased slaves could be embarked out of Alexandria only upon a permit and payment of a passport fee.[3] In contracts for nursing of children the wet nurse selected for a slave child might be either a free woman or a slave, just as for a free child.[4]

Whether the child were free or slave the same demands were made with respect to satisfactory food for the nurse. Specifications of the food to be supplied to the nurses are found in a number of contracts, olive oil, for example, and other things, in a contract of A. D. 50.[5] It is clear from a similar document from Alexandria, dated

as of 13 B. C.,[6] in the provision requiring the nurse to take adequate care of herself and the child and not to injure the flow of milk, that the intention is to preserve the health of the nurse as it affects the child.[7] In *BGU* 4: 1106, 49 ff. the nurse, a free woman, agrees to bring the slave child several times each month for inspection by its owner.[8] Although the primary purpose of these arrangements was the protection of the slave child, as object of value, the humanitarian result of adequate care was, nevertheless, attained. Manual training or other educative preparation of a slave was a matter of the owner's decision.

A number of contracts deal with the training of slaves, either as apprentices or under a direct teaching contract.[9] These contracts show no difference in the formulary and reciprocal engagements between slave-owner and the apprentice master or teacher, whether the apprentice or pupil be slave or free. The obligation of supplying food and clothing to the slave or free child who was under instruction, was handled in different ways. In the pure teaching contracts it falls upon the slave-owners, while in the apprentice contract it falls upon the teacher.[10] In *BGU* 4: 1021, 14 f. and *P. Oxy.*

---

[1] Calderini, Aristide, *Liberi e schiavi nel monde dei papiri*, 18, Milan, 1918.

[2] Schubart, Wilhelm, and Emil Seckel, *Der Gnomon des Idios Logos*, *BGU* 5: 1, 67, Berlin, Weidmann, 1919.

[3] *Ibid.* 5: 64-66, 69.

[4] *Papiri della Società Italiana* 10: 1131, 26-27; *Michigan papyri* 2: 123 recto, 14, 31-32; *BGU* 4: 1106, 3, 12, 1108, 4, 7. *Bouriant papyri* 14: 4 ff. In the *Reinach papyri*, 2111 (Mel. Glotz 1: 243) and in *BGU* 4: 1107, 9 we have cases mentioned of free women acting as nurses of abandoned children rescued into slavery. For instances of free children nursed by slave women see the *Oxyrhynchus papyri* 1: 91, 16-17 and *BGU* 4: 1109, 6, 9-10 as well as *Papiri della Società Italiana* 9: 1065, 10-11.

[5] *BGU* 1: 297, 13. *Cf.* the olive oil, in the nursing contract of a free child in *BGU* 4: 1109, 13, also 4: 1058, 12, reproduced in Mitteis-Wilcken, *Grundzüge* 2: 2, M no., where olive oil and bread are mentioned. In *Papyri Bouriant,* 14, 13 we find wine and four fowls listed in the food furnished to the nurse.

[6] *BGU* 4: 1106, 27-30. *Cf. BGU* 4: 1108, 13-15, Alexandria, 5 B. C.

[7] *Cf.* the receipts for completed nursing in *Oxyrhynchus papyri* 1: 91, 16-20 and in *BGU* 4: 1108, 25-28.

[8] *Cf. P. Oxy.* 4: 1107, 27-29, where provision is made for nurse and child to stay with the owner for four days each month for inspection. Inspection by the owner three times each month is mentioned, *ibid.* 1108, 25-26.

[9] See Berger, Adolf, *Die Strafklauseln in den Papyrusurkunden*, 169, Leipzig, Teubner, 1911. Also Mitteis-Wilcken, *Grundzüge* 1: 1, 261; see further Taubenschlag, Rafael, *Zeitschrift der Savigny-Stiftung* 50: 156, and *Studi in onore di Salvatore Riccobono* 1: 512, Palermo, G. Castiglia, 1936; see also Westermann, W. L., Apprentice contracts and the apprentice system in Roman Egypt, *Classical Philol.* 9: 295-315, 1914.

[10] Taubenschlag, Rafael, *Studi Riccobono* 1: 512. This arrangement is also implied in the *Oxyrhynchus papyri* 4: 724. See further *Studien zur Paläographie und Papyruskunde* 22:

14: 1647, 16 f. it devolves upon the slave-owner.[11] The importance of these examples lies in the conclusion that the proper feeding and clothing of a slave was socially and legally mandatory.

When the observance of holidays was contractually agreed upon, either in the apprentice or teaching contracts, there was no distinction made as between free persons and those of servile status. In teaching contracts, like that in which a slave boy is to be taught shorthand signs, the holidays were no doubt set aside in the interest of the teacher;[12] but in a weaving contract the eighteen holidays stipulated for the year fall to the advantage of the apprentice.[13]

The granting of feast days to slaves had already become customary in the Aegean area in the Hellenistic period.[14] At Lampsacus a capital endowment was established in the second century B. C. for celebration of the festival of Asklepios; it contained the provision that the school children should be released from their studies and the servants from their work.[15] At Magnesia the arrangement for school holidays was based upon ancestral precedents; but the provision for the release of slaves from all their tasks upon these holidays seems to be a novelty.[16] This type of concession to the slaves continued in the Greek world under the Empire. At Gythium in the Peloponnesus in A. D. 161-169 an endowment was set up for supplying oil for the gymnasium for the citizens and strangers, with a special provision that slaves were to enjoy this privilege on two occasions of festivals of three days duration each year.[17]

In Roman Egypt the death of a slave from other than natural causes required official investigation and report as to whether it was accidental or homicidal, just as in the case of a free person. Thus the accidental death of a slave boy, which occurred while watching the dancers at a festival, was reported to the strategus, who in turn ordered his assistant, accompanied by a public physician (*dēmosios iatros*), to investigate and send in a written report upon the case.[18] At the time of the fourteen-yearly census which was introduced into Egypt by the Roman administration, slaves received a classification for fiscal purposes corresponding to that of their owners.[19] Slaves who belonged to owners of the poll-tax-paying group, (*laographoumenoi*) were subject to the poll tax. Those belonging to persons of the privileged class of the *epikekrimmenoi* were exempt from the poll tax as their masters were.[20] The financial classification of the slave-owner, with its privileges and burdens, which was taken over from his master by the slave, was transmitted to his offspring, even if he remained in slavery,[21] and fixed his status if he were emancipated.[22] Although the unfree had no political status it is nevertheless apparent from the well-known letter of the Emperor Claudius of A. D. 41 to the city of Alexandria that slave-born sons of Alexandria citizens by servile mothers had been slipping into the register of the *ephebi* and thus attaining Alexandrian citizenship[23] contrary to the exacting law which strictly forbade that practice.[24]

No special type or quality of clothing was worn by the slaves in Egypt which would distinguish them in appearance from the poorer free population. This is clear from the lack of reference to a particular kind of clothing for slave boys or girls in the apprentice and teaching contracts which would differentiate these documents in respect to the amounts allocated for *himatismos* (clothing allowance) from those which deal with free children.[25] The dwelling conditions of slaves who lived with their owners were determined by the economic status of the owners, the slaves no doubt receiving the less habitable rooms. In the documents of Heracleides, amphodarch at Arsinoe in A. D. 72-73, the house owner, Apollonius, occupied his house with a single slave;[26] and two women house owners also appear who lived each with a single male slave.[27] Free men of the class of the *epikekrimmenoi* (those on the enrollment lists not sub-

40, 18-19, and *cf.* the alimentation money supplied by the weaver for a free apprentice, in *Papyrus Tebtunis* **2**: 385, 13-14.

[11] *Cf.* the testamentary arrangement for annual payment of ten artabs of wheat and a money payment for clothing made by his former owner in behalf of a freedman, as found in *P. Ryl.*, 153, 2-4. The will provides, also, for a friend of the deceased who was free.

[12] An example of this is found in *Oxyrhynchus papyri* **4**: 724, 6.

[13] *Ibid.* **14**: 1647, 36-39. There it is a slave girl apprenticed to a weaver that is discussed. *Cf.* the twenty days set aside for holidays for a free weaver's apprentice, *ibid.* **4**: 725, 35.

[14] Robert, Louis, Sur des inscriptions de Chios, *Bulletin de Correspondance Hellénique* **57**: 505-543, 1933.

[15] *Corpus Inscriptionum Graecarum* **2**, no. 3641b, Addenda, pp. 1130-1131. Reproduced in Laum, B., *Stiftungen in der griechischen und römischen Antike* **2**: 66, 18, Leipzig and Berlin, Teubner, 1914.

[16] *Die Inschriften von Magnesia am Maeander* (Otto Kern, editor), 100 *b*, 11-13, Berlin, W. Spermann. *Cf.* also 29-33 and Dittenberger, *Syll.* 3, no. 694, 54-55, in which slaves and school children at Elaea (or possibly Pergamum) were granted holiday from their tasks and from school attendance on the occasion of a newly established festival.

[17] LeBas-Foucart, *Voyage Arch.* **2**, suppl., 243a. Reproduced in Laum, *Stiftungen* **2**: 9, 38-40.

[18] *Oxyrhynchus papyri* **3**: 475. *Cf. ibid.* **1**: 51 for a similar case regarding a free person.

[19] Mitteis-Wilcken, *Grundzüge* **1** (1) : 192-197.

[20] Schubart, Wilhelm, *Archiv für Papyrusforschung* **2**: 158, Leipzig, Taubner, 1903. Taubenschlag, R., *Zeitschrift der Savigny-Stiftung* **50**: 162, 7.

[21] *Rylands papyri*, 103, n. 4.

[22] *Oxyrhynchus papyri* **3**: 478; *cf.* **2**: 222; **4**: 714. Also *BGU* **1**: 324.

[23] Bell, H. I., *Jews and Christians in Egypt*, 24, 56, London, Oxford Univ. Press, 1924.

[24] μὴ ὦν δὲ νόμιμος υἱὸς τοῦ πατρὸς ὄντος, Ἀλεξανδρέως Ἀλεξανδρεὺς οὐ δύναται εἶναι, Cattaoui papyri, 1 + *BGU* **1**: 114, col. 5, 6-7. See also *Archiv für Papyrusforschung* **3**: 60.

[25] *Studien zur Paläographie und Papyruskunde* **22**: 40, 14; *BGU* **4**: 1021, 14; *Oxyrhynchus papyri* **14**: 1647, 17. *Cf.* the labor contract involving a slave girl as weaver in *Studien zur Paläographie und Papyruskunde* **22**: 36, 11, and the obligation imposed upon the guardians for the slaves of a minor heir, in *Rylands papyri*, 153, 29-30.

[26] *Stud. Pal.* **4**, pp. 62-63. Also in *P. Lond.* **2**: 261 (pp. 53-61).

[27] *Ibid.*, line 178; *Stud. Pal.* **4**, p. 68, lines 301-302.

jéct to the poll tax) who were not related to the house owners occupied living quarters upon the street, obviously as renters of rooms.[28] In like manner slaves who were the property of other men than the house owners with whom they lived had living quarters upon the same street.[29] Two of the houses were occupied each by a group of slaves who, so far as ascertainable, did not belong to the house owner. One of these apartments supplied the living quarters of seven slaves, the other of six slaves.[30] This would indicate crowded tenement conditions for the slaves who "lived away" from their owners (*chōris oikountes*), assuming that the houses were of about the same size. There is a case, however, when, by the will of his patron, a freedman was assigned the use of a single room in a house of four stories for the remainder of his life.[31]

The question whether, in Roman law, a slave was conceived of, in any sense, as a *person* has been the subject of discussion among the modern scholars versed in the doctrines of ancient law. There seems to be little doubt that in Roman jurisprudence, as in the Greek concept, the slave was regarded as a person as well as a *res*. Certainly this was true in the Greco-Roman law of Egypt.[32] The principle of partial manumission of a slave held in co-ownership was not admissible under the Roman law;[33] but it was freely practised in Roman Egypt.[34] The social result of this difference was to introduce into Egypt between the full slave and the freedmen a new group, partly slave and partly free, intermediates in status who had the legal right to dispose of a portion of their time and energies. The introduction of this partially servile group must have served to level further the falling barriers between the condition of freedom and slavery under a system in which the distinctions of status were not strongly founded in recognized differ-

ences of dress or color or race. For a remarkable example of the lack of race feeling based upon distinctions of color we have a metrical inscription in which a Negro slave is praised by his master.[35] It is significant of the narrow line which separated them, that a free servant might be mistaken for a slave.[36]

The relations existing in Egypt between slaves and their owners, and freedmen and their patrons, as attested by the papyri, were on the whole intimate and cordial rather than strained.[37] There is a case where the obligation of caring for the tomb of his master, without hindrance on the part of his heirs, is assigned for the remainder of his life to a slave by will of his deceased owner.[38] In another instance we have a former high priest of the temple of Hadrian who manumitted eight of his slaves because of the fellowship and solicitude which existed between them and himself.[39] Significant, also, is the will of a Roman veteran of the end of the second century by which three female slaves were manumitted and instituted as the heirs of their former owner.[40] With the above-mentioned Egyptian example compare the manumission of all of his slaves of both sexes by a public-spirited citizen of Gythium in lower Greece in A. D. 161-169, with the injunction laid upon the city and the members of the city council that the freedom of these former slaves is to be protected in every way.[41]

In the area of the eastern Mediterranean a tendency is apparent to admit slaves, upon stated occasions, to participation in the public sacrifices and festivals. The differences which existed in the Greek city-states in respect to the concessions to be granted them must be due to localized conditions which can no longer be explained. At Cos slaves were excluded from the sacrifices and the meal at the festival of Hera,[42] whereas at Pagai in the Megarid they were permitted to participate in the public meals along with the citizens, non-citizen residents, and the resident Roman citizens.[43] Under Trajan the gymnasium at Argos was made accessible to all the population, both slave and free;[44] and at Pana-

[28] *Stud. Pal.* 4, pp. 73 and 76, lines 532, 608; reproduced in *P. Lond.* 2: 260 (pp. 42-53), lines 25, 101.

[29] *Stud. Pal.* 4, p. 68, lines 299, 303-304.

[30] *Ibid.*, lines 313-326.

[31] *Rylands papyri*, 153, 6-8.

[32] Girard, Paul F., *Manuel élémentaire de droit Romain*, 93-94, Paris, Rousseau, 5th ed., 1911, definitely asserts that the slave was not a *person* in Roman law though accepted as a human being. Buckland, W. W., *Roman law of slavery*, 3-4, Cambridge, Univ. Press, 1908, has refuted Girard's thesis. For the slave as person and subject of the law in Greco-Roman Egypt see Taubenschlag, R., *Law of Greco-Roman Egypt*, 57, 72, New York, Herald Square Press, 1944.

[33] Mitteis, L., *Archiv für Papyrusforschung* 3: 253-254. Taubenschlag, *Zeitschrift der Savigny-Stiftung* 50: 166-167; *Law of Greco-Roman Egypt*, 75-76. See the interpretation of Gaius, in *PSI* 11: 1182, 38-44, which asserts that, by the manumission of a part of a slave who is jointly owned, freedman status is acquired in respect to the parts of all the remaining owners.

[34] Arangio-Ruiz, *Persone e famiglia nel diritto dei papiri*, 9, Milan, Vita e Pensiero, 1930. For examples see *P. Oxy.* 4: 716, 17-18; 722, 14-18, and the *Edmondstone papyrus* of the fourth century, reproduced in *P. Oxy.* 4: 202-203 and in Mitteis-Wilcken, *Grundzüge* 2 (2), no. 361. An agreement is entered into in *Stud. Pal.* 2, 2, 43, 20-24 not to dispose of a part ownership in a slave. For a petition in the case of a partial manumission allegedly obtained by fraud, see *PSI* 5: 452, 10-21.

[35] This inscription from Egypt is found in Georg Ebers' Festschrift, *Aegyptiaca*, Leipzig, Engelmann, 1897. The inscription reads: "The darkness of the negro's skin was caused by the rays of the sun; but his soul bloomed with white blossoms."

[36] As in *P. Oxy.* 10: 1294, 9. *Cf.* the list of payments of the weaver's tax in *Papiri della Società Italiana* 10: 1154, 8, in which a man is registered as Εὔπορος, ὅ[ς] φη(σὶ) δοῦλος 'Α[....]; "Euporus, slave of A———, as he asserts."

[37] See the affectionate letter of a girl who was presumably a slave of Apollonius, strategus in the Heptakomia, to her absent master, *P. Giessen* 17, reproduced in Mitteis-Wilcken, *Grundzüge* 1 (2), 481. *Cf.* Calderini, *Liberi e schiavi*, 19.

[38] *BGU* 7: 1685, col. 2, 26-33, col. 3, 57-59.

[39] *P. Teb.* 2: 407, 6.

[40] *BGU* 1: 326, reproduced in Mitteis-Wilcken, *Grundzüge* 2 (2), 316.

[41] Laum, *Stiftungen* 2: 9, 53-55.

[42] Athenaeus, 14: 639 D from Philetus, see Powell, J. U., *Collectanea Alexandrina*, 95, no. 25, Oxford, 1925.

[43] Wilhelm, Ad., *Jahreshefte des österreichischen archäologischen Instituts* 10: 19, 22-25, 1907.

[44] παντὶ ἐλευθέρῳ καὶ δούλῳ, *IG* 4: 597, 17-18.

mara in Lycia in the time of Marcus Aurelius a citizen asserts with pride that he had furnished wine upon two days of the festival of Zeus Komyrios to citizens, alien residents and slaves.[45]

In Egypt testimony from slaves in the courts continued to be taken under torture;[46] and the right of physical chastisement of their slaves remained with the owners.[47] Although there is surprisingly little evidence of it in the papyri, brutal punishment of slaves no doubt occurred at times. The great Pergamene physician, Galen, speaks with horror of the kicking of slaves, beating them with fists, knocking out their teeth, or gouging out their eyes. He refers to the blinding of a slave with a reed pen as an incident which he had actually witnessed.[48] He himself had learned from his father never to strike a slave with the hand, advocating the use of a reed whip or a strap instead. His eye-witness account of the brutal wounding of two slaves by a traveling companion in Attica furnishes a most circumstantial and trustworthy example of the possible results of the master's right of punishment as applied in moments of unrestrained passion.[49] The genuine sorrow and self-abasement of the slave-owner is sufficient proof that such exhibitions were individual, not socially countenanced, and probably of infrequent occurrence.[50] The often quoted stories of cruelties towards slaves shown by sadistic members of the imperial household, such as the order issued by Commodus, when a boy of twelve, that a slave bath attendant be thrown into the furnace (*Script. hist. Aug., Commodus*, 1, 9) may well be true. It is to be observed in this case that the command was not carried out.

The position of the slave class in Egypt in respect to the social stigma arising from physical punishment was mitigated by the fact that free persons were not exempt from it, because military punishment of free persons was now permissible, though this was restricted to the use of sticks or switches,[51] whereas punishment by whips[52] was reserved for slaves alone.[53] A *praeses* of the Thebaid of the fourth century rendered an opinion that the use of whips (*himantes*) was illegal in the corporal

punishment of free persons. Though permissible in the case of slaves it was nevertheless to be deplored.[54]

Some degree of freedom of movement was certainly accorded to slaves by their owners in Egypt.[55] Possibly under the influence of the law of ancient Egypt[56] the sexual cohabitation of servile and free persons might be regarded, under the common law, as legitimate marriage,[57] although the offspring was of slave status if the mother was a slave.[58] Social pleasure clubs or associations of other kinds which received slaves and freedmen in their membership, which attained a high stage of development on Roman soil, seem to have been lacking in Egypt.[59]

Although it is apparent that the right of asylum did not disappear altogether from Egypt under Roman domination[60] no instance of a flight to a temple or to a statue of the Emperor on the part of a slave has thus far appeared in the papyri. The failure of the contracts dealing with slaves to provide against flight or sanctuary by the inclusion of an *emphaneia* clause[61] would imply that this right, so far as slaves were concerned, had completely disappeared. This may be a further evidence that the type of slavery existing in Egypt was not so brutal that it required protective sanctuary for its slave class. Despite the general impression of a considerate treatment of slaves in Egypt, the lot of a domestic or industrial slave could not have been enviable at best. Instances of flight of slaves from their owners, and the provisions in *parmonē* documents and other contracts for protection against the possibility of flight indicate a widespread dissatisfaction with their lot among the slaves themselves.[62] In addition to these indications of

[45] *BCH* 11: 380, 17.

[46] Taubenschlag, *Strafrecht im Rechte der Papyri*, 125. In the local Egyptian law the application of torture was restricted, Taubenschlag, *Law of Greco-Roman Egypt*, 62.

[47] In *P. Oxy.* 4: 1643, 11, dealing with A. D. 298, we have a case where the owner delegated the right to arrest and chastise a runaway slave to his representative. *Cf. P. Oxy.* 6: 903, 5-6, of the fourth century. For the beating of slaves in other districts of the eastern Mediterranean see Lucian, *Demonax*, 46; *Menippus*, 17; *Timon*, 22.

[48] Galen, *De animi morbis*, 4, Kühn edition, 5: 17.

[49] *Ibid.*, 18-19.

[50] *Ibid.*, 19.

[51] ῥάβδοις or σπάθαις (*virgis*).

[52] μάστιξι, cf. the verb μαστιγοῦν in *Oxyrhynchus papyri* 14: 1643, 11, *flagellis caedere*.

[53] See the instance at Philadelphia in the Fayum of the actual beating by two policemen of a Roman citizen and veteran of the *ala Apriana* in A. D. 153, in *Papyri Berlin*, inventory 13877, A, 4, ῥάβδοις καὶ κόμμασι, *Aegyptus* 12: 129-140.

[54] *Oxyrhynchus papyri* 9: 1186. For the imperial law see Just., *Digest* 48: 19, 10 *ex quibus causis liber fustibus caeditur, ex his servus flagellis caedi. Cf.* 19, 28, and see Mommsen, Theodor, *Römisches Strafrecht*, 983-985, Leipzig, Duncker and Humblot, 1899.

[55] *Oxyrhynchus papyri* 2: 262, 3-6: ὁ δοῦλός μου 'Απολλοφάνης ----ἐτελε(ύτησεν) ἐν τῆι ξένηι.

[56] Diodorus, 1: 80: cf. Lumbroso, Giacomo, *Recherches sur l'économie politique de l'Égypte*, 49, Turin, 1870.

[57] *Rylands papyri* 2: 103; cf. Lumbroso, *ibid.*, 49-51.

[58] Taubenschlag, *Zeitschrift der Savigny-Stiftung* 50: 144, 1.

[59] San Nicolo, Mariano, *Ägyptisches Vereinswesen zur Zeit der Ptolemäer und Römer*, *Münchener Beitrage zur Papyrusforschung* 2: 32-33, Munich, 1915.

[60] *Oxyrhynchus papyri* 10: 1258, 8-9; von Woess, *Asylwesen Ägyptens*, 212-215, Wilcken, *Archiv für Papyrusforschung* 6: 419, against the older view of Rostovtzeff, M., *Göttingische gelehrte Anzeigen*, 640, Berlin, 1909; found also in Rostovtzeff, M., *Studien zur Geschichte des römischen Kolonates*, 217, Leipzig, B. G. Teubner, 1910; see also Mitteis-Wilcken, *Grundzüge* 1: 1, 114.

[61] See *Oslo papyri* 2: 40, 10-11, of A. D. 150. Cf. 96.

[62] Harboring a runaway slave was a punishable offense, *Oxyrhynchus papyri* 12: 1422. Instances of fugitive slaves or of the possibility of flight occur in *BGU* 4: 1149, 33-37, and *Papiri della Società Italiana* 6: 710, 7, has provision against flight or death of the slave. *Oxyrhynchus papyri* 3: 472, 14; 12: 1422. In *Geneva papyri* 5, 4-5, a slave is listed as ἀφανής, and cf. *Oxyrhynchus papyri* 14: 1643, 5-9. Kalén, Ture, *Berliner Leihgabe griechischer papyri*, 15, Uppsala, 1932. From

callow brutality toward slaves cited above we have many reports which lay a higher claim upon our belief and our recognition as historical incidents.[63] The attitude of the slave towards his servitude was no doubt one of a constant desire for freedom such as appears in a letter to his patron written by a freedman who seems to have been in charge of some slave weavers: "but you know in your soul that I, desiring your affection, have conducted myself blamelessly just as a slave wishes to be conciliatory in the interest of his freedom." [64]

The traditional belief in the cruelty of treatment accorded to the slave class under the Roman Empire and in the general bitterness of their lot [65] has its inception in the acknowledged ruthlessness displayed toward them in Italy and Sicily under the Republic. It finds some support, also, in the Roman satire and other literature of the first century in the depiction of acts of cruelty which, although imaginative, may be accepted as indicative of the treatment received by some slaves in individual cases in the highest social circles at Rome.[66] One instance is recorded of the crucifixion of a slave because he had blasphemed by the *genius* of Gaius.[67] In another case a slave adulterer was thrown to wild beasts,[68] and the poet, Propertius, speaks of the punishment of a slave girl by being hung up by the hair.[69] Of greater historical significance are the concern expressed regarding the effects upon Roman children of the sight of punishments inflicted upon slaves [70] and the general statements and admonitions against abuse of the master's powers of punishment which appear in Seneca.[71] This is in complete conformity with a popular attitude of the time

which expressed itself in favor of the egalitarian position of all people, whether bond or free. With his genuine gift of rhetorical expression Seneca has stated this inner equality of every great and upright soul, irrespective of its civil status. "What else might one call this (soul) than God dwelling as a guest in a human body? Such a soul might chance to descend into a Roman knight as well as into a freedman or into a slave." [72] Actual cases of crucifixion of slaves are reported in two other reliable sources.[73] Galen's eye-witness tale of a bloody attack upon two slaves must be literally acceptable,[74] but his story that Hadrian put out the eye of a slave in anger [75] is not trustworthy. In addition to these there are other instances of brutality.[76] It may be assumed that under some slave-owners the quality of the food served to slaves was not good and the quantity insufficient.[77] The appearance of suicide among the slaves in the period of the Empire [78] must, however, be regarded as an evidence of the penetration into the lower classes of the custom of self-destruction as an accepted method of escape from the difficulties of life [79] rather than as additional evidence of the great cruelty of the slave system of that time.[80]

There was no special and distinguishing type of garment worn by the slaves, even in the West.[81] The proposal of Alexander Severus to establish a distinctive type of dress for the slaves of the imperial court was connected with an attempt to introduce uniforms through all ranks of the imperial staff and to discipline the slaves by preventing them from mingling with the free-born population. Because of the opposition of the jurists Ulpian and Paulus the idea was abandoned.[82]

The amount of our information upon the housing

---

the fourth century, see *London papyri* 2: 14, 317, where the slaves who are being sold are called "faithful and not given to running away," ἀδράστους.

[63] In Suetonius, *Augustus*, 67, 2, we have a case of a slave put to death for adultery. Cf. Suetonius, *Caligula*, 32, 1-7 and Tacitus, *Annals* 4: 54 and 16: 19. The story of Vedius Pollio who ordered a slave, because of a minor accident, to be thrown into a fish pond to be eaten alive was well known in antiquity. The slave was saved by action of Augustus, as seen in Pliny, *Natural history* 9: 77; Seneca, *De ira* 3: 40; *De clementia* 1: 18; and Dio Cassius, 54: 23, 1-2.

[64] *BGU* 4: 1141, 23-25, of 14 B.C.

[65] Allard, Paul, *Les esclaves chrétiens* (6th ed.), 127-132, Paris, J. Gabalda, 1914. Halkin, Leon, *Les esclaves publics chez les Romains*, 221-222, Brussels, 1897. Gordon, M. L., The nationality of slaves under the early Roman Empire, *Jour. Roman Studies* 14: 93-111, 1924.

[66] See this chapter, p. 105. For alleged instances of flogging and branding see Petronius, 30, 69. Martial, 2: 66; 3: 94; 8: 23. Apuleius Madaurensis, *Metamorphoses* 3: 16. Juvenal, *Satires*, 6, 475-485. Cf. 4, 179-180. For the criticism regarding acceptance at face value of the picture drawn by Juvenal see Schneider, A., *Geschichte der Sclaverei*, 20-21.

[67] Petronius, *Satyricon*, 53. Cf. Juvenal, *Satires* 6: 219, 475-485; 8: 179-180. Martial, 2: 82.

[68] Petronius, *Satyricon*, 45.

[69] Propertius, 4: 7, 45.

[70] Juvenal, *Satires*, 14, 23-24.

[71] Seneca, *De ira* 3: 19, 2; 32, 1; *De constantia* 5: 1. For cases of slaves forced by cruelty to flight or suicide see *De ira* 3: 5, 4; *De clementia* 1: 13, 2. Cf. *De beneficiis* 2: 35; *Ad Marciam*, 20, 2.

[72] Seneca, *Epistulae morales*, 31, 11.

[73] Tacitus, *Histories* 2: 72, and Dio Cassius, 54: 3, 7.

[74] Galen, *De animi morbis*, 4, edition Kühn 5: 18.

[75] *Ibid.*, 17.

[76] *Cf.* Dio Cassius, 59: 13, 2; 60: 12, 1; 61: 31, 1-2; 33, 8. See also *Scriptores historiae Augustae, Commodus*, 1, 9, and *Macrinus*, 12, 10.

[77] See the statement of the Italian brigand, Bulla, that the slaves must be fed if the officials wished to put an end to brigandage, in Dio Cassius, 77: 10, 5.

[78] Seneca, *De ira* 3: 5, 4; *Epistulae* 4: 4; 70, 20; 77, 14; Dessau, *ILS*, 8511. Just., *Digest* 21: 1, 23, 3. *Cf. ibid.* 1: 17, 5.

[79] Hirzel, Rudolph, Der Selbstmord, *Archiv für Religionswissenschaft* 11: 417-476, 1908. *Cf. the statement of Seneca, Ad Marciam*, 20, that suicide was an easy avenue of escape from slavery.

[80] As presented by Allard, *Les esclaves chrétiens*, 139-145.

[81] Seneca, *De clementia* 1: 24, 1. Daremberg-Saglio, *Dictionnaire des Antiquités* 4 (2), 1279. No distinction by costume as between the slaves and the free was made by the Roman artists of the Empire, *see JRS* 14: 96.

[82] *Script. hist. Aug., Alexander Severus*, 23, 3; *cf.* 27, 1. In the price edict of Diocletian the assignment of certain types of clothing to peasants and slaves, as was done by Blümner, Hugo, *Der Maximaltarif des Diocletian*, 169, 172, Berlin, Reimer, 1893, was based upon an unwarranted restriction of the words φαμιλιάριος and φαμιλιαρικός to the slaves of the *familia*. For the inclusive meaning see Pauly-W., *RE* 6: 1981-1982. *Cf. IG* 3, nos. 2511 and 3213; *P. Oxy.* 14: 1712, 3 and *BGU* 1: 816, 10.

conditions of slaves in Italy, particularly for the cities, is not great. At Pompeii no living quarters especially intended for the slaves have been found, even in the better houses, except in the Casa del Menandro. They apparently lodged where it happened to be convenient, perhaps in the upper stories of the houses when they lived with their owners, and in the quarters of the city in which the poorer artisans lived when they lived apart.[83] In the Casa del Menandro the quarters of the servants were constructed upon one side of the building cut off from the remainder of the house except for a long corridor which connected the two parts,[84] and with separate entrances for admission and departure of the slaves without the necessity of going through the atrium and peristyle.[85] Their lodging rooms were on the second floor, opening upon a rustic court which contained below stable and store rooms, a kitchen and latrines for the slaves.[86] In the Laurentine villa of Pliny, also, the quarters of the slaves and freedmen were set apart so that the voices of the *familia* could not be heard in the rooms used by the free members of the household.[87] Pliny considered them pleasant enough to receive his guests.[88] His slaves slept in groups, in dormitory fashion.[89] It is probable that the lodging conditions provided for slaves on these wealthier estates were more comfortable than those of the servile class resident in the towns and cities.

The treatment of sick slaves was dependent upon the individual kindness or callousness of the owner. The lack of humanity toward sick slaves on the part of some of the slave-owners called forth the decree of Claudius providing that sick slaves who had been exposed and recovered were to be free.[90] In contrast with this practice stand notable instances of solicitude for the health of slaves which were motivated by intrinsic kindness as well as by economic interest. Pliny's statement that free persons in ill health received gentler treatment from their medical attendants than slaves proves that slaves customarily received medical care.[91] He writes to a friend[92] that he had again sent into the country a favorite freedman, his reader, whom he had previously sent to Egypt because of lung trouble. An insane slave who attacked Hadrian with a sword was turned over to the

care of a physician.[93] Pliny the Younger furnishes a notable example of liberality in the treatment of the members of his slave *familia*. He permitted them to make wills, leaving their property *intra domum*; and he faithfully executed the terms of these wills, although they were not legally valid testaments.[94] There is also further evidence of kindly treatment or affectionate relations between masters and slaves.[95]

Unusual cruelty on the part of the masters was often met by the retribution of murder,[96] or by the flight of the abused slave. The problem of the runaways (*fugitivi, errones*) was a serious one in all parts of the Empire, constituting a loss of property and of valuable services to the owners of slaves and a general public menace through the increase in brigandage.[97] The imperial legislation defining the *fugitivus* and fixing the terms and methods of his arrest and return to his owner[98] testifies to the extent of slave desertions and the administrative difficulties involved in their apprehension. The aedilian edicts directed that, in sales of slaves in the open market, a declaration must be made that the slave was inclined to run away if he had shown this tendency,[99] the vendor being liable to redhibitory action in case this defect should appear within a limited period.

The search for slaves in *fuga* became under the Empire an organized business conducted by private *fugitivarii*[100] who delivered the apprehended runaways either directly to the owners or to the nearest municipal magistrate. The magistrate was required to guard the slave until he could be delivered to the *praeses* or *praefectus vigi-*

[83] As in Arsinoe in the Fayum in Egypt, see this chapter, notes 26-31.

[84] Maiuri, A., *Casa del Menandro* 1: 186-188, Rome, 1933. Cf. ibid. 2, pl. 1.

[85] *Ibid.* 1: 187.

[86] *Ibid.* 2, pl. 1, no. 39. For similar lodging conditions for slaves on the estates in Campania consult della Corte, M., in *Notizie degli scavi di antichità* 22: 459, 1922: *l'angolo sud est del atrio servile*; and see villa no. 8 in *Notizie degli scavi* 23: 277, fig. 4, 1923. Consult, also, Rostovtzeff, M. I., *Soc. and econ. hist. Roman empire*, 504, n. 21 to chap. 2.

[87] Pliny, *Epistles* 2: 17, 22.

[88] *Ibid.* 2: 17, 9.

[89] *Ibid.* 7: 27, 13.

[90] Suetonius, *Claudius*, 25; Just., *Digest* 40: 8, 2.

[91] Pliny, *Epistles* 8: 24, 5.

[92] *Ibid.* 5: 19, 1-4.

[93] *Scriptores historiae Augustae, Hadrian*, 12, 5. See Seneca, *De beneficiis* 2: 21, 2. Cf. Jacoby, *Fr. GH* 2A: 426, no. 139.

[94] Pliny, *Epistles* 8: 16, 1-2. Note his sadness at the death of young slaves and his desire to free them before death occurred.

[95] See Petronius, 57, 9, *nemo tamen sciit utrum servus essem an liber.* Cf. the inscription to a house-born slave child who was held *in loco filii*, in Dessau, *Inscriptiones*, 8554. See also Florus, Lucius Annaeus, 3: 20, and Dio Cassius, 60: 12, 2, 4. There is a poetic picture of the relations of house born slave children and their masters in Tibullus, Albius, 2: 1, 21; 1: 5, 25.

[96] Seneca, *Ad Neronem de clementia* 1: 26, 1, *crudelitatem privatorum serviles quoquo manus sub certo crucis periculo ultae sunt.* Cf. *Epistles* 4: 8, and the case of the freedman Largius Macedo whom Pliny, in *Epistles* 3: 14, 1, describes as *superbus alioqui dominus et saevus.* Cf. 7: 6, 8, where the slaves were suspected of murdering their owner. Killing of a master at Moguntiacum, followed by suicide of the slave murderer is cited in Dessau, *ILS*, 8511.

[97] For the connection of runaway slaves with robber bands, see Dio Cassius, 77: 10, 5. Cf. Juvenal, *Satires*, 8, 173-182, who associates a decadent noble with *nautis et furibus ac fugitivis inter carnifices.* Further references showing the prevalence of desertion of slaves are to be found in Petronius, 98, 107; Juvenal, *Satires*, 10, 3; Pliny, *Epistles* 9: 21, 1. Lucian, *Juppiter Tragoedus*, 42, and *Alexander seu Pseudomantis*, 24 who discovered fugitive slaves for their owners. Apuleius, *Metamorphoses* 6: 8; Martial, 3: 91; Epictetus, 3: 26, 1.

[98] Buckland, W. W., *The Roman law of slavery*, 267-274, Cambridge, Univ. Press, 1908.

[99] Gellius, Aulus, *Noctes Atticae* 4: 2. *Digest* 21: 1, 1, 1. Cf. Karlowa, Otto, *Römische Rechtsgeschichte* 2: 1220-1221, Leipzig, Veit, 1901.

[100] Florus, 3: 19; *Digest* 21: 1, 17, 12.

lum.[101] The case of the slave-owners was further strengthened by the imposition of a penalty upon anyone who might discover a *fugitivus* upon his land and did not report the fact within twenty days.[102] In the early years of the Roman Empire, possibly under the principate of Augustus,[103] the right of the slaves to flee for refuge to the statue of the Emperor afforded some measure of protection to them through the assurance of a hearing for their grievances.[104] In Bithynia a slave who had formerly belonged to Labirius Maximus, *legatus pro praetore* in Moesia in A. D. 100, took refuge at the statue of Trajan.[105] In Greece the old practice of sanctuary at the altars of the gods against abuse by a master (*dominus*) with the right to demand sale to another owner [106] still remained in force.[107] Although the Roman imperial law did not grant the right of temple asylum for slaves,[108] the provision that a slave might demand sale out of the possession of an abusive master was accepted in the later Roman law.[109]

Slaves were not exempted from enjoying many of the pleasures which the time afforded. They could attend the theatre, the gladiatorial games, and the races [110] and might, upon occasion, share in municipal banquets.[111]

In the funerary clubs [112] the slaves of Italy enjoyed both social pleasures while living and an assurance of honorable funeral rites after death. They were accepted as members of the occupational clubs also, in so far as these were not professional colleges of men working for the Roman state,[113] and much more freely in the *collegia tenuiorum*. The permission of the slave-owner was required before the slave could accept membership in an association; [114] but this seems to have been granted

readily. A funerary college is mentioned [115] as having its locality where the association held its meetings for sacrifices and banquets connected with the place of burial; [116] but the *collegia domestica* of the wealthy families were customarily supplied with a meeting place in the houses of the owners.[117] In those *collegia* into which the slaves were admitted in association with freedmen and free persons they held a position of social equality with their fellow members.[118] In certain of the associations of initiates into the mysteries of Bacchus all the social distinctions of the profane world were so completely effaced that all members of the spiritual confraternity,[119] without distinction as to freedom or servitude, were called by their surnames alone.[120] In these *collegia*, and even in those which were composed of slaves alone, they found satisfaction for the innate human desire for social preferment in group activities, in serving in the elective offices of *magistri* and *magistrae, curatores, decuriones,* or *praefecti*; in the arrangements for banquets; in the imposition of fines and the offering of sacrifices; in distributions of surplus funds; and in presiding over meetings.[121] In the *collegium funeraticium* of Lanuvium, which contained both slaves and free,[122] it was ordained that, if any slave member should die and his body should not be handed over by his owner to the *collegium* for burial, the association would pay him the honor of a fictitious burial (*funus imaginarium*). Each slave member was required, when he attained his freedom, to donate an amphora of good wine to the college.[123]

Concluding this survey of improvement of the position of the slave class during the first three centuries of the Empire, it should be emphasized that the movement was not uniform in the direction of a softening of the social attitude. Nor was it consecutive in its retrogressive phases. So far as the ancient contemporary evidence goes the overall trend clearly favored a better treatment of the slave population. This is apparent from a number of legal enactments which reflect and incorporate elements of the popular change. In the fol-

---

[101] Lenel, Otto, *Das Edictum perpetuum,* 4, Leipzig, B. Tauchnitz, 1927.

[102] Apuleius, *Metamorphoses* 6: 4. *Celare fugitivum* paid a double penalty, as cited by Woess, Friedrich von, *Das Asylwesen Ägyptens in der Ptolemäerzeit,* 178, from the *Digest* 11: 4, 1, 1.

[103] Barrow, R. H., *Slavery in the Roman Empire,* 59.

[104] Seneca, *De beneficiis* 3: 22; *De clementia* 1: 18, 1-3; *Digest* 1: 12, 1, 1 and 8, entire; 21: 1, 17, 12.

[105] Pliny, *Epistles* 10: 74. See the complaint against abuse of this privilege at Rome under Tiberius, Tacitus, *Annals* 3: 36, 2.

[106] See above chap. 3, pp. 17-18.

[107] Plutarch, *Moralia,* 166, D, E.

[108] See the remark of Juno in Apuleius, *Metamorphoses* 6: 4, *legibus quae servos alienis profugas invitis dominis suscipi vetant prohibeor.*

[109] *Digest* 21: 1, 17, 12.

[110] Columella, 1: 8, 2; Petronius, 45, 70; Dio Cassius, 69: 16, 3.

[111] Dessau, *ILS,* 5672, cites an instance where money left for bathing facilities at Praeneste could be used for all, including slaves. At Suasa in Umbria, *ibid.,* 5673. At Ferentinum slave children were included with free children in a distribution of nuts arranged for by bequest of a citizen, 6271. Cf. Barrow, *Slavery in the Roman Empire,* 169-170.

[112] Schiess, Traugott, *Die römischen Collegia Funeraticia,* Munich, Askermann, 1888.

[113] Waltzing, J.-Pierre, *Les corporations professionnelles chez les Romains* 2: 245; 1: 346-347, Louvain 1895-1900. Rostovtzeff, *Gesellschaft und Wirtschaft* 1: 147, 304, n. 22.

[114] *Digest* 47: 22, 3, 2; Pauly-W., *RE* 4: 417.

[115] *CIL* 6: 10237.

[116] Waltzing, *Les corporations professionnelles* 1: 214.

[117] *CIL* 3: 4017, 4799, 7357; 6: 7458, 8750, 9148, 9149, 9404, 10251a, 10260-10264; 12: 4449; 14: 2875.

[118] Barrow, *Slavery in the Roman Empire,* 165.

[119] *Fratribus suis* in Dessau, *ILS,* 3360.

[120] Cumont, Franz, La grande inscription bachique du Metropolitan Museum, *Amer. Jour. Arch.* 37, 232-236, 1933. Among the *cultores Dei Solis Invicti Mithrae* of Sentinum, *CIL* 11: 5737 (reproduced in Dessau, *ILS,* 4215) appear a freedman (col. 1, 5), and a public slave of the municipality of Sentinum (col. 3, 3).

[121] Waltzing, *Les corporations professionnelles* 4: 251 ff. Barrow, *Slavery in the Roman Empire,* 165. For women holding offices as *magistrae* see Waltzing, 4: 3, 41, and Dessau, *ILS,* 7882d. Cf. the *magistrae* in the cult associations of Minturnae under the Republic in Johnson, J., *Excavations at Minturnae* 2 (1): 120.

[122] Bruns-Gradenwitz, *FIR*[7] no. 175, reproduced in Dessau, *ILS* 7212, 2, 4.

[123] *Ibid.* 2 (2), 7212, frag. II, 6.

lowing chapters, which are to deal with both slavery and some attendant features of bondage relations in the post-Diocletian period, it should become clear that the analyses of these subjects emanating from nineteenth-century scholarship were dominated by two powerful social interests of that time. These were the flow of the abolitionist movement and a strong belief in the softening influence of Christianity upon the manners and activities of the two and one-half centuries from Diocletian's reign to the death of Justinian.

In the discussion of enslavement in the first three centuries of the Empire it is necessary to establish and analyze separately the popular attitude toward the slave group and the imperial legislation which was required to give sanction to the popular feeling. The difference between them is aptly illustrated by an incident which occurred at Rome under the principate of Hadrian. Dio Cassius is our primary source for the tale.[124] Upon the occasion of one of the spectacles at Rome the populace in attendance shouted their demand that a favorite charioteer who was a slave should be set free. Hadrian refused this request in a posted pronouncement expressed in these approximate terms:

It does not befit me, nor is it fitting to request of me, that I should free a slave belonging to another person, or compel his owner to do this.

It is clear that the decision of Hadrian in this instance was based upon a constitutional question of the extent of the imperial authority as against the right of private-property interest in slave ownership. If this was the influence motivating Hadrian's refusal, the clash between the popularity of a slave charioteer and the constitutional limits upon the imperial authority is clear. They did not necessarily coincide or move *pari passu*, even with Hadrian, although his usual attitude, as disclosed in his slave legislation, tended to conform to the popular movement of his time by limiting the jurisdic-

tion of the owners over their slaves rather than the reverse.[125]

From evidence which comes from the slaves themselves there is ample testimony that, even in Roman Italy, a new popular respect for the family relations of slaves had arisen. For in their grave inscriptions the slaves speak of their deceased wives or of their husbands, or of their brothers and the sisters whom death has taken from them, in the same terms of relationship as those used by the free. Particularly revealing in this regard is a Latin burial inscription from the region about Locri in southern Italy. In it, with permission of her owner, the death of a slave woman at the age of thirty is recorded by her " father and fellow slave." [126]

One may respect Seneca as an early and a bold exponent of this general change in feeling regarding slavery which was so characteristic of the early Empire. But the sources out of which this transformation arose in the acceptance of slaves lay deeper than the teachings of the Roman Stoicism of Seneca. Chronological reasons regarding the spread of Christianity, and the acceptance of the institution of slavery by the new religion, make it apparent, also, that the new attitude did not spring from Christian doctrine.[127] This does not mean, however, that Christian teaching did not contribute, within the limits of its own communities, to the feeling of equality between slave and free labor which appeared in the early Empire.[128]

---

[124] Dio Cassius, 69: 16, excerpted from Dio by Zonaras, *Annals* 11 : 24.

[125] Bernard d'Orgeval, *L'empereur Hadrien*, 71-72, Paris, Douort,, 1950.

[126] Dessau *ILS* **2** (2) : 8438 (*CIL* **10** [1] : 26.)

[127] Barrow, R. H., *Slavery in the Roman Empire*, 158, London, Methuen, 1928, although he is judicious and restrained in his presentation of the humane tendency of the Roman legislation of the early Empire, ascribes a greater influence for this trend to Stoicism than I would venture to do.

[128] The legal uplifting of the slave class in the economic-legal sense during the first century appears, for the period of Vespasian, in a wax-tablet receipt from Herculaneum published by Giovanni P. Carratelli as tablet VIII in *La Parola del Passato* **1** : 383-384, 1940. A slave named Venustus acknowledges receipt in full for 1,000 *denarii* due to a fellow slave owned by the same person, a woman.

XVII. IMPERIAL SLAVES AND FREEDMEN OF THE EMPERORS

AMELIORATION OF SLAVERY

One of the outstanding features of slavery under the Roman Empire is the great importance which fell to the slaves of the imperial family (*servi Caesaris*) posted throughout the Empire during the first two centuries after Christ. The importance attained by them while in slave status was in many instances continued throughout the rest of their lives as imperial freedmen, as is attested by many inscriptions found in all parts of the Empire and by the literature of the period. It is explained by the accepted position which slaves had assumed during the late Republic as trusted and capable

agents of the great Roman *familiae* [1] and by the great amount of the personal properties and patrimonial inheritances of the Emperors. Under Augustus these two sources of revenue played an important part in his benefactions.[2] His private wealth was increased during his principate by large bequests of friends, relatives, and

---

[1] See above, p. 74.

[2] Monumentum Ancyranum, 18: *ex privato et patrimonio meo*; cf. Wilcken, U., in *Sitzungsb. Akademie der Wissenschaften, Berlin, ph.-hist. Klasse* **27** : 773, 777, 780, Berlin, 1931.

dependents.[3] Many additional slaves were incorporated among the *servi Caesaris* as parts of such bequests.[4] Absorption of slaves into the group of the *servi Caesaris* is also recorded under Vitellius.[5] The growing extent of the imperial domains and other properties of the Emperors, both in the imperial and in the senatorial provinces, and the increasing ceremony and luxury of the imperial household [6] encouraged the use of slaves or freedmen in the confidential and personal duties which were involved.

The Greek city-states and Republican Rome had long been familiar with the use for municipal services of slaves owned by the state.[7] Because of the predominant position of the Emperors in Rome itself and their interest in the city it is difficult to establish any important difference between the *servi publici populi Romani* of Rome and the *servi Caesaris* who were in service there, except in the budgetary provisions for their maintenance. While Octavianus Caesar, during the years 40-30 B. c., was gradually assuming power, and still more in the period after he took full control in 27 B. c., it was natural that he should turn to the body of slaves and freedmen of his *familia*, with whose competence he was familiar, for the accomplishment of the details of management of his great personal fortune.[8] Because of the lack of clear definition between his own properties and those which accrued to him as Emperor it was a simple and natural expedient for him to employ men from the group of his slaves for the administration of his imperial properties.[9] In so far as the services which these slaves rendered were kept within the bounds of work directly connected with the imperial household and its investments and did not encroach upon actual magisterial duties or involve titles identified with these duties [10] there was nothing inherently opposed to the custom of the time in such use of slaves of the *Princeps*.

The history of the *cura aquarum* of the city of Rome is characteristic of this development.[11] This service in the later period of the Republic had been thoroughly organized and placed under the administration of the censors, aediles, and quaestors. They leased the conduct of the water service to entrepreneurs who used their own slaves for the work, although these slaves were kept under quasi-official oversight.[12] When Agrippa was made aedile in 33 B. c. he followed this procedure in forming a group of his own slaves which he placed in charge of the water system as a permanent body. Upon his death they were incorporated by will of Agrippa among the slaves of Augustus, hence became *servi Caesaris*. When Augustus Caesar died he left this group to the state in his will [13] so that they were transferred to the classification of *servi publici* of Rome [14] and placed under the direction of appointees of senatorial rank called *curatores aquarum*.[15] Claudius, when he added new aqueducts to the city water supply, reorganized the administration of the system by installing freedmen of the imperial family as *procuratores aquarum* [16] and by adding a supplementary body of *servi Caesaris* to the existing *servi publici populi Romani*, so that the entire system under Nerva was composed of 240 *servi publici*, developed from the original group established by Agrippa, and 460 *servi Caesaris*.[17] To this considerable group must be added the six hundred slaves whom Augustus had put under the direction of the curule aediles as a permanent *familia publica* [18] in 22 B. c. when he organized a city fire department. The assignment of these public firemen for duty was made in accordance with the regions of the city.[19]

In the actual management of the household of the imperial palace slaves and freedmen of the Emperors are attested by many dedicatory inscriptions as engaged in those types of occupations for which they were customarily used in any great Roman household, either as attendants of members of the imperial family or as assistants assigned by the emperors to their administrative agents. Among these we find the " footmen " (*pedisequi*) who were probably attendants of an imperial procurator at Carthage; *paedagogi puerorum*, teachers of the pages in attendance at the imperial court; physicians; chamberlains; litter-bearers; overseers of the furniture; overseer of lighting of the palace, *ex peculiaris lampadaris*; slaves in charge of ointment (*unctores*) and of the selection of jewelry to be used with particular costumes (*ornatores, ornatrices*); valets of several types of clothing; tailors and clothing menders; a butler in charge of wine for the imperial table (*adiutor a vinis*); an official taster; a slave in charge of the sacred implements; and a steward in charge of supplies [20] (*dispens[ator] a frumento*).

---

[3] *Ibid.* 783; Hirschfeld, Otto, in *Klio* 2: 45-50, 1902 (= Hirschfeld, *Kleine Schriften*, 516-521).

[4] Hirschfeld, *Klio* 2: 51-53; Dessau, *ILS*, 1821: *Diogneto Ti. Au(gusti) ser(vo) Alypiano*. The slave of Tiberius had formerly belonged to Alypius. Cf. 1535, 1824, 1773, 1789; Hirschfeld, *Klio* 2; 49-50.

[5] Tacitus, *Hist.* 2: 92.

[6] Hirschfeld, Otto, *Die kaiserlichen Verwaltungsbeamten bis auf Diocletian*, 307-317, Berlin, Weidmann, 1905.

[7] For the importance of the *servi publici* at Rome under the Republic see L. Halkin, *Les Esclaves publics chez les Romains*, 15-32, Brussels, Société belge de librairie, 1897.

[8] Suetonius, *Augustus*, 67, 2.

[9] Hirschfeld, Otto, *Verwaltungsbeamten*, 458-459; Rostovtzeff, M. I., *Soc. and econ. hist. Roman Empire*, 55.

[10] Hirschfeld, *Verwaltungsbeamten*, 412, 1; 413.

[11] Pauly-Wissowa, *RE* 4: 1784.

[12] Frontinus, *De aquaeductibus urbis Romae*, 96; Halkin, L., *Esclaves publics*, 80.

[13] Frontinus, *De aquaeductibus*, 98.

[14] E. g., *Laetus publicus populi Romani aquarius*, Dessau, *ILS*, 1775 = *CIL* 6: 2345; cf. 2343, 8489.

[15] Halkin, *Esclaves publics*, 80-81.

[16] Frontinus, *De aquaeductibus*, 105.

[17] *Ibid.*, 116; cf. Hirschfeld, *Verwaltungsbeamten*, 273-276.

[18] Dio Cassius, 54: 2, 4; Halkin, *Esclaves publics*, 85-86.

[19] *CIL* 6: 2342, *Barnaeus de familia public(a) reg(ionis)* VIII; Halkin, *Esclaves publics*, 87.

[20] The references to the occupations are here given in the order in which they are enumerated in the text above. Dessau, 1789, 1819, 1820, 1821, 1823, 1824; Friedlaender, Ludwig, *Dar-*

The large group of slaves which would fall to a new emperor could be used as his property, as gifts to friends, out of political considerations or for the purpose of winning popular favor.[21] It is also readily understood that the emperors as the richest capitalists and largest slave-owners of the Roman world, would, as any other wealthy proprietor, use the slaves who were trained in special handicrafts to augment the income of the imperial house by practice of their trades or by sale.[22] *Servi Caesaris* are, therefore, to be found in the weaving industry,[23] in the jewelry trade, in silversmithing and goldsmithing[24] and in the building trades, in which they seem to appear in greater numbers as the powers of the emperors increased.[25] A *praepositus* of the apprentice mirror-makers of the imperial household is also mentioned.[26]

The powers which were gained in the first two centuries by some of the slaves of the imperial domestic service through their necessarily intimate connection with the persons of the emperors are illustrated by the cases of Helicon, slave[27] of the Emperors Tiberius and Gaius. He was the man whom the Jewish embassy from Alexandria under Philo accused of hatred of their race and of accepting a bribe from their opponents.[28] These powers are to be seen in the cases of Asiaticus, freedman of Vitellius;[29] of Parthenius, *cubiculo praepositus*,[30] and Sigerus, *cubicularius*, both of these in the time of Domitian;[31] and in the example of the Phrygian slave, Cleander, who became *cubicularius* when a freedman under Commodus.[32] He was said to have enrolled freedmen in the Senate, to have sold appointments to the provinces and to have made twenty-five persons consul in one year.[33] The reports of the scandalous conduct of

Elagabalus and the slaves of his household[34] were followed by an attempt under Severus Alexander to re-establish the old distinctions between slaves, freedmen, and equites.[35] A reduction of the number of the *aulicum ministerium* occurred,[36] and the use of them was limited to the duties recognized in earlier days as befitting that class, such as those of messengers, cooks, bakers, fullers and bath-keepers.[37] The employment of eunuchs was entirely eliminated except in the women's baths.[38] The moral implications of this position taken by Alexander Severus are more severe respecting the rich and noble ladies of the high circles of Rome than upon the slaves owned by the same class since the slaves must have been few who dared run the risk of refusing their favors under solicitation of women in positions of power. During the period of anarchy and of the re-establishment of the imperial power in the third century, there was little opportunity for the return to power of the *servi Caesaris* of the imperial palace in the rough service of the soldier emperors of that time.

In the provincial administration the use of the *liberti Augusti*, also called *liberti Caesaris*, was restricted in the main to those positions which were open to direct appointment by the emperors of men who were to act as their personal representatives. Although the title of *procurator* was in general use in application to the position of freedmen managers of the properties of any private Roman of wealth,[39] the emperors were, on the whole, chary of its use by freedmen because of its high political associations. Augustus himself made several appointments of freedmen to high posts, as in the case of Licinius[40] who carried on the duties of a *procurator* in Gaul although probably without the title.[41] Under Tiberius an imperial freedman is known to have carried on, as an interim assignment, the duties of the Prefect of Egypt.[42] He was not, however, vested with the command of the legions stationed there.[43] The increase of the numbers and the political influence of these ex-slaves was rapid. Under Claudius a brother of the powerful freedman Pallas, named Felix, was appointed as procurator of Judaea with command over its troops.[44]

stellungen aus der Sittengeschichte Roms 1: 64, Leipzig, Hirzel, 1922; Dessau, *ILS*, 1825; 1827; 1830; 7811; 1843; 1746; 1751; 1753; 1772; 1773; 1774; 1780; 1784; 1785; 1786a; 1789; 1790; 1791; 1759; 1760; 1787 *sutor*; 1788 *sarcinatrix*; 7428; 7429; 1794; 1795; 7886; 376; 410 *dispens(ator) a frumento; cf.* Friedlaender, *Sittengeschichte Roms*, 68-74; E. Fairon, L'organisation du palais impérial a Rome, *Le Musée Belge* 4: 5-25, Louvain, Charles Peeters, 1900.

[21] Offer made by Vespasian to Vitellius of a retreat, money and slaves, Tacitus, *Hist.* 3: 66; slaves given to the audience in the theatre by Titus, Dio Cassius, 66: 25; *Script. Hist. Augustae, Severus Alexander*, 58, 3, 5; retinue of fourteen slaves assigned to a tribune in a letter to a procurator of Syria, *ibid., Claudius*, 14, 7-11.

[22] Dio Cassius, 59: 28, with respect to Caligula. Sale of gladiators by Caligula, *ibid.*, 14.

[23] Gummerus, Herman, Industrie und Handel, Pauly-W., *RE* 9: 1457.

[24] *Ibid.*, 1458, 1504.

[25] *Ibid.*, 1461.

[26] *CIL* 6: 8659; *cf.* Gummerus, Pauly-W., *RE* 9: 1493.

[27] ἀνδράποδον, Philo, *De legatione ad Gaium*, 166.

[28] *Ibid.* 172.

[29] See article Asiaticus, Pauly-W., *RE* 2: 1578-1579.

[30] Suetonius, *Domitian*, 16, 2.

[31] Pauly-W., *RE*, 2nd ser., 2: 2277; Martial, 4: 78, 7-8; Dio Cassius, 67: 15, 1; Tertullian, *Apology*, 35.

[32] *Script. hist. Aug., Commodus*, 6, 2.

[33] *Ibid.*, 9-13; *cf.* Friedlaender, *Sittengeschichte Roms* 1: 61-62.

[34] *Script. hist. Aug. Elagabalus*, 6, 1; 11, 6; 25, 5; 26, 6. Hierocles the charioteer, a Syrian slave, was supposed to be the lover of Elagabalus, 6, 5; Dio Cassius, 7: 10, 3.

[35] *Script. hist. Aug., Severus Alexander*, 19, 4; 23, 3.

[36] *Ibid.*, 41, 3.

[37] *Ibid.*, 42, 2.

[38] *Ibid.*, 23, 5-8.

[39] *Cf.* the *libertus*, Agathopous, who in the time of Tiberius was προνοητὴς πάντων (= *procurator omnium negotiorum*) of his patron, *OGI* 2: 660.

[40] Suetonius, *Augustus*, 67: *multos libertorum in honore et usu maximo habuit, ut Licinium et Celadium aliosque.*

[41] Despite his designation by Dio Cassius, 54: 21, 7 as ἐπίτροπος τῆς Γαλατίας; *cf.* Hirschfeld, *Verwaltungsbeamten*, 377, n. 7.

[42] Dio Cassius, 58: 19, 6; *cf.* Philo, *In Flaccum* 1: 2.

[43] Hirschfeld, *Verwaltungsbeamten*, 379-380.

[44] Suetonius, *Claudius*, 28, 1. *Cf.* the threat made by Nero that he would turn over the provinces and the military commands to the Roman *equites* and freedmen, Suetonius, *Nero*,

The position of importance which might be attained by such freedmen is illustrated by the fact that sixteen slave assistants (*vicarii*) assigned to Musicus Scurranus, freedman of Tiberius and former paymaster attached to the *fiscus* in Gallia Lugdunensis, were in attendance upon Scurranus when he died at Rome.[45] The names and careers are well known of the powerful freedmen who served in the central administration at Rome. They include Polybius, *a studiis*, Pallas, *a rationibus*, Narcissus, *ab epistulis*, and Castor, *a memoria et a cubiculo*.[46] In the inscriptions freedmen appear in the islands and in other districts of minor importance, especially in Africa, vested with complete administrative control.[47] The Emperor Trajan made use of his freedman, Lycormas, in the period immediately preceding his Parthian Wars, upon a confidential diplomatic mission which had to do with the Bosporan king, Sauromates.[48] Freedmen connected with the conduct of the *patrimonium* in the provinces were later permitted to assume the title of procurators, but their activities were confined chiefly to the finance department.[49] The activities of the actual slaves of the emperors, so long as they remained of that status, were restricted to posts as subordinates and assistants of the provincial magistrates, such as *tabularii* in the different accounting bureaus, *proximi* and *adiutores* of the proconsuls, *dispensatores* and *arcarii* in the provincial paymaster departments, and in other like positions of a clerical and subordinate character.[50] One slave is mentioned, however, as *vicarius* (subordinate) of his owner who was himself a *servus Caesaris* connected with the paymaster's department in the province of Achaea.[51]

The sepulchral inscriptions which give their occupations of these imperial freedmen indicate their pride in the positions which they had attained. In the Palmyrene tariff regulations of A. D. 136-137 a freedman of Caesar named Kilix had, while collector of the *portoria* at Palmyra, fixed the rate to be paid upon unloaded camels.[52] His name continued to be cited as author of that rate. From the statement in the Institutes of Gaius, *si quis . . . servum procuratoris habendi gratia . . . apud consilium manumittat*,[53] and from the absence in the inscriptions of examples of slaves who acted as procurators the conclusion is to be drawn that the *servi Caesaris* were rarely permitted to hold the procuratorial title. It is improbable [54] that in Egypt a nome strategus could be represented by an imperial slave.

Despite these limitations in the first century after Christ, in combination with the imperial freedmen the *servi Caesaris* formed a new and important group in the society of the Empire.[55] The power which they could wield is shown by the statement of Dio Cassius where he enumerates, as those whose positions enabled them to act as informers under Macrinus, the soldiers and the slaves and freedmen of the imperial household as well as knights, senators, and prominent women.[56]

Distinctions of rank appear among these servile bureaucrats, the *servi ordinarii* taking a higher position than the *vicarii*.[57] In accordance with the provisions of the Gnomon of the Idios Logos in Egypt an imperial *vicarius* was not permitted to acquire property or to marry a freedwoman.[58] This regulation obviously did not apply to a *servus ordinarius*.[59] When Hadrian established the policy of displacing the imperial freedmen from all higher administrative posts by the use of the *equites* [60] some diminution of the power and position of the imperial slaves must also have occurred. Except in the case of a temporary reaction under Marcus Aurelius in favor of the use of *servi Caesaris* as procurators,[61] both slaves in the imperial service and freedmen in the higher positions appear with increasing rarity.[62] During the latter half of the third century both imperial slaves and imperial freedmen disappear from the lower administrative posts of the Empire, displaced by a new bureaucracy taken from the free population.[63]

The large number of sepulchral inscriptions set up in the first two centuries of the Empire in memory of imperial slaves, or by them in memory of members of their families, offers the best evidence of their prosperity, of their sense of family solidarity, and of their

37, 3. Under both Claudius and Nero imperial freedmen appear in command of the fleet at Misenum, Hirschfeld, *Verwaltungsbeamten*, 225-226.

[45] Dessau, *ILS* 1: 1514; *cf.* Pliny, *Natural history* 33: 145 upon the display of his wealth by the slave Rotundus, *dispensator Hispaniae citerioris*, in the time of Claudius.

[46] Suetonius, *Claudius*, 28; Dio Cassius, 60: 14, 3-4; 76: 14, 2. *Cf.* Friedlaender, *Sittengeschichte* 1: 52-57; Daremberg-Saglio, 3²: 1218.

[47] Hirschfeld, *Verwaltungsbeamten*, 380, with references to *CIL* 10: 6785, Metrobius as prefect of Pandateria, and 7494, *Chrestion Aug(usti) lib(ertus) proc(urator) insularum Melitae et Gauli*.

[48] Pliny, *Letters to Trajan* 10: 63, 67.

[49] Hirschfeld, *Verwaltungsbeamten*, 381, n. 4.

[50] *Ibid.*, 460-462; *CIL* 3: 6082, 19, *ab iis qui sunt in tabulario Ephes(i)*; 6077, 7-10, *collegia lib(ertorum) et servorum domini n(ostri) Aug(usti)—Magnum et Minervum tabulariorum*; Dessau 1: 1421, *Salvianus Aug(usti) n(ostri) vern(a) dispensator rationis extraord(inariae) provinc(iae) Asiae*; 1516, *Piero Caesaris vern(ae) a commentariis fisci Asiatici*.

[51] Dessau 1: 1503, *cf.* 1504. For multiple references to imperial slaves in such subordinate functions see Dessau 3 (1), *indices*, 414-435.

[52] *OGI*, 629, 90.

[53] Gaius, *Institutes* 1: 19.

[54] *P. Lond.* 2: 98, 12; *cf.* Wilcken's statement in *Archiv für Papyrusforschung* 1: 145.

[55] Rostovtzeff, *Soc. and econ. hist. Roman empire*, 99.

[56] Dio Cassius, 68: 2.

[57] Hirschfeld, *Verwaltungsbeamten*, 462, n. 3; 463, n. 2.

[58] *BGU* 5: 1, 110; *cf.* Meyer, Paul M., *Juristische papyri*, 344, Berlin, Weidmann, 1920.

[59] Examples of marriage with freedwomen, *CIL* 10: 529; Dessau, 1787; *cf.* Taubenschlag, *Zeits. Sav.-Stift.* 50: 161, 7.

[60] Hirschfeld, *Verwaltungsbeamten*, 478.

[61] *Ibid.*, 381, n. 4.

[62] For a freedman procurator of the *praedia Quadratiana* in Phrygia in the principate of Alexander Severus see Buckler, W. H., W. M. Calder, and C. W. M. Cox, Monuments from Iconium, Lycaonia and Isauria, *Jour. Rom. Studies* 14: 28, n. 7, 1924.

[63] Hirschfeld, *Verwaltungsbeamten*, 486.

consciousness of an acknowledged social position. The following examples are selections from a long list: a dedicatory inscription from Carthage by a wife who is not a slave to her husband, a *verna Augustorum*; a sepulchral inscription from Bithynia by a *verna Caesaris* in praise of his wife, a free woman; by a wife, not a slave, to herself and her husband, a slave of Nero; by a woman who is not slave to a slave of Tiberius; from Carthage by a slave to his wife, who is not a slave; a funerary inscription by a *vicarius*, named Thyrsus, presumably slave of Diognetus Alypianus, to Diognetus, who was himself a slave and chief *pedisequus* of Tiberius; another inscription set up by a slave *pedisequus* and his colleague to the mother of the first slave; by one slave of the imperial court to another; from Rome, by his wife, who is not a slave, to a *servus Caesaris* who was a teacher of the boys at the imperial court, whom she calls her *coniunx*; by a slave surgeon of Antonia, wife of Nero Drusus, to Chreste, his fellow slave and his wife; another by a slave consort who calls herself " wife " (*coniunx*), and her slave son to her husband who was a tenant upon the Paccian estate (*fundus Paccianus*) in central Italy.[64]

Memorial inscriptions set up for imperial slaves employed upon the domains of the emperors customarily employ the terms of persons of free status in respect to their family relations.[65] Although their right to claim a legal marriage may be doubted,[66] socially they did not feel themselves to be under the compulsion of the Roman legal principle that their children were *nullo patre* or that their marriages were not upon the same footing as those of free persons.[67] They did not share the privilege of the sustenance allotment which was paid to the *servi publici*[68] although such stipends were paid from the treasury to the public slaves who were connected with the aqueduct system of Rome.[69] This difference between the two types of slaves is explained by Mommsen upon the basis that the stern limitations set by the Roman law upon private slaves were strictly applied to the *servi Caesaris*.[70] Despite their lack of salary payments the *servi Caesaris* must have had money in considerable amounts at their disposal. This is proved in the case of the slave of Domitian's wife who paid for the tiles and the gilding of the roof panels in a temple of Apollo Laermenus in Asia Minor.[71]

It is generally conceded that the condition of the slaves of Italy and the public attitude toward them, as compared with that which had existed previously in Italy and Sicily, had undergone a marked change during the first two centuries of the Empire in the direction of an increased humanity in respect to them.[72] At this time the philosopher Apollonius of Tyana states that everyone except barbarians accepts the fact that slavery is degrading, and that only barbarians will heedlessly sell their children into slavery. This indicates that the society of the time had reached the humanitarian realization that, in the institution of slavery, damage other than that of a purely material kind was inflicted upon a human being by the simple fact of his enslavement.[73] This movement may be connected with the growth of the prerogatives gained by the *servi publici* throughout Italy and in the Roman and Latin colonies of the West:[74] it was probably abetted by the honorable position attained by the slaves and freedmen of the imperial household through their efficient services in the administration of the Empire.[75]

The attitude of subservience toward the *servi Caesaris* displayed by men of the senatorial class at Rome, the great public benefactions made by the group of imperial slaves, their marriages into the highest Roman families and even with the daughters of kings as in the case of Felix, imperial freedman and procurator of Judea,[76] all of these evidences of the power and prosperity to which some slaves might attain must have had their effect upon the public attitude toward the slave class throughout the Empire and particularly at Rome.

In the first century after Christ the changed social consciousness in this respect found expression in three writers of the upper class who represent totally different

---

[64] The references to the descriptions are given in the order in which they appear in the text: Dessau, 1510; 1539; 1760; 1773; 1820; 1821; 1823; 1826; 1830; 7811; 8555.

[65] From Asia Minor, Ἀσκληπιάδη πατρὶ καὶ Μομία μητρί, *Monumenta Asiae Minoris antiqua*, 1: nos. 26 and 28, ἀνδρὶ γλυκυτάτῳ. At Rome the son of parents who were slaves of Nerva at the time of his birth and, therefore, a *servus Caesaris*, is called *filius eorum*, Dessau, 1763.

[66] Mommsen, Th., *Römisches Staatsrecht* (in Marquardt, Joachim and Theodor Mommsen, *Handbuch der römischen Alterthümer*) 2: 836, note 5, Leipzig, Hirzel, 1887.

[67] Ramsay, William Mitchell, Pagan revivalism under the Roman Empire, *Aberystwyth Studies* 4: 11, n. 2, Aberystwyth, Univ. of Wales Press, 1922; cf. Allard, Paul, *Les Esclaves Chrétiens*, 6th ed. 271, Paris, Librairie Le Coffre, 1914.

[68] See Halkin, L., *Esclaves publics*, 112-125 for this and other privileges of the *servi publici*.

[69] Frontinus, *De aquaeductibus*, 118; cf. Pliny, *Letters* 10: 31, 2.

[70] Mommsen, Theod., *Staatsrecht* 2: 826.

[71] *MAMA* 4: 293.

[72] Schneider, Albert, *Zur geschichte der sclaverei im alten Rom*, 20 Zürich, Schulthess, 1892; Vollmann, Franz, *Über das verhältnis der späteren Stoa zur Sklaverei im römischen Reiche*, 5-6 and *passim*, Diss., Erlangen, 1890; Meyer, Eduard, *Kleine schriften*[2] 1: 209; Barrow, R. H., *Slavery in the Roman empire*, 30, 50; Rostovtzeff, *Soc. and econ. hist. Roman empire*, 323; Duff, Arnold M., *Freedmen in the early Roman Empire*, Oxford, Clarendon Press, 194-197, 1928.

[73] Philostratus, *The life of Apollonius of Tyana* 8 (7): 161 (*Loeb Classical Library* 2: 335-337).

[74] Halkin, L., *Esclaves publics*, 229-230.

[75] Cf. Ciccotti, Ettore, *Il tramonto della schiavitù nel mondo antico*, 317-373, Udine, Istituto delle edizioni academiche, 1940. Ciccotti has emphasized, perhaps too strongly, however (372), the importance of the wealth and social position attained by the freedmen in bringing about the change in the public attitude toward the institution of slavery under the Empire. Manumission had always been common and cannot have suffered a change in its effects under the Empire.

[76] Suetonius, *Claudius*, 28; Tacitus, *Histories* 5: 9; Josephus, *Antiquities* 20: 141-143; cf. Friedlaender, *Sittengeschichte Roms* 1: 46-51.

interests and background, namely, Seneca, Petronius, and Pliny the Younger. Other external causes which, combined with the power and responsibilities placed in the hands of the imperial freedmen, produced the change, are to be found in the decrease of slave numbers together with the fact that manumission still continued upon a wide scale,[77] and in the growth of liturgical services exacted from the free population in the third century which ended in a leveling of the standards of living as between the poor free and the slave group.[78] This leveling process in the lower classes of labor was further encouraged by the sacrifice of the lower ranks of the free population of the municipalities and villages throughout the Empire to the fiscal demands of the bureaucracy set up by the central government [79] which brought about a growing sense of community of interest as between the poor free, the freedmen, and the slave populations. An example of this may be noted as early as A. D. 61 when a decision was taken at Rome to put to death all the slaves of Pedanius Secundus who had been murdered by one of their number. The report of this determination, however, caused a tumult among the Roman population of sufficient seriousness to call for the use of armed forces to put it down.[80] Even in the time of Tiberius the people at a theatrical performance had forced the Emperor to manumit an actor.[81] Eventually manumissions of this type, gained by pressure of the people in the theatre, became an abuse which had to be met by imperial legislation against it.[82] In the third century the leveling of the class barriers between free and slave became open and recognized among the Christians when the Pope Calixtus officially sanctioned the cohabitation of Christian free women and Christian slaves because legal marriage for them was impossible.[83]

The gradual change thus noted in the social consciousness toward slaves is best represented in a series of imperial enactments passed in the first three centuries of our era which attempted to better the social and legal status of the unfree.[84] By a lex Petronia de servis of A. D. 19 the former right of life and death held by the slave owner was restricted by the provision that the use of slaves in deadly combat with animals was only permissible by magisterial approval.[85] In A. D. 20 the same

procedure was established by a *senatus consultum* for the trial of slave criminals as was followed in the case of free criminals.[86] By an enactment passed under Claudius the killing of sick or crippled slaves by their owners was placed in the same catagory as murder; and if sick slaves were exposed by their masters upon the island of Aesculapius in order to avoid the responsibility of medical care for them, these were to be free in case they recovered.[87] Under Domitian the castration of slaves to be sold as eunuchs was forbidden.[88]

In practical affairs as well as in the increased kindness of attitude toward slaves as exhibited in social speculation regarding them, the lines of class cleavage between free and slave tended to disappear. This trend becomes noticeable in the craft of medicine. Contrary to the legal prohibition known to have existed in some of the Greek polities which did not permit slaves to practise the medical *technē* except upon fellow slaves it had become the habit of the rich and powerful at Rome under the late Republic to use their own slaves and freedmen as practical nurses and for household doctoring. Augustus Caesar himself employed one of his freedmen named Antonius Musa as health adviser and practitioner in his own frequent illnesses.[89] Galen, the eminent Pergamene physician of the second century, bitterly attacked the methods used by a Greek physician named Thessalus who practiced at Rome in Nero's time. He accused him of being a charlatan and an unscrupulous critic of his medical predecessors in promoting his own personal reputation. Among his angry accusations against Thessalus, Galen includes him among the group of doctors who, for the sake of the money to be earned thereby, accepted superannuated slave chamberlains of the houses of the rich among their medical students.[90]

The necessary conclusion of the uplifting of slaves into the higher echelons of the *technai*, such as medicine, is confirmed by the discovery in 1934, in the lower city of Pergamum in Asia Minor, of a rescript of the Emperor Domitian, dated A. D. 93-94. Although the rescript, which is written in Latin, is badly damaged its general context is certain. The Emperor states that many slaves were being admitted to training, meaning apprentice instruction, in the " art " of medicine. The

[77] Persson, Axel, *Staat und Manufaktur im römischen Reiche*, 54-55, Lund, Blom, 1923.
[78] Rostovtzeff, *Soc. and econ. hist. Roman empire*, 431-432.
[79] *Ibid.*, 451.
[80] Tacitus, *Annals* 14: 42, 45.
[81] Suetonius, *Tiberius*, 47.
[82] Decree of Marcus Aurelius, Just., *Digest* 40: 9, 17; *cf.* Jonkers, E. J., De l'influence du Christianisme sur la législation relative à l'esclavage dans l'antiquité, in *Mnemosyne, Bibliotheca Classica Batava*, 3d ser. 1: 242, 1934.
[83] Hippolytus, *Philosophumena* 9: 12, Migne, J. P., *Patrologiae Graecae* 16³: 3386-3387; Harnack, Adolf von, *The mission and expansion of Christianity in the first three centuries* 1: 170, n. 5, New York, Putnam, 1908; Jonkers, *Mnemosyne*, 3d ser. 1: 262-263.
[84] Schneider, Albert, *Zur geschichte der sclaverei im alten Rom*, 28.
[85] Pauly-W., *RE* 12: 2401; *cf.* the alleged example of con-

demnation of a slave to the arena in Gellius, *Noctes Atticae* 5: 14, 27.
[86] Just., *Digest* 48: 2, 12, 3.
[87] Suetonius, *Claudius*, 25; Just., *Digest* 40: 8, 2.
[88] Suetonius, *Domitian*, 7. This was extended in its application by a rescript of Hadrian, who forbade castration of free or slave, with or without consent, Just., *Digest*, 48: 8, 4, 2. The law of Domitian against castration probably applied to Egypt also. See *BGU* 5: 112; *cf.* Schubart, W., Galli und Spadones im Gnomon des Idios Logos, *Aegyptus* 14: 89, 1934.
[89] Pauly-W., *RE* 1: 2633, *s. v.* Antonius, no. 79.
[90] Galen, On the method of healing (*Therapeutikē technē*), 1, in Kühn, C. G., *Claudi Galeni Opera* 10: 4, Leipzig, Cnobloch, 1825. Upon Thessalus of Tralles consult the article of Ernst Diehl in Pauly-W., *RE* 6 A 1: 168-182. Diehl rehabilitates the reputation of Thessalus. Pliny, *Naturalis historia* 29: 1, 4 (9) presented the same critical attitude regarding him as Galen showed later.

reason assigned by the decree for the lowering of the bar against slaves in medical practice was the same, apparently, as that assigned by Galen in the case of Thessalus, the " greed " of the doctors who accepted them as pupils. Domitian's rescript forbade the continuation of this practice with sanctions to enforce obedience to his decision.[91] From two widely separated parts of the Empire, therefore, Rome and Asia Minor, the evidence has been given us that in the latter half of the first century after Christ slaves and freedmen moved upward into the higher occupations of the " liberal arts " and were there accepted in numbers which seemed to require legislation to retard the movement. This is the important conclusion left by the data presented above.

Although the elder Pliny clearly expressed himself in the middle of the first century as opposed to the use in agriculture of chained slaves from the prisons of hard labor [92] the practice was still prevalent in his time.[93] The younger Pliny, however, writing somewhat later in that century, states that he and his neighbors in the Po valley had ceased to use them.[94]

By legislation passed under Hadrian the *ergastula* were abolished in the punishment of slaves as well as of free persons.[95] Hadrian also forbade the sale of a male slave to a trainer of gladiators, or of a female slave to a procurer, without a definite statement of the reason.[96] The procedure of taking testimony by torture from the slaves of a murdered master was modified in his principate to the extent that only those slaves who were near enough to have had knowledge of the crime should be thus examined.[97] Hadrian is known to have banished for five years a Roman matron who had been cruel to her slaves without cause.[98] He also took away the right of slave-owners to kill their slaves and gave it over to the courts.[99]

Under Antoninus Pius the slaying of his own slave by the owner without a reason was placed in the same legal category as the killing of a slave of another master.[100] This incursion into the right of life and death granted to the *dominus* by the *ius gentium* was justified by the jurist Gaius on the basis of the spirit of the time: " but in these times it is not permissible either for Roman citizens or for any other persons who are under

the rule of the Roman people to exercise severity against their slaves beyond measure and without cause." [101] A slave who claimed to have suffered injustice at the hands of his master might find refuge in flight to a temple or to the statue of the Emperor.[102] This temporary relief was to be followed by a complaint addressed to the Prefect of the City.[103]

Diocletian forebade the exposure of infant slaves.[104] It remained for Constantine to take the humanitarian step of providing that, in the division of estates in inheritance, slaves belonging to the property of the deceased were to be allocated in such a manner as not to separate parent and child, husband and wife, brother and sister.[105] It is to be deduced from a constitution of Diocletian promulgated in A. D. 294 against the sale of children by their parents [106] that there had been a trend, during the economic misery which marked the last half of the third century, to return to that practice. Permission was granted to parents by Constantine in A. D. 329 in cases of extreme poverty and want that they might sell their children, under the proviso that they should always retain the right to buy them back.[107] This seeming reversal of the liberalizing slavery policy of the imperial period is to be explained as a necessary concession to the realities of the economic pressure of the time.[108]

As justification for his pleasure in making frequent manumissions Pliny [109] states that he desired to see his fatherland increased in respect to the number of its citizens. A similar motivation for manumitting slaves which is placed in the mouth of Augustus Caesar by Cassius Dio [110] must be referred to Dio's own time, since it is well known that the legislation of Augustus himself [111] tended to place restrictions upon manumissions, at least those arranged by testamentary grant, rather than to encourage them. A suggestion has been made that encouragement of the custom of freeing slaves in periods of financial difficulties in the later centuries of the Empire rested upon the desire of the state to keep up the number of the free population who were compelled to shoulder the fiscal obligations imposed by the state; [112] but other tendencies and other considerations were probably more important.

---

[91] Herzog, Rudolf, Urkunden zur Hochschulpolitik der römischen Kaiser, *Sitzungsb. Berl. Akad.*, no. 32, 967-1019, 1935. Herzog's conclusions should be checked in W. Hartke's review of his article in *Gnomon* 14: 507-512, 1938.

[92] Pliny, *Natural history* 18: 7, 4.

[93] *Cf.* Seneca, *De ira* 3: 3, 6.

[94] Pliny, *Letters* 3: 19, 7.

[95] *Script. hist. Aug., Hadrian*, 18, 9.

[96] *Ibid.*, 18, 8.

[97] *Ibid.*, 18, 11; Just., *Digest* 48: 18, 1, 1.

[98] Just. *Digest* 1: 6, 2.

[99] *Script. hist. Aug., Hadrian*, 18, 7.

[100] Gaius, *Institutiones* 1: 53. For further legislation under Antoninus designed to lighten the burdens of slavery see Pauly-W. *RE*, 2d ser., 2, 1831, article *servitus poenae*. Under Diocletian the extreme penalty could be demanded of an owner who killed his slave, Theod., *Codex* 9: 12, 1.

[101] Gaius, *Institutiones* 1: 53.

[102] *Ibid.* 44: 1.

[103] Just., *Digest* 1: 12, 1, 1; *cf.* Schneider, Albert, *Geschichte der sclaverei*, 25.

[104] Theod., *Codex* 5: 9, 1.

[105] *Ibid.* 2: 25.

[106] *Codex Justinianus* 4: 43, 1.

[107] *Ibid.* 4: 43, 2.

[108] Jonkers, E. J., De l'influence du Christianisme, *Mnemosyne* 1: 270. For legislation in protection of manumission and the interests of freedmen, similar to that established above for the servile classes, see Schneider, A., *Geschichte der Sclaverei*, 34-44; Brassloff, Stephan, *Sozialpolitische Motive in der römischen Rechtsentwickelung*, 32, n. 52, Vienna, Perles, 1933.

[109] Pliny, *Letters* 7: 32, 1.

[110] Dio Cassius, 46: 7, 6.

[111] *Lex Fufia Caninia* and *Lex Aelia Sentia.*

[112] See Jonkers, E. J., *Economische en Sociale Toestanden in het Romeinsche Rijk*, 134-135, Wageningen, Weennionn and sons, 1933.

A traditional view in respect to the legislation of the first two centuries of the Empire ascribes to the later Stoa a powerful influence upon the spirit and character of the imperial enactments, especially of those which had to do with the protection of the interests of slaves.[113] The idea has initially in its favor the fact that the Roman jurists of the last century of the Republic were adherents of one or the other of the Greek philosophic schools[114] and that the Stoa was held by them in high esteem.[115]

The belief which the classical jurists accepted, that slavery was grounded in the common practice of all peoples but was *contra naturam*, may, indeed, be Stoic in origin.[116] The Stoa deserves also the chief credit for deciding definitively the old Sophistic problem whether slave status was one imposed by nature or by human enactment ($\phi\acute{v}\sigma\epsilon\iota$ or $\theta\acute{\epsilon}\sigma\epsilon\iota$) in the sense of the latter alternative, namely that it was a condition imposed by law ($v\acute{o}\mu\omega$).[117] But the juristic concept must be clearly distinguished from the legislative enactments. These were based upon practical considerations and reflected the adjustments of the state to immediate needs and to local or more general pressures of smaller or larger groups representing a public attitude. One must begin with the initial fact that the outstanding figures of the Middle Stoa, Panaetius, Posidonius, and Hecato, in so far as the fragmentary knowledge of them permits a decision, maintained an unsympathetic attitude toward labor in general, including slaves and slave labor.[118] Bernhard Kuebler went even further than this in his scepticism about the Stoic influence upon the ancient institutions of slavery in his statement that it was the opponents of Stoicism, not the Stoics themselves, who were responsible for the insistence, in the classical period of Roman jurisprudence, upon *aequitas* as the basis of legal interpretation.[119]

The beginning of the imperial legislation in correction of current abuses of the slave class is, in fact, to be placed before the maturity of Seneca's views upon the necessity of a merciful treatment of them[120] and at a time when the Stoics were out of favor with the rulers of the Empire.[121] The notable lack of enactments for the protection of slave interests emanating from the eight years when Seneca held political power[122] gives sufficient evidence of the sterility of his teaching as measured by direct and practical results in legislation. As author, however, rather than as philosopher[123] Seneca deserves the credit, as a man of great wealth and, therefore, a great slaveholder, of having accepted a forward-looking movement popular in his day. However much this attitude was dictated in the first two centuries of the Christian era by the spiritual egalitarianism of the Roman type of Stoicism, as well as by Christianity, Seneca nevertheless gave a strong and appealing formulation to the doctrine of the equality of all men and insisted upon the application of this doctrine to the slave class.[124] Out of this generalized doctrine of equality Seneca drew the logical conclusion that slaves should be treated with the same kindness as their fellow men of free status.[125]

Proof of the general adoption in the time of Seneca of the idea that slaves were human beings is apparent in the statement placed by Petronius in the mouth of the parvenu freedman, Trimalchio,[126] that slaves also are men, nurtured upon the same milk as the free and differing only in the *malus fatus* which besets them. Juvenal, likewise, regarded the abuse of slaves as a serious evil in the life of his day.[127] Pliny the Younger made it a point to treat the wills of his slaves as valid and the bequests made by them as obligations, the fulfillment of which rested upon him, provided the beneficiaries were members of his *familia*. The restriction to his own

[113] Laferriére, M. F., Mémoire concernant l'influence du Stoicism sur la doctrine des jurisconsultes Romains, *Mémoire de l'Académie du Science Morales et Politiques*, 601-603, Paris, Durand, 1860; Wallon, H., *Histoire de l'esclavage* 3: 19-46; Vollmann, Franz, *Über das Verhaltnis der späteren Stoa zur Sklaverei im römischen Reiche*, 35-53.

[114] Kuebler, B., Griechische Einflüsse auf Entwickelung der römischen Rechtswissenschaft, *Atti del Congresso Internazionale di Diritto Romano* 1: 84, 1934. For an extensive bibliography see his n. 4.

[115] *Ibid.* 92.

[116] Stroux, J., *Römische Rechtswissenschaft und Rhetorik*, 51-52, 71, Potsdam, Stichnote, 1949, reprint of *Summonum Ius Summa Iniuria*. Stroux has successfully combatted an imbedded idea that the Roman jurists of the early classical period took over their general scientific method from the Stoa.

[117] Braun, Martin, *Griechischer Roman und hellenistische Geschichtschreibung*, in *Frankfurter Studien zur Religion und Kultur der Antike* 6: 32, Frankfurt am Main, 1933.

[118] Lichy, Joannes, *De servorum condicione quid senserit L. Annaeus Seneca*, 35, Münster, Monasterii Westfalorum, 1927, quoting Cicero, *De officiis* 2: 7, 24: *sit sane adhibenda saevitia ut heris in famulos si aliter teneri non possunt.*

[119] *Voluntas* as against the strict Stoic interpretation by *verba*. See Kuebler, *Congr. Inter. Dirit. Rom.*, 92-98. If I understand the brief statement of Bernard d'Orgeval, *L'empereur Hadrien, Œuvre législative et administrative*, 65, Paris, Editions Domat

Montchrestien, 1950, an increasing rigor of treatment of slaves manifested in the time of Hadrian should be ascribed to the authoritarian spirit of the imperial rule of that principate and should *not* be attributed to Stoic influence.

[120] Lichy, Joannes, *De servorum condicione quid senserit Seneca*, 37, 43.

[121] Kuebler, B., *Atti Congresso Internazionale di Diritto Romano*, 98.

[122] Jonkers, E. J., *Econ. Soc. Toestand. Rom. Rijk*, 135, n. 2.

[123] Pauly-W., *RE* 1: 2243.

[124] Seneca, *Epistulae morales*, 47, 1: *Servi sunt. Immo homines. Servi sunt. Immo contubernales. Servi sunt. Immo humiles amici*; 47, 10: *istum, quem servum tuum vocas, ex isdem seminibus ortum eodem frui caelo, aeque spirare, aeque vivere, aeque mori. Cf. loc. cit.*, 31, 11; *Dialogorum* 4: 24, 3; *De beneficiis* 3: 20, 2: *corpus itaque est, quod domino fortuna tradit: hoc emit, hoc vendit; interior illa pars mancipio dari non potest. Ab hac quidquid venit, liberum est*; 6: 16, 1.

[125] *Servi liberine sint hi . . . quid refert? Ubicumque homo est, ibi benefici locus est: Dialogorum* 7: 24, 3; *cf. Epistulae morales*, 47, 5, 6, 13.

[126] Petronius, *Cena Trimalchionis (Satyricon)*, 71, 1.

[127] Juvenal, *Satires*, 6, 219-223: *meruit quo crimine servus supplicium? Quis testis adest?* On the necessity of proof of the guilt of slaves before punishment is inflicted see Pliny, *Letters* 8: 14, 13.

familia was justified by Pliny on the conviction that in the case of slaves the master's house was the substitute for commonwealth and city-state allegiance.[128] In two discourses of Dio of Prusa upon the subject [129] slavery is accepted as an existing organization. The interest of Dio is not regarding the genesis of slavery or whether it is against the dictates of nature, but it centers upon a precise definition of slavery and freedom. Freedom is not the mere right to liberty of action.[130] Nor can slavery be defined in terms of the purchase price paid for a man,[131] or in terms of chains or tattoo marks or of work done at a grinding mill.[132] Nor is it a matter of birth from a slave parent or a question of race.[133] Freedom is a derivative of character, the noble in spirit being free. The ignoble are slaves.[134]

In the West the formulation of the late Stoic attitude as it appears in Seneca reappears with little alteration in Epictetus.[135] Epictetus would regard as a slave a man who had even twice been consul and could call himself a friend of Caesar if he were under the compulsion of the power of Caesar.[136] In Epictetus the Stoic view that all men derive their descent from God is clearly stated.[137] Although the legislation of Marcus Aurelius upon slavery was more probably dictated by practical demands than by philosophic doctrines, the influence of Epictetus upon his personal and philosophic attitude is not to be doubted.[138] In Phrygia the teachings of this Phrygian slave, Epictetus, regarding true freedom and true slavery were quoted in a metrical inscription still extant which was set up by one who appears to have been himself a slave. Certainly he was a disciple of the Stoic school.[139]

With the exception of the small Jewish sect of the Essenes, no religious or other organization of antiquity failed to accept slavery.[140] The early Christians accepted the institution as they did the Roman sway and the conditions which it set for them, for the reason that mundane distinctions, including questions of legal and social status, were of no consequence to them and because, when once baptized as Christians, all believers were regarded as equal.[141] In the letters of the Apostles slaves who were Christians were strictly enjoined to render obedience to their masters in fear and trembling as they did to Christ.[142] The direct influence of early Christianity toward an increased humanity *within its own communities* should not, however, be minimized. From the outset of its missionary activity the appeal of Christianity to the slave class was marked.[143] A salutary effect upon the spirits of slaves who became Christians and upon their treatment must have resulted from the equality granted them in the early congregations which gave them equal right of receiving sacrament, of taking part in the meetings, of rising into the ranks of the clergy, and of burial in the cemeteries.[144] Although the bishops advised their followers against the employment of slaves in luxury services [145] it is probable that the Christians continued to own and employ them in much the same degree and manner as their pagan contemporaries of similar economic standing.[146]

---

[128] Pliny, *Letters* 8: 16, 2. *Cf.* 8: 24, 5. Although free men receive better treatment from physicians than do slaves, in reality a slave does not differ in his sickness from a free man. The idea that the master's house is the city state of the slave can be traced back to Menander. See fragment 581 in Kock, Theodor, *Comicorum Atticorum fragmenta* 3: 127.

[129] Dio of Prusa, *Orations*, 14, 15.

[130] *Ibid.*, 14, 3-8, 13-14.

[131] *Ibid.*, 14, 11; 15: 29.

[132] *Ibid.*, 14, 19.

[133] *Ibid.*, 15, 30.

[134] *Ibid.*, 15, 31.

[135] Lichy, Joannes, *De serv. condic. quid sens. Seneca*, 36; cf. Bonhöffer, Adolf, *Die ethik des stoikers Epictet*, 99. Stuttgart, Ferdinand Enke, 1894.

[136] Epictetus, *Discourses* 4: 1, 6-14; *cf.* 57.

[137] *Ibid.* 1: 3, 9.

[138] Lichy, Joannes, *De serv. cond. quid sens. Seneca*, 36, n. 1.

[139] Kaibel, Georg, Inschriften aus Pisidien, in *Hermes* 23: 542-545, 1888.

[140] Philo, *Quod omnis probus liber sit*, 79 = Cohn, Leopold, and Paul Wendland, *Philonis Alexandrini opera quae supersunt* 6: 23, 2-3. Josephus, *Jewish Antiquities* 18: 1, 5, gives about four thousand as the limit of their number.

[141] I Corinthians, 12, 13: ἐν ἑνὶ πνεύματι ἡμεῖς πάντες εἰς ἓν σῶμα ἐβαπτίσθημεν, εἴτε Ἰουδαῖοι εἴτε Ἕλληνες, εἴτε δοῦλοι εἴτε ἐλεύθεροι. See the decision of von Harnack, Adolf, *Mission and expansion of Christianity* 1: 168, n. 1, that the question of slavery did not arise as a problem in the early church.

[142] Ephesians, 6, 5. cf. Colossians, 3, 23; Titus, 2, 9-10, 19. The attitude of submission, even to cruel masters, is motivated in I Peter, 2, 19 on the ground that patient endurance is pleasing to God.

[143] For slaves in the early communities see the intercession of Paul, written to the slave's owner, for the runaway Onesimus, whom he had baptized, NT, Philemon, 15-16: αὐτὸν ἀπέχῃς οὐκέτι ὡς δοῦλον, ἀλλ᾽ ὑπὲρ δοῦλον, ἀδελφὸν ἀγαπητόν. A similar request for merciful treatment of a delinquent freedman was made by the pagan Pliny and granted by his pagan friend, Sabinianus, Pliny the Younger, *Letters* 9: 21, 24. For Roman citizens mingling with slaves in the Christian communities in Bithynia in A. D. 112, see Pliny, *Letters (to Trajan)* 10: 4, 8.

[144] Von Harnack, Adolf, *Mission and expansion of Christianity* 1: 168-170; Allard, Paul, *Esclaves Chrétiens*, 6th ed., 185-215. The overemphasis placed by Allard upon the part which Christianity played in the amelioration of slave conditions is obvious.

[145] Clement of Alexandria, *Paedagogi* 3: 7, 9 (= Migne, *Patr. Graec.* 8: 609-620).

[146] Ignatius, *To Polycarp*, 4 (= Migne, *Patr. Graec.*, 5: 723); Irenaeus, *Contra haereses* 4: 9, 1 (= Migne, 7: 996).

XVIII. THE MORAL IMPLICATIONS OF IMPERIAL SLAVERY AND THE "DECLINE" OF ANCIENT CULTURE

Slavery continued under the Empire to exercise its influence upon the moral life and standards of the time,[1] presumably diminishing in the degree of its social impact in a ratio corresponding to the relative decrease in slave numbers. The slaves of the imperial household and of the senatorial families at Rome were peculiarly subject to debasement of character through the deteriorations arising from the exercise of political power without public responsibility and from the intrigues which were rife in the imperial circles. The prevalent system of delation also influenced their characters adversely because information against their masters might always be exacted through fear of torture or encouraged by the hope of rewards.[2] Although the immediate circle of slaves was limited to which these temptations applied, the influence of their example must have been widespread. This is indicated by the numerous cases of delation cited, and the importance ascribed in the historical literature of the Empire to them and to related actions of slaves in the higher social families at Rome.[3] The severe discipline of silence often imposed upon slaves of the larger households in the presence of their owners tempted them the more to gossip about their masters when opportunity offered.[4]

A strong reaction against the evils of delation by slaves occurred in the second and third centuries.[5] The Emperor Tacitus refused to accept the testimony of slaves in cases of *majestas*[6]; and Constantine the Great, in a further attempt to abate this evil, ordered the crucifixion of any slave or freedman who presented such an accusation against his master or patron.[7] Under Gratian accusations of treason presented by slaves were admitted; but the slave who accused his master upon any other charge was to be punished with death by fire.[8]

There can be no doubt that the right of free disposition of slaves possessed by the owners resulted in a great amount of sexual indulgence with slave women, and, less generally, between free women and slaves.[9] The decree of Hadrian, which restricted the right of sale of a slave girl to a *leno* to those cases in which a just cause for such sale could be advanced[10] obviously left open a wide field of exploitation for purposes of prostitution.[11] One method of circumvention of the charge of *infamia*[12] was to rent a locality to one's slaves and have them set up brothels on their own account.[13] The general acceptance of the attitude that slave women were, in respect to debauchery, upon a different legal and moral plane from free women appears clearly in the view expressed by Ulpian that if a slave woman had been used as a prostitute by her master, her reputation should not suffer because of this after she had been freed,[14] and in the decree of Aurelian that free born women could not be kept as concubines, with its obvious implication that this was permissible in the case of freedwomen and slaves.[15]

Homosexual indulgence was unquestionably encouraged by the institution of slavery because of the diminished resistance on the part of slaves and their economic as well as social dependence.[16] *Stuprum* with free men was condemned by public opinion although the punishment therefor lay with the family; but debauchery with slaves aroused no great objection.[17] It is probable that slaves are to be included with the members of the lowest classes of the free population who were engaged in the

---

[1] Kroll, W., Römische Erotik, *Zeitschrift für Sexualwissenschaft und Sexualpolitik* 17 : 147, 1930.

[2] Tacitus, *Annals* 15 : 54; *nam quum secum servilis animus praemia perfidiae reputavit, simulque immensa pecunia et potentia obversabantur, cessit fas et salus patroni et acceptae libertatis memoria.* Cf. idem, *Histories* 4 : 23.

[3] Tacitus, *Annals* 2 : 30. Cf. the maltreatment of Drusus by imperial slaves recorded by Dio Cassius, 57 : 19, 5-7. Delation under Claudius, *ibid.*, 60 : 15, 1-4; the treatment of Britannicus, Tacitus, *Annals* 12 : 26, and cf. his *Histories* 1 : 7; 2 : 84; Suetonius, *Galba*, 10. The prosecution of a senator on the charge of a slave was not, however, admitted by Nero, see Tacitus, *Annals* 13 : 10. On the harm resulting from the gossip of slaves, see also Juvenal, *Satires*, 9, 102-123; 10, 87-88, *sed videant servi, ne quis neget et pavidum in ius cervice obstricta dominum trahat.* Torture of slaves in obtaining evidence against their masters was used by Caracalla, according to Dio Cassius, 77 : 2, 2.

[4] Seneca, *Letters*, 47, 4.

[5] *Script. hist. Aug., Pertinax*, 9, 10 where a slave was crucified for bringing an accusation against his master. Cf. 10, 7; *Severus Alexander*, 66, 3-4. Elimination of the sale of favors by *spadones*, *ibid.*, *The three Gordians*, 24-25.

[6] *Ibid., Tacitus*, 9, 4.

[7] *Ephemeris Epigraphica* 7 : 416, Rome, 1892, or Bruns-Gradenwitz, *FIR*, no. 94, 28-34.

[8] Theod. *Codex* 9 : 6, 2.

[9] Lucian, *The tyrant*, 11.

[10] See chap. 17; *Scrip. hist. Aug., Hadrian*, 18, 8.

[11] Allard, P., *Esclaves Chrétiens*, 147, n. 5. Just., *Digest* 3 : 1, 1, 4, 2.

[12] *Ibid.*

[13] *Ibid.* 3 : 2, 4, 3.

[14] *Ibid.* 2 : 2, 24.

[15] *Script. hist. Aug., Aurelian*, 49, 8, cf. Seneca, *De beneficiis* 3 : 19: *servus autem non habet negandi potestatem*; [Quintilian], *Declamationes*, 307; Just., *Digest* 25 : 7, 1; *Codex* 9 : 9, 20, 25.

[16] Ciccotti, E., *Tramonto della schiavitù*, 180. For laudations of the virtue of slaves see Seneca, *De beneficiis* 3 : 19, 2-4. In the Cynic-Stoic propaganda and the novelistic literature of the Empire, the retention of *virtue* on the part of slaves under temptations is a common theme. Cf. Braun, M., *Griechische, römische und hellenistische Geschichtschreibung, Frankfurter Studien zur Religion und Kultur* 6 : 44, 1934.

[17] Kroll, W., Römische Erotik, *Zeitschrift fur Sexualwissenschaft* 17 : 157-158, 1930. Cf. Petronius, 63, 3; Tacitus, *Annals*, 11 : 2; 14, 42; 15, 37; Dio Cassius, 79 : 21, 1; *Script. hist. Aug., Macrinus*, 4, 3; *Elagabalus*, 6, 4.

practice of homosexuality as it appears in the graffiti found upon the walls at Pompeii.[18]

In contrast with this picture stands the impression of a fairly decent standard of life and of action among the slaveholding families and the slaves themselves which is gained from the sepulchral inscriptions from all parts of the Empire and from the papyri from Egypt. There is no example in the numerous contracts of slave sales thus far published from Egypt of the insertion of a clause providing against the use of the slave for purposes of prostitution by the purchaser such as appeared in some of the sales under Roman law.[19] The papyri are, on the whole, remarkably free from indications of the coarser forms of debauchery. Although many of the children of female slaves which appear in wills in the papyri may have been born of extramarital relations between masters and slave women,[20] observation of the house-born slaves (οἰκογενεῖς) in Roman Egypt leads to the conclusion that a considerable number of them were children of slave parents upon both sides who had been permitted to live in quasi-marital relations. Considerations of a higher economic return from the slaves through a decrease in restlessness and dissatisfaction, as well as through the rearing of additional slave children, must have urged such a course.

In Italy both Varro[21] and Columella[22] had advocated this practice of supplying consorts for the agricultural slaves for the purposes stated above. The idealized picture of country life drawn by the poets of the Empire[23] leads to the same conclusion. The considerable proportion of the *vernae* in Italy[24] suggests that the slaves of the towns and the cities who were engaged in industrial and other urban occupations were frequently permitted to establish families of their own. A study of three thousand inscriptions from miscellaneous *columbaria* of slaves and ex-slaves of the menial classes at Rome,[25] which include a few inscriptions dealing with poor citizens of free status, shows that from twenty-six and one-half per cent to *ca.* thirty-nine per cent report quasi-marriages of the slaves concerned. Fifteen and one-half per cent of these cases report children born of such unions. Such children were, of course, of servile status. In the inscriptions from the *columbaria* of the aristocratic families, from twenty-four to forty per cent show family unions of slaves, with fifteen per cent recording children born to these slave parents. In the inscriptions which deal with the imperial slaves the proportions of

quasi-marital unions, with use of terms *coniunx* and *contubernalis*, is still higher.[26]

The extent of the vicious practices attendant upon the slave system in the period of the Roman Empire, even in the groups owned by the nobility of Rome, has obviously been given an undue importance in the literature of the time; and the impression of widespread debauchery is unavoidably increased by the necessary accumulation of its instances when these are assembled, as has been done above. The best available check upon this exaggeration lies in the data furnished by Tenney Frank upon the family life established between slaves in Rome and in the prevalence of relations between free men and slave women, or male slaves and free women, which corresponded to mixed marriages.[27]

The system of ancient slavery has frequently been brought into connection with the " decline " in ancient culture. This " decline " is usually ascribed to the alleged moral degeneration caused by slavery or to the economic conditions which slave employment is thought to have brought about.[28] A variant of this theme is to be found in Otto Seeck's view[29] which ascribes to the slave system the development of a character quality of subserviency which the Greco-Roman population of the later Empire received as an inheritance from its freedmen ancestors. Granting that the opportunities for sex indulgence outside of the marriage relation were considerably increased by slavery, there is still no method of proving the total moral and physical effects of this fact upon ancient society.

The economic approach to the height and decline of ancient civilization customarily exaggerates the numbers of slaves in antiquity and the effects of slavery.[30] E. Heitz attributes the decline of ancient civilization to slavery because the slave system had finally forced free labor out of almost all spheres of economic life.[31] Sig-

[18] *CIL* 4: 1882; 3375; 4024; 4126; 4816. Kroll, W., *Zeitschrift für Sexualwissenschaft* 17: 156.

[19] Just., *Digest* 18: 1, 56. *cf.* Just., *Codex* 4: 56, 1-3.

[20] Taubenschlag, R., Das Sklavenrecht im Rechte der Papyri, *Zeitsch. d. Savigny-Stift.* 50: 144, 1930; Sudhoff, K., *Ärztliches aus griechischen Papyrusurkunden*, 149, Leipzig, Barth, 1909.

[21] Varro, *De re rustica* 2: 10, 6.

[22] Columella, *De re rustica* 1: 8, 19.

[23] Tibullus, 2: 1, 21; 1: 5, 25.

[24] See above, chap. 13, p. 86.

[25] Frank, T., Race mixture in the Roman Empire, *Amer. Hist. Rev.* 21: 698, 1916.

[26] Fifty-one to *ca.* fifty-nine per cent of the family relations recorded. There is a reduction to thirteen per cent if we include only those documents which record children of these unions, *ibid.*, 697. *Cf.* the interesting data upon the occupations of the men and women concerned in these relations, *ibid.*, 696.

[27] *Inscriptiones Graecae ad res romanas pertinentes* (= *IG Rom*) 1: 492; *CIL* 5: 1071; Dessau, *ILS*, 8553, 8555; and see the numerous examples cited by Ciccotti, *Tramonto della schiavitù*, 261, n. 2.

[28] For the view that the moral turpitude resulting from slavery helped to bring about the deterioration of Greek culture see Barbagallo, C., *La fine della Grecia antica*, 3-76, Bari, Laterza, 1905, and Wallon, *L'esclavage* 1: 452, 457. For traditional view of its blighting effects upon Roman culture see *ibid.*, 2: 325-326, 383; 3: 335, and Adams, G. B., *Civilization during the Middle Ages*, 80, New York, Scribner, 1904.

[29] Seeck, O., *Geschichte des Untergangs der antiken Welt* 1: 314-318, 327-328, Berlin, Siemenroth & Troschel, 1897.

[30] Bücher, K., *Industrial evolution*, 98, New York, Holt, 1912: " The artificers in the early records are not freemen engaged in industry, but artisan slaves who receive from the hands of the agricultural and pastoral slaves the corn, wool or wood which are to be transformed into bread, clothing or implements."

[31] Heitz, E., *Neue Grundsätze der Volkswirtschaftslehre*, 8-9, Stuttgart, Kohlhammer, 1897.

wart[32] explains the failure of capitalistic production methods to develop in antiquity on the ground that slave labor was a costly form of enterprise, owing to the fact that the slaves were poor workmen and lazy and needed expensive supervision, except when their diminished economic productivity was counterbalanced by abnormally low market prices for them after great wars had thrown large numbers upon the slave market.[33] Although there is a complete absence of statistical data upon which the relative productivity of slave and free labor may be ascertained on the basis of investment cost of the slaves and wages of the hired labor, Rostovtzeff's view is to be accepted that slave labor was, on the whole, neither cheap nor docile.[34]

The conclusion that the use of slaves in the handicrafts prevented the development of improved technical procedures[35] must also be rejected[36] because there is no warrant for the belief that a system of complete free labor would have changed in the slightest degree the development of the industrial techniques from that course which they actually followed in antiquity. The guarded implication of Ciccotti[37] that the sullen rancor of slaves resulted in careless workmanship, which, in the ceramic handicraft particularly, lacked the patient skill required for an artistic output, is completely refuted by ceramic evidence available to us which can definitely be assigned to individual slave artists. This is the relief pottery of the slave workmen at Arretium. It shows a fine feeling for craftsmanship, great technical skill, and an especial patience in detail.[38]

The gradual quantitative decline in the slave system during the imperial period[39] must be regarded as an outcome, rather than a cause, of the social, economic, and political changes of the time. The causes which conditioned the reduction in the use of slaves in agriculture and industry were: the cessation of war and kidnapping, which were the main sources of a large and cheap supply; the high cost of slave labor as provided by the rearing of slave children and the mortality risk involved in this method of supply; and the downward grading of the mass of the agricultural population from the position of free tenants to that of *coloni* or *adscripticii*, bound to the soil which they cultivated.[40] Their purchasing power must have declined notably; and any ability of the *coloni* as a class to buy slaves of their own must have decreased slowly toward the vanishing point.[41]

Two suggestions may be added to these reasons for the constantly diminishing importance of slavery. The first is that, in the decentralization of industrial activity out of Italy into Gaul and the Rhenish provinces as exemplified in the shifting of manufacture of relief pottery from Arretium to the north,[42] the new centres of industry lay in localities in which slave labor on a large scale did not take hold because it was neither indigenous to the region nor adapted to the spirit of the people who dwelt there.[43] The second is that, in the combined slave and free labor situation of antiquity, manumissions had constantly occurred upon a wide scale and the barrier between slavery and freedom had never been a rigid one. In consequence of this the decrease in the use of slaves could occur gradually, almost imperceptibly, and without violent disorganization of the labor market.

---

[32] Sigwart, C., Kapitalismus, Pauly-W., *RE* 10: 1905.

[33] *Cf.* Ciccotti's belief, expressed in *Tramonto della schiavitù*, 37, 282, 285, in the low return from slave labor.

[34] Rostovtzeff, M., *Soc. and econ. hist. Roman emp.*, 303, with exaggeration, however, of the number of slaves employed in the Hellenistic period. See chap. 8, p. 48.

[35] Salvioli, G., *Il capitalismo nel mondo antico*, 75, Bari, Laterza, 1929, which has been accepted by Heichelheim in a review of Salvioli's book in *Historische Zeitschr.* 143: 95, 1931, but later was wisely modified by him in his *Wirtschaftsgeschichte des Altertums* 1: 401-403, Leiden, A. W. Sijthoff, 1938.

[36] Rostovtzeff, M., *Soc. and econ. hist. Roman emp.*, 303.

[37] Ciccotti, E., *Tramonto della schiavitù*, 283.

[38] In Oxé, A., *Arretinische Reliefgefässe vom Rhein*, Frankfurt am Main, Baer, 1933, observe the signed vase of the slave potter, Pylades, pl. 5, 12 *a*, *b*; those of Pantagathus, pl. 22, 108 *a*, *b*; pl. 36; that of Hilario, slave in the factory of L.

Avillius Sura, pl. 52; and that of Dardanus, slave of Q. Ancharius, pl. 55, no. 282.

[39] Ciccotti, E., *Tramonto della schiavitù*, 33, 285, 314. See chap. 13, p. 84.

[40] Rostovtzeff, M., *Gesch. des röm. Kolonates*, 396-398, and his *Soc. and econ. hist. Roman empire*, 472-473; Seeck, O., Colonatus, in Pauly-W., *RE* 4: 495-496.

[41] Rostovtzeff, M., *Soc. and econ. hist. Roman empire*, 470, where he speaks of the impoverishment of the peasants and the decline in the numbers and in the purchasing power of the urban *bourgeoisie*.

[42] Dragendorff, H., *Gnomon* 10: 360, 1934, in his review of Oxé, *Arretinische Reliefgefässe vom Rhein*.

[43] See chap. 14, pp. 93-94.

XIX. IN THE EASTERN PROVINCES OF THE ROMAN EMPIRE

The assumption of Ed. Meyer[1] that in Egypt real slavery, as opposed to serfdom, did not at any time in its history attain important proportions has been fully substantiated for the period of the Roman domination by the evidence of the papyri.[2] The percentage of slaves

owned in the villages was very low.[3] They were not strongly employed in agricultural operations, for which paid hands in continual service were preferred or labor-

---

[1] Meyer, Ed., Sklaverei im Altertum, *Kleine Schriften*, 2nd ed., 1: 191, n. 1.

[2] Wilcken, U., *Griechische Ostraka aus Ägypten und Nubien*

1: 681-704; Reil, Th., *Beiträge zur Kenntnis des Gewerbes im hellenistischen Ägypten*, 170-174, diss. Leipzig, 1913.

[3] One or two per cent in the smaller places to seven per cent in the town of Ptolemais Hormos, see above, Wilcken, *Griechische Ostraka* 1: 683.

ers were hired by the day as needed.[4] Slaves occasionally appear, however, in agricultural production in some documents. In A. D. 23 a slave reports the transfer of a large flock of sheep and goats, which are his personal property,[5] from the Oxyrhynchite to the Cynopolite nome.[6] Again a slave belonging to a Roman veteran [7] managed some of his owner's farms, in the manner of a Roman *vicarius*.[8] In the long agricultural account from Karanis of A. D. 191-192,[9] out of a total of more than one hundred persons who appear in connection with the activities of this large farm only three are slaves.[10] A fourth-century papyrus [11] shows two farmers (*geōrgoi*) and one donkey boy who are slaves.

In view of the small number of the enslaved who appear in agricultural occupations on the large estates it must be doubted that the farmers of small parcels employed slave labor in any large amount. Although the total evidence on the use of *douloi* in handicrafts in the Egyptian *chōra* has been materially increased since the references gathered by U. Wilcken,[12] his conclusion has not been altered that the amount of industrial use of slave labor was not great or vitally important. The method of its employment did not differ from that of paid free labor. The slave might work in his own home or in his master's home or shop. He might be bought and trained to a trade as pure capital investment,[13] to be hired out as a skilled workman to a handicraft shop-owner; or he might work independently at his trade, paying a part of his earnings to his master [14] as in the case of the pay-earning slaves (*misthophorounta sōmata*) known at Athens in the fifth and fourth centuries B. C. In view of the great activity in the weaving trades and the constant demand for qualified laborers in this field [15] it is not surprising to find that slaves appear in Egypt

as weavers in larger numbers than in other handicrafts.[16] Still, the predominance of free labor over slave labor even in the weaving trade, where the slaves were most strongly represented, is quite clear in the papyri.[17]

Other occupations of the enslaved appear infrequently from the towns and villages of Egypt. A *rhētorikos doulos* appears who was either owned by a *rhētōr* or one who taught rhetoric.[18] In another papyrus the *paidiskē* who delivered beer to a house may be a slave;[19] and in an apprentice contract a slave boy was placed with a writer of shorthand (*sēmiographos*) for two years for instruction in that *technē*.[20] In one lease of services of a slave boy the occupation is lost.[21] A papyrus of the second or third century contains a lease of services of a boy who worked a hand mill;[22] another one of the third century [23] mentions a slave apprenticed to a wool carder;[24] and one of A. D. 252 introduces a slave copper-smith and a slave fisherman.[25] An enslaved girl was used by two brothel keepers, probably at Arsinoe, ca. A. D. 265.[26] In a papyrus of A. D. 338 [27] it is possible that the *paidia* are slaves. Official receipts are preserved for taxes paid by slaves who apparently worked indepen-

---

[4] See the expenditures recorded as payments for workmen (μισθὸς ἐργάτων) in the accounts of an estate in the Hermopolite nome, *P. Lond.* 1: 131, pp. 170-188. *Cf. Varro, De re rustica* 1: 17: *quos obaerarios nostri vocitarunt ut etiam nunc sunt in Asia atque Aegypto et in Illyrico complures*; Wilcken, *Griechische Ostraka* 1: 698-700.

[5] Greek: ἃ ἔχω ἐν ὑπογραφῇ.

[6] *P. Oxy.* 2: 244, 3, 15, 19-20.

[7] *Stud. Pal.* 4: 117: διὰ Ἐπ[α]γά[θ]ου π[αι]δαρί[ου]. *Cf. P. Fayum*, no. 110, p. 262.

[8] Westermann, W. L., *Univ. of Wisconsin Stud. in Lang. and Lit.* 3: 172, n. 9, Madison, 1919.

[9] *P. Goodspeed*, no. 30 in Goodspeed, E. J., *Greek papyri from the Cairo Museum*, Chicago, 1902.

[10] *Ibid.*, col. XII, 22; XV, 18; XVI, 23. In Meyer, P. M., *Griechische Texte aus Ägypten*, no. 57, 6, Berlin, Weidmann, 1916: τῇ ἐμῇ παιδίσκῃ perhaps refers to a slave girl. *Cf. BGU* 1: 7, col. II, 9; 6: 1490, 7.

[11] *P. Leip.*, no. 26, 7-9 in Mitteis, L., *Griechische Urkunden der Papyrussammlung zu Leipzig*. *Cf. ibid.*, no. 111, 9-12, where some slaves belonging elsewhere were hired to work on a small farm as workmen (ἐργάται).

[12] Wilcken, *Griechische Ostraka* 1: 687-695. *Cf.* Reil, Th., *Beiträge zur Kenntnis des Gewerbes*, 171-172; Taubenschlag, R., *Zeitsch. d. Savigny-Stift., Rom. Abt.* 50: 149, n. 7.

[13] Reil, *op. cit.*, 172.

[14] *Ibid.*, 171.

[15] *Ibid.*, 172.

[16] *P. Oxy.* 2: 262 of A. D. 61, death notice of a slave weaver who was at the time of death resident at a distance from his owner (ἐν τῇ ξένῃ); *Stud. Pal.* 4: 311; *Papyrus Erzherzog Rainer*, no. 33 of A. D. 72/73. *Papiri della Società Italiana* 10: 1139, 3, of A. D. 134/135, receipt for payment of weaver's license of a freedman; *BGU* 7: 1564, 2, 23 of A. D. 138, two freedmen paid for deliveries of woven goods; *Stud. Pal.* 22: 36, 8-9 of A. D. 145, a slave γερδίαινα contracted to work out interest upon a debt, the creditor being permitted to let out her services to any weaver whom he desires for two years; *P. Lond.*, no. 311, 12-13, 2: 220, of A. D. 149, a female slave weaver is used with another slave, as pledge for a debt, the value resting in her industrial skill; *P. Lond.* 3, no. 1269b: LXX, of A. D. 159, weaving license paid for a slave; *P. Grenfell*, no. 59 in Grenfell, B. P., and A. S. Hunt, *Greek Papyri, Series II*, 94, Oxford, Clarendon Press, 1897, of A. D. 189, contract for hire of a slave for twenty months who is ἀθλητὴν γερδιακὴν τέχνην; *P. Oxy.* 14: 1647, contract of apprenticeship of a girl slave to a weaver for four years; *BGU* 2: 617, 3-4, payment of weaving tax by a slave woman who was probably working independently on an understanding with her owner, *cf.* Wilcken, *Griech. Ostraka* 1: 688; *Papiri della Società Italiana* (*PSI*) 3: 241 is an apprentice contract of the third century (ὁμολογία διδασκαλική) for teaching the weaving trade ([γερδιακῆς ἢ] ὑφαντικῆς τέχνης) to a slave girl aged fourteen years.

[17] Apprenticing of free children to the weaving trade, *P. Oxy.* 2: 275; *P. Teb.* 2: 385, 442. *Cf.* the παραμονή contracts of free boys with weavers in *P. Teb.* 2: 384; Vitelli, G., *P. Flor.* 1: 44, 16-21.

[18] *Stud. Pal.* 4: 67; *P. Erzherzog Rainer*, no. 11 of A. D. 72/73.

[19] *P. Teb.* 3: 401, 12.

[20] *P. Oxy.* 4: 724 of A. D. 125. *Cf.* Westermann, W. L., *Class. Philology* 9: 295-315, 1914.

[21] *PSI* 6: 710, 13.

[22] *Stud. Pal.* 22: 60, 14.

[23] *BGU* 4: 1021, 6-18.

[24] Greek: κτενιστής; see Reil, Th., *Beiträge zur Kenntnis des Gewerbes im hellenistischen Ägypten*, 66, 99.

[25] Wessely, K., *P. Leipz.*, 11, in *Berichte sächs. Gesell. der Wissensch., ph.-hist. Klasse* 37: 252, 1885.

[26] *PSI* 9: 1055a.

[27] *P. Leipz.*, no. 97, col. X, 7, 9, in Mitteis, *Griechische Urkunden der Papyrussammlung zu Leipzig*.

dently.[28] A slave woman who had recently borne a child was used by her owner for wet-nursing, both in the cities and in the towns.[29] At Alexandria a slave girl belonging to a freedman was hired out as a nurse.[30]

The knowledge attainable upon the economic life and the industrial system in Alexandria is greatly restricted by the lack of papyri which deal with that city; but its wealth and its importance as a center of handicraft industries and of commerce [31] would justify the assumption that slaves were to be found in much larger numbers in domestic service among its wealthy inhabitants than in the Egyptian small towns and villages. It is certainly not warranted to assume, from the analogy of the moderate use of slaves in handicrafts in the *chōra*, that industrial employment of slaves in Alexandria was equally limited; [32] but it is also impossible to prove the statement [33] that any considerable body of slaves was used there in the handicrafts. Against the assumption of a large industrial slave class stands the fact that slave labor is obviously not considered of outstanding importance in Alexandria in a letter ascribed to Hadrian,[34] and that the small number of papyri now extant from Alexandria and its environs [35] indicate the use of free men on a much larger scale than slaves. The documents dealing with the slave group in or about Alexandria include a letter, presumably written by a freedman, dealing with a household in which some slaves were engaged in weaving;[36] a papyrus in which a woman who leased a house used her slave as collecting agent for the rent; [37] another document in which a slave appears as property mortgaged to secure a loan; [38] and one in which a slave boy was apprenticed to a music master for instruction in flute accompaniments.[39] The Roman merchants who in the first century A. D. engaged in export commerce from the Red Sea ports of Myos Hormos and Berenice, introduced there the Roman custom, already known from the methods they employed in their operations at Delos before 88 B. C., of conducting their business *in absentia* and of using highly trusted slaves and freedmen as their agents.[40]

A greater flexibility in the theoretical approach to-

ward slavery distinguished the Greek and Oriental lands of the eastern Mediterranean from the rigidity of the earlier Roman legal attitude toward slaves. This difference can best be followed in the papyri from Egypt. Whereas the slave, according to Roman law, was in principle incapable of owning property other than that assigned to him as his *peculium*,[41] in Egypt under Roman sway slaves had the right of property ownership just as they had had this right under the Babylonian, old Egyptian, Assyrian, and Talmudic law, and as the *oikeis* or *dōloi* under the Greek law of Gortyn,[42] the *chōris oikountes* at Athens [43] and some of the slaves at Pergamum had held it.[44] In the Roman province of Egypt recognition of this pre-Roman right of property ownership is shown in the fact that slaves frequently appear as paying their own trade licenses [45] and in definite indications of properties held in the names of slaves. In a papyrus of the time of Antoninus Caesar [46] the property belonging to a runaway slave was officially confiscated. In another document [47] a certain " Cerinthus, slave of Antonia, daughter of Drusus," requested permission to transfer sheep and goats which were registered in his own name.[48]

Divided ownership in slaves was permissible both under Roman law and in the peregrine law of Egypt; but the idea of a person being half-free and half-slave, which was readily accepted in Egypt, because of the practice of partial manumission, was irreconcilable with Roman legal principles.[49] From the Roman legal view of the slave the logical conclusion was derived that a slave as *res* was incapable of introducing or defending a civil action, whereas in Egypt as Roman province slaves were empowered to start actions before the police authorities, either in their own names or in behalf of others, in cases of personal injuries or of property damages.[50]

A group of documents found in the excavations at

[28] Wilcken, *Griechische Ostraka* 2: 235, 1400; cf. ibid. 1: 688; and *P. Lond.*, 1269a, *Greek papyri in the British Museum* 3: LXX.

[29] *BGU* 4: 1058 of 13 B. C.; *P. Oxy.* 1: 91; *P. Teb.* 2: 399.

[30] *BGU* 4: 1112, 11 of 4 B. C. Cf. ibid. 4: 1109, 11, 17 of 5 B. C.

[31] Rostovtzeff, M., *Soc. and econ. hist. Roman empire*, 167, 170.

[32] *Ibid.*, 507, n. 35.

[33] Reil, Th., *Beiträge zur Kenntnis des Gewerbes*, 173.

[34] *Script. hist. Aug., Saturninus*, 8, 5. Cf. Wilcken, *Griech. Ostraka* 1: 681.

[35] Notably the papyri from Abusir el Mäläg, edited by W. Schubart in *BGU* 4: 1098-1209.

[36] *BGU* 4: 1141, 20-22, 33-34, of 13 B. C.

[37] *BGU* 4: 1116, 38-42.

[38] *BGU* 4: 1139, 26, 33-34, of 1 B. C.

[39] *BGU* 4: 1125 of 13 B. C.

[40] For slaves as agents, see Tait, J. G., *Greek ostraca from the Bodleian Library* 1: 240, 252, 267, 275, 276, London, 1930, all dated within the years A. D. 34 to A. D. 50. Cf. Rostovtzeff's Review of Tait's book in *Gnomon* 7: 24-25, 1931.

[41] Taubenschlag, R., *Studi in onore di P. Bonfante* 1: 406, Pavia, 1929, with references to *BGU* 1: 96, 14-16, and *PSI* 9: 1040, 18-19: σὺν πεκυλίῳ παντί.

[42] See above, p. 16.

[43] See above, p. 12.

[44] Cf. Taubenschlag, R., *Zeitschr. d. Savigny-Stift., Rom. Abt.* 50: 156-157, 1930.

[45] Taubenschlag, *loc. cit.*

[46] *P. Geneva*, no. 5 in Nicole, Jules, *Les papyrus de Genève* 1, no. 5, 5-8, reading in line 8: οὐ τὰ [ὑ]πάρχοντα ε[ἰ]σπρα-[χθ . . . . . κτλ]. Cf. Preisigke, *Berichtigungsliste der griechischen Papyrusurkunden aus Ägypten* 1: 157, Leipzig, Walter de Gruyter und Co., 1922.

[47] *P. Oxy.* 2: 244, 15, 2.

[48] *Ibid.*, 5. Cf. Wenger, L., *Die Stellvertretung im Rechte der Papyri*, 167, n. 7.

[49] Mitteis, L., *Arch. f. Pap.* 3: 252-256; Arangio-Ruiz, V., *Persone e famiglia nel diritto dei papiri*, 8-9, Milano, Vita e Pensiero, 1930; Taubenschlag, R., *Studi in onore di P. Bonfante* 1: 405. Out of the possibility of pledging against a debt a part of a slave held in joint ownership the legal problem arose as to whether, under failure to pay the debt, the entire slave might be seized by the creditor. See *P. Lond.*, inventory no. 1983, edited by Bell, *Studi in onore di P. Bonfante* 3: 64-65.

[50] Taubenschlag, *Zeitschr. d. Savigny-Stift., Rom. Abt.* 50: 163.

Dura-Europus on the Euphrates River has brought to light information of great importance upon the legal institutions, including slavery, appertaining to the easternmost borders of the Roman Empire. *Parchment Dura*, no. 2 [51] is a fragmentary register of contracts of the end of the first century B. C., the second of which [52] records the dowry assignment of two slaves by a prominent citizen to his daughter.[53] A document of the year A. D. 86-87 [54] is in effect a foreclosure upon three slaves because of failure on the part of their owner to repay a loan. The transaction appears in the form of a Greek *dosis* in which the debtor had given over her entire property in satisfaction of the creditor's claim but received everything back with the exception of the three slaves whose value presumably covered the amount of the loan.

A document of A.D. 121 [55] is a contract embodying a loan made to a man who bore the Aramaic name, Barlaas, and lived in the village of Paliga near Dura. The interest upon the loan was to be met by personal antichretistic services of the debtor [56] with definition of the services to be rendered as *doulikas chreias*. In case of nonpayment at the end of the term of the loan execution is provided for, both upon the property and upon the person of the debtor, so that the limited antichretistic services of the debtor might be extended into *de jure* slavery.[57]

Parchment Dura, no. 23,[58] dated in A. D. 180, is a contract of sale in which a half of a vineyard held in divided ownership by two brothers was sold by one brother to the other, along with a slave, aged twenty years, whom the vendor had held in full ownership. It is important to note that the slave was transferred with the vineyard,[59] obviously as a part of the labor inventory attaching to the property, and was enumerated in the contract of sale in the same manner as the fruit trees, the wine vat and other appurtenances of the property [60]

which were necessary to the successful operation of the vineyard.

These documents have brought proof that the law upon slavery, as it appears in the Mesopotamian area of the Empire in the documents formulated in the Greek language, was decidedly more Hellenistic than Oriental, with no adoption of the principles of the Roman law of slavery.[61] The Hellenistic character of the slave law is particularly indicated in the restriction upon the freedom of movement of the debtor in the *paramone* clauses of *Parchment Dura*, no. 10,[62] and in the non-Roman right of execution upon the person of the debtor and consequent enslavement in case of eventual non-payment.[63] A deed of sale of a female slave, designated as a captive, dated in A. D. 243 and written in the Syrian language,[64] seems to show, however, non-Hellenistic elements in the legal background which is behind it. This document will unquestionably be of great importance in the future discussion of the law of slavery in the eastern area of the Roman Empire. The penetration of the Roman law upon slavery into this region and further eastward into the Sassanid Persian kingdom occurred in the post-Constantine period during the eastward advance of the Christian missionary activity out of Antioch.[65] Its acceptance appears in the Syrian-Roman law book of the fifth century [66] and in the compilation made by Archbishop Jesubocht in Persia in the Mohammedan period. It is manifested in the statement, " Concerning slaves male and female thus it is written in the law of the Romans: a man may free one third of his slaves, etc." [67] and in the principle that in a manumission *inter vivos* the peculium must be expressly bestowed upon the freed slave.[68] Possibly also the regulations which appear there regarding the status of children born from the union of a free woman and a slave go back to the *Senatus Consultum Claudianum* of A. D. 53.[69]

The tolls levied upon the export and import of slaves which appear in fragmentary form in the Palmyrene

[51] Cumont, F., *Fouilles de Doura-Europos*, 296-297, Paris, 1926; Johnson, J., *Dura studies*, 35-37, diss. Pennsylvania, 1932.

[52] *Parchment Dura*, no. 2, 11-19.

[53] [σώματα δο]υλικὰ δύο. *Cf.* Johnson, J., *Dura studies*, 40, 44.

[54] *Parchment Dura*, no. 21, unpublished. See Welles, C. B., *Münchener Beiträge*, 19: 395-396.

[55] *Parchment Dura*, no. 10, first published by Rostovtzeff, M. and C. B. Welles, *Académie des Inscriptions et Belles-lettres, Comptes rendus*, 158-181, 1930; republished by Rostovtzeff, M. and C. B. Welles, *Yale Classical Studies* 2: 1-78, 1931; Rostovtzeff and Welles, *Excavations at Dura-Europus, Second Season*, 201-215, New Haven, Yale Univ. Press, 1931; Koschaker, P., *Abh. sächs. Akad., phil.-hist. Klasse* 42 (1): 2-9.

[56] *Parchment Dura*, no. 10, 7-8.

[57] *Ibid.*, 17-18. See the discussion by Rostovtzeff and Welles, *Excavations at Dura-Europus, Second Season*, 211-215; Koschaker, P., *Abh. sächs. Akad., phil.-hist. Klasse* 42 (1): 2-9.

[58] Welles, C. B., *Münchener Beiträge*, 19: 382-389.

[59] *Parchment Dura*, no. 23, 12-21, *ibid.* 382-385. The Greco-Macedonian tradition presented by this document, unaffected by the Roman law of slavery, is emphasized by C. B. Welles, *ibid.*, 387-388.

[60] *Ibid.*, 14-15: ἀκροδρύοις λημῶνι καὶ τοῖς ἄλλοις τοῖς συνκυροῦσι καὶ καθήκουσι πᾶσι.

[61] Koschaker, P., *Chronique d'Égypte, Bulletin périodique de la fondation Reine Élisabeth*, 13-14: 205, Brussels, 1932. The Greek character of the law, particularly as displayed in *Parchment Dura*, no. 10, is more strongly stressed by Schönbauer, E., *Zeitschr. d. Savigny-Stift., Rom. Abt.* 53: 449, 1933.

[62] *Parchment Dura*, no. 10, 8-11.

[63] Koschaker, P., *Abh. sächs. Akad.* 42: 17-18; *Chronique d'Égypte* 13-14: 207-209.

[64] *Parchment Dura*, no. 20, noted by Welles, C. B., *Münchener Beiträge*, 19: 297-298, and published by Torrey, C. C., *Zeitschrift für Semitistik und verwandte Gebiete* 10: 33-45, 1935. *Cf.* Welles, C. B., and A. Bellinger in *Yale Class. Studies* 5: 95-154, 1935.

[65] Taubenschlag, R., *Zeitschr. d. Savigny, Stift., Rom. Abt.* 45: 495.

[66] Bruns-Sachau, *Syrisch-römisches Rechtsbuch*, 184, n. 4, Leipzig, 1880.

[67] Sachau, E., *Syrische Rechtsbücher* 3: 177, 1a, Berlin, 1914, excerpted from the *lex Fufia Caninia*, Gaius 1: 43; Bruns-Sachau, *loc. cit.*; Sachau, *Syrische Rechtsbücher* 3: 334.

[68] Sachau, *op. cit.* 3: 179, 3.

[69] *Ibid.*, 77, 5c; 302. *Cf.* Taubenschlag, R., *Zeitschrift der Savigny-Stiftung, Rom. Abt.* 45: 496-497.

gate tolls (the *portoria Palmyrenorum*) of A. D. 137 [70] prove certainly the passage of slaves in the first half of the second century A. D. in both directions over the caravan route Babylon-Dura-Palmyra-Damascus and Palmyra-Petra; [71] but, in view of the observation that only a small number of Asiatic slaves actually appear within the Roman Empire and that the number of the home-bred slaves [72] was increasing, it is inadvisable to establish conjecturally a great slave importation into the Empire via Palmyra. [73] The toll exacted upon each slave at Palmyra was twenty-two *denarii*, with special arrangements for *veterani* [74] and for one other type of slave. Because the rate of the tolls cannot be ascertained, no conclusions as to slave prices at Palmyra can be drawn from the inscription.

The material available on labor conditions in Syria and Palestine, either for agricultural or industrial lines, is very slight. Lucian presumably was reflecting the situation in the handicrafts in northern Syria when he spoke of both free men and slaves who were endowed with technical skill of some kind. [75] The use of slaves in wealthy homes of the city dwellers is attested by his account of a slave messenger whom it was necessary to tip when he brought an invitation to dinner. [76] In the glassware production of Sidon in the first century of the Empire [77] the workmen whose names appear embossed upon the glass designate themselves as the responsible craftsmen by the simple name, " Artas a Sidon(ian)," " Aristo a Sidon(ian)," " Nikon a Sidon(ian)," or by the statement " Eirenaeus a Sidonian made (it) " or " Megas," or " Ennion made (it) " as the case may be. [78] Sidonian glass cups in the Metropolitan Museum in New York show, in addition to the names of Megas and Ennion above, a workman named Jason and another incomplete name. [79] Some of these glassworkers were unquestionably free men, as is proved by their designation as Sidonians. In the cases with the name of the workman alone embossed on the glassware it is not possible to assume that they were slaves in view of the fact that they were permitted to sign the cups or vases without any indication either of the name of the shop owner or of the owner of the slave. [80] In Syrian agrarian oc-

cupations slaves were no doubt employed to some extent; [81] but, as in Palestine, farm and vineyard labor was largely supplied by a free peasantry. [82]

In the case of the Jews, both in Palestine and in the Diaspora, the unusual conditions set by religious law for the early Hebrew economic life in its attitude on slavery continued into the Empire with little change. A distinction was constantly maintained between Jewish and non-Jewish slaves under Jewish ownership, the former appearing as *ĕbed* (slave), the latter as *ĕbed kanaăni* (Canaanite slave) both in the Old Testament and in the Talmud. This distinction is clearly continued in the retention of the ancient enactment that a Jewish slave in Jewish ownership must be given his freedom in the seventh year. [83] Those Jews who were so unfortunate as to fall into bondage were to be treated as one treats hired servants. [84] The forbiddance of labor upon the Sabbath, which applied even to domestic animals, [85] no doubt affected the working conditions of all slaves owned by Jews, of whatever religion they might be. According to the Talmud, [86] if the relatives of a Jew who had become enslaved to a Gentile could not purchase his freedom, it was the duty of the Jewish local community to ransom him. [87]

It is in manumission practice that the nature and the degree of the acceptances and rejections of the Hellenistic slave system by the Jewish Diaspora communities are most clearly lighted up for us. This occurs only in one localized area, in the Russian Black Sea ports now called Kertsch (ancient Panticapaeum) and Anapa. The information is restricted to four documents; [88] but

---

[70] Dittenberger, W., *Orientis Graeci inscriptiones selectae* 2: 629, 17-24.

[71] *Cf.* Rostovtzeff, M., *Caravan cities*, 109-110, Oxford, Clarendon Press, 1932.

[72] οἰκογενεῖς, *vernae, cf.* above pp. 32-33.

[73] As is done by Février, J. G., *Essai sur l'histoire politique et économique de Palmyre*, 47, Paris, Vrin, 1931.

[74] [Ἀνδράποδα] οὐετερα[νά], restored from the *vᵗᵗrᵗn* of the Aramaic version.

[75] Lucian, *De parasito*, 1.

[76] Lucian, *De mercede conductis*, 14.

[77] So dated from the letter forms by Kisa, A. C., *Das Glas im Altertume* 3: 704, Leipzig, Hiersemann, 1908.

[78] Kisa, *op. cit.* 3: 704-716.

[79]].ειϰα.s, *cf.* Richter, G. M., *The room of ancient glass*, 16, New York, Metropolitan Museum, 1930. No. I. 2465. 94 of the J. P. Morgan Collection, New York, is also signed by Jason.

[80] *Cf.* the Arretine *sigillata* pottery from Italy upon which the name of the factory owner always appears when the stamp

of the slave workman is on the vase. Also the slave-owner's name always appears in the genitive. See Oxé, A., *Arretinische Reliefgefässe vom Rhein*, 118, Index IV, *Topferverzeichniss I*, Frankfurt, Baer und Co., 1933; Dragendorff, H., *Gnomon* 10: 358.

[81] A slave vinedresser appears in Lucian, *Philopsend.*, 11.

[82] Rostovtzeff, M., *Soc. and econ. hist. Roman empire*, 245, Oxford, Clarendon Press, 1926. In the New Testament there is no evidence of agricultural slavery.

[83] Exod., 21, 2. Bertholet, Alfred, *A history of Hebrew civilization*, 166, London, Harrup and Co., 1926. This contrast between Jew and non-Jew is implied by Philo in his discussion of the Jewish coreligionists in debtor bondage, the Jews being οἱ μὴ γένει δοῦλοι, " those who by birth are not slaves," Philo, *On the virtues*, 122-123. In his *De Josepho*, 248, it is stated that Joseph was not a slave by birth.

[84] Leviticus, 25, 39-40.

[85] Deuteronomy, 5, 14.

[86] Baba Bathra, fol. 8 *ad fin. Cf.* Krauss, Samuel, *Talmudische Archäologie* 2: 98, Leipzig, G. Fock, 1910-1912.

[87] Note the case from Egypt of ransom of a Jewess with her two children in A. D. 291 by the local synagogue; *P. Oxy.* 9, no. 1205.

[88] *Inscriptiones orae septentrionalis Ponti Euxini* 2, nos. 52, 53, 400, 401, edited by Latyschev, B., Petropolis (Petrograd), 1890. Number 52 of Latyschev is to be found, also, in Dareste, R., B. Haussoullier, Th. Reinach, *Recueil des inscriptions juridiques grecques* 2 (2-3), no. 34: 208-209, Paris, Leroux, 1904. Latyschev nos. 52 and 400 are reproduced by Minns, Ellis, *Scythians and Greeks; Appendix*, nos. 46 and 43, pp. 653-654, Cambridge, Univ. Press, 1913. We follow Latyschev's decision, *op. cit.*, no. 54, in omitting that fragmentary record from the dis-

these, when closely analyzed, permit several deductions upon the tendencies of Hellenistic-Jewish syncretisms as expressed in this limited field of the institution of slavery. The four documents clearly demonstrate that in this Jewish Diaspora group in lower Russia, of the latter half of the first century after Christ, the traditional Hebrew attitude as it expressed itself in slavery was maintained, but that in the formal and external features both of procedure and of publicity of the event, Greek practices and models were copied almost completely.[89]

The records of the acts of manumission were published in the same general form and in the same sequence of events as were the *anagraphai* (the posted records) at Delphi where they were incised upon various structures in the sacred precinct. The Jewish grants of freedom were presumably set up in the synagogue, imitating in this respect the Delphic practice, but converted into terms of the Jewish community religious center.[90] The following features of the documentation and procedure in these liberations from slave status are Greek, not Jewish:

1. By traditional Jewish law and custom the slaves of these Jewish manumittors must have been, originally, of the Gentile religious beliefs, and they could not be released from their enslavement. In the later Talmudic law this forbiddance of manumission of the slaves of Jews was re-enforced. Probably manumission of Gentile slaves was not acceptable to all in the first century under a strict interpretation of Jewish law.

2. The language of these synagogue grants of liberty is Greek. The records reproduce, with a fair degree of accuracy, the terminology and the sequence of the formulas employed in the Delphic manumissions.

3. The Jewish manumissions diverge from the Delphic type in the fact that they profess to be consecrations. Most of the Delphic grants of liberty appear in the form of trust sales to Apollo. In their aspect of consecrations (*anathemata*) the South Russian liberations follow the symbolic dedicational type which is well known from central Greek towns other than Delphi. In both cases the manumissions were really consummated by civil action.[91]

4. The arrangement for a continuation by the new freedman of some part of his former services for his former owner, under a contract called a *paramonē*, is Greek, completely.

5. The oath taken " by Zeus, earth and sun " has no possible place in a Jewish civil or religious act.[92]

6. The clearance of the new freedman's title to his liberty by assent of the heirs of the slave-owner is entirely Greek.[93]

7. The most important, and most complete, adoption of a Greek feature in these manumissions is represented in the acceptance in them of three of the four elements which appear in the Delphic trust sales to Apollo as those basic possessions of a free man which make him free. These are: *eleutheria*, legal freedom; the fact that he is not subject to unwarranted seizure or subject to harassment; [94] and that, now being free, he is at liberty to go wherever he (or she) wishes.[95]

The practice and the ethos of Hebrew enslavement are, on the other hand, maintained without impingement of Greek models or spirit in several of the fundamental attitudes manifested in the four emancipations from

---

cussion as offering nothing in the preserved portion to indicate that the manumittors belonged to the Jewish community.

[89] Lipinsky, H., Über einige Inschriften in Südrussland, *Jüdisch-litterarische Gesellschaft, Jahrb.* 1: 324, Frankfurt, Kauffmann, 1903. Baron, Salo, *The Jewish community*, 1: 88, Philadelphia, Jewish Publ. Soc., 1945, has briefly and correctly stated the general conclusion upon the Greek and Jewish elements involved.

[90] Krauss, Samuel, Sklavenbefrieiung in den jüdisch-griechischen Inschriften aus Südrussland, *Festschrift zu Ehren des Dr. A. Harkavy*, 65, St. Petersburg (no publisher named), 1908. The phrase *manumissio in hierodulismum*, which goes back to Krauss, should be abandoned. It confuses the understanding of the widespread Greek custom of manumission by a simulated divine dedication.

[91] Latyschev, 2: 52, and 401 are purely civil acts and without any religious implications as shown by the phraseology in no. 52,

6-8 and no. 401, 15-16; ἀφείημι ———— Ἡρακλᾶν ἐλεύθερον in the first case, and ἀφείομεν τὴν θρεπ[τὴν] ἡμῶν ἐλευθέραν in the second. In Latyschev, *Ins. orae sept. Pont. Eux.* 2, no. 54, 6-7 and 400, 8-14 a slight, religious tincture is present in the use of the verb ἀνατιθέναι, "to dedicate." Krauss in the *Festschrift Harkavy* was misled by his lack of knowledge of the Greek manumissions by dedication to a god in which the consecration of the slave to the god was a mere phrase. The opening lines of the documents are mere invocations, like the ἀγαθῆ τύχῃ of Greek inscriptions. Krauss himself, in fact, suspected (*op. cit.*, 65) that the manumission in the prayer house might be nothing more than a fictitious procedure. The civil act of granting freedom was the important element, which stated that the slave-owner made the consecration to the god through the city council as the law required: τὴν ἀνάθεσιν ποιόμενος διὰ τῶ συνεδρίω κατὰ τὸν νόμον. See *IG* 7: 3301, 3302 and many other examples up to 3406.

[92] Latyschev, 2, no. 400, presents a manumission by dedication in the prayer-house, therefore by manumittors who were Jews (lines 8-10: ἀνέθηκεν (ἐν) τ[ῆ]ι [προσ]ευχῆι.). In this record the oath of protection of the slave's liberty is taken " by Zeus, earth and sun," which is a Greek oath. Lieberman, Saul, *Hellenism in Jewish Palestine*, 214, New York, Jewish Theol. Seminary, 1950, emphasizes the depth of the assimilation represented by the unconscious Jewish assimilation of these Gentile formulas.

[93] The waiver of claim to the slave and the document which incorporates it customarily appear in the Greek manumissions in a genitive absolute clause stating that the possible future heirs join in " approving," " feeling satisfaction with," or " commending." Westermann, W. L., Extinction of claims in slave sales at Delphi, *Jour. Juristic Papyrology* 4: 51, 1950, Warsaw. In Latyschev's 2, no. 52, lines 15-17 (Ellis Minns, *Scythians and Greeks*, App., no. 46) the phrase states that " my heirs Heraclides and Heliconias, join in nodding assent," (συνεπινευσάντων). See Westermann, as above, p. 52, n. 9, for the use of this verb, συνεπινεύειν in *IG* 7: 3386, the liberation of a slave by dedication, from Chaeronea in Boeotia.

[94] Latyschev, *Ins. orae sept. Pont. Eux.* 2, no. 52, 9-10: ἀνεπίλημπον καὶ ἀπα[ρ]ενόχλητον. This feature appears, also in no. 400, 11-12.

[95] *Ibid.* 52, 13-14: [τ]ρέπεσθαι ὅπου ἂν βούλ[η]ται.

the Jewish community. (1) There is, implicit in the documents though not subject to direct proof, a retention of the Hebrew distinction, arising from an intrinsic tribal-religious approach, between actual enslavement for Gentiles and six-year bondage services for core-ligionists.[96] (2) The granting of liberty took place before the synagogue, the religious community, and in the prayer house itself.[97] (3) The records of the manumissions were posted in the synagogue as the center of life of the Diaspora community. (4) The manumission resulted from a vow ($\kappa\alpha\tau$' $\epsilon\dot{\upsilon}\chi\dot{\eta}\nu$) taken by the slave-owner and with the assent of the community.[98] This is a West Asiatic and non-Greek element which expressed itself, in a different psychological form, in the dream motivation of the child oblations to a god as they are known from Asia Minor.[99] The statement of the right of the new freedman to physical mobility has been isolated above as Greek. The expression of this right of movement appears, however, with a religious restriction which has no similarity to anything known to me in a Greek parallel. The freedman released from Jewish slavery may, indeed, go wherever he may desire to go without hindrance " according as I have made my vow, except (that he must go) into the prayer house for his devotions and to spend his time," $\chi\omega\rho\grave{\iota}\varsigma$ $\epsilon\dot{\iota}\varsigma$ $\tau\dot{\eta}\nu$ $\pi\rho\sigma\epsilon\dot{\upsilon}\chi\eta\nu$ $\theta\omega\pi\epsilon\dot{\iota}\alpha\varsigma$ $\tau\epsilon$ $\kappa\alpha\grave{\iota}$ $\pi\rho\sigma\sigma\kappa\alpha\rho\tau\epsilon\rho\dot{\eta}\sigma\epsilon\omega\varsigma$.[100]

The materials presented by Rostovtzeff in his penetrating studies of the agricultural organization which prevailed in Asia Minor under the Roman Empire need not be reproduced here.[101] The conditions of land ownership and the methods employed in production had been taken over by the Roman emperors in the forms which they had developed in the Hellenistic period.[102]

The cultivation of the imperial domains was done chiefly by tenant serfs (coloni) who lived in villages, as they had formerly done in Hellenistic times.[103] The great stretches of land owned by the temple organizations of the Anatolian gods were cultivated by a peasantry attached to the temples but not subject to sale. They were, therefore, serfs rather than slaves in any true sense.[104] The servitia received by Hadrian for work in the camps of Cappodocia [105] were serfs, not slaves.[106]

We have direct testimony regarding the burdens which rested upon the agricultural peasantry attached to the imperial estates in Phrygia in the third century and upon the low economic condition to which they had been reduced in the complaint of the imperial tenants (paroikoi kai geōrgoi) of the village of Arague to the Emperor Philip.[107] Under the conditions attested by that document the use of slaves in agriculture on a large scale seems highly improbable. The farm lands attached to the Greek city states in Asia Minor were either owned by small-farm peasants who cultivated their own holdings in person,[108] or, upon the large estates, they were cultivated by tenants.[109]

Information in small quantity is available upon labor employment in the handicrafts in Cilicia from the period of the Empire. At Tarsus in the first century the linen weavers, dyers, leather cutters, and carpenters were free workmen.[110] In the necropolis inscriptions of the Empire and the Byzantine period, collected in Cilicia by J. Keil and Ad. Wilhelm,[111] among the large number of tradesmen and artisans who appear [112] none are slaves.[113] For Cilicia it would probably be right to assume that the use of slaves never again attained large proportions after the suppression of Cilician piracy by Gnaeus Pompey. The inscriptions from eastern Phrygia show a number of imperial slaves and freedmen attached to the imperial estates about Laodicea Combusta,[114] with a very small number of slaves in private ownership.[115]

[96] Lipinsky, op. cit., 323, quoting the Talmud, Gittin 38a.

[97] $\epsilon\pi\grave{\iota}$ $\tau\hat{\eta}\varsigma$ [$\pi\rho\sigma$]$\sigma\epsilon\dot{\upsilon}\chi\eta\varsigma$ in Latyschev, 2, no. 52, 6. Cf. ibid., no. 400, 8-9 and 53, 20.

[98] Latyschev 2: 52, 8: $\sigma\upsilon\nu\epsilon$[$\pi\iota\tau$]$\rho\sigma\pi\epsilon\dot{\upsilon}\sigma\eta\varsigma$ $\delta\grave{\epsilon}$ $\kappa\alpha\grave{\iota}$ $\tau\eta$[ς] $\sigma\upsilon\nu\alpha$-$\gamma\omega\rho\hat{\eta}$[$\varsigma$].

[99] Buckler, W. H., W. M. Calder and Guthrie, Monumenta Asiae Minoris Antiqua 4, nos. 275 II—277 B, Manchester, Univ. Press, 1933.

[100] $\chi\omega\rho\grave{\iota}\varsigma$ $\epsilon\dot{\iota}\varsigma$ $\tau\dot{\eta}\nu$ $\pi\rho\sigma\epsilon\dot{\upsilon}\chi\eta\nu$ $\theta\omega\pi\epsilon\dot{\iota}\alpha\varsigma$ $\tau\epsilon$ $\kappa\alpha\grave{\iota}$ $\pi\rho\sigma\sigma\kappa\alpha\rho\tau\epsilon\rho\dot{\eta}\sigma\epsilon\omega\varsigma$, Latyschev 2, no. 52, 10-15; no. 53, 16-21. I have understood this cryptic passage in the sense of Lipinsky's translation in Jüdisch-literarische Gesellschaft, Jahrb. 1: 322. These would necessarily be Gentile slaves by origin, who had been converted to the Jewish faith. The translation of Latyschev 2, no. 52, in Dareste-Haussoullier-Reinach, Recueil 2: 299, presents it as a prohibition of the presence in the synagogue of the new freedman, Heraklas, and against his paying his devotions in the prayer house. Krauss in Festschrift Harkavy, 58, has wrongly concluded that the slaves in all of the four Jewish manumissions had been converted to the Jewish belief. This decision is warranted only in Latyschev's nos. 52 and 53 where the persons freed are required, as I interpret it, following Latyschev and Boeckh, to pay their homage in the synagogue. See Latyschev's commentary upon no. 52.

[101] Rostovtzeff, M., Studien zur Geschichte des römischen Kolonates, 283-312.

[102] Ibid., 292-294. See Rostovtzeff, Soc. and econ. hist. Roman empire, 563, n. 4, for the evidence upon this subject which has accumulated since 1910.

[103] Kornemann, E., in the article Domänen, Pauly-W., RE, Supplementb. 4: 247.

[104] The lands of the temple state of Komana, established by Pompey, were worked by hierodules who were under the control of its ruling priest " except for the right to sell them "; Strabo 12: 3, 34.

[105] Script. hist. Aug., Hadr., 8, 7.

[106] Rostovtzeff, M., Soc. and econ. hist. Roman empire, 564, 7.

[107] OGI, 519, 7. Cf. Rostovtzeff, ibid., 622-623, 26.

[108] They are similar to the $\gamma\epsilon\omega\rho\gamma\sigma\hat{\upsilon}\nu\tau\epsilon\varsigma$, also designated as $\mu\acute{\epsilon}\tau\sigma\iota\kappa\sigma\iota$ on the island of Cos. IGR 4: 1087. Cf. Rostovtzeff, M., ibid., 562 n. 3, and in Anatolian studies presented to Sir William Ramsay, 376, Manchester, Univ. Press, 1923.

[109] Possibly they were cultivated by slaves in some instances as claimed by Rostovtzeff, Soc. and econ. hist. Roman empire, 236, although proof of farming with slave labor is lacking.

[110] Dio Chrys., 34, 23.

[111] MAMA 3, Index III (trades).

[112] Twenty-one retailers, twenty-three potters, fifteen bronze workers.

[113] $\sigma\grave{\upsilon}\nu$ $\tau\hat{\omega}$ $\delta\sigma\upsilon\lambda\iota\kappa\hat{\omega}$ in 795 may refer to a single slave attendant.

[114] Calder, W. M., MAMA 1: 17.

[115] Ibid., 28, 30; $\dot{\alpha}\pi\epsilon\lambda\epsilon\dot{\upsilon}\theta\epsilon\rho\sigma\iota$, as also in 107; and cf. 133; (threptoi) 44, 91.

Omitting consideration of the imperial slaves, who belonged to a special category which did not affect the local problem of free and servile labor, in the inscriptions from the eastern section of the province of Asia and western Galatia, six documents appear which deal with manumissions of slaves who were privately owned.[116] One inscription [117] shows both free men and slaves occupied as sheep grazers. All the craftsmen, retail dealers, and hired laborers who are found in these Galatian inscriptions were free men.[118] The consideration might well be advanced that slave laborers or craftsmen, being the humblest of the local inhabitants, would not have had their names recorded upon burial stones and might have been present in these regions without being so honored after death. Against this idea stands the fact that freedmen's names, also, occur very seldom in these grave monuments.[119]

The limited information brought by the inscriptions of Sardis upon the status of workers in manufacturing and retail lines leads to the same conclusion, that during the Empire few of them were slaves.[120] The frequent occurrence of strikes in the Asia Minor cities [121] also speaks strongly for a predominant body of free workmen in that region in the period of the Empire. Household slavery in the homes of wealthy city dwellers and upon the large country estates unquestionably persisted.[122] In the cities of Asia Minor, as distinguished from the towns, the villages and the rural districts, the total of the slave population may have been about one third of the entire body of residents, as intimated by Galen for Pergamum.[123] This proportion of slaves probably included assistants of local selling and distributing agencies, owners of retail stores,[124] and the slaves connected with household services.

The character of the economic life of the Danubian and Balkan provinces precludes the probability of a large use of slaves in those sections of the Roman Empire. This decision is based upon the inscriptions, limited in their number, which offer any testimony of value upon slave conditions. Throughout this region industrial life was not highly developed. The great stretches of arable land in southern Russia were cultivated by serfs rather than slaves.[125] The ten thousand men who were offered in A. D. 49 by Zorsines, King of the Siracians, in exchange for his free subjects who had been captured, although designated as slaves by Tacitus,[126] were probably serfs.[127] Serfs of similar type furnished the labor for agricultural production in Dacia, Moesia and Istria.[128] The supposition advanced by Rostovtzeff,[129] of a lively trade in slaves from beyond the Danube who furnished the labor upon the large estates in the Danubian provinces, finds no support in the list of those slaves whose *origo* can definitely be ascribed to that region. The slaves and freedmen who appear in the documents from Serbia and Macedonia [130] were connected with the imperial household and used in the collection of tolls and in similar services. There is no indication of the type of labor used in the ironworks of Noricum.[131]

The use of slaves continued, of course, in Macedon, Thessaly, and the Greek mainland, but a gradual and decided decrease in their numbers and a change in the use of them may safely be postulated as a result of the continued economic decline of the Greek peninsula. The disappearance of industrial activity in all but a few lines of production is the outstanding feature of this change.[132] With the elimination of the handicraft production which had had the entire Mediterranean area as its potential market, the industrial slavery which had featured the life of Athens and Corinth during the fifth and fourth centuries B. C. must have disappeared almost entirely.[133]

---

[116] *MAMA* 4: 275B; 276A II and B; 277A II; 278; 279. θρεπταί are mentioned in 354; 355.

[117] *Ibid.*, 297, 8-9.

[118] *MAMA* 4: 73; 100; 113a; 343, 349. When slaves appear in funerary inscriptions their status seems to be given, as in nos. 32, 279 and 293.

[119] One freedman, whose occupation is not recorded, appears *ibid.*, 336.

[120] Buckler and Robinson, *Sardis* 7 (1), *Greek and Latin inscriptions*, Leyden, 1932: 56, a sculptor in relief; 94, a barber; 159, a dealer in swine; 167, a maker of breeches. All of these are free men. Freedmen appear in no. 165, an inscription found upon a sepulchre erected by a citizeness of the Lydian town of Tabalis who was then residing in Sardis.

[121] The instances are gathered by W. H. Buckler, *Anatolian studies presented to Sir William Ramsay*, 27-50. Cf. Rostovtzeff, *Soc. and econ. hist. Roman empire*, 540, n. 4.

[122] See the honorary inscriptions of the Rhodians to Nicostratus, the sophist, with particular mention of his efforts, upon an embassy to Rome, to obtain concessions regarding the *eikostē*, which was probably the five per cent tax on manumissions. *Ann. della Reg. Scuola Arch. di Atene* 2: 147, 1916. A similar embassy sent for the same purpose is recorded from Thyatira in Lydia. *IGR* 4: 1236. Cf. Rostovtzeff, *ibid.*, 539, n. 42, who cites the inscription honoring a slave dealer, σωματέμπορος, at Thyatira, set up by workmen and middlemen agents in slave transfers (προξενηταὶ σωμάτων), Dittenberger, *Or. Gr. Ins.* 2: 524.

[123] Kühn, Gottlob, *Claudii Galeni opera omnia* 5: 49, Leipzig, Cnobloch, 1823.

[124] Rostovtzeff, *ibid.*, 569, 31.

[125] Rostovtzeff, M., *Iranians and Greeks in South Russia*, 161, Oxford, Clarendon Press, 1922.

[126] Tacitus, *Annals* 12: 17: *servitii decem milia offerebant. Quod aspernati sunt victores, . . .*

[127] Rostovtzeff, M., *Soc. and econ. hist. Roman empire*, 562, n. 2 and 565, n. 12. For the Bosporan Kingdom, *ibid.*, 241.

[128] *Ibid.*, 229-230.

[129] *Ibid.*, 229.

[130] Published by Premerstein and Vulic, *Jahresh. Wien* 6, *Beiblatt* 36: 44.

[131] The development of this began after the establishment of the province *ca.* 15 B. C., Strabo, 6: 8, σιδηρουργεῖα.

[132] For the use of slaves by the prosperous classes in the Greek cities as teachers, farm laborers, agents in business relations, and moneylenders, see Plutarch, *De lib. educ.*, 6-7. Industrial slaves are not mentioned in Plutarch's list.

[133] Rostovtzeff, *ibid.*, 161, 235. Artistic bronze ware was still produced in Corinth, Aegina and Delos, women's wear in linen near Elis and Patrae, and perfumes in Boeotia, Fr. Oertel in *Camb. Anc. Hist.* 10: 403. Upon the specious appearance of prosperity of the city of Athens in the second century, consult

In the more isolated parts of Greece, such as Arcadia, slave employment had apparently reverted to a situation

somewhat like that which had existed in the Homeric period.[134]

Day, John, *Economic history of Athens under Roman domination*, 196, New York, Columbia Univ. Press, 1942; for the third and following centuries, *ibid.*, 258, 263 and 267-268. The abandonment of land and the depopulation of Euboea are probably presented in exaggerated form by Dio Chrys., *Or.*, 7, 34. Thessaly is depicted by Dio as deserted, Arcadia as ruined (*Or.*, 23,

25). On the poverty of the Arcadian town of Lycosura in A. D. 42, see *Or. Gr. Ins.* 2: 800; upon the depopulation of Greece, Plutarch, *De defect. orac.*, 8.

[134] Philostratus, *Vita Apoll. Tyan.* 8: 7, 161, speaks of slaves in Arcadia as farm hands and herders of goats, swine, cattle and horses.

XX. FROM DIOCLETIAN TO JUSTINIAN

PROBLEMS OF SLAVERY

The tendencies of the legislative enactments in the three first centuries of the Roman Empire and of the administrative activities in the provinces had slowly and constantly been moving in the direction of lowering the economic and legal position of free handicraftsmen and agrarian labor toward that which had formerly been held by workers of slave status. Some of the detailed expressions of these trends have been touched upon in passing in the preceding chapters.[1] It is difficult to detect and to evaluate with certainty the original causes of these labor movements because of the scarcity and the inconclusive nature of the evidence. The actuality of the changes involved is apparent enough, however, in the labor system as it developed in the centuries from the accession of Diocletian (A. D. 284) to the death of Justinian. Gradually free hired labor had increased in numerical strength over slave labor in the first century of the Empire during the period of the continuation of its imperial expansion, upon the North, toward the West, and at the western end of North Africa. Under Hadrian the system changed to one of defense at the wall and ditch *limites*, the riparian defenses of the Rhine and Danube, and upon the shifting defensive lines in the desert areas of Africa and Arabia. The demand for slaves might still have seemed to be constant; and the supply to be dredged up out of the pools of border warfare might still have appeared in the first century of the Christian era[2] to have been inexhaustible. It was during the first half of the nineteenth century that the modern scholarly understanding, and the corresponding popular ideas of the slave institutions of antiquity, assumed the standardized form which, in many circles, they have steadily maintained to the present day. The earlier period of the nineteenth century was characterized by an increasing reaction away from the system, as a form of labor employment inadequate to the demands created by the industrial movement and as a moral degradation of a part of humanity which was unworthy of the Christian and the liberal ethic of that time. Even then the fact of the decrease in slave numbers during the first three centuries of Roman imperial history and of the continuation of the numerical decline in the slave

population of the early Byzantine era was clearly recognized.[3] The explanation of this quantitative decline was beclouded, however, by the conviction reached by Henri Wallon that Christianity was the primary cause which bettered the conditions of slavery in the centuries of the early Empire. Great praise is due to the French scholar for establishing the importance of the acceptance of slaves into the Christian communities, from the outset of the Christian missionary activity under the Apostle Paul, on a basis of complete equality with their masters so far as the group itself was concerned. Within the community faith in Christ obliterated caste.

Wallon's study responded to the needs of the century during which it dominated the field of its interest. Nevertheless, the moralistic tone of a militant abolitionist bedimmed the conclusion that the early Christian leaders, however much they deplored the essential doctrine of enslavement, accepted its practice *in toto* as a part of the divine dispensation working in society as God had established it for His own ends. It served to obscure, also, the observation that the early Church fathers, in their counsels to their charges, and the later Church canons, in urging Christian slave-owners to manumit their Christian slaves, failed to reject the fundamental moral concepts of the system itself.[4]

Paul Allard also, in his celebrated study of early Christianity and slavery, accepted as a historical fact a general diminution, for the fourth and fifth Christian centuries, in the number of the slaves. This he regarded as an incident of the general " decline " of the Empire attributed to those centuries.[5] He also adopted the view that a deterioration had occurred in the fourth century in the freedom of physical movement granted to free

---

[1] See above chap. 19, pp. 120-127.
[2] Oertel, Friedrich, in *CAH* 12: 237, 253.

[3] For Wallon's idea of a serious proportional decline in slave labor as contrasted with free labor see his *L'esclavage* 3: 110-116. This belief was accepted by Meyer, Eduard, *Die Sklaverei im Altertum*, 49, Dresden, Zahn und Jaensch, 1898, (= *Klein Schriften* 2: 212, Halle, Niemeyer, 1924); by Lot, Ferdinand, *The end of the ancient world*, 80, New York, Knopf, 1931; and by Segrè, Angelo, The Byzantine Colonate, *Traditio* 5: 108, 1947, as by all important scholars of the present century whether their approach be from the previous period of antiquity or from the later historical developments of the Middle Ages.
[4] Wallon, *L'esclavage* 3: 361-362.
[5] Allard, Paul, *Les esclaves Chrétiens*, 6th ed., 429, Paris, Lecoffre, 1914.

labor along with other free men and in the " movement of labor " in its modern meaning of the individual's right of changing the locality of his employment and the nature of his occupation. These two conclusions, each true in itself, were combined with a third belief, the theological assumption that a moral revolution had been brought about through the Christian idea that a nobility of character was engendered and fostered by the fact itself of honorable physical effort. This was considered to be particularly beneficial in its results for those engaged in manual labor. In Allard's analysis the working classes seem to have profited morally under Christian influence and discipline, but the middle class to have suffered thereby.[6]

A change in the discussion of the slave system in the early Byzantine era became apparent when John Bagnall Bury published, in 1889, his study of the later Roman Empire. Bury based his meagre analysis of the institution as it was in that time [7] upon the reasons advanced by the German legal historian, Rudolph von Ihering, for the pauperism which then prevailed in the Roman Empire.[8]

Under the Empire even the number of the slaves decreased.

. . . This diminution in the number of the slaves led to the rehabilitation of free labor; but the freemen were soon involved in the meshes of the caste system which reduced them not to slavery, but to serfdom.[9]

Bury's treatment of Byzantine labor relations did not pretend to be an adequate presentation of the subject; but the mere assumption made by the Irish scholar of a " rehabilitation " of free labor, even without any attempt to define that phrase, was an important step forward. Since the publication of Bury's work one helpful synthesis of the slave system of the early Byzantine period has appeared, that of the Italian scholar Ettore Ciccotti.[10] His analysis is limited in its usefulness because of its concentration upon the problem of the decline of slavery as an element of Byzantine labor organization. Despite the polemic engendered by Ciccotti's study, upon the ground that it was too deterministic in its approach and too scornful of the eventual values of moral, philosophic, and religious considerations,[11] his

work has its own value, in its emphasis upon the gradual elimination of the differences, in the centuries after Christ, of the economic and social statuses which had previously existed between free and slave. It was further valuable in directing attention to the material factors in the life of the Empire which affected the slave system. These were the elements which, in conjunction with an undeniable spiritual shift in the attitude towards enslavement, introduced ideas weakening to the slave system as a fixed factor of the culture of the Mediterranean world where it had for two millennia been imbedded as an accepted mechanism of labor control.

The formulation of this and the following chapter has been conditioned by the present lack of a balanced synthesized approach to the shift in the economic importance of slavery in the three centuries of the Empire following the reign of Diocletian. No pretense is made here to finality upon a subject which is still insufficiently explored and must be studied in its local details as it has been done for Spain by Charles Verlinden.[12] Since 1920 much interest has been shown in one phase of the subject. This was the shift in agrarian production and in the handicrafts from free and slave employment to a labor system under state impressment and control, with a marked effort to ascertain the reasons which determined the change. Most of these studies have been conducted from the medieval point of view, retrospectively, and as an approach to the understanding of the industries and the land-tenure system which characterized the European situation in the later Middle Ages.[13]

By this approach the morphology of slavery, its social impacts in the Diocletian-Constantine period, and the mechanics of liberation from it are presented out of the conditions and experiences of a time still unknown to the generations which lived under the system as it was or suffered under its compulsions. The living agents under the system had some knowledge of the past of the institution and personal acquaintance with its operation under their own eyes. They had none of its future. To cite one example of the results of this retrospective

---

[6] *Ibid.*, 432-440. For a general estimate of the basic attitude of Allard consult Verlinden, Charles, L'esclavage dans la monde iberique médiéval, *Anuario de Historia del Derecho Español* 11: 288-289, 291, 299, 1934.

[7] Bury, J. B., *History of the later Roman empire from Arcadius to Irene* 1: 26, n. 1, New York, Macmillan, 1889.

[8] Jhering (Ihering), Rudolph von, *Geist des römischen Rechts,* 3d ed., 2 (1): 234-259, Leipzig, Breitkopf und Härtel, 1874.

[9] Bury, J. B., *Roman empire from Arcadius to Irene* 1: 27.

[10] Ciccotti, Ettore, *Il tramonto della schiavitù*, 2nd ed., Udine, Istit. delle Edizioni Accademiche, 1940. Ciccotti's collection, in the notes upon pages 420-423, of the epigraphical evidence bearing upon the proportional decline of slave employment in the second and third centuries after Christ is particularly useful.

[11] The polemic appears in the preface to the fifth edition of Paul Allard's *Esclaves Chrétiens*, repeated in the sixth edition, pp. viii-xii. A favorable view of Ciccotti's work is to be found

in Seligman, Edwin R. A., *The economic interpretation of history*, 82, New York, Columbia Press, 1902. The summary dismissal of Ciccotti's book—" beaucoup d'hypothèses, peu de faits " —by Verlinden, *Anuario del Derecho Español* 11: 298, n. 4, is in my judgment much too harsh. Ciccotti's version of the diminution in slave numbers in the face of the colonate is upon pp. 434-439 of the second edition, 1940, of the *Tramonto della schiavitù*.

[12] *Cf.* Verlinden, Ch., *Anuario del Derecho Español* 11: 291, n. 31, for the method which must be followed.

[13] Among the recent studies which should be mentioned are: the article of E. J. Jonkers, De l'influence du Christianisme sur la législation relative à l'esclavage, *Mnemosyne*, 3d ser., 1: 241-280, 1933-1934; the brilliant work of Marc Bloch in *Cambridge economic history* 1: 224-271, Cambridge, Univ. Press, 1941, and the incompleted article published after his death, Comment et pourquoi finit l'esclavage antique, *Annales* 2: 30-44, 1947; and Verlinden, Ch., *Anuario del Derecho Español* 11: 283-448, 1934. The interest of Marc Bloch centered upon the problem of the transition from an agrarian system, resting primarily upon a small freehold tenantry and praedial slave labor, to the later colonate and the far-reaching restrictions upon the forces of production which it entailed.

approach to the Byzantine period, the Christian manu-mission in the Church (*manumissio in ecclesia*) some-times becomes a mechanism of freedom which was es-tablished by an edict passed A. D. 316, under Constan-tine's reign. The realities of a wide and deep back-ground are thus ignored.[14] This right to manumit in the Church should be explained as an assignment to the Christian organization, at the time of its acceptance as a legalized religion, of a privilege long held by the Greek and Roman pagan temples and still longer practised in the Jewish synagogues. For the newly licensed religion it was an important concession. Even though Christi-anity had adopted human enslavement as an instrument of labor control, the right to manumit in its sanctuaries established for the Church a legal basis for the develop-ment of an attitude toward slavery which in the distant future must ultimately destroy the institution as a system of labor control. For when the Church, at the outset, adopted the slave institution as a part of the world in which it lived as a going concern so ordained by God,[15] it accepted also the moral weakness structurally in-herent in the social edifice of enslavement. This was the dichotomy implied in Aristotle's observation that a slave was a *ktēma ti empsychon,* a kind of possession with a soul.[16]

The need of a scholarly synthesis covering the Medi-terranean experience with enslavement in the three cen-turies following Diocletian's reign has become increas-ingly urgent because of a new approach to the problem which appears in combination with a new assessment of the social structure and the fate of the later Roman Em-pire in Asia Minor and Armenia and in the region south of the Danube River. Contrary to the accepted attitude of western scholarship the agrarian structure of Armenia in the Hellenistic period, according to this new view, was primarily based upon slavery. Later this type of organization was transformed into a semifeudal frame-work which left the Greco-Roman slave labor system in an incompleted and presumably subordinate and weak-ened stage.[17] A second article of this nature depicts the

Visigoths in their invasions of the provinces of the Roman Empire lying south of the Danube as liberators who came to release an enslaved population from the oppressions of the Roman Empire. According to the picture drawn by the Russian author of this study, the Empire seems to have been filled with Sarmatian slaves.[18] The barbarian invasions of the region below the Danube become conscious liberation movements. The persecutions of the Aryans assume the deterministic aspect of an effort upon the Roman side to suppress uprisings among the sub-Danubian peoples caused by the economic and social malevolence of the ruling Romanized classes. On the part of the northern tribes the invasions become planned efforts to succor the op-pressed peasantry and the enslaved workers of the Danubian provinces.[19]

The problems which face the search for a correct synthesis of the labor situation, including slave labor, in the period from the beginning of Diocletian's reign are only put out of their true perspective, in my judgment, by the approach and the method described above. In the attempt to estimate slave numbers in comparison with those of the *coloni* and the free and half-free workers in the handicrafts fantastic exaggerations of the manumis-sions by rich Christians will be found; but no material adequate for a comparative estimate has come down to us. The quantitative problem can, therefore, be an-swered only by a process of cautious rationalization. A second problem, that of the influence both of the secular and the canon law toward the equalization of slave and free workmen in respect to their social and economic situation, offers some evidence bearing toward a solu-tion. The deepening of the concern, both of State and Church, is manifested in the legislation of these two powers. Upon which side any specific attempt at amelio-ration originated it is sometimes difficult to determine. Its answer is to be found in further research along the lines already set by E. J. Jonkers [20] and Charles Ver-linden,[21] who have studied the reciprocal influences of the two organizations. Canon and secular legislation seem to have moved somewhat *pari passu* under a com-pulsion which forced them to collaborate toward the betterment of social conditions, each working in its own interest and in its own manner.

Two problems remain open to investigation. These,

---

[14] Admirable as his study of slavery in Visigothic Spain seems to be, Verlinden, *Anuario* 11: 306, gives no indication that the *manumissio in ecclesia* was a re-enactment in favor of the newly accepted religion of a right which had long adhered to the pagan religious organizations. Jonkers, E. J., in *Mnemosyne,* 3d ser., 1: 265, 1933-1934, shows an awareness of the pagan precedents for this privilege.

[15] Saint Augustine, *De civitate Dei* 19: 15, represents slavery as an expression of the will of God which took the form of a punishment inflicted upon mankind for human sin. The ethical problem of human slavery is integral in the conception of it as a penalty. The general attitude of the Church Fathers is well presented by Verlinden, Ch., *Anuario* 11: 305. The Church could close its eyes to prevalent social inequalities and still, in the abstract, recognize and advocate the moral equality of slave and free, *ibid.,* 307.

[16] Aristotle, *Politics,* 1: 2, 4. It is characteristic of the Greek habit of mind that this is an observation and a description, not a definition of what a slave is.

[17] Eremian, S. T., Upon slavery and slaveholding in ancient Armenia (in Russian), *Vestnik drevnei istorii* 1 (31) : 26, 1950.

Since I do not read Russian I must here express my obligation to my colleague in History, Mr. J. M. Thompson, for his kind-ness in translating for me this article and the following one of A. D. Dmitrev. Despite their fixation to the land and their transference with the land upon its sale, Eremian regards the Armenian agricultural workers of the first century B. C. as slaves.

[18] Dmitrev, A. D., The rising of the west Goths on the Danube and the slave revolt, *ibid.,* 66-80.

[19] *Ibid.,* 77-80.

[20] Jonkers, E. J., *Mnemosyne,* 3d ser., 1: 265-266, 273-275, 1933-1934.

[21] Verlinden, *Anuario del Derecho Español* 11: 313-322. See, also, Mor, C. G., Manumissio in ecclesia, *Rivista del Diritto Italiano* 1: 80-150, 1928. Verlinden's treatment lays the heavier stress upon the economic practices advocated by the legislation.

by the complexity of the forces involved, will be difficult of solution. The effect of the quantitative diminution of slavery upon the intrinsic nature of the institution has not been approached so far as I know. Nor has the constant failure of the institution of slavery to thrive as vigorously in the physical and mental climate of northern lands as it did in the Mediterranean countries received proper explanation. Certainly it is not an adequate explanation to ascribe the different quantitative employment of slaves in the northern and southern tiers of states of the North American Union solely to the material cause of dominant industry as against a dominant plantation economy. For the Greek and Roman experiences of the slave system have shown that industrial and plantation and ranch slavery can flourish for long periods side by side although complicated in both fields of production by the use of free and slave labor working together. Some more deeply lying cause is involved than purely mechanical differences between manufacturing and farm work. What this difference may be is unknown to me. In the historical perspective of western labor history the fact as such seems to be evident.

One incident, ascribed to A. D. 206 or 207 of the principate of Septimius Severus, throws a stronger beam of light upon the continuity of slave labor in Italy than the enumeration of the funerary epitaphs of slaves and freedmen can possibly do, instructive as these may be. For two years an engaging brigand named Bulla, who had taken to himself the Sullan title of Felix (Lucky), defied the Roman detachments sent by so adroit and experienced a military leader as Severus himself to capture him. The clearest insight into the contemporary conditions of slavery in Italy which the tale of Bulla gives us lies in a message which he sent back to his pursuers through a captured centurion of the Roman army: " Give this message to your masters. ' Pay your slaves their maintenance wages [22] in order that they may not become brigands.' " The group of six hundred followers of Bulla included, it is reported, numerous recruits, possibly freedmen, from the household of Caesar who were " in part ill paid, in part not paid at all." [23] The artisans whom the bandit leader seized he held for a time, making use of their skills. He then dismissed them with rewards for the work they had done. There is nothing in the passage to indicate that they were slave workmen. They are spoken of merely as *technitai*, persons technically equipped. Tertullian supplements this picture a few decades later by his statement that military stations were posted throughout all the provinces " to guard against robbers wandering about them." [24]

For the province of Syria and its eastern border we have a situation which is symptomatic of the disruption of the central imperial control in the first years of the principate of Septimius Severus. After the death of Pescennius Niger in Antioch, A. D. 193, Severus found that his severity toward the adherents of Niger had caused a great number of the soldiers of his army to take refuge with the enemy east of the Tigris River. Many of these, as we are told explicitly by the historian Herodian,[25] were artisans who could be useful to the Parthians in other ways and particularly by instructing them in the production of war materials. As soldiers in the imperial armies these craftsmen were necessarily freemen, not slaves.

In Egypt the signs of the breakdown of orderly government, characteristic of the Empire as a whole in the central fifty years of the third century, became increasingly frequent in the early decades of that period. A drastic proof of the impending internal collapse of Egypt is to be seen in a proclamation issued by Baebius Juncinus, a prefect ruling that country, whose period of office fell in the years 213-215 after Christ.[26] He enjoined upon the nome governors of central Egypt to give the greatest attention to the suppression of the robbers who were roaming about, offering rewards for diligence displayed in carrying out his orders and punishments for slackness in this duty. Thus far the prefect's directive is couched in the terms of customary administrative routine. It is the appended general proclamation to the people which is so revealing of the gravity of the disorders.

Lucius Baebius Aurelius Juncinus, prefect of Egypt, speaks. To purge robbers apart from those who shelter them is impossible. That is clear to all. But we will quickly punish them if they are deprived of those round about (who assist) them. There are many ways of sheltering them. Some who are participants in their unjust actions give them shelter; others who do not have a part in them. . . .

The papyrus is here broken off.[27] The continuance of the administrative collapse is clarified for us by occasional glimpses afforded by contemporary records among the papyri. In A. D. 202 a prosperous Egyptian in the Oxyrhynchite nome advanced the money for purchase of an estate so that the income from it might be used to assist his neighbors in the nome in meeting the obligations which they had to incur in the conduct of the local offices taken over by them under government compulsion.[28] From A. D. 216 we have evidence from the

---

[22] The verb *trephete* is used here by Dio Cassius. They were to be paid their " rations " (*tropheia*).

[23] Dio Cassius, *Roman history* 76: 10 (Loeb Library edition, 77: 10).

[24] Tertullian, *Apologeticum* 2, 8.

[25] Herodian, *From the death of the deified Marcus* 3: 7-8. See Miller, S. N. in *CAH* 12: 8-9.

[26] The dates of the prefecture of Baebius Juncinus are those given by Reinmuth, O. W., *Klio*, Beiheft 34: 137, 1935.

[27] *P. Oxy.* 12: 1408, 21-26. From the year A. D. 215 we have an edict of Caracalla (*P. Giessen* 40, reproduced in Hunt, A. S., and C. E. Edgar, *Select papyri* 2, no. 215, Loeb Classical Library) which ordered the expulsion from Alexandria of people from the villages of the *chōra* who had sought refuge in that city.

[28] *P. Oxy.* 4: 705, 65-79 (= Wilcken, U., *Papyruskunde, Chrestomathie*, No. 407).

Fayum of the flight of men burdened under this compulsory system of office holding and of the leniency employed by the higher magistrates in enticing them to return to their local obligations.[29]

The progressive character of this administrative breakdown is demonstrable for Egypt.[30] In the rest of the Empire it is to be assumed as developing in aggravated form and in accelerated tempo under the " soldier Emperors " through the two middle quarters of the third century. The economic destruction caused by the contending armies, living off the provinces as they moved back and forth, cannot be estimated. The point which is here to be stressed is the displacement of labor which necessarily occurred. " Displacement " is here used in the sense of the lessened degree of the self-controls permitted to the labor groups in the face of new rigidities imposed by government regulations and the shifting of the composition of the labor element as between the enslaved and the free.

For the early Byzantine history of slavery as a component part of the labor resources of the time the famous edict of Diocletian upon maximal prices and wages, the *edictum Diocletiani de pretiis rerum venalium*, offers a valuable point of departure.[31] It was promulgated A. D. 301 with the avowed object of controlling the rise in prices of food and manufactured products, particularly in those regions through which the imperial troops were compelled to move.[32] In an early discussion of the frag-

ments then extant Karl Bücher was convinced that the wage rates, and the piecework rates established for some types of skilled labor, were to apply to slaves leased by their owners for the particular tasks required or to freedmen workers.[33] This view arose out of Bücher's exaggerated conception of the prevalence of slaves in manual labor under the Roman Empire. Bücher's conclusion in this respect was almost immediately refuted [34] and has long since been abandoned by most scholars acquainted with the ancient evidence.

In its application to the slave problem the important observations to be made in Diocletian's decree are two. No maximal prices for slave sales have appeared in any of the fragments discovered up to the present time, and there is no trace of differences established in the daily wages or piecework payments as between slave labor, freedmen's work, and free labor. The only word connected with slavery which has occurred in the fragments is the incomplete form *andrapod-*. It appears in a section which deals with silversmithing. Presumably the broken word is an adjectival form; [35] but its application cannot be determined.

The few impressions of slavery conveyed by the decree upon maximal prices and wages are these. (1) When the services of slaves were leased out under contract by their masters the slaves must have been paid at the same scale as the freedmen and free workers hired for corresponding manual or skilled services. (2) Ettore Ciccotti, toward the close of his career, maintained his early point of view that the edict of Diocletian on prices of goods offered for sale demonstrated the activity and preponderance of " hired labor " (presumably as against slave labor) at the time of the promulgation of the edict.[36] If slave labor had not seriously declined in numbers relatively to hired free labor, and consequently in importance, at least it must be said that no distinction was made by Diocletian's economic advisors regarding

---

[29] *BGU* 1: 159 (= Wilcken, *Chrestomathie*, no. 408).

[30] This is briefly sketched by Bell, Sir Harold, in his admirable book upon *Egypt from Alexander the Great to the Arab Conquest*, 93-97, Oxford, Clarendon Press, 1948. Bell lays stress upon the unbroken flow of the stream of ordinary life even under the distressing conditions which prevailed in the third century. Professor Allan C. Johnson published an article upon the situation in Egypt in the third century, *Jour. Juristic Papyrology* 4: 151-158, 1950, in which he comes to an opinion directly opposed to that of Bell. Johnson states that his survey "would seem to indicate that Egypt in the third century did not share in the misfortunes of the rest of the Empire." The article was unconvincing to me.

[31] Theodor Mommsen published the Latin and Greek texts, put together from numerous fragments, found in many places, in the *Corpus Inscriptionum Latinarum* (*CIL* 3, *Supplement* 3: 1911-1953); also with Blümner, Hugo, *Das Maximaltarif des Diocletian*, Berlin, Reimer, 1893. A convenient presentation of the bilingual text with English translation is given in Frank, Tenney, *Economic survey of ancient Rome*, 5 (*Rome and Italy of the empire*): 307-422, with references for the fragments found since 1893. This work was done by Elsa Rose Graser who has more recently published new fragments found in Italy in 1937 and in Aphrodisia in Caria, *Trans. Amer. Philol. Assn.* 71: 157-174, 1940. She has followed the text of Jacopi, G., *Gli scavi della missione italiana a Aphrodisiade nel 1937*, *Monumenti Antichi* 38, 1939. In the translation by Miss Graser the shirts, tunics and the like which are said to be " from Tarsus " or " from Laodicea " were probably soft goods fabrics which might have been processed into shirts or tunics in Alexandria or anywhere else. This is shown by the listing of clothing " from Tarsian [cloths]—Alexandrian." For this, consult Reil, Th., *Beiträge zur Kenntnis des Gewerbes*, 98, Borna-Leipzig, 1913, and Miss Graser's statement, *TAPA* 71: 161.

[32] *CIL* 3, *Suppl.* 3: 1919, sect. 1, line 30—sect. 2, 5; Mickwitz, Gunnar, *Geld und Wirtschaft im römischen Reich des vierten*

Jahrhunderts, 71-72, Helsingfors, 1932; Frank, Tenney, *Economic survey* 5: 314.

[33] The wage and piece rate series appears in section 7 of the edict in Miss Graser's translation in Frank, *Economic survey* 5: 336-345. Bücher's point of view was presented in *Ztsch. für die gesammte Staatswissenschaft* 50: 674, 1894.

[34] See Hugo Blümner in Pauly-Wissowa, *RE* 5: 1945.

[35] *CIL* 3: 31, 6; Frank, T., *Economic survey* 5: 413 where the meaning ascribed to the word φαμελιαρικῶν, lines 386, 389, 392, 395, 398, as referring to yarns to be used in the production of garments for " slaves," seems to me to be incorrect as translation. According to its use in the later centuries of the Empire the word probably refers to yarns for garments of " individuals and members of household organizations." In *BGU* 1: 316, 10, in a slave sale from Egypt of A. D. 359, the *familia* of the vendor means nothing more than a group of young reservists in a garrison, according to Wilcken in *Hermes* 19: 422 (1884). In *P. Oxy.* 14: 1712, the φαμέλια of the prefect is his household. Even as applied to domestic service the word does not appear to carry any idea of servile status despite the meaning ascribed to the equivalent Latin *familiaricus* in the *Thesaurus Linguae Latinae* 6: 246.

[36] Ciccotti, Ettore, *Tramonto della schiavitù*, 424, Udine, Bianco e Figlio, 1940 (p. 304 in the first edition of 1899).

the labor cost involved in the production of handicraft goods on the basis of status of the workmen, whether they were free or bond.

Support for these observations made upon the study of Diocletian's edict which indicate that the importance of slavery in the Empire had already decreased is to be found in the continuance of its decline as evidenced by sporadic signs in the material of the succeeding period. Some slaves unquestionably were still used in the imperial manufactories in the fourth and fifth centuries. In large part, however, the government shopworkers were free men so far as their legal status went.[37] Again, legislation passed by Constantine the Great in preparation for the census of A.D. 327 ordained that slaves employed in agriculture could be sold only within the same province.[38] The restriction of this provision to agrarian slaves warns us against the conclusion that ease of census taking was the chief consideration involved in the promulgation of the decree. For, in that case, the unfree among the urban and village handicrafters would have been included. The ordinance seems to imply that the number of slave workmen employed in agriculture was not abundant and that such slaves were to be kept at their tasks within those provinces which were important to the general food supply. The permanent attachment of the *coloni*, the tenant farmers, to the estates upon which they were registered was established by the terms of a famous decree of Constantine of October 30, A.D. 332. This, too, warrants the conclusion that large groups of slaves were not available for rural

tasks except for the possibility that they were to be found upon the domains of some of the biggest land barons.[39]

In direct contradiction of the conclusions which I have just expressed stands a statement of the redoubtable Max Weber which he derived from a passage of Palladius.[40] This is to the effect that the owners of large domains in the late period of the Empire maintained their own slave artisans, as carpenters, ironworkers, and potters, to supply their estates with the needed tools and products of their craft skills. There is nothing in the cited passage of Palladius which necessitates the decision that the workmen referred to were slaves. The Finnish scholar, Herman Gummerus, has shown, on the other hand, that the slave workmen upon the estates of the early Empire did not include trained industrial personnel and that the manufactured articles required by the estates were bought in the neighboring towns or cities. In the lifetime of Palladius, in the fourth century, these conditions were still prevailing in respect to manufactured goods. We know that Palladius depended for much of his information upon Varro and Columella. In this case his dependence upon these previous writers makes no difference because the fact of the purchase of farm tools and the like in the cities was still the same as in the earlier period.[41]

---

[37] The probative references are cited in the excellent article by Herman Gummerus upon Industrie und Handel in Pauly-W., *RE* **9**: 1532-1533. See, also, Persson, Axel, Staat und Manufaktur im römischen Reiche, *Publications of the New Society of Letters at Lund* **3**: 83, 1923.

[38] Theod., *Codex* 11: 3, 2. Seeck, Otto, *Untergang der antiken Welt*, 2nd ed., **2**: 324.

[39] Theod., *Codex* 5: 17, 1; Seeck, Otto, Colonatus, Pauly-W., *RE* **4**: 498.

[40] The passage of Palladius, *Opus agriculturae* 1: 6, 2, reads: *ferrarii, lignarii, doliorum cuparumque factores habendi sunt.*

[41] According to Gummerus, Herman, Der römische Gutsbetrieb, *Klio, Beiträge zur alten Geschichte*, Beiheft **5**: 49, 1906, there were no slaves upon the estates who were professionally trained in the crafts. His view is accepted by Dopsch, Alfons, *Economic and social foundations of European civilization*, 328-329, London, Kegan Paul, 1937.

XXI. FROM DIOCLETIAN TO JUSTINIAN

THE EASTERN AND THE WESTERN DEVELOPMENTS

For Egypt during the period from Diocletian's accession to the Arab conquest the evidence upon the use of slaves and that upon the tendencies in the functioning of the slave system are much less abundant than they are for the first three centuries of the Empire. Enough papyri which in some way mention slavery have, nevertheless, been published so that it is possible to follow with satisfactory results some of the trends in the institution in these later centuries. Primarily we can be certain that the employment of slaves, in the strict legal meaning of the word, continued upon a considerable scale in the province of the Nile valley where, traditionally, demographic conditions have always worked against their presence in great numbers. In the face of a normal abundance of crops the large population of

the valley and Delta has always tended to exert a constant pressure upon the food supply. For the time of Augustus Caesar, Diodorus of Sicily is our authority for the statement that the density of population in Egypt surpassed that of any other region of the cultured world, the *gē oikoumenē* of the Greeks and Romans.[1] The abundance of free labor, thus available, lowered the rate of wages required, thereby minimizing the demand for slave employees in agriculture and the handicrafts.[2]

---

[1] Diodorus Siculus, 1: 31. 6.

[2] For a correct presentation of this situation consult Johnson, Allan C., and Louis West, *Byzantine Egypt, economic studies*, Princeton University Press, 1949. The book is to be used with some caution according to the review by Sir Harold Bell in *Jour. Roman Studies* **40**: 123-128. The discussion of the eco-

The problem of estimating, even in gross terms, the relative numbers of the slaves owned and employed in agriculture upon the great estates in Egypt of the fifth and sixth centuries is not completely insoluble. The " boys " (*paides*) who appear in the records from the Hermopolis portion of the Apion-Strategus estates in these centuries are probably not to be regarded as slaves as E. R. Hardy considered them to be.[3] I would judge that they were free boys hired to work in the fields. Despite his assumption that these *paides* were slaves, for which the Greeks preferred the term *douloi*, which is unmistakable in its meaning, Hardy has rightly concluded that there were few slaves used upon these estates except those employed in domestic services. There is some support from other nomes for the correctness of this decision. An Oxyrhynchus papyrus of the sixth century, presumably from one of the Apion properties, presents a long account of kiln-burnt bricks used in the repair of water reservoirs and buildings upon the estate complex.[4] One entry of the long list shows the assignment of bricks " for the use of—emius, slave of Matreu." Matreu was the name of one of the many small holdings of the estate and the slave must have been its tenant.[5] Against this one instance of a slave—and he a tenant—the number of the peasant holders of free status in the account is eighty-two.[6]

In the Egyptian papyri of the period from the fourth to the eighth centuries slaves of foreign origin and stock appear but rarely.[7] In A.D. 359 a slave boy aged fourteen was purchased by an army officer stationed in the

Arsinoite nome, the present Fayum oasis. In the instrument of sale the boy is designated as a " Gaul by birth," and the officer who sold him bore the Frankish name of Augemundus.[8] The surmise suggests itself, therefore, that the previous owner had brought the Gallic slave boy with him when his army service caused him to come to Egypt. Synesius, bishop of Ptolemais, in one of his letters which is to be dated about A.D. 400 tells of a storm which the ship encountered when he was sailing out of the harbor of Alexandria for Cyrene. He speaks of a Pontic slave girl who was on board.[9] Though this girl was not his property, Synesius, born of a rich North African family, assuredly owned slaves; but the reflection from his letters is that the slave numbers maintained by the prosperous citizens of Libya as represented by persons of his position might possibly be estimated in tens rather than in hundreds. This is the impression one gains despite Synesius' own statement that " there is not a house, however modest it may be, in which one does not find a Scythian slave," the term " Scythian " meaning, as usual in Synesius, a Goth.[10]

Two further observations present themselves in the reading of Synesius' letters. Both of them suggest caution in assuming large slave numbers among the Cyrenaeans. The wealth of the Cyrenaean landowners " for the most part was our cattle, our herds of camels and horses which grazed on the prairie. All are lost. All have been driven away." [11] There probably were some slaves as well as free herders who attended these animals; but there is no mention of the slaves who would normally be among the booty which bandits would carry off. Indicative, also, is a second fact which strikes one in his letters. In Libya, in the life as it is vividly depicted in his correspondence, letters sent to distant friends were customarily delivered by traveling acquaintances.[12] In Cicero's day, at Rome and elsewhere, the normal method of delivery in a prosperous household corresponding to that of Synesius would have been by sending one's own slave.

It is here assumed that labor conditions, as affecting slaves and their numbers and use, were fairly similar in Cyrene and in Egypt. In the Nile valley the demand for slave labor was still strong enough in the sixth

nomics of Egypt in the study of Johnson and West begins with A.D. 297 which the authors accepted as the date of the inauguration of the indiction cycle, following in this the German scholar, Otto Seeck. The proof of its inception in A.D. 312, as fixed in the *Chronicon Paschale*, was, however, presented from a Princeton papyrus in the dissertation of Kase, E. H., *A papyrus roll in the Princeton collection*, 25-31, Baltimore, Furst, 1933. The ancient dating in 312, thus re-established by Kase, was accepted, contrary to his previous belief, by Ulrich Wilcken, Mitteilungen aus der Würzburger Papyrussammlung, *Abh. preuss. Akad., ph.-hist. Klasse*, no 6: 97, 1934.

³ *P. Baden*, 95, lines 62, 74-75, 408, 503-504; Hardy, *Large estates*, 104, n. 5, and 112. These are actual payments in barley as " wages," ἐξ(οδιασμοῦ) ὑπὲρ ὀψωνί(ων) τῶν παιδῶν.—Or they were the customary advances in money for clothing or olive oil. In either case, slaves of the estate would not have been paid wages.

⁴ *P. Oxy.* 18, no. 2197, published in 1941 and therefore not yet known to E. R. Hardy. Note 1 of the editors gives its probable connection with the Apion estates.

⁵ *Ibid.*, line 40. The holding called " Matreu " appears also in nos. 2196, 4; 2197, 34, 38; 2207, 5.

⁶ The personal names of these tenants must be checked in Index Vc of *P. Oxy.* 18 in order to differentiate the names given to the watering apparatus (*mēchanai*) from the names of the farmers.

⁷ In using the list of references in Johnson and West, *Byzantine Egypt*, 149, to foreign slaves in Egypt one must note that there is nothing to show that the " Moor " of *BGU* 3: 728, or the Sarmatians in *PSI* 3: 211, were in fact slaves. The editors of *Byzantine Egypt* have correctly recognized, p. 119, n. 2, that the " Gothic boys " (*paidariois Goth-*) of *PSI* 8, nos. 953, 17, 46, 47, 84 and 956, 26, may or may not have been slaves.

⁸ *BGU* 316, 13: γένι Γάλλον. For the name Augemundus see Wilcken, U., *Hermes* 19: 422 (1884). *P. London* 2: 251, pp. 316-318, presents a deed of sale of two slaves from the fourth century.

⁹ Synesius, *Epistles*, 4, at the end. Other references to slaves in Synesius are to be found in *Epistles*, 32, a drunkard whom Synesius was willing to deport to his own country, apparently without recompense; and in 79 and 125. The numbers of the letters are here cited as they appear in the edition of Dionysius Petavius, Paris, Drouart, 1612.

¹⁰ This is quoted from Bloch, Marc, Comment et pourquoi finit l'esclavage antique, *Annales. Économies-Sociétés-Civilisations* 2: 31, 1946.

¹¹ Synesius, *Epistles*, 130 in the translation of Fitzgerald, Augustine, *Letters of Synesius of Cyrene*, London, Oxford Univ. Press, 1926.

¹² *Ibid.*, 133, 144.

century to warrant the existence of slave merchants (*sōmatemporoi*) as a specialized group. In the Egyptian villages and cities the private sale of African slaves was conducted by local dealers. The importation of them from central Africa was in the hands, apparently, of Ethiopian slave traders. This is indicated for the sixth century in an agreement from Hermopolis by which a negro girl, twelve years old, called a " Moor," was sold into private ownership by two local slave dealers. They declared that they, in turn, had purchased the girl from " Ethiopian " slave merchants.[13] Back of these dealers we must still envisage the age-old system of enslavement by seizure or by tribal warfare in inner Africa which, though hidden from our knowledge, had been the source of delivery of the young negress to the Ethiopian market. The contract throws a flash of light which is rare upon the conduct of the slave trade in antiquity in a specific zone.

The methods of recruitment of slaves as these are reflected in the Greek papyri of the Byzantine period remained the same as they had been in the previous history of the business. The scanty information which we have does not permit an exact statement, or even a rough guess, of the proportion of the slave numbers supplied by each of the different ways of obtaining them. These were the constant and changeless methods characteristic of the slave institution—primarily inheritance of the status by birth from a slave mother, captivity in war or by kidnapping, sale of children by impoverished parents,[14] self-sale into the slave class, rearing of abandoned children, and enslavement for debt.[15]

Two of these ways of increasing the slave population, as they present themselves in the Greek papyri from Egypt, need special discussion. The revolt of a certain Achilleus, also called Lucius Domitius Domitianus, which was suppressed in A. D. 296 by Diocletian, caused damage enough in Alexandria, but little in the countryside of the Delta or the actual valley. Probably the enslavements which resulted from this internal disturbance were not many. For two full centuries thereafter, until the incursion of the Persians into the Delta at the beginning of the sixth century and that of the Nubian Blemmyes across the southern frontier, Egypt was not troubled by military attacks from without. Additions to the slave element of the population from wars must, therefore, have been indirect, by importation, for example, of individual Goths captured in the defeats in

the Balkans suffered by these invaders.[16] There is proof, as we have seen, of the presence of slaves in Egypt who were of barbarian birth; but their number, so far as the papyri go, is small.

There is more evidence furnished by the papyri that enslavement for debt and parental sale of children induced by poverty were on the increase in the period now under survey. This is true, also, of the Empire as a whole in spite of the fact that it was not consistent with the Roman legal attitude which opposed slavery through debt.[17] This becomes clear in the concession to the realities of the time which is shown in an edict of Constantine of the year 329. It granted to parents the right to sell their children under the following considerations: " if any person because of excessive poverty and want shall have sold a son or daughter of his own blood for the sake of sustenance the sale is to be valid, in such a case only." This permissive decree is further restricted in the finality of its legal consequences by granting to the parent the right of redemption, either at a satisfactory price or by substitution of a slave of the same kind.[18] As for Egypt the *mores* of that country both under Ptolemaic and under Roman rule had always countenanced the pledging of the children's services under the *paramonē* relation against debts incurred by their parents.[19] But it is scarcely open to doubt that this often resulted, in Egypt, in complete enslavement. We have, indeed, two examples of the sixth century of the enslavement of free-born children with the expressed right of redemption by payment of the debt,[20] just as was guaranteed in the Constantinian edict of A. D. 329.

In making the attempt to arrive at a credible estimate of maximal slaveholdings by individual owners in the eastern provinces one is justified in leaving out of consideration the reports of mass manumissions by Christian martyrs which have come down to us through the hagiographers. Their exaggerations include the following instances: 1,250 slaves granted their freedom at Eastertide by a certain Hermes who is otherwise untraceable though stated to have been a prefect of Rome under Hadrian; 5,000 manumitted by a certain Ovinius; and 8,000 granted their freedom by Saint Melania the

---

[13] *P. Strassb.*, inv. no. 1404, edited by Preisigke, Friedrich, Ein Sklavenkauf des 6. Jahrhunderts, *Archiv für Papyrusf.* 3: 414-424, notably line 24 of the contract.

[14] *P. Oxy.* 9: 1206 (A. D. 335) is a certain example of this practise. *P. Théadelphie*, no. 16, 18-20, of A. D. 307, is a probable one, and *PSI* 6: 709, 6-9, is a possible instance of it in the sixth century, Taubenschlag, R., *Law of Greco-Roman Egypt*, 56, and n. 33-37. The author gives a general discussion of the sources of slave supply in the early Byzantine period, *ibid.*, pp. 52-57.

[15] Bell, H. I., *Jews and Christians in Egypt,* nos. 1915 and 1916, published a fourth-century example of child enslavement for debt of the parents. See no. 1915, 27-28, 35-36, and 1916, 16-18.

[16] Verlinden, Charles, L'esclavage dans le monde iberique médiéval, *Anuario de Historia del Derecho Español* 11: 317-319, 1934, has come to the conclusion that the number of the slaves introduced by the Gothic invasions was in no way comparable to those furnished by the wars of expansion of the late Republic and early Empire.

[17] Meyer, Paul M., *Juristische papyri*, 29; Taubenschlag, R., *Zeit. Sav.-Stiftung, rom. Abt.* 50: 146.

[18] Just. *Codex* 4: 43, 2: *propter nimian paupertatem egestatemque victus causa.*

[19] Such earlier examples of *paramonē* pledging of their children's services as security for debt are: *PSI* 4: 424, third century B. C.; *P. Oxy.* 10: 1295 of the second or early third century after Christ; *P. Flor.* 1: 44, A. D. 158.

[20] *P. Jandanae*, part 2, 62 in Speisse, G., *Instrumenta Graeca publica et privata*, Leipzig, Teubner, 1916, and Maspero, Jean, Papyrus grecs d'époque byzantine, 67023 (A. D. 569), *Catalogue général du Musée du Caire*, Cairo, Institut Français, 1911.

Younger.[20a] The thousand slaves, or " twice as many," which wealthy residents of Antioch boasted of possessing, according to Saint John Chrysostom,[21] possibly fall within the range of the maximal possibility for the fourth century. Much more plausible is the number of 310 slaves which had been owned by a Babylonian Jew according to a statement of his daughter.[22]

In the Jewish communities in Palestine and in Babylon the ownership of slaves persisted, just as it continued to do among the non-Jewish elements of that area. The basic features of the old Jewish attitude toward enslavement remained unaltered. Following the tribal-national approach which had so long dominated the Semitic attitude in slave legislation, still under Talmudic law a Hebrew coreligionist could not become an actual slave to a fellow Hebrew.[23] The limit of the labor control to be exercised in such a case was still the six-year bondage period of the old days, succeeded by unconditional release in the year of the Jubilee.[24] Still, as of old, the duty rested upon the Jewish community of ransoming enslaved fellow Jews out of their enslavement, wherever they might be. In the Talmudic law this obligation was extended so as to cover, also, any non-Jewish slaves who had been torn away from the Jewish households to which they belonged.[25]

A slave purchased from a non-Israelite theoretically could enter into the legal ownership of a Jew only after his circumcision and baptismal bath. The performance of these two actions were the symbols of the acceptance of the person, as slave, into the Jewish household group and as participant in the family rites, including the feast of the Passover. Despite his low status he had thus been recognized as an accredited member of the family [26] and, thereby, a member of the Hebrew religious community. This policy of immediate and direct affiliation of a newly purchased slave of non-Hebrew associations into the civil and ritual fellowship of his owner did not become widely effective by adoption from the Hebrew example into the Gentile institutions of antiquity, notably as represented in Christian slavery. Two reasons may be suggested for this singularity. First, the Jewish religion as organization had neither the numbers nor the social acceptance accorded to Christianity. Second, it lacked the emotional appeal which was the dominant force in the participation of slaves who were converted to the Christian belief and became conscious of its equalizing effects. For the equality of the Christian groups had its roots deeply imbedded in the idea of membership in a mystical brotherhood. The lowliest of its participants shared in the transcendencies of the celebration of the mass and of the communion.

The fact of the compulsory ritualistic acceptance of the non-Hebrew slave into religious fellowship with his Hebrew master and the feeling of equality which in many cases it must have brought with it cannot, however, be overlooked. The new slave now became regarded as a man born in the image of God and a member of the brotherhood of God.[27] The closely knit organization of Jewry, despite its areal dispersion, gave to the idea of this participation of the slave in the observances of the Jewish community, as symbolized by circumcision and baptism of the human chattel, a continuing, though limited, value and importance in the history of slavery. After the Jewish revolts in the principates of Vespasian and Hadrian the conversion of purchased Gentiles must have seemed dangerous to the Jews and to the ruling authorities in some degree potentially subversive of the Roman power. Under this rationalization one may find an adequate reason for the passage of a law under Antoninus Pius forbidding Jews to practice circumcision except upon their own sons. This law was fortified by the savage, though effective sanction of emasculation of the offender in case of transgression of the decree.[28]

Under stress of the dangers imposed by the decree of Antoninus and by similar anti-Jewish legislation it is understandable that the Jewish slave law should attempt to make concessions to bring about a viable adjustment to the society within which it had to operate, particularly as suggestions for change would find themselves expressed in the Roman law of slavery of that time. According to an interpretation of Rabbi Ismael, presumably resulting from the restrictions of the right of circumcision cited above, it was permissible for members of the Jewish communities to own slaves who were not circumcised.[29] Under another Rabbinical interpretation a slave freed by his Jewish master, if he had received his liberty under a Roman form of manumission, obtained a freedom of a second grade. A distinction in the quality of freedom of this sort had been unknown in the earlier slave law of Jewry. It has been explained by Simon Rubin in his study of the Talmudic law as an example of the influence of the Roman *lex Junia*. Under this law the slaves of Roman citizens might become citizens of a lower grade under the name of " Junian Latins." As freedmen of this designation they enjoyed all the legal protections which Latin citizenship offered, with the restrictions which that degree of citizenship carried with it. One of these restrictions was the lack of the right of marriage (*conubium*) with persons of the full Roman citizen group.[30]

[20a] Quoted by Wallon, Henri, *L'esclavage* 3 : 359, who regarded them as exaggerated.

[21] Saint John Chrysostom, In *Matth. homilia*, 63, 4.

[22] Graetz, H., *History of the Jews*, 2 : 555, Philadelphia, Jewish Publ. Society, 1893.

[23] Rubin, Simon, *Das Talmudische Recht. Die Sklaverei*, 8, Vienna, 1920.

[24] Chap. 7 above, p. 43.

[25] Rubin, *Talmudische Recht*, 61, with the necessary references.

[26] *Ibid.*, 17-18.

[27] Rubin has a clear statement of the Rabbinical attitude upon this point, *ibid.*, 64, n. 12.

[28] Just., *Institutes*, 48, 8, 11.

[29] Rubin, Simon, *Talmudische Recht*, 18, with a translation in n. 47, p.28, of Baraitha Yebamoth, 47b.

[30] Rubin, *Talmudische Recht*, 103-104. *Cf.* Buckland, W. W., *Roman law of slavery*, 533-534.

Among the non-Jewish residents of Palestine, even into the seventh century, Greek attitudes affecting bondage still appeared. An example of this is to be seen in a release from a general service (*paramonē*) labor contract, which is to be dated in the years 679-688. It is a bilingual document in Arabic and Greek, found at Nessana in southern Palestine. By the original contract of *paramonē* a father had indentured his son's services as security for a debt he had incurred. The son was to work for the creditor until the loan was repaid. This is a characteristic feature of the Greek *paramonē* relation under such circumstances.[31]

The problems of slavery in Armenia during the later period of the Roman Empire actually lie beyond the scope of this survey. The recent article written in Russian by S. T. Eremian, which was mentioned in the preceding chapter, nevertheless challenges attention in this treatment because it brings in the slave procedures in Cappadocia of the Byzantine era when that area still remained a portion of the Roman Empire of the East. The author acknowledges that the ancient Armenian sources themselves present Armenia of the Hellenistic period as a feudal structure; but this view of the local contemporary historians Eremian rejects as untrue. It arose, as Eremian seems to be convinced, because of the adoption by the Armenian writers of antiquity of the feudal preconceptions then current.[32] Eremian, therefore, concludes that the economic and political power of the Armenian nobility of the Hellenistic era was based upon the exploitation of slave labor.[33] Later, by the process of the transfer of the crown lands to the nobility, the feudalizing of Armenian society really occurred. This is the argument advanced.

It is not within my own linguistic scope to estimate the value of the philological discussion of the ancient Armenian terms relating to land tenure as presented in this article. Its analysis and its use of a statement of the geographer, Strabo, is, however, open to question. In dealing with the tenure and labor system in Cappadocia, Strabo states that Pompey in 63 B. c. turned over to Archelaus of Cappadocia the priesthood of the Zeus temple at Comana and the jurisdiction over the land appertaining to it. Archelaus, by virtue of the appointment by Pompey, became *hēgemōn*, that is, official head of the district " and lord over the hierodules inhabiting the city [of Comana] except for the right to sell them." [34] Eremian understands these hierodules, numbering some

six thousand according to Strabo, to be slaves, despite the specific statement of Strabo that they could not be sold. Under a precise analysis of their status they should be regarded as a group attached to the service of the god; but they are not actually unfree in the legal sense. Perhaps the most precise designation would be " temple bondsmen," which is the term applied to them by Walter Otto.[35] In its application to Cappadocia, at least, the decision of Eremian is to be rejected. The generally accepted view of modern scholarship, which has the fundamental support of the ancient evidence, is still valid. Crop production in Cappadocia and Armenia was not predominantly due to the labor of slaves, but was the work of semi-free peasants attached to the soil of the princely and temple domains of the time. The system resembled the colonate of the earlier Roman Empire and the serf labor of medieval society.[36]

A second article emanating from recent Russian scholarship also relates to the slave problem of the Roman Empire in the period after Constantine, which demands consideration in this survey. It appeared in the same journal as the reconstruction of the ancient Armenian historical evidence by Eremian. In this study the incursion of the West Goths into the Danubian provinces which culminated in the disastrous defeat of the army of Valens in A. D. 378 is coupled closely, and even fundamentally explained, as a revolt of the slaves of that region.[37] The Roman difficulties of the time are stripped of all the connotations of military revolts of the Roman armies which have usually been ascribed to them.[38] One must agree that there was a considerable group of German and Gothic slaves in Moesia and Thrace in the closing decades of the fourth century; but the Gothic element among them had been sold to the resident slave merchants, *by the Goths themselves*, it is to be noted. This had occurred during the months which immediately preceded the Gothic uprising, at a time when the Goths had been cheated out of the food supplies which had been promised them.[39] It is understandable that many of the Goths within the Empire who had recently become enslaved would readily join their invading countrymen when the opportunity offered.

Despite these agreements with the argument of the

---

[31] Nessana Papyrus, inv. no. 13306, published and discussed in Hebrew by Professor M. Schwabe of the Hebrew University of Jerusalem in *Magnes Anniversary Book*, 224-235 (English summary, p. XXX), Jerusalem, Hebrew Univ. Press, 1938. Professor Schwabe regarded the document as a manumission out of slavery whereas I feel confident that it is a release from a *paramonē* arrangement incurred by debt. See Westermann, The *paramone* as general service contract, *Jour. Jur. Papyrology* 2: 47-50, 1948.

[32] Eremian, S. T., *Vestnik Drevnei Istorii* 1: 13, 1950.

[33] *Ibid.*, 26.

[34] Strabo, 12: 34 (Casaubon's p. 558): καὶ τῶν τὴν πόλιν οἰκούντων ἱεροδούλων κύριος πλὴν τοῦ πιπράσκειν.

[35] Otto, Walter, Beiträge zur Hierodulie. *Abh. bayer. Akad.*, n.f., **29**: 9-12, 1950.

[36] Grousset, René, *Histoire de l'Arménie*, 294, Paris, Payot, 1947. For the tendency in Asia Minor in the Hellenistic period toward an increase in free peasant holdings rather than toward large domains worked by slave labor, see Magie, David, *Roman rule in Asia Minor* 1: 144.

[37] Dmitrev, A. D., The rising of the West Goths on the Danube and the slave revolt, *Vestnik Drevnei Istorii* 1: 66-80, 1950.

[38] *Ibid.*, 66.

[39] Ammianus Marcellinus, 31: 6, 5: *ex eadem gente multitudo dudum a mercatoribus venundati*; Seeck, Otto, *Untergang der antiken Welt* 5: 102, Berlin, Siemenroth, 1913. Synesius, *De regno*, 22, tells of the Gothic slaves put upon the market later by Theodosius. He states that they were good workmen as table-makers, kitchen servants and carriers of camp stools for their masters.

Russian writer, Dmitrev, his total concept of the Gothic movement must be discarded. In his depiction it becomes a class struggle in which the poor peasantry, the *coloni* and the slaves in the Danubian provinces combined against the rich. This belief is then used to support a dictum of Friedrich Engels to the effect that the barbarian invaders were awaited by the Romanized population of the provinces as their saviors.[40] This is far different from the picture of the devastation of the countryside, of the resultant distress and confusion, and of the terror of the local inhabitants as these manifestations of their sufferings have come to us from Hieronymus and Eunapius.[41]

So far as its applications to this investigation is concerned the article of Dmitrev does not in the slightest weaken the established view that the colonate was still the prevailing agrarian mechanism of production operating in the Danubian regions. Nor can it in any respect be regarded as proving that a " slave revolt," or even a popular liberation struggle, actually occurred in that area. Above all it does not warrant the contention that the danger of slave revolts was more strongly feared by the Romanized population than the invading barbarians themselves were feared.[42]

IN THE WESTERN MEDITERRANEAN AREA

The changes in labor economics which fall in the period from Diocletian to the Moslem conquest came about gradually, with differing intensities and in different tempos, in the East and West, and with different results. The meagre materials which are available upon the continuation and the extent of the use of rural slaves in North Africa have been assembled and admirably discussed by Stéphane Gsell.[43] According to the *Expositio totius mundi*, slaves were still being exported from Mauretania in the fourth century.[44] Some legislation is extant from the fourth and early fifth centuries which mentions the *mancipia rustica* and *servi* employed upon the large African domains.[45] If more data were at our

disposal it would probably be found that slave numbers had declined in North Africa even though the exploitation of the domains of that area by slave labor, although in lessened degree, continued to persist.[46] In contrast to the Apion domains in Egypt of the fifth and sixth centuries, which obtained their bricks by hiring brickmakers from outside the estate[47] and supplied their large demand for wine jars by the same method,[48] some of the North African estates maintained their own artisans in these crafts.[49] They may, however, have been free workmen or of the borderline group between free and slave which became characteristic of the time.

In their movement into Illyricum and later into Italy the warriors of the Visigoths were settled upon the land in the depopulated parts of Italy.[50] It is difficult to draw the line of the status of these barbarians placed upon the soil of Italy as between outright slavery and a position like that of the semi-free *coloni*. Salvianus speaks of them under the designation *servi*; but he continues his explanation of their tendencies to steal and to run away by referring to the low wages paid them. These wages, he says, might meet the customary payments for labor of that time; but they did not meet the requirements of a living sufficiency.[51] The expectation of money payments on the part of these agrarian workers necessarily makes their assignment to the slave category questionable. It is, nevertheless, not to be denied that a fairly large group of Gothic, German, and Hunnish were to be found in Italy who must be classified as legally enslaved persons, subject to transfer by sale and lacking recognized legal personality. This becomes clear from the terms dictated in A. D. 410 by Alaric, the Visigothic chieftain, to ensure his withdrawal from Rome. This lay in his demand that all the barbarians held as slaves in Rome must be turned over to him if he were to leave the city. This stipulation would have no meaning if these captives were men free to move and so to join the forces of Alaric.[52]

[40] Dmitrev, *Vestnik Drevnei Istorii* 1 : 76, quoting Engels.

[41] Hieronymus, *Epistola* 60, 16, in Migne, J.-P., *Patrologiae Latinae Cursus* 22 : 1, 600 : *Scythiam, Thraciam, Macedoniam, Dardaniam, Daciam, Thessaliam, Achaiam, Epiros, Dalmatiam, cunctasque Pannonias; Gothus, Sarmata, Quadus, Alanus, Hunni, Vandali, Marcomanni vastant, rapiunt. Quot matronas, virgines Dei et ingenua nobiliaque corpora his belluis fuere ludibria?* Cf. Eunapius, 464, on the Goths in A. D. 395, in Wright, W. C, *Philostratus and Eunapius*, Loeb Classical Library, New York, Putnams, 1922.

[42] Dmitrev, *Vestnik Drevnei Istorii* 1 : 71; Engels, *Origin of the family, private property and the state*, 137, New York, International Publishers, 1942, expresses the idea in this way, that the " Romans " who had fled into areas held by the barbarians and those who remained within Gaul " feared nothing so much as a return to Roman rule."

[43] Gsell, Stéphane, *Esclaves ruraux dans l'Afrique romaine, Mélanges Glotz* 1 : 407, Paris, Presses Universitaires, 1922.

[44] Riese, Alexander, *Expositio totius mundi*, 122, in *Geographi Latini Minores*, Heilbronn, Henning Brothers, 1878.

[45] Theod., *Codex* 10 : 8, 4; mentioned in connection with the

Donatist schism, 16 : 5, 52, 4-5 and 16 : 6, 4. *Cf.* St. Augustine, *Epistulae*, 108, 6, 18; 185, 4, 15, in Migne, J.-P. *Patrologiae Latinae Cursus* 33 : 2, Paris, 1865.

[46] Gsell, *Mélanges Glotz* 1 : 407.

[47] *P. Oxy.* 16, no. 1910, 5; no. 1913, 45, 63.

[48] *Ibid.* 16, no. 1911, lines 181, 185, 187, 191; no. 1913, lines 29, 33, 49, 51; Hardy, E. R., *Large estates*, 122-123.

[49] Gsell in *Mélanges Glotz* 1 : 404.

[50] For information upon the provinces of Gaul and Spain I have depended largely upon Verlinden's account in *Anuario de Historia del Derecho Español* 11 : 1934. Consult the *Cambridge medieval history* 1, *The Christian Empire*, 233, Cambridge Univ. Press, 1924, for the prisoners captured by the Roman general Frigeridus, A. D. 377. See, also, the account of the plan envisaged by the Emperior Aurelian (A. D. 270-275) of planting captured families of the enemy in Etruria upon lands lying uncultivated, in *Script. hist. Aug., Aurelian*, 49, 2. The translation in the Loeb Library of *familias captivas* as " families of slaves captured in war " is an inadvertent mistake.

[51] Salvianus, *De gubernatione Dei*, 4, 14, *Monumenta Germaniae Historica* 1 : 14, p. 38, Berlin Weidmann 1877. The word used by Salvianus for the payments is *stipendia*.

[52] Emerton, E. E., *Introduction to the study of the middle ages*, 31, New York, Ginn and Co., no date.

In Gaul and Spain in the three centuries following Diocletian's reorganization of the imperial structure the dwindling slave population seems to have been absorbed in large measure into agrarian life. As elsewhere in the Empire in general, the difficulty arises in these provinces, also, of establishing a sharp distinction between the restricted peasants of the colonate and the enslaved workmen upon the estates.[53] There are indications applying to the first quarter of the fifth century that the number of slaves needed in agrarian work in lower Gaul and in northern Spain was not excessive. About the middle of the fifth century Paulinus of Pella removed from Aquitania to Massilia. After he had done so he had not enough money remaining to acquire a farm staffed with an adequate complement of cultivators. He therefore took a garden of about two and a half acres which he could cultivate with the aid of his house slaves. Of these he had a sufficient number for the required work.[54] Obviously there could not have been many of them.

When the Visigoths settled in Spain they did not bring slaves with them. In their arrangements with the local Romanized population they agreed to a division of the land on the basis of the rule of hospitality, called the

tertia. By this division the Visigoths received two-thirds of the tenures and one-third of the slaves. The Spanish proprietors retained two-thirds of the slaves.[55]

A lack of slaves also in the area of the upper Rhone at the time of the Germanic invasions is indicated by the observation that the Burgundians when they entered that territory were compelled to purchase their slaves from Germany.[56] Continuance thereafter of the trade in slaves is attested by numerous manumissions of the Merovingian period and by regulations governing the purchase of slaves in the laws of the tribes of central and eastern Germany.[57] According to Alfons Dopsch, it is probable, however, that the additions to the numbers of slaves obtained by purchase did not keep pace with the manumissions in the period which followed the breaking down of the Roman Empire.[58]

---

[53] Verlinden, *Anuario del Derecho Español* 11: 320: *nous voyons aussi les proprietaires user de leurs esclaves comme des colons.*

[54] Paulinus of Pella, *Eucharisticus*, lines 520-538. The text and translation is given by White, H. G. Evelyn, (Loeb Classical Library) *Ausonius* 2: 344-345, New York, Putnams, 1921.

[55] Lot, Ferdinand, Du régime de l'hospitalité, *Rer. Belge de Philologie et d'Histoire* 7: 975-1011, 1928. For the two-thirds of the tenures see p. 983 and *cf.* Dopsch, Alfons, *Wirtschaftliche und soziale Grundlagen der europäischen Kulturentwickelung* 1: 213-214, Vienna, Seidel und Sohn, 1918; English version, *Economic and social foundations of European civilization,* 99-100, London, Kegan Paul, Trench, Trubner, 1937.

[56] Dopsch, *Grundlagen* 1: 89. The Roman landowners in Gaul under the Franks retained their freedom and their lands, *ibid.,* p. 218.

[57] *Ibid.* 2: 175-176 (= *Economic and social foundations,* 232), 2nd ed., 1924.

[58] Dopsch, *Grundlagen* 2: 177, 2nd ed. (= *Economic and social foundations,* 233), in contradiction of the opinion of Wopfner, H., *Historische Vierteljahrschrift* 21: 199, 1922-1923.

XXII. FROM DIOCLETIAN TO JUSTINIAN

LEVELING OF POSITION BETWEEN FREE WORKERS AND SLAVES

The preceding two chapters have reopened an old question of the decrease or the relative stability in the proportion of slaves to free in the later Roman Empire. A recent attempt has been made to picture the trend of slavery in the post-Diocletian period as one in which widespread and highly oppressive use of slaves in agriculture resulted in slave revolts sparked and guided by invading armies from the North. The study of the available source material in my judgment warrants the rejection of this result as unjustified in its basic assumption and deceptive in its conclusions.[1] It is to be granted that the problem of a decline in slavery in the fourth to the sixth century after Christ cannot be established by statistical computations because of the insufficiency of the evidence available. It has seemed advisable, therefore, to shift the aim of the inquiry to a different objective which offers the hope of giving results more susceptible of proof and more important than the mere numerical proportion of slave to free labor would in itself grant.

Such an inquiry as is here followed cannot lay claim to the interest of complete novelty;[2] but it seems to deserve a more patient and complete analysis than it has yet received. Did not a gradual leveling off occur between the economic and social privileges granted to enslaved labor and those held by the free working population of the Empire, those working in the lower echelons of labor such as the farming groups, the transporters, and the free craftsmen?

In the summation of his discussion of the social and economic trends which marked the first three centuries of Roman imperial history Michael I. Rostovtzeff stated that, after the reforms instituted by Diocletian and carried forward by Constantine, there was no social leveling, " nor was there even equality in the common slavery to the state." He grants that a " negative " equality was reached through the elimination of all self-govern-

---

[1] These conclusions have been outlined and discarded in the two chapters XX and XXI.

[2] E. g., Wallon, Henri, *L'esclavage* 3: 249-251; Piganiol, André, *Histoire Romaine,* 2, *l'empire Chrétien,* 285, Paris, Presses Universitaires, 1945: *mais la plupart de ces travailleurs libres ne sont libres qu'en apparence.*

ment and of all political freedom; that this extended upward even to the ranks of the great landed proprietors of the period; and that there were different shades of bondage—but there was no equality.[3] It is difficult to differ with the great authority of the late Professor Rostovtzeff upon social and economic problems of the Hellenistic and Roman periods of antiquity; and any difference of opinion here ventured may be no more than a semantic one. The insistence here is that there occurred a standardizing of privileges and demands among the lower sections of the laboring classes of the Empire, in the sense of a decline in the liberties accorded to the free and a rise in the position of the slaves in like employments, accompanied by a bettered social attitude toward the latter group. The legal distinction between free and slave was maintained. The trend was toward a general standard of uniformity in the treatment of slave and free. This displayed itself in the extent of the established controls operating upon these labor groups and in the methods of application of these controls, whatever the legal terms might be which differentiated the one group from the other.

This process of flattening off the uneven terrain of differences between workers of divergent status[4] was but one phase of a transformation of much wider scope which was taking place in the entire economic, religious, social, and cultural experience of the Mediterranean world of that time. In their ultimate legal formulation the changes found expression in the codes of Theodosius and Justinian. There they are displayed in enactments which loosened the strict controls by which the slave element had formerly been bound to the will of the master group. In their application to the upper element of the free workers they appear as restrictions upon the rights and privileges which had once been theirs. Juristically considered, practices which had long operated in the pre-Roman legislation of the provincial areas, or had been accepted without legal sanction in the daily economy of these localities, had been taken over into the constitutions of the Emperors. This system of folk practice, developed in the various sectors of the Empire, has recently been designated " the vulgar law " to distinguish it from the " peregrine " written law which had continued to determine many of the legal relations arising between non-Roman populations until the passage of the *constitutio Antoniniana* in A. D. 212.[5] In the

post-Diocletian period some part of these *leges extra legem* had received acceptance and had been drafted into the law of the Empire by those who counseled the emperors in legal matters.

On the side of the laboring groups of free and slave workers the trend toward a sympathetic understanding that in the economic field their interests coincided had been a matter of long and slow development.[6] The feeling had undoubtedly been fostered in the western Mediterranean sphere by the brutality of the praedial system of slavery which had long been indigenous there and by its contrast with the Greek system of handicraft slavery which had been spreading in the West after the second Punic war. This communion of slaves and free interests had manifested itself in the slave revolts which took place in Sicily and Italy in the second century B. C. and in the " war of the gladiators " led by Spartacus in 72-71 B. C. In the first century after Christ some credit has been granted to the position of power attained in imperial affairs by the freedmen of the Emperors for the rise of the slave class in popular regard. A striking display of the sympathy and feeling of unity which had grown up between the free and the slave group occurred in Rome itself in 61 B. C. Following the precedent of an old law the Roman Senate had condemned to death all the enslaved members of the household of a prominent Roman who had been murdered by one of his slaves. When the condemned men were led to their execution, because of previous rioting of the city populace, the streets had to be guarded by soldiers lining the way. Apparently this expression of solidarity was a spontaneous one which disregarded all the lines of status.[7]

The drawing together of slave and free labor can be most clearly followed as it expressed itself in the depression of the legal position of the tenant farmers, the *coloni*, to a state of semi-bondage. This trend has been so frequently and so effectively presented that it needed no more than a brief restatement here. From the end of the Carthaginian wars onward through the first three centuries of the Empire the tendency was toward a gradual decrease in the number of the small peasant owners, noticeably so in the Italian peninsula. It had been precisely these owners of " dwarf farms " in Italy

---

[3] Rostovtzeff, *Social and economic history of the Roman empire,* 473.

[4] In the interest of verbal accuracy I have avoided a temptation to use the modern terms " upgrading " and " downgrading " which are now widely employed in the discussions of American labor conditions. Their applications should be limited, as, in fact, they usually are, to financial advantages which are sought for members of the labor unions; particularly in respect to the employment of Negroes in the more skilled operations of their particular fields of work.

[5] Levy, Ernst, *West Roman vulgar law, The law of property,* Mem. Amer. Philos. Soc. **29**, 1-17, Philadelphia, 1951. Ludwig Mitteis in his *Reichsrecht und Volkrecht,* Leipzig, Teubner, 1921 used the term " folk law " to cover this type of unwritten

social practice. He it was who formulated the modern distinctions and analyzed the different elements of the Roman imperial law in his famous statement in *Reichsrecht,* 5 (as translated by Ernst Levy, *West Roman vulgar law,* 5): " Vulgar law and peregrine law do not coincide. The first is degenerate Roman law, the second is not Roman law at all." The Introduction of Professor Levy's book is a masterly condensation of a new approach to the western development of the Roman law.

[6] See chap. XI above; Westermann, W. L., Industrial slavery in Roman Italy, *Jour. Econ. Hist.* **2**: 149-163; for some of the contributions of the freedmen to Roman society in the early Empire, Barrow, R. H., *Slavery in the Roman Empire,* 189-207, London, Methuen, 1928. Barrow failed to note the retroactive effect of the positions of power attained by freedmen upon the class from which they rose.

[7] Tacitus, *Annals* 14: 42: *concursu plebis;* 14, 45, *conglobata multitudine . . . Tum Caesar populum edicto increpuit. Cf.* chap. XVII above at n. 82.

who had originally furnished the sturdy strength of the Roman Republic.[8] The middle decades of the third century were characterized by a constant succession of civil wars. Some of these were between military leaders whose claims to the imperial seat had been sanctioned by the recognition accorded them by the Roman Senate. In other cases heavy battles took place because of the disastrous pretensions of generals who had sought the great responsibility of ruling the Empire without grace of the Senate's acceptance. The anarchy in the administrative functioning of the Empire caused by these civil wars was aggravated by barbarian incursions into the northern provinces. In the distortion of the total economy of the Mediterranean area brought about by these factors one must reckon with a dislocation of agricultural labor which must have assumed some importance, particularly in the invaded provinces west of the Rhine and south of the Danube.

These external factors of disturbance were contemporary with deeper internal movements which have been admirably presented by M. I. Rostovtzeff. Together the internal and external agencies of dislocation set the stage for a marked decline in the position of the *coloni*, the tenant farmers of the Empire. The papyri have shown that in Egypt the response of the small farmers to their despair was to desert in flight the lands which they owned or worked as tenants.[9] The reaction of the Roman government to this form of refusal by the Egyptian farmers to fulfill their customary task of tilling the soil was to re-enact its measures restricting the right of movement of the peasants and to add police action aimed at the prevention of further flight and restoration of the fugitives to their places of work.

The reduction of the free agrarian workers to a state of actual bondage is officially recorded in a mandate of Constantine I issued A. D. 332. It provided that the *coloni* who might flee or might plan to flee from their overlords must be returned to them and be shackled in irons—" so that they might fulfill, under the compulsion of a merited condemnation to servitude, the obligations which befitted them as free men." [10] This enactment

presupposes that, before its publication, the *coloni* had already lost their freedom of moving away from the locality of their census enrollment. Deprived of the free man's privilege of going where they wished, they had lost in some measure the attendant liberty of " doing what they wished." These are two of the four liberties which, according to the Delphic manumissions by sale to the god, distinguished the free man from the slave.[11]

If there was a specific enactment which attached the *coloni* irrevocably to their farming functions and made these compulsory and hereditary at the definite place of the registration this constitution is lost to us. Certainly the fact of this attachment to the job and its official acceptance as practice is to be placed before A. D. 332, under Diocletian himself or under one of his successors. There are, in fact, several indications which recommend Ensslin's conclusion that the tax system inaugurated by Diocletian, which was designed to meet a great increase in the income required for government expenditures, set the stage for the acceptance of the restrictions which legally bound the *coloni* to their farming tasks.[12] For the increase in the administrative payroll expenditures of the Empire necessitated by Diocletian's division into four prefectures, each with its own court, its own bureaucracy and its own army, we have the testimony of the brochure ascribed to Lactantius upon the deaths of the persecutors of the Christians.

He[Diocletian] divided the *orbis* [the circuit of the Roman Empire] into four parts and set up three assistants of his rule. The armies were multiplied since each one of them strove to have a far greater number of soldiers than the previous emperors had had when they, singly, had carried on the republic. The number of recipients [of the state's money] even began to be greater than those who gave it so that the *coloni* were devoured by the enormity of the tax requirements, the fields were deserted, and the cultivated lands were turned into forests.[13]

The series of legislative enactments which brought the

---

[8] The fundamental study of the deterioration of position of the free agricultural forces of the Empire has been, notably, the work of Rostovtzeff, M. I. (Rostowzew in the German transliteration of the Russian name), *Studien zur Geschichte des römischen Kolonates* in *Archiv für Papyrusforschung*, Beiheft 1, Leipzig, Teubner, 1910. The results of that study have been incorporated in his *Soc. and econ. hist. of the Roman empire*, 190-222, and more simply stated in his Origin of serfdom in the Roman empire, *Jour. Land and Public Utility Economics* 2: 198-207, 1926.

[9] Bell, H. Idris, The Byzantine servile state in Egypt, *Jour. Egypt. Archaeology* 4: 96, 1917.

[10] Theod., *Codex* 5: 17, 1; Ensslin, W., in *CAH* 12: 402 and n. 1. Ensslin's phrase, "bound to the soil" (*adscripti glebae*), is to be understood as a later usage, transferred to an earlier period. In the legislation of the fourth century they were called *coloni censiti*, or *adscripti censibus*. See Seeck, Otto, article Colonatus in Pauly-W., *RE* 4: 498-499.

The deprivation of the right of movement as a central factor in the bondage inflicted upon all the elements of the working

population of the Empire was briefly, but quite clearly, stated by Hartmann, Ludo, and H. Kromayer, *Römische Geschichte, Weltgeschichte im gemeinverständlicher Darstellung*, 2nd ed., 3: 215-216, Gotha, Perthes, 1921. See, also, Hartmann, *Untergang der antiken Welt*, 2nd ed., 22, Leipzing, Heller, 1910. Hartmann went too far in confining the right of free movement to the ruling classes only in his *Römische Geschichte*, 215.

[11] The recognition in the Delphic manumissions of mobility and choice of work as two of the four most important elements of liberty permitted to free men has been briefly presented in chap. 6 of this book. Otto Seeck, Die Schätzungsordnung Diocletians, *Ztsch. für Social- und Wirtschaftsgeschichte* 4: 281-395, 1926, emphasizes the widespread system of corruption which prevailed under the land-tax system. Those who could pay the bribes demanded of them had their financial obligations lowered. Those who could not do so, endured the entire burden of the tax. The summary nature of Diocletian's division of the land into *juga* brought it about, according to Otto Seeck, *loc. cit.*, that 449 olive trees paid the same tax as 225 olive trees, since both fell below the number of 450 which began the second *jugum* unit. Seeck's observation is accepted, though with some hesitation, by H. Idris Bell, *Jour. Egypt. Arch.* 4: 96, 1917.

[12] Ensslin, W., *CAH* 12: 401-402.

[13] Lactantius, *De mortibus persecutorum*, 7.

economic and social permissions and restrictions of the lower strata of free workmen toward a similarity with those granted to slaves or imposed upon them appeared slowly and at widely spaced intervals. The bestowal upon the landowners, by the enactment of Constantine I in A. D. 332; of the right of punishing their *coloni* as they might punish their own slaves is clear.[14] Under the Emperor Constantius (A. D. 350-360) transfer of *coloni* was forbidden when a property was sold or otherwise changed hands.[15] By an enactment of Valentinian and Valens of A. D. 366 governors of provinces were to compel all fugitives everywhere, registered tenants or dwellers in houses upon the estates (*adscripticios colonos vel inquilinos*) to return to their old homes (*penates*) where they were registered, where they had been reared and were born.[16] By this legislation two groups connected with the large estates which had previously been differentiated were now merged in respect to their permanent attachment to the place of their work or of their habitation. Although they continued to be differentiated formally from the "rustic slaves" (*servi rustici*), the *coloni* later come to be referred to as "slaves of the land itself to which they were born."[17] This change in terminology expresses realistically the degree of the descent toward enslavement which the *coloni* had undergone.

Two contemporary witnesses from Gaul can be cited who give an insight into this determination of position of the lesser landholders of that area and its end in the complete deprivation of their freedoms. They are Salvianus, Bishop of Arelate in the middle of the fifth century, and Apollinaris Sidonius, Bishop of Massilia at the same time. Speaking of the poor but free landowners in Gaul, Salvianus says that some of them had lost their herds and their homes, either through the Gothic invasions or because of their flight from their farms to escape the tax collectors. The more astute among them sought the estates of the landlords who were powerful and rich and became their tenant farmers (*coloni*). Having lost the security afforded by free birth they fled in desperation to some protective asylum. Similarly those who could not any longer keep either the home of their native freedom, or retain the dignity (it conferred), submitted themselves to that dependence which characterized the homeless residents (*inquilinae*

abjectionis). They were lost—both they themselves and all that they had owned. *Deprived of the ownership of everything, they lost, also, the rights of their former status of liberty.*[18]

The letter of Apollinaris Sidonius tells, in the account of a criminal assault of that day, of the finesses of distinction between a slave and an *inquilinus* (a homeless "squatter"), between a taxpaying subject and a client, and that between a bondage tenant (*colonus*) and a plebeian. The situation described by the terminology of Sidonius leaves a clear impression of the narrowness of the space between these groups.

Since the woman in the case was free, that is, of freedman status, Sidonius felt that he could concede that the guilty male slave might remain unpunished—upon one condition. His friend must release the rapist from slavery and stand thereafter as *patronus* to him instead of master over a slave. Thus advanced by his manumission to the initial stage of liberty as an *inquilinus*, the guilty man would be in a position to marry the injured woman without contravening the law. The marriage having been performed the rapist was then to be advanced to the status of a clientage dependency instead of a taxpayer. He would then "begin to have the [legal] personality of a plebeian rather than that of a *colonus*."[19] Here again the slight gradations in position between these legal personalities in the upward scale from "slave" to "plebeian," as Apollinaris Sidonius saw them, are clear. They are given in the ascending scale—slave, *inquilinus*, tribute-paying subject, client, *colonus*, plebeian. In the downward scale these gradings would merely be stated in reverse order. The sole distinction between the plebeian and the *colonus* seems to be that the *colonus* was enrolled upon the tax register.[20] The difference between the *inquilinus* and the man enslaved was, in this period, that the slave could not legally marry a free woman. Even that distinction between them was soon to disappear in the practice of daily life through the acceptance of the continuance and legality of such intermarriages in so far as they had been consummated before the law forbidding it was passed.[21]

---

[14] Theod., *Codex*, 5: 17, 1 (*Breviarium*, 5:9, 1); Just., *Codex*, 11: 53, 1: *si abscesserint ad alienosve transierint, revocati vinculis poenisve subdantur.*

[15] Theod., *Codex* 13: 10, 3.

[16] Just., *Codex* 11: 48, 6. Gaius explained the distinction between the *coloni* and the *inquilini* as one between tenants who enjoyed the usufruct of the land they worked and those who had dwelling rights thereon, Just., *Digest* 19: 2, 25, 1: *colono frui et inquilino habitare liceat.* Cf. Leonhard, R., Pauly-W., *RE* 9: 1559. Rostovtzeff also, *Kolonat*, 342, understood that the *inquilini* had some claim of ownership upon the places in which they lived.

[17] *Servi tamen terrae ipsius cui nati sunt*, in Just., *Codex* 11: 52 (51), 1. *Inserviant terris . . . nomine et titulo colonorum*, *ibid.*, 11: 53 (52), 1.

[18] Salvianus, *De gubernatione Dei* 5: 8 (106), in Migne, J.-P., *Patrologiae Latinae* 53: 103, Paris, 1865.

[19] Apollinaris Sidonius, *Epistulae*, 5: 19, 2: *mox cliens factus a tributario, plebeiam potius incipiet habere personam quam colonariam.*

[20] Seeck, Otto, Pauly-W., *RE* 4: 505, and *Untergang der antiken Welt*, Anhang 1: 585-589.

[21] In the year 468 an edict of the Emperors Leo and Anthemius declared existing marital relations between free women and their slaves to be legitimate marriages, not affecting adversely the inheritance rights of children born to such unions. It added, however, a prohibition against them for the future, Novella 1 of Anthemius in Paul M. Meyer, *Leges novellae ad Theodosianum pertinentes*, Theod., *Codex* (Mommsen edition) 2: 203-204. For slave and free intermarriage as a practice of the "vulgar" law in Egypt in the fourth century, see Taubenschlag, R., *Atti di Congresso Internazionale di Diritto Romano* 11: 1, for the acceptance of a completely servile attitude toward the big landlords by the Egyptian *coloni* of the sixth century in the excerpts from

The ability of the government to enforce the regulations which undermined the liberties of free men was methodically effected by binding the subjects to the places of their duties and by enforced inheritance, at the place of their registration, of the obligations when they were once thrust upon the heads of families. As early as the first quarter of the third century the application of these agencies of control were being extended upward also upon the more prosperous classes as well as upon the lower. For the *decuriones*, the men appointed to fill the membership ranks of the municipal councils, this appears in an opinion given by Ulpian, the Roman jurist of Tyre, which has fortunately been preserved in the *Digest* of Justinian. It states that the *praesides* of the provinces were to call back to the places of their paternity those decurions who could be proved to have left their homes and moved to other regions. They were further to see to it that these decurions were to carry out in their old home localities the official obligations appropriate to them.[22] About two hundred years later, A. D. 415, the official duties which had once been undertaken voluntarily by these leaders in their municipalities had become heavy burdens, imposed under compulsion and hereditary in the male line: " if any person shall be descended from a decurion family he shall be obligated to the bonds of the municipal council by birth status or blood descent." [23]

The same long period which experienced both the binding of the middle classes of curial ranks to their home localities and its duties and the decline of small landholders and free farm tenants to the position of *coloni adscripticii* saw, also, the deterioration of the freedoms of the craftworkers, the tradesmen, and the transporters.[24] In the treatment of these groups two elements of the previous background must be kept in mind. Under the free-contract system men following these occupations were accustomed to accept restrictions upon their mobility and their right to work at other

tasks; but these personal sacrifices were temporary, limited to the terms of the contractual agreement, and entered into voluntarily by the work-takers. The second feature to be remembered is that voluntary associations of workmen, meeting for purposes of religious worship, entertainment, and social welfare, were widespread in the Greek and Roman world. It is the hardening of these accepted temporal infringements upon the time and efforts of the work-takers into inescapable regulations of governmental control which brought the freedom of these groups close to the level of bondage. In the voluntary associations of the working classes the Roman Empire found ready at its hand instruments useful for the direct application of its regulatory enactments.

In the nature of their occupation the shipowners associated in the transport guilds could not be permanently fixed at a definite locality by imposing restrictions upon their right of movement. They were controlled, however, as functionaries necessary to the problems of the imperial food distribution, by an early insistence upon life-long duration of their collegial obligations (A. D. 334) and upon its inheritance as a state burden (*onus publicum*).[25] A government demand is later recorded by which the shipowners were required to hand in lists of the members of their associations (*collegia naviculariorum*) accompanied by the names of their wives and children.[26] Through the listing of their wives in the towns of their husbands' registration the officials could keep their hands sufficiently well upon the male members of the shipping associations.[27]

The narrow range of assignment of their personnel to the function to which they were allocated becomes apparent in an official letter of A. D. 400 from Hermopolis on the Nile. A man who served in the state galley of the governor of the Thebaid asked for the release of one of his rowers who had been compelled to undertake some other state obligation. The complainant who asked for the release of his oarsman based his claim upon the fact that the man's father and his grandfather had served as rowers upon the government galleys. His requisition for another liturgical function was, therefore, unwarranted.[28]

Oxyrhynchus Papyri 1, no. 130 and *P. Cairo Maspero* 1: 67002 (*Catalogue général des antiquités égyptiennes*, Cairo, 1911) as translated by H. Idris Bell, *Egypt from Alexander the Great to the Arab conquest*, 125-126, Oxford, Clarendon Press, 1948.

[22] Just., *Digest* 50: 2, 1.

[23] Theod., *Codex* 12: 1, 178, as translated in Pharr, Clyde, *The Theodosian code*, Princeton, Univ. Press, 1952.

[24] Only a few out of the long list of important references upon the history of the artisan guilds and the imposition of government controls upon them can here be cited. Wallon, H., *L'esclavage* 3: 158-207 (with mention on pp. 115 and 188 of the importance of the legal restraints placed upon labor mobility); Villard, A., *Histoire du proletariat*, 189-192, Paris, Guillaumin, 1882; Waltzing, J-P., *Les corporations professionelles chez les Romains* 2: 259-348, Louvain, Peeters, 1896; Gummerus, Herman, in Pauly-W. *RE* 9: 1532-1535; Oertel, Friedrich, *Die Liturgie*, 417-426, Teubner, Leipzig, 1917; the same in *CAH* 12: 265-281; Rostovtzeff, M. I., *Soc. and econ. hist. Rom. empire*, 470-474, with his references upon pp. 629-630, n. 6 to chap. 12 to many other treatments of the binding of the workingmen; Piganiol, André, *Histoire romaine* 4(2), *l'empire Chrétien*, 285-293, Paris, Presses Universitaires, 1947, presents a succinct statement of this development of the artisan, trade and transport associations.

[25] Theod., *Codex* 13: 5, 1 of A. D. 314. In his important study of the problem of cartel functions among the guilds in late Roman antiquity and in the earlier Byzantine era Gunnar Mickwitz, Kartellfunktionen der Zünfte, *Finska Vetnskaps-Societeten, Commentationes Humanarum Litterarum* 8: 3, 167 and 172, has correctly divested the controls exercised over the *collegia* in the later Roman Empire of any other purposes than those dictated by its financial needs. See in particular his rejection of the idea of Doren, Alfred, *Italienische Wirtschaftsgeschichte*, 102, Jena, G. Fischer, 1934, that the later Roman Empire was motivated. in the pressure of its controls upon agrarian and handicraft associations, by far-reaching plans of state socialistic character directed toward reanimating the fading powers of its subject population.

[26] Theod., *Codex* 13: 5, 14, 2 (A. D. 371).

[27] Theod., *Codex* 13: 5, 12 (A. D. 369). I have here followed the article by Albert Stöckle upon *navicularii* in Pauly-W., *RE* 16: 1918.

[28] P. Grenfell 2, no. 82.

The several hundred single local *collegia* which have been found throughout the Mediterranean area, as these were known before the appearance in 1900 of his impressive publication upon the associations, have been assembled by J.-P. Waltzing in the fourth volume of his study of the corporations.[29] In the period of the late Republic we may be certain that slaves, freedmen, and free-born members were occasionally to be found, even then, mingled together in some of the funerary and cult associations in Italy and elsewhere.[30] When freedmen and slaves only are recorded as members of these social groups, as in the lists of the *magistri* and *magistrae* from Italian Minturnae of about 90 to 64 B.C., several explanations for the lack of free members may be suggested. Perhaps the freedmen and slave officials alone were enumerated as an expression of pride on the part of these groups in the position of social importance which their humble colleagues had attained. More plausible, perhaps, is the suggestion that freedmen and slaves were permitted to enter the cult associations along with free members only in those places, like Minturnae, where the number of the craftsmen which could be recruited from these groups did not warrant the maintenance of separate associations for the slaves and ex-slaves.[31]

For Egypt the papyri now show that the system of collective payment of the weaving license (the *gerdiakon*) and corporate responsibility for other governmental requirements were already beginning to appear in the first quarter of the second Christian century. A receipt of A.D. 123 has been published which records the payment *by a single representative of the weaver's association of Philadelphia* of what looks to be the total of the weaving licenses (*gerdiaka*) of the entire membership of that group for the full year. The system was apparently in a transitionary stage from the liturgical system of collection to one of direct payment by the local associations of weavers in which they became responsible for the total amount due. For the payment, in this instance, went " into the account of one Lucius, who is also called Serenus, and his associates, receivers of the weavers' [license]." This tendency of the government, in its own fiscal interest, to impose upon the craftsmen *collegia* these administrative functions had its beginnings in the second Christian century, as was long ago assumed by Theodor Reil.[32] Reil's decision has, more recently, been

strengthened by a receipt of the year 128 from the village of Socnopaei Nesus.[33] It is an attestation by " the receivers of public clothing " that nineteen tunics, destined for some guards, and five short cloaks (*palliōla*) had duly been delivered for some soldiers who were at that time posted in Judaea. I see no way, as the evidence now stands, of determining whether corporate responsibility was first applied to the Egyptian weavers in the delivery of the clothing requisitions destined for the armies or to the payment of money taxes by their *collegia*.

It is in the fourth century that the system of collegiate responsibility of the artisans, small tradesmen and transport groups is met in its full development. In comparison with the farm workers the members of the associations engaged in these occupations were able to retain distinctly more of their private rights and the legal capacities appertaining to free men than did the *coloni*, bound as these were to their agrarian work and to the places of its fulfillment. The losses of independence sustained by the tradesmen and handicrafters lay solely in the range of the last two of the four basic criteria of freedom as these had been noted and set forth in the Delphic manumissions by sale to Apollo of the years 200 B.C. to about A.D. 75. These two were the customary privileges accorded to the free, that of physical mobility and that of changing both the type of their work and its location, as opposed to the two inherited rights of free men, those of legal status and protection from arbitrary seizure. Under the aegis of their free status, the *collegiati*, if of free birth or if made free by manumission, retained the rights of testamentary disposition and sale of what they owned, or of giving it away if they so wished. The deprivation of their freedom of movement after Diocletian's time is sharply expressed in a Novella of A.D. 458 by Majorian: " to these regulations the provision of Our Serenity adds that the guildsmen shall furnish services to the municipality at alternate times in accordance with the decision of the curials, and they shall not be permitted to reside outside the territory of their own municipality." [34]

Although the associations of the shipowners, by virtue of their wide-ranging activities, were especially privileged, we none the less have rescripts of Valentinianus and Valens from the middle of the fourth century which

[29] Waltzing, J.-P., *Corporations professionelles* 4, Louvain, Peeters, 1900. The lists of the guilds presented by Waltzing under A and B in 4: 1-128 include the artisans, shippers, hunters and traders along with other types.

[30] *Ibid.* 1: 346-347. This is contrary to the belief expressed by Theodor Mommsen and Heinrich Dirksen, *ibid.*, 347, n. 2. For the public slaves it is attested by Halkin, Leon, *Esclaves publics chez les Romains.* Consult, also, Johnson, Jotham, *Excavations at Minturnae* 2 (1), *Republican magistri*, 118-119, Univ. of Penn. Press, 1933.

[31] The latter explanation is that advanced by Halkin, L., *Esclaves publics*, 209.

[32] *Berl. Griech. Urkunden* (*BGU*) 7, no. 1591; Reil, Theodor,

Beiträge zur Kenntnis des Gewerbes im hellenistischen Ägypten, 185, Borna-Leipzig, R. Noske, 1913.

[33] Johnson, J. de M., V. Martin, and A. S. Hunt, *Greek papyri in the John Rylands Library* 2, no. 189, Manchester, Univ. Press, 1915. A translation of the receipt appears in Frank, T., *Economic survey* 2, *Egypt*, 626, no. 372, where the editor, through a confusion with *BGU* 7: 1564, placed in Cappadocia the troops who were to receive the five white cloaks. *BGU* 7: 1564, dated A.D. 138, is a similar requisition of military clothing to be supplied by the total group of the weavers of Philadelphia.

[34] *Novellae* of Majorianus, 7: 1, 3 in the *Codex Theodosianus*. The translation is adapted after that of Pharr, *The Theodosian Code*, 557.

prescribed that the length of services rendered by their members had no bearing upon the problem of their cessation.[35] Because of the nature of their duty of providing an adequate meat supply for the towns in which they operated it is not surprising that we find the sausage makers and pork butchers known to us from Egyptian papyri bound to the cities and towns in which they served the state. From Antinoopolis upon the Nile there has come an oath of A. D. 566, taken by their sponsors, that the members of these *collegia* would not leave the place during the year in which they were to serve.[36]

The tendency toward local fixation of the association members is more drastically expressed in a new law of the Emperor Majorian, A. D. 457-461, which runs to this effect: for them (the *collegiati*) Our Serenity has added a proviso that the association members who in alternating periods carry on their services at the disposition of the local senators shall not be permitted to dwell outside of the city of their services.[36a]

Respecting the *collegia* of the city of Rome we have a letter of Symmachus of A. D. 384 asking for remission of a new burden which was being projected for the population of the city. " It is manifest that in effect the Romans are paying a great price for what, in ancient times, was their privilege. They are buying an immunity, in name only, by submitting to a yoke [of servitude]." [37]

In the year 530 under Justinian he or his advisors were responsible for the declaration that the old law of inheritance of status was still in application. This provided that children born of a slave father and of a mother of colonate status, or, conversely, of a free man of colonate registration (*adscripticius*) and a slave mother, inherited the condition of the mother—*matris suae ventrem sequatur*: " for what difference can be established between slaves and *adscripticii* since each of them has been placed in the power of his master and it may be possible for him [the *dominus*] to manumit the slave with his *peculium* and to reject out of his control the registered *colonus* with his land? "

In following the trend toward a leveling off of the practical distinctions between free transporters, the farm tenant class, the artisans, and the small tradesmen of the markets it must be kept in mind that equality, as between them and slaves engaged in the same occupations, was never attained. Mommsen long ago threw off the brief suggestion that a distinction always was maintained by the Romanized population of the Empire between voluntary entrance into the colonate relation and self-sale into slavery. This belief seemed to be based by Mommsen upon the psychological factor that colonate

position did not completely destroy the personal pride in one's free status or the legal recognition of its continuance.[38]

The nature and the degree of the decline in the personal liberties of the tenant who went into the colonate class is made clear in a deed of surety from Oxyrhynchus in Egypt which is dated A. D. 579. Therein a lead-worker accepted the obligation of acting as surety for a farmer registered upon one of the scattered Apion estates. The lead-worker gave bond that the *colonus* would remain (*paramenein*) continuously on his holding with his friends, his wife, his herds, and all his possessions; " and I will be answerable for all that pertains to his person or to his fortune as registered cultivator, and that he will not leave this holding or remove to another place." [39]

The registered tenant was under a lifelong contract to stay upon the estate.[40] In agreeing to his position as *enapographos geōrgos* (registered farmer) he had sacrificed his option of moving away and had undertaken to be at hand when called upon for any duty upon the estate of his registration. His choices had been narrowed down to his farm labors and to any further tasks demanded by the estate management.[41] With the loss of his mobility went, also, much of his personal control of his own working capacity.

Wilhelm Schubart has intimated that this later Roman period was marked by a feeling of insecurity which rested upon all the lower orders of society. The humility expressed in their approach to their overlords and to the government officials gives evidence enough of this slavish mentality of the unprotected and the oppressed of the fifth and sixth centuries.[42] The tone of self-abasement, whether or not it may in some degree be considered a mere literary fashion of the time, was foreign to the Greek and Roman slave populations of the pre-Diocletian era. In this facet of expression the downward movement in spiritual freedom toward an acceptance of the attitude of servility had reached its completion.

A distinct tendency to lessen the old Roman Republican harshness in the treatment of slaves had already become evident in special enactments of the first two centuries of the Empire. Generally these took the form

---

[35] Theod., *Codex* 13: 6, 5; 13: 6, 3.

[36] Preisigke, Friedrich, *Griech. Papyrus zu Strassburg (P. Strass.)*, nos. 46-51, Leipzig, Hinrich, 1912.

[36a] *Novellae* of Majorianus, 7: 1, 3, in Theod., *Codex*.

[37] Symmachus, *Epistles*, 10, 14 [*Relationes* 14], in Seeck, Otto, *Monumenta Germaniae Historica* 6: 290-291, Berlin, Weidmann, 1883; Waltzing, J.-P., *Les corporations officielles de l'ancienne Rome*, Gand,, Vanderhaeghen, 1912.

[38] Mommsen, Theodor, *Gesammelte Schriften: Juristische Schriften*, 3: 14, Weidmann, Berlin, 1907.

[39] *P. Oxy.* 1, no. 135, lines 10-21.

[40] *Ibid.*, line 16: αὐτὸν ἀδιαλείπτως παραμεῖναι. The verb is here to be understood in its general sense of " remaining " upon the place, as in the following διάγειν ἐν τῷ αὐτοῦ κτήματι, rather than as expressing an agreement to carry out any services required of him. See Westermann, Paramone as general service contract, *Jour. Jurist. Papyr.* 2: 9-50, 1948.

[41] *Ibid.*, lines 21-26. The *colonus* (line 26) is to be " in the keeping of your honored house," as the editors translate it, rather than to be brought to the estate prison by the surety as Hardy, E. R., understands it in his *Large estates of Byzantine Egypt*, 69, n. 2, New York, Columbia University Press, 1931.

[42] Schubart, Wilhelm, Vom Altertum zum Mittelalter, *Archiv für Papyrusforschung* 11: 85, 1935.

of legislation designated to better specific external conditions of enslavement practice which obviously needed to be changed.[43] The continuation into the post-Diocletian period of legislation of this type may be regarded both as an indication and as a result of the drying up of the older sources of the slave supply. A more decisive measure of the upward swing in the treatment of the slave group can be seen in several legal opinions given in the first quarter of the third century. A creditor, according to the eminent jurist, Papinian, could not take away his *peculium* from a slave who had been turned over to him as a pledge unless this action had been directly specified in the debt agreement.[44]

Before Ulpian's time juridical opinion had been divided upon the point whether free workmen upon an estate were, or were not, to be regarded as instruments of the agricultural production of the property, which, upon a transfer of the estate, should go over with it to the new owner. Approximately a decade after Papinian had given the decision cited above upon a slave's *peculium* Ulpian posed the problem whether it followed that a slave working upon an estate in the position of a *colonus* (*quasi colonus*) would be included as part of its working inventory in a legacy of the estate. In the opinion which he gave, Ulpian's decision agreed with the older concept of the slave as personal property of his owner, not as a tool of the productive capacity of the soil, therefore not subject to a transfer by legacy as a component part of the productive organization.[45] It is the statement of the problem as it was put by Ulpian which here displays the rise of the estate slave toward the position of the *colonus* and away from the legal view that he was the complete possession of the slave-owner. A constitution of A. D. 293, or of a few years earlier, points in the same direction. It provided that a public slave who had been freed but continued, after his manumission, to serve as a notary was not affected in respect to his liberty by the continuation of his former servile activity. If a son were later born to this manumitted *servus publicus* the fact of notarial service on the father's part would not debar the free-born son from selection into the municipal council at the place of his residence.[46]

The movement toward similarity of the demands placed upon estate slaves to those expected from the *coloni* worked toward the application of governmental controls over the enslaved farm workers which tended to assimilate the procedural treatment accorded the two groups. In a rescript of Valentinian II, Valens, and Gratian, falling somewhere in the years 374-378, one finds that some of the slaves were registered in the lists of estate workers just as were the *coloni* who were native to the place (the *originarii*). The *domini* could no longer sell such slaves apart from the estate.[47] The

importance of this is evident. The central organization of the Empire, in respect to these " registered slaves," had, therefore, reversed the opinion advocated by the jurist, Ulpian, so far as the decision was now to apply to these " registered slaves," by taking away from the estate owners their unconditional right to dispose of this element of the working force of the estate. One may again assume that this was done in the interest of constant production from the estates, by fixation of as much of its labor force as possible. The rustic workers, the *coloni*, and now the farm hands of slave status had become recognized as part of the inventory of the estates.

It is scarcely to be believed that the conditions of living of these slave hands were thereby bettered; but their assimilation toward the position held by the *coloni* of the time is apparent. In much the same way the master moldmakers of the Arretine pottery works of the early first century in Italy were sometimes transferred with the sale of the pottery shops themselves. A closer analogy may lie with the Helots of Sparta in that the " census-listed slaves " of the post-Diocletian period, like the *coloni* and the *rustici*, were not alienable from the jobs which their registration entailed. As Sparta had done in the case of the Helots, the later Roman Empire had assumed legal control of the slave farm hands, so far as transfer by sale was concerned. In Roman terms, the *servus privatus* had risen to something like the level of the *servus publicus*. He had been raised one further step upward toward the constricted freedom to which the *colonus* had been demoted when he became fixed upon the estate which he served.

The last title of the Digest of Justinian contains a legal maxim which declares that, in cases of doubt, the preference in the decision should be given to the more benevolent view. A recent discussion has shown, conclusively in my opinion, that this maxim, as legal directive, goes back in its practical application to Gaius and Marcellus, and beyond them to Marcus Aurelius and even to Hadrian.[48] The step taken by Justinian and his collaborators was merely to raise the idea from the plane of an advice to that of a rule.[49]

The enunciation of the rule—*in dubiis benigniora*—furnishes another important link in the series which marks the breaking down of the barriers of distinction in the treatment of the enslaved as compared with the free-born. A practical example is to be seen in an opinion of the time of Justinian regarding the status of a single child, or of children of a multiple birth, born to a female slave after her manumission. In this instance a testator had freed in his will a slave woman who was with child, specifying that the child as yet unborn should

[43] Chap. 17 above, pp. 114-116.
[44] Just., *Digest* 20: 1, 1.
[45] *Ibid.* 33: 7, 12, sections 2-3; Piganiol, *Histoire romaine, l'empire Chrétien,* 275.
[46] Just., *Codex* 7: 9, 3; Wallon, *L'esclavage* 3: 160.
[47] Just., *Codex* 11: 48, 7: *quemadmodum originarios absque*

terra, ita rusticos censitosque servos vendi omnifariam non licet; Verlinden, Ch., *Anuario de Historia del Derecho Español* 11: 321.
[48] Berger, Adolf, In dubiis benigniora, *Seminar* 9: 37, 41, 1951, which is a condensation of a fuller presentation in *Atti del Congresso Internazionale di Diritto Romano* 2: 187-205, 1951.
[49] Berger, *Seminar* 9: 48.

also be free when the will went into effect. When the birth was a multiple one the problem of the freedom of more than one child arose. The decision was that both of the twins, or all the offspring in the case of a multiple birth, should be free because, in a doubtful case, it were better that the more humane decision should be followed.[50] It should be noted in reference to the guiding criterion, *melius est—humaniorem amplecti sententiam*, that the passage of the Codex urges its application "especially in matters appertaining to freedom." The meaning seems to be plain that the ameliorating effect of the *benigniora* rule was to be observed particularly in the frame of reference of the dwindling numbers of the slave population.

Legislation passed in the fifth and sixth centuries upon the unions of slaves and upon mixed cohabitations of slaves with free persons was constantly, though intermittently, moving toward a softening of the rigidities which had formerly been slackened in their enforcement rather than in their legal acceptance. An example offers itself in an edict passed in A. D. 468 by the Emperors Leo and Anthemius which sanctioned as legal unions (*matrimonia*) marriage relations entered into with their own freedmen by women of noble birth. They were to be *justae nuptiae*, and the children born of such unions were assured of inheritances from their parents. For the freedman-husband identity of *status* with the free wife was not attained; but he *was* moved upward in the scale of economic and social relations to a position approaching parity with her.

A further section of this edict is still more significant. As from the year of its passage women patrons could not contract legal marriages with their dependants, nor women slave-owners with their slaves,[51] "so that the illustrious nobility of distinguished families may not be cheapened by the befoulment of an unworthy association."[52] The edict warrants the conclusion that such relations *were* being established, presumably on a wide scale, before its promulgation: "first, therefore, we decree, with the assurance of the edict, that if it shall be proved that marriage relations of this kind have been entered into, even up to our second consulship, they shall not be deprived of legal stability." One must conclude that such conjugal relations were fully accepted by the public opinion of the time. The words used in the edict to describe them are *matrimonia* and *similia conjugia*.

The upward trend of the slave group toward a parity of social and economic position with that held by freedmen and workers of free birth can be seen in a pronouncement of Justinian of the year 529. It had reference to abandoned male children, whether they were of free birth, born of freedwomen, or the sons of mothers of slave status. Any person who had taken over and reared a male child of any one of these derivations could not enter a claim for control over the child as his property, either under the guise of ownership, of registration status, or of *colonus* condition. Whatever their birthright might have been, such male children were to be considered free, with the right of transmitting later to their own children or to other heirs whatever property they might have acquired. Since bishops, along with the provincial magistrates, were enlisted in the enforcement of this pronouncement it is likely that Christianity had exerted its influence upon the decision thus formulated.[53]

The normal juristic attitude of the early Empire respecting status as established by marriage was succinctly expressed by Celsus: in legal marriages the children follow the father; in non-legalized unions they follow the mother.[54] In either case, as in political classification affecting citizenship before the passage of the *Constitutio Antoniniana*, the decisive factor was birth.[55] To repeat an observation already insisted upon, which needs still further insistence, the post-Diocletian legislation upon labor and the working classes brought about a depression of the members of the trade and transport associations and of the registered tenants (*coloni adscripticii*) to a plane of empirical restrictions not far above those applied in the case of slavery. Free labor lost two of the privileges which appear in the Delphic formula of manumission as basic to the idea of freedom—the capacity of working as they wished (similar to the modern idea of the right of contract) and that of moving about as they desired.

These deprivations affecting the functioning of labor in the society of the time can be stated in the more generalized social and economic terms of a long development. A fundamental *credo* of Greek and Roman polity had been the inheritance of political status, as citizen or non-citizen, through birth. The *Constitutio Antoniniana* of A. D. 212 had spread citizenship privileges over the world of the Mediterranean to the thinness of a veneer which, in the first two centuries of the Empire, had gradually lost its glitter and its civic meaning. The fundamental idea of inheritance of privileges by birth, and its reverse—the deprivation of them by a less fortunate birth—had now moved over from the political sphere to cover the field of the economic functions of the subjects of the Empire. In this application to the laboring personnel of the time the status of the father was still dominant, as it had originally been in the field of polity status.

---

[50] Berger, *ibid.*; Just., *Codex* 7: 4, 14, 2: *In ambiguis sensibus melius est, et maxime in libertate, favore eius humaniorem amplecti sententiam.*

[51] Theod., *Leges novellae* (*Anthemius*) 1: 1, edited by Paul M. Meyer.

[52] *Ibid.* 1: 2.

[53] Just., *Codex* 1: 4, 24: *nemini licere volumus — — — eum puerum in suum dominum vindicare sive nomine dominii sive adscripticiae sive colonariae condicionis.*

[54] Just., *Digest* 1: 5, 19 (Celsus). *Cf.* Marcianus in *Digest* 1: 5, 5, 2, and Ulpian, *ibid.*, 24.

[55] Francesco De Robertis in his *Diritto associativo Romano dai collegi della republica alle corporazioni del basso impero*, 434-441, Bari, Laterza and Sons, 1938, has emphasized the inheritance of economic function in the *collegia* through the father.

The regression of slavery as well as the loosening of the complete control over slaves which was once vested in their owners may be observed in several aspects of the changed relations between the masters and the human property which belonged to them. Noteworthy in this respect is the repeal of the *Senatus Consultum Claudianum* by an enactment of Justinian which falls in the years 531-534. The senatorial decree thus repealed had been passed under Claudius in A. D. 52. It had provided that a woman of the rank of Roman citizeness might live with a slave belonging to some other person, if the slave's owner consented. With that consent the Roman woman was to remain free; but any children resulting from the union were to be non-free and the property of the owner of the slave.[56] Tacitus gives the gist of the law, emphasizing the negative aspect of it, that if the owner of the slave had not been apprised of the liaison and had not come to an agreement with the woman concerned, she herself would lose her freedom [57] and her property.[58] Though repealed under Hadrian it was shortly thereafter re-enacted. In the fourth century this law governing unions of free women with slaves was extended, both in its permissive and in its punitive aspects, quite beyond its application to women of Roman citizen classification so as to include any free women.[59] Although subjected to these changes the senatorial decree of the first century had stood for almost five hundred years as the basic rule of guidance in respect to unions of free women and male slaves.

By the repeal of the *Senatus Consultum Claudianum* under Justinian it became permissible that marital relations might be established, for any reason at all, by a free woman with a slave, with a freedman, or with a registered land tenant (an *adscripticius*). Even if the woman, according to the wording of the act of repeal, in making her union had been motivated solely by physical desire her action no longer was to threaten any deterioration in her status.[60] The reasons assigned for the repeal of the enactment are two. The first is the devotion of Justinian to the idea of the liberty of his subjects. The second is the feeling that it would be unworthy of that age if the relatives of the woman concerned, who might well be prominent persons, should be disgraced indirectly by her degradation to slavery under the provisions of the old *SC Claudianum*. This justification of the act of repeal reveals not the slightest trace of Christian influence or Christian sentiment.

At the end of the opinion a limitation is placed upon these mixed unions which has its importance in the study of the elimination of social disparities between the slave class and the *coloni*. It provides that if a union of this type, now recognized as legal, should have been brought about by the conniving of the slave or of the registered tenant in the case—which was particularly to be feared in the case of the *adscripticii* [61]—the overlord was empowered both to chastise the culprit and to break off his association with the woman concerned in the alliance. The merging of the slave element toward a parity of treatment with the registered tenant group becomes evident, both in the application to both classes of the constitution upon cohabitation with free women and in the right of the *dominus* to punish members of either group in the same way and to dissolve the mixed unions in either case.

It is in Egypt, through the papyri, that case records appear which illustrate this trend toward similarity of treatment and toward the sloughing off of the sharp distinctions which had separated the *collegiati* and the *coloni*, bound by the state regulations, from the slave class. A striking instance of the disappearance of the clear lines of separation is presented in a document which is to be dated a short time before the repeal of the *Senatus Consultum Claudianum*.[62] Legally the instrument is probative only. It alleges that a certain woman named Martha, who had herself stated that she was a slave, was, in fact, a free woman. In a few particulars the circumstances remain uncertain; but the general situation is quite clear.

This Martha, who stood in some relation of dependency upon the writer of the document, had made a statement, in the hearing of the writer, that she was not a free woman, but a slave. This she had done in connection with a difficulty, which is not explained, about a sum of money belonging to her. Her patron, the deponent, was shocked by her assertion of her slave status. In refutation of it he recited the history of her family, including her sisters, through her parents and back to her grandparents. He presented his conviction of her free status so that this Martha might not, at a later time, be oppressed by anyone as a slave: " And at no time have I ever found any indication [in the attitude] of my father or of anyone else, nor have I found any agreement, [showing] that they [the parents and grandparents of the woman Martha] had become slaves under any kind of legal title whatsoever." [63]

It is because of the vagueness of the lines which separated freedom from slavery that we find, in a Christian

---

[56] Gaius, *Institutes* 1 : 84.

[57] Tacitus, *Annals* 12 : 53.

[58] Just., *Institutes* 3 : 12, 1.

[59] Theod., *Codex* 4 : 12, 1. *Cf. ibid.* 4 : 12, 6 : " if in the estimation of a lustful woman her concupiscence is of more importance than her freedom, she is made a slave, not by war or by purchase, but by cohabitation, so that her children shall be subject to the yoke of slavery." The translation is that of Pharr, *The Theodosian code*, p. 93.

[60] Just., *Codex*, 7 : 24, *De senatus consulto Claudiano tollendo*.

[61] *Ibid.: quod maxime in adscripticios verendum est.*

[62] *Catalogue général des antiquités égyptiennes* 9 (1), *Papyrus grecs d'époque byzantines* (= P. Cairo Cat.), no. 67089, with a duplicate copy, *ibid.* 9 (3), no. 67294. The document has been admirably presented and evaluated for its legal and social implications by Wenger, Ein Christliches Freiheitszeugnis, in *Beiträge zur Geschichte des christlichen Altertums* (*Festgabe Albert Ehrhard*), 451-478, Bonn, Schroeder, 1922. The probable dating and the connection with the *SC Claudianum* are discussed by Wenger, pp. 464-466.

[63] *P. Cairo Cat.*, 19 (1), no. 67089, 5-8.

deed of surety of A. D. 551, that the son of a deacon living upon an Oxyrhynchus estate is said to have served the estate " in the capacity of a free slave." [64] The same difficulty of distinguishing slave from free in the terminology employed is shown in a contract for household services of the year 569 entered into in Antinoopolis in middle Egypt. A man who is definitely designated by his surety as possessing his freedom [65] made a contract to act in domestic service of some kind, possibly as a house manager, in the home of a resident of the city who was a personage of some importance, as we must assume. Despite his free status, made more certain by his right of contract, the man who let out his services speaks of himself thus : " I, the above mentioned Colluthus, son of Victor, family slave ' boy ' in fixed service, hereby agree, etc." [66]

In the case of the woman, Martha, discussed in the second paragraph above, it is not a matter of consequence whether her assertion that she was not free was motivated by guile, by fear, by ignorance of her rights, or by indifference. In any case the claim itself, which apparently had no documentary or other support, attests the beclouded state of the boundary which, at that time, separated slavery from free status.[67] In fact, the case of Sophia, a cousin of this Martha, again attests the vagueness of the lines of status which then prevailed. Although she was apparently as free as the woman

Martha, Sophia and her children had been " dragged into slavery " ; and those who did this injustice would know what it was to come before the bar of justice of a Mightier Power,[68] as the Christian deponent of this protest piously declared.

In the period of Arab control the treatment of the government workers, who were legally still free, took on the aspect of a grim brutality. In the eighth century some caulkers had taken to flight who had been working upon ships which were being constructed at Babylon on the Canal of Trajan which connected the Nile in the Delta with the northern end of the Red Sea. Orders were sent out that they were to be confined in wooden fetters and thus returned to the place of their work assignment. From A. D. 710, presumably, we have a letter ordering the use of these same fetters upon fugitives from the Arsinoite nome, probably peasants, who were thus to be returned to their own places of residence.[69] This was requisitioned labor, with payment for the services rendered; but there was no choice left to one who was levied for a task.[70] Any attempt to escape was treated as desertion.

---

[64] *P. Oxy.* 19: 1348, 11: καὶ πρὸ τούτου παραμένοντα αὐτῇ ἐν τάξει δουλελευθέρου.

[65] Preisigke, Friedr., *Greich. Papyrus ---- zu Strassburg (P. Strass.),* no. 40, line 29: καὶ τῆς αὐτοῦ ἐλευθερίας.

[66] *Ibid.,* lines 23-24: φαμιλιάριος ἑδραῖος κατάδουλος παῖς.

[67] Leopold Wenger, *Festgabe Ehrhard,* 463 and 466, has shown the looseness of these relations.

[68] *P. Cairo Cat.* 9 (1), 67089, 11-13. *P. Cairo Cat.* 9 (1), 67023 of A. D. 569 is a characteristic example from the sixth century of bondage for debt. Members of the family of debtors could be handed over as sureties for payment. Where the area of separation between liberty and enslavement was so vaguely defined and self-sale was legally permissible, the outlook for many of such free children, when given over as pledges for debt, must often have been enslavement.

[69] *PSI* 12 (1), no. 1266. Again consult H. Idris Bell in *Greek Papyri in the British Museum (P. Lond.)* 4: 1384, 26-28, and Index 7, under καλαφάτης.

[70] See Bell's introduction to *P. Lond* 4: xxxi, xxxii.

XXIII. UPON SLAVERY AND CHRISTIANITY

The following homely and convincing description is given in the gospel of John of the scene in the room and of the persons present when Jesus of Nazareth was taken before the High Priest in Jerusalem to be questioned. Among those present was Peter. " The slaves and the attendants had made a charcoal fire and stood close to it, warming themselves because it was cold. And Peter, also, was there standing among them, warming himself." [1]

Just as simple and just as true is the picture which is drawn for us of the time when Jesus went to see the sick slave of a Roman centurion at Capernaum. The centurion apologized for his presumption in asking Jesus to come to his house. He explained that he was a captain of a military company, and as such accustomed to give orders to soldiers—when they were to come and where they were to go; and they came and went,

he said, as he bade them. " Also to my slave [I say] ' do this,' and he does it." [2]

To the Apostle Paul slavery and freedom were facts of everyday life which were to be accepted and which could be expressed in simple terms and grasped readily by simple people. His letter to the Galatians is addressed to a group located rather remotely from the great highways of traffic. In it he wrote:

For, as many of you as have been baptized into [union with] Christ have clothed yourselves in Christ. There is no

---

[1] *NT,* John, 18, 18.

[2] *NT,* Matthew, 8, 9; Luke, 7, 8. It may here be noted that the orders to the slave correspond to the third of the four freedoms of the free man which the slave lacks, according to the Delphic manumissions by sale to the god Apollo, to wit, the right to work at what he wished to do. It is expressed, for example, in *GDI* 2, no. 1766, of 174-173 B. C., in these words that, after the trust sale to the god, the freedman is at liberty to do whatever he wishes: ὥστε ἐλεύθερον ὄντα ---- ποιοῦντα ὅ κα θέλῃ. See above, chap. 5 (no. 53-68), and in chap. 6, *passim.*

place for Jew or Greek, nor is there place for slave or free—And I say that [in the matter of a legacy] so long as the heir is a minor, though he be lord of all [the inheritance], he differs not at all from a slave; but he is under guardians and house managers.—So also, we when we were minors were enslaved under the principles which guide the world order set for us. But when the fulness of time came God sent his Son, born of a woman and subject to law, that he might buy us out [of enslavement] under the law so that we might receive adoption as his sons.—No longer, then, are you a slave, but a son; and if you are a son, you are an heir of God through Christ.—Look, then, brother; we are not children of the slave girl, but of the free woman.[3] Stand fast, therefore, for the freedom for which Christ has liberated us and be not again held in the yoke of slavery.[4]

What Paul had done for slavery as it applied to Christian believers was to accept it as a physical fact, but to spiritualize that acceptance so that it became almost, if not fully, meaningless for those who were imbued with his own fervent conviction that Jesus of Nazareth was the ordained Savior of mankind.

In simple analogues and pictures such as these, drawn out of the life of their time by the apostles and Paul, slaves move in and out of the pages of the New Testament, appearing quite casually in the midst of free laborers and servants of the local Palestine area and the general East Mediterranean scene. There is little evidence of antagonism to the system itself which produced them.[5] Apparently without any concern about the matter, certainly without arousing the hostility of the pagan world of the time for doing so, the early Christians admitted slaves into their midst as readily as free persons. The numbers of slaves to be found in any group of converts would presumably approximate the proportion of slaves to free which existed in the particular town or city of each Christian congregation. This is necessarily an opinion only; but the rationalization is, at least, a sensible one.

With certainty we may accept the statement of Adolf Harnack that it is false to ascribe to the early Church any consciousness of a " slave problem." [6] It would be self-deception if one failed to see that Jesus of Naza-reth,[7] the apostles and the Church, both in its formative period and in its later development, accepted the going system of labor of its time, including the slave structure, without hesitation or any expressed reluctance. It was there, and they took it. It did not occur to the early Christians to attempt to justify or even explain the slave institution. There is in the New Testament no expression of that cold social logic characteristic of a Greek philosopher like Aristotle which demanded a description of the system and a consideration of its place in the economic world of the time. Nor does one find anything of the frigid sympathy towards slaves characteristic of the Stoic Seneca with his advice that, after all, they were men with the same teeth as other human beings and that they should be treated as men. To the early Christians like Paul slaves were human personalities, not economic tools and not " things "—not *res* as in Roman law—but men and women with souls which would be saved if they could be convinced of Christ. Against this one must put the fact, made quite certain by Paul's letter to Philemon about the slave convert, Onesimus, that early Christianity did not object to the ownership of Christians as slaves by their own brethren. This lack of concern about the enslavement of fellow Christians continued into the second century.[8] It is a direct corollary of the doctrine that enslavement was spiritually meaningless under the all-embracing hope of salvation.

In the long range of the history of slavery in antiquity many divergences of detail, and sometimes of basic principle, had developed among different peoples of the pre-Christian world in the treatment of slaves, in the uses to which they were put, and in the number and kind of the privileges which were permitted them. One of the dominant legal and social attitudes had been to refuse them the privileges of group association and organization which were regarded as among the rights customarily permitted to men of free birth.[9] By the complete break with this tradition which was advocated by the early congregations the accepted social distinctions of legal status ceased to exist in their communities

---

[3] The allegory refers to Galatians, 4, 22-26. Of the two sons of Abraham one was born of a slave girl, the other of a free woman. The Hebrews had been children of God; but being born of the slave woman they were slaves under the covenant of Mt. Sinai. Those now converted, though of Hebrew faith, had been freed by the sacrifice of Christ.

[4] These extracts are translated from Galatians, 3, 27 to 5, 1.

[5] Further examples of this simple acceptance of slavery are given in Steinmann, Alphons, *Sklavenlos und alte Kirche,* 66-67, München-Gladbach, Volksvereins Verlag, 1922. Martin Luther's mistake in translating the Greek word *doulos* as " *Knecht* " became ossified in the tradition of the modern renditions and caused modern confusion about slavery as it existed in the world of New Testament times, as Adolf Deissmann has shown in *Licht vom Osten,* 3rd ed., 240, Tübingen, 1909.

[6] Harnack, Adolf, *Mission und Ausbreitung des Christentums in den ersten drei Jahrhunderten,* 3rd ed., 1 : 174, Leipzig, Hinrichs, 1951 (in the English translation, *Expansion of Christianity* 1 : 207, New York, Putnams, 1904).

[7] P. R. Coleman-Norton has recently presented the correct view that Jesus made no move toward the abolition of slavery as an institution. See his article upon the Apostle Paul and the Roman law of slavery in *Studies in Roman economic and social history,* 158-159, Princeton Univ. Press, 1951. He has, however, read considerably more than is warranted into this simple and tender letter of a Roman citizen, Paul, to a provincial, Philemon. It has nothing to do with the *Lex Fabia* or with the Roman law of slavery as Professor Coleman-Norton, *ibid.,* 170 and appendix, 173, suggests that it has. The correct approach to this very simple and purely Christian letter is to be found in Deissmann, Adolf, *Paul,* 19-20, New York, Doran, 1926.

[8] Harnack, Ad., *Expansion of Christianity* 1 : 207, using the *Didachē tōn Apostolōn* (*The Teaching of the Apostles*), 4, 11, which is of the late first century or of the middle period of the second centry according to Oscar von Gebhardt-Adolf Harnack, *Texte und Untersuchungen zur Geschichte der altchristlichen Literatur* 2 (2) : 159.

[9] *Ibid.* 1 : 207.

along with the differences of racial origin and former religious belief. This may be ascribed, in part, to the conviction which they held that the Day of Judgment, and with it the end of the existing world, was not far distant. Whatever the explanation, the fact remains that the Christians freely admitted slaves to baptism and so into their organizations; and this fact is important. A paradox existed between the Christian teaching of sympathy for the poor and wretched and the apathetic attitude toward the slave institution as such. This becomes evident in a statement of Paul in his first letter to the Corinthian congregation.[10] Each believer was to remain in that calling in life in which he had belonged when he accepted the faith. You were converted when a slave? Do not worry about it; but if you have an opportunity to become free, take advantage of it.[11]

From Egypt in the second Christian century we have advice upon the relations which should prevail between Christian masters and their slaves of the same faith. It shows that Christian assent to the system still persisted, presumably still to be explained by indifference to it.

Do not give orders to your slaves in bitterness, whether they be male or female who place their hope in the same God. . . . He has not come to summon us according to personal distinction. He comes to those in whom the spirit has been prepared. And you, slaves, do you give obedience in modesty and fear to your master as to one patterned after God.[12]

These admonitions upon master and slave relations may safely be generalized to apply to all the Christian communities of that time.

So long as the Christian communities were unconcerned about the underlying justice and injustice of enslavement as a part of the labor system it was impossible for Christian doctrine to conceive the idea of its abandonment, much less to formulate a plan to that end. A contradiction was thus established, which continued for many centuries, between Christian acceptance of slavery and its tenet of the equality of all in the sight of God. Anti-Christian writers had been conscious of the paradox between Christian ownership of slaves and their tenet of the equality of all who accepted Jesus as the Anointed One. Also the pagan polemic denied that their Christian claim to an egalitarian attitude was justified which the converted based upon the liberality of their membership practice and upon the treatment of their slaves by Christian slave owners.[13] It was, in fact,

an epistolary custom of the time, as the pagan opponents rightly pointed out, for correspondents who were totally unrelated to address one another as " brother " (adelphos). Pagans of the laboring classes could, also, point out, quite correctly, that fellow members of their funerary and social guilds often spoke of each other as " brothers ";[14] and they could assert just as truly that this usage was to them something more than a polite affectation.[15]

Despite these counterclaims one may still believe that in the early days of Christianity the feeling of brotherhood among the members of their congregations of believers was especially deep and effective in their group relations. The very denial of this in the anti-Christian polemic of the second and third centuries may be construed by us as proof, rather than as disproof, of its actuality.

The first three centuries cover the period of the popular hostility toward the Christians and that of their own dread of the spasmodic prosecutions set on foot by imperial decrees—carried out in the various provinces or not put into effect according to the religious zeal or the desire for uniformity which moved the particular governors there appointed. So long as the Christian communities were closely united by the fires of their danger all of the communicants felt themselves equal in the sight of God. In this period slavery or freedom remained unimportant considerations. So long as this was true, condemnation of slavery could not easily arise as a part of Christian doctrine.

In the fourth century the new faith passed rapidly through the stage of equality of tolerance with its older religious competitors into a position, in the fifth and sixth centuries, of being the favored hieratic system of the Empire. It was in this process that the problems of adaptation to the old currents of life arose before the Church, along with the responsibilities which, as a great institutional organization, it had to assume in behalf of its members. From the papyri found in Egypt we have received fresh evidence of the nature and the methods of its assimilation, or its adaptation, of old religious ceremonials and of magical and devotional practices long and deeply imbedded in the life of that province.[16]

An example of the change in Christian thought respecting slavery brought about by the necessities of

[10] Coleman-Norton in *Studies in Roman economic and social history*, 171.

[11] *NT*, First Corinthians, 7, 20-24; Westermann, The freedmen and the slaves of God, *Proc. Amer. Philos. Soc.* 92: 16, 1948.

[12] From *The Teaching of the Apostles* (Didachē tōn Apostolōn), chap. 4, 11, in Gebhardt-Harnack, *Texte und Untersuchungen* 2: 1 .

[13] Some of their arguments are repeated by Lactantius, *Institutiones divinae* 5: 10: " Someone will say: ' Among you are not some paupers, others rich—some slaves, others masters? ' " The answer given by Lactantius runs something like this: we are

all equals, free and slaves, rich and poor in humility of spirit; but before God we are divided on the basis of character.

[14] Ziebarth, Erich, *Das griechische Vereinswesen*, 100, Leipzig, Hirzel, 1896; Waltzing, *Les corporations professionelles* 1: 329-330.

[15] Waltzing, *Les corporations* 1: 331.

[16] Some of the documentary evidence upon the early spread of Christianity in Egypt will be found in Ghedini, Giuseppe, *Lettere Cristiane*, Milan, Vita e Pensiero, 1923.

H. Idris Bell has discussed the evidences of Christianity in Egypt in *Harvard Theol. Rev.* 37: 185-204, 1944. B. R. Rees presents a fresh approach to the transition to Christianity in Egypt in *Jour. Egypt. Arch.* 36: 86-100, 1950.

adaptation is indirectly illustrated by a potsherd upon which a narrative is written of the baptism of Jesus by John the Baptist. The ostracon presumably came from a monastery in Upper Egypt and has been dated as of the sixth century by two well-equipped papyrologists, Sir Harold I. Bell and Wilhelm Schubart. In the main the story of the baptism follows the account found in the gospel of Matthew; [17] but it has one addition to the words of John which is of interest for the change in the Christian attitude toward slavery. John protested, in this version, that *he* should be baptized by Jesus, not the reverse. " Shall the master be under his slave, the shepherd under his sheep? How shall the Creator be under his Creator? " [18] The inferiority of the slave to his master which is here implied is in marked contrast to the early Christian doctrine that there was no difference between them. In the theory of the early communities of the first half of the third century they were equals. This is shown in a discussion of the baptism of Jesus written by Hippolytus, presbyter and schismatic Bishop of Rome. In his narrative of the baptism all of the rhetorical trappings of the baptismal story as it appears in the ostracon are present—the sheep and the shepherd, the Creator of all things, and the slave.[19]

The change in the Christian attitude towards slavery indicated by these divergent narratives of the baptism contrasts sharply with the equalization movement affecting the relative positions of free and slave labor which has been emphasized as characteristic of the post-Diocletian era. It does not conform, in fact, with the general trend of the time as shown both by the civil legislation and by the Church canons which tended prevailingly toward an amelioration of slave conditions. Modern attempts of the past two centuries to resolve the tangled skein of the enactments upon slavery in the period from Diocletian to Justinian have generally been based upon the conviction that the Christian religion, openly at the outset, always unequivocally by virtue of its equalitarian position as universal religion, must, in the end, inevitably have destroyed the slave institution. The line followed by the earlier modern writers who dealt with the Roman imperial experience with enslavement was either charted for them by their devotion to the abolitionist movement itself or, thereafter, they were still tossed about in the turbulent wake of its emotional appeal.

In the group of studies directed by antislavery fervor falls a brochure of the Abbé Thérou. He ascribed to

Christianity a compelling enthusiasm, displayed in intangible efforts to maintain the idea of equality in its membership, which discredited the entire concept of human enslavement. The whole slave structure would have collapsed, in his opinion, had not the barbarian invasions come to retard its fall.[20] Under the same cover with this essay appeared a treatise which was similar in tone, of a noted German professor of Theology, Johann Adam Moehler. Moehler ascribed the origin of slavery to the fall of man, the development of its gentler aspects in the post-Diocletian era to the powerful ethical force inherent in the Christian religion. The love of Christ for mankind, in Moehler's view, broke the chains of enslavement which brother had imposed upon brother.[21]

A book written by Charles Schmidt about a decade later displayed an unusual balance, for its time, in the place which it assigned to pagan thought upon slavery. Nevertheless, Schmidt arrived at substantially the same conclusion as his predecessors. For him it was " the mysterious and gentle breath of the evangelical ideas" of Christianity which caused the change in the public attitude toward slavery.[22] For the Comte de Champagny it was the slave system and pagan immorality which, in their combination, ruined the health of the Roman Empire. Only the flame of Christianity could bring to completion a progress which the Christian faith alone could inspire.[23]

Two of the French studies of ancient slavery call for especial consideration because of their enduring influence upon the subject. The first is the three volume work of Henri Wallon.[24] Although it has left a deep impression upon the entire development of the modern study of ancient slavery among the Greeks and Romans its influence in establishing the modern religious-moralistic assessment of the ancient institution has probably been the most harmful and the least challenged. The second French study of permanent authority, that of M. Paul Allard, confined itself to the investigation of the structure and the ideas of the slave system as it was affected by the Christian practice of it and Christian teaching.[25] Of the two the work of Wallon was the more strongly oriented by the abolitionist prejudices of the time of his first edition, that of Allard the more biased in laying emphasis upon the services rendered by the teaching of Christianity toward the amelioration of slave conditions in the later Roman Empire. Both writers maintained that the decline in slave numbers

[17] Matthew, 3, 13-17. *Cf.* Mark, 1, 9-11; Luke, 3, 21.
[18] Turner, Eric G., Catalogue of Greek and Latin papyri and ostraca in the possession of the University of Aberdeen, *Aberdeen Univ. Studies* 110, no. 3, Aberdeen Univ. Press, 1939. The use of the genitive with the meaning " under the orders of " appears already in the Ptolemaic papyri according to Mayser, Edwin, *Grammatik der griechischen Papyri* 2 (2): 511-512, Berlin, De Gruyter, 1934.
[19] Hippolytus, εἰς τὰ ἅγια θεοφάνεια, Achelis, Hans (editor), in *Die griechischen christlichen Schriftsteller der ersten drei Jahrhunderte* 1 (2nd part), 258, Leipzig, Hinrichs, 1897.

[20] Thérou, l'Abbé, *Le Christianisme et l'esclavage*, 33, Paris, Langlois et Leclercq, 1941.
[21] Moehler, J. H., *De l'abolition de l'esclavage, ibid.*, 223. The essay is known to me only in its French form as published together with that of l'Abbé Thérou cited in the previous note.
[22] Schmidt, Charles, *Essai sur la société civile dans le monde romain*, 431, 439-449, Paris, Hachette, 1853.
[23] De Champagny, Francois Joseph, *Les Antonins* 3: 285, 308, Paris, Bray, 1863.
[24] Wallon, H., *L'esclavage dans l'antiquité*, 2nd ed., in volume 3.
[25] Allard, Paul, *Les esclaves Chrétiens*, 6th ed., Paris, Lecoffre, 1914.

resulted from the exhortations to manumit their slaves addressed to their Christian followers by the clergy.

Despite the wider sweep and control of slave history which he had Wallon was, nevertheless, a strong advocate of the moral force which Christianity exercised for the betterment of social conditions of the later period. In his view the eventual realization of the work of universal emancipation was reserved for Christianity because that cause found its sanction in the sacred law, which the conscience of mankind obeys.[26] This conviction of Wallon brought in its train a number of misconceptions. Among these one must include his belief that Christianity was conscious of its purpose of bringing about the end of usury and clear as to the methods to be employed to attain that end; and that, in condemning usury, it closed one important source of slave recruitment, namely that through debt.[27] A similar error, strangely illogical in a scholar who had intensively studied the ancient evidence upon slavery, was adopted from Wallon by Paul Allard. This is Wallon's assertion that the command given to the early Christians by their leaders that they should sell their possessions and give the money to the poor implied that they were to manumit their slaves.[28] Certainly if their slaves had been intended in the injunction that they sell their properties and if they had followed this advice, the Christians would merely have confirmed the slave status of their own dependents by transferring them to another owner. If they had manumitted them by acceptance of a redemption price from their slaves they would have merely been robbing a poor slave Peter to pay an equally poor Paul of free status.

An improbable deduction arising from the theological approach to Christianity and slavery has been accepted by Paul Allard in connection with the epistle of Saint Paul to Philemon regarding the return to his master of the converted slave Onesimus. It lies in the belief that Paul implored Philemon, the slave owner, and persuaded him indeed, to manumit Onesimus. In fact, Paul requested Philemon merely to take him back forever, not as a slave, but as a brother. This seems to mean nothing more than that Onesimus be welcomed by his master and treated as a fellow Christian—a " brother " in Christ.[29]

A more recent attempt to explain the relation of Christianity to slavery in the late period of the Empire has proceeded from more material considerations of the economic aspects affecting both parties of this equation. Ernest Renan was one of the early exponents of the view that the Christian apologists of the late second and third centuries prepared the way for a reconciliation between the Christian acceptance of slaves and the general rule of pagan society of excluding them from their organization by insisting upon the idea that the interests and the lot of the two elements involved, paganism and Christianity, actually coincided.[30]

An unusually balanced and unbiased presentation of the gradual adjustments between the secular legislation which bettered the lot of the slave class and the movement toward the same end which had its inception in Christian doctrine appeared over a half century ago in a book by the eminent American scholar, Henry C. Lea, which discussed the early Church in several of its relations.[31] Definitely socialist and strongly materialistic in its approach is the work of Ettore Ciccotti in which he dealt with the slave system of the post-Diocletian era as a phenomenon of general decline and sought to explain the reasons for that fact.[32] He has overstressed the hostility of the slave class in the imperial period to their owners, which after all is a latent or active accompaniment of any slave system. In addition, he overemphasized his belief that the depth of this feeling at the time was caused by the devotion of the slave element to paganism. Despite these criticisms Cicotti's work has its own value.

An important contribution to the study of the economic pressures upon Christianity as a determining force in the development of its attitude upon slavery throughout the history of the Roman Empire was published in 1934 by the Dutch legalist, Engbert Jan Jonkers.[33] His conclusion is not to be doubted that other sentiments than that of *caritas* alone (their sensitivity toward the poor and the wretched) played an equal part in establishing the Christian attitude toward enslavement.[34] He presents one interesting suggestion which seems to me to be untenable, that during the first four centuries after Christ the successive measures taken by the Roman imperial government to better the lot of the slave population came to be interpreted by the slaves themselves as a manifestation of weakness on the part of the State. This had the psychological effect, according to Jonkers, of making them conscious of their own

---

[26] Wallon, *L'esclavage* 3 : 295.

[27] *Ibid.* 3 : 365-367. For the refutation of this idea consult Jonkers, E. J., De l'influence du Christianisme sur la législation relative à l'esclavage dans l'antiquité, *Mnemosyne*, 3rd ser., 1 : 267-271, 1934.

[28] Wallon, *L'esclavage* 3 : 7-8 ; Allard, *Esclaves Chrétiens*, 201-202.

[29] The warning of Deissmann, Paul : a study in social, religious history, 19-20, against reading implications into this simple letter is well taken. The problem for Paul was whether Onesimus would be punished if he was sent back to his owner, and if so, how severely. There is a possible vague hint at manumission in the statement that Paul knew that Philemon would do more than Paul asked. The idea is not urged upon the slave-owner—not even suggested clearly.

[30] Renan, Ernest, *The influence of Rome on Christianity*, 187-199, London, Williams and Norgate, 1880.

[31] Lea, Henry C., *Studies in church history*, 540-553, Philadelphia, Henry C. Lea's Sons, 1883.

[32] Cicotti, Ettore, in the German translation, *Untergang der Sklaverei im Altertum*, 202-203, Berlin, Buchh. Vorwärts, 1910 and *Il tramonto della schiavitù*, 392-393, Udine, 1940.

[33] Jonkers, E. J., De l'influence du Christianisme, *Mnemosyne*, 3rd ser., 1 : 241-280, 1934.

[34] *Ibid.*, 260.

power and thus of encouraging them to seek further advantages.[35]

Against this view several factors must be advanced. Among them are: the lack of sufficient evidence in the Christian pagan literature of the time which points to such a consciousness of the slave power on the part of the enslaved; the lack of any slave revolts, such as occurred in the second century B. C., which would have been the probable result of such a feeling; and the continuing ease of manumission. For it is the fluidity of status from enslavement to personal liberty which, above all, in any slave society, eases the tensions of hostility between slave-owners and the enslaved. The equalization of social and economic position between the lower free and the slave group, as presented in the previous chapter, would have seemed a distinct advance, so far as enslavement was concerned, in a society which had so completely, and for so long, adjusted itself to all the implications of combined free-and-slave labor. In my opinion Jonkers' conclusion is questionable that the legislation of the Roman state favorable to slave labor was not influenced by Christian theory, but that it followed primarily, in each instance of its expression, the interests of the State authority.[36] His article lacks the thoughtful balance attained by Henry C. Lea [37] between the spiritual influence of Christian teaching and the practical requirements of the world into which Christianity came and within which it must live. Despite these reservations the study of Jonkers is stimulating. It deserves greater attention than it seems to have received.

In any community which has adopted slave employment as an integral part of its labor organization the harshness of the rules of control imposed upon the enslaved and the resulting bitterness which develops are largely dependent upon two factors. The first is the number and variety of the methods of liberation provided [38] and the ease with which their procedures may be set in motion.[39] The second factor depends upon the spontaneity of the acceptance of former slaves into some group of the free population and the lack of discrimination against these new freedmen which is manifested in the social class within which they are to be assimilated. Proof of this observation is to be found in two outstanding slave structures, both of the latifundian type. In the first of these, the Italian-Sicilian type of plantation-ranch slavery of the late third, the second and first centuries B. C., manumission was not made easy for the agricultural slaves. The second of these two systems was that which was to be found in the southern tier, that is, the slaveholding states, in the North American Union. The legislation and the public attitude in these states created social and legal barriers against the freed Negroes which made extremely difficult any acceptance of them as equal, or even reputable, members of mixed communities of white- and dark-skinned subjects.[40]

In the years 311 and 313 after Christ the Christian religion was granted tolerance by the Roman state and was received among the worships legally permissible for subjects of the Empire. By edicts promulgated by Constantine I in the years 316 and 323 the Christian communities were authorized to manumit slaves in their churches.[41] The procedure followed received the official title of *manumissio in ecclesia*. In origin it probably goes back to the Greek method of manumission by herald's call, for in the Greek polities it had taken place before the popular assemblies just as the Church manumission was now carried out before the congregations.[42] The procedure followed was simple. Members of the clergy were even permitted to free their own slaves by a mere declaration of that intention without the customary requirement of witnesses or of written documents.[43]

It has been suggested that the grant of the rights to manumit *in ecclesia*, as given by the State and accepted by the Church, was symbolic of an ideological rejection of the entire slave system or that it was an unexpressed protest of Christianity against an institution which was inherently contrary to the humane doctrines which it represented. Quite the opposite seems to be true. Manumission in the Church furnishes another proof, if that were needed, of the complete adoption of the institution of slavery with all of its mundane formulas and practices. Nor should the fact of liberation in the Church be ascribed to a greater feeling of concern on

[35] *Ibid.*, 242-244.

[36] *Ibid.*, 280.

[37] Lea, Henry C., *Studies in church history*, 540-549.

[38] Grupp, George, *Kulturgeschichte der römischen Kaiserzeit* 1: 277, Munich, Allgemeine Verlagsgesellschaft, 1903-1904, maintains in respect to manumission that it represents an ever-present protest against the intrinsic folly of enslavement. This is no more true than it would be true to describe a pension arrangement as a proof of the injustice of the contract and wage system or a door as a symbol of, or a protest against, the architecture of a house.

[39] Charles Verlinden, in *Anuario del Historia del Derecho Español* 11, places too much weight upon the sources of slave recruitment in contrast to his neglect of the procedures of manumission to the point that it becomes a major weakness in his entire discussion of the transition from slavery to serfdom in Spain. The slaves had always before them a possible exit from the regulations under which they lived. For the *coloni adscripticii* of the Empire there was no similar legal outlet from their status.

[40] Olmstead, Frederick L., *The cotton kingdom* 1: 307-308, New York, Mason Bros., 1861. For the laws prohibiting intermarriage of Negroes with whites see Hurd, John C., *Law of freedom and bondage in the United States* 2, index under " Negro, marriage with white," Boston, Little Brown, 1862.

[41] Just., *Codex* 1: 13, 1; Lea, *Studies in church history*, 542-543. For an elaborate discussion of the edicts of Constantine see Mor, Carlo Guido, *Rivista di storia del diritto Romano* 1: 87-108, 1928. A brief, but clear, statement will be found in Jonkers' article in *Mnemosyne*, 3rd ser., 1: 265.

[42] Partsch, Josef, Mitteilungen aus der Freiburger Papyrussammlung, *Sitzungsberichte der Heidelberger Akad. der Wissensch.* 7, Abh. 10: 44, 1916.

[43] Just., *Codex* 1: 13, 2; Theod., *Codex* 4: 7, 1.

the part of the Christians for the unfree than that which the pagan Greek cults had shown before them in their temple manumissions by entrusted sale to a god or by consecration of a slave to one of their deities. Further, it is not warranted to suppose that any noteworthy increase in the volume of manumissions followed because of the practice of Church manumission. For the three long-established processes of granting freedom were, of course, always available to the Christians if they wished to set their slaves free, just as they were to non-Christian subjects of the state. These were the grant of freedom by testament,[44] the *manumissio* by trial with a predetermined outcome, and the form of liberation called the *manumissio inter amicos*. In fact the method of manumission *in ecclesia* seems to have spread slowly after Constantine's reign. It was not obtained in the province of Africa, for example, until A. D. 401.[45] Why this was so we do not know; but knowledge of the fact does not suggest either a widespread use of the right by the Church or even a deep interest in it.

In the attainment of the right of asylum as it applied to the oppressed or to fugitive slaves the Church was either not so insistent upon parity with the old pagan temples or was less fortunate in exercising its insistence than in the case of manumission in the churches. For it was not until the fifth century that the custom becomes noticeable, in the sources we now have, that slaves sought sanctuary at the altars or in the church precincts. It was not until A. D. 399 that a Carthaginian synod decided to send two bishops on a mission to the Emperor Honorius to obtain a decree which would protect anyone, whatever the charge against him might be, from being dragged away from a church if he had there sought asylum.[46] In the fifth century Schenute of Atripe, a militant Patriarch in Upper Egypt, was granting protection to slaves in the White Monastery in the Thebaid by receiving them within the walls and under the regulations of its organization.[47]

As with the free suppliants for protection it may be assumed in the case of the slaves that the pressures of bad economic conditions, rather than the depths of their devotion to the faith often motivated their desire to accept the monastic regime.[48] Whatever be the causes among the slaves for seeking Church asylum, the grant of the right to accept them into the monastic life assumes

a special importance because it seems to have been gained against the opposition of the State. For we know of four enactments of the imperial Government, passed during the period A. D. 398 to the death of Justinian, forbidding this right to the Church or restricting it. The first of these was passed in 398 when the eunuch, Eutropius, was minister of state at Constantinople. The fourth, promulgated under Justinian, denied the right of asylum to the churches and monasteries, but only in its application to the protection of slaves.[49] The reason for this special restriction is not clear; but similar restrictive laws with reference to them appear in Justinian's reign. The attitude toward the enslaved element which had been traditional in the first three centuries of the Empire, which had regarded them as property (*res*) only, seems to have re-established itself, after a long period of reversal, under Justinian.[50] The injunction that enslaved persons must be well treated was pragmatically based upon the consideration that the slave population, considered as labor, still constituted a valuable asset to the State.[51]

However varied the reasons may be which have been assigned by modern scholars for the declarations upon slaves and slavery by the ante-Nicene Fathers and the enactments of the post-Nicene canons regarding them, upon one point there has been no reasonable disagreement. Even in the first three centuries of its spread, much more so in the following post-Nicene period, Christianity made changes and adjustments affecting its pristine teaching upon slavery which brought its attitude and practice into a nearer conformity with the conditions of the world about it. The recent materialistic inclination of scholarly opinion upon the early Christians and the Church in the post-Nicene period has been useful as a corrective to the previous dominance of the theological-abolitionist view; but the new determinism carried its advocates too far.

In the past two decades support has come from an unexpected source for the older point of view that Christianity exercised a powerful influence upon the direction taken by the thought of the Roman Empire upon slavery as it displayed itself in civil legislation enacted in the post-Diocletian era. The reaction toward the older belief, that of a strong influence exercised by Christianity, has come from scholars who have devoted their abilities to a new interpretation of the Roman law. Among them one finds an unobtrusive, but firm, insistence upon the influence of Christian doctrine upon later Roman legislation affecting the institutions of the time

---

[44] The freeing of slaves in the wills of Christians in Egypt is attested by Groningen Papyrus no. 10 (of the fourth century judging by the script), published by Roos, A. G., Papyri Groninganae, *Verhandelingen der Akademie te Amsterdam* 32, no. 4, 21-31, 1933, and in *P. Cairo Maspero* 3, no. 6731, lines 99-104, of A. D. 567, Maspero, Jean, *Catalogue général du Musée du Caire*, 1916.

[45] Lea, Henry C., *Studies in church history*, 543.

[46] Mansi, Giovane D., *Sacrorum conciliorum collectio* 3, col. 752, Florence, 1759.

[47] Leipoldt, Johannes, Schenute von Atripe, in Gebhardt, Oscar von, and Adolf Harnack, *Texte und Untersuchungen zur Geschichte der altchristlichen literatur*, **25** (n. f. 10) : 1, 1904.

[48] *Ibid.* 11 : 1.

[49] Just., *Codex* 1 : 12, 4, 6 for the churches; *Novellae* 5 : 2, for the monasteries. Woess, Friedr. von, Das Asylwesens Ägyptens, *Münchener Beiträge zur Papyrusforschung und Rechtsgeschichte* 3 : 229-236, Munich, Beck, 1923.

[50] Just., *Digest* 48 : 18; *Codex* 9 : 41, 18. See Jonkers, *Mnemosyne*, 3rd ser., 1 : 290.

[51] Just., *Institutes* 1 : 8, 2 : *expedit enim rei publicae ne quis re sua male utatur.* Jonkers, *Mnemosyne*, 1 : 280, rightly states that this civil legislation was passed in response to the needs of the time, not because of any Christian connection.

in which the Church was directly, and necessarily, interested. These include the family organization, the law of property, slavery, and other matters remote from ritualistic and theological preoccupations.[52] An example of the direct influence of Christianity upon Roman civic legislation is to be recognized in the abolition, under Constantine I, of punishment by crucifixion. This enactment, as Ernst Levy has plausibly pointed out, is to be ascribed to the Christian abhorrence of its use evoked by the memory of the crucifixion of Jesus of Nazareth.[53] A later constitution, passed under Justinian in A. D. 529, may also be directly attributed to the influence of the Church. It provided that exposed male children who had been picked up and reared by anyone were not to be assigned to them in slave status. The detection of such cases, presumably also the obligation of bringing about enforcement of the law, was committed " not only to the governors of the provinces, but also to the most holy bishops." [54]

An unexpressed feeling of malaise about the institution of slavery was neither new to Christianity in antiquity nor peculiarly the result of its teachings. In the history of the system of slave labor, from the time of the earliest written records of man's experience with it, a certain discomfort about it can be detected in the applied or suggested restrictions which were imposed upon its operation. In the pre-Greek world, particularly in the areas of the Semitic cultures, a realization of the incompatibility of the system with the existing standards of social morals expressed itself vaguely in the compromises imposed upon it. In the Semitic world these took the form of a tribal-religious restraint upon its application. The members of the " national " group, as determined by the preference shown to his devotees by their special tribal god and by the protection which he afforded them, might fall under a temporary bondage to their fellow worshippers; but this condition was not slavery. For it was restricted to a fixed term of years and it was not a heritable situation.[55]

It has been maintained throughout this study that the practice of slavery among the Hellenic polities was dominantly of the handicraft and domestic types and was, in consequence, of a relatively mild form. Despite the comparative decency of its application, from the Homeric period onward the passionate adherence of the

Greeks to the desire for political and personal liberty made it difficult for them to find a satisfactory explanation of their own slave organization and its relation to the general social system in which it was involved. In the Homeric epics the day of enslavement was the day of the loss of full manhood. In the fifth century drama the slave was a standard stage type used to incite compassion in the audiences at the religious festivals. Plato's reaction took the form of a mild protest that Greeks should not enslave their fellow Greeks while, as a matter of fact, the Hellenes of his day were using their fellow Hellenes as slaves, and without much compunction about it. Aristotle's explanation of the origin of slavery was rationally based upon the then accepted theory of congenital and heritable differences in human capacities, as displayed both individually and in national totalities. The weak and the inefficient were servile by nature. This might be considered acceptable as a logical consequence of Aristotle's presupposition that acquired characteristics are heritable. His definition of a slave in the *Politics* is not so admirable. *Doulos organon empsychon*—a slave is a tool with a soul. Only in the most superficial and materialistic sense is this true. The slave, as a human being, is not a tool; and a tool has not a soul.

In the early and middle periods of the Stoa its reaction toward slavery was one of social negation. Liberty and enslavement were to the Stoics conditions external to the development of the soul. As such they were to be regarded by the wise man, the philosopher, as factors of no importance since they did not contribute to the Stoic ideal of virtue—*aretē* in the Greek, to which one must ascribe a certain connotation of " efficient character." Since the opposites of freedom and slavery did not affect the attainment of virtue, just as the contraries of wealth and poverty or of sickness and health did not do, so enslavement also was to be regarded as an *adiaphoron*, something neutral and external. The determining factor so far as all of these " indifferences " were concerned, including slave condition, was the use to which they were put. Only the way in which they were met could determine whether they would contribute to the character development of the individual and so to his happiness or unhappiness.[56]

In the formulation of the Christian attitude toward slavery the discussion of it by the Apostle Paul was the determining factor. Fundamentally, Paul's view of the institution did not diverge widely from that of the early and middle Stoic teaching. For those converted to the belief in Christ, free or slave status was not a matter of consequence. But the reason for reaching this similarity of conclusion was completely different. To the Stoic it was an " indifference " because it did not affect the betterment or the deterioration of the soul in its struggle to attain, in this world, the calmness of spirit which was

[52] Koschaker, Paul, *Ztsch. der morgenländische Gesellschaft*, **89** (n. f. **14**) : 31, n. 2, 1935; Riccobono, Salvatore, Cristianesimo e diritto Romano, in *Rivista di Diritto Civile, Scienze Giuridiche* 43 : 46-64, 1935, and in *Atti del Congresso Internazionale di Diritto Romano* 2 : 61-78, 1935; Bruck, Eberhard F., Political ideology, propaganda and public law, *Seminar* 7 : 19, 1949. To these one might add, with recognition of the accuracy of his decisions, the much earlier view of the non-legalist Henry C. Lea, *Studies in church history*, 545-549.

[53] Levy, Ernst, *Ztsch. der Sav.-Stiftung* 49 : 253, 1929.

[54] Just., *Codex* 1 : 4, 24; chapter XXII above, n. 53.

[55] Consult the discussion of the fundamental differences between the pre-Greek approaches to slavery and the Greek in chapter VII, above.

[56] Diogenes Laertius, *Lives of the philosophers, Zeno*, 7, 65 (126-128), gives this as a summation of the views of Zeno, Chrysippus, and Hecato.

to be derived from the practice of goodness for its own sake. To Paul it was only salvation and happiness in the world to come which counted; and this was only to be attained through complete faith in Jesus as the Savior.

In a letter which came to him from the community at Corinth several requests for guidance were presented to Paul to which he wrote specific answers. These were problems of marriage and divorce, the necessity of circumcision for the converts, and whether manumission must be granted to, or sought for, slaves who had embraced the faith. The answers which Paul gave were characterized by a preeminent common sense and were expressed with an admirable clarity. Upon the question of the necessity of liberation of a Christian slave his answer was:

> Regarding the matters of which you wrote me.—The slave who is called in the Lord is a freedman of the Lord. Likewise the free man who is called is the slave of Christ. You have been bought for a price; be not slaves of men. Let each man, brothers, remain beside God in that status in which he was called.[57]

As Aristotle and the Stoics before him, and as so many others since his day, Paul was under the compulsion of finding an explanation for the employment of slave labor in a world formed and controlled by an all-merciful Deity. In the matter of contractual free labor no other explanation was needed or attempted than that man was forced to earn his livelihood, because of Adam's sin, through the sweat of his brow. The slave system, also, was to Paul the result of the offense of Adam, a punishment for the original sin. But through the beneficence of God's sacrifice of Christ for mankind the way of mercy had been clearly designated for those who sought union with God through conversion.[58] To Paul, as to the Stoics, the slave system was a part of the cosmos; but in the Stoic concept it was a manifestation of the Reason which fixed the rules by which the universe was swayed. It is this intellectualized interest in the slave system which dictated the rhetorical, but essentially unemotional approach to the subject displayed by the Roman Stoic, Seneca. To Paul, in each new initiate into the brotherhood of the believers a new self had been created. " Here what matters is not ' Greek ' or ' Jew,' the circumcized or the uncircumcized, barbarian, Scythian, slave, free-born, but Christ is everything and in us all." [59]

With the growing success of Christianity and the increase in its strength and responsibilities an increased sophistication appears in the explanations offered for the acceptance of slavery in practice and its rejection as a determining factor affecting community membership. Even in the latter half of the second century Irenaeus, Bishop of Lyons, displays the need of a more complicated explanation of the contradiction which is imminent in the slave system. For Irenaeus, offerings in the Church are required by divine authority; but he makes a distinction between two types of offering, the " servile " and the " pure " sacrifice. The offering of a slave, which has been made in simplicity of heart and in righteousness, is acceptable to God. True! But the distinction between free and servile offerings had been present in the system since first these were made by Cain and Abel.[60]

After Christianity became a *religio licita* through the enactments of Galerius and Constantine its difficulties in meeting the ambiguities of its own practice of slave-holding and the all-embracing nature of God's mercy, as shown in the acceptance of slaves in the congregations, became more urgent. In the fourth century Gregory of Nyssa emphasized for Christian practice some aspects of the civil legislation of his time which may have been enacted by the state authority under the influence of Christian pressure. However remote this connection may be, he declared that Jews, Samaritans, and newly converted Christians were not to be allowed to own slaves who had been baptized.[61] Saint John Chrysostom, the famous Bishop of Constantinople, ascribed the origin of enslavement to the insatiable greed of man and insisted upon Paul's view that in the Church the social distinction of free and slave did not exist.[62] This must mean that it was not admissible to regard slavery as a part of the spiritual structure of the Church. But he, Chrysostom, had already recognized Christian enslavement by attributing its origin to sin.[63] Elsewhere, also, he shows a confusion of mind regarding slavery. This is particularly noticeable in his involved attempt to explain the paradox of Saint Paul that all Christians alike were equal as being slaves of God and that those who were legally slaves were freedmen of Christ.[64] These attempts to resolve the Christian difficulty as displayed by Chrysostom have been plausibly ascribed to the swiftness of his mental processes, to the number and the rapidity of his digressions, and to his urgent need for immediacy of expression of any idea.[65]

---

[57] First Corinthians, 7, 1 and 7, 24. For Christ's sacrifice as the redemption price paid for the believing slave, which is here patterned after Greek procedure, and the Semitic idea of all believers as the slaves of the Lord, see Westermann, The freedmen and the slaves of God, *Proc. Amer. Philos. Soc.* **92**: 61-62, 1948.

[58] NT, Romans, 5-6.

[59] Colossians, 3, 11. The translation is that of Goodspeed, Edgar J., *The New Testament, An American translation*, 288, Chicago, Univ. Press, 1923.

[60] Irenaeus, *Contra haereses* 4: 18, 2-3 in Migne, *Patrologiae Graecae* 7, col. 1025; *ibid.* 4: 13, 4, col. 1009.

[61] Gregory of Nyssa in Migne, *Patrolog. Graecae* **44**, col. 644.

[62] Jonkers, E. J., in *Mnemosyne*, 3rd ser., 1: 249; John Chrysostom, *In epistulam ad Ephesios homilia*, 6, 22, 2, Migne, *Patrologiae Graecae* 62: 156-158.

[63] *Idem, In epistulam ad I Corinthios homilia*, 12, 7, in Migne, *Patrolog. Graecae* **61**, col. 105.

[64] John Chrysostom, *In epist. ad I Corinthios homilia*, 19, 4-5, Migne, *Patrologiae Graecae* 61: coll. 156-158.

[65] Laistner, M. L. W., *Christianity and paganism in the later Roman empire*, 76.

To Saint Augustine, also, the explanation of the system of slavery in the world at large, presumably including enslavement of Christians to fellow Christians, lay in the fact that it existed by the decision of God as punishment for original sin. In God there is no injustice. Therefore the slave system is justified since God knows how to assign different punishments according to the deserts of the wicked.[66] In striking antithesis to this stands his assertion that a slave ought not to be regarded by a Christian owner as his property in the same sense in which he regards a horse or money as his possession. This statement was justified by Augustine on the scriptural precept that one should love another man as himself, even one's enemies.[67] But Augustine's reiteration of the old Christian idea that slavery arose from man's transgression shows, in itself, the disturbance of mind brought about by the attempt to bring the justice of the Divine Being into logical conformity with the system of slavery which was so manifestly unjust in many of its individual applications. Henri Wallon has attempted to resolve this dichotomy of the Church Fathers upon the subject of slavery into a unity of concept. Although it is written with a wide knowledge of the ancient sources and carried along upon the strong current of the abolitionist and theological convictions of his time the result is not convincing.[68]

The difficulty which faced organized Christianity in its desire to collaborate with the State upon the question of slavery was sharply outlined in one particular issue of Church policy. This was the decision upon the admission of slaves into the ranks of the clergy and under the protecting aegis of the monastic life. The problem apparently had not arisen in the early second century in respect to clerical positions in the lower frames. From A. D. 112 or 113 we have the famous letter of the Younger Pliny written when he was governor of Bithynia to Trajan regarding what he should do with those persons who were brought before him as Christians. Pliny mentions two *ministrae*, or deaconesses, from whom he had taken testimony, employing violence to that end. Since the third degree was used upon them in obtaining their testimony these two women were un-

doubtedly slaves.[69] Clearly there was at that time no settled attitude of objection to the acquiring of lower positions in the Christian communities even by female slaves.

The natural expectation would be that this early policy of admitting slaves into the lower ranks of assistants would be extended in the later second and third centuries. If the dating of the *Teaching of the apostles* (*didachē tōn apostolōn*), is correct, as given by Adolph Harnack, that is, around tne middle of the second century, this is not the case. For in the *didachē* we already find the beginning of the compromises of the Christian communities with the demands set by slave-ownership under the civil laws of property. The adjustment made by Christianity appears in the eighty-second canon of the *Apostolic teaching*. It provides that slaves should not be appointed to clerical positions in the Christian congregations without the consent of their masters. If this consent had been granted such slaves must be freed by their owners and dismissed from their homes.[70]

The Canons of the Council of Elvira are now customarily dated in A. D. 306. At this meeting it was provided that freedmen whose patrons were of the laity should not be appointed to positions in the clergy.[71] This is a retrogressive movement, presumably in protection of the property interests of slave-owners, whether they be Christians or non-Christians. The same type of decision, in this case respecting the admission of slaves into the monastic life, was taken by the Council of Chalcedon held in 451. At that meeting it was provided that slaves should not be accepted by the monasteries except with the express consent of their owners. Anyone concerned in an evasion of this canon was threatened with excommunication.[72]

So far as the record goes upon receiving slaves into clerical and monastic life the civil legislation came later than the Church decisions regarding it. By a constitution of Arcadius and Honorius of A. D. 398 slaves, both male and female, public debtors, members of the local councils (*curiales*) and others subject to state obligations were forbidden to enter the Church to escape their worldly impositions.[73] The civil law and the canons of the Church upon this point run almost side by side in the fifth century. In both cases, as Henry C. Lea has suggested, the reasons seem to have lain in the economic field. In the view of the government, admission to

---

[66] Saint Augustine, *De civitate Dei* 19 : 15 : *quod non fit nisi Deo judicante apud quem non est iniquitas*; Migne, *Patrologiae Latinae* 41 : coll. 643-644.

[67] *Idem, De sermone Domini in monte*, book 1 : 59, in Migne, *Patrologiae Latinae* 34 : col. 1260. Lea, Henry C., *Studies in church history*, 538. In my judgment Lea has read too much into this statement.

[68] Wallon, *L'esclavage*, 2nd ed., 3 : 307-342. A specific example of Wallon's unconscious distortion of the Christian attitude toward slavery is to be seen on pages 362-363. The ransoming of prisoners to save them from sale as war booty was a constant accompaniment of enslavement practice throughout Greek and Roman pagan history. It should not be used as proof of any special zeal for liberation aroused by the exhortations of the clergy. A more balanced and cooler recognition of the difficulty of Saint Augustine's attempt to reconcile slavery, as a punishment for sin, with God's goodness is given by Henry C. Lea, *Studies in church history*, 538.

[69] Pliny the Younger, *Letters* (to Trajan) 10 (9) : 96, 8.

[70] The Harnack dating of the *Didachē* is given in von Gebhardt-Harnack, *Texte und Untersuchungen zur Gesch. der altchrist. Literatur* 2 : 2, 159. See n. 8 of this chapter. For the canon itself see Krüger, G., *Sammlung ausgewählter kirchen- und dogmengeschichtlichen Quellenschriften* 12 : 82, 12.

[71] Council of Elvira in Mansi, G., *Sacrorum Conciliorum Collectio* 2 : 19, canon 80.

[72] Canones Chalcedonenses, in Mansi, *Sacror. Concil. Collectio* 7 : col. 394. *Vide*, also, Granič, B., Das Klosterwesen in der Novellengesetzgebung Kaisers Leons des Weisen, *Byzantinische Zeitschrift* 21 : 63-67, 1931.

[73] Theod., *Codex* 12 : 45, 3.

monastic and clerical life was being used as a ready avenue of escape from burdens which the civil organization imposed. On the side of the Church, in A. D. 443, Saint Leo had complained that owners had been entering their slaves in the Church orders to obtain the revenues accruing from the offices which these slaves might obtain. A constitution of A. D. 484 conceded to slaves the right to enter the monasteries if this was done with the knowledge and consent of their masters. The latter were to be deprived of their ownership rights so long as the slaves remained in the monasteries. When they abandoned the life of solitude they were to be returned to their former status of servitude.[74] Under the

legislation passed by Justinian the pressure of the Church regarding its rights to accept slaves into the monasteries and into the clergy was obviously increased. If a slave, after a probationary novitiate of three years, had become a monk his owner's claim upon him was irrevocably gone unless, as monk, the former slave should leave the monastery of his own accord.[75]

---

[74] Just., *Codex* 1 : 3, 37 (38) (*De episcopis et clericis*) : *si ser-*

---

vis suis ad monasteriorum cultum migrandi tribuerint facultatem (eorum domini). . . . alioquin si relicta forte vita solitaria ad aliam se condicionem transtulerint, certum est eos ad servitutis iugum, quam monachicae professionis cultu evaserant, reversuros.
[75] Lea, Henry C., *Studies in church history*, 571-575, has an admirable, though brief, sketch of this development. The legislation of Justinian upon the matter appears on pp. 573-575.

XXIV. CONCLUSION

One problem remains which presses insistently for an answer, however tentative it may be. It arises out of a conviction which has often been expressed both by students working in the field of the development of the early Church and by several of the scholars who have interested themselves specifically in the slave system as it operated in the final centuries of the Roman Empire. This is the belief that the tenets of Christianity should have led to the overthrow of the slave institution, perhaps in the sixth century. If not then it must have occurred eventually at some unspecified period in which the conjunction of circumstances became favorable to that outcome. Among the reasons for the final success of the antislavery movement in the nineteenth century, however pragmatic the approach of interested writers upon the subject may have been, some part of the change in social conscience which brought about the abolition of slave labor and enslavement is usually ascribed to Christian influence.

Accepting this concurrence of opinion as justified, the problem of interest may be stated in this form. What were the elements inherent in Christian doctrine, whether original in Christianity or borrowed, and what were the factors in the later structure of Christian power which sanction the opinion that Christian teaching, the Christian way of life, and Christian organization must, in the final analysis destroy slavery? For one starts with full knowledge that Christianity, like all of the religious beliefs which it overcame, had inherited the going slave system, and had accepted it as unquestionably as the pagan worships had done before it.[1] There is another facet of the problem which must also be evaluated. If

Christian thought was, from its origin in the teaching of Jesus, invested with ideas so incompatible with slavery that it must in the end break the long hold upon human societies which the system had held, why was this inevitable consequence delayed for eighteen centuries after the brief mission of the Nazarene?

A lesser, but attendant, question concerns the slave trade. Why was it that the early Church Fathers were as indifferent to the traffic in slaves as all the pagan writers were before them who concerned themselves with slavery and with the fate of those who were involved in its meshes? To this minor problem a possible solution is, indeed, available. No criticism of the Church Fathers is implied in the statement of this problem because it is modern in origin, having arisen out of the black shadow of horrors which sometimes attended the system of transporting slaves from Africa to the Americas over what was called " the middle passage." This was the central stretch of a triangle of journeys—from the upper eastern coast of the present United States to West Africa, the " middle " passage from Africa to the ports of slave distribution in the two Americas, and the return journey to the home port. As contrasted with the frightful conditions ascribed to the " middle passage " the ancient transportation of slaves was bearable. The hauls were relatively short, in distance and in time. The food supplied the slaves was probably neither good nor too abundant. We hear no complaint about it in the ancient literature—which may not mean much. Despite the comparison, favorable as it may be to antiquity in this one respect, one still misses in the Christian literature some note of protest against the trade in slaves or against those who participated in it. For in the *pagan* literature, both that in Greek and that in Latin, the slave trader stood in low esteem.

Even the casual reader will not fail to note that the early Christian leaders were not entirely happy regarding the situation which the acceptance of slavery created

---

[1] Henri Wallon, in his *L'esclavage* 3 : 364, states that the Church worked zealously for the suppression of slavery, externally by ransoming captives, internally by elimination of some of the sources of the wretchedness which slavery caused. The idea is misleading if it means to imply that any intention or suggestion of eliminating the slave system came to expression in the writings of the Church Fathers.

for them.[2] This feeling of uncertainty shows itself in a conversation which Gregory of Nyssa imagined as occurring between himself and a slave-owner. The man regarded himself, so Gregory depicts him, as lord and master of enslaved persons who were, in fact, of the same race as he was. " For," as this slave master is made to say, " I owned male slaves and slave girls; and there came to me [presumably from their unions] house-born slaves." The reply of Gregory reads as follows: " Do you not see the magnitude of your flatulent boasting? - - - [Do you not see] that you condemn to slavery a man who is by nature free and self-empowered, and that you set up laws in rivalry with God, overthrowing His law which is based upon nature? " [3] God had, Himself, put human enslavement in the world. Nevertheless the rhetorical question of Gregory of Nyssa, if not a challenge to the moral validity of slavery, stands at the least in clear opposition to the slave system of that time.

A second illustration of the clash between the traditional practice and the unexpressed feeling of moral rejection of enslavement is the more impressive because it appears in a legal action taken by an ordinary, apparently middle-class, Christian believer in Egypt in the sixth century. The man had made an official declaration, in the case of a woman dependent of his family, that she was a free woman, in opposition to her own assertion that she was of slave status.[4] The overtones of the declaration are unmistakably non-pagan. When he heard that the woman, Martha by name, had declared that she was not a free woman, " on account of this, fearing the judgment of God and, mindful of the Savior's love of mankind, I groaned aloud." [5] Earlier in the document the declarant had threatened any persons who might attempt to drag away the woman and her children into slavery with the warning that they might then " see themselves brought before the fearsome bar of judgment of a Mightier Power." For this Christian there was a higher power than the civil law or the Church itself whose awful punishment would ensue against anyone who essayed to enslave a man or woman of free status. There may be extant some literary or documentary evidence showing that one or another of the multiple deities of Greece or of the Romans could be accredited with an equal concern for the maintenance

of the liberty of a free person; but if there is some similar example of it, it has escaped my memory.

In the attempt to analyze the problem created for the practice of enslavement by Christianity one point of departure must be assumed. Both the idea of slavery and the organization through which it operated have always rested upon two quite different foundations. Upon one side it has been built upon the rock bottom of a solid reality, that of the advantages which it offered in antiquity in the simplification of labor relations and production in that degree in which slave labor was used. Theoretically and legally the slaveowner, as work-giver, had complete control over the working capacity of his slaves, the hours of their labor per day, the nature of their work assignments and the restrictions to be imposed upon their goings and comings. In the analysis of these controls as implied in the Delphic manumissions by trust sale to Apollo the slave was divested of four freedoms which were available to free workmen. His legal personality was vested in that of his master. He was subject to seizure without right of protest against it. He had no choice in the matter of the type of work he desired to do. He lacked all personal privileges of going where he might wish to go. In terms of work this last deprivation meant that, in the discretion of his owner, he was always tied to the locale of his labor assignments. So far as production of goods was concerned, under the master's concept of it, this last advantage of slave labor over free labor was an enormous one.

The opposite foundation of the structure of slave labor, the weak one, was that upon the side of the human relations necessarily involved. Some of the numerous speculations advanced in antiquity by the heritors of the traditional system of slave labor, in its combination with dominant free and contractual labor, have been presented in previous chapters of this study. In the pre-Greek period the appeasement of the mental discomfort which slavery created took the form of a tribal-religious decision, so far as the Semitic reaction was concerned. Fellow tribesmen and coreligionists were not to be subjected to servitude under their fellow " nationals "— using " nationals " in the sense indicated. Bondage to their coreligionists—yes! But not enslavement!

The Hellenes, when they began to subject all human problems to the searching inquiry of reasoned discussion, did not adopt this half-solution which the Semitic peoples accepted. That is, they did not exempt from servitude under themselves either fellow subjects of their own city-state communities, fellow believers in the tutelary gods of their own polities, or " culture Greeks " whom they associated with themselves under the broad concept of Hellenic cultural affinities. This broadening of the possibility of enslavement of Greeks to Greeks brought the dichotomy of the slavery concept all the closer home to them. Their recognition of the rational inadequacy of the system formulated itself in time into the conviction that slavery was contrary to nature, and

[2] Whitehead, Alfred North, in *Adventures of ideas*, 15, New York, Macmillan, 1946, has made this general statement upon the point: " In those days (that is, in antiquity) the penetrating minds found a difficulty in reconciling their doctrine of slavery to certain plain facts of moral feeling and of sociological practice."

[3] Gregory of Nyssa in Migne, J.-P., *Patrologiae Graecae* **44**: col. 644. A similar thought appears in Gregory of Nazianzus, *De pauperum amore, ibid.* **35**: col. 892: " freedom and riches lie solely in the observation of God's commandment. True poverty and enslavement are the transgression of that command."

[4] Maspero, Jean, *Cairo Catalogue général* **9**(1): no. 67089. It has been cited in the text which accompanies n. 62 of chap. XXII. There the appropriate references are given.

[5] *Cairo Catalogue* **9**(1): no. 67089, lines 27-29.

that the slave structure was man-made and legalized only by human laws.

By Saul of Tarsus and the early Christians who followed him this solution was transmuted into the theological explanation that slavery was instituted by God's justice as punishment for sinful man. Through the operation of one of the inexplicable chances of history the practice of admitting slaves, without reservation or restriction, into the Christian communities coincided with the economic and social leveling between the *coloni*, who tilled the soil under durance, the free members of the handicraft guilds, the free transport workers, and the slaves who might be working beside them in any of these fields of labor. For eighteen hundred years this remained the traditional basis for the moral acceptance by Christian society of the continuing use of slaves in labor employment. The abandoning of slavery was the result of many converging forces. Among these was something deeply latent in Christian ethics which could become fully operative only after material changes had been brought about through different methods of production and within a new frame of labor relations which these new methods established.

In the course of a prolonged investigation connected with the practice of enslavement in antiquity and with the problems arising out of the slave institution in other times and places the following suggestions have taken form relating to Christianity and slavery. They center upon a single query. Why did Christian ideals and the Christian way of life, though generally regarded as having become a strong influence toward the elimination of slavery, so long countenance a system of labor control which its own ideals rejected? The answers which have presented themselves to me are here put down for consideration.

1. The inability to feel at ease with the slave system was not, in antiquity, confined to Christian doctrine. A special strength was, however, given to Christianity in respect to this feeling through its claim to universality. All who accepted the belief in the God of the Christians as the sole and all-embracing divine power were His children. This universalism left no avenue of escape to Christian leaders, by way of tribal preference or of religious or racial " nationalism," from the inherent inconsistency of enslavement.

2. The belief that all men were of one human brotherhood was nothing new or startling. In pre-Christian days it had already been expressed in the ancient world, notably as a dogma of Stoic thought.

A new element was, however, injected into the Christian concept of the brotherhood of all men. This was the idea that all those who embraced the Christian faith, open as it was to adoption by anybody, were members of a family in which God was the Father of all. With this belief there came into the Christian relationship between men and their God an intimacy which cut across all lines of caste or status. This had been absent from the pagan worships.[6]

3. The Christian assertion of the innate equality of all men was a conspicuous feature of its membership program. It was not unlike the practice long followed in the social clubs of earlier antiquity and in the associations of the *coloni* and the handicraft *collegia* which became so prominent under the Empire. What the Christians did that was new was to emphasize this factor of equal association and to transform it from the horizontal scale of occupational association to a vertical application in depth which united the lowly with the fortunate. All who were baptized in the faith, including the slaves, became by that symbolic act equal participants in the plan of Divine salvation.

4. By emphasizing a group of the gentler virtues, those of obedience, resignation, humility, and patience, Christianity gave a new strength and a new place in life to the slave class. According to William Lecky these virtues were " servile " qualities which stood in marked contrast to those characteristics embodied in the ideal of the *virtue* of the Roman citizen of the old Republic. The concept of *virtus*, according to Lecky, had stressed the attributes of dignified demeanor, self-reliance, strength, endurance in difficulties, and the like. The assemblage of character qualities which were emphasized by Christian teaching, gave a moral dignity to the enslaved which, in Lecky's view, helped to undermine the structure of slavery in European life until, in the fourteenth century, it had in that area been almost eliminated.[7] The following period of the expansion of slavery to meet the demand created in the Americas for a tractable type of labor does not, in my judgment, weaken the validity of this idea advanced by Lecky.

5. The constant emphasis by Christianity upon the miraculous, the emotional, and the mystical aspects of the religious experience which it offered were powerful forces operating toward acceptance of the new faith by all those groups which had been economically and socially disadvantaged in ancient life.[8]

The effects of the mystical elements of Christian theology toward the ultimate result of a direct effort to discard the entire system of slavery must necessarily have developed slowly. The weakening of the principle of enslavement brought about by these elements was due

[6] Rees, B. R., *Jour. Egypt. Arch.* 36 : 97-98, 1950. Rees ascribes to Hebraism the origin of this family concept of the divine and the human relationship.
[7] Lecky, William E. H., *History of European morals*, 3rd ed.. 2 : 65-71, New York, Appleton, 1927.
[8] This idea was clearly expressed by Henry C. Lea, *Studies in church history*, 526. He restricted the effects of these Christian views of life upon the eventual antislavery outcome to Christian believers. But the concept of the universality of God and the zeal displayed in the dissemination of their faith by the Christians must have given a wider effect to the consequences of their opposition to enslavement through penetration beyond the scope of Christian conversion, than Lea seems to have ascribed to them.

to the participation together of slaveowners with their slaves in the symbolic devotional practices of the Mass and the Eucharist. The sharing of the emotional experiences evoked by them were potent influences in breaking down within the Christian communities the barriers which had been erected by slave classification. This agency of spiritual equalizing had been present in the Christian belief and organization from the outset.[9]

Such were some of the qualities and practices inherent in Christianity which helped, in the passage of the centuries, to transform an original acceptance of slavery into a widespread ethical rejection of it. Important as these inner elements have been in the consideration of the pressure of Christian belief toward an eventual conflict with slavery they could never have succeded in eliminating the institution of slavery apart from the strength of the external organization of "institutional Christianity."

6. One must grant to the pre-Christian religions, and to the pagan philosophies as well, the germination of ideas of the essential equality of all men similar, on the whole, to those which Christianity expressed. None of them, however, developed an organization comparable to that through which the Christian faith expanded over the western world, either in the geographical spread of its power or in the centralization of its authority. Despite its sectarianism the Christian doctrine was actively preached and spread by vigorous missionary activity. When the time of its movement against slavery arrived

it had, in all its sectarian differences, the organizations which could make its attack upon slavery effective.

The failure of Christianity over the succession of the centuries to bring the inner opposition of its ideals into an open conflict with the stark realism of slavery must be acknowledged and faced. It can only be explained in terms of time-conditioning and of difference of environment. In each separate historic period since Justinian the problem involved is complex, much too intricate to be ventured upon in a study which is devoted solely to the slave institution of the Mediterranean world in the time of its domination by the Greeks and Romans.

In his book, *Adventures of Ideas*, Alfred North Whitehead has outlined his view of the origins and development of the moral objection to the use of slaves, from the birth of the idea to its culmination in the abolitionist movement. His understanding of ancient slavery is subject to criticism, in places even to outright rejection. The lines upon which he has sketched the moral bases of the antislavery feeling are, nevertheless, boldly and correctly drawn. He ascribes its beginnings to Plato's evaluation of the supreme importance of the human soul and carries it through the long period of the influence of Christian thought in developing it. The outline is clear and impressive.[10]

To Professor Whitehead "the great transitions [caused by moral ideas] are due to a coincidence of forces derived from both sides of the world, its physical and its spiritual natures.[11] - - - In the Middle Ages institutional Christianity - - - became an instrument of conservatism instead of an instrument of progress."[12] It was the convergence of the effects of different ideas—those of Christianity, the humanitarianism of the eighteenth century, and finally the idea of democracy—which eventually brought about the abolishing of human enslavement. It was the necessity of the development of these ideas, and the long wait for their convergence until the time arrived when material conditions were favorable to it, which best explain the failure of the antislavery feeling for so many centuries to culminate in abolition.

---

[9] The brief rejection of the influence of mysticism and magical formulae expressed by Arnaldo Momigliano in *Jour. Roman Studies* **34**: 109,, 1944, in which he is followed by Ronald Syme, *ibid.* **36**: 149, 1946, may not have been intended to apply to the religious satisfactions which they give. For the criticism of Momigliano see Bruck, Eberhard F., Political ideology, propaganda and public law of the Romans, *Seminar* **7**: 19, 1949. Other discussions of the powerful effects of mystic practices and beliefs are to be found in Farnell, Lewis R., *Greek hero cults and ideas of immortality,* 275, Oxford, Clarendon Press, 1921 ("it was easier for the new religion to foster the miraculous than the scientific tradition"), and in Rees, B. R., *Jour. Egypt. Arch.* **36**: 96, 1950. Rees lays stress upon the emotional appeal of Christianity to the common man through the spiritual medium of prayer and through the adoption of pre-Christian magic, but as a means toward faith, not as an end in itself, *ibid.,* 89-90.

---

[10] Whitehead, Alfred North, *Adventures of ideas,* 15-31.
[11] *Ibid.,* 21.
[12] *Ibid.,* 22.

BIBLIOGRAPHY

AUTHORS OF ANTIQUITY AND OTHER ANCIENT SOURCES

AELIAN. Varia historia.
AESCHINES. Orations.
—— Pseudo-Aeschines, Letters.
AESCHYLUS. Tragedies.
ANDOCIDES. Orations.
ANTIPHON. Orations.
APOLLINARIS SIDONIUS. Epistulae.
APPIAN. Civil Wars.
—— Foreign Wars.
APULEIUS. Apologia.
—— Metamorphoses.
ARISTOPHANES. Acharnians; Birds; Clouds; Ecclesiazusae; Frogs; Knights; Lysistrata; Plutus; Thesmophoriazusae; Wasps.
—— Fragments, Meineke, August. Poetae comici. Fragmenta comicorum Graecorum. 5 v. Berlin, Reimer, 1847-1857.
ARISTOTLE. Eudemian ethics. Nicomachean ethics. Politics.
ARRIAN. Anabasis of Alexander.
—— Discourses of Epictetus.
ATHENAEUS. Deipnosophists.
AUGUSTUS CAESAR (emperor). Monumentum Ancyranum (Res gestae divi Augusti).
AUGUSTINE, SAINT. De civitate Dei.
—— De sermone Domini in monte.

CAESAR, GAIUS JULIUS. Civil War.
—— Gallic War.
CALLIMACHUS. Aetia.
CATO, MARCUS PORCIUS. De agricultura.
CATULLUS, GAIUS VALERIUS. Poems (Carmina).
Chronicon Paschale.
CHRYSOSTOM, SAINT JOHN. In epistulam ad Ephesios homilia.
—— In epistulam ad I Corinthios homilia.
CICERO, M. TULLIUS. Letters: to Atticus; to his friends; to his brother Quintus.
—— Orations.
—— Philosophical writings; the divisions of oratory (Partitiones Oratoriae); on moral duties (De officiis).
—— In Caecilium divinatio (preliminary examination in the prosecution against Verres).
CICERO, QUINTUS TULLIUS. De petitione consulatus (on canvassing for the consulship).
Codex Justinianus.
Codex Theodosianus.
COLUMELLA. De re rustica.
CURTIUS = QUINTIUS CURTIUS RUFUS. History of Alexander the Great.

DEMOSTHENES. Orations.
DIO CASSIUS. Roman history.
DIO CHRYSOSTOM (DIO OF PRUSA). Orations.
DIODORUS SICULUS. World History.
DIOGENES LAERTIUS. Lives of the philosophers (Vitae philosophorum).
DIONYSIUS OF HALICARNASSUS. Antiquitates Romanae.

EPICTETUS. Discourses (see Arrian, above).
EUNAPIUS. Histories.
EURIPIDES. Alcestis, Hecuba, Helena, Ion, Iphigenia in Aulis, Medea, Orestes, The Phoenician women, Suppliants.
Expositio totius mundi: in Riese, A., Geographi Latini Minores.

FESTUS, SEXTUS POMPEIUS. De verborum significatione.
FLORUS, LUCIUS ANNAEUS. Epitome of Roman history.
FRONTINUS, SEXTUS JULIUS. De aquaeductibus urbis Romae.

GAIUS. Institutes.
GALENUS, CLAUDIUS. Ed. Kühn, Carl.
GELLIUS, AULUS. Noctes Atticae.
GREGORY OF NAZIANZUS. De pauperum amore.
GREGORY OF NYSSA. Treatises.

HARPOCRATION. Lexicon of the ten orators.
HERONDAS (Herodas). Mimes.
HERODOTUS. History of the Persian wars.
HESIOD. Works and days.
HESYCHIUS, lexicographer. Dictionary.
HIERONYMUS (Jerome), EUSEBIUS. De viris inlustribus. Ad Jeremiam. Ad Zachariam.
HIPPOCRATES. De aere aquis locis.
—— Epidemiai (sick visits).
HIPPOLYTUS. *Eis ta hagia theophaneia.*
HOMER. Iliad; Odyssey.
HORACE. Epistles.
—— Odes.
—— Satires.
HYPEREIDES. Orations.

IGNATIUS. Epistles, in Migne, J.-P., Patrologiae, series latina, 55.
Inscriptions: Greek. Corpus inscriptionum Atticarum.
—— Fouilles de Delphes 3 (1-6). Epigraphie. École française d'Athènes.
—— Inscriptiones Graecae.
—— Inscriptiones Graecae² (editio minor).
—— Inscriptiones Graecae ad res Romanas pertinentes, Cagnat, R., *et alii.*
—— Monumenta Asiae minoris antiqua.
—— Orientis Graeci inscriptiones selectae. Dittenberger, W.
—— Recueil des inscriptions juridiques grecques. Dareste-Haussoullier-Reinach.
—— Sammlung der griechische Dialektinschriften, Collitz, H., J. Baunack, F. Bechtel et alii.
—— Supplementum epigraphicum Graecum, Hondius, J. J. E.
—— Sylloge inscriptionum Graecarum, Dittenberger, W. 3rd ed.
Inscriptions: Latin.
—— Corpus inscriptionum Latinarum.
—— Corpus inscriptionum Latinarum, 2nd edition, 1 (1) and 1 (2).
—— Inscriptiones Latinae selectae, ed. Dessau, Hermann.
IRENAEUS. Contra haereses.
ISAEUS. Orations.
ISOCRATES. Orations.

JOSEPHUS. On the Jewish War.
—— Jewish Antiquities.
JUSTINIAN. Corpus Juris Civilis: Codex.
—— Digesta.
—— Institutiones.
—— Novellae.
JUSTINUS. Epitome of Pompeius Trogus.
JUVENAL. Satires.

LACTANTIUS. Institutiones.
—— De mortibus persecutorum.
Laws of Gortyn.
Laws of the XII Tables.
Lex Julia. Bulletino della Commissione archeologica comunale di Roma, **36**, 1908.
Lex municipalis Salpensana.
LIVY, TITUS. History of Rome (Ab urbe condita).
—— Periochae.
LUCAN. Bellum Civile (Pharsalia).
LUCIAN. Adversus indoctum.
—— Charon.
—— De Mercede conductis.
—— Navigium sive vota.
—— Piscator.
—— Toxaris.
—— Tyrannos.
LYCURGUS. Orations.
LYSIAS. Orations.

MACCABEES. OT, Apocrypha.
MACROBIUS. Saturnalia.
MARTIAL. Epigrams.
MENANDER. Comedies.
—— The arbitrants (*Epitrepontes*).
—— The girl with the shorn locks (*Perikeiromenē*).
—— The hero.
MINUCIUS FELIX. Octavius.

NEPOS, CORNELIUS. De viris illustribus.
NICOLAUS OF DAMASCUS. Life of Augustus.
NONIUS MARCELLUS. De compendiosa doctrina.

OROSIUS. Historiae.

PAUSANIAS. *Periēgēsis* (Guide to Greece).
Papyri, publications. Aramaic.
—— Aramaic papyri discovered at Assuan, by Sayce, A. H., and A. E. Cowley.
—— The Brooklyn Museum Aramaic papyri, ed. Kraeling, E. G.
Papyri, publications. Greek.
  P. Aberd. Catalogue of Greek and Latin papyri in the University of Aberdeen, ed. Turner, Eric G.
  P. Baden. Veröffentlichungen aus den badischen Papyrus-Sammlungen, Spiegelberg, W., F. Bilabel, G. A. Gerhard.
  BGU. Ägyptische Urkunden aus den staatlichen Museen zu Berlin. Griechische Urkunden.
  P. Bouriant. Les papyrus Bouriant, Collart, P.
  P. Cattaoui. Bulletin de l'institut français d'archéologie orientale 3, Barry, L.
  P. Cairo Maspero. Maspero, Jean. Catalogue général des antiquités égyptiennes du Musée du Caire. Papyrus grecs d'époque byzantine.
  P. Cairo Zenon. Catalogue général des antiquités égyptiennes du Musée du Caire. Zenon papyri, 5 v, Edgar, C. C.
  P. Cornell. Greek papyri in the library of Cornell University, Westermann, W. L., and C. J. Kraemer.
  Corpus Papyrorum Raineri 1. Vienna. 1895.
  P. Eitrem 7. A Greek papyrus concerning the sale of a slave. Jour. Egypt. Arch. **17**: 44-47, 1931.
  P. Flor. Papiri greco-egizii. Comparetti, D., and G. Vitelli.
  P. Freiburg. Mitteilungen aus der Freiburger Papyrussammlung, Aly, W., M. Gelzer, J. Partsch, U. Wilcken.
  P. Giessen. Greich. Papyri im Museum des Oberhessischen Geschichtsvereins zu Giessen, Eger, O., Ernst Kornemann, P. M. Meyer.
  P. Giessen, no. 20. Büttner, H., in Schriften der Hessischen Hochschulen. Universität Giessen.
  P. Goodspeed. Greek papyri in the Cairo Museum, Goodspeed, E.

P. Grenfell 1. An Alexandrian erotic fragment and other Greek papyri, Grenfell, B. P.
P. Grenfell 2. New classical fragments and other Greek and Latin papyri, Grenfell, B. P., and A. S. Hunt.
P. Gron. Papyri Groninganae. Griechische Papyri der Universitäts-bibliothek zu Amsterdam, ed. Roos, A. G.
P. Halensis 1. Graeca Halensis. Dikaiomata: Auszüge aus alexandrinische Gesetzen und Verordnungen.
P. Ham. Griechische Papyrusurkunden der Hamburger Staatsund Universitätsbibliothek, ed. Meyer, P. M.
P. Harris. The Rendel Harris papyri of Woodbrooke College, Powell, J. E.
P. Jandanae. Papyri Jandanae, Kalbfleisch, C. and students.
P. Leipzig. Griechische Urkunden der Papyrussammlung zu Leipzig, ed. Mitteis, Ludwig.
P. Lille. Papyrus grecs. Jouguet, Pierre, P. Collart, J. Lesquier, M. Xoual.
P. Lond. Greek papyri in the British Museum, ed. Kenyon, F. G., H. I. Bell.
P. Michigan. Michigan Papyri. 8 v. Boak, A. E. R., E. M. Husselman, W. F. Edgerton, J. G. Winter, H. C. Youtie, O. M. Pearl.
P. Michigan Zenon. Zenon papyri in the University of Michigan collection (P. Michigan 1), by Edgar, C. C.
P. Oxy. Oxyrhynchus Papyri. 21 v. to date. Ed., Grenfell, B. P., H. I. Bell, E. Lobel and others.
P. Paris. Notices et extraits des papyrus grecs du Musée du Louvre et de la bibliothèque imperiale, Brunet de Preslé, W.
P. Petrie. The Flinders Petrie papyri. 3 v. Mahaffy, J. P., J. G. Smyly.
P. Princeton. Papyri in the Princeton University collections. 3 v., ed. by Johnson, A. C., H. B. Van Hoesen, E. H. Kase.
P. Rainer 281. Papyrus Erzherzog Rainer, in Wessely, C., Studien zur Paläographie und Papyruskunde 4: 58-83, and P. London, 260 and 261, in Kenyon, F. G., Greek papyri in the British Museum 2: 42-61.
CPR. Corpus papyrorum Raineri, by Wessely, C.
P. Reinach, inv. no. 2111. Un papyrus inedit et P. Rylands 178, by Collart, Paul, in Mélanges Gustave Glotz 1: 241-247.
P. Revenue Laws. Revenue laws of Ptolemy Philadelphus, Grenfell, B. P.
P. Ross. Georg. Papyri russischer und georgischer Sammlungen, 5 v., Zereteli, G., O. Krüger, P. Jernstedt.
P. Rylands. Catalogue of the Greek and Latin papyri in the John Rylands library, 4v., Hunt, A. S., J. de M. Johnson, V Martin, C. H. Roberts, E. G. Turner.
P. Schow. Charta papyracea graece scripta mus. Borgiani, Schow, N.
P. Società Italiana. Pubblicazioni della Società italiana. Papiri greci e latini, 13 v., Vitelli, G. and Medea Norsa.
P. Strassburg, inv. no. 1409. Ein Sklavenkauf des 6. Jahrhunderts, Archiv. für Papyrusforschung 3: 419.
P. Strassb. Griechische Papyrus der kaiserlichen Universitäts- und Landesbibliothek zu Strassburg. ed. Preisigke, Fr.
P. Tebtunis. The Tebtunis papyri. 3 v. Grenfell, B. P., A. S. Hunt, J. G. Smyly, E. J. Goodspeed, C. C. Edgar.
P. Theadelphia. Papyrus de Théadelphie, by Jouguet, Pierre.
Urkunden der Ptolemäerzeit, by Wilcken, Ulrich. 2 v.
Parchment Dura, no. 23, in Münchener Beiträge zur Papyrusforschung und antiken Rechtsgeschichte 19: 382-383.
Periplus maris Erythraei.
PETRONIUS. Satyricon.
PHILEMON, edited by Kock, Theodor (1884), Comicorum Atticorum fragmenta.
PHILO JUDAEUS. De legatione ad Gaium.
—— De virtutibus.
—— De somniis.
PHILOSTRATUS. Life of Apollonius of Tyana.

PINDAR. Odes.
PLATO. Dialogues.
—— Gorgias
—— Laws.
—— Lysis.
—— Phaedo.
—— Republic.
—— Symposium.
—— Theaetetus.
PLAUTUS. Captivi.
—— Casina.
—— Curculio.
—— Menaechmi.
—— Mercator.
—— Miles gloriosus.
—— Mostellaria.
—— Poenulus.
—— Pseudolus.
—— Rudens.
PLINY, THE ELDER. Natural history.
PLINY, THE YOUNGER. Letters.
PLUTARCH. Lives.
—— Alexander.
—— Aratus.
—— Caesar.
—— Cato the Elder.
—— Cato the Younger.
—— Cimon.
—— Coriolanus.
—— Crassus.
—— Flamininus.
—— Lucullus.
—— Pericles.
—— Philopoemen.
—— Pompey.
—— Solon.
—— Moral essays.
—— De fortuna Alexandri.
POLLUX. *Onomastikon.*
POLYBIUS. Universal history.
POLYAENUS. *Stratēgēmata.*
POSIDONIUS. Histories.
PROPERTIUS. Elegies.
PSEUDO-ARISTEAS. Epistula ad Philocratem.
PSEUDO-ARISTOTLE. De mirabilibus auscultatibus.
—— Oeconomica.
PSEUDO-PLUTARCH. De vita decem oratorum.
PSEUDO-XENOPHON. Polity of the Athenians.

[QUINTILIAN]. Declamationes.
SALLUST. Bellum Jugurthinum.
—— Catilina.
SALVIANUS. De gubernatione Dei.
Scriptores historiae Augustae.
SENECA. Controversiae.
—— Dialogues.
—— De beneficiis.
—— De clementia.
—— De ira.
—— De vita beata.
—— Epistulae morales.
SERVIUS, grammaticus. In Vergilii carmina Aeneidos.
STATIUS. Silvae.
SOPHOCLES. Philoctetes.
—— The Women of Trachis.
STOBAEUS. Florilegium.
Stoic fragments, in Arnim, Hans von, Stoicorum veterum fragmenta. 4 v.
STRABO. Geography.
SUETONIUS. Lives of the twelve Caesars.
—— De grammaticis et rhetoribus.
SYMMACHUS. Epistles.
SYNESIUS. Epistles.
TACITUS. Agricola.
—— Annals.
—— Germania.
—— Histories.
TERENCE. Comedies.
—— Eunuchus.
—— Andria (The girl from Andros).
TERTULLIAN. Ad nationes.
—— Apologeticum.
TIBULLUS. Elegies.
VALERIUS MAXIMUS. Facta et dicta memorabilia.
—— De paupertate.
VARRO. De lingua latina.
—— De re rustica.
VELLEIUS PATERCULUS. Historia Romana.
VITRUVIUS. De architectura.
XENOPHON. Agesilaus.
—— Cyropaedia.
—— Hellenic history.
—— Memorabilia.
—— Oeconomicus.
—— *Poroi* (Ways and means).
ZONARAS. Annals.

ARTICLES AND BOOKS OF MODERN AUTHORS

A century of population growth. 1909. U. S. Department of Commerce and Labor.
ADAMS, G. B. 1904. Civilization during the middle ages. New York, Scribners.
Aegyptiaca. Festschrift für Georg Ebers. 1897. Leipzig, Engelmann.
Ägyptische Urkunden aus den staatlichen Museen zu Berlin. Griechische Urkunden. 1895- 9 v. Berlin, Weidmann.
AFFOLTER, FRIEDRICH. 1913. Die Persönlichkeit des herrenlosen Sklaven. Leipzig, Veit.
ALLARD, PAUL. 1914. Les esclaves Chrétiens depuis les premiers temps de l'église jusque à la fin de la domination romaine, 6th ed. Paris, Lecoffre.
Anatolian studies presented to Wm. H. Buckler. Edited by Calder, W. M. and Josef Keil. 1939. Manchester, Univ. Press.

ANDREADES, A. M. 1928-1931. Ἱστορία τῆς Ἑλληνικῆς δημοσίας οἰκονομίας. Athens, Tzaka.
—— 1933. A history of Greek public finance, trans. by Carroll N. Brown. Cambridge, Harvard Univ. Press.
ANDRONIKOS, M. 1950. Αρχαιαι επιγραφαι Βεροιας. Thessalonica (Greece), Dept. of Hist. Monuments and Archaeology.
ARANGIO-RUIZ, V. 1930. Persone e famiglia nel diritto dei papiri. Milan, Vita e Pensiero.
ARDAILLON, E. 1897. Les mines du Laurion dans l'antiquité. Paris, Thorin.
ARNIM, HANS VON. 1921-1924. Stoicorum veterum fragmenta. 4 v. Leipzig, Teubner.

BANG, M. 1910. Die Herkunft der römischen Sklaven. *Mitteilungen des kaiserlichen deutschen archaeologischen Instituts, Römische Abteilung* 25: 223-251.

BARBAGALLO, C. 1905. La fine della Grecia antica. Bari, Laterza.

BARKER, ERNEST. 1947. Greek political theory. London, Methuen.

BARON, SALO. 1945. The Jewish community. 2 v. Philadelphia, Jewish Publ. Society.

—— 1947. Modern nationalism and religion. New York, Harper.

BARROW, R. H. 1928. Slavery in the Roman empire. London, Methuen.

BAUR, P. V. C., M. I. ROSTOVTZEFF, A. R. BELLINGER, C. HOPKINS, C. B. WELLES. 1929-1946. The excavations at Dura-Europus. 9 v. New Haven, Yale Univ. Press.

BEAUCHET, L. 1897. Histoire du droit privé de la république Athénienne. 4 v. Paris, Marescq.

BEKKER, IMMANUEL. 1814-1821. Anecdota Graeca. 3 v. Berlin, Nauck.

BELL, H. I. 1917. The Byzantine servile state in Egypt. Jour. Egypt. Arch. 4 : 87 ff.

—— 1924. Jews and Christians in Egypt. London, Oxford Univ. Press.

—— 1948. Egypt from Alexander the Great to the Arab conquest. Oxford, Clarendon Press.

—— 1950. The acts of the Alexandrines. Jour. Jur. Papyrology 4 : 19-42. Warsaw.

BELOCH, K. J. 1886. Die Bevölkerung der griechisch-römischen Welt. Leipzig, Duncker und Humblot.

—— Griechische Geschichte. 1912-1927. 4 v. Strassburg, Trübner.

BERGER, ADOLF. 1911. Die Strafklauseln in den Papyrusurkunden. Leipzig, Teubner.

BERGK, TH. 1872-1878. Poetae lyrici Graeci, 4th ed. 3 v. Leipzig, Teubner.

BERNEKER, E. 1932. Zu einigen Prozessurkunden der Ptolemäerzeit. Études de Papyrologie 2 : 59-72.

BERTHOLET, ALFRED. 1926. A history of Hebrew civilization. London, Harrap.

BI(c)KERMAN, ELIAS. 1938. Les institutions des Seleucides. Paris, Geuthner.

—— 1949. The name of Christians. Harvard Theol. Rev. 42.

—— 1951. The maxim of Antigonos of Socho. Harvard Theol. Rev. 44 : 150-165.

BIDEZ, J. 1932. La cité du monde et la cité du soleil. Paris, Belles Lettres.

BIEBER, MARGARETE. 1950. Bronze statuette of a comic actor. Record of the Art Museum, Princeton University 9 (2) : 5-12.

BISSINGER, JOSEF. 1925. Der Agrarstaat in Platons Gesetzen. Klio, Beiheft 17 (n. f. 4).

BLASS, F., and C. C. JENSEN. 1917. Hyperidis orationes sex cum ceterarum fragmentis. Leipzig, Teubner.

BLOCH, MARC. 1947. Comment et pourquoi finit l'esclavage antique. Annales. Économies. Sociétés. Civilisations 2 : 30-44 ; 161-170.

BLOCH, MORITZ. 1914. Die Freilassungsbedingungen der delphischen Freilassungsinschriften. Strassburg, Singer.

BOAK, A. E. R. 1933. Papyri from Tebtunis. Part I. Ann Arbor, Univ. of Michigan Press.

BOECKH, AUG. 1886. Die Staatshaushaltung der Athener. 3rd ed. 2 v. Berlin, Reimer.

BONHÖFFER, ADOLF. 1894. Die Ethik des Stoikers Epictet. Stuttgart, Ferd. Enke.

BONSIRVEN, J. 1934. Le judaisme Palestinien. Paris, Beauchesne.

BONWETSCH, G. N., HANS ACHELIS, and others. 1896-1916. Die griechischen christlichen Schriftsteller der ersten drei Jahrhunderte. 3 v. Leipzig, Hinrichs.

BRADY, THOS. A. 1935. Reception of the Egyptian cults by the Greeks. Univ. of Missouri Studies 10 (1). Columbia, Univ. of Missouri.

BRASSLOFF, STEPHAN. 1933. Sozialpolitische Motive in der römischen Rechtsentwickelung. Vienna, M. Perles.

BRAUN. MARTIN. 1934. Griechischer Roman und hellenistische Geschichtschreibung. Frankfurter Studien zur Religion und Kultur der Antike 6. Frankfurt am Main, Klostermann.

BREHAUT, E. 1933. Cato the Censor on farming. New York, Columbia Univ. Press.

BRUNS, C. G.-O. GRADENWITZ. 1909. Fontes iuris Romani antiqui. 7th ed. Tübingen, Mohr.

BRUNS, IVO. 1880. Die Testamente der griechischen Philosophen. Zeitschrift. d. Savigny-Stiftung, Rom. Abt. 1 : 1-52.

BÜCHELER, FRANZ-E. ZITELMANN. 1885. Das Recht von Gortyn. Rheinisches Museum, 40, Ergänzungsheft.

BÜCHER, KARL. 1912. Industrial Evolution, translated by S. M. Wickett. New York, Henry Holt.

BÜCHSENSCHÜTZ, B. 1869. Besitz und Erwerb im griechischen Alterthume. Halle, Waisenhaus.

BUCKLAND, W. W. 1908. The Roman law of slavery. Cambridge, Univ. Press.

BUCKLER, WM. H., W. M. CALDER, C. W. M. COX. 1914. Monuments from Iconium, Lycaonia and Isauria. Jour. Roman Studies 14 : 24-84.

BUCKLER, WM. H., and D. M. ROBINSON. 1932. Sardis. Leyden, Brill.

BURMESTER, O. H. E. KHS. 1948. The temple and cult of Aphrodite at Paphos. Farouk I University: Bull. Faculty of Arts. Alexandria.

BURY, JOHN B. 1889. History of the later Roman Empire from Arcadius to Irene. New York, Macmillan.

BÜTTNER, H. 1931. Mitteilungen aus der Papyrussammlung der Giessener Universitätsbibliothek. Griechische Privatbriefe, III. Schriften der hessischen Hochschulen, Univ. Giessen, Giessen, Töpelmann.

CAGNAT, RENÉ, G. LAFAYE, J. F. TOUTAIN, V. HENRY. 1901-1927. Inscr. Graecae ad res Romanas pertinentes. Vs. 1, 3, 4. Paris, Leroux.

CALDERINI, A. 1908. La manomissione e la condizione dei liberti in Grecia. Milan, Hoepli.

—— 1918. Liberi e schiavi nel mondo dei papiri greco-egizii. Milan, R. Accad. Scientifica-litteraria.

Cambridge ancient history. 1923-1939. Editors, Bury, J. B., S. A. Cook and F. E. Adcock et al. 12 v. Cambridge, Univ. Press.

Cambridge economic history of Europe. 1941-1952. Clapham, J. H. and Eileen Power, editors. 2 v. Cambridge, Univ. Press.

Cambridge medieval history 1. The Christian empire. 1924. Gwatkin, H. M., J. P. Whitney, editors. Cambridge, Univ. Press.

CAMERON, A. 1939. ΘΡΕΠΤΟΙ and related terms in the inscriptions of Asia Minor. Anatolian Studies Presented to Wm. H. Buckler. Manchester, Univ. Press.

CARL, GERTRUD. 1926. Die Agrarlehre Columellas. Vierteljahrsch. f. Soz. und Wirtschaftsgesch. 19 : 1-47.

CHEESMAN, G. L. 1914. Auxilia of the Roman army. Oxford, Clarendon Press.

CICCOTTI, E. 1899. Il tramonto della schiavitù nel mondo antico. Torino, Bocca.

—— 1940. 2nd ed. Udine, Edizione Accademica.

—— 1931. Il problema demografica nel mondo antico. Metron 9 : 111-165.

COLEMAN-NORTON, P. R., ed. 1951. Studies in Roman economic and social history in honor of Allan Chester Johnson. Princeton, Univ. Press.

COLLART, PAUL. 1926. Les papyrus Bouriant. Paris, Champion.

—— 1932. Un papyrus inédit et P. Rylands 178. Mélanges Gustave Glotz 1 : 241-247. Paris, Presses Universitaires.

COLLITZ, HERMANN, J. BAUNACK, F. BECHTEL et al. 1899-1915.

4 v. Sammlung der griechischen Dialektinschriften. Göttingen, Vandenhoeck-Ruprecht.

COMPARAETTI, D., and G. VITELLI. 1906-1915. Papiri Greco-Egizii. Papiri Fiorentini. 3v. Milan, Hoepli.

Corpus inscriptionum latinarum. 1863–. Berlin, Prussian Acad. of Letters.

DELLA CORTE, M. 1922. Pompeii: La villa rustica di Ti. Claudi Eutychi Caesaris liberti. *Not. degli scavi di antichità* **22**: 459-485.

CUMONT, FRANZ. 1919. Comment la Belgique fut romanisée. Brussels, Lamartine.

—— 1933. La grande inscription bachique du Metropolitan Museum: Commentaire religieux de l'inscription. *Amer. Jour. Archaeol.* **37**: 232-263.

—— 1926. Fouilles de Doura-Europos. Paris, Geuthner.

CURCIO, GAETANO. 1929. La primitiva civiltà latine agricola e il libro dell' agricultura di M. Porcio Catone. Firenze, Vallecchi.

DARESTE, R., B. HAUSSOULLIER, TH. REINACH. 1891-1904. Recueil des inscriptions juridiques grecques. 2 v. Paris, Leroux.

DAUX, GEORGES. 1945. Chronologie Delphique. Paris, de Boccard.

DAY, JOHN. 1932. Agriculture in the life of Pompeii. *Yale Class. Studies* **3**: 166-208.

—— 1942. An economic history of Athens under Roman domination. New York, Columbia Univ. Press.

DEISSMANN, ADOLF. 1926. Paul; a study in social and religious history. New York, Doran.

DELBRÜCK, H. 1900. Geschichte der Kriegskunst im Rahmen der politischen Geschichte. Berlin, G. Stilke.

DESSAU, H. 1892-1916. Inscriptiones latinae selectae. 3 v. Berlin, Weidmann.

DIEHL, E. 1942. Anthologia lyrica Graeca. 2nd ed. 2 v. Leipzig, Teubner.

DINDORF, L. 1832. Chronicon Paschale. 2 v. Bonn, Weber.

DITTENBERGER, W. 1903-1905. Orientis Graeci Inscriptiones. 2 v. Leipzig, Hirzel.

—— 1915-1921. Sylloge inscriptionum Graecarum. 3rd ed. 4 v. Leipzig, Hirzel.

DMITREV, A. D. 1950. The rising of the West Goths on the Danube and the slave revolt (in Russian). *Vestnik Drevnei Istorii* **1**: 66-80.

DONINI, AMBROGIO. 1951. The myth of salvation in ancient slave society. *Science and Society* **15**: 57-60.

DOPSCH, ALFONS. 1937. Economic and social foundations of European Civilisation. London, Kegan Paul.

DOUGHERTY, R. P. 1932. The shirkutu of Babylonian deities. *Yale Orient. Studies* **5** (2).

DRAGENDORFF, H. 1912. Westdeutschland zur Römerzeit. Leipzig, Quelle und Meyer.

DRAGENDORFF, H., and CARL WATZINGER. 1948. Arretinische Reliefkeramik mit Beschreibung der Sammlung in Tübingen. Reutlingen, Gryphius-Verlag.

DUCATI, P. 1925. Etruria antica. Turin, Bibl. Paravia.

DUFF, ARNOLD M. 1928. Freedmen in the early Roman Empire. Oxford, Clarendon Press.

DUREAU DE LA MALLE, ADOLPHE. 1840. Économie politique des Romains. Paris, Hachette.

EDGAR, C. C. 1925. Records of a village club. *Raccolta di scritti in onore di Giacomo Lumbroso*, 369-376. Milan, Aegyptus.

—— 1925-1931. Zenon Papyri, *Catalogue général des antiquités égyptiennes du Musée du Caire*. Cairo, Institut Français.

—— 1931. Zenon papyri in the University of Michigan collection. *Univ. of Mich. Studies, Humanistic Ser.* **24**. Ann Arbor, Univ. of Mich. Press.

—— 1934. A new group of Zenon papyri. *Bull. John Rylands Library* **18**: 111-130.

EHRENBERG, VICTOR. 1932. Der griechische und der hellenistische Staat. Leipzig, Teubner.

EMERTON, E. E. 1916. Introduction to the study of the Middle Ages. New York, Ginn and Co.

ENGELS, FRIEDRICH. 1942. Origin of the family, private property and the state. New York, International Publishers.

ENSSLIN, W. 1939. The reforms of Diocletian. *Cambridge Ancient History* **12**: 383-408.

EREMIAN, S. T. 1950. Regarding slavery and slaveholding in ancient Armenia (in Russian). *Vestnik Drevnei Istorii* **1**: 12-26.

EUSSNER, A. 1872. Commentariolum petitionis. Würzburg (dissertation), Thein.

FAIRON, E. 1900. L'organisation du palais impérial a Rom. *Musée Belge: Revue de Philologie Classique* **4**: 5-25. Louvain, Charles Peeters.

FARNELL, LEWIS R. 1921. Greek hero cults and ideas of immortality. Oxford, Clarendon Press.

FERGUSON, W. S. 1907. Researches in Athenian and Delian documents. *Klio* **7**: 213-240.

—— 1911. Hellenistic Athens. London, Macmillan.

FÉVRIER, J. G. 1931. Essai sur l'histoire politique et économique de Palmyre. Paris, Vrin.

FITZGERALD, AUGUSTINE. 1926. Letters of Synesius of Cyrene. London, Oxford Univ. Press.

FITZLER, KURT. 1910. Bergwerke u. Steinbrüche in röm. Aegypten. *Leipziger historische Abhandlungen* **21**.

FOUCART, PAUL. 1867. Mémoire sur l'affranchissement des esclaves par forme de vente a une divinité. Paris, Imprimerie Impériale.

Fouilles de Delphes. 1909-1943.
3(1) Epigraphie. Bourguet, E. Inscriptions—du sanctuaire au trésor des Athéniens. 1929.
3(2) Colin, G. Inscr. du trésor des Athéniens. 1909-1913.
3(3, 1) Daux, Georges et A. Salac. Inscr. depuis le trésor des Athéniens. 1939.
3(3, 2) Daux, Georges. Inscr. depuis le trésor des Athéniens. 1943.
3(6) Valmin, Natan. Les inscriptions du théâtre. 1939. Paris, de Boccard.

FRANK, TENNEY. 1916. Race mixture in the Roman empire. *Amer. Hist. Rev.* **21**: 689-708.

—— 1927. Economic history of Rome. Baltimore, Johns Hopkins Press.

—— 1930. Life and literature in the Roman republic. Berkeley, Univ. of Calif. Press.

—— 1932. The sacred treasury and the rate of manumission. *Amer. Jour. Philol.* **53**: 360-363.

—— 1933-1940. Economic survey of ancient Rome. 5v. Baltimore, Johns Hopkins Press.

FRIEDLAENDER, LUDWIG. 1920-1922. Darstellungen aus der Sittengeschichte Roms. 4v. Vs. 1-2, 10th ed.; vs. 3-4, 9th ed. Leipzig, Hirzel.

FUCHS, KARL. 1935. Die alttestamentliche Arbeitsgesetzgebung im Vergleich zum Codex Hammurapi. Heidelberg, Evangelisches Verlag.

GARDINER, A. H. 1935. A lawsuit arising from the purchase of two slaves. *JEA* **21**: 140-146.

GEBHARDT, OSCAR VON, and ADOLF HARNACK. 1904. Texte und Untersuchungen zur Geschichte der altchristlichen Literatur, **27**. Leipzig, Hinrichs.

VAN GELDER, H. 1900. Geschichte der alten Rhodier. The Hague, Nijhoff.

GERNET, LOUIS. 1923. Antiphon. Paris, Belles Lettres.

GHEDINI, GIUSEPPE. 1923. Lettere Cristiane. Milan, Vita e Pensiero.

GINSBURG, M. 1928. Rome et la Judée. Paris, Povolosky.

GIRARD, PAUL F. 1929. Manuel élémentaire de droit Romain. 8th ed. Paris, Rousseau.

GLOTZ, G. 1906. Études sociales et juridiques sur l'antiquité grecque. Paris, Hachette.

GLOTZ, GUSTAVE. 1920. Le travail dans la Grèce ancienne. Paris, Alcan.

—— 1926. Ancient Greece at work. New York, Knopf.

—— 1925. Histoire ancienne, deuxième partie. Histoire grecque. Paris, Presses Universitaires.

—— 1929. The Greek city and its institutions. New York, Knopf.

GOMME, A. W. 1933. The population of Athens in the fifth and fourth centuries B. C. Oxford, Blackwell.

GOODENOUGH, ERWIN R. 1929. Jurisprudence of the Jewish courts in Egypt. New Haven, Yale Univ. Press.

GOODSPEED, E. J. 1902. Greek Papyri from the Cairo Museum. Chicago, Univ. of Chicago Press.

—— 1923. The New Testament. An American translation. Chicago, Univ. of Chicago Press.

GORDON, MARY L. 1924. The nationality of slaves under the early Roman empire. Jour. Roman Studies 14: 91-111.

Graeca Halensis. 1913. Dikaiomata: Auszüge aus alexandrinischen Gesetzen und Verordnungen. Berlin, Weidmann.

GRAETZ, H. 1893. History of the Jews. 6v. Philadelphia, Jewish Publ. Society.

GRENFELL, BERNARD P. 1896. The revenue laws of Ptolemy Philadelphus. Oxford, Clarendon Press.

—— 1896. An Alexandrian erotic fragment and other Greek papyri. Oxford, Clarendon Press.

GRENFELL, BERNARD P., and A. S. HUNT. 1897. New classical fragments and other Greek and Latin papyri. Oxford, Clarendon Press.

GRENFELL, BERNARD P., ARTHUR S. HUNT, and others. 1898-. The Oxyrhynchus papyri. 21 v. to date. London, Egypt Exploration Society.

GRENFELL, BERNARD P., A. S. HUNT, J. G. SMYLY, E. J. GOODSPEED, et al. 1902-1938. The Tebtunis papyri. 3v. London. Vs. 1, 2, 3¹, Oxford Univ. Press; v. 3², Cambridge Univ. Press.

GRENIER, A. 1938. Sur la "coutume ouvrière" des potiers gallo-romains. Festschrift für August Oxé. Darmstadt, Wittich Verlag.

GRIFFITH, F. L. 1909. Catalogue of the demotic papyri in the John Rylands Library. Manchester, Univ. Press.

GROUSSET, RENÉ. 1947. Histoire de l'Arménie. Paris, Payot.

GRUPP, GEORG. 1903-1904. Kulturgeschichte der römischen Kaiserzeit. 2 v. Munich, Allgemeine Verlagsgesellschaft.

GSELL, STÉPHANE. 1914-1928. Histoire ancienne de l'Afrique du Nord. 8 v. Paris, Hachette.

—— 1922. Inscriptions latines de l'Algérie. Paris, E. Champion.

—— 1932. Esclaves ruraux dans l'Afrique romaine. Mélanges Gustave Glotz 1: 397-415. Paris, Presses Universitaires.

GUIRAUD, PAUL. 1893. La propriété foncière en Grèce jusqu'à la conquête romaine. Paris, Imprimerie Nationale.

GUMMERUS, H. 1906. Der römische Gutsbetrieb als wirtschaftlicher Organismus. Klio, Beiträge zur alten Geschichte. Supplb. 1, Beiheft 5. Leipzig, Dieterich.

GUMMERUS, HERMAN. 1916. Industrie und Handel. Pauly-W., RE 9: 1381-1535.

HALKIN, L. 1897. Les esclaves publics chez les Romains. Brussels, Société Belge.

HARDY, EDWARD R. 1931. Large estates of Byzantine Egypt. New York, Columbia Univ. Press.

HARNACK, ADOLF VON. 1908. The mission and expansion of Christianity in the first three centuries. 2 v. New York, Putnam's Sons.

HARTMANN, LUDO. 1910. Untergang der antiken Welt. Leipzig, Heller.

HARTMANN, LUDO, and H. KROMAYER. 1921. Römische Geschichte, Weltgeschichte in gemeinverständlicher Darstellung 3. Gotha, Perthes.

HASEBROEK, J. 1931. Griechische Wirtschafts- und Gesellschaftsgeschichte bis zur Perserzeit. Tübingen, Mohr.

HATZFELD, JEAN. 1919. Les trafiquants Italiens dans l'Orient hellénique. Bibliothèque des Écoles Françaises d'Athènes et de Rome 119. Paris, de Boccard.

HAUSSOULLIER, B. 1902. Études sur l'histoire de Milet et du Didymeion, Bibliothèque de l'École des Hautes Études, Sciences Historiques et Philologiques 138. Paris, Bouillon.

HEADLAM, WALTER. 1922. Herodas. The mimes and fragments. Cambridge, Univ. Press.

HEICHELHEIM, F. 1931. Review of Salvioli, Capitalismo. Historische Zeitschrift 143: 94-96.

HEICHELHEIM, FRITZ. 1938. Wirtschaftsgeschichte des Altertums. 2 v. Leyden, Sijthoff.

HEITLAND, W. E. 1921. Agricola; a study of agricultural life in the Graeco-Roman world from the point of view of labour. Cambridge, Univ. Press.

HEITZ, E. 1897. Neue Grundsätze der Volkswirtschaftslehre. Stuttgart, Kohlhammer.

HELLEBRAND, WALTER. 1939. Arbeitsrechtliches in den Zenon-Papyri. Festschrift Paul Koschaker 3: 241-251.

HERMET, FRÉDÉRIC. 1934. La Graufesenque. 2 v.
1. Vases sigillés.
2. Graffites.
Paris, Leroux.

HERZFELD, E., S. GUYER, W. M. CALDER, J. KEIL, ADOLF WILHELM, W. H. BUCKLER and others. 1930-1939. Monumenta Asiae Minoris antiqua. 6 v. Manchester, Univ. Press.

HERZOG, RUDOLPH. 1935. Urkunden zur Hochschulpolitik der römischen Kaiser. Sitzb. Akad. Berlin 32: 967-1019.

HETTICH, E. 1933. A study in ancient nationalism, the testimony of Euripides. Williamsport (Penna.), Bayard Press.

HIRSCHFELD, OTTO. 1902. Der Grundbesitz der römischen Kaiser in den ersten drei Jahrunderten. Klio: Beiträge zur alten Geschichte 2: 45-72, 284-315.

—— 1905. Die kaiserlichen Verwaltungsbeamten bis auf Diocletian. Berlin, Weidmann.

—— 1913. Kleine Schriften. Berlin, Weidmann.

HOGARTH, D. G. 1908. The Archaic Artemisia. British Museum Excavations at Ephesus. London, British Museum.

HOHL, ERNST. 1950. Zeit und Zweck der Pseudoxenophontischen Athenaion Politeia. Class. Phil. 45: 26-35.

HOMOLLE, TH. 1884. Les Romains a Délos. BCH 8: 75-158.

—— Comptes et inventaires des temples Déliens. BCH 14: 389-511.

HOW, W. W., and J. WELLS. 1928. A commentary on Herodotus. 2nd ed. Oxford, Clarendon Press.

HUME, DAVID. 1882. Of the populousness of ancient nations. Essays moral, political and literary 1: 381-443. London, Longmans, Green.

HUNT, A. S., J. DE M. JOHNSON, V. MARTIN, C. H. ROBERTS, E. G. TURNER. 1911-1952. Catalogue of the Greek and Latin papyri in the John Rylands library. 4v. Manchester, Univ. Press.

HUNT, A. S., and C. C. EDGAR. 1932-1934. Select Papyri. 2 v. Loeb Classical Library. New York, Putnam's Sons.

HURD, JOHN C. 1862. Law of freedom and bondage in the United States. 2 v. Boston, Little Brown.

IHERING, RUDOLPH VON. 1874. Geist des römischen Rechts. 3 v. Leipzig, Breitkopf and Härtel.

ILBERG, J. 1930. Rufus von Ephesos. Ein griechischer Arzt in trajanischer Zeit, Abhandlungen der sächsischen Akademie der Wissenschaften, phil.-hist. Klasse 41 (1) : 1-53.

Inscriptiones Graecae. 1873-. Königliche Akademie der Wissenschaften, Berlin, 14 v. at present.
—— Inscriptiones Graecae,² (editio minor). 1913-. König. Akad. der Wissenschaften, Berlin. 1-4 and 9 (1).

JACOB, O. 1928. Les esclaves publics à Athènes. *Bibliothèque de la Faculté de philosophie et lettres de l'Université de Liège* 35.

JACOBY, FELIX. 1923-1950. Die Fragmente der griechischen Historiker. 5 v. Berlin, Weidmann.

JOHNSON, ALLAN C., H. B. VAN HOESEN, E. H. KASE, S. P. GOODRICH. 1931-1942. Papyri in the Princeton University collections. V. 1, Baltimore, Johns Hopkins Press; v. 2-3, Princeton, Princeton Univ. Press.

JOHNSON, JOTHAM. 1933. Excavations at Minturnae 2(1). Philadelphia, Univ. of Pennsylvania Press.
—— 1932. Dura Studies (Thesis). Philadelphia, Univ. of Pennsylvania.

JONKERS, ENGBERT JAN. 1933. Economische en sociale toestanden in het Romeinsche Rijk blijkende uit het corpus juris. Wageningen, H. Weinman.
—— De l'influence du Christianisme sur la législation relative à l'esclave dans l'antiquité. *Mnemosyne. Bibliotheca Classica Batava*, 3rd ser., 1 : 241-280.

JOUGUET, PIERRE. 1911. Papyrus de Théadelphie. Paris, Thorin et Fils.
—— 1912-1928. Papyrus de Lille. 2 v. *Institut Papyrologique de l'Université de Lille*. Paris, Leroux.

JULLIAN, CAMILLE. 1913. Histoire de la Gaule. Paris, Hachette.

KAIBEL, GEORG. 1888. Inschriften aus Pisidien. *Hermes* 23 : 531-545.

KALÉN, TURE. 1932. Berliner Leihgabe griechischer Papyri. *Uppsala Universitets Arsskrift* 1.

KARLOWA, OTTO. 1901. Römische Rechtsgeschichte. Leipzig, Veit.

KASE, E. H. 1933. A papyrus roll in the Princeton collection. Baltimore, J. H. Furst.

KEIL, B. 1902. Anonymus Argentinensis. Strassburg, Trübner.

KENYON, FREDR., H. I. BELL. 1893-1917. Greek papyri in the British Museum. 5 v. London, British Museum.

KERN, OTTO. 1900. Die Inschriften von Magnesia am Maeander. Berlin, Spermann.

KISA, A. C. 1908. Das Glas im Altertume. Leipzig, Hiersemann.

KOCK, THEODOR. 1884. Comicorum Atticorum fragmenta. 3 v. Leipzig, Teubner.

KOHLER, JOSEF, and E. ZIEBARTH. 1912. Das Stadtrecht von Gortyn. Göttingen, Vandenhoeck und Ruprecht.

KÖRTE, ALFRED. 1929. Hellenistic Poetry. New York, Columbia Univ. Press.
—— 1912. Menander, Epitrepontes. Leipzig, Teubner.
—— 1932. Eine Verlustliste aus der Schlacht bei den Agrinusen. *Philologische Wochenschrift* 52 : 1027-1031.

KOSCHAKER, PAUL. 1931. Über einige griechische Rechtsurkunden aus den östlichen Randgebieten des Hellenismus. *Abh. d. sächsisch. Akad. der Wissensch., philol.-hist. Klasse* 42 (1), 1934.
—— 1935. Keilschriftrecht. *Ztsch. der morgenländischen Gesellschaft* 89 (n. f. 14) : 1-39.

KRAELING, EMIL G. 1952. New light on the Elephantine colony. *The Biblical Archaeologist* 15 (3), 50-67.
—— 1953. The Brooklyn Museum Aramaic Papyri. New Haven, Yale Univ. Press.

KRAUS, SAMUEL. 1908. Sklavenbefreiung in den jüdisch-griechischen Inschriften aus Süd-Russland. *Festschrift zu Ehren des Dr. A. Harkavy*, 52-66. St. Petersburg.
—— Talmudische Archäologie. *Schriften von der Gesellschaft zur Förderung der Wissenschaft des Judentums* 5.

KROLL, WILH. 1930. Römische Erotik. *Ztschr. f. Sexualwissenschaft* 17.

—— 1933. Die Kultur der ciceronischen Zeit. Leipzig, Dieterich.

KUEBLER, B. 1934. Griechische Einflüsse auf Entwicklung der römischen Rechtswissenschaft gegen Ende der republikanischen Zeit. *Atti del Congresso Internazionale di Diritto Romano, Roma* 1 : 79-98. Pavia, Successori Fusi.

KÜHN, CARL. 1821-1833. Claudii Galeni opera omnia. 20 v. Leipzig, Cnobloch.

LAFERRIÉRE, M. F. 1860. Mémoire concernant l'influence du Stoicism sur la doctrine des jurisconsultes Romains. *Mémoires de l'Académie des Sciences Morales et Politique* 10 : 579-685.

LAISTNER, M. L. W. 1951. Christianity and pagan culture in the later Roman empire. Ithaca, Cornell Univ. Press.

LANGER, C. 1919. De servi persona apud Menandrum. Bonn (diss.), Georgi.

LAQUEUR, R. 1924. Hellenismus. *Schriften der hessischen Hochschulen, Universität Giessen* 1.

LAUM, BERNHARD. 1914. Stiftungen in der griechischen und römischen Antike. 2v. Leipzig and Berlin, Teubner.

LEA, HENRY C. 1883. Studies in church history. Philadelphia, Henry C. Lea's Sons.

LE BAS, PHILIPPE, and W. H. WADDINGTON. 1847-1887. Voyage archéologique en Grèce et en Asie Mineur. 3 v. Paris, Didot.

LECKY, WILLIAM E. H. 1927. History of European morals. 3rd ed. New York, Appleton.

LECRIVAIN, C. 1904. Études sur l'histoire Auguste. Paris, Fontemoing.

LEIPOLDT, JOHANNES. Schenute von Atripe. *Texte und Untersuchungen zur Geschichte der altchristlichen Literatur* 25 (n. f. 10).

LENEL, OTTO. 1927. Das edictum perpetuum. Leipzig, Tauchnitz.

LEON, H. J. 1927. The language of the Greek inscriptions from the Jewish catacombs at Rome. *TAPA* 58 : 210-231.

LEVY, ERNST. 1951. West Roman vulgar law. The law of property. *Memoirs Amer. Philos. Soc.* 29. Philadelphia.

LEWALD, HANS. 1910. Zur Personalexekution im Rechte der Papyri. Leipzig, Veit.

LICHY, JOANNES. 1927. De servorum condicione quid senserit L. Annaeus Seneca. Münster, Monasteria Westfalorum.

LIEBESNY, HERBERT. 1936. Ein Erlass des Königs Ptolemaios II Philadelphos. *Aegyptus* 16 : 257-264.

LINFORTH, I. M. 1919. Solon the Athenian. Berkeley, Univ. of Calif. Press.

LIPINSKY, H. 1903. Über einige Inschriften in Südrussland. *Jüdisch litterarische Gesellschaft, Jahrbücher* 1 : 321-324. Frankfurt, Kauffman.

LOT, FERDINAND. 1931. The end of the ancient world. New York, Knopf.
—— 1928. Du regime de l'hospitalité. *Rev. Belge de Philol. et d'Histoire* 7 : 975-1011.

LOTH, JOSEPH. 1924. Le graffiti de Blickweiler dans la Palatinat occidentale. *Académie des Inscriptions et Belles-lettres. Comptes rendus*, 67-75.

LURIA, S. 1933. Frauenpatriotismus und Sklavenemanzipation in Argos. *Klio* 28 (n. f. 8) : 211-228.

MAGIE, DAVID. 1950. Roman rule in Asia Minor. 2 v. Princeton, Univ. Press.
—— 1922-1924. Scriptores historiae Augustae. 3 v. *Loeb Classical Library*. New York, Putnam's.

MAHAFFY, JOHN P., and J. G. SMYLY. 1891-1905. The Flinders Petrie papyri. 3 v. *Cunningham Memoirs 8, 9, 11*. Dublin, Academy House.

MAIURI, A. 1933. La casa del Menandro. 2 v. Rome, Libreria dello stato.

MANSI, GIOVANE D. *et al.* 1759-1927. *Sacrorum conciliorum collectio.* 53v. Arnhem, Welter.

MAROI, FULVIO. 1925. Intorno all'adozione degli esposti nell'

Egitto romano. *Raccolta di scritti in onore di Giacomo Lumbroso*, 377-405. Milan, "Aegyptus."

MARQUARDT, J. 1884. Römische Staatsverwaltung. Leipzig, Hirzel.

MASPERO, JEAN. 1911-1916. Papyrus grecs d'époque byzantine. *Catalogue général des antiquités égyptiennes du Musée du Caire* 9 (1, 2, 3). Cairo, Institut Français.

MAYSER, EDWIN. 1923-1934. Grammatik der griechischen Papyri aus der Ptolemäerzeit. 2 v. Berlin, de Gruyter.

MEINEKE, AUGUST. 1847-1857. Poetae comici. Fragmenta comicorum Graecorum. 5 v. Berlin, Reimer.

MEISSNER, BRUNO. 1920-1925. Babylonien und Assyrien. 2 v. Heidelberg, Winter.

Mélanges Gustave Glotz. 2 v. 1932. Paris, Presses Universitaires.

MENDELSOHN, ISAAC. 1949. Slavery in the ancient Near East. New York, Oxford Univ. Press.

MEYER, ED. 1898. Die Sklaverei im Altertum. Dresden, v. Zahn und Jaensch.

—— 1924. Die Sklaverei im Altertum. *Kleine Schriften* 1 (2nd ed.) : 169-212. Halle, Niemeyer.

MEYER, PAUL M. 1920. Juristische Papyri. Berlin, Weidmannsche Buchhandlung.

—— 1924. Griechische Urkunden der Hamburger Staats- und Universitätsbibliothek. Leipzig, Teubner.

—— 1916. Griechische Texte aus Ägypten. Berlin, Weidmann.

MICHELL, H. 1940. The economics of ancient Greece. New York, Macmillan.

MICKWITZ, GUNNAR. 1932. Geld und Wirtschaft im römischen Reiche des vierten Jahrhunderts, *Societas Scientiarum Fennica, Commentationes Humanarum Litterarum* 4 (2).

—— 1936. Die Kartellfunktionen der Zünfte. *Finska Vetenskaps-Societeten. Commentationes Human. Litterarum* 8 (3) : 1-250.

MIGNE, JACQUES-PAUL. Patrologiae cursus completus. 1844-1880, 221 v., Series Latina ; 1854-1866, 161 v., Series Graeca, Paris.

MINNS, ELLIS. 1913. Scythians and Greeks. Cambridge, Univ. Press.

MITTEIS, LUDWIG. 1891. Reichsrecht und Volksrecht in den östlichen Provinzen des römischen Kaiserreichs. Leipzig, Teubner.

—— 1906. Griechische Urkunden der Papyrussammlung zu Leipzig. Leipzig, Teubner.

MITTEIS, LUDWIG, and U. WILCKEN. 1912. Grundzüge und Chrestomathie der Papyruskunde. 2 v. Leipzig, Teubner.

MOMMSEN, THEODOR. 1884. Die italische Bodentheilung. *Hermes* 19 : 393-416.

—— 1887. Römisches Staatsrecht, 2, in Marquardt, Joachim, and Theodor Mommsen, *Handbuch der römischen Alterthümer*. Leipzig, Hirzel.

—— 1878-1905. History of Rome. 3 v. New York, Scribner.

—— 1899. Römisches Strafrecht. Leipzig, Duncker and Humblot.

—— 1905-1907. Juristische Schriften. 3 v. Berlin, Weidmann.

MOMMSEN, THEODOR, and H. BLÜMNER. 1893. Der Maximaltarif des Diocletian. Berlin, Reimer.

Monumenta Asiae Minoris Antiqua. 1930-1939. Edited by E. Herzfeld, S. Guyer, W. M. Calder, J. Keil, Adolf Wilhelm, W. H. Buckler *et al.* Manchester, Univ. Press.

MOORE, ELLEN W. 1935. Neo-Babylonian business and administrative documents. Ann Arbor, Univ. of Michigan Press.

MOORE, GEORGE FOOTE. 1927. Judaism. 2 v. Cambridge, Harvard Univ. Press.

MOR, CARLO G. 1928. La " manomissione in ecclesia." *Rivista di Storia del Diritto Italiano* 1 : 87-108. Rome, Tip. " Leonardo da Vinci."

MORROW, GLENN. 1939. Plato's law of slavery. *Univ. of Illinois Stud. in Lang. and Lit.* 25 (3).

MÜLLER, CARL. 1841-1875. Fragmenta Historicorum Graecorum. 5 v. Paris, Didot.

NELSON, BENJ. N. 1949. The idea of usury. Princeton, Univ. Press.

NOTOPOULOS, J. A. 1941. The slaves at the battle of Marathon. *Amer. Jour. Philol.* 62 : 352-354.

OERTEL, F. 1917. Die Liturgie. Leipzig, Teubner.

—— 1927. Review of Laqueur, R., Hellenismus. *Gnomon* 3 : 94-96.

—— 1930. Zur Frage der attischen Grossindustrie. *Rheinisches Museum* 79 : 230-252.

OLMSTEAD, FREDERICK L. 1861. The cotton kingdom. New York, Mason Bros.

D'ORGEVAL, BERNARD. 1950. L'empereur Hadrien. Œuvre législative et administrative. Paris, Editions Domat Montchrestien.

ORMEROD, H. A. 1914. Piracy in the ancient world. Liverpool, Univ. Press.

OTTO, W. 1905. Priester und Tempel im hellenistischen Ägypten. 2 v. Leipzig, Teubner.

OTTO, WALTER. 1928. Beiträge zur Seleukidengeschichte. *Abh. Bayer. Akad., philos.-philol. Klasse* 34 (1).

—— 1950. Beiträge zur Hierodulie im hellenistischen Ägypten. *Abh. Bayer. Akad. der Wissensch., philos.-hist. Klasse,* n. f., **29.**

OXÉ, A. 1925. Die Töpferrechnungen von der Graufesenque. *Bonner Jahrbücher* 130 : 38-99. Bonn, Marcus and Weber.

—— 1933. Arretinische Reliefgefässe vom Rhein. Frankfurt am Main, Baer.

—— 1934. Frühgallische Reliefgefässe vom Rhein. Frankfurt am Main, Baer.

PAOLI, UGO. 1930. Studi di diritto attico. Florence. Bemporad.

Papyrus Halensis 1. 1913. Dikaiomata, Auszüge aus alexandrinischen Gesetzen und Verordnungen. Berlin, Weidmann.

PARK, MARION E. 1921. The plebs in Cicero's day. Cambridge, (Mass.), Cosmos Press.

PARTSCH, J. 1908. Review of L. Wenger, Die Stellvertretung. *Archiv für Papyrusforschung* 11 : 495-502.

—— 1920. Die alexandrinischen Dikaiomata. *Arch. f. Pap.* 6 : 34-76.

—— 1909. Griechisches Bürgschaftsrecht. Leipzig, Teubner.

PARTSCH, JOSEF. 1916. Mittheilungen aus der Freiburger Papyrussammlung. *Sitz. d. Heidelberger Akad.* 7, *Abh.* 10.

—— 1921. Die Lehre vom Scheingeschäfte im römischen Rechte. *Zeitschrift der Savigny-Stiftung, Rom. Abt.,* **42** : 227-252.

—— 1921. Die griechische Publizität der Grundstücksverträge im Ptolemäerrecht. *Festschrift für Otto Lenel.* Leipzig, Tauchnitz.

PERDRIZET, PAUL. 1896. Mèn. *BCH* 20 : 55-106.

PERNICE, ALFRED. 1886. Zum römischen Sacralrecht. *Sitzb. preuss. Akad. Berlin,* 1169-1203.

PERNICE, (LOTHAR) ALFRED. 1895-1900. Marcus Antistius Labeo. 2nd ed. 2 v. Halle, Niemeyer.

PERSSON, AXEL. 1923. Staat und Manufaktur im römischen Reiche. Lund, Blom.

PETAVIUS, DIONYSIUS. 1612. Synesii episcopi Cyrenes opera. Paris, Drouart.

PETERSEN, EUGEN. 1896. Die Marcussäule auf Piazza Colonna in Rom. Munich, Bruckmann.

PETROPOULOS, G. A. 1933. An unpublished Greek papyrus of the Athens collection. *Aegyptus* 13 : 563-568.

PFEIFFER, RUDOLF. 1949. Callimachus. Oxford, Clarendon Press.

Picard, Ch. 1921. Fouilles de Thasos (1914 et 1920). *Bull. Correspondance Hellénique* 45 : 87-173.

PIGANIOL, ANDRÉ. 1947. Histoire générale. Histoire romaine 2. *L'empire chrétien.* Paris, Presses Universitaires.

PIRENNE, JACQUES. 1932-1935. Histoire des institutions et du droit privé de l'ancienne Égypte. 3 v. Brussels, Fondation Égyptologique.

PLAUMANN, GEBHARD. 1914. Griechische Papyri der Sammlung Gradenwitz. *Sitzb. Heidelb. Akad., phil.-hist. Klasse* **5**, *Abh.* 15.

PÖHLMANN, ROBERT VON, and FRIEDR. OERTEL. 1925. Geschichte der sozialen Frage und des Sozialismus in der antiken Welt. 3rd ed. Munich, Beck.

POLAND, FRANZ. 1909. Geschichte des griechischen Vereinswesens. *Preisschriften der jablonowskischen Gesellschaft* **23.** Leipzig, Teubner.

POWELL, J. Ü. 1925. Collectanea Alexandrina. Poetae graeci minores. Oxford, Clarendon Press.

POWELL, J. ENOCH. 1936. The Rendel Harris papyri. Cambridge, Univ. Press.

PRÉAUX, CLAIRE. 1939. L'économie royale des Lagides. Brussels, Fondation Égyptologique.

PREISIGKE, FRIEDRICH. 1906. Ein Sklavenkauf des 6. Jahrhunderts. *Arch. f. Pap.* **3**: 414-424.

—— 1912. Griechische Papyrus der kaiserlichen Universitäts- und Landesbibliothek zu Strassburg. Leipzig, Hinrich.

—— 1922. Namenbuch. Heidelberg, Selbstverlag.

—— PREISIGKE, F. BILABEL and EMIL KIESSLING. 1915-1950. Sammelbuch griechischer Urkunden aus Ägypten. 5 v. Strassburg, Trübner; Selbstverlag Bilabel, Heidelberg; Harrassowitz, Wiesbaden.

—— Preisigke and E. Kiessling. 1925-1944. Wörterbuch der griechischen Papyri. 4 v. Vs. 1-3, Heidelberg, Selbstverlag; v. 4, Berlin, Selbstverlag (Kiessling).

PREUSCHEN, ERWIN. 1893. Analecta. Kürzere Texte zur Geschichte der alten Kirche und der Kanons. *Sammlung ausgewählter kirchen- und dogmengeschichtlicher Quellenschriften* **8.** Leipzig, Mohr.

PRINGSHEIM, FRITZ. 1950. The Greek law of sale. Weimar, Böhlaus.

PRITCHARD, JAMES B., ed. 1950. Ancient Near Eastern texts relating to the Old Testament. Princeton, Univ. Press.

PROTT, HANS VON, L. ZIEHEN. 1896-1906. Leges Graecorum sacrae. 2 parts. Leipzig, Teubner.

PUGLIESE CARRATELLI, GIOVANNI. 1940. Tabulae Herculanenses. *La Parola del Passato* **1**: 379-385.

RABEL, E. 1902. Die Haftung des Verkäufers wegen Mangels am Rechte. Leipzig, Veit.

RAMSAY, SIR WILLIAM M. 1922. Pagan revivalism under the Roman empire. *Aberystwyth studies* **4**: 1-11. Aberystwyth, Univ. of Wales Press.

—— 1928. Asianic elements in Greek civilization. New Haven, Yale Univ. Press.

REES, B. R. 1950. Popular religion in Greco-Roman Egypt. Part 2: The transition to Christianity. *JEA* **36**: 86-100.

REIL, THEODOR. 1913. Beiträge zur Kenntnis des Gewerbes im hellenistischen Ägypten. Borna-Leipzig, Noske.

REINACH, THÉODORE. 1920-1921. Un code fiscal de l'Égypte romaine. Le gnomon de l'idiologue. *Nouvelle revue historique de droit français et étranger* **44**: 5-134.

RENAN, ERNEST. 1880. The influence of Rome on Christianity. London, Williams and Norgate.

RICCOBONO, S. 1935. Cristianesimo e diritto Romano. *Rivista di Diritto Civile, Scienze Giuridiche* **43.**

—— 1935. L'influsso del Cristianesimo sul diritto Romano. *Atti del Congresso Internazionale di Diritto Romano, Roma* **2**: 61-122.

RICCOBONO, SALVATORE, JR. 1950. Il gnomon dell' idios logos. Palermo, G. Mori.

RIESE, ALEXANDER. 1878. Expositio totius mundi. *Geographi Latini Minores.* Heilbronn, Henning Brothers.

ROBERT, LOUIS. 1933. Sur les inscriptions de Chios. *BCH* **57**: 505-543.

ROBERTIS, FRANCESCO DE. 1938. Diritto associativo Romano dal collegi della repubblica alle corporazioni del basso impero. Bari, Laterza and Sons.

ROBERTS, E. S., and E. A. GARDNER. 1905. Introduction to Greek epigraphy, Part II. Cambridge, Univ. Press.

ROHDEN, P. VON. 1895. Asiaticus. Pauly-W., *RE* **2**: 1578-1579.

ROOS, A. G. 1933. Papyri Groninganae. *Verhand. d. Akad. Amsterdam* **32.**

ROSTOVTZEFF, M. I. 1904. Die Geschichte der Staatspacht in der römischen Kaiserzeit bis Diokletian. *Philologus,* Supplementband **9.**

—— 1910. Studien zur Geschichte des römischen Kolonates. *Archiv für Papyrusforschung,* Beiheft **1.** Leipzig, Teubner.

—— 1916-1918. Pontus, Bithynia and the Bosporus. *Annual Brit. School at Athens* **22**: 1-22.

—— 1923. Economic policy of the Pergamene kings. *Anatolian Studies Presented to Sir Wm. Ramsay,* 359-390. Manchester, Univ. Press.

—— 1926. Social and economic history of the Roman empire. Oxford, Clarendon Press.

—— 1931. Review of Tait, J. G., Greek ostraca from the Bodleian library. *Gnomon* **7**: 21-26.

—— 1932. Caravan cities. Oxford, Clarendon Press.

—— 1932. Seleucid Babylonia. *Yale Class. Studies* **3**: 1-114.

—— 1941. The social and economic history of the Hellenistic world. 3 v. Oxford, Clarendon Press.

RUBIN, SIMON. 1920. Das Talmudische Recht. Die Sklaverei. Vienna, Nibur-Verlag.

SALVIOLI, G. 1929. Il capitalismo nel mondo antico. Bari, Laterza.

SARGENT, RACHEL L. 1924. The size of the slave population at Athens. *Univ. of Illinois Stud. in Social Sciences* **12** (3).

SAYCE, A. H., and A. E. COWLEY. 1906. Aramaic papyri discovered at Assuan. London, Moring.

SCHACHERMEYR, F. 1930. Die römisch-punischen Verträge. *Rh. Mus.* **79**: 350-380.

SCHÄFER, DIEDRICH. 1950. Pistis. Pauly-W., *RE* **20** (2): 1812-1813.

—— 1933. Zu den ptolemäischen ΠΙΣΤΕΙΣ. *Philologus* **88**: 296-301.

SCHIESS, TRAUGOTT. 1888. Die römischen collegia funeraticia nach den Inschriften. Munich, Ackermann.

SCHILLER, A. A. 1935. The Coptic ΛΟΓΟΣ ΜΙΝΟΥΤΕ documents. *Studi in memoria di Aldo Albertoni.* 3 v. Padua, Tipografia del Seminario.

SCHILLER, LUDWIG. 1847. Die Lehre des Aristoteles von der Sklaverei. *Jahresbericht von der königlichen Studienanstalt zu Erlangen.* Erlangen, Barfus.

SCHLAIFER, ROBT. 1936. Greek theories of slavery from Homer to Aristotle. *Harvard Stud. in Class. Philol.* **47**: 165-204.

SCHMIDT, J. 1892. Der Sklave bei Euripides. *Wissenschaftliche Beilage zum Jahresberichte der Fürsten- und Landesschule zu Grimma.* Grimma, Schiertz.

SCHNEIDER, A. 1892. Zur Geschichte der Sclaverei im alten Rom. Zürich, Schulthess.

SCHÖNBAUER, E. 1924. Beiträge zur Geschichte des Liegenschaftsrechts im Altertum. Leipzig, Graz.

SCHOFF, WILFRED H. 1912. The Periplus of the Erythraean Sea. New York, Longmans, Green.

SCHOW, N. 1788. Charta papyracea graece scripta Musei Borgiani. Rome, Ant. Fulgonium.

SCHUBART, W. 1918. Einführung in die Papyruskunde. Berlin, Weidmann.

—— 1920. Rom und die Ägypter nach dem Gnomon des Idios Logos. *Zeitschrift für ägyptische Sprache und Altertumskunde* **56**: 80-95.

—— 1925. Oikogeneia. *Raccolta di scritti in onore di Giacomo Lumbroso*, 49-67. Milan, "Aegyptus."

—— 1934. Galli und Spadones im Gnomon des Idios Logos. *Aegyptus* **14**: 89-92.

—— 1935. Vom Altertum zum Mittelalter. *Arch. f. Pap.* **11**: 74-106.

SCHUBART, W., and EMIL SECKEL. 1919. Der Gnomon des Idios Logos. *Berliner Griechische Urkunden* **5**. Berlin, Weidmann.

SCHÜCK, JULIUS. 1875. Über die Sklaverei bei den Griechen. *Programm des städtischen Johannes-Gymnasiums zu Breslau.* Breslau, Grass, Barth.

SCHULTEN, A. 1930. The Romans in Spain. *Cambridge Ancient Hist.* **8**: 306-324. Cambridge, Univ. Press.

SCHWABE, M. 1938. P. Nessana inv. 13306. *Magnes Anniversary Book*, 224-235. Jerusalem, Hebrew Univ. Press.

SCHWAHN, WALTER. 1930. Gehalts- und Lohnzahlung in Athen. *Rhein. Mus.* **79**: 170-177.

SCHWARTZ, EDUARD. 1885. Hekataios von Teos. *Rh. Mus.*, n. f., **40**: 221-262.

SECKEL, EMIL, W. SCHUBART, and UXKULL VON GYLLENBAND. 1919 and 1934. Der Gnomon des Idios Logos (*BGU* 5). Berlin, Weidmann.

SECKEL, E., and P. M. MEYER. 1928. Zum sogennanten Gnomon des Idios Logos. *Sitzb. der Akad. der Wissenschaften, Berlin, phil.-hist. Klasse*, 424-456.

SEECK, OTTO. 1913. Geschichte des Untergangs der antiken Welt. 6 v. Berlin, Siemenroth.

SEGRÈ, A. 1922. Circolazione monetaria e prezzi nel mondo antico ed in particolare in Egitto. Rome, Libreria di Cultura.

—— 1944. Liberi tenuti in schiavitù nella Siria etc. *Archivio Giuridico* **11**: 161-182.

SEIDL, ERWIN. 1935. Übersetzungen und Abhandlungen zum vorptolemäischen Rechte Aegyptens (1930-1934). *Kritische Vierteljahrschrift für Gesetzgebung und Rechtsgeschichte*, 3rd ser., **27**: 268-277.

—— 1940. Römische Rechtsgeschichte und römisches Civilprozessrecht. Hannover, Wissenschaftliche Verlagsanstalt.

SELIGMAN, EDWIN R. A. 1902. The economic interpretation of history. New York, Columbia Univ. Press.

SETHE, KURT, and J. PARTSCH. 1920. Demotische Urkunden zum aegyptischen Bürgschaftsrecht. *Abh. Sächs. Akad., phil.-hist. Klasse* **32**: 433-438.

SEYMOUR, THOS. D. 1907. Life in the Homeric Age. New York, Macmillan.

SIEGEL, BERNARD. 1945. Some methodological considerations for a comparative study of slavery. *Amer. Anthropologist* **47**: 357-390.

—— 1947. Slavery during the third dynasty of Ur. *Amer. Anthropologist* **49**: 1-8.

STARR, C. G. 1941. The Roman Imperial Navy. Ithaca, N. Y., Cornell Univ. Press.

STRACK, MAX L. 1901. Inschriften aus ptolemäischer Zeit. *Archiv für Papyrusforschung* **1**: 200-210.

STROUX, JOHANNES. 1926. Summum jus summa injuria; ein Kapitel aus der Geschichte der interpretatio juris. Leipzig, Teubner.

—— 1949. Römische Rechtswissenschaft und Rhetorik. Potsdam, Stichnote.

Studi in onore di P. Bonfante. 1936. 4 v. Palermo, Arti grafiche G. Castiglia.

SUDHOFF, K. 1909. Ärztliches aus griechischen Papyrusurkunden. Leipzig, Borna.

SWOBODA, HEINRICH. 1905. Beiträge zur griechischen Rechtsgeschichte. *Zeitschrift der Savigny-Stiftung, Rom. Abt.* **26**: 149-284.

TAEGER, FRITZ. 1928. Untersuchungen zur römischen Geschichte und Quellenkunde. Tiberius Gracchus. Stuttgart, Kohlhammer.

TARN, W. W. 1938. The Greeks in Bactria and India. Cambridge, Univ. Press.

TAUBENSCHLAG, R. 1916. Das Strafrecht im Rechte der Papyri. Leipzig, Teubner.

—— 1930. Das Sklavenrecht im Rechte der Papyri. *Ztsch. Sav.-Stift., Rom. Abt.* **50**: 140-169.

—— 1936. Die Alimentationspflicht im Rechte der Papyri. *Studi in onore di Salvatore Riccobono* **1**: 505-518. Palermo, Castiglia.

—— 1938. The ancient Greek city laws in Ptolemaic Egypt. *Actes du Ve Congrès Internat. de Papyrologie*, 471-489. Brussels, Fondation Égyptologique.

—— 1944. The law of Greco-Roman Egypt in the light of the papyri. New York, Herald Square Press.

—— 1951. Periods and terms in Greco-Roman Egypt. *Atti del Congresso Internazionale di Diritto Rom.* **3**: 363-366.

TURNER, ERIC G. 1939. Catalogue of the Greek and Latin papyri in the University of Aberdeen. *Aberdeen Univ. Studies*, **110** (3). Aberdeen, Univ. Press.

URE, P. N. 1922. The origin of tyranny. Cambridge, Univ. Press.

VERLINDEN, CHARLES. 1934. L'esclavage dans le monde ibérique médiéval. *Anuario de Historia del Derecho Español* **11**: 283-448.

VILLARD, A. 1882. Histoire du proletariat. Paris, Guillaumin.

VITELLI, G., and D. COMPARETTI. 1906-1915. Papiri Greco-Egizii. Documenti pubblici e privati dell'età Romana e Bizantina. 3 v. Milan, Hoepli.

VITELLI, G., and M. NORSA. 1912-1951. Pubblicazioni della società Italiana. Papiri greci e latini. 13 v. Florence, Tipografia Ariani.

VOLLMANN, FRANZ. 1880. Über das Verhältnis der späteren Stoa zur Sklaverei im römischen Reiche. Diss., Erlangen.

WALBANK, F. W. 1946. The decline of the Roman empire in the West. London, Corbett Press.

WALLON, HENRI. 1879. Histoire de l'esclavage dans l'antiquité. 3 v. Paris, Librairie Hachette.

WALTZING, J.-P. 1895-1900. Étude historique sur les corporations professionelles chez les Romains. 4 v. Louvain, Peeters.

WASZYNSKI, S. 1898. De servis Atheniensium publicis. Diss., Berlin, G. Schade.

WEBER, M. 1924. Gesammelte Aufsätze zur Sozial- und Wirtschaftsgeschichte. Tübingen, Mohr.

WEINREICH, OTTO. 1919. Stiftung und Kultsatzungen eines Privatheiligtums in Philadelphia in Lydien. *Sitzb. Heidelberg. Akad., phil.-hist. Klasse, Abh.* **16**: 1-68.

WEISS, EGON. 1923. Griechisches Privatrecht. Leipzig, Meiner.

WELLES, C. BRADFORD. 1936. A Yale fragment of the acts of Appian. *Trans. Amer. Philol. Ass.* **67**: 7-23.

WENGER, L. 1906. Die Stellvertretung im Rechte der Papyri. Leipzig, Teubner.

—— 1922. Ein christliches Freiheitszeugnis. *Beiträge für Geschichte des christlichen Altertums (Festgabe Albert Ehrhard)*, 451-478. Bonn, Schroeder.

WESSELY, CARL. 1902. Die Stadt Arsinoe (Krokodilopolis) in griechischer Zeit. *Sitzungsberichte der Wiener Akademie der Wissenschaften, phil.-hist. Klasse* **145** (4): 1-58.

—— (ed.). 1905-1924. Studien zur Paläographie und Papyruskunde. 23 parts. Leipzig, Avenarius.

WEST, L. 1917. Phases of commercial life in Roman Egypt. *Jour. Roman Stud.* **7**: 45-58.

WESTERMANN, W. L. 1925. The Greek exploitation of Egypt. *Pol. Science Quart.* **11**: 517-529.

—— 1929. Upon slavery in Ptolemaic Egypt. New York, Columbia Univ. Press.

—— 1933. Slave transfer: deed of sale and affidavit of vendor. *Aegyptus* **13**: 229-237.

—— 1935. Sklaverei. Pauly-W., *RE*, Supplb. **6**: 894-1068.

—— 1938. Enslaved persons who are free. *AJP* **59**: 1-30.

—— 1941. Athenaeus and the slaves of Athens. *Harvard Studies in Classical Philology*. Special vol., 451-470.

—— 1942. Industrial slavery in Roman Italy. *Jour. Econ. Hist.* **2**: 149-163.

—— 1943. Slavery and the elements of freedom in ancient Greece. *Quart. Bull. Polish Inst. Arts and Sciences* **2**: 1-14.

—— 1945. Between slavery and freedom. *Amer. Hist. Rev.* **50**: 213-227.

—— 1945. Slave maintenance and slave revolts. *Class Phil.* **40**: 1-10.

—— 1946. Two studies in Athenian manumissions, *Jour. Near Eastern Studies* **5**: 92-104.

—— 1947. The paramone as general service contract. *Jour. Juristic Papyrology* **2**: 9-50. Warsaw.

—— 1948. The freedmen and the slaves of God. *Proc. Amer. Philos. Soc.* **92**: 55-64.

—— 1949. Alexandria in the Greek papyri. *Bull. Soc. Royale d'Archéologie d'Alexandrie* **38**. Alexandria, Soc. Publications Égyptiennes.

WESTERMANN, W. L., and CLINTON W. KEYES. 1932. Tax lists and transportation receipts from Theadelphia. New York, Columbia Univ. Press.

WESTERMANN, W. L., CLINTON KEYES, and H. LIEBESNY. 1940. Columbia papyri 4 (Zenon papyri 2). New York, Columbia Univ. Press.

WESTERMANN, W. L., and C. KRAEMER. 1926. Greek papyri in the Library of Cornell University. New York, Columbia Univ. Press.

WHITE, H. G. EVELYN. 1921. Ausonius. 2v. *Loeb Classical Library*. New York, Putnams.

WHITEHEAD, ALFRED NORTH. 1946. Adventures of Ideas. New York, Macmillan.

WIEGAND, THEODOR. 1941. Milet, Dephinium. Berlin, Reimer.

WILAMOWITZ-MÖLLENDORFF, ULRICH VON. 1923. Staat und Gesellschaft der Griechen und Römer bis zum Ausgang des Mittelalters. 2nd ed. Leipzig, Teubner.

—— 1927. Heilige Gesetze. Eine Urkunde aus Kyrene. *Sitzb. preuss. Akad.* **19**: 155-176.

WILCKEN, U. 1899. Griechische Ostraka aus Ägypten und Nubien. 2 v. Leipzig, Giesecke und Devrient.

—— 1920. Zu den κάτοχοι des Serapeums. *Arch. für Papyrusf.* **6**: 184-212.

WILCKEN, ULRICH. 1927-1935. Urkunden der Ptolemäerzeit UPZ). 2v. 1. Papyri aus Unterägypten. Berlin, De Gruyter and Co., 1927. 2. Papyri aus Oberägypten. Berlin, De Gruyter, 1935.

—— 1934. Mitteilungen aus der Würzburger Papyrussammlung. *Abh. preuss. Akad. Berlin* **97**(6).

WILLOUGHBY, H. R. 1929. Pagan regeneration. Chicago, Univ. Press.

WILSON, JOHN A. 1951. The burden of Egypt. Chicago, Univ. Press.

WOESS, FRIEDRICH VON. 1923. Das Asylwesen Ägyptens in der Ptolemäerzeit. *Münchener Beiträge zur Papyrusforschung* **5**. Munich, Beck.

WOPFNER, H. 1922-1923. Critique of Dopsch, Alfons, Wirtschaftliche und soziale Grundlagen. *Historische Vierteljahrschrift* **21**: 196-206.

WRIGHT, W. C. 1922. Philostratus and Eunapius. *Loeb Classical Library*. New York, Putnams.

ZELLER, EDUARD. 1876-1889. Die Philosophie der Griechen. 3rd ed. 3 v. Leipzig, Fues's Verlag.

ZERETELI, G., O. KRÜGER, and P. JERNSTEDT. 1925-1935. Papyri russischer und georgischer Sammlungen. 5 v. Tiflis, Georgisches Museum.

ZIEBARTH, ERICH. 1896. Das griechisches Vereinswesen. Leipzig, Hirzel.

—— 1929. Beiträge zur Geschichte des Seeraubs und Seehandels im alten Griechenland. *Hamburgische Universität; Abhandlungen aus dem Gebiet der Auslandskunde* **30**.

ZUCKER, FRIEDRICH. 1910. Urkunde aus der Kanzlei eines römischen Statthalters von Ägypten. *Sitzungsberichte der königlich preussischen Akad. der Wissenschaften, Berlin* **27**: 710-730.

INDEX